# CONTEMPORARY EUROPE SINCE 1870

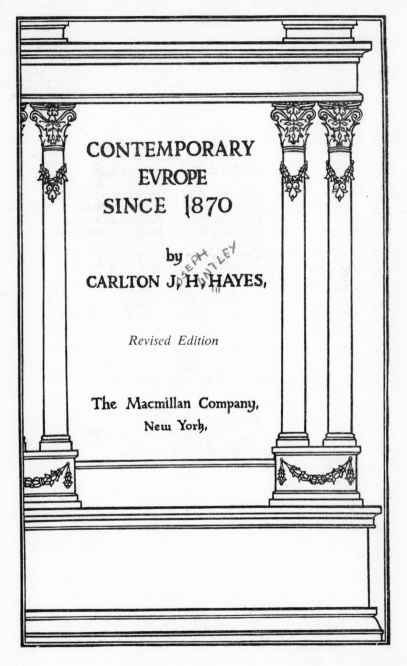

# CONTEMPORARY EVROPE SINCE 1870

## by
### CARLTON J. H. HAYES,

*Revised Edition*

### The Macmillan Company,
### New York,

Library of Congress catalog card number: 58-8571

Some of the material in this book is from Hayes, *A Political and Cultural History of Modern Europe*, Volume II, shorter revised, copyright 1939 by Carlton J. H. Hayes. Previous edition copyright 1953 by Carlton J. H. Hayes.

12-28-70

# FOREWORD

This volume treats of two brief related epochs that might be described as the "grandeur" and the "decline" of Europe. The former covers the last three decades of the nineteenth century and the first decade of the twentieth. It was then that Europe seemingly climaxed its historical evolution with world supremacy in industrial production, military might, and imperial domination, and with phenomenal progress in wealth and social betterment, in democracy and education, in the arts and sciences.

Yet amid Europe's "grandeur," events were leading to the "decline" which has become increasingly apparent during the last four decades, with two world wars of unprecedented vastness and violence, with spread of totalitarian dictatorship, with world-wide nationalist revolt against western imperialism, with grave weakening if not collapse of European great powers and bipolarizing of the world between America and Eurasian Russia, and with fateful crisis, both spiritual and material, in our traditional civilization. For these developments, *Contemporary Europe since 1870* furnishes both foreground and background.

The present volume, like its companion *Modern Europe to 1870,* is interpretative as well as factual. It not only records political and military happenings but explains them by reference to their social, economic, and ideological setting. The two volumes together should prove useful for general courses on modern European history in colleges and universities. Or this volume may be used separately for more specialized courses in recent history; and it also offers to non-academic persons some explanation of the troubled Europe—and world—of today.

Care has been taken to make the book clear and accurate and readable, and to provide it with appropriate maps and up-to-date bibliographies. In its preparation, the author acknowledges with deep gratitude the advice and help he has had for many years from hundreds of colleagues and students, and most recently from the publishers, from the Columbia University libraries, and, for the maps, from Mr. Theodore R. Miller.

C.J.H.H.

JERICHO FARM
AFTON, NEW YORK.
January 28, 1953

## NOTE ON REVISED EDITION

The period since World War II has now lengthened and assumed such crucial character as to merit fuller treatment than it received in the original edition. Hence in place of a single chapter on post-war developments in Europe and the world, *three* are here presented. They constitute a whole new Part V entitled "Two Worlds, Communist and Free, since 1945."

In addition, minor corrections have been made elsewhere in the volume. The selective bibliography has been brought up to date. Seven new or amended maps have been helpfully provided by Mr. Theodore R. Miller.

C.J.H.H.

JERICHO FARM
AFTON, NEW YORK.
March 7, 1958

# CONTENTS

ix

## PART II

### BACKGROUND OF TWENTIETH-CENTURY WORLD WARS

# PART III

## THE "FIRST" WORLD WAR AND ITS PROMISING AFTERMATH, 1914–1929

# PART IV

## LENGTHENING SHADOWS AND THE "SECOND" WORLD WAR

# PART V

## TWO WORLDS: COMMUNIST AND FREE, SINCE 1945

## MAPS

### *by Theodore R. Miller*

# PART I

## FRUITION OF THE NINETEENTH CENTURY: INDUSTRIAL AND DEMOCRATIC PROGRESS, 1871–1905

# CHAPTER I

## INDUSTRIAL FOUNDATIONS OF CONTEMPORARY EUROPE

### I. THE SO-CALLED INDUSTRIAL REVOLUTION AND ITS ORIGINS IN ENGLAND

ONTEMPORARY Europe's (and America's) most striking feature is the prevalence of large-scale mechanized industry and transportation. This is the result of technological developments which occurred first in England and subsequently on the European Continent and overseas, and which radically changed the conditions of popular working and living.

Until the nineteenth century the large majority of Europeans, like the vast majority of inhabitants of other Continents, had lived in rural communities, worked on farms, and been agriculturally minded. By the beginning of the twentieth century, however, a large majority of the population of western and central Europe (and of the United States) were living in urban communities, working in factories or foundries, and becoming industrially minded. Railways and steamships and practical applications of electricity, which were unknown prior to the nineteenth century, were now commonplace, and soon also would be automobiles and airplanes, cinema and television, and the harnessing of atomic energy.

So far-reaching has been the mechanical progress of the last hundred and fifty years, and so profound its social consequences, that the term "Industrial Revolution" is customarily employed to describe it. A more accurate term would be "Industrial *Evolution*," for "revolution" is apt to connote a sharp, sudden upheaval,

3

with results immediately apparent, as in the case of the political revolutions in England in the seventeenth century or in America and France in the eighteenth century or in central Europe in 1848. In contrast with these, the so-called Industrial Revolution was not sudden, nor were its effects speedily appreciated. The process of improving manufacturing techniques, developing the factory system, and increasing industrial output has been long and evolutionary, whether in England or in the world at large. It can be traced back at least to the fifteenth century,[1] and it is still continuing and spreading. What has developed through five centuries is hardly a "revolution."

*An Evolutionary Process*

If the term "Industrial Revolution" is to be used at all, it should be applied to the period in which a country is fairly quickly changed from predominantly agricultural and commercial pursuits to those of mechanized industry. In England such a change occurred, roughly speaking, between 1830 and 1870. On the European Continent, in the United States, in Japan, and elsewhere, it occurred at various times after 1870.

That the change—the so-called Industrial Revolution—began in England, is attributable to the fact that certain prerequisites for it had been more completely fulfilled there than in any other country. These prerequisites may be listed under six heads: capital, labor, techniques, resources, transportation, and markets.

*Why Notable Change First in England*

(1) *Capital.* For intensive industrialization, capital in large quantities is necessary to build factories and machines, to hire workers, and to buy raw materials. This was available in England as profit from the successful British commerce of the seventeenth and eighteenth centuries and from the capitalist type of agriculture which grew up especially after 1740 in connection with the enclosure movement.[2] In England, moreover, the use of capital was expedited by the Bank of England, by efficient handling of governmental finances and by the rise of a London money market where bills could be discounted and shares bought and sold. The British coinage and paper money were on a sound basis from the early eighteenth century onwards, save for a brief period during and after the Napoleonic wars. Just when the need for financing

---

[1] There had been considerable technological advance in medieval Europe, especially in Italy, Germany, and the Netherlands.

[2] See *Modern Europe to 1870*, pp. 79-91, 121-122, 459-460, 463.

industry was becoming great, joint stock banks, other than the Bank of England, were legalized (1826). In the ensuing decades the formation of joint stock corporations for industry, commerce, and finance was made simple and easy. It must be noted, however, that much of England's industrial capital was self-generated. That is, a manufacturer, starting with a small capital, enlarged his plant by plowing back a considerable part of his profits into the business.

(2) *Labor.* Workers for the new English industries of the nineteenth century came from a number of sources. The British population was growing rapidly. It almost doubled in the eighteenth century and doubled again in the first half of the nineteenth, despite considerable emigration. There was some immigration into England of Continental European labor in the eighteenth, and of Irish in the nineteenth, century. Perhaps most important of all, labor was made available for factory production through the gradual destruction of the old peasant farming as a result of the enclosure movement.

(3) *Techniques.* England, in the late eighteenth and early nineteenth centuries developed techniques, processes, and machines necessary for large-scale industry. France was probably ahead of England in technology as late as 1750. Afterwards England rapidly outstripped all rivals. The story of the cotton textile inventions is familiar, though it has probably been unduly conventionalized, and the work of a number of inventors has been attached to a single name. In any case, the flying shuttle (John Kay, 1733), the spinning jenny (James Hargreaves, about 1767), the water frame (Richard Arkwright, 1769), the spinning "mule" (Samuel Crompton, 1779), the power loom (Edmund Cartwright, 1785), the cotton gin (Eli Whitney, 1792, in the United States), the cylindrical calico printing machine (Thomas Bell, 1785), and chemical bleaching and chemical dyes—all these had been developed before the end of the eighteenth century. They had been successfully grouped in factories operated by water or even steam power, and cheap large-scale production in factories had put out of business the small-shop and the home production of cotton thread. In the early nineteenth century, the factory cotton industry grew by leaps and bounds. By 1835 there were nearly 106,000 power looms in the British Isles.

The story of the metal industries is almost as familiar. Shortage of wood to make charcoal for the smelting of iron ore impelled experimentation with coal, which had been mined in ever increasing quantities in England since the sixteenth century. The Darbys at Coalbrookdale, in the first half of the eighteenth century, attained success in this endeavor by transforming coal into coke and then using a strong blast of air in the smelting process. English iron production had been declining for lack of charcoal; it was rejuvenated after the mid-eighteenth century by the use of the Darbys' coke-blast process and by a series of other inventions and improvements: John Smeaton's air pump (1760), the reverberatory furnace, "puddling," and the rolling mill (all developed by Henry Cort and Peter Onions about 1783), James Watt's steam hammer, Huntsman's steel process (about 1740), the hot blast (Nielson, 1828). By the early nineteenth century, iron was being produced in rapidly increasing quantities. From it were made the new machines. Enthusiasts were urging the use of iron for bridges, for ships, and even for coffins.

In the eighteenth century the power most generally used was, as in the past, that of man, mules, wind, or water. A steam (or atmospheric) engine—the Newcomen—had been invented in the early 1700's, but its use was restricted to pumping water out of mines. It was vastly improved upon by James Watt's engine, patented in 1769 and first put to industrial use in 1776. By the first decade of the nineteenth century, steam was becoming a major motive force.

No longer did a mill have to be located beside a running stream. Steam engines were being put on boats (Robert Fulton's *Clermont* was one of the first, 1807), and the first moderately successful locomotive was made by George Stephenson in 1814. Watt had encountered difficulty in making his early engines for lack of proper machine tools. But gradually this was surmounted by the development and use of drills, lathes, the slide rest, and stamping presses.

(4) *Resources.* England was well endowed with just the resources needed for industrialization. Its climate was damp enough to be highly suitable for mechanical spinning and weaving. Its water power was ample. More important, England was abundantly endowed with iron and coal.

(5) *Transportation.* With its many ports and extensive shipping, England was well equipped, by the eighteenth century,

for sea-borne transport. Then, during the latter half of that century, England modernized its medieval inland transportation by the construction of a network of roads and canals. Since no part of the country is much more than sixty or seventy miles from salt water, these roads and canals soon put many inland towns in a position to share directly in the growing British trade.

(6) *Markets.* England and Scotland, under the Act of Union of 1707, constituted a consolidated open market, free of tariffs. To them, Ireland was united in 1800, giving English industry a still more extensive home market. English merchants had already opened up channels of trade to all Europe, to North America, to Africa, and to Asia. Afterwards, British markets continued to expand. The United States purchased more British goods after they became politically independent than they had purchased previously as colonies. India bought a steadily mounting quantity of British wares, especially the new cheap cottons. The Spanish American colonies were opened to British commerce in the period of the French Revolution and Napoleon, and Britain increased its trade with them when they became independent countries in the 1820's. All over the world, from Canton to Buenos Aires, and from Capetown to North Cape, British commerce, from the beginning of the nineteenth century, was unrivaled.

Thus by 1830 England had all the prerequisites for the rapid growth of large-scale factory production. By this time, too, England was already well advanced in the mechanizing of certain key industries, such as cotton textiles and metallurgy.

### 2. DEVELOPMENT IN GREAT BRITAIN AND SPREAD TO WESTERN CONTINENTAL EUROPE, 1830–1870

The industries already developed in Britain expanded with amazing rapidity after 1830. For example, British exports of cotton goods rose in value from 19 million pounds sterling in 1830 to 56 million in 1870. In 1870, moreover, 88 per cent of all workers in the cotton industry were employed in factories and living in towns.

Progress in the iron industry was almost as fast. British production of pig iron rose from 750,000 tons in 1830 to six million in 1870. Coal production similarly increased from 26 million tons in 1830 to 110 million in 1870. In the metal industries, the biggest advance was the improvement of methods for large-scale conversion of iron into steel. The Bessemer process, introduced in 1856, was rapid and relatively inexpensive. It made steel available for machinery, rails, and ships, and steel was stronger and more durable than iron. Then to the Bessemer process was added the Siemens-Martin "open hearth" process in the 1860's, while in the 1870's the Thomas-Gilchrist developments made it possible to use iron ores with a high phosphorus content. Between 1856 and 1870, the price of steel was cut in half in Great Britain.

**British Industrialization Prior to 1870**

In the same period, factory organization and machine production were applied to such old and formerly small-scale industries as shoe-making, brewing, flour-milling, and furniture-making. Production of arms and munitions was likewise revolutionized both by mechanization and by new inventions such as the percussion cap (as against the flintlock), the rifle (as against the musket), and breech-loading (as against muzzle-loading). In 1862 an American, Richard Gatling, invented a machine gun which would fire 350 shots a minute. With the "Gatling gun," the "industrial revolution" was carried into warfare.

New industries came into existence alongside the older ones. In the 1840's, growing urban demand, increasing scientific knowledge, and better methods of making glass jars and tin receptacles permitted the introduction of canned foods. By the 1860's, fresh fruits, fish, and vegetables were being canned in considerable quantities, and "extract of beef," just invented by the German scientist Liebig, was enjoying a popularity quite out of line with its nutritional value. Gail Borden in America had just patented "condensed milk," and dried milk was first made in England in 1855.

From the making of coke for iron smelting, there developed a new industry, for, in producing coke, coal gas is released. A gas-lighting company was incorporated in London in 1812, and gas was first used for cooking in 1832. By the mid-century many streets and many homes were being lighted by gas, and "gas works" disfigured most of the larger cities.

But scientific progress in the field of electricity was already preparing a rival for gas. The invention of the carbon arc light and improved dynamos made electrical lighting practicable by

1870, and the invention of the incandescent lamp in 1878 put it in widespread use. Meanwhile, electricity was being employed for the electroplating of metals as early as the 1850's, and in the previous decade the telegraph had spread a network of wires not only over Great Britain but into central Europe and in the United States. Together with a submarine cable successfully laid from Britain to America in 1866, the telegraph made it possible to get news transmitted with unheard-of rapidity and gave a stimulus to newspapers, which were likewise aided by mechanical steam presses and cheaper paper.

A new industry that arose between 1830 and 1870 was photography. Though the first crude photograph had been made in 1822, it was a Frenchman, Daguerre, who rendered the process practicable. By 1839 he could "take pictures" in thirty minutes; and "daguerreotype" was long a synonym for photograph. In 1841 Fox Talbot, an Englishman, developed a faster process; and a decade later, almost instantaneous photography was realized. Henceforth the new art developed swiftly as a major commercial industry.

The invention, by the American Charles Goodyear in 1839, of a process of vulcanizing rubber in order to make it stronger and more elastic laid the foundation of another new industry. By the 1860's there was a marked growth of factories for the production of rubber articles, but the great days of rubber still lay ahead. Similar was the story of petroleum products. In the 1850's a Scottish industrial chemist, James Young, discovered how to make naphtha, lubricating oils, paraffin, and kerosene by distilling crude oil. Gradually these new products found a market, and kerosene or "coal oil" was especially popular for use in lamps. World production of petroleum, a mere two thousand barrels in 1857, rose to five and a half million barrels in 1870. Only ten years later it would be thirty million.

The mechanization of industries, old and new, produced what amounted to another profession—that of engineer. Originally, engineers had been men who designed and constructed fortifications and engines of war. But as industrial in- **Engineering** vention proceeded and became more complicated, it gave rise to "civil engineers" trained to plan and build roads, docks, canals, aqueducts, drainage systems, lighthouses, etc. In 1828 the civil engineers of London formed a society. But rather rapidly the engineers became more specialized. Some, dealing with steam engines, machine tools, mill work, and moving machinery in general, became "mechanical engineers." Others, busying themselves with the technical problems of mines, became "mining engineers." By 1870 there were "marine engineers," "sanitary engineers," "chemical engineers," and "electrical engineers." In a way the engineers were a link between industry and science. Many of them were competent scientists and some of them made significant contributions. Gradually science and industry became closely interlocked.

Probably even more "revolutionary" than the rapid progress of industry, between 1830 and 1870, were the startling improvements in transportation. In 1830 men still went afoot, **Mechanical Transport** or rode on horseback or in carriages. In 1870 they and their goods could be whisked about at previously unheard-of speeds over shining roads of rails. The first steam railway was that between Stockton and Darlington in England, opened in 1825, with stationary engines to draw the cars over the hills and locomotives to pull them on the level stretches. In 1830, the Liverpool-Manchester line was opened, and on it Robert Stephenson's improved locomotive, the *Rocket,* covered the forty-mile distance in an hour and a half. The success of this venture ushered in a period of extensive railway building. There were forty-nine miles of steam railways in England in 1830. In 1870 there were 15,300 miles. Small lines were consolidated into larger systems, and London was linked with all the major English and Scottish cities. Locomotives were vastly improved, railway building techniques developed, and both speed and safety increased.

The revolution in ocean transportation was slightly slower. In 1838 two ships crossed the Atlantic under steam power, the *Sirius* in eighteen days, and the *Great Western* in fifteen days. Two years later Samuel Cunard inaugurated the first regular trans-Atlantic steamship service. In the 1850's, the screw propeller was widely adopted in place of the earlier paddle wheels, and iron began to replace wood as the building material for the larger ships. In 1858, when an iron liner, the *Great Eastern,* was constructed with a gross tonnage of 18,337, a horsepower of 11,000, and a speed of thirteen knots, it was regarded as a triumph of marine engineering. The number of British steamships increased from 298 in 1830 to 3,178 in 1870, and their net tonnage rose in the period from 30,339, to 1,112,934. But it was not until the 1880's that the tonnage of Britain's steamships surpassed that of its sailing vessels.

Not only was there a shift from sail to steam. There was a remarkable growth of the merchant marine as a whole. The tonnage of British ships more than doubled between 1830 and 1870, and just at the end of the period the opening of the Suez canal in 1869 gave another impetus to sea-borne transport. The swift decrease of the costs of shipping goods by water made it possible for England to sell its wares, even bulky ones of iron, all over the world, and also made it easier and less expensive to import both raw materials like cotton and wool, and food like wheat.

The impact of industry, science, and cheap transportation on English agriculture worked first in one direction, then in the other. By the enclosure movement and the new techniques of the eighteenth century, British farming had **Agriculture** been changed over into a large-scale, profit-making enterprise. High prices in the Napoleonic era had brought wealth to the landowners, but in the twenty-five years after 1815, prices were relatively low, workers were drawn off into the growing factories, and competition of cheap food from the Continent was increasing. For a while, agricultural profits were low, and the agricultural classes suffered.

But from 1840 to 1870, British farming became very profitable once more, despite the repeal of the corn laws in 1846.[1] Machinery, applied to agriculture, drastically cut labor costs. In 1853 the "Crosskill reaper" was perfected in England, and at about the same time the "McCormick reaper" began to be imported from America. Moreover, Liebig's work on fertilizers had practical effect. Manufacture of superphosphate of lime was begun in England (1846), use of nitrate of soda grew, and guano from Peru was imported in swiftly increasing amounts. With the advance of chemical and mechanical agriculture, the crops of British landlords rose while their labor costs dropped. They did very well until the 1870's, when a combination of diseases among their animals and cheap food imports on steamships from overseas brought depression.

[1] See *Modern Europe to 1870*, pp. 650–651.

So far in this section we have concentrated on the prime development of British industry. But Great Britain was so closely connected with the European Continent that the mechanized industrialization of the former was certain to affect the latter. Machines, such as water frames of the Arkwright type, were introduced sporadically into France and the Belgian Netherlands in the latter part of the eighteenth century. As early as 1781 an English iron master founded the famous metal and munitions works at Creusot north of Lyons and installed a steam engine there. Coke smelting was employed at Creusot in 1810, and though the enterprise declined when munitions orders fell off at the close of the Napoleonic wars, it was later revivified by the Schneider family and became one of the most famous metal works in Europe.

**Continental Industrialization Prior to 1870**

Another Englishman, William Cockerill, mechanic and inventor, constructed in Belgium (at Verviers) in 1799 the first wool-carding and wool-spinning machines on the Continent. In 1807 he established a large machine shop at Liége and made a handsome fortune from it. After the peace settlement of 1815, machine production was quickened and extended.

Though the process of industrialization was begun in Belgium well before 1830, it was the ensuing decades that witnessed its triumph. By 1870, Belgium, aided by British investments and engineers, was a nation of foundries, factories, and mines. It was the most densely populated country in Europe. The majority of its inhabitants lived in cities and got their livelihood from industry or trade. As early as 1834, the Belgian parliament adopted a plan drawn up by George Stephenson for the construction of a national system of railways radiating from Liége and Brussels. Through loans floated in England, the plan was speedily carried into effect.

**Belgium**

France was more slowly and less completely industrialized. Its traditions of hand-work and luxury manufacture had become solidly entrenched before the political revolution of 1789. Its system of small-scale agriculture had been reinforced by that revolution. It had lost both colonies and markets during the long wars. It lacked adequate supplies of coking coal, and much of its iron ore had too much phosphorus in it to be useful before the development of the Thomas-Gilchrist

**France**

process in 1878. Yet the "industrial revolution" gradually penetrated France. First it affected mining and metallurgy. The output of coal rose from 800,000 tons in 1815 (about the same as in 1770) to 1,800,000 tons in 1830, and of pig iron from 100,000 to 300,000 tons, while the number of steam engines (still used mainly for pumping water out of mines) increased from 16 to 625.

After 1830, with the aid of the business-minded government of Louis Philippe and later subsidies and assistance from Napoleon III, French industries developed behind a wall of tariffs which were maintained at high levels till 1860. Especially vitalizing for industry was the construction of railways, which was begun in 1842 with a line from Paris to Rouen and thence to Le Havre (built by an English company, with English capital, and English engineers and workmen). By 1870 a network of main lines radiated north, south, east, and west from Paris.

From 1830 to 1870 the output of French coal increased from 1,800,000 to 16,000,000 tons, and of pig iron from 300,000 to 1,400,000 tons, while the horsepower of steam engines, other than locomotives, rose from 20,000 to 336,000. After 1840, power-driven machinery began to compete with hand-work in the French textile industries. Most of the new factories were concentrated in the north of the country, in Alsace and Lorraine or near Lille, Rouen, and Paris. By 1870, many an urban Frenchman was a machine-tender in a factory, although small shops and the putting-out system still flourished and the bulk of the population was still definitely agricultural.

Germany, despite vast resources of coal and iron, was originally more backward than France. Although some machinery was brought in from England and a few factories were built *Germany* prior to 1830, there was scarcely a beginning of industrialization till after that date. The formation of a customs union (*Zollverein*), including by 1833 most German states (except Austria), removed many trade barriers. It had been designed primarily to help landowners by enlarging markets for agricultural goods, but it also served to stimulate commerce and to create a desire for improved means of communication. In 1839, with aid from British capital, the first important German railway was built from Dresden to Leipzig, and by the time of the political revolutions of 1848, there were some 4,000 miles of railway connecting Berlin with Hamburg, the Rhine, Prague, and Vienna. In Germany, in contrast to England, Belgium, and France, railway building preceded real beginnings of industrialization, but just as railways speeded up the foundries and factories of those countries, it served to create them in Germany.

German coal output, less than that of France in 1850, rose to 16 million tons in 1860 and to more than 37 million in 1870. Production of pig iron jumped to half a million tons in 1860 and soared to almost two million tons ten years later. Meanwhile, steam-driven machinery was being applied to cotton spinning, and textile factories were springing up in Saxony, Silesia, Westphalia, and the Rhineland. Cotton weaving and the manufacture of other textiles were, however, as late as 1870, still predominantly hand industries, and almost two thirds of the population of Germany were still classed as rural and agricultural. Germany was clearly beginning to experience an "industrial revolution." But its sweeping consequences were to become obvious only after 1870.

Elsewhere on the Continent, large-scale manufacturing, with the factory system and industrial capitalism, appeared only **Elsewhere** spottily before 1870. There were a few instances in Holland, Sweden, and Spain. There were considerably more in Russian Poland, particularly near Warsaw. Bohemia (especially Prague) and German Austria (especially Vienna) participated somewhat in the new mechanized industry. In the 1850's a few steam engines were brought into northern Italy (Piedmont), and Count Cavour acquired wealth and his first fame as a promoter of industrialization. But, by and large, the European Continent, with the exception of Belgium, France, and Germany, was almost as solidly agricultural in 1870 as it had been a century or two earlier.

Overseas, the only region significantly affected, before 1870, by the new industrialization was the northeastern part of the United States. Here there was a good deal of mechanical invention. There was also a considerable importation of both machinery and capital from Great Britain. Factories for large-scale production of textiles and shoes sprang up in New England, while extensive building and operation of railways led to a big development of coal mining and iron working in Pennsylvania. By 1870 the United States gave promise of becoming a great industrial nation, comparable with Britain, France, or Germany.

### 3. INDUSTRIAL EXPANSION AFTER 1870

The forty years from 1830 to 1870 had seen a veritable "industrial revolution" in Great Britain, and the preparatory stage of one in western and central Europe and in eastern North America. The next forty years, from 1870 to 1910, were marked by a progressive output of industries already largely mechanized, a rapid evolution of novel industries, and a swift transformation of agricultural into industrial population. Nor were these developments restricted mainly to Britain (and Belgium). They now became characteristic of Germany and the United States, and, in only lesser degree, of almost all countries of the European world. They penetrated the Russian Empire and helped to revolutionize faraway Japan.

All the industrial advance of the preceding period continued from 1870 to 1910 with quickening pace over wider areas. Engineers and scientists—physicists and chemists—became ever more numerous and allied themselves ever more helpfully to machine industry. The establishment of "polytechnical" schools and schools of "applied science" was now epidemic in all countries which aspired to be "civilized" and "progressive." Tools of precision were multiplied and rendered ever more "precise" and useful.

The production of coal and iron, the twin bases of machine industry, was speeded up by mounting demand on the one hand, and by improving methods of supply on the other. The British production of coal increased from 110 *Coal, Iron, and Steel* million tons in 1870 to 265 million tons in 1910, and of pig iron from six to nine million tons, but these figures tell only a part of the story. For whereas up to 1870 Britain produced more coal and iron than all the rest of the world, its production in 1910 was only twenty-six per cent of the coal and fourteen per cent of the iron. In the meantime the output of coal increased in Germany from $37\frac{1}{2}$ million tons to 222, in France from 16 to 40, and in the United States from 35 to 415; while the output of pig iron grew in Germany from 2 million tons to almost 15, in France from $1\frac{1}{2}$ to 5, and in the United States from $1\frac{2}{3}$ to $27\frac{1}{3}$.

There was steady progress in perfecting and utilizing the Bessemer and Siemens processes for the manufacture of steel. There was marked improvement of steam locomotives and of all accessories to railway transportation, and noteworthy extension of railway mileage. Not only was the network of rails in western and central Europe elaborated, but it was extended into eastern Europe, and railway construction went on apace outside Europe. In the United States the mileage increased from 30,000 in 1860 to 250,000 in 1910. In Canada and Australia, it increased proportionately. Long lines were built and more were projected in Latin America, in Asia, and in Africa. By 1905 a trans-Siberian railway linked Moscow (and western Europe) with Vladivostok on the Pacific Ocean. There was corresponding development of steamships, in numbers, size, and speed. Regular services were multiplied for passengers and goods from London and Liverpool, Hamburg and Bremen, Le Havre and Marseilles, Antwerp and Rotterdam, Genoa and Trieste, New York and Montreal, Yokohama and Shanghai, Bombay and Melbourne, Cape Town and Buenos Aires.

The cotton industry, whose mechanization had been an important aspect of early industrial development in Britain, kept on

**Textiles**    growing. In Britain itself, the number of spindles increased from 36,700,000 in 1870 to 53,500,000 in 1910 and the number of power looms from 475,000 to 700,000. But, while Britain possessed far more spindles and power looms than all the rest of the world put together in 1870, in 1910 it had only about forty per cent of the spindles and thirty per cent of the power looms. By this time there were 37,200,000 spindles on the Continent of Europe, 27,800,000 in the United States, and 10,000,000 in other parts of the world (chiefly in India and Japan).

It was similar with the other textile industries of wool and linen. These, following the lead of cotton, had been pretty largely put on a machine and factory basis in Britain before 1870, and after 1870 the same basis was firmly established for them on the Continent of Europe and in the United States, with similar results. The silk industry of France and Italy was likewise mechanized and expanded, and gradually the search for an "artificial silk" led to the emergence of still another large-scale textile industry—that of "rayon" as it is called in the United States.

Another noteworthy addition to the mechanized textile industry during the period following 1870 was the steady progress in applying chemistry to the dyeing of fabrics. A profusion of chemical dyes were derived from coal tar, and were used as cheap substitutes for natural dyes.

Comparable with the advance of the textiles was that of other significant industries whose production had already been speeded up by machine and factory. With improving machines, enlarging factories, and increasing markets, there was a mounting output, in Britain, on the Continent of Europe, and in the United States, of cutlery, porcelain, tinware, boots and shoes, paper, furniture, tools, firearms and other war implements. *Other Established Industries*

The machine-gun which Gatling had invented in America in 1862, was improved and rendered automatic in 1889 by Sir Hiram Maxim, an American who acquired a British title. Sir Hiram also invented, in 1908, the "Maxim silencer" for suppressing the noise of the discharge of firearms; and his brother, Hudson Maxim, perfected a smokeless powder. Rifles were much improved and were produced in great quantities by the ever expanding factories of the Vickers and the Armstrongs in Britain, the Krupps in Germany, the Schneiders (Creusot works) in France, the Du Ponts and the Remingtons in the United States. Of high explosives, an outstanding inventor was Alfred Nobel, a Swedish chemist and engineer, who introduced dynamite in 1867 and amassed an immense fortune from its manufacture.[1] The first practical "submarine" was the invention of an American, John Holland, in 1875.

Essentially new industries arose. The rayon industry, already mentioned, was one of these. Among many others of special importance, were (1) those connected with the increasing knowledge and exploitation of *electricity;* (2) those having to do with a miscellany of mechanical aids to *individual comfort,* such as heaters, refrigerators, the sewing machine, the typewriter, the bicycle, wood-pulp paper, etc.; (3) those evolving from *photography;* and (4) those dependent on novel types of engine, especially on the *internal-combustion* engine. *New Industries*

From 1870, electricity and its applications came to occupy a central industrial position similar to that held previously by the

---

[1] The bulk of his fortune Nobel left in trust for the support of the "Nobel prizes," which have been awarded since 1901 for distinguished work in physics, chemistry, medicine, literature, and international peace.

steam-engine. This did not signify a lessening number or importance of steam-engines. It meant merely that, side by side with the omnipresent steam-engine, there appeared now a wide range and great variety of electrical devices. Nor was the development of "applied electricity" confined to one country as the early development of the steam-engine had been. It occurred simultaneously in Britain, in America, and all over the European Continent. It was closely associated everywhere with the general advance of physics and chemistry.

**Electricity**

Electrical dynamos and motors were rapidly improved and multiplied. Moreover, the successful transmission of electrical power fostered the establishment of central power plants for ever extending systems of electric lighting and traction. Lighting by gas or kerosene lingered for some time, but eventually it was largely supplanted by electric lighting.

Almost simultaneous with the invention of the incandescent electric light by Thomas Edison (1878) was the invention of the telephone by Alexander Graham Bell (1876). This proved immediately successful, and with improvements and modifications it was quickly adopted throughout Europe and America.

Close upon the heels of the telephone came electric trams and street cars. The first regular line, a short one with a single motor-car, was opened in Germany in 1881. By the end of the 1880's, most cities in Europe and America were being provided, or were taking steps to be provided, with systems of electrically powered street railways. Subsequently, electric railways began to parallel steam railways between populous centers, and certain steam railway companies "electrified" some of their lines.

Meanwhile, a theoretical foundation was being laid for wireless telegraphy and telephony by British and German physicists; and in 1895 a youthful Italian, Guglielmo Marconi, devised a practical system of wireless telegraphy. A year later Marconi patented his device in Britain and began the organization of a company for its commercial exploitation. In 1898 wireless telegraphic communication was established across the English Channel, and in 1901 across the Atlantic.

As the nineteenth century ended and the twentieth began, the applications of electricity, especially for domestic purposes, became ever more numerous. There were electric lights and telephones, and small electric motors for vacuum cleaners, for sewing machines, and for washing machines. And, on a large scale, there was rapid progress in electroplating, in electrotyping, and in the use of electric furnaces for making steel. The "age of electricity" was even marked by New York's substitution in 1888 of "electrocution" for hanging as the legal death penalty for criminals.

Parallel with the rise of electrical industries was the development of special mechanical aids to the comfort of people at home and in shop or office. For example, artificial heating was provided by a variety of "furnaces"—coal-burning or (later) oil-burning—while higher standards of sanitation and better methods of plumbing contributed to a rapidly growing vogue of bathrooms, lavatories, and all manner of accessories. *Aids to Personal Comfort*

For lightening the labor of housekeepers and ensuring to populous centers a copious and varied supply of foodstuffs, refrigeration was developed. It depends, of course, on a plentiful supply of ice; and this was rendered possible and comparatively cheap by the ingenuity of chemists and engineers. Certain chemicals were found useful for making ice, as well as for preserving tinned or potted goods, and engineers eventually learned how to apply electricity to refrigeration.

A big aid to domestic economy was the sewing machine. The first practical design had been patented by an American, Elias Howe, in 1846, and the first commercial exploitation of it, with some modifications, had been undertaken by another American, Isaac Singer, in the 1850's. It was not until 1863, however, that the "Singer Manufacturing Company" was solidly established and not until 1872 that it erected its first large factory. Thereafter, the production and improvement of sewing machines went on apace. The "electric" sewing machine was patented in 1889.

A special aid to office economy was the typewriter. There had been several early experiments with mechanical writing devices in England, America, and France; but the first really successful typewriter was made jointly by three ingenious residents of Milwaukee, Wisconsin, in 1867–1872, and its commercial manufacture was inaugurated by Remington and Sons, gunmakers of Ilion, New York, in 1874. Other firms soon took to making typewriters, in America and in Europe, and there was steady improvement in the "Remington" and its competitors.

A special aid to individual locomotion (and a special stimulus to outdoor exercise and "sport") was the bicycle, whose manufacture developed steadily after 1870. For several years, the front wheel was made big and the rear wheel small. Gradually, however, a "standard" form was evolved. Ball bearings were introduced in 1877. Pneumatic rubber tires were added in 1889. By the 1890's the bicycle was widely used in Europe and America. It was helpful to workers going back and forth to the factory and to young people going back and forth to school; and it provided incentive and opportunity for all sorts of persons to escape from home and town into the open spaces.

Many ends were served by a remarkable contemporary utilization of wood pulp or "cellulose." One form of it, "celluloid," was first made in the United States in 1869. Other forms came to be employed for the new "artificial silk," for explosives, for photographic films, and most quantitatively from the 1880's for print paper. Indeed, the extensive manufacture of cheap wood-pulp paper was of primary significance in the evolution of journalism during the years from 1870 to 1910. Not only did the constantly improving printing machines, powered by electricity as well as steam, permit of much swifter printing of news. Not only did the telegraph, telephone, and wireless and the perfected means of transport greatly facilitate the collection of news and the distribution of newspapers. But the substitution of cheap wood-pulp paper for the more expensive (and durable) cotton or linen paper enabled publishers to print more in their newspapers and to sell them more widely. These developments, together with the marked increase of "advertising" which attended industrialization, ushered in the distinctive popular and "sensational" journalism of the twentieth century.

Photography made remarkable progress after 1870. In 1884 the film-roll was invented, and in the following year George Eastman laid the foundations of his great photographic industry at Rochester, New York, by patenting a machine for the manufacture of films. In 1888 the Eastman Company marketed the first Kodak, a small portable roll-film camera, which enabled amateurs, as well as professionals, to "take pictures." By 1900 photography was an important and widespread industry. Cameras and Kodaks were used everywhere for artistic and scientific purposes, for individual diversion, for journalistic illustration.

**Photography**

The idea of "moving pictures" had been toyed with in France, Britain, and America since the 1860's, but it did not lead to practical results until after Eastman began the manufacture of roll-films in the 1880's. In 1891 Thomas Edison patented a peep-show device known as the "kinetoscope," which was put to commercial use for the first time in New York City in 1894. Then, in 1895, two brothers by the name of Lumière, in Lyons, France, patented the "cinematograph," a mobile machine, combining a camera, a film-printing device, and a projector; and this marked the real beginning of the motion-picture industry. True, there was some delay in exploiting the "cinema," in part because of lawsuits over patent rights. But after 1900 the display of motion pictures became a regular feature of most vaudeville shows in the larger cities throughout the world, and in 1905 the first exclusively motion-picture theater was opened at Pittsburgh. Though the enormous growth of the motion-picture industry was to come afterward, the preparation for it was made before 1910.

A particularly important feature of the era from 1870 to 1910 was the devising of the steam turbine and internal-combustion engines, the application of the latter to motor car, **Internal-** motor boat, and aviation, and a consequent prodigious **Combustion** rise of the petroleum, rubber, and cement industries. **Engine** The turbine is a rotary motor in which the shaft is rotated steadily in its bearings, not by means of cranks, as in the earlier "reciprocating" engine, but directly by a current of water, air, or steam. The principle of the turbine had long been embodied in the windmill, but its utilization for a steam-engine was the master invention of a British engineer, Sir Charles Parsons, who patented his steam turbine in 1884 and labored on its perfecting for many years thereafter. In 1889 Parsons established at Newcastle a large factory for the manufacture of steam turbines, and by 1910 they were being extensively employed for the running of electrical dynamos and steamships.

The internal-combustion engine is a device for the direct translation of energy into mechanical power by means of gas explosion behind a piston; it "puts the furnace into the cylinder." There had been much experimentation with "gas" engines throughout the nineteenth century, but not until the last quarter of the century did it produce practical results in the oil-burning engine evolved by a German, Rudolf Diesel. The "Diesel engine" was patented in 1892 and publicly demonstrated for the first time in 1898. By 1910 it was being employed in electrical works, ocean liners, and locomotives.

Another German engineer, Gottlieb Daimler, devised in 1885–1886 a small, portable internal-combustion engine, fueled with light oil and capable of propelling vehicles and boats. This was the "gasoline engine," destined speedily to rival Watt's steam engine in revolutionizing transportation and stimulating industry. Daimler applied the gasoline engine to a bicycle in 1886 and to a wagon in 1887, but, being much more interested personally in water travel, he sold his patents for motor cars to a French concern and devoted himself to the manufacture of motor launches.

In the meantime, in the late 1880's and during the 1890's, mechanics and "promoters" were producing varieties of motor cars in France, Germany, England, and the United States. At first, more cars were manufactured in France than elsewhere, but by 1910 three-fourths of the world's output were being produced in the United States. Here, the output of four cars in 1895 increased to 181,000 in 1910, and this figure was only a little augury of the monster production, twenty years later, of pleasure cars, business cars, trucks, buses, and tractors. Probably the most famous popularizer of the motor car was Henry Ford, an American mechanic, whose company, founded at Detroit in 1902, began a large-scale production of cheap "Ford" cars in 1909.

Aviation also was rendered practicable by the gasoline engine. Man had long dreamed about flying, and in the 1780's Louis XVI of France had been edified, and his courtiers and countrymen elated, by several sensational balloons—round or egg-shaped, filled with hot air or hydrogen—pulling courageous human beings, in attached "cars," up toward heaven and then depositing them in earthly fields or trees. In the nineteenth century, balloon ascents—sometimes with parachute drops—became a sport in many countries, at local fairs and at international expositions; and balloons were occasionally used for military reconnaissance, as in the American Civil War and in the Franco-Prussian War.

In the 1890's Daimler's engine was utilized for "airships." The pioneers were an elderly German, Count Ferdinand von Zeppelin, and a youthful Brazilian, Santos-Dumont. The latter, coming to

Paris, inaugurated the building of dirigible motor airships in 1898 and in 1901 won a prize for the first definite flight in a given time from St. Cloud to the Eiffel Tower. Count Zeppelin, a retired army officer who devoted many years to the scientific study of aeronautics, designed dirigibles of larger size and with a framework of aluminum. The first "zeppelin" was constructed in 1900, and the first successful flights with one were made in 1906.

While Zeppelin and Santos-Dumont were building motor airships (lighter than air), various mechanics and engineers were devising motor airplanes (heavier than air). Among the pioneers of the latter, the most successful were two American brothers by the name of Wright. They were associated in the business of repairing bicycles at Dayton, Ohio, and in the early 1890's, as a recreation, they took up "gliding" with a winged contrivance. Gradually they learned how to adjust and control the wings, and in 1903, after intensive study and much manual labor, they installed a gasoline engine in a glider and made a successful short flight with it. In 1905 they made forty-five airplane flights, in the longest of which they kept their machine in the air half an hour and traveled twenty-five miles. These feats of the Wrights were soon excelled by others. Santos-Dumont at Paris turned from gas dirigibles to flying machines. In 1909 Bleriot, a French aviator, flew across the English Channel from Calais to Dover. The age of aviation was dawning.

From the invention of the internal-combustion engine and its rapidly extending utilization for motor cars, motor boats, and airplanes, and likewise, through the Diesel engine, for dynamos, ocean liners, and locomotives, there arose a great, and essentially new, petroleum industry. The output of crude oil throughout the world, amounting to half a million bar- **Petroleum and Rubber** rels in 1860, reached a total of 325 million barrels in 1910. Almost all the output of petroleum, prior to 1880, was from the United States; after 1880, though at least two-thirds of it continued to be from the United States, sizable quotas were obtained from Russia, Rumania, Mexico, South America, Persia, and the Dutch East Indies. It was a large industrial undertaking to refine the crude oil and to transport it from industrially backward areas, where it was produced, to industrially advanced regions, where it was used.

There was a corresponding development of the rubber industry,

in general because of the steadily growing manufacture of miscel-
laneous rubber goods, and specifically because of a suddenly
mounting demand for rubber tires for motor cars. The world's production of crude rubber rose from 10,000 tons in 1870 to 75,000
tons in 1910. The supply from wild rubber trees of Brazil proved
insufficient and was supplemented, and after 1900 surpassed, by
the supply from rubber plantations in the Dutch East Indies, Ceylon, Borneo, French Indo-China, and various regions of tropical
Africa.

The motor car was an important factor in stimulating the
rubber and petroleum industries and also the building of cement
("concrete") roads. Lime cements had been made back in the
eighteenth century, and about 1825 a particularly good kind was
invented in Great Britain and named "Portland cement" by
reason of its resemblance in color to Portland limestone. The
manufacture of this Portland cement was carried on in Britain
and France in the 1850's. After 1870, the manufacture was
notably improved, through a lessening of the water content, and
was extended to many countries on a scale commensurate with the
growing demand for "concrete construction," in which Portland
cement was a principal ingredient.

With all the strictly industrial progress of the era from 1870
to 1910 went hand-in-hand the steady mechanizing and indus-
**Agricul-**      trialization of agriculture. Farm machinery, which had
**tural De-**     appeared in preceding decades, continued to be im-
**velopment**    proved and multiplied. To bigger and better drills,
seeders, cultivators, and harvesters, were now hitched gasoline
engines; and to an ever greater knowledge and use of chemical
fertilizers, which immensely increased the yield of crops, were
now added novel means of marketing them, at a great distance as
readily as near by. All these developments meant that the
countries of western and central Europe and the eastern part
of the United States, as they became more intensely industrialized and urbanized, were becoming more dependent for foodstuffs and many raw materials on those regions of the world
which undertook large-scale agriculture—Russia, Argentina, Canada, and the Middle-West and South of the United States. Of
course, small-scale farming remained fairly important in France
and Germany, in Italy and Scandinavia, in the eastern United
States, in Ireland and even in England, but it was relatively static,

and at its best, as in France, it hardly sufficed to meet local demands.

To the preponderant industrialization of Britain and Belgium, which had occurred between 1830 and 1870, the era from 1870 to 1910 added a similar industrialization of other countries— Germany and the United States most strikingly; France, less so, but still to large extent; and, in lesser and varying degree, Italy, Austria, Bohemia, the Dutch Netherlands, Sweden, Spain, Russia, Canada, Australia, New Zealand, and Japan. In 1870, England and Belgium were the only countries in the world having more people engaged in manufacture and mining than in agriculture. In 1910 Germany and the United States could be ranked with England and Belgium in this respect, and in all the above-named countries there was a marked lowering of the percentage of farmers and a corresponding raising of the percentage of day laborers.

### 4. ENHANCEMENT OF CAPITALISM AND SOCIAL CHANGE

Capitalism had long been an important feature of European economy,[1] but prior to the nineteenth century it was managed and directed chiefly by landed nobles and upper middle-class persons, whose activities did not radically undermine the traditional society of Europe. This was still a society of landlords and peasants, of bourgeoisie and artisans; and capitalism was mainly agricultural or commercial in source and use. It is true that capitalism had been applied, fairly early, to the "heavy" industries of mining and metallurgy, which were owned by wealthy employers and manned by wage earners who were neither farmers nor guild artisans. But such industries were exceptional.

It is also true that throughout the eighteenth century there was a notable growth of a kind of industrial capitalism in the form of "putting-out" and "domestic" systems, in which an employer furnished raw material, such as wool for instance, to peasants to work up for a wage and then sold the finished product for profit to himself. Yet under those systems, peasants did the manufacturing in their own homes and in combination with farm-work. And in most industries a premium was put upon skilled artisans, while in most countries guild regulations about apprenticeship were respected.

[1] See *Modern Europe to 1870*, pp. 79–91, 337–338, 365, 463.

The development of industrial machinery, say in England at the close of the eighteenth and the beginning of the nineteenth century, sharply altered matters. It greatly enhanced capitalism and gave it a distinctively *industrial* character. Most of the new machinery was far too expensive to be owned by peasants or artisans and much too cumbersome and complicated to be housed in their cottages or operated by them without superintendence. Hence it was purchased by wealthy men, or by "promoters" with the backing of wealthy men, and it was installed and operated in special buildings—factories or foundries—which the same wealthy men put up and to which they could bring numerous workmen to tend the machines under expert central guidance.

**Industrial Capitalism**

In other words, the factory (or mill) came with industrial machinery. It is true that there had been some mills or factories before the large-scale mechanizing of industry, and some factory-like foundries and collieries in connection with metallurgy. The fact remains, however, that only with the advent of much machinery at the end of the eighteenth century did the factory become a common and usual center of industrial production. Thereafter, we may speak of a *factory system* prevailing in the "great industry" and carried on by machines in capitalists' factories. It was obviously very different from the *domestic system* of the older, and still continuing, "little industry" conducted by hand or with simple tools in the workers' houses. For a long time the new factory system and the old domestic system existed side by side, and even today the latter has not wholly disappeared in England or anywhere else. But in measure as an industry has been mechanized, the factory system has tended to dominate and then to supplant the domestic system.

**Factory System**

Another important fact to be borne in mind is that the owners of machinery and factories were in a position to make far greater profits than the middlemen who utilized the hand-work and home-work of artisans and peasants. The domestic worker usually labored hard for a very small wage, but his employer could get from him only what he actually made with his own hands and tools, and he frequently alternated work for his industrial employer with agricultural work for himself. On the other hand, the factory worker, usually divorced from the land and deprived of any income from that source, labored exclusively for his industrial employer, and labored in such a way that his employer got from him much more than he could possibly have produced with his own hands. In the factory, it was the machine which really did the work, and it did an amount of work which, before its invention, could only have been done by ten, or a hundred, or a thousand human beings. The machine was thus equivalent to so many human beings; they were "iron men" because they were mechanical; and they were "iron slaves" to the employer because he owned the machine. The factory worker was merely an overseer of gangs of iron slaves; he tended them and made them work; and their multiplying production accrued less to his profit than to the capitalists who owned them.

Machine-owning capitalists were at first of two kinds. Some were persons who had already been enriched by the earlier commercial capitalism and who belonged to the upper middle class or the landed nobility. These were enabled by their ownership of extensive estates, as well as by their association with banks and their familiarity with joint-stock companies, to apply new machinery and new processes to coal mining and iron working. Such a gentleman as the Duke of Bridgewater, coal magnate and canal builder, is a good example of the aristocratic agricultural capitalist who turned industrial capitalist. Other machine-owning capitalists, however, were "self-made men," drawn from the lower classes, without previous name or fame. These came to the fore, particularly in the textile industry, by reason of inventive genius and ability as "promoters." Arkwright, an ex-barber, was such a "self-made man," and such too, with the assistance of Matthew Boulton, was James Watt. In numerous like cases, the "self-made man" shared profits of factory production with established capitalists and often became an outstanding capitalist himself.

Early industrial capitalists were likely to be in close and direct contact with their business enterprises. Richard Arkwright, for example, was not so much a passive capitalist as an active "promoter," manager, superintendent, and dealer. As "promoter" he contracted loans, built factories, and installed machinery. As manager, he hired workmen and sought profits with which he could pay off the loans and amass wealth for himself. As superintendent, he sped from mill to mill in his "coach and four," seeing that the work was done properly, that the laborers were not idle, that the machines were in good order. As dealer, he purchased the raw cotton and sold the finished goods. Richard Arkwright, like many other industrial capitalists of his day, was both shrewd and hard-working; the title of knighthood which King George III conferred upon him seemed an appropriate reward for his abundant qualities of assiduity and ambition.

As time went on and the factory system became more complicated, and especially as larger industrial enterprises, like railways, were undertaken, the individual capitalist tended to play a less active role. Ownership of large-scale industry "Big Business" passed from individuals and partnerships to joint-stock companies and corporations, which entrusted the superintendence and dealing, even the management and promotion, to salaried employees and which contented themselves with floating the necessary loans (in the form of stocks or bonds) and distributing the ensuing profits (in the form of dividends or interest) among their directing officers and among "investors" outside. In this way, many industrial capitalists came to have no personal relationship with the business from which their profits were derived. They were mere investors, delivering profits which they had obtained from one industry to a banker or broker for investment in another industry and receiving income, perhaps from several different industries, without serious expenditure of mental or physical energy on their part. There was, of course, a considerable element of gambling in this procedure. Individual investors might lose, as well as make, fortunes. Not knowing first-hand much about a given enterprise, they might invest in one which was badly conceived or badly managed. Even well-managed and normally profitable enterprises might occasionally experience "hard times" and suffer reverses. In such instances directors of large means could afford, better than small investors, temporarily to forego profits and patiently to await a revival of business.

By means of machinery and the factory system, the capital wealth of Great Britain increased prodigiously during the nineteenth century and into the twentieth; and similar increases accompanied the spread of industrialization in Increase of Wealth other countries. Especially after 1870, the rise of great new industries, the big expansion of old industries, the rapid extension of manufacturing and commerce, vastly enlarged the fields in which persons of wealth could make lucrative investments. At the same time it enabled many a pushing, ingenious, and sometimes unscrupulous individual to emerge from economic and social obscurity into monopolistic ownership of mines, petroleum wells, electrical works, motor-car factories, dynamite manufacture, or other key-business, and thence into front rank among the world's captains of industry. The opportunities for "self-made men," as well as for professional bankers (and corporation lawyers), were now golden.

According to estimates for the years 1870 and 1910, capital investments increased in Great Britain from 35 to 70 billion dollars, in France from 28 to 55 billion, and in German from 17 to 70 billion, while British foreign investments grew from 5 to 20 billion dollars, French from 2½ to 8 billion, and German from none to five billion. Of this augmenting wealth, a growing proportion, especially in Germany and the United States was owned or controlled by great industrial combinations—"cartels" as in Germany, or "trusts" as in the United States. They represented consolidations or federations of formerly competing businesses in a given industry, for the purpose of reducing "overhead" expenses, securing a practical monopoly, and thereby increasing profits for managers and stockholders. There were national "trusts" or "cartels," sometimes with international affiliates, of steel, of petroleum, of copper, of sugar, of electrical works, of chemical works, etc. And the directors and heavy stockholders of such combinations or pools were the great "barons"—in some cases, in public opinion, the "robber barons"—of the new industrial era.

Attendant upon the mechanizing of industry, and the enhancement of capitalism, was a remarkable growth of population. For centuries up to the eighteenth, the population of Europe had been relatively static. Afterwards, it rapidly increased. The inhabitants of England numbered about **Growth of Population**
9 million in 1800; 14 million in 1830; 22 million in 1870; and 36 million in 1900. In Europe as a whole, the growth was from about 187 million in 1800 to 305 million in 1870 and on to 440 million in 1910. By this last date, there were ten Europeans for every four a century previously; and Europe, the smallest of the four major continents, now contained a quarter of the human race. It should be borne in mind, moreover, that the increase of population in Australia and in the American continents, particularly

the increase in the United States from 6 million in 1800 to 92 million in 1910, was largely of European stock.

Most of the population increase went to the growth of cities and towns. The birth rate remained as high in rural as in urban areas, but in country districts a stationary or even dwindling population, with the aid of agricultural machinery and foreign imports, sufficed to feed larger aggregations of people, and the excess of country-born persons naturally sought and usually found employment in factory towns or mining centers. There was much emigration from populous regions of Europe to more sparsely settled areas in America. There was much more migration, within industrialized nations of Europe, from farms to cities.

In Great Britain, London expanded into an urban colossus; old cities like Bristol or Glasgow grew, while new ones, which had been mere villages in the eighteenth century, came to be busy, densely populated centers, as in the case of Liverpool, Leeds, Sheffield, Manchester, or Birmingham. Similar changes occurred on the Continent, with sensational growth of such cities as Brussels, Paris, Lille, Milan, and Berlin. In Germany, the urban population increased from thirty-five per cent in 1870 to sixty per cent in 1910.

The rapid growth of industrial towns betokened a significant change in the structure of society. The familiar division of landowner and peasant, merchant and artisan, persisted. But to it was added another division of industrial capitalists (with dependent managers, foremen, engineers, lawyers, etc.) and industrial proletarians. The most numerous type of the latter was the "factory hand," who owned no property and made his living by daily labor at some kind of machine. It was this type which most commonly left farming and went to swell the population of cities.

In the first stages of the new industrialization, the lot of the urban wage-earner, the "proletarian," was hardly a happy one. While the average peasant or rural artisan of the eight-**Urban Workmen** eenth century had most likely worked long hours and been ill housed and ill clad, he had been, to a considerable degree, his own master. He often owned some land, some tools, and a cottage. He had some security. He was part of a friendly community that felt some responsibility for him. On the other hand, the mid-nineteenth-century worker in factory, forge, or mine had few such advantages. He labored twelve or fourteen hours a day at a machine in dismal, unsanitary, and unsafe factories, or, if he was a miner, he worked underground and scarcely saw the light of day. He went to work at the sound of a whistle. He was fined for absence or lateness. He was clad in rags or shoddy cloth. He ate unwholesome food. He lived in a rented room in some sort of human rabbit-warren with much dirt and little or no sanitation. His work was intensely monotonous and he had few amusements. He was often unemployed because the factory owner found it cheaper to hire his wife and children. Even six-year-olds were found useful because of their nimble fingers. The bad living and working conditions of industrial laborers, in grimy factory towns, appeared first in Great Britain, but they were duplicated on the Continent wherever machine industry developed.

In earlier rural life, there had always been work to do. But in the newer industrialized life there were usually a considerable number of jobless men—the unemployed. And every few years, there recurred a business "crisis" or "depression" which produced widespread mass unemployment, with intense suffering for the hapless urban proletarians. Such depressions occurred, for example, in 1847–1848, 1857–1858, 1866–1867, 1873–1878, 1893–1894, 1907–1908.

In course of time, and especially after 1870, as industrialization deepened and broadened, a gradual betterment of working and living conditions was brought about, in part through the agitation of the urban proletariat itself, and in part through the sympathetic support of humanitarians among the middle and upper classes. Eventually, "*social* politics" and "*social* reform" became major concerns of the government of every industrialized country.

Altogether, the industrial evolution of Europe (and America) in the nineteenth and twentieth centuries has been responsible for much that differentiates the contemporary world from the world of earlier times. Not only did it enhance capitalism and create a big and essentially new class of proletarians. It greatly forwarded the efforts of man to subdue nature and make it serve his ends. He could henceforth produce a wide range of luxuries as well as necessities, and he could produce them in a fraction of the time which had been required by previous hand-work. He could travel much faster and more cheaply. He could live more comfortably, with electric lights, steam heat, and a profusion of mechanical conveniences.

*Distinguishing Features of Material Advance*

He could feed on the most varied products of the whole world. He could know quickly what was happening throughout the world. From routine toil he could gain leisure for recreation and self-cultivation, mental and spiritual as well as physical. Material advance held out to the masses, not less than to the classes, an inspiring and substantial hope.

Moreover, the material advance was strikingly dynamic in character and effect. So long as the masses lived on the soil and worked at farming, they were likely to be enrooted in ancestral customs and habits and ideas. From these they were largely and rather suddenly uprooted when they migrated to town and worked in factory, foundry, or shop. In contrast with the domestic system which kept industrial workers apart, the factory system brought them together and led them to form trade unions for the promotion of their common interests. Then, too, the urban proletariat was a far more vocal and effective force than the rural workers had been in denouncing abuses and demanding reforms. And there can be little doubt that life in a factory town, even with its early misery and squalor, was preferred to country life by a large number of persons. It was at once more sociable to those who liked company and more concealing to those who wished to live aloof. It was more casual and, to many, more exhilarating.

For better or for worse, urbanism—the "city spirit"—became dominant over the rural and the local. It made for mass movements: mass nationalism, mass democracy, mass education, mass socialism; eventually for totalitarian dictatorship and totalitarian war.

### 5. ECONOMIC LIBERALISM AND ECONOMIC NATIONALISM

By 1870, the conflict which had been going on throughout western and central Europe between conservatives and liberals,[1] seemed to issue in the triumph of the latter. Liberal principles and practices of individualism, constitutional government, and national self-determination were now dominant not only in Britain, France, and the other western countries, but also in Italy and Germany. The explanation lies principally in the fact that the urban middle classes—the bourgeoisie —which from the start had been the chief supporters of liberalism, were now greatly strengthened in numbers and influence by the

**Economic Liberalism**

[1] See *Modern Europe to 1870*, pp. 577–579, 607–680.

process of industrialization with its attendant growth of cities and rise of industrial capitalists.

The new "captains of industry," in espousing political liberalism, usually allied it with an economic liberalism which had been expounded by a series of British economists of the "classical" or "Manchester" school in the first half of the nineteenth century to explain the way in which industrialization was then developing. All these economists were deeply influenced by the laissez-faire doctrines of Adam Smith's *Wealth of Nations*, though they made distinctive additions. Malthus promulgated a "law of population," that the number of persons tends to grow faster than the food supply, and that over-population can be prevented only by "positive checks" of famine, war, and disease, or by "preventive checks" of continence and abstention from marriage. The poor, said Malthus, were "the authors of their own poverty"—they had too many children. Ricardo argued that "rent" is determined by population growth, forcing use of ever more sterile land for the production of food. He also enunciated an "iron law of wages," that wages tend to fall toward the level of bare subsistence.

*Liberal Political Economy*

Nassau Senior demonstrated to his own satisfaction—and to the satisfaction of many employers—that daily hours of factory labor should not be reduced from fifteen to fourteen, because it was the fifteenth hour which gave the capitalist his needed profit. McCulloch advanced a "wage fund" theory, that there was just so much money to pay the laborers of a country; if one group of workers succeeded in raising their wages, they were merely reducing the pay of some of their fellow laborers. Meanwhile Jeremy Bentham, philosopher of "utilitarianism," maintained that the application of *laissez-faire* and the ideas of economic liberalism would result in the greatest good for the greatest number of people.

As developed by such British writers, economic liberalism became by the 1830's a well-organized body of doctrine. Like political liberalism, it stressed the individual. It made individual self-interest the motive force of economic life. Again like political liberalism, it stressed freedom—freedom of trade (no tariffs or subsidies), freedom of contract between individuals (no labor unions), freedom from government interference or regulation (*laissez-faire*), freedom of competition (no monopolies, especially none chartered by governments). The economic liberals were the heirs of eighteenth-century thought in that they believed that economic life was guided by supposedly "natural laws," such as "laws" of rent and wages and population. Man could not prevent, though he might impede, the operation of such "laws." The best thing to do was to remove all man-made restrictions and let the "laws" work automatically.

Despite growing pessimism of "classical" economics from the time of Malthus and Ricardo (which earned for it the title of "the dismal science"), its doctrine of economic liberalism won many followers. Industrial capitalists found in it justification for the system under which they were growing wealthy, and many statesmen were quite convinced of its validity. Economic liberalism gained firmest foothold and most victories in Great Britain. Between 1800 and 1860, almost all the long-standing British restrictions on private industry and trade were repealed by parliamentary action. Thus disappeared the statute of apprentices, laws regulating woolens, leather, and linens, the assize of bread, navigation acts, tariffs, usury laws, monopolies of East India Company and Hudson's Bay Company, and the Elizabethan poor law. By the time the last of the English import duties (except a few retained for revenue) were removed by the Cobden treaty with France in 1860, Great Britain had adopted free trade and *laissez-faire* as thoroughly as any nation has ever done.

In France and Germany, economic liberalism won a considerable number of converts. Yet it never triumphed completely, and those who advocated it usually did so because it seemed consonant with the political liberalism they favored.

It must be emphasized that in the 1860's and 1870's, at the very time when "big business" was becoming enrooted on the Continent of Europe (and in America), a series of wars was eventuating in the erection of national states for Italians, Germans, Magyars, and Balkan peoples (and the repression of sectionalism in the United States) and was promoting an intensification of national spirit and rivalry all over Europe (and America). In the circumstances, it was but natural that this spirit and rivalry should find expression in the economic and industrial field as well as in strictly cultural and political domains. The fostering of a country's machine industries, the exploitation of its natural resources, the

Economic
Nation-
alism

stimulation of its domestic and foreign trade, the increase of the security and purchasing power of its citizens, became central objects of concern to the statesmen (and the masses) of every nation.

In other words, industrial progress was attended, after 1870, not so much by governmental policies of *laissez-faire*—giving free rein to individual competition, respecting the "laws" of supply and demand, and establishing the freedom of profession, trade, and "contract"—which had been especially urged during the era from 1830 to 1870, as by a return of most national governments to the mercantilist, regulating policies of the seventeenth and eighteenth centuries before the advent of liberalism. In brief, economic liberalism gradually gave way after 1870 to economic nationalism.

The new trend was a result, at least in part, of differences among nations in degree of industrialization. So long as large-scale mechanized industry was mainly confined to Great Britain, as was the case before 1870, this industrialized nation and likewise the other nations, predominantly agricultural, could readily perceive mutual advantages in international free trade. British manufactured goods could be freely exchanged for the rest of the world's raw materials and foodstuffs, to the profit of all concerned. But after 1870, with the extension of machine industry in one country after another—the United States, Germany, France, Italy, Austria, Russia, etc.—the argument for free trade was not so convincing. If all these countries had remained agricultural, or if all of them had been industrialized equally with one another and with Britain, free trade might conceivably have continued as an ideal and a practical policy.

Britain, it is true, did cling to free trade during the era from 1870 to 1914. Its industrialization was so much more complete than that of any other nation. It had so much more capital, so much more experience in mechanical pro- **British Free Trade** duction, so many more customary markets, so much greater need for raw materials and food supplies, that its "national interests" did not appear to be seriously endangered by foreign competition.

Other nations, nevertheless, were in a different position. They were undergoing a novel industrialization. Their developing mechanical industries were "infant industries," varying greatly from

country to country in lustiness and promise, and yet everywhere creating unusual strains for traditional agriculture. In these na-
**Continental Tariffs** tions, consequently, tariff protection was sought for "infant industries" against more highly developed foreign industries, and likewise for agriculture against both rising domestic industry and mounting importation of foreign foodstuffs and raw materials. And intensified popular nationalism helped interested manufacturers and farmers to obtain what they sought.

The trend away from economic liberalism (or *laissez-faire*) and toward economic nationalism (or "neo-mercantilism") was most marked in Germany. Here it was promoted by the agitation of a "national school" of economists, by the swift industrialization of the country, and by the patriotic fervor which accompanied the successful issue of the struggle for political unity. And here it found a twofold expression: in the inauguration, in 1879, of protective tariffs; and in the elaboration, during the 1880's, of a system of compulsory insurance for the nation's wage-earners.

Among the industrialized states of Europe (and America), Germany was only a pioneer in the pursuit of economic nationalism. Others quickly followed. In the three decades from 1880 to 1910 almost every such state enacted neo-mercantilist legislation. Some, such as France, the United States,[1] and Russia, specialized in tariff legislation in behalf of manufacturers and farmers and were relatively backward in labor legislation in behalf of workmen. A few, such as Britain and the Dutch Netherlands, abstained wholly from tariff legislation but adopted a good deal of national labor legislation. The countries which imitated the example of Germany in stressing both major features of neo-mercantilism—tariff and labor legislation—were Austria-Hungary, Italy, Belgium, and the Scandinavian kingdoms.

In the following chapters, we shall see in specific detail how and in what varying circumstances the several countries of Europe applied the new economic nationalism. What we are doing in this place is to point out the general fact that the *laissez-faire* principle which had been regarded as a natural and ideal accompani-

---

[1] The United States actually preceded Germany in the adoption of tariff protection and, after 1879, greatly surpassed Germany in the height of national tariff walls. France, too, had never been a completely free-trade country, but its moderate tariff protection of the 1860's and 1870's was considerably stiffened in the 1880's and thereafter.

ment of industrial progress in Europe during the era from 1830 to 1870 was replaced to a large extent during the era from 1870 to 1910 by neo-mercantilism, by governmental attempts to treat industry and agriculture, commerce and labor, as "national interests."

The transition from economic liberalism to economic nationalism roughly synchronized with the advent of political democracy in western and central Europe. Back in the 1830's and 1850's liberalism had been, politically as well as socially, a middle-class movement, and few liberals had sponsored a political democracy in which the mass of men without property or education might participate in voting and office-holding. A handful of "radicals," like John Bright in England and Mazzini in Italy, had represented, it is true, a democratic left wing of the liberal movement, but for a long time they had been unable to prevail upon the majority of liberals to democratize the Victorian Compromise in Britain, the bourgeois monarchy in France, or the severely restricted suffrage in Belgium and Italy. Wherever liberalism was strongest, there was parliamentary government, but a parliamentary government of upper and middle classes.

Adoption of the form of democratic government, at least of universal manhood suffrage for parliamentary elections, occurred widely in western and central Europe between 1867 and 1885. This resulted less from the activity of convinced middle-class liberals than from the agitation of working-class leaders and the opportunist tactics of professed conservatives like Disraeli in Britain and Bismarck in Germany. It was usually acquiesced in, and even applauded, by liberals—which was a sign that they were weakening in their devotion to a major political tenet of earlier liberalism. Of course, they thought they could afford to acquiesce and applaud. For, now that the bourgeois spirit was permeating upper and lower classes, the whole citizenry of an industrialized nation might be expected to share the basic concern of the bourgeoisie for industry and commerce, for property rights and material prosperity.

So political democracy, or important concessions to it, attended the advance of industrialization. Gradually, almost imperceptibly, this one departure from earlier liberalism was attended by other departures. One was in the field of popular education. Liberals had always been friendly to the idea that while education should be "free," the secular state should broaden the opportunities for popular education by subsidizing private schools and supplementing them, if necessary, by a system of public schools, attendance at which, however, would be voluntary. With the advent of political democracy, nevertheless, the movement for popular education took a new turn and became more insistent. Trade unionists and working-class people generally demanded a radical extension of public schools, and the upper and middle classes, intent upon preparing the masses for "enlightened" and patriotic exercise of their new political rights, heeded the demand.

Almost immediately, under democratic auspices, great systems of state-maintained and state-directed schools were inaugurated or strengthened. And eventually, still under democratic auspices, **Increase of State Functions** school attendance ceased to be voluntary and was made compulsory, while public secular schools were preferred to private religious schools. This might involve, theoretically, an abridgment of individual liberty. Practically, it was a response on the part of liberals themselves to the insistent demand of a machine age for the training of the masses.

Similar to the increase of state power in education was the parallel extension of state control over matters of public health and charity. The more industrialized a nation became, the more extensive and rigorous was its exercise of "police powers" over individual conduct, even over individual property rights, affecting the health and physical well-being of the community. Statute followed statute, regulating, in one country after another, the treatment of communicable disease, the disposal of sewage, the sanitation, ventilation, and lighting of factories and shops and private dwellings. Simultaneously, governmental appropriations multiplied for the establishment and maintenance of public hospitals and sanitariums, as well as of prisons and reformatories. In all these developments, professed liberals, full of humanitarian zeal, cooperated with conservatives and radicals and thereby helped to bring about a situation in which the old liberal ideal of the state as a "passive policeman" gradually receded before the new reality of the omnipotent state.

Just as economic liberalism was transformed, in the latter part of the nineteenth century, into economic nationalism, so the latter started a trend toward the "welfare state" of the twentieth century. To this trend, socialism—particularly that of Karl Marx —contributed in important ways. Marxian socialism was indeed a product of the latter part of the nineteenth century; and, like nationalism, it was at least an indirect stimulus to the changing economic thought and policies after 1870. But it did not achieve revolutionary results until 1917 and then only in eastern Europe. We shall therefore defer an account of its rise and growth until a later chapter.

# CHAPTER II

## PREEMINENCE OF GREAT BRITAIN

### I. WORKSHOP AND BANKER OF THE WORLD

IGHT through the nineteenth century and until the world wars of the twentieth, Great Britain enjoyed a preeminence among the nations comparable with that of Spain in the sixteenth century or of France in the seventeenth. But while the preeminence of Spain and France had been a result in chief part of political and dynastic developments, that of Britain is primarily attributable to economic factors. Britain underwent large-scale industrialization two or three generations before any other country, and its consequent lead in manufacturing, commerce, and banking was retained at least to 1914.

Other countries, to be sure, underwent progressive industrialization after 1870: Germany and the United States, most notably; France and Austria and Italy, considerably; and, in varying degrees, all the countries of western and central Europe—and Russia and Japan, Canada and Australia, and even India. But while Britain no longer had a monopoly of industrial machinery, while it felt the increasing competition of industrial rivals, while its commerce and capital constituted a gradually lessening proportion of the world's total, the loss to Britain was relative and not absolute. Despite new competition, it continued to be, par excellence, the workshop and the banker of the modern world.

Britain's population grew and shifted proportionately with its industrialization. In the island of Great Britain (embracing **Increase of Population** England, Wales, and Scotland), where the bulk of big industry was carried on, the population almost quadrupled between 1801 and 1911; and the increment was concentrated in urban centers.

In the adjacent island of "Little" Britain (that is, Ireland), only industrialized Belfast greatly increased in population. The population of Ireland as a whole, largely agricultural and once almost as numerous as that of Great Britain, declined from eight million in 1841 to four and a quarter in 1911. This decline is accounted for by the stream of emigration which flowed from agricultural Ireland to industrial centers in America, Scotland, and England.

One British industry suffered serious loss. That was agriculture. For three decades previously, the tide of British agricultural prosperity had been rising, but after 1874 it turned and rapidly ebbed. At first, the ebb was viewed as a temporary phenomenon, a natural but passing effect of a widespread economic "depression" of 1873–1874, which adversely affected manufacturing as much as agriculture. But while British manufacturing soon recovered and again forged ahead, the ebb of British agriculture became chronic. From the 1870's British farmers were staggered by an astounding rise of grain-growing in the United States and Argentina, Canada and Australia, and by still more astounding expansion of overseas shipping whereby the plentiful cheap grain of those hitherto distant countries came flooding into British cities and underselling British-grown grain. In the circumstances, the grain area of England and Wales shrank from eight and a quarter million acres in 1871 to five and three-quarters in 1901; and the financial profits from what remained tended to disappear.

*Decline of Agriculture*

British farmers simply could not meet the newer foreign competition. They were handicapped by an aristocratic land-holding system under which most of them were tenants rather than owners [1] and hence were expected to make enough money from farming to support themselves and to pay rents to noble landlords. And the one advantage which they had possessed of proximity to their markets was now being overcome by the speed and cheapness of ocean transportation.

The decline of British agriculture was platonically lamented,

[1] The number of persons in England and Wales owning more than one acre of land was about 150,000, or less than 1/170 of the total population, and of this number 2,250 were landed aristocrats who owned almost a half of all the cultivated land. It is noteworthy that at the same time France, with a population only a third larger, had some 5,600,000 landed proprietors, and Belgium, with a population of but 7,000,000, had as many as 1,000,000 landowners.

but little was done to arrest it. Already when it began, the agricultural population was too small a fraction of the total population of Great Britain—about a sixth—to be able to exert any great or decisive influence, as a class, upon governmental policy or legislation. The land-holding aristocracy, though still very influential in government, was now as much identified with banking, trade, or manufacturing as with agriculture. Landlords complained that they could not make their ancestral estates "pay," but the persons who suffered most were usually their tenants and farm laborers. These persons might better their lot only by migrating to industrial towns or foreign fields. Landlords, on the other hand, could continue to derive pleasure, if not profit, from their country estates; they could transform them into parks and hunting grounds with the profits which they reaped from urban business. British noblemen and gentlemen—and social pretenders among the middle class—might play on country estates, but their work was more and more in urban offices, in the management of factories, collieries, foundries, railways, steamship lines, public utility corporations, insurance companies, banks and brokerage houses, in the maintenance of Britain's premier position in industry and trade.

For Great Britain was the leading commercial as well as industrial country; and the value of its foreign commerce steadily **Commercial Supremacy** rose. Already in 1865 it was 418 million pounds sterling, much in excess of any other country's. In 1890 it was 600 million, and in 1910 it amounted to 1,085 million. London was the greatest commercial port in the world, and Liverpool did the greatest exporting business. Moreover, the bulk of the shipping to and from Great Britain, together with the largest part of the whole world's carrying trade, was in British hands, and it showed a similar gain. The net tonnage of the British merchant marine went up from five and a half million in 1870 to eleven and a half million in 1910; and whereas sailing vessels constituted over four-fifths of the tonnage in 1870, steamships accounted for over nine-tenths of it in 1910.

Great Britain was the wealthiest country in the world, with the largest accumulations of capital at home and the largest investments abroad. Its domestic wealth was roughly estimated at 6,000 million pounds sterling in 1865, and at 14,000 million in 1910, representing a rate of increase considerably in excess of the rate of population increase. And Britain was the chief lending country in the world, the foremost exporter of capital. By 1913, its external investments aggregated at least 3,760 mil- lion pounds sterling, comprising 1,825 million in the British overseas empire, 755 million in the United **Financial Supremacy** States and a like amount in Latin America, 110 million in Russia, 65 million in Japan, 25 million in the Ottoman Empire, and 225 million elsewhere. Wherefore from all parts of the world and from a variety of public and private undertakings a stream of annual tribute flowed to Britain in the form of interest on stocks and bonds. London was the unquestioned financial capital of the world, the pivot of the world's money and banking and stock exchange.

As the national wealth increased, the British government could and did increase its revenues and expenditures. The central government more than doubled its expenditure from 71 million pounds in 1867 to about 150 million in 1910, while local authorities multiplied their expenditures almost fivefold from 36 million in 1867 to about 168 million in 1910. The expense of past wars and of preparedness for future wars was still the principal item in Britain's public budget, but it was not increasing quite so fast as the expense of the civil service. The state was being called upon to do more for its citizens than to provide armed protection for them.

About Britain, there were certain peculiar, almost paradoxical, facts which were intimately associated with its position as workshop and banker of the world and which are fundamental to an understanding of its political and social development. One was the striking contrast between the waxing industrial wealth of the country as a whole and the continuing poverty of **Poverty** the majority of its inhabitants. It is true that the misery **amid** prevalent among the masses during the earlier stage of **Wealth** industrialization was gradually mitigated. But it is also true that there was no general diffusion of wealth at all comparable with its quantitative increase. The economic condition of farm tenants and agricultural laborers grew steadily worse; and, if the lot of urban workmen as a class showed some improvement, most of them still owned no property, had no permanent homes, and were expected to work long hours for mere subsistence wages, while some of them remained chronically idle and on the verge of starvation. The profits of British industry, we must remember, went on accruing primarily to a minority of Britishers rather than to the majority.

A second curious fact about Britain was the evolutionary, rather than revolutionary, character of its politics and society,

**Political and Social Stability** It had had no "French Revolution." Side by side with its impressive and very modern machine industry, Great Britain retained a form of government and a class society which dated from the middle ages and which a series of compromises had adapted, slowly and imperfectly, to changing conditions. By the latter part of the nineteenth century, "compromise" was an almost sacred word in the English language, and "muddling through" a favorite way of describing the process by which compromises were effected. There was a monarch who reigned "by grace of God," but did not rule. There was a privileged national church whose communicants constituted only a fraction of the nation. There was a small privileged nobility which prided itself on land-holding but profited mainly from bond-holding. There was a powerful House of Commons, elected by the masses but actually dominated by the classes. And, despite a persistent tradition of individualism and personal liberty, despite an extraordinary frankness of discussion and criticism, the great majority of Englishmen were wont to respect their social "betters" and to obey their political rulers. On the whole, they were intensely patriotic, and, however poor or unromantic they might be individually, they were disposed to glorify the "wealth of Britain" and British "common sense." They might demand "reform," but they were not likely to participate in "revolution." All of which gave internal solidity and external fame to the "workshop of the world" and to its political and social institutions.

A third remarkable fact was that Great Britain, as workshop and banker of the world, seemed to be so small a part of the

**Small Homeland and Big Empire** world. We say, "seemed to be." In a literal sense, "Great Britain" was one of two relatively small islands lying off the coast of the smallest of the five continents, and its population, even when reaching the figure of forty million, was dwarfed by the sixty-five million in Germany, the ninety-three million in the United States, the hundred and forty million in Russia, the three hundred million in India. In

a metaphorical and truer sense, however, "Great Britain" was
not a mere island with a puny population; it was a huge imperial
domain. And this domain was not confined to the political British
Empire where the British flag waved over a fourth of the earth's
habitable area and a fourth of the human race. It embraced an
economic empire of all lands and seas and of all peoples wherever British shipping and trade or British investment extended.

### 2. OPERATION OF PARLIAMENTARY GOVERNMENT AND ITS GRADUAL DEMOCRATIZING

A new era in British politics was ushered in by the Reform
Act of 1867.[1] Previously, voting for members of Parliament
had been confined to upper and middle classes. Afterwards,
most urban workers could vote. Thereby the earlier "Victorian
compromise" between noble landlords and bourgeois capitalists
was succeeded by a new compromise between aristocracy and
democracy. On the one hand, the upper and wealthier **Aristoc-**
classes retained their prime position in public life. They **racy and**
provided the leadership for both Liberal and Conserva- **Democracy**
tive parties. They occupied nearly all cabinet offices and supplied the heads and much of the staff for the governmental services, military, naval, and civil. On the other hand, this continuing
political ascendancy of the classes was newly and radically conditioned by the enfranchisement of the masses. Government had
to function within a democratic framework, with the result that
while it remained predominantly aristocratic in personnel it became increasingly democratic in method and policy.

The first parliamentary elections under the new dispensation
returned a majority of Liberals, and their leader, William E.
Gladstone, formed a ministry which lasted from 1868 **Gladstone**
to 1874.[2] Gladstone stuck to the Liberal tradition of **Ministry,**
"peace and retrenchment," economizing on expendi- **1868–1874**
tures and obtaining necessary revenues from free-trade budgets,
and pursuing a pacific policy in foreign and colonial affairs. He
preserved a strict neutrality during the Franco-Prussian War
of 1870–1871. He submitted to arbitration the claims of the
United States for damages growing out of the depredations of
British-built Confederate vessels during the American Civil

---

[1] See *Modern Europe to 1870*, p. 701.
[2] On Gladstone and his earlier career, see *Modern Europe to 1870*, pp. 699–703.

War.[1] He patronized the extension of self-government to several parts of the overseas British Empire. He sponsored the disestablishment of the Anglican Church in Ireland and an ineffectual land reform there.

But the most significant legislation of the time was in response to demands of the recently enfranchised workmen. It represented an evolution of British liberalism toward putting greater emphasis on social welfare.

One of the major popular demands was met by the Education Act of 1870. Since 1833 the state had been subsidizing elementary schools maintained by the church (chiefly by the Anglican Church), and the subsidies, at first very slight, had gradually been increased. Until 1870, nevertheless, there had been no real state schools in Britain, and almost half of the nation's children had no regular schooling. Now, provision was made for larger public subsidies to private schools, and also for the establishment of a supplementary system of state schools ("board schools," as they were called) which would be financed entirely by public taxation and managed by public "boards of education" and in which no denominational religion should be taught. Under the operation of these new "board schools" and of the continuing church schools, and with the added requirement (in 1880) that every child must attend some school, illiteracy in England rapidly decreased from twenty-four per cent in 1871 to one per cent in 1910. By 1910 more than 5,500,000 English children were attending school (3,000,000 in "board schools" and 2,500,000 in "church schools"), and government (central and local) was expending £25,000,000 on elementary education.

Another major demand of British workmen was partially met by the Trade Union Act of 1871. This formally and finally legalized trade unions, by empowering them to hold property and to maintain and defend actions at law, but it contained drastic provisions against "picketing" and every form of "violence" in connection with strikes and other labor disputes. Trade unionism grew rapidly in Britain after 1871, but its rank and file were not satisfied with the Act of that year.

Still another popular demand was met in 1872 by the abolition

---

[1] The most famous of these vessels of the Southern Confederacy was the *Alabama*. The arbitration of the so-called "Alabama Claims" resulted in the payment (in 1872) of 15 million pounds sterling by Great Britain to the United States.

of public voting in parliamentary and municipal elections, and the substitution of the secret ballot—called the "Australian" ballot in reference to the place of its origin. This nicely supplemented the Reform Act of 1867 by enabling urban workmen to vote as they pleased without oversight or possible retaliation on the part of their employers. It was a democratic step forward.

Yet in the election of 1874 Gladstone and the Liberal party lost their majority in Parliament. The Conservative party, under the adroit leadership of Benjamin Disraeli,[1] exploited to its advantage a contemporary economic depression and likewise working-class dissatisfaction with Gladstone's Trade Union Act and popular criticism of his "inglorious" foreign policy.

*Disraeli Ministry 1874–1880*

The resulting Conservative ministry of Disraeli lasted from 1874 to 1880. It put through Parliament in 1875 the repeal of the restriction which the Trade Union Act of 1871 had imposed on "peaceful picketing," and in 1878 the enactment of a comprehensive code of factory laws. But while it thus catered to British workmen, its chief interest—and significance—was in the nationalist domain. It was extremely patriotic, even jingoistic, and it displayed a tender regard for the unity, the dignity, and the greatness of the British Empire. Disraeli knew how, by flattery and cajolery, to manage his somewhat difficult sovereign, Queen Victoria, and he did much to render the crown the outstanding symbol and object of British patriotism. He did much, too, to reassert and revivify Britain's imperial traditions. He emphasized the union of Ireland with Great Britain and refused to make any concessions to what he termed the "rebellious elements" in that island. He stressed the importance of India to Great Britain by adding to the titles of his sovereign that of "Empress of India." He obtained for Britain the financial control of the Suez Canal. He intervened decisively in the Russo-Turkish War of 1877–1878, helped to dictate the terms of peace at Berlin,[2] and, as a kind of brokerage-fee, secured for his own country the island of Cyprus.

Disraeli's government was turned out of office by the general election of 1880, and he himself died the following year. But Gladstone, whose second Liberal ministry extended from 1880

[1] On Disraeli and his earlier career, see *Modern Europe to 1870*, pp. 699–701.
[2] See below, pp. 161–162.

to 1885, was unable to breast the current of nationalism and imperialism which Disraeli had set in motion and which the Con-

**Gladstone,**
**and Par-**
**liamentary**
**Reform of**
**1884–1885**

servative party now exploited to the full. Though the
Liberal prime minister was a shrewd politician and a
resonant orator, his principles and prejudices were
more consonant with mid-century liberalism than with
late-century nationalism. He was still a "little Englander," dubious about foreign entanglements and distant undertakings and
sure that the noble ends of peace and material prosperity could
best be attained through a continuous proliferation of such domestic "reforms" as had been effected by previous Liberal governments.

Gladstone talked so much and so eloquently about "reform"
that he acquired the reputation of being more radical than he
really was. He alarmed many conservatively minded persons, and
Queen Victoria disliked him on personal grounds (she said he
talked to her as if she were a mass-meeting) and deemed his
"principles" highly dangerous. Yet it was the irony of fate that
the only memorable domestic "reform" which Gladstone accomplished during his second ministry was the extension of the parliamentary suffrage to farm tenants and agricultural laborers
(1884), and this he accomplished through an understanding with
the Conservative party that there should be a new and equitable
rearrangement of electoral districts (1885). Thereby the political
democratizing of Great Britain, begun by the Reform Act of
1867, was greatly forwarded.

Gladstone permitted, it is true, an armed intervention in Egypt,
but he insisted that it would be only temporary, and he so weakened it that it came perilously near to disaster. For Ireland he
contented himself with another Land Act (1881) and a renewal
of coercive measures.

There was increasing popular opposition to the Liberal government. Workmen complained that it did nothing to improve their
lot. Patriots denounced its concessions abroad as weak and un-
dignified, if not traitorous. Men of means were alarmed by the
restrictions which its Irish Land Act placed upon the rights of
private property. The Irish were not satisfied; they wanted a
more radical land reform, they opposed coercion with redoubled
violence, and they intensified their agitation for "home rule." In
1885 Gladstone, outvoted in the House of Commons, resigned;

and until a new general election could be held, a Conservative ministry under the Marquess of Salisbury took office.[1]

The first general election in which the agricultural as well as the industrial masses participated was held in 1885. It returned a slightly greater number of Liberals than of Conservatives but a sufficiently large number of Irish National-
ists to give them the balance of power between the two
major parties. Gladstone at once perceived the advan-

*Liberal Split over Irish Home Rule*

tage of "home rule" to Ireland and to his own political fortunes. In alliance with the Irish Nationalists, he voted Salisbury out of office and in 1886 formed his third ministry, pledged to set up a separate Irish parliament at Dublin.

Gladstone's third ministry was brief. Its one proposal was a home-rule bill for Ireland, and the bill was defeated in the House of Commons. Though the Irish Nationalists and a majority of the Liberals voted for it, a minority of Liberals who called them-selves "Liberal Unionists," and who proved themselves more na-tionalist than liberal, joined the Conservatives in rejecting the bill. Gladstone immediately resigned, and Salisbury, with Liberal Unionist backing, formed his second and more lasting Conserv-ative ministry.

The year 1886 thus registered a schism within the Liberal party as significant for British politics and as symptomatic of a social and intellectual shift as the schism of 1846 within the Conserv-ative party had been. Back in 1846 economic and political liberal-ism had been so much in the ascendant that a considerable num-ber of Tory Conservatives (including their leader, Sir Robert Peel) had repudiated the traditional agrarian policies of their party and joined the Liberals in repealing the corn laws and in-stituting the regime of free trade. And during the forty years from 1846 to 1886, the Liberal party, reinforced by the "Peelites," was usually the major political party in the realm and was in power most of the time. Now, in 1886, nationalism and imperial-ism were so much in the ascendant that a considerable number of professed Liberals cooperated with the Conservatives to pre-

[1] Robert Cecil, third Marquess of Salisbury (1830–1903), was an aristocrat of the aristocrats. He had been a bitter opponent of the Reform Act of 1867 but had subsequently accepted it as "irrevocable" and had been one of Disraeli's chief colleagues in the Conservative ministry from 1874 to 1880. His principal interest was in foreign affairs, and he succeeded to the leadership of the Conservative party on the death of Disraeli in 1881.

vent Gladstone from tampering with the Union between Britain and Ireland. And during the ensuing twenty years, the Conservative party, supported by Liberal Unionists, controlled the government almost continuously. For only three years (1892–1895) out of the twenty were the Gladstonian Liberals in office, and then with a most precarious majority in the House of Commons.

Nationalistic imperialism was not the only factor in the disintegration of the Liberal party. A goodly number of professed Liberals, especially among the younger generation, were impatient with Gladstone's "old-fashioned" leadership and ideas and desirous of a "new liberalism" which should be less doctrinaire and which should realistically face the practical social and economic problems of the day. The most conspicuous of such Liberals and the leader of the "Liberal Unionists" was Joseph Chamberlain, a highly successful manufacturer of Birmingham and a "radical" in religion and in the cause of social reform. Chamberlain made a reputation for himself as a "socialistic" mayor of Birmingham in the 1870's: he cleaned up the city slums and established municipal ownership of gas and water supply. Gradually, as he became more active in national politics, he evinced an interest not only in social legislation but in imperialism and tariff protection; in other words, in the neo-mercantilism which was spreading out from Germany and which was obviously at variance with the economic liberalism that had long been the guiding principle of British public policy. The question of "liberating" Ireland and loosening its ties with the British Empire was the occasion, rather than the basic reason, for the secession of Chamberlain and his followers from the Liberal party of Gladstone.

The Conservative ministry of Salisbury from 1886 to 1892 conducted the British government along the nationalist and im-

**Salisbury's Conservative Ministry, 1886–1892** perialist paths already pointed out by Disraeli. It celebrated in 1887, with befitting pomp, the fiftieth anniversary of Queen Victoria's accession to the throne and utilized the occasion to inaugurate a series of semi-ceremonial, semi-advisory "colonial conferences," in which the chief ministers of the overseas self-governing colonies discussed with representatives of the home government matters of general concern to the British Empire as a whole. It sponsored in 1889 a sensational strengthening of the British navy, ostensibly for the protection of the Empire, and it greatly enlarged the territorial extent of the Empire by securing, through treaties of 1890–1891 with Germany, France, and Portugal, the principal share in the pending general partition of Africa. In respect of Ireland, it consistently opposed all "home rule" and "separatist" agitation, but in an effort to reconcile the Irish peasants to political union it sponsored a type of land reform more fundamental in character and eventually more beneficent in operation than the Gladstonian land reforms of 1870 and 1881. Whereas Gladstone had undertaken merely to restrain landlords from oppressing their tenants, the Salisbury government enabled peasants, by advancing money to them on easy terms, to buy out their landlords and transform themselves from tenants into small landed proprietors. By a series of such "land purchase acts," the number of peasant proprietors in Ireland was materially increased.

Salisbury was scarcely more interested than Gladstone in social reform within Great Britain. The Conservative party was still more agrarian than the Liberal, though by the 1880's—thanks to the striking industrialization of the country—many Conservative landlords were as much identified as any Liberal with manufacturing, commerce, and banking, and quite as reluctant to endanger capitalistic profits by legislation in behalf of workmen. Nevertheless, the Conservative party, unlike the Liberal, had a tradition of *noblesse oblige,* a memory of the stand which some of its most honored members, such as Shaftesbury and Disraeli, had previously taken in behalf of factory legislation. This tradition, this memory, was kept alive by the agitation of a special group of young Conservatives—the so-called "Tory Democrats"—under the leadership of the brilliant Lord Randolph Churchill,[1] and was reinforced by the pressure of Joseph Chamberlain and his Liberal Unionists. In the circumstances, the Salisbury ministry was induced to grant some working-class demands. It put through a mines act in 1887, forbidding the employment of children under twelve years of age. In 1891 it practically abolished tuition fees in elementary schools.

The general election of 1892 gave the Liberals, in combination with the Irish Nationalists, a slight majority in the House of

[1] Churchill was a younger son of the seventh Duke of Marlborough and a strenuous advocate of the doctrine that the Conservatives ought to adopt, rather than oppose, reforms of a popular character and to challenge the claims of the Liberals to pose as the champions of the masses. Lord Randolph was the father of Winston Churchill.

Commons. Gladstone, now a very old man, formed his fourth ministry and tried again to realize the one and only "reform"
Last<br>Gladstone<br>Ministry,<br>1892
which filled his mind: home rule for Ireland. This time he got a home-rule bill through the House of Commons, but it was thrown out by the House of Lords, and in 1894 the "Grand Old Man" of nineteenth-century British liberalism turned over the premiership to a younger and more imperialistic colleague, the Earl of Rosebery, and withdrew, at the age of eighty-four, to his country estate. Here he lingered on, charming visitors with his conversation and edifying them with his piety, and bursting into the public limelight once more, and for the last time, with a clarion call to Britain to aid Armenians against the Turks. He died in 1898.

In the general election of 1895, the coalition of Conservatives and Liberal Unionists won an overwhelming victory. Salisbury
Conserv-<br>ative<br>Rule and<br>Imperial<br>Expansion,<br>1895–1905
resumed the premiership and Joseph Chamberlain entered the cabinet as colonial secretary. In 1900 another election prolonged the coalition's sway, and, though Salisbury's age and infirmity caused him in 1902 to surrender the headship of the cabinet to his kinsman, Arthur J. Balfour, a placid academic person and former disciple of Lord Randolph Churchill, the regime endured until 1905. These ten years of Salisbury and Balfour government witnessed some social legislation, inspired mainly by Chamberlain and including, most notably, a "Workmen's Compensation Act," the insurance of workmen against accidents in certain specified trades. They also witnessed an important Education Act (1902), increasing the facilities for popular schooling and especially strengthening the church schools.

But what the decade preeminently witnessed was an extraordinary advance of nationalism and imperialism and a startling agitation for protective tariffs. It was the time when economic—and imperial—rivalry was fast developing among the Great Powers, when Great Britain was feeling acutely the industrial competition of Germany and the United States and was becoming alarmed by the ambitious projects of Russia in Asia, France in Africa, and Germany in the Near East and in the Pacific. It was the time, too, when Cecil Rhodes was dreaming about an Africa which would be solidly British, when Rudyard Kipling was composing poems about "the white man's burden" and "the manifest destiny" of imperial Britain, when Joseph Chamberlain was zealously enlisting popular and governmental support in furtherance of just such dreams and just such a destiny.

The Conservative government which busily concerned itself with imperial projects abroad neglected no opportunity to enhance patriotic pride at home. It celebrated the sixtieth anniversary of Queen Victoria's reign in 1897 as a magnificent national fête; and with emotional intensity, colorful processions, and a grandeur reminiscent of antique Rome, it buried the Queen in 1901 and crowned her son and successor, Edward VII (1901–1910). Edward, it is interesting to note, added to the sovereign's titles of "King of Great Britain and Ireland, Defender of the Faith, and Emperor of India," the new and appropriate title of "King of the British Dominions beyond the Seas."

In 1903 the restless Joseph Chamberlain began a campaign for "tariff reform." Alike as an imperialist and as a manufacturer, he felt that the circumstances of the twentieth century necessitated a departure from those "liberal" policies of the nineteenth century which had involved free trade, a comparatively slight expenditure on national armaments, and a progressive loosening of ties, economic and political, between the mother-country and her colonies. Instead, he would have Great Britain reestablish import duties on foodstuffs and manufactures, according preferential treatment to foodstuffs coming from other parts of the Empire as these lowered their tariffs on British manufactures. He prophesied that such all-around "imperial preference" would cement the Empire and profit both British industry and colonial agriculture. Simultaneously he called upon the colonies to share with the mother-country in the maintenance of armaments sufficient to assure the unity and integrity of the Empire as a whole. "Imperial preference," "imperial defense," and "imperial conference" were convenient slogans for ideas which were closely intertwined in Chamberlain's mind, and among these, the substitution by Great Britain of tariff protection for free trade was central.

Joseph Chamberlain had disrupted the Liberal party in 1886. In 1903–1905 he weakened, if he did not disrupt, the Conservative party. For, while most of the Liberal Unionists and a considerable number of their Conservative allies endorsed his tariff proposals, a somewhat larger number of Conservatives were so accustomed

to free trade or were so fearful of the effect of tariff protection in
raising the cost of living, and hence the wages of industrial and
agricultural laborers, that they denounced his proposals as un-
sound and "radical" and practically forced him out of the cabinet.
In vain, Balfour, the prime minister, tried to keep peace within
the coalition and prevent party warfare. There was a growing
enmity between "free traders" and "tariff reformers"; and at
length, late in 1905, Balfour resigned, and King Edward VII
invited the Liberal leader, Sir Henry Campbell-Bannerman, to
form a ministry. The ensuing general election, early in 1906, was
a "landslide" for the Liberal party, the acknowledged party of
free trade. Campbell-Bannerman had the biggest backing in the
country and in Parliament that any British minister had ever had.
Chamberlain was rebuked, tariff reform was shelved, and the
Conservative party was discredited. It was a peaceful kind of
democratic revolution.[1]

### 3. NATIONALIST IRELAND

For more than a century after the "Act of Union" of 1801, the
British Isles constituted a political unit—the "United Kingdom
of Great Britain and Ireland"—with a common sovereign and
with a single Parliament at Westminster. To the bulk of the
population of Great Britain, whether English, Welsh, or Scottish—and to a minority (the so-called "British garrison") in
Ireland, especially in Ulster—this centralized state appeared
natural and desirable, but not so to the large majority of native
Irishmen. And the intensification of British nationalism (and imperialism) after 1870 spurred the development of a rival, separatist nationalism in Ireland.

Irish nationalism had roots reaching into the distant past, and
prior to 1870 it had produced chronic protests and periodic revolts.[2] Then in the decade of the 1870's it received fresh impulse
from two new apostles. One was Charles Stewart Par-
**Parnell
and Davitt** nell, an "Anglo-Irish" landowner, aristocratic and Protestant, who imbibed from his mother, an American
woman, an almost fanatical hatred of England, and who, elected
to Parliament in 1875, organized among his Irish colleagues in the
House of Commons a political party—the Irish Nationalist party

[1] On the Liberal government after 1905, see below, pp. 318–330.
[2] See *Modern Europe to 1870*, pp. 480, 576–577, 702–703.

—with the purpose of insisting upon the reestablishment of "home rule" in Ireland.

The other apostle was Michael Davitt, an untutored Irish peasant, who, after his father's eviction from the land, had worked in cotton mills in England, participated in Fenian riots, and been jailed for seven years. Released in 1877, Davitt went to the United States, where, in concert with other exiles, he worked out a plan for organizing the Irish peasants into a "Land League" to agitate for radical agrarian reform. Then, returning to Britain, he prevailed upon Parnell to accept his ideas, and in 1879 he formally launched his Land League.

At once the Irish nationalist movement assumed new vigor and prominence. In the British Parliament of 1880, nearly eighty of the hundred Irish members belonged to Parnell's "home-rule" party and strictly obeyed his orders to render themselves such nuisances at Westminster, in obstructing debates, as might induce their British colleagues to heed their demand. At the same time, in Ireland, the peasant masses were being organized through Davitt's Land League as well as through Parnell's Nationalist party, to support the latter's political aims and to forward the former's economic purposes. And from Irish-Americans across the Atlantic was coming invaluable financial aid for the interconnected causes of home rule and land reform.

In 1881 Gladstone sought to halt the movement by putting through Parliament a new Land Act: fair rents were to be determined by a special land court; provision was made against unjust evictions and in behalf of free sale of **Land Act of 1881** land. But, though the land court reduced the average rents in Ireland by a fourth, Davitt and the Land League were by no means satisfied. They were now insisting that the peasants should own, rather than rent, the land. The Act of 1881, they said, was only a sop, and it did not touch the central problem of home rule. So both the Land Leaguers and the Nationalist party redoubled their protests, and in Ireland peaceful agitation was succeeded by systematic "boycotting" [1] and an epidemic of acts of violence. Gladstone's only response for the next five years was

---

[1] The word "boycott" was first employed in 1880, when a certain Captain Boycott, an agent for an Irish landlord, was made to suffer for refusing demands of the landlord's tenants. His life was threatened, his servants were compelled to leave him, his fences torn down, his letters intercepted, and his food supplies interfered with. In a word, he was "boycotted."

coercion. Ireland was put under martial law. Parnell was arrested and temporarily jailed. Davitt spent two years in prison. Rioting was sternly repressed.

In 1886, by a strange balancing of political forces in Great Britain, Gladstone had to choose whether he would retire from office or try to remain in office by conciliating the Irish Nationalists. He chose the latter alternative, and submitted to Parliament a home-rule bill acceptable to Parnell. It was a very modest measure, which would transfer Irish administration to an Irish ministry appointed by a separate local parliament at Dublin, but which would leave all "imperial" matters and most of the taxing power to the central Parliament at Westminster. Nevertheless it aroused furious opposition both in England and in Ulster. A large group of Liberals —the Liberal Unionists—deserted Gladstone, and violent resistance was threatened in Ulster. The bill was rejected in the House of Commons. Gladstone was compelled to retire from office. The Conservative party, foes of "home rule," dominated the British government during the next six years. And, as a seemingly final blow to the cause of "home rule," a domestic scandal clouded the career of Parnell and split his Nationalist followers into two quarreling factions.

*Gladstone's Home-Rule Bills*

In 1893 Gladstone, again in office, introduced into the Parliament at Westminster a second "home-rule" bill, which passed the Commons by a close vote but was rejected by the Lords. It was the last serious effort of England's veteran Liberal statesman. His colleagues advised him that it would be suicidal to their party to appeal to the country at large on the question, and he withdrew from public life. The extended sway of Conservatives and Liberal Unionists from 1895 to 1905 appeared to seal the doom of Irish hopes.

In fact, however, these very years of Unionist domination proved a fertile seed-time for a luxuriant new crop of Irish nationalism. Something of an agricultural revolution occurred in Ireland, attributable in part to the series of land acts which transformed numerous tenant-farmers into peasant proprietors, and in part to the tireless activities of Sir Horace Plunkett and the Irish Agricultural Organization Society which he founded in 1894 for the development of cooperative enterprises among Irish farmers. Peasant proprietor-

*Economic and Cultural Nationalism*

ship and the cooperative movement combined to improve the condition and to promote the solidarity of the rural masses.

Simultaneously, a literary renaissance began. In 1893 Douglas Hyde inaugurated a Gælic League for the preservation and extension of the native Irish language, and around it soon clustered a galaxy of poets, essayists, and dramatists. They wrote mainly in English, but they dealt largely with Irish themes, and, in conjunction with the Gælic League, they were intent upon reviving among the masses of the Irish people a knowledge of the national language and an appreciation of traditional Irish character, customs, and culture. Gradually it became fashionable for the younger generation to receive some instruction in Gælic.

Neither Plunkett's agricultural society nor Hyde's Gælic League was political in character or purpose. Both sought to weld together the whole Irish population, regardless of their religious affiliation or "racial" stock, and irrespective of their attitude toward "home rule." The one organization was economic; the other, cultural. Both Plunkett and Hyde were Protestants, and Plunkett in politics was a Unionist rather than a Nationalist. Unwittingly, nevertheless, the fruitful labors of these men served to stimulate a new kind of political nationalism which would triumph in Ireland in the twentieth century.

#### 4. THE BRITISH EMPIRE AND ITS SELF-GOVERNING DOMINIONS

The British Empire was a creation of modern times, almost wholly since the seventeenth century; and its greatest expansion and development occurred in the nineteenth century. The Napoleonic wars markedly enlarged it; and though from the 1840's to the 1870's English Liberals seemingly weakened its bonds by according self-government to important parts of it and by adopting a censorious attitude toward imperialism in general, it actually suffered no diminution in size, and at least in the case of India was expanded by conquests and solidified by the transference of control from commercial company to crown. After 1874, when the government of the mother-country passed from the liberal Gladstone to the imperialistic Disraeli and when the industrial advance was revitalizing overseas ambition, the British Empire grew by leaps and bounds. By the end of the nineteenth century, it embraced approximately a quarter of the Earth's land surface and a quarter of its population, repre-

*Growth of British Empire*

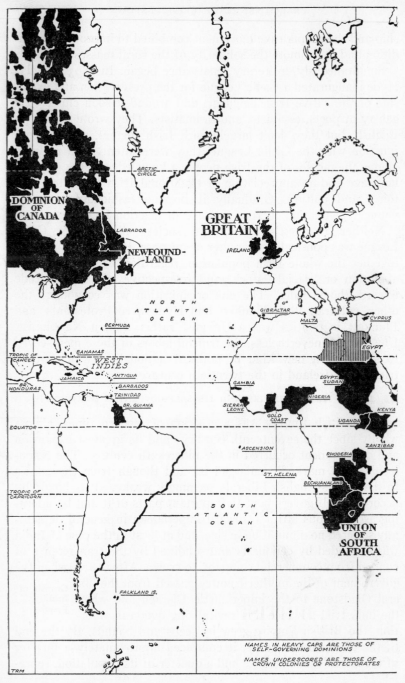

DOMINION
OF
CANADA

GREAT
BRITAIN

LABRADOR

NEWFOUND-
LAND

IRELAND

ARCTIC
CIRCLE

NORTH
ATLANTIC
OCEAN

GIBRALTAR

BERMUDA

MALTA

CYPRUS

TROPIC OF
CANCER

BAHAMAS

WEST
INDIES

JAMAICA

ANTIGUA

BARBADOS

TRINIDAD

BR. GUIANA

BR.
HONDURAS

GAMBIA

SIERRA
LEONE

GOLD
COAST

NIGERIA

EGYPT. SUDAN

EGYPT

UGANDA

KENYA

EQUATOR

ASCENSION

ZANZIBAR

RHODESIA

ST. HELENA

BECHUANALAND

TROPIC OF
CAPRICORN

SOUTH
ATLANTIC
OCEAN

UNION
OF
SOUTH
AFRICA

FALKLAND IS.

NAMES IN HEAVY CAPS ARE THOSE OF
SELF-GOVERNING DOMINIONS

NAMES UNDERSCORED ARE THOSE OF
CROWN COLONIES OR PROTECTORATES

TRM

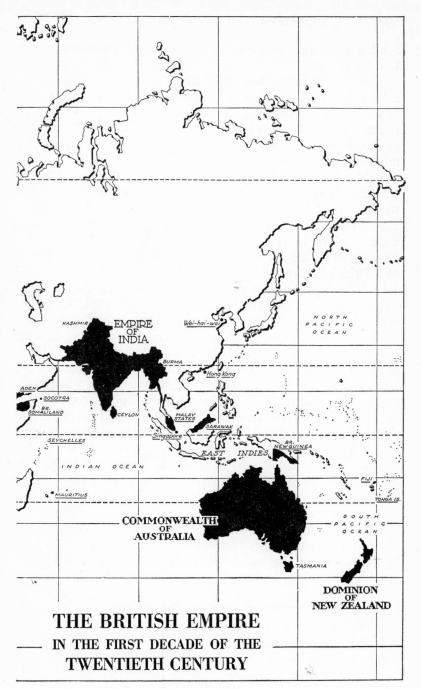

THE BRITISH EMPIRE
IN THE FIRST DECADE OF THE
TWENTIETH CENTURY

senting every race and every phase of culture from Cambridge to cannibalism.

This growth of the British Empire was partially a growth of such colonies as were peopled mainly by persons of European stock—Canada, Australia, New Zealand, South Africa. Much more, however, it was a growth of British political and economic sway over non-European peoples in Asia and Africa, a growth by military conquest or diplomatic negotiation.

British India was designated an "empire," and Queen Victoria was proclaimed Empress of it, in 1877; in the 1870's Baluchistan, to the west of it, was finally conquered and annexed, and in the 1880's Burma, to the east. The Malay states adjoining Singapore were obtained in 1874. From China were taken Hongkong in 1842 and Wei-hai-wei in 1898, and presently Tibet was treated as a British "sphere of influence." In the Pacific Ocean, the Fiji Islands were appropriated in 1874, southeastern New Guinea (Papua) in 1884, northern Borneo (Sarawak) in 1888, Tonga (or the Friendly Islands) in 1900. Nearer home, in the Mediterranean, Cyprus was occupied in 1878. And with amazing rapidity the British Empire expanded in Africa. Here, prior to 1880, it comprised only Cape Colony and Natal in the extreme south and a few trading posts on the west coast. After 1880, a large part of the continent came under British rule. Egypt was occupied in 1882, and protectorates were established in Bechuanaland in 1885, in Somaliland in 1887, in Zanzibar in 1890, in Uganda in 1896. Chartered commercial companies acquired Nigeria in 1886, British East Africa (Kenya) in 1888, and Rhodesia in 1889. Conquest was made of Zululand in 1887, of Ashanti in 1896, of the Egyptian Sudan in 1897, and of the Dutch republics of Transvaal and Orange Free State in 1902.

It was but natural that an Empire so large and heterogeneous should not be administered according to any one pattern. Indeed, it displayed, as it expanded, a growing differentiation in government, so that in the latter part of the nineteenth century at least three distinct types of dependency were generally recognized: (1) the self-governing colonies, or "dominions"; (2) a miscellany of crown colonies, naval stations, and "protectorates"; and (3) the so-called "empire" of India.

The self-governing colonies, or "Dominions," included by 1902 a trifle more than half of the territory in the British Empire. It would be most misleading, however, to infer that half of the Empire possessed the right of self-government; for in respect of population the Dominions constituted only a twentieth **Self-** part of it. Self-government was a special privilege con- **Governing** ferred by Great Britain upon a small minority of **Dominions** colonial subjects, not a natural right granted freely to all. It is noteworthy, moreover, that the privileged minority was almost exclusively of European stock, that the colonies enjoying home rule were precisely the colonies in which relatively large numbers of Britishers had settled—Canada, Newfoundland, Australia, New Zealand, and South Africa.

When Queen Victoria ascended the throne in 1837, there was no self-governing colony in the British Empire. When her son, Edward VII, died in 1910, there were twenty-one.

As Canada had been the first colony to obtain self-government,[1] so also it was the pioneer in another important movement, the formation of confederations among self-governing colo- **Canada** nies. In 1867 the colonies of Nova Scotia and New Brunswick joined with Quebec and Ontario to form a confederation styled the "Dominion of Canada." The Dominion was technically created by enactment of the British Parliament at Westminster—the British North America Act of 1867—but the plan had originated in Canada and been formulated by a convention at Quebec in 1864. The government of the Dominion was modeled after that of the mother-country, with a Governor-General acting for the monarch, a Senate in place of the House of Lords, and a democratically elected House of Commons, to which the cabinet of ministers was responsible. Although each of the four provinces preserved its separate legislature, there was little question of "states' rights" in Canada. With the terrible example close at hand of the United States in civil war over "states' rights," the framers of the Canadian constitution restricted the powers of the several provinces.

For a long time the dominant political party in Canada was the Conservative, strongly British in sympathy, though resolved to promote an economic nationalism within the Dominion; and its leader, Sir John Macdonald, was prime minister from 1867 to his death in 1891 (excepting the five years 1873–1878). The Dominion organized its own militia and police, civil service, and

[1] See *Modern Europe to 1870*, pp. 652–653.

systems of banking, currency, and posts. It established a protective tariff for the fostering of Canadian industries. It promoted
agricultural settlement in the great Northwest.

The growth of the Dominion was remarkably swift. First, from
the Hudson's Bay Company were purchased extensive lands from
which the new province of Manitoba was carved (1870). Then
British Columbia (1871) and Prince Edward Island (1873) were
brought into the confederation. Finally a decree of 1878 proclaimed that the Dominion of Canada should have jurisdiction
over all British territory north of the United States, with the
exception of Newfoundland (and its dependency of Labrador),
which remained a separate colony until 1949. The fertile prairies
and rich mines of western Canada attracted a steady stream of
settlers, particularly after the construction of the Canadian
Pacific Railway (1886), some from Great Britain and others from
the United States, and the ensuing economic development of the
West received political recognition by the creation (1905) of two
new prairie provinces, Alberta and Saskatchewan.

Meanwhile, following the death of Sir John Macdonald, the
Conservative party declined and was supplanted in power by the
Liberal party, whose gifted leader, Sir Wilfred Laurier, held the
premiership continuously from 1896 to 1910. Laurier was a native
of Quebec, French in nationality and Catholic in religion, and
he proved that a French Canadian could be as loyal both to the
British Empire and to the Dominion of Canada as anyone of
British extraction. While he lowered the protective tariff and
sought to promote closer commercial relations with the United
States, he was a staunch supporter of British imperial interests.
He sympathized with Joseph Chamberlain's proposals for "imperial preference," and he dispatched a Canadian army to South
Africa to help the English in the Boer War.

Notwithstanding the evident success of the confederating movement in Canada, the Australian colonies hesitated three decades
before they finally decided to form a similar union. There were
**Australia**   five of these (Victoria, Queensland, South Australia,
Western Australia, and Tasmania), besides the original
colony of New South Wales, which had been founded as a penal
station back in 1788 and had since developed into a free, prosperous community. In the early part of the nineteenth century
the introduction of sheep-raising, and in the middle of the century

the discovery of gold, attracted British emigrants to the Australian colonies and enabled them to mature rapidly.

They would doubtless have been federated as early as 1885, had they not been divided on the tariff question. While New South Wales clung stubbornly to free trade, the younger colonies were reluctant to surrender the revenues which they obtained from their customs duties. But the advantages to be gained from confederation—especially the advantage of concerted action in excluding Chinese immigrants and maintaining British supremacy in the South Pacific against French and German intruders—finally outweighed the disadvantages. After long discussion, the colonists agreed upon a plan which was enacted by the British Parliament as the Commonwealth of Australia Act (1900). New Zealand, physically separated from Australia by 1,200 miles of water, refused to join the Commonwealth, just as the island of Newfoundland had held aloof from the Dominion of Canada.

The six Australian colonies became states in the Commonwealth.[1] The federal or Commonwealth legislature, like the American Congress, was composed of a Senate, in which each state had the same number of seats, and a House of Representatives, in which the seats were distributed according to population. The High Court of the Commonwealth, like the American Supreme Court, was the guardian and interpreter of the constitution. Besides, by delegating only specified powers to their federal government and reserving all others to the respective states, the Australians imitated the political structure of the United States rather than the more centralized system of Canada. In two important respects, however, the Australian Commonwealth was essentially British. First, its highest magistrate was a Governor-General, who, like the monarch whom he represented, reigned but did not rule. Second, its cabinet of ministers was responsible to the parliament rather than to the chief magistrate. Australia preceded both Great Britain and the United States in the enfranchisement of women.

An outstanding feature of Australian development was the rapidity and extent of its industrialization and urbanization. Sheep-farming and agriculture in general, which, along with mining, had originally been the basis of the continent's economic and

---

[1] Subsequently the Commonwealth took over the government of two "territories" —Papua or British New Guinea (1905) and Northern Australia (1911).

social life, were eclipsed after 1871 by manufacturing and commercial enterprise. One result was that, while the population tripled between 1871 and 1914, the country as a whole remained sparsely settled and urban centers absorbed the entire increment. Another result was that the governments of the several states, and the government of the Commonwealth after its creation in 1900, had to cope with a serious land problem and with even more serious labor problems.

The latter were made acute by increasingly radical demands from the masses of urban workmen. After a furious but futile fight for the principle of the "closed shop" (in a widespread strike of 1890), workers became convinced that they must use the ballot box as well as the trade union to better their lot. Labor parties consequently sprang up in the several states and demanded socialistic legislation. Between 1890 and 1910 the state of Victoria, coming under the control of the Labor party, enacted a series of laws providing, among other things, for the creation of trade boards to regulate the wages and hours of industrial labor. Labor influence and legislation soon spread to Queensland, South Australia, and New South Wales.

The Commonwealth government followed the lead of the states, establishing in 1904 a federal arbitration court for the settlement of interstate industrial disputes, and in 1908 a system of old-age pensions. In the general election of 1910 the Labor party swept the country, and their leader, Andrew Fisher, a former Scottish coal miner, formed a ministry which, with a brief interruption and some changes in personnel, endured for the next seven years. It failed to induce the people to pass constitutional amendments which would have enabled it to forward its socialistic program, but it succeeded in introducing, in 1911, compulsory military training for all young Australian men—a significant innovation in the army traditions of the British Empire.

New Zealand, the Australasian colony which remained apart from the Commonwealth, had been self-governing since 1856, and **New Zealand** in 1907 was styled a "Dominion" and accorded equal rank with the confederations of Canada and Australia.

Its internal development was strikingly similar to neighboring Australia's. There was a similar increase of population, with the majority settled in cities. There was similar legislation of a democratic and socialistic sort. In respect of this legislation, New Zealand was even more radical than Australia. Not only were women enfranchised; not only were old-age pensions provided, workmen insured against accident, and special courts set up to arbitrate disputes between employers and employees; but the government, in the spirit of "state socialism," undertook to own and operate railways, life- and fire-insurance, and coal mines. Nor was New Zealand much if any behind Australia in adopting the principle of compulsory military training, and in evidencing both a proud nationalism of its own and an intense loyalty to the Empire.

In South Africa, two grave problems developed in the nineteenth century. One was racial, arising from the fact that white settlers of European stock were greatly outnumbered by native Negroes and colored immigrants from India. **South Africa** The other was nationalistic, resulting from rivalry among the white settlers between British and Dutch. For a long time the second of these problems bulked bigger than the first, for both Dutch and British resolutely maintained "white supremacy" and sternly repressed the blacks.

Side by side were two colonies dominated by the British—Cape Colony and Natal—and two republics dominated by the Dutch (the so-called Boers)—the Transvaal and the Orange River Free State. Between Boers and British there had been armed conflict in the 1850's,[1] and, following a reassertion of British claims to sovereignty over the Transvaal in 1877, hostilities were renewed. In 1881 the defeat of a British force at Majuba Hill induced the pacific Gladstone to recognize anew the virtual independence of the Transvaal.

Elated by their success, the Boers increased their truculence toward the British, and some of their leaders dreamed of uniting the Dutch-speaking minorities in Cape Colony and Natal with the forces of the two republics in a war to make all South Africa Dutch. On the other hand, British imperial ambitions were stimulated by the activities of Joseph Chamberlain in England and by the sensational projects and achievements of Cecil Rhodes in Africa. Relations of the Boers with the British were not improved when thousands of British fortune hunters and adventurers flocked into the Transvaal following the discovery there (in the

[1] On developments in South Africa prior to 1870, see *Modern Europe*, pp. 66, 336, 589, 696.

Rand region, 1886) of the world's richest gold mines, or when the British shut off the Transvaal from all access to the sea by annexing Zululand and the territory just south of Delagoa Bay (which was Portugese), or when Dr. Jameson, an associate of Rhodes and a fanatical imperialist, led a filibustering expedition into the Transvaal (1895) with the avowed intention of over-throwing its Boer government and incorporating it in the British Empire.

The "Jameson raid" failed of its immediate purpose, and its leader, captured by the Boers and turned over to the British government, underwent a brief imprisonment at London. But the raid greatly embittered the situation in South Africa. Jameson was lauded by Britishers in measure as he was reprobated by Boers. From 1895 to 1899 the Transvaal government, headed by Paul Kruger, a hardened old Dutch pioneer, assumed an ever more implacable attitude toward the British and especially to-ward the "Uitlanders," the British immigrant miners within the Transvaal. These immigrants were very vocal in criticism of the oligarchical character of the Transvaal government and stentorian in demands for recognition of their political rights under it. The refusal of the Boers to enfranchise the "Uitlanders" (except after seven years' residence) was the grievance which these most fully exploited.

In 1899, the republics of the Transvaal and the Orange River Free State, feeling that peaceful measures had failed to check British pressure and aggression, formed an alliance and went to war with Great Britain. At the outset, the Boers took **Boer War** the offensive, invading Natal and striking at the Kim-berley diamond fields in Cape Colony, and they won several brilliant victories. Their armed forces were not large, probably fewer than 40,000 men, but they had resourceful commanders in Louis Botha, Jan Smuts, and Christian De Wet, and the rank and file knew how to get about the country and to shoot straight. In time, however, they were borne down by weight of numbers. The regular British army was reinforced by volunteers from England and Scotland and by detachments from Canada, Aus-tralia, and New Zealand, until the British had some 350,000 men in the field under the command of Lord Roberts and Lord Kitchener. In a year the Boers seemed to have lost the war: they were compelled to retire from Natal and Cape Colony;

Pretoria, the capital of Transvaal, fell; President Kruger fled to Europe; and the British annexation of both the Transvaal and the Orange River Free State was proclaimed. Nevertheless, Boer resistance was not yet broken, and two years of fierce and trying guerilla warfare ensued. Not until May 1902, by the treaty of Vereeniging, did the Boer generals agree to lay down their arms and then on condition that the British government should respect the Dutch language in South Africa and grant self-government to the former Dutch republics. That was done in 1906–1907.

In 1909 the Union of South Africa was formed, modeled after the Dominion of Canada, and including Cape Colony, Natal, the Transvaal, and the Orange Free State. In a sense, the **Union of South Africa** Union was a triumph for the Boers. They outnumbered the British as a whole, and inasmuch as they enjoyed equal political rights with the British they elected a majority of the members of the Union parliament, and one of their number, General Louis Botha, became the first premier of the Union. Botha loyally accepted the new order. While safeguarding Boer interests in respect of language, education, agriculture, and the subject native races, and maintaining that South Africa was a "nation," he was conciliatory toward the British inhabitants of the Union and willing to keep it within the British Empire. He had some difficulty with extremists on both sides, but the masses acquiesced in his policy of moderation.

Thus by 1910 Great Britain was mistress—or ally—of five "colonial nations"—the Union of South Africa, the Commonwealth of Australia, the Dominions of Canada, New- **Britain and the Dominions** foundland, and New Zealand—whose territorial extent and natural resources promised them a bright future. Politically, the ties between them and the mother-country were loosening. They managed their own internal affairs as they saw fit through parliaments and ministries of their own choosing, and the Governors-General whom the British government at Westminster sent out to reside in their midst were symbols, rather than directors, of imperial rule. The mother-country still claimed certain rights over the Dominions: to pass upon their constitutions; to veto acts of their parliaments; to control their foreign relations; and to decide in its own Privy Council at London judicial cases which might be appealed from their law courts. In practice, however, the British government interfered less and less with the legislative freedom of the Dominions and even permitted them on occasion to negotiate treaties with foreign countries.

Economically, too, the self-governing Dominions went their own way, sometimes against the interests and policies of the mother-country. To forward their own industrial development, they levied tariffs on imports from foreign countries and likewise from Great Britain. To raise the standard of living of their citizens, as well as to insure that they would remain "white" countries, they imposed restrictions on immigration, particularly of Orientals, even where the immigrants might be from British dependencies such as India and Hongkong.

Despite the growing political and economic cleavage between mother-country and self-governing colonies—or, as some persons said, *because* of the lessening sources of friction—there was a marked increase of sentimental devotion on the part of these colonies to the British Empire. Significant of the new spirit of voluntary, but very real, cooperation was the fact that Canada could have a French prime minister in Laurier, Australia a socialistic premier in Fisher, and South Africa a Dutch premier in Botha, and yet all be proud to own themselves "British."

Various proposals were made, especially in England, for establishing some "system" of inter-dominion relationship. One of the most celebrated was Joseph Chamberlain's triple scheme of "imperial conference, imperial preference, and imperial defense." Formal imperial conferences were actually inaugurated in London in 1887, and henceforth, at more or less regular intervals, the prime ministers of the several Dominions met personally with the prime minister of the United Kingdom and discussed matters of mutual concern.

"Imperial preference" was recognized by some of the Dominions in lowering their tariffs on commodities imported from Great Britain, though the rigid adherence of the mother-country to free trade prevented her from favoring colonial imports and hence militated against the full fruition of "imperial preference." "Imperial defense" remained a matter of voluntary action on the part of the several self-governing sections of the British Empire; in peace times it was sluggish, but at critical moments, as in the Boer War or in the later World Wars, it was remarkably cooperative and prompt.

## 5. COLONIES, PROTECTORATES, AND THE INDIAN EMPIRE

In addition to the self-governing Dominions which we have just been discussing, the British Empire embraced a miscellany of crown colonies, naval stations, and protectorates, that were as far-flung and considerably more numerous but which were inhabited chiefly by non-European stocks and were ruled more or less despotically by agents of the British government.

The "crown colonies" represented a continuation of the type of colonial administration which had flourished in the earlier days of the British Empire, before the revolt of the United States and the grant of self-government to Canada. **Crown Colonies** They were presided over by governors who were named by, and responsible to, the colonial ministry in London and who might be "advised," but could hardly be dictated to, by assemblies or councils elected or appointed from British residents in the several colonies.

The oldest group of crown colonies comprised the remaining British possessions in tropical America—British Honduras, British Guiana, and West Indian islands—the large majority of whose inhabitants were descendants of Negro slaves; and the West African coastal lands (almost wholly Negro) which Britain had held since the eighteenth century—Gold Coast, Gambia, and Sierra Leone. As crown colonies were administered, also, the series of naval stations which Britain had gradually acquired in the Mediterranean—Gibraltar, Malta, and Cyprus. Of these, the native population was respectively Spanish, Italian, and Greek, and at least in the cases of Malta and Cyprus there was such a lively local nationalism that the British government thought it unsafe to entrust them with self-government. Among still other crown colonies were Ceylon, Hongkong, the Straits Settlements, the Falkland Islands, and British East Africa (or Kenya).

The "protectorates" represented, as a rule, larger areas, more recently acquired and less civilized, in which native princes were allowed to retain the trappings of power but were **Protectorates** obliged to exercise it in harmony with instructions or "advice" of a resident British agent. In some instances, a crown colony acquired a protectorate over its hinterland; such was the case with the crown colonies in West Africa. In other instances, a commercial company, specially chartered by the

British government, gained and exercised a protectorate. Such was the case with Cecil Rhodes's "British South African Company" (chartered in 1898), which, by virtue of wars and treaties with native chieftains, opened up and actually governed the huge territory of Rhodesia. Such, too, was the case with the "Royal Niger Company" (chartered in 1886) whose activities added the equally huge tract of Nigeria to the British Empire. In still other instances, protectorates were established directly and exercised from the outset by the British government. Such was the case with the Federated Malay States, with Sarawak (whose rajah was an Englishman), with Tonga, with Zanzibar and Uganda and British Central Africa (renamed Nyasaland in 1907).

A kind of informal protectorate Great Britain established in Egypt. This country, in theory, was still a vassal state of the Ottoman Empire, but in the first half of the nineteenth century an ambitious and bellicose Turkish governor (or pasha), Mehemet Ali, had wrung from the government at Constantinople the recognition of a privileged position for Egypt and for himself and his family.

**Egypt**

For a time, under Mehemet Ali's grandson, Ismail (1863–1879), Egypt appeared to be advancing toward full independence and national well-being. Ismail, with the consent of the Ottoman Sultan, assumed the title of "Khedive" (1867); and, full of admiration for European material civilization, he labored to "modernize" his country. He remodeled the administrative system. He promoted cotton culture. He employed European engineers to build railways, telegraph lines, a breakwater at Alexandria, and harbor works at Suez. He subsidized the researches of European scholars in Egyptian antiquities and founded a museum at his capital city of Cairo. In 1869 he celebrated with gala fêtes the opening of the Suez Canal, which had been financed by a French company (with liberal aid from the Khedive) and constructed by a distinguished French engineer, Ferdinand de Lesseps.

Unfortunately, all these undertakings were very expensive. Ismail was notoriously prodigal, while the mass of Egyptians were notoriously poor. The result was a rapid accumulation of indebtedness to foreign bankers, especially French and British; a crushing burden of taxation on the Egyptian peasants in order to meet the interest-charges to foreigners; and, eventually, national bankruptcy and foreign intervention.

In 1875 Ismail sought relief by selling to the British government for about twenty million dollars the block of stock which he owned in the Suez Canal Company. The canal thus came permanently under British control, but the financial relief to Egypt was transitory. In 1876 Ismail submitted Egyptian finances to a "dual control" of British and French agents, and when, three years later, he tried to get rid of the foreigners, he was deposed. His successor had to submit anew to the "dual control," but some of his subjects resented it and in 1882, under the leadership of Ahmed Arabi, they revolted. The French declined to use force against the rebels, but a British fleet bombarded Alexandria and a British army occupied the country.

From 1882 Egypt was virtually a British dependency. It continued to have a native Khedive, but a British army remained and British will was law. There can be no doubt that under the guidance of British "advisors," notably Lord Cromer and Lord Kitchener, many helpful reforms were instituted. Finances were gradually put on a solid footing. The administration of justice was bettered. The Egyptian Sudan, long a seat of disorder, brigandage, and religious fanaticism, was reconquered and policed. Important irrigation works were undertaken, culminating in the construction of the magnificent Assuan dam. Moreover, an advisory assembly was created in 1883, and in 1913 it was intrusted with limited legislative powers. Notwithstanding such benefits, many Egyptians, particularly young men who had studied in Europe and learned lessons in nationalism, were discontented. Arabi's insurrection of 1882 had been crushed, but the echoes of his slogan, "Egypt for the Egyptians," resounded.

India was the greatest of all British imperial possessions in the nineteenth century. Within it, at the close of the century, were four-fifths of the population of the whole British Empire. For every square mile of territory in the **India** United Kingdom, India could show fifteen; and as the British Isles had only 45 million inhabitants as against India's 315 million, every man, woman, and child in the former might be thought of as having seven subjects in the latter. And no other country in the world purchased so large an amount of British merchandise as did India.

The foundation of British supremacy in India had been laid,

and much of its superstructure reared, by a succession of mer-
chant-adventurers and empire-builders of the English East
India Company during the seventeenth, eighteenth, and early
nineteenth centuries.[1] Not until the Sepoy Mutiny of 1857 and
the resulting passage of the "Better Government of India Act"
by the British Parliament in 1858 did the East India Company
cease to function and the British government assume direct and
full responsibility for India. Eighteen years later—in 1876—
Parliament enacted that British India should be designated an
"Empire" and the British sovereign should be styled "Empress
(or Emperor) of India."

British India was extraordinarily heterogeneous in geography,
race, language, religion, and culture. It was truly an "empire"
and not a "national state." Geographically it comprised four
fairly distinctive areas: the triangular peninsula-plateau of
southern India (usually called the Deccan); the broad belt of
lowlands forming the Ganges and Indus river valleys to the
north of the Deccan; the mountainous region still farther north
reaching into the Himalayas and extending westward past the
frontiers of Afghanistan into Baluchistan; and the northeastern
area of Burma.

Racial divisions corresponded roughly with the geographical,
the so-called Dravidians dwelling in the Deccan, the Hindu
Aryans in the lowland belt, the descendants of Moslem invaders
(Arab, Afghan, and Persian) in the northern hill region, and
Mongoloid peoples in Burma. In many localities, however, different races lived side by side in neighborly hostility, and everywhere was plentiful evidence of racial intermixture.

Religious differences and antagonisms accentuated the racial
and cultural contrasts. About two-thirds of the entire population adhered to the Brahmanic or Hindu religion, with its poly-
theism, its sacred laws, its distinctive ceremonies and pilgrimages,
and its rigid caste system. Three sizable religious groups derived
originally from Hinduism but had long been quite separate:
Buddhists, numbering about eleven million, chiefly in Burma;
Jains, a million and a quarter, recruited principally from the
commercial class in cities on the Malabar coast; and Sikhs,
some three million, compactly settled in that part of the Indus

---

[1] On the history of the British in India during these centuries, see *Modern Europe to 1870*, pp. 343–344, 349, 353–355, 356–362.

valley known as the Punjab. Over against these was a fairly large number of militant Moslems—some seventy million—whose stronghold was in northern India, though influential Moslem princes were to be found elsewhere in the country. Among Moslems, and even more among Hindus, were innumerable sects; while the religious hodge-podge was increased by the activity of Christian missionaries, Catholic and Protestant, whose converts by 1914 totaled about five million.

To the confusion of religion was added the confusion of language. Over two hundred languages were spoken in British India, and while three-fourths of the whole population employed Aryan languages derived from ancient Sanskrit (akin to Latin, German, and Slavic), there were wide dialect differences among them, and, in addition, certain languages of basically different derivation, such as the Dravidian (spoken by sixty million persons in the Deccan) and the Tibeto-Chinese (in Burma).

It was but natural, in the circumstances of divergent languages, religions, races, and geographical features, and in the face of a widespread and deeply rooted caste system, that cultural contrasts should be sharp. Some natives were highly cultured. Others were extremely primitive. Some, among the Moslem aristocracy and the Hindu upper classes, were inordinately wealthy and lived a life of luxury. Others, the vast majority of the native population, worked hard in field or shop for bare subsistence and had first-hand experience with poverty and famine.

In the realm of politics, even after the British had created their "Empire of India," governmental uniformity was notably lacking. There were two major parts of British India —two major methods by which the British government dealt with the heterogeneous country. On the one hand was the "Empire of India" in its technical sense, the portion ruled directly by British officials. It embraced three-fifths of the area and seven-ninths of the population of British India, and was divided into nine provinces, comparable in size with countries in Europe, each presided over by a governor and all subject to central direction by the "Viceroy of India" named by the government at Westminster and responsible in turn to the "Secretary of State for India" in the British ministry. The Viceroy was practically a dictator, and through the governors in the several provinces and also through a vast staff of civil and military

*Indian Empire and Native States*

officials he ruled the "Empire." On the other hand were some 600 "native states," including several fairly large ones [1] and many very small ones, each governed directly and usually quite despotically by a Hindu or Moslem prince (with some such title as "rajah" or "gaekwar"), though all these princes were obliged to acknowledge British suzerainty, to live on friendly terms with the "Empire of India," and to submit to "supervision" by the Viceroy.

As a part of the British Empire, India experienced an internal peace and an economic development which it had not known for centuries. The British civil service was generally of a high order of intelligence and integrity, and British officials displayed no little resourcefulness in coping with the traditional animosities and conflicting interests of the vast and heterogeneous native people. Roads and railways were built, agricultural production was stimulated, industrial machinery was introduced, harbor works were undertaken, and throughout the huge territory sanitation and public health were promoted and some educational opportunities provided. An Indian army was organized with British officers and utilized to protect as well as to extend India.

Nevertheless it seemed as though the more the British tried to do for the well-being of India, the more the natives found fault. To be sure, most of the princes, favored by British rule, were undoubtedly devoted to it, and the vast masses of the ignorant peasantry were as indifferent to it as they had been to the less benevolent despotism of native potentates. But many of the younger generation of Indian intellectuals, especially those who were educated at European schools in their own country or at universities in England, gradually adopted and propagated a kind of nationalism. Why not India for the Indians? Why not a welding together, through their own efforts, of Hindus and Moslems, of Aryans and Dravidians, of high-born and low-born castes, of rich and poor, of the cultured and the untutored, to fashion a real and free Indian nation? Why not a fairly rapid transition to self-government? In 1885 ardent nationalists formed an "All-India Congress" whose subsequent sessions were ever more largely attended and ever more vociferous in demanding self-government.

**Rise of Indian Nationalism**

---

[1] Such as Hyderabad, Mysore, Kashmir, Gwalior, and Baroda. The Himalayan native states of Nepal and Bhutan, also fairly large, were recognized by the British as fully independent though they were in practical alliance with British India.

Eventually in 1909, in an attempt to reconcile the nationalist Indian desire for self-government with the British determination to rule, the British Parliament enacted an "Indian Councils Act," providing for native election (by a very restricted suffrage) of a minority of members of the advisory councils which were set up in six of the nine provinces and of the "legislative council" which would advise the Viceroy. This act did not satisfy the Indian nationalists. They termed it a sham and redoubled their agitation for radical constitutional reform. To stifle the rancorous criticism, the government curtailed the freedom of the press, censored the mails, and forbade "seditious" meetings. Extremists replied with attempts at rioting and terrorism. Opposition was undoubtedly intensifying.

We must not forget that important economic considerations strengthened the determination of Great Britain to retain India and to exercise real authority over it. India was Britain's largely an agricultural country, a cheap producer of Economic foodstuffs and raw materials for export to Britain and Status a big consumer of manufactured goods imported from Britain. Of the country's rapidly growing trade, which increased fivefold from the Mutiny in 1857 to the World War in 1914, Great Britain had almost a monopoly. On the eve of the war, the United Kingdom exported to India ten times as much merchandise as did the rival industrial nation of Germany; and three-fourths of India's seaborne commerce was carried under the British flag. British shipping interests were naturally eager to maintain British rule.

So, too, were many industrialists in Great Britain, particularly in the cotton and iron industries, who derived profits from the Indian market. There was also a large number of Britishers who drew their livelihood from civil or military service in India; they were likely to be apologists and propagandists for the British regime. There was an even larger number of Britishers who invested savings, much or little, in Indian government securities (of which some 600 million dollars' worth were held in England), or in private enterprises in India.

These investors, together with all the other interested Britishers, were prone to dilate upon the civilizing "mission" of Great Britain in India. Some persuaded themselves—and others—that Britain was a kindly schoolmistress, teaching material well-being and the higher Anglo-Saxon virtues to her class of rather back-

ward Hindu students and preparing them for the noble but difficult task of establishing a parliamentary government and a material prosperity according to English models. It should be remarked, however, that Britain as yet appeared more anxious to
promote its own economic interests than to educate the native
population. The British "Empire of India" spent almost sixty
million dollars on railways and canals and almost a hundred
million on army, but only thirty million on schools. It was hardly
surprising, therefore, that of the total population of the immense
Indian Empire more than 94 per cent could neither read nor
write.

On the whole, nevertheless, Great Britain was enviably successful throughout the nineteenth century in gaining and holding
overseas dominion. As Britain was the workshop of the world, so
its Empire was the premier economic and political association.

### 6. BRITAIN AND THE EUROPEAN STATE SYSTEM

British preeminence was primarily industrial and maritime and
was conditioned by Great Britain's relationship to the European
state system. At least superficially this state system remained
about what it had been since the seventeenth century: a congeries
of sovereign powers, theoretically equal in right and dignity and
regularly maintaining formal diplomatic relations with one another as professed members of a "European family of nations."
Actually, of course, the powers were very unequal and diverse.
A select number, distinguished from the others by superior resources and armaments, were customarily styled *great powers*.

These great powers had not always been the same. Their
ranking had fluctuated according to military successes or reverses. Some of those in early modern times, like Spain and
the Ottoman Empire, had subsequently declined to the status of
**European** second-rate powers, while others, like Prussia and
**Balance of** Russia, had correspondingly risen. But whatever their
**Power** number and individual strength at any given time,
they always tended toward a "balance of power." If one became
too aggressive or expansive, others would oppose it.

A central feature of Britain's foreign policy had long been the
maintenance of a balance which would prevent any Continental
power from dominating Europe or the high seas. It was exemplified in successive struggles, from the sixteenth to the nineteenth

century, with Spain, with the Dutch Netherlands, and, longest of all, with France.

In the latter part of the nineteenth century, and particularly as an outcome of nationalist wars between 1859 and 1871, a noteworthy shift occurred in the balance of power. For some time previously, Great Britain and France had cooperated in checking Russia, with Austria and Prussia neutral. Now France as well as Austria suffered defeat and humiliation at the hands of Prussia, with the result that Italy, through its political unification, emerged as a new great power, while Prussia merged its might in a still mightier German Empire. Henceforth this Germany held a primacy among the Continental great powers, and Berlin succeeded Vienna and Paris as the military and diplomatic center of Europe.

Both Britain and Russia were neutral during the stirring events of the 1860's, but neither was indifferent to the consequent shift of the European balance. Both displayed a special eagerness to secure new laurels comparable with what Germany had just obtained. Russia sought them in renewed extension of its influence and sway in the Balkans and in Asia; Great Britain, in the big new wave of overseas imperialism which supplanted "little England" Liberals with expansionist Conservatives and raised Queen Victoria to the dignity of Empress of India. Thus the rivalry between Britain and Russia became increasingly imperialistic, and it was complicated by efforts of Austria and France to obtain compensation for their recent losses in Europe by embarking upon imperialist enterprises of their own: Austria in the Balkans, in competition with Russia; and France in Africa, in competition with Great Britain.

In later chapters we shall follow in detail the development of international relations after 1871.[1] Here it suffices to point out that throughout the latter part of the nineteenth century, and into the twentieth, the preeminent position which Great Britain held in industry, commerce, wealth, and overseas imperial- **Britain's** ism enabled and encouraged its government, whether **"Splendid** Liberal or Conservative, to pursue a policy of "splendid **Isolation"** isolation" from entangling alliances with other great powers. During most of the time, Britain was less concerned with the military might of the new German Empire and the defensive

[1] See below, pp. 134–138, 264–267, 306–317, 352–356.

# EUROPE IN 1871

alliance it formed with Austria and Italy than with the imperial ambitions of Russia in Asia and of France in Africa. Only when Germany added to its military primacy on the Continent a serious rivalry in naval power and overseas empire-building, and when, during the Boer War, the Continental great powers concerted together to limit British expansion, only then did Great Britain abandon isolation and negotiate agreements with France and Russia calculated to restore a balance of power. This did not occur until the twentieth century, and then it proved a prelude to world war.

Meanwhile, Great Britain exerted a remarkable influence on the internal development of Europe and its state system in two important respects. First, it furnished the model and set the pace for well-nigh revolutionary growth of machine-industry all over the Continent (and in America and Japan), and its material wealth came to be generally regarded as the chief measure of "progress." Every "progressive" nation endeavored to strengthen itself, in imitation of Britain, by promoting large-scale industrialization, domestic and foreign trade, and capitalistic enterprise.

**British Prestige: Economic**

Second, most peoples abroad looked upon Britain as the exemplar of what was highest and best in political achievement. It seemed to have happily solved all those governmental problems which had caused so much domestic strife and so many rebellions in the rest of Europe prior to 1871, and to have solved them by peaceful evolution rather than through violent revolution. No "French Revolution," with its divisive consequences, had happened in Britain, nor any such revolutionary disturbance as shook many other European states in 1830 and still more in 1848. As late as 1871 Paris experienced a bloody insurrection, but not London.

**Political**

No wonder that the British were widely thought of as possessing a political genius! No wonder that other nations perceived in the British political system the means of peacefully reconciling liberty and authority, monarchical and constitutional government, aristocracy and democracy. By 1871, this British system, with its complement of a bill of rights, a king who reigned but did not rule, a popularly elected parliament which levied the taxes and made the laws, and a ruling ministry responsible to the parliament and manned alternately by liberals and conservatives, was consciously copied, in full or in part, by almost every country of western and central Europe, as well as by the self-governing dominions of the British Empire.

With the spread of industrialization and constitutional government, the European states showed during the thirty years after 1871 a stability and a domestic peace which they had **Apparent** scarcely had in previous years of the nineteenth cen- **Stability** tury. The earlier bitter feud between "Left" and **on the** "Right" was assuaged, as liberals became more con- **Continent** servative, and conservatives more liberal. True, minorities of radical Marxian socialists were vocally critical of existing government, and their numbers grew, but they attempted no revolt, preferring to adopt the party name of "social democrats" and to act accordingly.

There can be no doubt that in the latter part of the nineteenth century, most European states were more governed and better governed than at any earlier period. Back in the eighteenth century, at the time of the "enlightened despots," for example, the functions of state government had been relatively few and inadequately discharged. Public finance had been disorderly; and state taxes, inequitably levied and badly collected, had barely sufficed to maintain the officials, the court, and the army. The state government as such had little surplus to spend on public works, schools, or social betterment.

Now, however, industrialization provided greatly increased wealth and hence greatly enlarged tax resources for the state; and the democratizing of politics led to increased expenditure for broadened state functions. In Great Britain, the earlier doctrine of liberal economists that the state should be only a "passive policeman," was gradually superseded by popular demands that the state should utilize its magnified resources not only to strengthen its armaments but to promote a wide range of social benefits; and such demands bore especially significant fruitage on the Continent.

Along with more functions of government in the European state system, went better administration. This was due to the nineteenth-century development of a trained and competent civil service, "open to talent," and usually requiring a university education. Its members were "permanent" officials and were treated as of almost equal social status with the military profession. They were apt to evince a strong corporate spirit; and, by remaining in office while the political complexion of parliaments and ministries changed, they contributed immeasurably to the stability of state and government. In some states the civil service was more fully developed, and hence more solid than in others—most in Britain and Germany, and generally more in western than in eastern Europe.

By and large, it was the western states of Continental Europe which most closely approximated Britain's political principles and practices during the latter part of the nineteenth century. Of these democratic states during this period we shall treat in the next chapter; and then, in a succeeding chapter, of the newly nationalist states of central Europe and the anomalous and "backward" empires of eastern Europe.

# CHAPTER III

## THE DEMOCRATIC NATIONS OF WESTERN EUROPE

### I. THE THIRD FRENCH REPUBLIC

ROCLAMATION of the Third French Republic was made at Paris by a self-constituted "provisional government" on September 4, 1870, two days after the disastrous defeat of the main French army by the Germans at Sedan and the surrender of the Emperor Napoleon III.[1] The leading figure in the new government was Léon Gambetta, who had risen to prominence in the latter years of the Second Napoleonic Empire as a flaming Republican orator and patriot. He was anxious to retrieve the military defeat and to ensure to a democratic "Third Republic" a permanence which the First Republic of 1792 and the Second Republic of 1848 had not had.

By 1870 the principle of political democracy was firmly enrooted in France. Its definite practice had begun in 1848 and been continued, at least nominally, throughout the reign of Napoleon III. Democracy was now professed not only by liberal Republican opponents of the Empire, but also by the majority of its Royalist critics.

In France as a whole there were more Royalists than Republicans when the Third Republic was proclaimed. But so long as the war with Germany lasted and the mass of Frenchmen perceived the necessity of presenting a united front to a common enemy, Royalists joined with Republicans in support of the "provisional government."

In January 1871, when Paris surrendered to the Germans and a truce was agreed to in order that the French people might elect a National Assembly to decide whether peace should be made or

[1] See *Modern Europe to 1870*, pp. 727, 757–758.

the war continued, a cleavage appeared between Republicans and
Royalists. The former, inspired by the oratory of Gambetta and
sharing his conviction that peace could be made with Germany
**National** only on terms humiliating to France and inauspicious
**Assembly,** for the endurance of the Third Republic, were bent on
**1871** continuing the war. The Royalists, on the other hand,
counseled the making of peace. On this issue the first electoral
campaign under the Third Republic was waged in February 1871,
with the result that, of the 650 deputies elected to the National
Assembly by universal manhood suffrage of the French nation,
about 400 were Royalists and only about 250 were Republicans.

The National Assembly, meeting at Bordeaux, naturally refused formally to sanction the Republic, contenting itself with
naming as "head of the executive power" Adolphe Thiers, the
Liberal Royalist who had been prominent in the bourgeois monarchy of Louis Philippe.[1] The Assembly then removed to Versailles and in due time ratified the treaty of Frankfurt (May
1871). Thereby France ceded Alsace and the greater part of
Lorraine to the newly created German Empire and promised, in
addition, to pay a war indemnity of five billion francs.

Meanwhile the National Assembly had to cope with a serious
insurrection of left-wing Parisian radicals, who had formed a
**Paris** "Commune" to govern the capital while it was besieged
**Commune** by the Germans and hence cut off from the rest of
France. The Commune included middle-class republican extremists and some workmen of socialist or anarchist pro-
clivities. Though they differed among themselves as to ultimate
purposes, they were one in hostility to the National Assembly—
its royalist majority, its sitting at Versailles instead of at Paris,
its willingness to conclude peace with Germany, and its unwillingness to do anything to relieve the continuing economic distress of
the Parisian lower classes.

So the Commune led a revolt against the National Assembly,
repudiating its authority, declaring that the city was self-governing, and summoning radicals in other localities to establish similar
communes and to federate them with that at Paris. "Communes"
were actually set up at Lyons, Marseilles, and a few other towns,
in imitation of Paris, but they were soon overthrown. Indeed,
the mass of the French people throughout the provinces seemed

[1] See *Modern Europe to 1870,* p. 654.

even more eager to suppress domestic strife than they had been to end the foreign war; they backed Thiers in ordering regular troops to capture Paris and end the Commune.

For two months—April and May 1871—Paris underwent a second siege, this time at the hands of French soldiers, and this time with notable ferocity on both sides but with success ultimately attending the national arms of France. The defending "Communists" fought furiously, but, overpowered by numbers and outplayed in generalship, they gave way little by little. In desperation, they slew the hostages they held (including the archbishop of Paris) and set fire to public buildings (destroying the City Hall and the palace of the Tuileries). On the heights of Montmartre they made their final futile stand. Nor did the victors display any leniency. Frenzied by the stubborn resistance they encountered, the troops of the National Assembly killed many of the prisoners they took. And after the Commune was ended and order restored, a kind of judicial terrorism continued.

The episode of the Paris Commune had significant consequences in France for at least a generation afterwards. It weakened extreme radicalism, by intensifying the dread of socialism and anarchism among the upper and middle classes and the peasantry, and also by silencing in death or banishment the chief propagandists of revolutionary violence among the urban working class. At the same time, it somewhat lessened the popularity of the Royalist cause. The Royalist Assembly and ministers had done a good work, it was generally conceded, in suppressing the Commune, but the stern measures they took gradually reacted against them. On the other hand, the Republican cause profited from the fact that it was purged of its extremist element and rendered "moderate."

By the end of May 1871, Thiers and the National Assembly had made peace with the Germans and restored order in France. The Republican minority contended that the Assembly **Presidency** had now complied with its mandate from the people **of Thiers,** and should therefore authorize the election of another **1871–1873** assembly to formulate a constitution for the Republic. The Royalist majority were not so anxious for new elections, however, and in August 1871 they passed the Rivet law, whereby the National Assembly assumed full power to prepare a constitution and conferred on Thiers the interim title of "President of the French

Republic." From 1871 to 1875 the Assembly remained the supreme governing and constitution-making body in France, and some important things it did.

In the first place, under the direction of the National Assembly, the government reorganized the public finances and floated additional loans, so that in 1873 the final installment of the war indemnity was paid to Germany and foreign troops were withdrawn from French soil. Secondly, army reforms were effected. Following the example of victorious Prussia, the principle of universal compulsory service was adopted, the term being fixed at five years in the active army.[1] New fortifications were constructed along the German frontier and the defenses of Paris were strengthened.

Thirdly, the National Assembly devised a constitutional government for France. This it did most painfully and after much delay. There was no serious division in the Assembly about reaffirming a democratic franchise or about continuing the highly centralized local government, under prefects and sub-prefects, which Napoleon had organized at the beginning of the nineteenth century, but about the headship of the central government conflict raged not only between the Royalist majority and the Republican minority, but also within the majority.

The Royalists in the Assembly (and in the country at large) were split into three factions. (1) The "Imperialists," as the supporters of the Bonaparte family were called, suffering from the odium of the recent disastrous war, were negligible. (2) More important were the "Legitimists," dyed-in-the-wool Royalists, who comprised most of the old nobility, many socially prominent persons in Paris and other towns, especially of northern France, and a large following among the Catholic clergy all over the country and among the peasants in certain regions, particularly Brittany and Vendée. They were faithful to conservative traditions and fearful of revolutionary change. Their candidate for the throne of France was Henry, Count of Chambord, grandson of Charles X.[2]

(3) At least as numerous as the Legitimists were the "Orleanists" (or "Liberal Royalists"), recruited mainly from liberally

*Division among Royalist Majority*

---

[1] The principle was not fully applied, however. It proved impractical to enforce a five-year term, and there were numerous exemptions.

[2] See *Modern Europe to 1870*, p. 639.

minded aristocrats, conservative bourgeois, and relatively well-to-do peasants, who were anxious to find a compromise—a "just mean"—between revolution and reaction, between democracy and monarchy, between church and modern society, and who thought it could be attained through a liberal, constitutional government similar to Great Britain's and presided over by the Count of Paris, grandson of King Louis Philippe.[1]

Between the Count of Chambord and the Count of Paris no love was lost, and between their respective partisans there was an obvious incompatibility of principles. It is not to be wondered at that the National Assembly, with its fundamentally divergent elements, made slow progress in framing a constitution for the Third French Republic. Republicans seemed to be hopelessly outnumbered by Royalists, and Royalists to be irreconcilably divided between Legitimists and Orleanists.

For a time in 1873 a Royalist agreement appeared likely. Legitimists and Orleanists were alike angered by the public confession of the supposedly Royalist President, Thiers, that a republican form of government was the only practicable way out of the *impasse*. They united to force his resignation and to elect as his successor Marshal MacMahon, famed soldier and convinced Royalist. Shortly afterwards, moreover, the Count of Paris paid an expiatory visit to his cousin, the Count of Chambord, then residing in Austria and childless, and reached an agreement with him whereby the latter should succeed immediately to the French throne as "Henry V," while the former would be next in line of succession. Royalist hopes quickened, and plans were laid for the speedy supplanting of the Third French Republic by a second restored Bourbon monarchy.

But Royalist harmony was short-lived. A pronouncement by the prospective "Henry V" in October 1873 that he was unalterably determined to maintain the principles of divine-right monarchy and to bring back to France the lilied white flag of the Bourbons shocked the Liberal Royalists and caused them to draw away from the Legitimists. And with renewed friction between rival groups of Royalists, the Republicans won several by-elections for filling vacancies in the Assembly and thus increased their representation in that body.

Henceforth but one practicable course presented itself to the

[1] See *Modern Europe to 1870*, p. 665.

Liberal Royalists, and that was to collaborate with the Republicans in organizing a government which could serve as a make-
**Republican** shift until such time as the Count of Chambord should
**Constitution** carry his white flag to the grave and leave the way open
to the more conciliatory Count of Paris. The first step
in such a course was taken by the National Assembly in November 1873, when a bill was passed bestowing upon Marshal Mac-
Mahon the title of President of the Republic for a definite term
of seven years. So great, however, was the distrust between the
factions of Republicans and Orleanists, on whose joint action
the adoption of even a makeshift depended, that the next step
was not taken until January 1875. Then, by the slender margin
of one vote, the Assembly made provision for the election of
future Presidents of the Republic. Two other "constitutional
laws" followed more rapidly in February, and a third in July
1875. These laws, thus voted piecemeal by a National Assembly
which had been elected four years earlier and in which Royalists
still outnumbered Republicans, proved to be, with few subsequent
amendments, the permanent constitution of the Third French
Republic.

The legislative power was vested in a parliament, consisting of
two elective chambers. These would combine in one body—called
the National Assembly—to elect the President of the Republic
or to amend the constitution; otherwise, they would meet separately. The upper chamber, the Senate, would comprise 300 members, chosen by indirect election for nine years.[1] The lower and
more numerous chamber, the Chamber of Deputies, would be
elected by direct universal manhood suffrage every fourth year
(or oftener, if its dissolution should meanwhile be decreed by
the President and the Senate).

The executive power was entrusted nominally to a President,
elected for seven years and eligible for reelection, but actually to
a Cabinet of Ministers. The ministers must have the backing of
a majority in the Parliament; if they failed to carry the measures
they proposed or if either chamber passed a vote of "lack of confidence," they must resign and leave to the President the task of
forming a new ministry which could command the chambers' confidence. This was virtually the British system of parliamentary

[1] Until 1884, the number of Senators elected for nine years was 225, and the remaining 75 were elected for life.

government with its ministerial responsibility. It appealed to Liberal Royalists as a convenient means by which, when they secured a majority in Parliament, they could easily substitute for the president a king according to their own heart, a king who would reign but not rule.

With the drafting of the constitutional laws, the National Assembly brought its labors to a close in 1875; and the first parliamentary elections under the new constitution of the Third Republic were held. The outcome was the return of a Republican majority to the Chamber of Deputies and of a Royalist majority to the Senate, and the continuation of partisan strife.

The President, Marshal MacMahon, with the support of the Senate, retained his office and utilized it along with his personal prestige to advance the Royalist cause. He encouraged army officers to participate actively in propaganda for **Royalist Activity** the restoration of the monarchy, and, in order to stimulate ecclesiastical cooperation to the same end, he appointed (under the Concordat) persons of strongly Royalist conviction to high church office and did what he could to satisfy Catholic requests. He contributed liberally to the fund for erecting, "as an expiation for the sins of revolution," the great basilica of the Sacred Heart on the heights of Montmartre, and he gave moral support to the agitation of prominent Catholics for French intervention in Italy in behalf of the Pope.

Against the President, the Republican majority in the Chamber of Deputies had a redoubtable leader in Gambetta, who allied the forces of anti-clericalism with those of republicanism. In the Chamber and in the country at large he assailed the Royalists because they aided the Church, and he attacked the Church because it was directed by and for Royalists. A bitter diatribe which he delivered in the Chamber early in May 1877, in the course of which he uttered the memorable phrase, "Clericalism, there is the enemy," was the immediate occasion for a test of strength between himself and the royalist President.

On May 16, 1877, Marshal MacMahon appointed a Royalist (and Clerical) ministry and adjourned the Chamber of Deputies for a month; then, with the sanction of the Senate, he dissolved the Chamber and ordered the holding of new elections throughout France. The resulting electoral campaign was exciting and spectacular. Both Gambetta and the President undertook speech-making tours. None could doubt MacMahon's sincerity, but few **Republican** could withstand Gambetta's oratory. The Republicans **Electoral** won a decisive victory, and as soon as the new Cham- **Success** ber met it forced the resignation of the Royalist cabinet and the appointment of a Republican ministry.

For another year Marshal MacMahon doggedly struggled on against a hostile Chamber and ministry, but partial elections to the Senate, early in 1879, assured Republican control of the upper house as well as the lower and left the Royalist President in a hopeless situation. He resigned, and in his place the Republican majority of the combined Chambers elected Jules Grévy, one of their own number. Thus, nine years after its beginning, the Third French Republic was at last in Republican hands. In the following year (1880), as token of Republican triumph, the seat of government was transferred from Versailles to Paris.

Gambetta did not long survive the triumph; after a brief term as prime minister he was accidentally killed in 1882. But though his following was already breaking up into a number of factional groups, France continued to be dominated by men loyal to the republican form of government. Royalists remained, but they lacked capable leaders and they gradually lost a good deal of their popular support. With the death of "Henry V," Count of Chambord, in 1883 the hopes of the Legitimists were dashed,[1] and the Orleanists were already too dispirited, and the masses too accustomed to the Republic, to admit of any immediate attempt to enthrone the Count of Paris. In 1886 parliamentary action expelled the Count and other Bourbon princes from French territory.

In following the history of the French Republic from the year 1879, when it came completely and finally under the control of **Bourgeois** professed Republicans, one is struck by the continu- **Prepon-** ously preponderant role of bourgeois politicians. The **derance** working majority in Chamber and Senate, the Presidents of the Republic, the ministers, the chief officers of local administration, all were "politicians" and almost all were of the middle class—lawyers or physicians, teachers or journalists, industrialists or financiers—well educated and comfortably well-

---

[1] Similarly, the prospects of the "Imperialists," or Bonapartists, which had been improving somewhat since 1875, were darkened by the death in 1879 of the Prince Imperial, "Napoleon IV," the youthful son and heir of Napoleon III.

to-do. There were no noblemen or clergymen among them, and, perhaps more surprising, few peasants or urban workmen. The latter classes voted for bourgeois office-seekers who promised them most, but otherwise they took little part in government.

One is struck by the perpetual factionalism among the politicians. Despite the fact that the Republic was established only after a nine-year political struggle with Royalists and was chronically threatened with subversion, its protagonists failed to maintain a comprehensive "republican party" and, instead, formed a bewildering variety of "groups" under rival "leaders."

The republican "Union of the Left," which had been formed under Gambetta's guidance to oppose Marshal MacMahon and turn him out of the presidency, dissolved as soon as victory was achieved. Several personal followings, or groups, emerged, representing divergent tendencies which were labeled "Moderate" and "Radical" respectively. The Moderates sought to reassure the propertied classes with the slogan of "liberalism truly conservative." The Radicals made special appeals to "the people," lauding the Jacobinism of the French Revolution and the First Republic. Both were intensely patriotic, the Moderates evincing somewhat greater enthusiasm for colonial expansion, and the Radicals for national concentration at home. Both were influenced by strongly anti-Catholic Freemasonry, and, under the banner of "anti-clericalism," most of their leaders campaigned against the Church.[1] For two decades, from 1879 to 1899, the Moderates usually outnumbered the Radicals, and one of the Moderates, Jules Ferry, a lawyer and journalist, was particularly influential in shaping the legislation of the Republic during the years from 1879 to 1885.

The outstanding leader of the Radicals was Georges Clemenceau, a physician who developed "radical" ideas about religion and society from a study of John Stuart Mill and Auguste Comte, and "radical" ideas about democracy from three years' observation in the United States (1866–1869), and who, by aid of peppery remarks in the Chamber and in the newspaper which he founded in 1880, exerted a gradually growing influence. Clemen-

---

[1] A leader of the "Right" during this period was Albert de Mun, nobleman, ex-army officer, brilliant speaker, and ardent apostle of Christian social reform. He was accustomed to say of himself and his Royalist and Catholic allies, "We are the counter-revolution."

ceau was a bitter foe of Ferry and most other Moderate Republicans (as well as of Royalists and conservatives of the "Right"), and he repeatedly declined to enter any ministry with them. There were not enough Radicals to take over the government themselves, but there were enough to embarrass other Republicans that might. This helps to explain why "ministerial instability" became a characteristic of French public life under the Third Republic. Ministries succeeded each other in kaleidoscopic fashion. From 1871 to 1914, while Great Britain had nine different ministries, France had not fewer than fifty!

Nevertheless, the administrative personnel of the centralized state remained and gave it continuity and stability. Moreover, a change of ministry did not usually involve a change in policy. One set of politicians might quickly succeed another in high office, but general tendencies would remain about the same in the omnipotent parliament and would be reflected in consistency of legislation over a relatively long period. For example, all Republican groups and some Royalists cooperated in enacting in 1881, and in retaining afterwards, important guarantees of individual liberty: a law establishing freedom of speech and the right of holding public meetings without any preliminary authorization on the part of the government; and a very liberal press law.

There was less unanimity about satisfying the demand of urban workmen that they be allowed full freedom to organize and conduct trade unions, but, largely through the efforts of Waldeck-Rousseau, an influential member of the Moderate cabinet of Jules Ferry, a law was put through parliament in 1884 according full recognition and protection to labor combinations.[1]

The conferring of material benefits upon the largest and most influential classes of the electorate was a constant care of the Material bourgeois politicians of the Third Republic—because Develop- they were especially interested themselves in economic ment "prosperity" and because they wanted the approval and votes of their constituents. The Republicans, no less than Napoleon III, perceived the desirability of encouraging commerce, industry, and agriculture. Some 30,000 kilometers of new railway were constructed. Harbors were deepened, and spacious

[1] A partial legalization of trade unions had been enacted in 1864 under Napoleon III. The French act of 1884 was analogous to the British acts of 1871 and 1875. See above, pp. 46, 47.

new ones were provided at Le Havre and St. Nazaire. The beautification and expansion of Paris went on, and here great international expositions were held in 1878, in 1889, and in 1900.

To the agricultural classes, still numerically preponderant in France, the parliament and the ministries were noticeably tender. With one hand they concealed from them the burden of taxation by substituting a host of indirect taxes for direct taxes on land; and with the other hand they extended many positive favors. A special ministry of agriculture was created (1881). Financial grants were made in aid of vine-growers (beginning in 1879). Bounties were voted for the culture of silk, flax, and hemp, and for the breeding of horses. Farmers were encouraged to form cooperative societies for collective buying and selling. Mutual loan banks and insurance agencies were established under state guarantees to assist peasant proprietors (1894). Agricultural schools were opened and endowed. And a system of tariff protection for French agriculture, which was partially constructed by the law of 1885, was capped by a comprehensive tariff act of 1892. That these measures had no little efficacy is indicated by the fact that the mass of the peasants, especially in southern and central France, became staunch advocates of the Republic, and also by the fact that the annual value of the country's agricultural product, which between 1800 and 1860 rose from four to six billion francs, mounted in 1913 to over eleven billion.

But the relative growth of French machine industry, and of French urban centers, was even more remarkable under the Third Republic. Machines in factories multiplied tenfold in horsepower, from 870,000 to 8,600,000. The output of coal mines was doubled, and that of blast furnaces sextupled. Though the principal market for French manufactures was the domestic market, foreign exports increased by 25 per cent. It was to protect infant industry, no longer quite infant, as well as to promote agriculture, that the tariff of 1892 was devised and adopted.

The accumulation of capital went on apace in France. The wealth of the country, roughly estimated at 200 billion francs in 1872, was calculated at 300 billion in 1913. This increase represented in part the growing profits of industrial enterprise accruing to a comparatively small number of manufacturers, and in considerable part the savings of peasants, artisans, and shopkeepers—the proverbially thrifty Frenchmen—who habitually invested in government bonds of their own country and of foreign countries too. Indeed, one reason for the "backwardness" of French industry as compared with that of Britain or Germany was the preference of French investors for putting their money into government securities rather than into business. France had the largest public debt of any country in the world, but practically all was owed to its own citizens, who thus, in the receipt of their interest, were pensioners of the state. Besides, French citizens drew more and more tribute from other countries, for the total of French foreign investments rose from twelve billion francs in 1871 to forty-five billion in 1914, a rate of increase much higher than that of the national wealth.

Another significant development under the Third Republic was the reemergence of France as a colonial power second only to Great Britain in the extent and richness of overseas

**Colonial Expansion**

dominion. When the Republicans took over the government in 1879, France possessed a few remnants of its empire of the eighteenth century,[1] together with Algeria, which had been "occupied" under Louis Philippe and subsequently "annexed" and "subdued," and certain other territories appropriated by Napoleon III in the Pacific and southeastern Asia.[2] Some of the Republicans, especially Clemenceau and his Radical following, were indifferent to this colonial heritage, and critical of further colonial expansion. They thought it would fritter away the energies of the mother-country and distract attention from radical reform at home.

But Jules Ferry and his Moderate associates were bent on pursuing a vigorous colonial policy. The extension of imperial dominion outside Europe would do much, they argued, to restore French prestige, sadly lowered in Europe by the outcome of the Franco-German War, and it would provide French business men and bankers with new fields for profitable trade and investment. In this matter Ferry and the Moderate Republicans found allies in Catholic conservatives, who perceived in French colonial expansion an opportunity to open up new areas for missionaries.

Jules Ferry was the chief champion of the "new empire." While

---

[1] Some islands in the West Indies and the Gulf of Newfoundland, the island of Réunion in the Indian Ocean, five commercial posts in India, a strip of Guiana in South America, a foothold on the Senegalese coast of Africa.

[2] New Caledonia, Cochin-China, and Cambodia.

he was prime minister in 1881 he dispatched a French expedition from Algeria into the troublesome neighboring state of Tunis and obliged its Moslem ruler, the Bey, to submit to a French protectorate. Then, in 1883–1885, when he was again prime minister, he shipped to the Far East another expeditionary force, which compelled China to consent to the establishment of a French protectorate over its vassal states in Indo-China—Annam and Tonkin. Likewise, by directing a bombardment of the chief port of Madagascar, he frightened the native sovereign into signing a treaty whereby that huge island in the Indian Ocean became virtually a French protectorate. By similar means he brought under French control a part of Somaliland on the African coast at the southern entrance to the Red Sea. Ferry, moreover, patronized French exploratory expeditions and trading companies in the interior of Africa, particularly along the Congo and Niger rivers.

The methods employed by Ferry in the acquisition of colonies were denounced by Clemenceau and other Radicals in France, but once colonies were acquired no French political group thought seriously of abandoning them. Indeed, from Ferry's active beginnings the expansion of the French colonial empire proceeded with accelerating speed, and, while many Frenchmen were accused of indifference to the heightening grandeur of their overseas dominion, outright opposition to it seemed to grow ever weaker. French Indo-China was steadily enlarged, mainly at the expense of Siam and China, and rapidly consolidated into a prized dependency with an area larger than the mother-country's and with a population half as large. In Africa, during the 1880's and 1890's French empire-building was especially ambitious and successful. Vast stretches of the Sahara and the western Sudan were explored and linked up with Algeria and Tunis on the north and with the Congo, Niger, and Senegal territories in the south and west. In 1892 the Negro kingdom of Dahomey on the west coast of Africa was conquered. In 1896 a revolt in Madagascar was suppressed and the island was transformed from a protectorate into a colony. In 1912, after protracted international negotiations and armed intervention, a French protectorate was established over the greater part of Morocco.

By 1913 the "empire" of republican France included not only the scattered minor colonies which were French before 1871 and the more recent acquisitions of Indo-China and Madagascar, but also a huge block of African territory constituting the five great administrative divisions of Algeria, Tunisia, Morocco, French West Africa, and French Equatorial Africa, and comprising an area of three and a quarter million square miles (almost fourteen times the area of France) and a population of approximately thirty million (about three-fourths the population of France).

This colonial empire of France was even less French in population than the British Empire was British. In not a single French dependency did persons of European stock outnumber persons of non-European stock. The large majority of French subjects on the African continent were Negroes, Berbers, or Arabs, mainly Moslem in religion; in Indo-China, Annamese and Chinese, almost wholly Buddhist; in Madagascar and the Pacific, Polynesians; and in the West Indies and Guiana, Negroes and mulattoes. Most of the colonies were sparsely inhabited, relative to the density of population in France or any other European country, and many of them, by reason of climate or soil, were unfit for European settlement. Moreover, the practically stationary population of France after 1871, together with a remarkable reluctance of Frenchmen to leave home, helps to explain why, even in regions suitable to European colonization, immigration from the mother-country was comparatively slight. In northern Algeria, the best developed of the French colonies and the most attractive to immigrants, some 500,000 Frenchmen settled between 1871 and 1914, but even here they were outnumbered six to one by native Berbers and Arabs. In Tunisia, the 75,000 colonists from France were fewer than those from Italy, and both together were outnumbered by the natives twelve to one. Elsewhere, there were hardly any French settlers at all—only French administrators, army officers, missionaries, and commercial agents.

There can be no doubt, however, that France surpassed Great Britain in the success with which the former stamped its own impress of language, manners, and culture upon alien "backward" peoples and gained their loyalty and cooperation. If France did not colonize its empire, it at least went far to "Gallicize" its indigenous population. It was assiduous in establishing French schools for its distant subjects, as well as in providing them with material things which would bring them within the orbit of European, and French, civilization. And French colonial governors were usually tactful in handling the natives; they were not so prone as British administrators to fix a gulf between "white" people and "black," between "God's people" and "lesser breeds without the law."

While no French colony was "self-governing" in the sense that British "Dominions" were self-governing, certain French colonies were treated as integral parts of France, and French colonists and "citizens" within them were privileged to elect Senators and Deputies to the central parliament at Paris. Colonies thus privileged were those which had been longest in French possession and were most "Gallicized": Guadeloupe, Martinique, and Guiana, in America; the trading posts in India; the island of Réunion; and northern Algeria. Elsewhere, throughout much the larger part of the French colonial empire, the authority of the republican government at Paris was exercised either indirectly through a native prince, as in the "protectorates" of Tunisia, Morocco, Annam, and Cambodia, who took orders from a "resident-general"; or directly through a "governor-general," as in West Africa, Equatorial Africa, and Madagascar.

From its overseas empire, France reaped considerable advantage, especially for its industrialists and financiers. The colonies were not permitted to levy tariffs against imports from the mother-country, but were required to give preference to French manufacturers, trade, and investment. The value of the annual commerce between France and its colonies steadily increased from 350 million francs in 1879 to nearly two billion in 1913; and by the latter year French capital investments in the colonies amounted to four billion francs. To be sure, the financial income which France derived from its colonies was exceeded by the expenditure made to acquire and hold them—expenditure on distant and frequent military expeditions, on police, on civil service, on navy. Yet there was some prospect and much hope that in the future, when the colonies were more fully developed, they would be a financial as well as a moral asset to France.

The imperialistic policy of the Third French Republic was shaped by the activity of Jules Ferry and the parliamentary support given him by Moderate Republicans, and also by Royalists and "Clericals," against the forensic criticism and electoral opposition of Radicals. The Moderates, however, were staunchly republican and inclined, as disciples of Gambetta, to be anti-clerical; and they were none too proud of appearing to be in alliance

with Catholic Royalists. On one issue, that of "clericalism," they
could heed the chief demand of their fellow Republicans, the
Radicals, and cooperate with them in combating the
clergy and restricting their influence. Hence the same
Jules Ferry, at the very time when he was alienating
Radicals by advancing imperialism abroad, was conciliating them
by launching a campaign against "clericalism" at home.

*"Anti-Clerical-ism"*

Education was a major issue in the campaign. Since the time of
the first Napoleon, Catholic religious instruction had been given
in most French schools, and under Napoleon III there had been
a marked increase in the number of schools conducted by Catholic
teaching orders. Now, under the Third Republic, two demands
for educational reform were insistently voiced. One was for a
compulsory extension of the country's school system so that every
French boy and girl, like every German boy and girl, should be
rendered literate and trained in citizenship. As Gambetta explained, the Prussian schoolmaster had won the last war, and the
French schoolmaster must win the next. The other demand, most
militantly insisted upon by Clemenceau and extreme Radicals,
was for the supremacy of lay (and Republican) over clerical
(and Royalist) influence throughout the primary school system,
so that every French boy and girl should be inoculated with
republicanism and immunized against "reaction."

In the early 1880's Jules Ferry, as minister of public instruction, heeded both demands and, through a coalition of Radical
and Moderate Republicans against the protesting minority of
Royalists and Conservatives, obtained parliamentary enactment
of a series of educational laws. Compulsory attendance at some
school was prescribed for all children. Parents might still elect
to send their children to "free" (church) schools, but if they
did they would have to support such schools out of their own
pockets. On the other hand, a system of "public" or "national"
schools was established, to be financed and directed by the republican government. Attendance upon them would be free, but
in them none but laymen acceptable to the government might
teach and no religious instruction might be given.

Ferry and his allies accompanied the reform of primary education with other anti-clerical measures. To remove a group of
Catholic clergymen who strongly denounced the public schools
as "godless" and "atheistical" and further to handicap the free

(church) schools, the government decreed the dissolution of the Society of Jesus (the Jesuit Order) and its expulsion from France. Moreover, it revived obsolescent eighteenth-century statutes against religious congregations of monks and nuns which had not been formally "authorized" by the state, ordering their dissolution and forbidding their members to conduct schools. And, in accordance with the demand of Radicals for a thorough laicizing of national life, the republican majority in parliament enacted a law prescribing that all marriages, to be legal, must be performed by civil magistrates, and another law empowering civil courts to grant divorces and annulments of marriage.

All these education and marital measures became known as "laic laws." By Frenchmen of the "Left" they were deemed necessary to check the reactionary influence of the Catholic Church in national life and to ensure the permanence of "progressive" republican institutions, while by Frenchmen of the "Right" they were interpreted as partisan maneuvers dictated by a "sect" of Freemasons and designed to spread a hatred of religion and especially of Catholicism under the cloak of "anticlericalism."

The majority of the French electorate seemed to acquiesce in the adoption and enforcement of the laic laws, but many Catholic clergymen and laymen were now more than ever convinced that the republican regime must be overthrown if the Church in France was to be saved from the destructive process of laicizing. These, therefore, redoubled their efforts to discredit the Republic, at the very time, in the late 1880's, when Socialist agitators, returning from exile (for participation in the Paris Commune of 1871) or springing up afresh in the wake of contemporary industrial progress, were prevailing upon urban workmen to resent their economic plight and to blame it upon the politicians of the Republic. There was little likelihood of any agreement between such Socialists and the Clericals except in general fault-finding, but herein lay a serious danger to the Republic. Socialists and Clericals might jointly create such widespread disaffection as to prepare the way for a dictatorship if not for a royal restoration.

This danger loomed large with the advent of George Boulanger on the political scene. He was a general who had fought in the Franco-German War and in Tunis and who, almost unique among his fellow army officers, had been an outspoken foe of monarchy and friend of republicanism. Professing devotion to radicalism in general and to the cause of radical social reform in particular, **The Boulanger Movement** he was appointed in 1886, on the recommendation of Clemenceau, to a seat in the cabinet as minister of war. He then used his public office for personal aggrandizement. He assumed a histrionic pose at military reviews. He talked about a war of revenge against Germany. He endeared himself to the rank-and-file of the French army. The increasing popularity of "the general on horseback" alarmed Clemenceau and other Republican leaders. Recalling how Napoleon had risen to power, they forced General Boulanger to resign his office (1887) and quit the army.

By opponents of the government the General was acclaimed a "martyr" to corrupt bourgeois politicians, and about him quickly crystallized a "revisionist party," demanding that he become a dictator and "revise" the constitution. The Bonapartist faction was prominent in the new party, and to it rallied most Royalists and many Moderates and even some Radicals whose nationalism was temporarily superior to their republicanism. The movement toward Boulanger was quickened by contemporaneous disclosure of financial scandals touching the family of the President of the Republic, Jules Grévy, who had been reelected to his high office in 1886 for a second term of seven years. Thoroughly frightened, the various Republican groups united, forced the resignation of Grévy (December 1887), and elected to the presidency of the Republic Sadi Carnot, an eminently respectable man who had avoided narrow partisanship and who possessed the additional advantage of being the grandson of the very famous Lazare Carnot who had organized the armies of national defense in the dark days of the First Republic.[1] For some time longer, nevertheless, the Boulanger excitement continued. The General stood for election to the Chamber of Deputies wherever a vacancy occurred and proved his widespread popularity by carrying one district after another, the climax being reached in January 1889 when he rolled up a big majority in Paris.

It was thought by his followers that had Boulanger acted promptly after his electoral victory in Paris, he might have overthrown the Republic by a *coup d'état*. But he preferred talk

[1] On Lazare Carnot, see *Modern Europe to 1870,* pp. 519–521, 527.

to action, and let slip the chance to make himself dictator. The republican government was more resolute; it immediately ordered his arrest and trial on charges of conspiracy. Whereupon Boulanger fled ignominiously across the border into Belgium, and was tried and condemned in his absence. Ensuing popular elections endorsed this verdict, and the Boulangist cause collapsed utterly when the "brave General" committed suicide at Brussels in 1891.

Several consequences of the Boulanger episode deserve mention. First, the republican government adopted new policies in respect of the army and foreign affairs. By reducing the period of active service in the army from five years to three (1889) and by retiring reactionaries from high command in the army, it reassured radical Frenchmen who had been fearful of the subversive influence of the military.[1] On the other hand, by contracting a close alliance with Russia (1891–1894), it countered the charge of zealous nationalists that the Third Republic was friendless and cowardly in foreign policy.

*Republican Defense*

Second, the prospect of monarchical restoration, whether of Bourbon king or of Bonapartist emperor, receded into the background. It had failed to materialize when the opportunity was seemingly most favorable, and the recurrence of a like opportunity was now rendered more dubious not only by the withdrawal of royalists from influential army posts, but also by a cleavage among the "clericals," who, up to this time, had been almost a unit in support of monarchy. For in 1892 Pope Leo XIII, convinced that French Catholics were making a grave mistake in identifying their religion with Royalist politics, addressed to them a famous encyclical letter urging them to desist from attacks upon the Republic, to accept the existing form of government, and to concentrate upon obtaining from it in constitutional manner the repeal of the laic laws. This advice served to split the French Catholics. It was spurned by many of them, especially among the religious orders, the secular clergy, and the nobility, who merely reemphasized their devotion to the Royalist cause. But on the other hand, the papal advice was heeded by a considerable num-

---

[1] The reduction of the term of service did not reduce the peace-strength of the army, for several classes of persons who had been exempt from five-year service were now obliged to perform three-year service. The Radicals were concerned with republicanizing the army rather than with reducing its strength.

ber of Catholics, including their chief spokesman in the Chamber of Deputies, Count Albert de Mun, who renounced monarchy and "rallied" to the Republic.

Finally, the outcome of the Boulanger "affair" produced a temporary reaction against republican radicalism as well as against monarchy. The Radical groups were relatively strong while the Republic was in obvious danger, but, as soon as the Republic appeared to be "saved," radicalism at least of the Clemenceau variety lost a good deal of backing. The feeling spread that, to allay partisan passions which the Boulangist movement had aroused, domestic concord should be promoted and that mild Moderates could do this better than belligerent Radicals. Then, too, the simultaneous rise and spread of Marxian socialism in France dealt a double blow to conventional radicalism. Some of its working-class followers deserted it to join outright socialist groups, while some of its bourgeois disciples united with moderates and conservatives to form a common front against socialism.

Marxian socialism was not indigenous to France,[1] and its development was retarded by the bloody suppression of the Paris
**Socialist Movement** Commune of 1871, the continuing predominance of agriculture and peasant proprietorship, the abiding tradition of individualism among French workmen, and the tendency of professed French Socialists as of other Frenchmen to split into factions rather than to constitute a unified party. In spite of handicaps, however, Marxian principles were gradually propagated among the proletariat in industrial centers by a number of middle-class intellectuals and radicals. One of the first and most tireless of such propagandists was Jules Guesde, a Parisian clerk and journalist, who, returning from the exile to which he had been condemned for participation in the Commune, founded in 1876 a "Labor party," which, four years later, adopted a characteristically Marxian platform. In the 1880's appeared several other Socialist groups, but Guesde was unable to unite them with his personal following, and not until the early 1890's did the movement achieve any noteworthy advance. By this time, Guesde's agitation was reenforced by the conversion of several young intellectuals, including Jean Jaurès, professor of philosophy in the University of Toulouse, and two brilliant young lawyers—Alexandre Millerand and Aristide Briand. In the general elections of

[1] On Marxian socialism in general, see below, pp. 214-220.

1893, the various Socialist groups together obtained fifty seats in the Chamber of Deputies.

Some labor legislation was adopted by the French parliament in the 1890's. It fell far short of the demands of Marxian Socialists and likewise short of the proposals of Count Albert de Mun and his group of Social Catholics among the Ralliés. But without pressure from both extremes, Catholic and Socialist, and also from a section of Radical Republicans who, sharing in the popular drift toward socialism, took the name of Socialist Radicals,[1] the Moderate Republican groups who at this time were most largely represented in parliament and in the ministries would hardly have sponsored the measures of social reform which they did. Three of these measures are noteworthy. (1) The "great act" of 1892 regulated the employment of women, forbade the employment of children under thirteen years of age, prescribed a maximum working day of ten hours for all laborers, prohibited manual labor on one day every week, preferably Sunday, and provided safeguards for miners. (2) An act of 1893 ensured free medical attendance to workmen and their families. (3) An act of 1898 obliged employers to pay compensation for personal injuries sustained by employees.

*Labor Legislation*

The "era of good feeling," which succeeded the collapse of the Boulangist movement and which was characterized by cooperation between Moderates and Ralliés and by the labor legislation just indicated, proved brief. It was rudely interrupted by the rise of anti-Semitism, and the disruptive development of the "Dreyfus affair." A certain Édouard Drumont, already of some notoriety as the author of diatribes against the Jews and their "pernicious" influence on French political and social life, founded at Paris in 1892 a sensational newspaper, *La Libre Parole,* whose stock-in-trade was frenzied appeal for "national union" against the "Jewish peril." Its appeal was adroit and many-sided. It was "socially minded," preaching to workmen that their real oppressors and the real foes of labor legislation were Jewish capitalists who dominated French industry and politics. It was "clerical," blaming the irreligious tendency of the Republic upon the influence of Jewish intellectu-

*The Dreyfus Affair*

---

[1] The French name for the group is *Radical Socialiste,* which is usually but faultily translated into English as "Radical Socialist." The emphasis is clearly upon Radical. In economics, the group was clearly conservative.

als and politicians. Above all, it was "patriotic," insisting that France could not wage war for the recovery of Alsace-Lorraine so long as Jews were suffered to honeycomb the French army and to betray its secrets to their kinsmen in Germany.

Fairly quickly, this hysterical anti-Semitic agitation became the means of reviving and extending the Nationalist party which had waxed and waned with Boulanger. Two notable events in 1894 gave impetus to the agitation: first, the exposure of grave financial scandals in connection with a corporation which had been chartered by the French republican government to construct a canal across the isthmus of Panama, involving several Jewish bankers and parliamentarians; and second, the disclosure that a certain Alfred Dreyfus, a Jewish officer in the French army, had been convicted by court-martial of selling military secrets to agents of the German government and consequently had been sentenced to degradation and to penal servitude for life on Devil's Island off the coast of Guiana. Here, apparently, was convincing substantiation of the charges of corruption and even of treason which Drumont and his kind were making against Jews and against the republican politicians. To the anti-Semitic Nationalist party flocked the elements which were traditionally hostile to the Third Republic, and also many republican patriots and a considerable number of workmen. The assassination of the President, Sadi Carnot, by an anarchist in the same eventful year of 1894, appeared to symbolize the fate that was closing in upon the Republic.[1]

Of the Panama scandals no exculpation could be advanced by ardent Republicans; these had to admit that the scandals, though most regrettable, were real. In the matter of the Dreyfus case, however, there was a different outcome. In 1897, after carefully investigating the matter, the head of the espionage section of the French army, Colonel Picquart, expressed his belief that the original court-martial had made a mistake, that the officer who had sold military secrets to Germany was not Dreyfus but a certain Major Esterhazy. Immediately, Radical Republicans backed Picquart's demand for a reopening of the case, while the

[1] Sadi Carnot was succeeded in the presidency by Casimir-Périer, a wealthy conservative, the grandson of a famous finance minister under Louis Philippe. He encountered so many difficulties with the Republican groups in parliament that he resigned in 1895. His successor was Felix Faure, a Moderate, who died in office in 1899.

higher military officers, feeling that the "honor" of themselves and the whole French army was at stake, refused to question the verdict of the original court-martial and some of them took to forging documents to strengthen the case against Dreyfus and to incriminate Picquart. Indeed, on the evidence of these documents, new military courts-martial tried both Esterhazy and Picquart, acquitting the former and disgracing the latter. Whereupon Émile Zola, the novelist, entered the lists in defense of Picquart and Dreyfus, by publishing a scathing denunciation of the anti-Semitic press and party, the alleged forgers of incriminating documents, and the army officers concerned. Though Zola was promptly convicted of libel, his open letter was a most effective means of arraying "Dreyfusards" against "anti-Dreyfusards." As against the latter, embracing Royalists, Clericals, and extreme Nationalists, and threatening to subvert the existing republican government, the former soon comprised those who would preserve the democratic, laic republic—Moderates, Radicals, Socialists.

The several groups of "Dreyfusards" in parliament created a political alliance, or *bloc*, agreeing to avoid subjects of controversy among themselves and to utilize their combined majority in "republican defense." The victory of their cause, foreshadowed by the zeal of Zola, was little in doubt after the confession and suicide of one of the army forgers and after Esterhazy's flight from France in 1898. In 1899 the *bloc*, with its parliamentary majority, secured the election of one of its supporters, Émile Loubet, as President of the Republic, and the choice of another, Waldeck-Rousseau, as head of a militantly Republican ministry. In the same year, several leading "anti-Dreyfusards," including the poet Paul Déroulède, were convicted of treasonable plotting against the Republic and were expelled from the country; and the French supreme court ordered the army to reopen the Dreyfus case and to accord him a new trial. Though the resulting court-martial still pronounced Dreyfus "guilty," it recommended, in view of "extenuating circumstances," that he be pardoned. This was promptly done by President Loubet, and not long afterwards the supreme court annulled unconditionally the conviction of Dreyfus and restored him to office in the army. Picquart also was vindicated and reinstated. Zola, who died in 1902, was given a state funeral and buried in the Panthéon.

Thus the democratic French Republic entered the twentieth

century triumphant over every effort to discredit and subvert it. It had already lasted longer than any regime which France had had since the eighteenth century; and, with its remarkably successful record in the conduct of foreign and colonial affairs and in the promotion of material progress at home, it bade fair, as time went on, to increase its popularity and strength.

Yet there was still no such popular or party agreement about political fundamentals in France as there was in Great Britain. Despite the apparent successes of the French Republic and its **Extremists** gains in electoral support, it continued to be confronted **of "Right"** with an extreme "Right," aspiring to some sort of **and "Left"** authoritarian government, and also with an extreme "Left," demanding a socialistic state and threatening violence to obtain it. The first decade of the twentieth century was to be marked, as an outcome of the Dreyfus affair, by severe punitive measures of the Republican *bloc* against the Catholic Church,[1] with intensified cleavage and bitterness between "Left" and "Right" and, in the long run, with mounting danger to the democratic Republic.

### 2. THE LOW COUNTRIES: BELGIUM, THE NETHERLANDS, AND LUXEMBURG

For a brief time after 1815, the Netherlands, under the Dutch King William I (of the historic Orange family), had constituted a fairly large kingdom, embracing all the Low Countries along the North Sea between France and Germany. In the 1830's, however, the southern (Belgian) provinces revolted and became the independent state of Belgium, under international guarantee of its neutrality and with Leopold of Saxe-Coburg as its constitutional King.[2]

Henceforth the kingdom of the Netherlands was confined to the northern (Dutch) provinces, although until 1890 its King was also Grand Duke of Luxemburg. Each of the separated kingdoms was small, but each had fertile soil, an industrious population, and no little economic importance.

Belgium's development in the nineteenth century was remarkable in three respects. First, unlike France or Britain, Belgium was not strictly a national state. It comprised two dif-

---

[1] See below, pp. 330–333.
[2] See *Modern Europe to 1870*, pp. 641–642.

ferent nationalities of almost equal size: (1) Flemish, in the north-west, whose language was essentially Dutch or "Netherlandish," and who were mainly agricultural and ardently Catho- **Belgium** lic; and (2) Walloon, in the southeast, whose language and culture were French and who were engaged chiefly in industry and trade. Yet the two regions and the two nationalities evinced a common Belgian patriotism and a like loyalty to principles of liberty and democracy. During most of the nineteenth century, the French or Walloon element, by reason of greater wealth and better education, exercised a preponderant influence, but gradually the Flemish people improved their lot and approached an equality with the Walloons.

A second characteristic of Belgium, especially of its Walloon provinces, was its comparatively early and thorough industrialization.[1] In this respect it most closely resembled England and was ahead of any other country on the Continent. Thickly studded with factories and foundries, it became the most densely populated country and, for its size, one of the wealthiest.

The third noteworthy feature of Belgium was the marked stability of its government and the orderliness of its political life. In politics, as well as in industry, Belgium kept pace with Great Britain. It was disturbed by no revolutionary upheaval or military *coup* and by no serious conflict between royalists and republicans. The liberal constitutional monarchy which had been instituted in 1831 in conscious imitation of the British—with a King who reigned but did not rule, with a bicameral parliament representing the upper and middle classes and making the laws, and with a cabinet of ministers conducting the administration and responsible to the parliamentary majority—this regime actually functioned more nearly like the British than did any of the other governmental systems which Continental nations copied from the "mother of parliaments." As in Britain, so in Belgium, there were two or three major political parties rather than a bewildering variety of "groups"; there was comparative stability of ministries; and there was gradual broadening of the franchise, with transition from oligarchy to democracy, within the general framework of the constitutional monarchy.

The principal controversy in domestic politics, for a long time, was over the relations of church and state, particularly in regard

[1] See above, p. 12.

to education. As the need for more schools grew apparent and the state attempted to meet the need, the question arose as to whether religious instruction should be given in public schools. On this question were formed, as early as 1847, two major political parties: the Catholic party, seeking to prescribe moral and religious instruction in the schools and to entrust it to the Catholic clergy; and the Liberal party, espousing the idea of neutral schools and inveighing against "clericalism." Between 1847 and 1884 Liberals controlled parliament and presided over ministries for terms aggregating twenty-eight years, and during this period of their supremacy they abolished religious instruction in the schools and for a time severed diplomatic relations with the papacy. In the latter part of the nineteenth century, however, the Liberal party lost heavily to a rising Socialist party, which, formally organized in 1885, soon attracted to its standards a large number of urban workmen and also a good many intellectuals eager to effect radical reform.

The Catholic party, benefiting from the rivalry between Socialists and Liberals and from its own championship of social reform, obtained a parliamentary majority in 1884 and retained it, together with the responsible cabinet, for the next thirty years. Not only was religious instruction restored in most of the public schools, but elementary education was so extended as greatly to reduce the percentage of illiteracy in the country. Under Catholic auspices, moreover, the government was largely democratized. In 1894 the property qualification for exercising the suffrage was removed, and every male Belgian who was over twenty-four years of age and had resided a year in the same commune was accorded the right to vote in national and local elections. At the same time the principle of plural voting was introduced by according one or two extra votes to an elector in possession of certain financial or educational qualifications. In 1898, in furtherance of popular democracy and to remove a handicap and grievance of the lower classes in northern Belgium who knew Flemish but not French, the former language was put on an equal footing legally with the latter. In 1899, by another electoral reform, proportional representation was instituted, whereby the parliamentary seats to be filled by a given district would be distributed among the several parties or candidates in proportion to the number of votes polled by each. In their op-

**Catholic Party**

position to the Catholic party, which had sponsored these reforms, both Socialists and Liberals attacked especially the clerical influence in education and the system of plural voting. In 1913 the Socialists conducted a brief general strike in behalf of "one man, one vote," but the elections of 1914 preserved a Catholic majority.

Some significant social legislation was enacted by the Belgian parliament, especially after 1890. Factories were regulated. Trade unions were fully legalized and their funds safeguarded (1898). A system of old-age pensions was adopted (1900). Considerable progress was made, moreover, in decently housing the working classes and in otherwise providing for their material well-being.

In a somewhat singular manner Belgium became a colonial power. Its second King, Leopold II (1865–1909), was an astute and none too scrupulous business man, to whom an Anglo-American journalist and explorer, Henry Stanley, pointed out in the 1870's the rich rubber resources of the huge Congo region in central Africa. The King proceeded to organize a private commercial company with himself as president and chief stockholder, to beguile native chieftains into turning over their lands to the company, and then to obtain international sanction (1884–1885) for the erection of the company's lands into the "Congo Free State," with himself as its personal sovereign. Leopold II invested heavily in the undertaking, and reaped rich rewards. By 1908, however, there were numerous disclosures of outrages and practical slavery visited upon the natives of the Congo to make them get rubber for the King and his "company," and insistent demands inside and outside Belgium for sweeping reforms in the Free State. Leopold II yielded to the pressure of public opinion sufficiently to propose in 1908 that the Congo Free State should be transformed into a Belgian colony—with liberal financial compensation to himself for his "sacrifice." The Belgian government, against the energetic opposition of a minority in parliament, accepted the proposal, and thus, in 1908, Belgium acquired an overseas empire with an area almost eighty times its own.

The kingdom of the Dutch Netherlands—or "Holland," as the country is commonly called—experienced, after its loss of Belgium, no corresponding intensive industrialization. It continued, rather, to be a land of burghers, farmers, and fishermen. Yet it held an economic importance out of all proportion to the

number of its square miles or of its factories and inhabitants.
The Dutch Netherlands, we must remember, still possessed a
large part of the colonial and commercial empire which
had been acquired in the seventeenth century.

**Nether-**
**lands**

Even after the loss of colonies to which the Dutch
had been subjected by Great Britain during the Napoleonic
wars,[1] they retained an East Indian empire—Java, Sumatra, the
Spice Islands (Celebes, etc.), most of Borneo, and half of New
Guinea—fifty-eight times as large as the mother-country and
six times as populous, and, in addition, the colonies of Guiana
(Surinam) in South America and Curaçao in the West Indies.
This imperial domain, especially the part of it in the East Indies,
was an unfailing source of wealth, as well as prestige, to the
Dutch. It provided handsome financial remuneration for many
Dutch citizens who carried on its administration and exploitation;
and it was so developed and regulated as to secure to Dutch
merchants and bankers a practical monopoly of its valuable
foreign commerce and of lucrative investments for its internal
development.

The commercial—and agricultural—significance of the Dutch
Netherlands was enhanced in the latter part of the nineteenth
century by the country's proximity to nations which were becoming highly industrialized.[2] It was at the crossroads of Great
Britain, Germany, and Belgium, whose mutual exchange of wares,
often effected across Dutch territory, was profitable to Dutch
carriers and middlemen, and whose rapidly growing urban populations provided an enlarging and increasingly gainful market
for the produce of Dutch truck-gardens, dairy farms, and deep-
sea fisheries.

In the circumstances, it was advantageous for the Dutch
Netherlands to remain a free-trade country at the very time when
policies of tariff protection and economic nationalism were being
adopted by all other countries of Continental Europe.

Perhaps because of the economic prosperity of the Netherlands,
the Dutch readily acquiesced in a political regime which was
notably conservative. It was not until 1848 that the King, Wil-

---

[1] Notably, South Africa and Ceylon.

[2] The foreign and colonial commerce of the Netherlands in 1913 had a value of
nearly three billion dollars, only a little less than that of France. More than a third
of Dutch commerce was with Germany.

liam II, was impelled to grant a constitution, transforming the Estates General into a bicameral parliament and making the royal ministers responsible to it, and also getting rid of serious limitations on religious liberty.

At the same time, however, an absolute veto over all legislation was retained by the monarch, while the imposition of heavy property qualifications restricted the parliamentary electorate to the wealthiest class of citizens. Although the qualifications for voting were subsequently lowered, political democracy made slower and more halting progress in the Netherlands than in any other country of western Europe.

During the long reign of King William III (1849–1890), the chief political debates had to do with popular education. On one side, a Liberal party contended for a system of free, public, secular schools in which no religious instruction should be given. On the other side, a Protestant Conservative party and a Catholic party made common cause in behalf of a system of public schools to be directed by the churches and supported by the state. For a time the Liberals appeared to have the upper hand; the state established and financed a system of "neutral" public schools. In 1889, however, Conservatives and Catholics secured governmental financial support for their respective denominational schools.

William III was succeeded on the Dutch throne by his daughter, Wilhelmina, who came of age in 1898 and three years later married a German prince, Henry of Mecklenburg. This marriage, in conjunction with the close commercial and cultural relations between Germany and the Netherlands, aroused apprehension among Dutch patriots and stimulated a popular movement for "national defense." The army was reorganized on the basis of general conscription and large sums were spent on fortifications.

The Kings of the Netherlands, of the House of Orange, had also been, from 1815 to 1890, Grand Dukes of Luxemburg, a diminutive state bordering on France, Belgium, and Germany. According to an arrangement within the **Luxemburg** Orange family, the grandduchy did not pass with the death of William III to his daughter, as the kingdom of the Netherlands did, but rather to a male kinsman, Adolphus of Nassau (1890–1905). It thus became an independent state, and since 1867 its territorial integrity and neutrality had been pledged by the

European great powers. Luxemburg was largely industrialized, like Belgium; and its constitutional government was similar to Holland's.

### 3. THE SWISS CONFEDERATION

Switzerland, in sharp contrast to the Low Countries, was a land of mountaineers, without seacoast or merchant marine. Even less of a "national state" than Belgium, it was a confederation of diverse peoples. It was not a monarchy, but a republic, famous for its advanced democracy.

Perched high upon the common Alpine watersheds of the Rhine, the Danube, and the Rhône, Switzerland was hardly larger in area than the Dutch Netherlands. Included in it, however, were some twenty-two republics, or "cantons," differing among themselves in language, religion, and customs, according to their geographical proximity to Germany, France, or Italy. In fifteen cantons, embracing two-thirds of the population of the whole Confederation, the German language prevailed. Of the remaining seven cantons, five were predominantly French in speech and two were Italian. Protestants were in a majority in twelve cantons, and Catholics in ten.

That such diverse populations, in an age of intensifying nationalism, could constitute a substantial political union and feel a common patriotic devotion to it is attributable in part to the continuing vital tradition of Swiss independence and in part to the nature of the Confederation. The population of any one canton was fairly homogeneous in nationality—it was German, or French, or Italian—and each canton had a government of its own and managed its domestic affairs. The powers of the federal government were limited, and were usually exercised so as not to wound the sensibilities of any canton or any linguistic group.

Of the Confederation, political democracy was an outstanding feature. A constitutional revision of 1874, though making no important change in the structure of government, intro-
**Swiss Democracy** duced the principle of the popular "referendum" in legislation and at the same time somewhat enlarged the powers of the Confederation, authorizing it, for example, to establish and supervise a system of free elementary schools for all Swiss children. In 1891 was adopted, as a corollary to the referendum, the "initiative," that is, the right of a specified

number of Swiss citizens to demand the submission of any measure of which they might approve to a referendum of the entire citizenry. By means of initiative and referendum, as well as through parliamentary action, much popular legislation was enacted for the whole of Switzerland, especially from 1890.

In the matter of military defense, the Swiss people, in view of mounting armaments of the surrounding great powers, and fearful lest their own neutrality, despite solemn pledges of the Congress of Vienna (1815), might not be respected in case of a general European war, deemed it necessary to authorize the compulsory training and service of all able-bodied young citizens for a certain number of days every year. This "militia," originally sanctioned in 1874 just after the Franco-Prussian War, was strengthened by several subsequent laws, most notably by one in 1907.

Throughout the forty years from 1874 to 1914 several factors contributed to the economic development of Switzerland. One, of long standing, was the habitual thrift of the hardy natives who still in considerable numbers herded flocks upon the mountain-sides or practiced the science of intensive cultivation in the narrow valleys. Second was the more recent but now steadily augmenting influx of foreign tourists who interspersed their Alpine-climbing and sight-seeing with liberal expenditure to inn-keepers and to purveyors of Swiss souvenirs. Third was the still more recent growth of manufacturing—and of industrialization in general—which was doubtless stimulated by tariff legislation and which was represented at the close of the nineteenth century by numerous establishments for the making of textiles, gloves, pottery, watches and clocks, and milk chocolate.

*Economic Development*

#### 4. THE SCANDINAVIAN KINGDOMS

Occupying the northernmost regions of Western Europe, the Scandinavian peoples—Danes, Swedes, and Norwegians—were much alike in origin, language, and religion, and in the nineteenth and twentieth centuries they passed through a similar social and political evolution. All three lived more by agriculture, commerce, and fishing than by machine industry; in Denmark and even more in Sweden the landed aristocracy was relatively important, while Norway was a "peasant nation." Among all three, though most in Sweden, some industrialization occurred, and socialism arose and spread its radical teachings. All three, while conservatively adhering to monarchy and avoiding any revolutionary disturbance, gradually modernized and liberalized their political institutions and eventually democratized them.

Denmark, by ceding Norway to Sweden in 1814 and by surrendering the duchies of Schleswig-Holstein to Germany in 1864,
**Denmark** was restricted to the peninsula of Jutland and its adjacent islands, and thus became, in European area, the smallest of the three Scandinavian countries. Alone of these countries, however, Denmark possessed a colonial empire outside Europe: Iceland, Greenland, the Faroë Islands, and some West Indian islands. By the constitution of 1849, revised in 1866, the King of Denmark shared his supreme political power with a parliament, the lower house of which comprised representatives of "popular" electors over thirty years of age and in possession of certain property qualifications. Throughout the long reign of King Christian IX (1863–1906) a political contest was carried on between this lower house, on one side, and the monarch and upper house, on the other. The former sought to liberalize the government by making the royal ministers responsible to parliament, and the King, intent upon strengthening the Danish army, long refused to make concessions to a body which would not vote the military appropriations requested by him and his personally appointed ministers. From 1872 to 1901 the constitution was hardly more than waste paper. Public funds were repeatedly obtained and spent by the government without parliamentary authorization.

During these years, however, the Danish peasants were steadily improving their economic condition through intensive cultivation of their small holdings and noteworthy development of dairy farming and cooperative enterprise. As they improved their economic position they took a more lively interest in politics, gradually swelling the complaints of middle-class Liberals against the arbitrary government of the crown, with the result that in 1901 the aged King finally yielded to popular pressure and installed a ministry representing the Liberal majority in the lower house of parliament.

The Danish government was now liberal but not yet democratic, and agitation for democratizing Danish political institutions eventually bore fruit in constitutional amendments of 1914–1915, reducing the age limit of voters from thirty to twenty-five, extending the franchise for the lower house of the parliament to all men and most women, and abolishing the appointive seats in the upper house. Already, measures of home rule had been enacted for the Faroë Islands and in 1903 for Iceland. In 1917 Denmark sold its West Indian islands, collectively called the Virgin Islands, to the United States.

Sweden had emerged from the Napoleonic wars at the beginning of the nineteenth century with the loss of Finland to Russia, with the gain of Norway from Denmark, and with a new royal dynasty stemming from Marshal Bernadotte **Sweden** of France who became Charles XIV (1818–1844).[1] All these happenings had important consequences for Sweden throughout the century. The Bernadotte dynasty, despite its French and revolutionary origin, proved to be even more stubbornly attached to royal prerogative and reactionary policies than were the Danish sovereigns. The loss of Finland stimulated popular apprehension about Russia and led to a more pronounced militarism in Sweden than in Denmark. And the artificial union of Norway with Sweden produced an unhappy feud between them.

Sweden and Norway were incompatible socially and politically. Sweden was a country of large landed estates with a well-to-do nobility and a dependent peasantry. Norway was a country of small farms, with a peasantry and fisher-folk accustomed to economic independence and to a feeling of contempt for titles of nobility. Moreover, as the nineteenth century advanced, Sweden underwent considerable industrialization with attendant growth of urban classes of capitalists and proletarians, while Norway remained overwhelmingly agricultural and commercial. Then, too, the political institutions of the two countries were divergent. Norway had a typically liberal constitution, which had been prepared just before the union with Sweden and which vested supreme authority in a parliament elected indirectly by taxpayers. In Sweden, on the other hand, the only constitutional check upon royal authority until 1863 was the clumsy old-fashioned Estates General with its four houses of nobles, clergymen, burghers, and peasants; and though in 1863 a modern bicameral parliament was substituted for the medieval Estates General, the aristocratic

[1] See *Modern Europe to 1870*, pp. 547, 563, 729–730.

classes controlled it and the King retained an absolute veto over its acts.

By the terms of the union of 1815, Norway had been formally recognized as "a free, independent, and indivisible kingdom, united with Sweden under one King." But while the joint King observed the letter of the agreement by tolerating the Norwegian parliament and allowing it to exercise jurisdiction over local affairs in Norway, he insisted on his own centralizing control of the army, the foreign relations, and a good deal of the civil administration of both his realms; and, backed by Swedish popular sentiment, he urged a closer union between the two states. The union was already too close to suit the Norwegians; and following the stubborn refusal of Oscar II (1872–1907) to sanction the appointment of Norwegian consular agents in foreign countries, the Norwegian parliament in 1905 unanimously decreed the complete separation of Norway from Sweden and the dethronement of the Bernadotte King. The decree was ratified by a plebiscite of the Norwegian people and grudgingly agreed to by the Swedish government. Whereupon the second son of the King of Denmark accepted the crown of Norway and assumed the title of Haakon VII. Thus was the union between Norway and Sweden dissolved.

**Separation of Norway**

The dissolution of the union between Sweden and Norway gave impetus to democratic agitation in both countries. In Norway, universal manhood suffrage had already been introduced (1898); direct elections were substituted for indirect (1906); the suffrage was extended to women, at first with property qualifications (1907) and presently (1913) on the same broad basis as to men; the royal veto was abolished (1913) and the crown rendered purely honorary.

**Democratic Measures**

In Sweden, shortly after the death of King Oscar II and the accession of his son, Gustavus V (1907), important constitutional amendments were adopted, providing for proportional representation in both chambers of parliament and establishing universal manhood suffrage for elections to the lower. Meanwhile, Sweden, more than any other Scandinavian country, was undergoing economic transformation and entering into rivalry with industrialized nations and was paying a price for it in dislocation and discontent of its lower classes. Some remedial social legislation was enacted, but that the masses continued to need economic betterment was attested by the spread of socialism among them and also by the large Scandinavian emigration to America. Sweden, the worst sufferer in this respect, lost between 1870 and 1914 one and a half million citizens, most of whom settled permanently in the United States.

### 5. THE KINGDOMS OF SPAIN AND PORTUGAL

Side by side in the Iberian peninsula, in the southernmost part of western Europe, were the two countries of Spain and Portugal whose histories and cultures, and whose nineteenth-century political developments, were, in most respects, strikingly similar. The whole peninsula had an area somewhat larger than France, though its total population was only about two-thirds the population of France. Of the Iberian peninsula, Spain embraced six-sevenths of the area; Portugal, the remainder.

Both Spain and Portugal were national states of long duration. Both had founded huge overseas empires and if the mother-countries had been bled of men and resources by their imperial undertakings they had the satisfaction of Similarities knowing that on the American continents were a Greater Spain and a Greater Portugal, whose populations retained the respective national languages and constituted, together with the population of the Iberian peninsula, aggregates of Spanish- and Portuguese-speaking peoples larger than those that spoke French or German.

Politically, neither Spain nor Portugal experienced any such steady and peaceful development of liberal democracy as did Britain, Belgium, or the Scandinavian countries. Ever since the Napoleonic Wars in the first decade of the nineteenth century, both Iberian kingdoms had suffered grievously from foreign intervention and tutelage and from civil war between rival claimants to the throne and bitter strife between partisans of revolution and those of reaction. A variety of liberal constitutions had been adopted between 1812 and 1865, but the parliamentary government for which they provided proved ineffectual and even farcical.[1] The peasant masses were generally illiterate, and they either followed blindly some local "boss" or were resentful of authority and inclined toward anarchism. Operation of constitutional government was left to a comparatively small number of professional

---

[1] See *Modern Europe to 1870*, pp. 561, 611–616, 642–645, 730–732.

politicians, who were apt to orate about liberty or democracy without doing much to achieve them and to put personal gain above national welfare. The real power in the state was wielded by the army. It was the principal bulwark against anarchy, and without the backing of its high officers no government, whether constitutional or not, could long endure in Spain or in Portugal.

In Spain, a half century of misgovernment was climaxed by a revolutionary upheaval which lasted from 1868 to 1876. This

**Spain after Revolution of 1868**
began with a military insurrection, headed by General Prim, which speedily led to the deposition and flight of the incompetent and profligate Queen Isabella II and the adoption, by a democratically elected Cortes (Assembly), of a new constitution providing for limited liberal monarchy of the British type.

For the next year or two, General Prim, while trying to induce this or that foreign prince to take the vacant Spanish throne, exercised practically dictatorial power and managed to maintain order in the country. Prince Amadeo of Savoy, a younger son of King Victor Emmanuel II of Italy, was finally persuaded to accept the dubious honor, but on the very day in December 1870 when the new King landed in Spain, General Prim was assassinated.

For two years King Amadeo strove unavailingly against many-sided opposition. Most Spaniards disliked him as a foreign intruder. The clergy and other militant Catholics denounced him as the son of an Italian sovereign who had despoiled the Pope, and they gave renewed impetus to the Carlist movement, particularly strong in Navarre and the Basque provinces, in behalf of the "legitimate" and reactionary claimant to the throne, Don Carlos.[1] At the other extreme, Amadeo was assailed by groups of radical revolutionaries who wanted to get rid of monarchy altogether and set up an anti-clerical republic. His only support came from middle-of-the-road liberal monarchists in the Cortes and in the army, of whom Marshal Serrano, a former lieutenant of General Prim, was chief. But Serrano, though successful in checking the Carlists, failed to unite the army as a whole in defense of the regime; and the Liberals in the Cortes engaged in factional disputes. Within two years there were six changes of ministry and

[1] This Don Carlos was the grandson of the Don Carlos who had fought his niece, Isabella II, in the 1830's. See *Modern Europe to 1870*, pp. 643–644.

three general elections. Amadeo, in despair, abdicated in February 1873 and returned to Italy.

The Cortes, as a next resort and in imitation of current action in France, proclaimed Spain a Republic. But this was going from bad to worse. Convinced Republicans comprised only a small minority of the country's population, and their leaders in the Cortes were theorists and talkers, unable to agree among themselves or to pursue any consistent policy. At first, the followers of Pi y Margall had the upper hand: they favored a "federal republic," that is, a loose union of local autonomous districts. Resulting anarchy soon discredited them, and they made way for the followers of Salmeron who favored a "unitary republic" with government centralized at Madrid.

**First Spanish Republic, 1873-1875**

Meanwhile popular riots multiplied throughout Spain; and in the northern provinces Don Carlos, returning from exile and recruiting an army of 75,000 men, precipitated civil war. Faced with this threat, the Cortes in September 1873 ousted Salmeron and entrusted the government to a less radical Republican, Emilio Castelar, who thereupon adjourned the Cortes and turned to the army for guidance.

An interim military government was set up with Marshal Serrano at its head; and one of its members, Marshal Martinez de Campos, worked out plans for ending the Republic and reinstating a liberal monarchy with Alphonso, the young son of Isabella II, as King. In December 1874, following the latter's promise that he would grant a full amnesty and insure constitutional government, he was formally proclaimed by Campos and in January 1875 he was installed at Madrid as Alphonso XII.

**Bourbon Restoration**

Weariness with the revolutionary turmoil of the preceding six years brought widespread popular acquiescence in the restoration of the Bourbon monarchy and enabled Spain to enjoy during the next two or three decades a period of relative calm. In 1876 armed opposition of the Carlists was finally crushed, and in the same year new constitutional guarantees of personal liberty and parliamentary government were affirmed. In 1878 a Cuban revolt, which had been a reflex of the Spanish revolution of 1868 and had smoldered ever since, was brought to an end by the arms and tact of Marshal Campos.

The actual functioning of constitutional government in Spain

was expedited after 1875 by the grouping of its political and
military supporters in two "parties": the Conservative, organized
by Canovas del Castillo, lawyer and journalist, and allied with a
set of army officers headed by Marshal Campos; and the Liberal,
formed by Mateo Sagasta, an engineer, and backed by another
set of army officers including Marshal Serrano. Difference in policy between Conservatives and Liberals was slight. The former
were a little more favorable to the Church and the aristocracy,
while the latter harbored some anti-clericalism and paid at least
lip service to the principle of political democracy. On major policies they were practically a unit; and, throughout the reign of
Alphonso XII (1875–1885) and the regency of his wife, Maria
Christina (the mother of Alphonso XIII), from 1885 to 1902,
Canovas and Sagasta nicely alternated in office without appreciable change of general tendencies.

Internal order was maintained. Republican criticism, on one
hand, and Carlist agitation, on the other, were repressed. Catholic support was obtained by respecting the concordat of 1851
with the papacy, by not restricting the religious orders, and by
leaving public education mainly under the control of the clergy.
A large army and a fairly large civil service, tasting the bounty
of the government, were seemingly quite loyal to it. "Regional-
ism," the separatist movement for home rule which persisted
among Catalans and Basques, was held in check.

Although Spain remained principally an agricultural country,
with large landed estates predominating in the south and west,
and peasant ownership of small farms in the north and east, it
underwent considerable industrialization. Barcelona, already the
country's commercial capital, became an important center of
textile mills; and large-scale mining and iron-working developed
around Bilbao. There was an accompanying notable growth of
Spanish cities and middle class and also of the number of urban
workmen in foundry and factory and on railway and dock.

To serve agricultural and industrial interests, a policy of
tariff protection was elaborated, mainly by Canovas and the Conservatives, though eventually acquiesced in by the Liberals. To
meet a political demand of "progressive" intellectuals and workmen, universal manhood suffrage for elections to the Cortes was
inaugurated by Sagasta and the Liberals in 1890, and then, to
balance the votes of interested urban dwellers with those of the

more indifferent rural population, the exercise of the suffrage was made compulsory for all male citizens by enactment of the Conservatives in 1907.

Externally, the principal effort of the royal government, whether Conservative or Liberal, was directed toward retaining the remnants of the once great Spanish empire overseas—Cuba, Puerto Rico, the Philippines, the Carolines, and a foothold in Morocco. The effort was very costly to Spain in men and money and it repeatedly invited disaster. Yet national pride and the prestige of the monarchy seemed to demand that the effort be made. In 1893 Marshal Campos, at the head of a large expeditionary force, suppressed a native outbreak in Spanish Morocco. In 1895 a second revolt began in Cuba, and presently the difficulty of putting it down was enhanced by an uprising in the Philippines and, more ominously, by the intervention of the United States. In the ensuing Spanish-American War (1898), Spain lost its navy, sacrificed the lives of several thousands of its citizens, and piled up a big national debt; and by the treaty of Paris which concluded the war, Spain was obliged to recognize the independence of Cuba and to cede Puerto Rico and the Philippines to the United States. The next year the Caroline Islands were sold to Germany.

*End of Overseas Empire*

At the turn of the century the Spanish kingdom faced a new crisis. Partially it was an outcome of the Spanish-American War, the substantial losses and even more the blow to patriotic pride and to faith in the existing government which the Spanish people thereby suffered. Partially it was a result of the passing of those veteran politicians who had had long experience in managing the country: Canovas del Castillo was assassinated by an anarchist in 1897, and Sagasta died in 1903. The result was a renewal of social unrest and partisan strife. Alphonso XIII, nominal King since birth in 1886, came of age in 1902 and assumed personal direction of affairs. A troubled reign lay ahead of him.

Portugal, unlike Spain, managed through its virtual alliance with Great Britain to retain and even enlarge its extensive colonial dominion. It was also less industrialized than Spain; its masses were equally agricultural, and its classes were more commercially minded. It escaped, too, the revolutionary commotion which afflicted Spain in the 1860's and 1870's.

*Portugal*

Otherwise, Portugal in the second half of the nineteenth century showed much the same trends and experienced much the same troubles as did Spain after the Bourbon restoration of 1875. There were two parties of constitutional monarchists, "Regenerators" and "Progressives," corresponding respectively to Spanish Conservatives and Liberals, and, like the Spanish parties, manipulating local officials and popular elections so as to take turns in holding office and dispensing patronage. There were the same opposition groups: reactionary Miguelists, corresponding to Carlists; revolutionary Republicans; and a slowly growing number of socialists and anarchists. There was the same indifference to politics on the part of the mass of peasants, and the same reliance on army and navy for vital support of the regime.

From the accession of King Pedro V in 1853 and through the reign of his brother, Louis I (1861–1889), liberal constitutional government seemed to function fairly well in Portugal. There was a respite from civil strife and an orderly operation of government. Nevertheless, the prevalence of corruption among officials, and the expense of maintaining and developing the large colonial empire,[1] gravely embarrassed the national finances and served to divert the attention of the government from other matters. Taxes were burdensome, popular education was neglected, needed social reforms were postponed, and tens of thousands of the most industrious and ambitious inhabitants of the country emigrated to the more prosperous Portuguese-speaking land of Brazil.

Under King Charles I (1889–1908) financial crises recurred with alarming frequency, opposition to the monarchy gathered headway, and factional quarrels developed among its professed supporters. The King himself was extravagant, and primarily intent, it seemed, on getting all the money he could from the national treasury to spend on personal pleasures. On several occasions, when he failed to get what he wanted from parliament, he dissolved it and ruled without it by means of "ministerial decrees." The last such occasion, and the most flagrant, was in 1907 when the King entrusted his faithful prime minister, João Franco,

---

[1] Portugal possessed in 1910 a colonial empire surpassed in area only by those of Britain, France, and Germany. It covered 800,000 square miles—almost twenty-five times the area of the mother-country—and comprised the following territories: in or near Africa—Guinea, Angola, East Africa (or Mozambique), and the Cape Verde Islands; in India—Goa, Damaun, and Diu; in China—Macao; and in the Malay Archipelago—part of Timor.

with dictatorial powers. Franco was determined to effect sweeping reforms, as well as to please the King in financial matters, but against him and his master the forces of opposition coalesced. In vain he filled the jails with political prisoners. In 1908 King Charles and the crown prince were assassinated while driving through the streets of Lisbon; Franco fled the country; and Manuel II, second son of Charles and an inexperienced youth, was soon faced with revolution.

# CHAPTER IV

## NATIONALISTIC CENTRAL EUROPE AND THE ANOMALOUS EMPIRES OF EASTERN EUROPE

IFFERENT from Western Europe, where national states had long existed and where liberal democratic government made steady advance throughout the nineteenth century, Eastern Europe continued to be characterized by despotic, polyglot empires—the Russian and the Ottoman Turk. The intervening belt of lands in Central Europe, including Italy, Germany, and Austria-Hungary, was culturally much more akin to the West than to the East, but, judged by Western standards, it was politically backward.

Only in the latter part of the nineteenth century did really national states emerge in Central Europe through the respective unifications of Italy and Germany, and even then Austria-Hungary still represented a curious compromise between imperial tradition and nationalist aspiration. Also, it was only in the latter part of the century that principles of constitutional government and liberal democracy were definitely adopted in Central Europe. Here, the newly created kingdom of Italy led the way and came closest to resembling France in political development. The nationalist German Empire followed with a more conservative regime. In the Dual Monarchy of Austria-Hungary, conflict among nationalities rendered the attainment of liberal democracy exceedingly difficult.

### I. THE KINGDOM OF ITALY

The kingdom of Italy was in 1871 a very recent creation. King Victor Emmanuel II of Savoy-Sardinia had taken the title of King of Italy only ten years previously, just after France had helped him to expel Austria from Lombardy and to annex the small duchies in the central part of the peninsula, and the "red-shirts" of Garibaldi had enabled him to appropriate Naples and Sicily. Then, in 1866, the kingdom of Italy had obtained Venetia by joining Prussia in the Seven Weeks' War against Austria; and in 1870 it had utilized an opportunity afforded by the Franco-Prussian War to overpower the Pope and to seize Rome.[1]

Formal political unity was thus achieved, but not yet a really national unity. Localism and sectionalism were rife, partly because the physical features of the country were divisive, and partly because different historical traditions had developed in the several regions through centuries of political separation and rivalry. Especially between North and South the contrasts were great. Italy as a whole was overwhelmingly agricultural, but what machine industry there was had been introduced into the North and was almost wholly confined to the North. The majority of the Italian people were illiterate, but the percentage of illiteracy was three times greater in the South than in the North.

The government of the Italian kingdom represented a continuation and extension of the Sardinian constitutional regime, which had been copied from Great Britain's, and embodied in the *Statuto* of 1848. The King reigned but **Liberal Regime** did not rule, and his theoretically broad powers were practically exercised by a ministry responsible to a bicameral parliament consisting of a Senate, partially hereditary and partially appointive, and a Chamber of Deputies elected by the upper and middle classes. The government was liberal, but not democratic.

The liberal regime had special difficulties with the Catholic Church. The minority of Italians who constituted the governing class of the kingdom were strongly inclined toward religious scepticism and radical anti-clericalism, by reason both of the general intellectual fashion of the time all over Europe and of the particular ecclesiastical complications attending the political unification of Italy. On the other hand, the Italian nation was Catholic by habit and tradition, and the large majority, however critical they might be of the administration and secular policy of the Church, were sincerely attached to its cult and sacraments. In the circumstances the royal government saw fit to maintain Catholicism as a kind of national institution. It continued the

[1] On Italian unification, see *Modern Europe to 1870*, pp. 733-742, 751, 760.

previous Sardinian practices of paying the salaries of the clergy, passing upon the appointment of bishops, permitting religious instruction to be given in the schools, and declining to sanction divorce. At the same time, it gradually reduced the number of monastic establishments throughout the country, repeatedly confiscated church property, and tolerated, at times actively promoted, anti-Catholic propaganda.

Special difficulty the kingdom had with the papacy. In 1871, shortly after the seizure and occupation of Rome by troops of King Victor Emmanuel II, the royal government sought to reconcile the position of the supra-national papacy with that

**Position of Papacy** of nationalist Italy by having the parliament enact a "law of papal guarantees." The law accorded to the Pope the ownership of the Vatican and Lateran palaces and the villa of Castel Gandolfo, the honors due a reigning sovereign, the right to communicate freely with governments and peoples abroad, and an annual subsidy of three and a quarter million lire from the national treasury as compensation for the loss of temporal possessions. But Pope Pius IX rejected the law, insisting that its acceptance would involve his recognition of a government which had unjustly invaded Rome and despoiled the papacy of needful temporalities and freedom, and furthermore that "papal guarantees" should be made by international treaty rather than by parliamentary act of Italy. So Pius IX would not accept any money from the Italian government or soften his hostility to it. He persisted in regarding himself as a "prisoner" and in calling upon foreign nations to intervene in his behalf. By the *non expedit,* he forbade Italian Catholics to vote or hold office under the royal government.

This uncompromising attitude of the Pope was undoubtedly advantageous to his international prestige, for, so long as he was not on friendly terms with the kingdom of Italy, foreigners could not suspect him of undue subservience to Italian interests. But in Italy the enmity between kingdom and papacy had unfortunate results for both. The Pope alienated from the Church a large number of patriotic Italians who resented his opposition to the nation's political unity and disregarded his injunctions, while the kingdom was deprived of the public services of many Italians who, obedient to the Pope, removed themselves from the nation's political life.

The Italian government and its electorate were, as we have said, a minority, but the minority, though for two decades remarkably homogeneous in its preponderantly bourgeois complexion and its uniform devotion to liberalism, nationalism, and anti-clericalism, was not a political unit. Rather, it broke up, like the Republicans in France, into a large number of "groups," each forming about some particular politician. In general, there were two conventional categories of such "groups," those of the "Right" and those of the "Left." The former were a trifle more aristocratic and a trifle less anti-clerical than the latter, but perhaps the significant differences were sectional and occupational. The leading politicians of the Right came mainly from the industrial upper and middle classes of Piedmont, Lombardy, and Tuscany, while those of the Left hailed principally from the professional and intellectual bourgeoisie of Sicily and Naples.

**Political Groups**

From 1870 to 1876 groups of the Right were in power. Then for two decades, from 1876 to 1896, groups of the Left usually controlled the government, at first under the leadership of Agostino Depretis, a native of Lombardy rather than of the South, who was prime minister, with two short interruptions, from 1876 to 1887, and afterwards under the direction of Franceso Crispi, an ambitious Sicilian, who presided over several ministries between 1887 and 1896. From 1896 to 1903 groups of the Right again predominated, and during the next ten years the kingdom was administered most of the time by a coalition of Left groups under the guidance of Giovanni Giolitti. The politicians mentioned—Depretis, Crispi, and Giolitti—were influential in fashioning Left groups into something like a party machine and also in determining major policies for the Italian nation. The difference between Left and Right about major policies, however, was more theoretical than real. Hardly appreciable change occurred, except in respect of political patronage, when a ministry of the Right succeeded a ministry of the Left, or vice versa.

The royal government, whether of Right or of Left, was sympathetic with industrial and commercial interests and did much to foster them. Thousands of miles of railway were built. Old roads were repaired and new ones constructed. Harbors were developed. Governmental bounties were given to merchant shipping; and, to encourage Italian

**Industrial Development**

industry and increase its financial profits, a system of tariff protection was instituted. In spite of the fact that Italy had no coal or iron of its own and had to import these basic necessities of modern industry, governmental solicitude helped to forward slowly but surely an economic transformation, most noticeably in the North but to some extent throughout the peninsula. The annual value of Italy's foreign trade, hovering around 440 million dollars from 1870 to 1897, rose steadily thereafter until it reached 1,200 million in 1913. Between 1897 and 1913, exports of manufactured goods almost tripled: Milan surpassed Lyons as the chief silk market in the world; and Italian cotton factories captured the home market and increased their foreign sales from five to fifty million dollars' worth. By 1914, moreover, the Italian merchant marine held sixth place among the commercial fleets of the several nations of the world.

While the Italian government, both of Right and of Left, was industrially minded, it was also nationalistically minded. It was the heir of that patriotic spirit which had actuated the country's political unification and which beckoned imperiously on to a great destiny for Italy in the world at large. Now that it was a sovereign power, it must be a great power. What Germany and France were doing with army and colonial empire, Italy likewise must do.

**National Ambition**

The Italian army was reorganized and enlarged, at least on paper, through the adoption of the principle of compulsory military training (1875). Large sums of money were spent on military equipment and fortifications and on a navy. In 1881 Italian nationalism—and imperialism—was markedly stimulated by the French occupation of Tunis, which was nearer to Italy than to France, which had more Italian than French residents, and which, as the land of ancient Carthage, possessed a greater sentimental interest for Italy than for France. Why had Italy, its patriots asked, been behindhand in appropriating Tunis? Because of Italy's international isolation, its government replied; and to put an end to that and to prevent any repetition of French "aggression," Italy in 1882 contracted with Germany and Austria-Hungary a famous Triple Alliance, which endured until 1915. Almost immediately Italy proceeded to establish a colonial empire in eastern Africa along the Red Sea. By commercial and military occupation and by treaties with native chieftains and with Great

Britain, it acquired, between 1882 and 1890, the sparsely peopled, blisteringly hot tracts of Eritrea and Italian Somaliland, and thence set out to subdue the Negro kingdom of Abyssinia (Ethiopia). The Abyssinians, however, put up such a stiff resistance, and at Adowa in 1896 routed an Italian army so decisively, that Italy agreed to make peace and respect Abyssinia's independence.

To elevate Italy to the position of a great power, to defray the expenses of army and navy, public works and colonial ventures, and incidentally to support the financial corruption which was fairly prevalent in Italian politics, the government imposed a heavy burden of taxation upon the nation and still found itself faced with recurrent threats of bankruptcy and with the necessity of economizing on expenditure for social and educational betterment. Thus, a law which the Italian parliament enacted in 1877 for compulsory schooling of children between the ages of six and nine was only partially and half-heartedly enforced because the government preferred to devote its financial resources to other objects. Illiteracy declined very slowly among the masses of the Italian people.

The economic condition of the mass of peasants and urban workmen was indeed sorry. The standard of living was low. The taxes were high. Population increased at a faster rate in Italy than in any other European country, and at a faster rate than did the opportunities for employment. **Popular Unrest**

In the circumstances, there was a good deal of popular unrest. Some of it was registered in a remarkable emigration of Italians, seeking a happier economic lot and an escape from military conscription, chiefly across the ocean to the United States, Argentina, and Brazil. In 1900 the number of emigrants was 350,000, and in 1910 it was 530,000. Not all these emigrants left home permanently. In fact, a large portion of them, in some years almost a half, returned to Italy after earning money abroad. Nevertheless, it was officially stated in 1910 that through emigration the kingdom of Italy had permanently lost to countries of the New World as many as five and a half million citizens, 80 per cent of whom were peasants, mainly from southern Italy.

Popular unrest was evidenced by this large-scale exodus of Italian peasants from the South, and also by the spread of Marxian socialism and revolutionary violence among the industrial proletariat in the cities, especially of the North. A Socialist party

was founded at Milan in 1891 and, taking advantage of a somewhat broadened suffrage which had been enacted in 1882, it managed to elect twelve members of the Chamber of Deputies in 1895.
The party, however, was more influential outside parliament than
inside, and outside among the proletarians its propaganda was
supplemented, and surpassed in extreme radicalism, by that of
anarchists who would have nothing to do with any parliamentary
regime and would concentrate, instead, on "class warfare," organization of labor, and acts of violence against employers and
government. In 1900 King Humbert, who had succeeded to the
throne on the death of his illustrious father, Victor Emmanuel II,
in 1878, was assassinated by an anarchist, and in 1904 the government of the succeeding monarch, Victor Emmanuel III, had to
employ the army to put down a general strike at Milan which
was being conducted with violence and obvious revolutionary
purpose.

Impelled from all sides, the Italian government, soon after the
setback to its imperialistic designs on Ethiopia and the resulting
retirement of Crispi (1896), began to devote more at-

**Labor
Legislation**
tention to internal reform. It gradually evolved a program of labor legislation. In 1898 old-age pensions
were provided, and workmen were compulsorily insured against
accidents and sickness. In 1902 an important factory law was
enacted. In 1908 a weekly day of rest was prescribed for labor.
In 1912 private insurance companies were nationalized. And
during this period, other measures of social significance were
adopted. The state took over from private companies the operation of the railways. Municipalities were authorized to own and
operate public utilities. Trade unions were legalized and their
funds and activities safeguarded. Some progress was made in
the arbitration of labor disputes. Cooperative societies for banking and for wholesale buying and retail selling were fostered,
particularly in the rural districts.

There was response, moreover, to the insistent popular demand
for the supplanting of restricted class government by full political
democracy. Back in 1882 an electoral reform had somewhat
broadened the suffrage by reducing the property qualification,
but until 1912 the retention of a literacy test and of some property qualification served to restrict the electorate to a comparatively small minority of the Italian nation. Now, at this

latter date, Giolitti and his coalition of groups of the Left were moved to enact a really drastic electoral law, establishing universal manhood suffrage as the method of choosing the Chamber of Deputies. In the general election of **Democratic Suffrage** 1913—the first under the new democracy—the Socialist party increased its representation in the Chamber from 43 to 78, and the bourgeois Left was so weakened that Giolitti resigned the premiership. A new "nationalist" ministry was formed under the leadership of Antonio Salandra.

Nationalism was arising anew in Italy. It was being stimulated among the masses by the concurrent rise of democracy and among the younger generation of intellectuals by literary and philosophical currents of which Gabriele D'Annunzio was a leading representative. It was already evident, side by side with socialist agitation, during the first decade of the twentieth century, when demands multiplied in parliament and in the country at large for greater armaments, larger colonies, more vigorous foreign policy, and more serious and sustained efforts to "redeem" those provinces of *Italia irredenta*—Trent, Trieste, and the eastern coast of the Adriatic—which were peopled by Italians but still ruled by Austria. It would shortly lead to war.

## 2. THE HOHENZOLLERN GERMAN EMPIRE

The German Empire, as fashioned in 1871 under the nominal headship of Prussia's Hohenzollern King, William I, and the actual guidance of his chief minister, Prince Bismarck,[1] comprised twenty-five states, besides the "imperial territory" of Alsace-Lorraine, each a sovereign state [2] with a government of its own and with control over many local matters, such as education and public health. For the Empire as a whole, no law **The Empire and Prussian Control** could be enacted without the consent of a Bundesrat (Federal Council) composed of personal agents of the several state governments. At the same time, popular—and democratic—participation in the central govern-

---

[1] On the creation of the German Empire, see *Modern Europe to 1870*, pp. 742–753, 756–760.

[2] Of the twenty-five states, four were kingdoms (Prussia, Bavaria, Saxony, and Württemberg); six were grandduchies (Baden, Hesse, Mecklenburg-Schwerin, Mecklenburg-Strelitz, Oldenburg, and Saxe-Weimar); five were duchies; seven were diminutive principalities; and three were republican "free cities" (Hamburg, Bremen, and Lübeck).

ment was guaranteed by the constitutional provision that all male citizens of the Empire, over twenty-five years of age, should have the right to vote for members of a Reichstag (Imperial Parliament), whose consent, as well as that of the Bundesrat, was requisite to the enactment of laws. Nevertheless, the democratic Reichstag could exercise no such control as the British or French parliament might exercise. It was estopped by the fact that the national ministry, headed by a Chancellor, was responsible not to it but to the Emperor and, more fundamentally, by the role which undemocratic Prussia was privileged to play in the Empire.

Prussia, it must be remembered, continued to be governed internally in accordance with the constitution which Frederick William IV had promulgated in 1850, with its formal recognition of the "divine right" of the King to choose his ministers at will and with its practical limitation of the Diet, or state parliament, to mere acceptance or rejection of royal proposals by representatives of the upper and middle classes.[1] This same Prussia was now become the most powerful and influential state in the German Empire. Prussia had made the Empire. Of the area and population of the Empire, Prussia embraced almost two-thirds, while the other twenty-four states together contained barely one-third. Naturally, Prussia—not so much its people as its government— occupied a commanding position in the government and administration of the Empire. The Hohenzollern King of Prussia headed the Empire; he bore the title of "German Emperor" and appointed or dismissed at will the Chancellor of the Empire. The Prussian military system had to be the Empire's military system. And enough votes were accorded to the agent of the King of Prussia in the Bundesrat to enable him to veto any reduction of army or taxes or any amendment to the imperial constitution which a majority in the Reichstag might approve.

For almost twenty years after 1871 William I was Emperor, and Bismarck was Chancellor, of the German Empire. Throughout this period Bismarck was the chief figure in the domestic politics of his own country and in the international politics of Europe. In the first years of his chancellorship, a large majority of the Reichstag (and, of course, the Bundesrat) supported the measures which he advocated for consolidating the Empire.

---

[1] On the Prussian constitution, as distinct from that of the German Empire, see *Modern Europe to 1870*, pp. 677, 679–680.

The legal systems of the several states were supplanted by uniform codes of law for the entire Empire. An act of 1873 created an imperial railway bureau, which did much to unify the various state railways and to coordinate them with the military, postal, and telegraphic organizations of the Empire. A Bank Act of 1875 transferred the control of banking from state governments to the Bundesrat, and the establishment of the Imperial Bank (Reichsbank) in 1876 expedited the financial operations of the central government and contributed to its stability and prestige.

**Bismarck as Chancellor, 1871–90**

Thanks to such legislation, and thanks still more to accompanying exploitation of great natural resources of coal and iron in the Ruhr and Saar basins and in newly acquired Lorraine, rapid progress was made after 1871 in all sorts of machine industry. Germany soon became the foremost industrial country on the Continent.

Germany was also the foremost military power. Successive triumphs in war over Austria and France had shown the Prussian-Germany army to be the best organized, the best equipped, and the most effective. And as Bismarck had used it with striking success to create the Hohenzollern German Empire, so he relied upon it to insure the Empire's preservation and international leadership. Accordingly, compulsory military service, which had been extended in Prussia in 1862, was applied in 1871 to the whole Empire, the "peace strength" of the German army being fixed at 400,000. On this matter Bismarck had some trouble with the Reichstag by reason of his proposal that the necessary financial appropriations should be made a permanent charge on the treasury. This the majority of the Reichstag refused to sanction, and Bismarck eventually had to accept a compromise whereby appropriations for the army were voted for a limited term of years—seven at first, and later five. From time to time, therefore, the government was obliged to submit its military policy to debate by the nation's representatives, but the Chancellor soon learned that by utilizing a "war scare" on the eve of any such debate, he could usually get from the Reichstag what he wanted for the army.

**Army Legislation**

Bismarck was well aware of the deep humiliation which France suffered in 1870–1871 and of its willingness to seize the first favorable opportunity to recover Alsace-Lorraine. With Germany's military superiority, he did not fear an attack by France single-handed, but he did fear a possible coalition of other great powers with France. Hence his foreign policy was directed toward keeping France isolated and deprived of potential allies.

In the main, the international situation from 1871 to 1890 was favorable to Germany, and the astute, and not too high-principled, Chancellor took full advantage of it. First **Foreign** of all, he adopted a most conciliatory attitude toward **Policy** Austria-Hungary. He had purposely been lenient in dictating terms of peace to the Emperor Francis Joseph in 1866; and after 1871 the internal exigencies of the Dual Monarchy, and the desire of the Habsburg family to recoup what they had lost in Italy and Germany by pursuing an expansionist policy in the Balkans, led the governing classes of Austria-Hungary to seek support of Germany's strong military arm and Bismarck's dexterous diplomatic hand. Then, too, Bismark could count upon the friendship of the newly formed kingdom of Italy. Many Italians remembered that it was through an alliance with Bismarck's Germany that they had been enabled to wrest Venetia from Austria in 1866. Besides, the Italian government was at feud with the papacy, and so was the German in the 1870's, at the very time when France was dominated by "clericals," many of whom favored intervention in Italy for the purpose of restoring the Pope's temporal rule.

With Great Britain, Bismarck sedulously avoided conflict. He insisted during the war of 1870-1871 upon the scrupulous observance of Belgian neutrality—an object dear to the British foreign office—and he hesitated for a decade and more about engaging in overseas imperialism. When eventually in the 1880's he yielded in this matter to the importunities of German merchants and patriots, he took pains to avoid quarrels with Great Britain. He knew that British imperialists were far more troubled by the aggressiveness of Russia in Asia and of France in Africa than by Germany's belated and relatively modest imperialism. He knew also that many English intellectuals admired the German people and extolled the "Teutonic race" which had produced the two leading states of the time—Germany, the master of the Continent, and Great Britain, the mistress of the seas. He knew that it had become a tradition of the British foreign office to avoid "entangling alliances" upon the continent of Europe so long as

British maritime supremacy was unquestioned. From all this, Bismarck felt confident that Germany need not fear an alliance between Great Britain and France.

Russia was a different quantity. Its growing rivalry with Austria-Hungary in the Balkans might prevent Germany from cultivating equally friendly relations with the two, and if Germany should favor Austria-Hungary, Russia would tend to gravitate toward an alliance with France. But several circumstances enabled Bismarck to forestall a Franco-Russian alliance. Politically, autocratic Russia was more sympathetic with monarchical Germany than with republican France. The Tsar Alexander II (1855–1881) detested the revolutionaries who were reputed to have learned their doctrines in France, and he gratefully remembered how Bismarck had offered him Prussian aid for the suppression of the Polish insurrection of 1863, and how again in 1871 Bismarck had graciously acquiesced in Russia's recovery of the right to maintain warships on the Black Sea.[1] He felt the need of German support in overcoming British opposition to Russian expansion whether in the Balkans or in Asia.

Of these considerations Bismarck took canny account. In September 1872, a meeting at Berlin of the Emperor William I, the Emperor-King Francis Joseph, the Tsar Alexander II, and their several ministers, advertised to the world that cordial and intimate relations existed among the three great Empires of central and eastern Europe. In 1873 the members of this so-called Three Emperors' League agreed to cooperate in the preservation of peace, and, in case war should threaten, to consult together "in order to determine a common course of action."

**Three Emperors' League**

For a moment in 1875 a press campaign in Germany against the military preparations then going on in France threatened the Russo-German friendship, for the Russian government (and likewise the British), suspecting that the campaign was inspired by Bismarck and was preliminary to a German assault upon France, protested against such a possible development. Bismarck declared with no little asperity that the suspicion was quite ill-founded. The press campaign was halted, and the excitement over the "affair of 1875" soon subsided.

A more serious difficulty for Bismarck was presented by the

[1] See *Modern Europe to 1870*, p. 761.

Russo-Turkish War of 1877–1878. The triumph of Russia, and its seeming ability to dictate a peace settlement giving it a dominant position in the Balkans, provoked the liveliest apprehension in Austria-Hungary as well as in Great Britain, and at the ensuing Congress of Berlin (1878) Bismarck undertook to play the role of "honest broker" in apportioning the Turkish spoils.[1] Thereby he satisfied Austria but displeased Russia.

In order to guard Germany against untoward results of Russian ill-feeling, Bismarck in 1879 concluded a defensive alliance between Austria-Hungary and Germany, in accordance with the terms of which each party bound itself to support the other with all the military forces at its command if either party or both should be attacked by Russia or by another power backed by Russia.[2] Then, in order still further to offset the danger of Russian hostility, Bismarck turned his attention to Italy. Italy, as has been remarked, was already naturally well disposed toward Germany, but Bismarck was unwilling to bind the two powers by an alliance unless Austria-Hungary were included, and relations between Austria and Italy were strained by the memory of recent wars between them, and also by conflicting ambitions as to Trent and Trieste and the mastery of the Adriatic. Nevertheless, the Italian government felt the weakness of diplomatic isolation; and in 1881 Italians were angered by French occupation of Tunis. In the midst of ensuing Franco-Italian recriminations, Italy responded cordially to the overtures of Bismarck, consented to banish anti-Austrian propaganda, and in 1882 signed a treaty of alliance with both Germany and Austria-Hungary. This treaty provided that if Italy or Germany were attacked by France without provocation these two allies would go to war with France; and that if any one or any two of the three allies were attacked by two or more great powers, all should engage in the conflict. The Triple Alliance, first formed in 1882 for five years, was renewed in 1887 with an additional stipulation that neither Austria nor Italy should attempt to occupy any territory in the Balkan peninsula without preliminary accord, and that such accord should be based on the

*Margin note: Triple Alliance with Austria and Italy*

---

[1] On the Russo-Turkish War, the Russian peace settlement of San Stefano, and the ensuing Congress of Berlin, see below, pp. 159–165.

[2] The existence of the alliance was widely advertised at the time, but its terms were not published until 1888.

principle of reciprocal compensation.[1] Moreover, in the 1880's the Balkan states of Serbia and Rumania became satellites of the Triple Alliance.

Danger of conflict between Germany and Russia had already subsided. The assassination of the Tsar Alexander II in 1881 and the accession of the ultra-reactionary Alexander III precluded any immediate understanding between autocratic Russia and democratic France; and the new Tsar decided to acquiesce in the Balkan settlement of 1878 and seek a renewal of the previous understanding with Germany and, if necessary, with Austria. Bismarck, of course, deemed the inclusion of Austria necessary; and consequently another Three Emperors' League was negotiated in 1881. By its terms, Russia, Germany, and Austria-Hungary mutually promised benevolent neutrality in case any of them should be involved in war with a fourth power. This arrangement, entered into for a period of three years, was renewed in 1884 for another three-year period.

Increasing friction in the Balkans between Russia and Austria led to the former's withdrawal from the Three Emperors' League in 1887, just when the agitation of General Boulanger was gathering headway in France for a war of revenge against Germany. The German Chancellor, greatly alarmed, took extraordinary steps to meet the situation. While renewing and strengthening the Triple Alliance with Austria-Hungary and Italy, he made a secret three-year pact, the so-called "Reinsurance Treaty," with Russia, pledging Germany's diplomatic support of Russian predominance in Bulgaria and even of Russian occupation of Constantinople, and obtaining in return a pledge of Russia's benevolent neutrality in case of a French attack upon Germany. At the same time (1887), in order to deter Russia from becoming too aggressive in the Balkans, as well as to hold France in check, he secretly encouraged a special agreement among Great Britain, Austria-Hungary, and Italy for the preservation of the *status quo* in the Mediterranean and the Near East. In 1889 he sought to bring Great Britain into direct alliance with Germany. In this he was unsuccessful, for, while the British government of the day was by no means anti-German, it was unwilling to commit Great Britain to definite participation in a Franco-German conflict.

[1] The Triple Alliance was subsequently renewed for continuous periods in 1891, in 1903, and in 1912. Its terms were not fully divulged until World War I.

At any rate during his tenure as Chancellor from 1871 to 1890, Bismarck managed by a remarkably complex series of alliances, and with the backing of a most powerful army, to keep France isolated and to insure the peaceful consolidation and development of the German Empire. International diplomacy, as well as military might, centered in Berlin during this period.

In the internal consolidation of the Empire in the 1870's and in the formulation of its domestic policies, Bismarck had the **German Political Parties** active support, in the Reichstag and in the country at large, of two nationalistic political parties. These were: (1) the National Liberty party, the party of the industrial and intellectual bourgeoisie whose nationalism (and devotion to material concerns) was fast eclipsing their liberalism, and whose popular following was the largest of any German party in the 1870's; and (2) the Free Conservative party, a party of "enlightened" landlords, chiefly Prussian but glad to forward nationalizing tendencies.

Of the two other political parties which had been in evidence in Prussia during the 1860's, the Conservative party was still the representative of numerous "old-fashioned" landed nobles and squires, Lutheran clergymen and army officers, eminently respectable and quite wedded to the "old monarchy," while the Progressive was a party of doctrinaire middle-class radicals whose liberalism was still superior to their nationalism. The Conservatives were too narrowly Prussian to sympathize fully with Bismarck's all-German mood after 1871 and too devoted to divine-right monarchy to evince any enthusiasm about his concessions to democracy, but inasmuch as they had long been in the habit of regarding Bismarck as one of themselves, they were not inclined to quarrel with him, and on some matters, notably on his army policy, they backed him vociferously. The Progressives, however, were a thorn in Bismarck's side. Not at all satisfied with the German constitution of 1871, they demanded its drastic revision in accordance with the British system of parliamentary government and ministerial responsibility. Being pacifist, too, they opposed Bismarck's pet army plans. And, with their lengthy discourses in the Reichstag, they wearied the Chancellor, who was more given to action than to speech.

The opposition to Bismarckian policies was not confined, in the Reichstag, to the Progressive party. It was voiced by several minor groups: (1) a few Socialists; (2) a few "Guelfs," deputies from the former kingdom of Hanover which Prussia had annexed in 1866 and who, led by Ludwig Windthorst, the last prime minister of that kingdom, were anxious to restore its autonomy; [1] (3) a Dane or two from northern Schleswig, demanding the retrocession of this province to Denmark; (4) a group from the Polish-speaking areas of Posen and West Prussia whom the rising German nationalism of the time only served to fire with Polish nationalism; (5) the deputies from Alsace-Lorraine, who, on their first appearance in the Reichstag in 1874, made solemn protest against the incorporation of their territory with the German Empire, and subsequently were quite critical of the Empire and its legislation; and (6) a somewhat larger group of deputies who, coming principally from the traditionally freer states of South Germany, were anxious to safeguard "states' rights" against too much Prussianizing or nationalizing, and who, being Catholic in religion, were fearful of intolerant interference from the Protestant majority in the Empire.

Bismarck was particularly nettled by the Catholic states' rights group, and his desire to repress it by striking at the Catholic Church was shared by the majority in both the imperial and Prussian parliaments. National Liberals and Free Conservatives thought the Catholics lacking in German patriotism and too much disposed to follow the dictates of a "foreign power"—the papacy—which, now fortified by the dogma of infallibility,[2] might be more dangerous than ever to German independence and unity. Many Conservatives, staunchly Lutheran, were ready to seize any opportunity to resume battle with Rome. And the Progressives, intent upon stressing the liberal and materialistic aspects of modern civilization, found themselves in the curious position of supporting Bismarck in his hostility to the Catholic Church. Indeed, it was a Progressive leader who applied the high-sounding phrase *Kulturkampf*—"battle for civilization"—to the struggle which was waged during the 1870's in Prussia and throughout the German Empire between the government and the Church.

In 1872 Bismarck fired the first guns in the *Kulturkampf* by expelling the Jesuits from Germany and breaking off diplomatic

*Conflict with Catholic Church*

---

[1] On the annexation of Hanover by Prussia, see *Modern Europe to 1870*, p. 751.
[2] See below, pp. 245–247.

relations between Prussia and the Vatican. Then followed, in May 1873 and May 1874, rounds of artillery fire from the Prussian parliament in the form of anti-Catholic enactments, sometimes styled the "May laws," and sometimes cited, from the name of the Prussian minister of education, the "Falk laws." The most significant of them prescribed that every official of the Catholic Church in Prussia—every bishop and every priest—must be a German citizen, a graduate of a German university, and duly "authorized" by the government; all ecclesiastical seminaries were placed under state control; and, as a special measure against Polish Catholics, all religious instruction must be given in German. Catholic bishops in Prussia, with the approval of their colleagues elsewhere in Germany and of Pope Pius IX, at once protested against the May laws and refused to observe them. Whereupon the Prussian parliament made refractory clergymen liable to loss of citizenship and to imprisonment or exile. With such severity were these penalties enforced, moreover, that within a single year six Catholic bishops were jailed, and in over 1,300 parishes Catholic worship ceased.

German Catholics fought back with unexpected unanimity [1] and increasing effectiveness. Encouraged by the papacy and by their "martyred" bishops, they rallied in support of the ecclesiastical "administrators" who by stealth took the place of the bishops and preserved a church organization in Germany, and likewise in support of political leaders, such as Windthorst, the Hanoverian "Guelf," who built up a distinctively Catholic party —the so-called Center party—to work openly at the polls and in parliament for the repeal of the anti-Catholic legislation. The Center party championed religious liberty and social reform, and soon commanded the suffrages of Catholic workmen as well as of other Catholics. In the general election of 1874 it polled one and a half million votes and increased its representation in the Reichstag from 60 to 90. And before long, within the Reichstag, Windthorst was skillfully aligning with the Center party most of

[1] The German government had counted on a good deal of indifference among the Catholic masses and on a large active secession from the Catholic Church to the so-called "Old Catholic Church," which had been set up by a few disaffected Catholics shortly after the definition of the dogma of papal infallibility in 1870 and which the government did its utmost to foster. The "Old Catholic Church," however, could not be nursed into vigorous life; its total membership in Germany reached a peak of 52,000 in 1878 and then declined.

the minor groups which for one reason or another were inimical to Bismarck—Poles, Alsatians, Guelfs, even Socialists. Eventually, when a section of the Conservatives took fright at the anti-religious implications of some of the legislation and began to cooperate with Windthorst, Bismarck grew alarmed and decided that the time had come to halt the *Kulturkampf*. Too many of his other policies were endangered by the coalition forming against him on his religious policy, and in Marxian Socialism he began to perceive a greater menace to what he held dear than in Roman Catholicism.

In 1880 the Prussian parliament, on Bismarck's recommendation, empowered the government to use its discretion in administering the May laws. Diplomatic relations were presently resumed with the Vatican; and in 1886 the most oppressive anti-Catholic measures were formally repealed. Bismarck thus confessed that his *Kulturkampf* had been a failure. It served to raise up and solidify a Catholic party which, under able leadership, persevered in what was to Bismarck an unholy alliance with democrats and socialists and all the other dissident groups who sought political change.

On the heels of the *Kulturkampf* came Bismarck's campaign against Socialism. As industrialization progressed in Germany, as mining and the metal industries developed in West- Conflict phalia and Silesia and the textile and other machine with industries in Saxony and the Rhineland and Alsace, Socialism Socialist propaganda made headway among the urban working classes. In the general election of 1874 Socialists obtained nine seats in the Reichstag. In 1875 they formed a compact "Social Democratic" party through the fusion of two previously rival groups. In the ensuing general election of 1877 they polled half a million votes and increased their representation in the Reichstag to twelve. The principles which the party preached were the antitheses of Bismarck's and were calculated, in his opinion, to subvert the state.

Making use of public horror attending two unsuccessful attempts in 1878 to assassinate the venerable Emperor William I, Bismarck dissolved the existing Reichstag and secured the election of a new one whose majority shared his opinion of Social Democrats and of what should be done with them. At once, despite the protests of a minority composed of Centrists, Progressives, and the minor dissident groups, the majority passed a severe law against Socialist propaganda. This law, originally enacted for a term of four years, was subsequently reenacted several times and remained in force until Bismarck's retirement from office in 1890. It forbade the circulation of Socialist literature, empowered the police to break up Socialist meetings, and removed the trial and punishment of Socialist offenders from the jurisdiction of the regular courts to that of the police.

Yet the Social Democratic party survived. It preserved its organization in Germany, conducted energetic propaganda from neighboring countries, and increased its representation and volubility in the Reichstag.

Socialists and Catholics were not the only groups that aroused Bismarck's ire and evoked repressive measures from him. He had the average Prussian noblemen's contempt for the Poles. He tried to force upon them the use of the German language during the *Kulturkampf* in the 1870's, and he sponsored in the 1880's certain enactments of the Prussian parliament directed, on the one hand, toward the curbing of Polish political activity and, on the other, toward the transfer of farms from Polish to German ownership. But his efforts against the Poles only intensified their opposition.

Alsace-Lorraine, which he had taken from France in 1871, Bismarck did his best to Germanize. He encouraged immigration into it from other parts of the Empire, and he secured from the Reichstag large appropriations for making the University of Strasbourg an important center of German intellectual life and cultural influence. Yet the attitude of the elected representatives from Alsace-Lorraine in the Reichstag was not reassuring, and Bismarck persisted in treating the provinces as conquered territory and denying them equality with the other German states.

Toward Jews, too, Bismarck was none too kindly disposed, though for political and financial reasons he refrained from public attacks upon them and actually rebuked a prominent Lutheran clergyman, Adolf Stöcker, for some of his anti-Semitic activities in the 1880's. Nevertheless, the bitterly anti-Jewish agitation of Stöcker and the National Socialist party which he founded, was quite consonant with the illiberal attitude and policies of Prince Bismarck toward most minority groups in Germany.

A very important change in national policy Bismarck wrought

with the aid of Conservatives and Centrists during the 1880's, and that was a change from economic liberalism to economic nationalism. The movement in behalf of such a change did not originate with Bismarck or with any particular person. It was a natural outcome of the demands of Economic National-ism German industry and agriculture, of the popular reaction to rising Socialism, and of the heightening political nationalism of the 1860's and 1870's in Germany. It manifested itself toward the close of the 1870's in the relative decline of those German political parties, National Liberal and Progressive, which had borrowed their economic doctrines from the English Liberals and stood for *laissez-faire,* and a corresponding gain of those parties, Conservative and Centrist, which were more inclined to paternalism. The resulting change in national policy which Bismarck was induced to favor was threefold. From being an essentially free-trade country, Germany became a leader in tariff protection. From being a purely European power, Germany became a world power with extensive overseas dominion. From being ostensibly unconcerned with relations between capital and labor, Germany became the chief exemplar of governmental intervention.

Tariff protection was inaugurated by act of the Reichstag in 1879. Bismarck's purpose in sponsoring this measure was to protect German "infant industries" against the competition of the older and more developed industries of Great Britain, to increase the taxable wealth of Germany, and to get enough income for the federal government from customs duties to relieve it of the necessity of levying assessments on the several states, as it had been obliged to do since 1871. The tariff act of 1879 did give new financial strength to the federal government, and, even more clearly, a marked impetus to Germany's industrial development. Indeed, the agrarian classes complained that the tariff of 1879 was too favorable to urban industry, and in order to redress the balance between industry and agriculture and to promote self-sufficiency for the Empire in foodstuffs as well as in manufactures, they secured by supplementary tariff acts of 1885 and 1887 greatly increased protection for agriculture without lessening the protection of industry.

Before the adoption of the policy of tariff protection Bismarck opposed overseas imperialism. In 1871 he rejected a French offer to cede colonies to Germany in lieu of Alsace-Lorraine; and throughout the 1870's he stuck to his belief that Germany should devote its energies to strengthening itself internally and on the **Overseas** continent of Europe and should avoid colonial under- **Imperialism** takings. But the merchant's desire to sell his goods, the capitalist's desire to make lucrative investments, the Christian missionary's desire to convert the heathen, and the patriot's desire to exalt Germany as a world power, all contributed to an irresistible national yearning for German colonies. Merchants led the way; missionaries soon followed. In 1879 a German trading company acquired privileges in the Samoan Islands. In 1882 an important German colonial society undertook, with much success, to unite business men in support of colonial ventures and to arouse popular interest in them. Within a brief time, commercial companies of Hamburg, Lübeck, and Bremen obtained concessions from native chieftains, and established trading posts in several areas in Africa—Southwest Africa, Togoland, Kamerun, and East Africa—and in several islands of the Pacific—the Marshall Islands, a part of New Guinea (flatteringly labeled Kaiser Wilhelmsland), and the group of islands presently christened the Bismarck Archipelago.

Prince Bismarck, in his new role as champion of German commerce and industry, conquered his earlier scruples and followed the merchants and missionaries with his official blessing. In 1884–1885 he prevailed upon the Reichstag to sanction formal protectorates over the distant trading posts in Africa and in the Pacific. In 1886 he secured governmental subsidies for regular steamship service between Germany and the protectorates. Before his retirement in 1890 the process was far advanced of delimiting the mercantile protectorates and transforming them into crown colonies, administered by imperial officials and policed by German troops. By this time Germany was in possession of a colonial domain of close to a million square miles—almost five times the area of the mother-country—though its population was relatively slight and almost entirely aboriginal, either Negro or Polynesian.

The pursuit of imperialism and the adoption of tariff protection were obviously intended primarily to increase the profits of German manufacturers and traders, and incidentally of German landlords, though it was frequently alleged that they served also to raise the wages of German workmen and to open to them new forms of employment. For the express benefit of workmen, however, significant social legislation was enacted. In 1883 a bill was passed insuring them against sickness, and in 1884 employers were compelled to insure their employees against accidents. In 1887 laws were enacted limiting the labor of women and children, establishing a maximum number of working hours for employees in various industries, and setting Sunday apart as a day of rest. In 1889 provision was made for insuring workmen against old age and invalidity. There can be no doubt that this labor legislation, together with a system of free labor exchanges which the government shortly set up, and with the development of trade unionism, prepared the German people from below, as protection and imperialism and governmental fostering of technological advance prepared them from above, to become one of the most efficient industrial nations.

*Labor Legislation*

Before his new economic policies were fully matured, the long period of Prince Bismarck's domination came to an abrupt close. He lost a sturdy friend when his Hohenzollern sovereign, the aged Emperor William I, died in March 1888. William's son and successor to the thrones of Prussia and the Empire was Frederick III, who was reputed to be "liberal," but whether he deserved the reputation and would have acted in accordance with it no one really knows, for he was a very sick man when he succeeded his father and he died in June 1888 after a reign of only ninety-nine days. Whereupon his son, the grandson of William I, became King of Prussia and German Emperor as William II.

William II (1888–1918) was a young man, twenty-nine years of age at the time, imbued with the same ideas of divine-right monarchy and the same predilection for militarism as had characterized William I, but with a vanity, a volubility, and an impulsiveness which were engaging to some people but irritating to Bismarck, who was now an elderly man quite used to handling the reins of government without much direction or advice from his sovereign. From William II's standpoint it soon became a question, as he subsequently expressed it, "whether the Hohenzollern dynasty or the Bismarck dynasty should rule." In March 1890 differences between the young Emperor and the old Chancellor reached a climax. Bismarck was anxious to retain close ties between Germany and Russia, while William II thought them incompatible with the

*William II's Dismissal of Bismarck, 1890*

alliance between Germany and Austria. William II refused to sanction Bismarck's plan to renew the repressive legislation against the Socialists and, if necessary, to frighten parliament and people into submission by armed force. Bismarck declined to accede to an order from William II which would have given to all cabinet ministers access direct to the Emperor instead of indirect through the Chancellor. So William II demanded Bismarck's resignation, and the "Iron Chancellor" withdrew to his large private estates. There the man who had done more than anyone else to create the Hohenzollern Empire and for twenty years to shape its policies lived in more or less open criticism of the Emperor and the new ministers until his death, at the advanced age of eighty-three, in July 1898.

From 1890 to 1914 the Emperor-King William II occupied the chief position in Germany and in Prussia, preserving Prussia's leadership in Germany and Germany's prestige in Europe. Politically, the basic ideas of William II were not essentially different from Bismarck's, though he talked about them more often and more loftily. He was fond of reaffirming with picturesque metaphors the historic Hohenzollern ideal of monarchy, established by God and in constant communication with Him. Militarism he constantly extolled—asserting on one occasion, in true Bismarckian style, that "the soldier and the army, not parliamentary majorities, have welded together the German Empire; my confidence is placed in the army." He accepted and forwarded the major domestic policies which Bismarck had developed; and, though he allowed the anti-Socialist legislation to lapse, he remained, like Bismarck, a pronounced foe of Socialists and "radicals."

Era of
William II

In foreign policy, there was a notable change. Bismarck, always haunted by the fear that some day France and Russia might unite against Germany, which would then have to wage war on two fronts, had successfully sought to bind Russia, as well as Austria and Italy, in alliance with Germany. But William II and the Chancellors who succeeded Bismarck felt that the latter's system of alliances was much too complicated and particularly that his "Reinsurance Treaty" with Russia was incompatible with Germany's obligations to Austria. Hence the treaty was allowed to lapse on Bismarck's retirement from office in 1890, and within the next three years what he had most dreaded came to pass—a military Dual Alliance of France and Russia.

Nevertheless, the new alignment of Continental great powers in supposedly competing Dual and Triple Alliances, was not as disturbing to Germany as had been anticipated. Russia exercised a restraining influence on French ambition to recover Alsace-Lorraine, and both France and Russia showed chief concern during the 1890's about imperialistic rivalry with Great Britain. Indeed, there was considerable cooperation between Germany, on the one hand, and France and Russia, on the other, in the Far East and in Africa; and at the time of the Boer War (1899) they even discussed the formation of a "grand alliance" against Britain. Not until 1905 did a dangerous cleavage appear.[1]

The reign of William II was especially marked by the accelerating tempo of Germany's industrialization. Between 1888 and 1913, the number of Germans engaged in manufacture and commerce increased from twenty million to thirty- *Industrial Progress* five million; the production of iron, from five million to fifteen million tons, and of coal, from 70 million to 200 million tons; Germany's share in the world's shipping, from six per cent to eleven per cent; and the annual value of its export trade, from 800 million dollars to 2,500 million.

Paralleling this industrial development, was a remarkable growth of population. Germany was not much more populous than France in 1871, but in 1913 it had three inhabitants to every two of France's. Besides, emigration, which had been heavy in the middle of the nineteenth century and which still amounted in the 1880's to a quarter million annually, decreased steadily afterwards until in the first decade of the twentieth century it averaged only about 25,000.

The forms of political action remained much the same under William II as under Bismarck. There were no important constitutional changes, though there was a good deal of agitation for the democratizing of the Prussian government. Of the five major political parties of the Empire, the Centrists, Conservatives, and National Liberals almost, if not quite, held their own; the Progressives decreased and the Social Democrats increased. In the general election of 1912 the Social Democrats polled four and a quarter million votes to two million polled by the Catholic Center,

[1] On this, see below, pp. 312–316.

one and three quarters million by the National Liberals, and one and a half million each by the Progressives and the Conservatives.

The large number of Social Democratic voters did not necessarily signify, however, that any revolution was imminent. Many such voters were trade unionists who desired no violent overturn of the existing regime but hoped rather to convince it that it should favor organized labor, while many others were middle-class "radicals," who, though not enthusiastic about the professed economic doctrines of the Social Democratic party, had come to feel that in the political sphere the party was the most promising agency for reforming imperial institutions and introducing real democracy into Germany. Which helps to explain why, as the German Socialists grew more numerous, most of their leaders and the majority of the rank and file were more prone to talk about reform than to engage in revolution.

Between 1890, when Bismarck retired from office, and 1914, when World War I began, the German Empire had four **Imperial Chancellors,** Chancellors: Caprivi (1890–1894), Hohenlohe (1894–**1890–1914** 1900), Bülow (1900–1909), and Bethmann-Hollweg (1909–1917). None of them had any such driving force or popular prestige as Bismarck possessed. They were spasmodically interfered with and dictated to by the mercurial William II, who appointed and dismissed them at will. It was but natural that many different, and even contradictory, tendencies were displayed by the German government from 1890 to 1914.

Count George von Caprivi, who succeeded Bismarck in 1890, was a Prussian army officer who had served with some distinction in the wars of 1866 and 1870–1871. Not being a great landowner like his predecessor, however, he was somewhat depised by the Prussian aristocracy and was inclined, perhaps for that reason, to like business men and to admire England. For political support in the Reichstag he relied less on the Conservatives than on the National Liberals and Progressives, in harmony with whose wishes he allowed the anti-Socialist laws to lapse, negotiated an important treaty with Great Britain, and modified the German tariff. By the treaty with Great Britain (1890), Germany abandoned certain colonial claims in Africa and obtained the cession of the island of Heligoland in the North Sea. By the new tariff enactment, the principle of reciprocity was approved; and in accordance with it commercial treaties were negotiated with Austria-Hungary, Russia, Rumania, and Italy, whereby Germany lowered its import duties on grain from these countries in return for the reduction of their tariffs on German manufactures. This arrangement was as unprofitable to German farmers as it was profitable to German industrialists and merchants; and the Prussian Conservatives, or "Agrarians," were moved mightily against Caprivi. In vain the Chancellor sought to humor them: They demanded his dismissal, and William II complied in 1894.

Caprivi's successor was Prince Hohenlohe-Schillingsfürst, an aristocrat from South Germany, who in his younger years had been the leading advocate in his native Bavaria of national unification under Prussian auspices, and who had then served successively in the Franco-German War, in the diplomatic service, and as governor of Alsace-Lorraine. Now, at seventy-five years of age, he was not much more than a distinguished figurehead, the actual conduct of the government being less in his hands than in those of the Emperor and of Prince von Bülow, secretary of state for foreign affairs and a polished versatile Prussian landlord. In domestic matters the government leaned heavily on the industrial and commercial classes for support in the Reichstag and in the country at large. It was in response to pressure from these classes, as well as in furtherance of a policy which Bismarck had inaugurated, that Hohenlohe and Bülow—and William II—devoted chief attention to the extension of A "World German dominion and trade overseas. The Emperor Empire" himself declared in 1895 that "the German Empire has become a world empire."

In 1897 the murder of two Christian missionaries of German nationality in China provided the pretext for landing German troops in the bay of Kiaochow and wresting from China some economic concessions for German merchants and bankers and the lease to Germany of some 200 square miles on the peninsula of Shantung. In 1899, following the Spanish-American War, Germany purchased from Spain the Caroline Islands in the Pacific. In 1899–1900, by agreement with Great Britain and the United States, Germany acquired the major part of Samoa.

In the meantime the German government was interesting itself in the Ottoman Empire. William II made a great show of visits to the Sultan at Constantinople, and presently the Turkish army was being reorganized and drilled by German officers, and Turkish war materials were being purchased in Germany. In 1899 a group of German bankers obtained from the Sultan a concession for the building of a railway across Asiatic Turkey from the Bosphorus to Bagdad.

Several factors conspired at this time to embark Germany on a policy of navalism, supplementary to its already highly developed militarism: the contention of many merchants and publicists that a powerful navy constituted the best surety of extended commerce and investment; the practical lesson of the importance of sea power learned from American triumph over the Spaniards and from British victory over the Boers; the propaganda of patriotic societies, especially the German Navy League; the personal enthusiasm of William II, whose art of phrase-making did excellent service to the cause in such pithy sayings as "Germany's future lies upon the water"; and, last but not least, the organizing ability of Admiral Alfred von Tirpitz, who was appointed secretary of state for the navy in 1897 and who retained that post until 1916. In 1898 was enacted the first, and in 1900 the second, of the important measures which built up for Germany an imposing navy, with a total tonnage second only to the British.

The retirement of the aged Prince Hohenlohe in 1900 and the advancement of Prince von Bülow to the chancellorship served to promote more cordial relations between the Imperial government and the Prussian Conservatives. Bülow had a suavity in handling Prussian reactionaries which Hohenlohe and Caprivi lacked; he was fundamentally more sympathetic with them; and he was freer to do what he wished as Chancellor than as a subordinate minister. He managed to yoke the agrarian Conservatives with the industrial National Liberals in a parliamentary coalition, or *bloc*, by prevailing upon the latter to consent to the abandonment of the policy of commercial reciprocity, which had been followed since the advent of Caprivi, and the adoption, in 1902, of a much higher tariff on agricultural imports.

In the Prussian parliament, to the delight of extreme German nationalists, Bülow sponsored the enactment of measures, more drastic than Bismarck's, against the Poles, limiting the use of their language and compelling them to sell land to German buyers. Yet, in spite of Bülow's best efforts to enforce his anti-Polish legislation, in spite of appropriations of a hundred million dollars to enable Germans to dispossess Poles, the provinces of Posen and West Prussia contained a larger—and more militant—Polish population in 1910 than in 1880.

As Bülow's domestic policy was dictated chiefly by Prussian Conservatives, so his foreign policy was determined mainly by imperialistically minded business men (particularly influential in the National Liberal party) and directed toward enlarging Germany's "place in the sun"—territorial and economic. This was attended by a series of spectacular threats and thrusts which aroused the distrust and hostility of Great Britain as well as of France and Russia. As we shall see in a later chapter, it produced the setting for world war.[1]

Here it should be noted that, within Germany, critics of Bülow's imperialistic policies were not wanting. Neither Socialists nor Centrists nor Progressives had ever taken kindly to the big financial outlays for army and navy; and in 1906, when Bülow asked of the Reichstag additional appropriations for the suppression of a native insurrection in German Southwest Africa, these parties seized the opportunity to put Bülow and his policies to a national test. They rejected the request, and, as they constituted for the moment a majority of the Reichstag, Bülow ordered its dissolution and the election of a new Reichstag. The ensuing electoral campaign of 1907 was hotly contested, but so stirring were the patriotic appeals addressed to the German people by the Emperor himself, and so clever were the political manipulations of the Chancellor, that, though the Centrists about held their own and the Socialists actually increased their popular vote, the government parties obtained a majority of the seats in the new Reichstag, the Socialist representation being cut in half. Henceforth, the opposition was considerably chastened. And it was an ironical commentary on the election of 1907 that the resignation of Bülow two years later was brought about by the hostility of patriotic Conservatives to his taxation schemes and by the clamor of a militarist group, led by the Crown Prince, against the Chancellor's "lack of forcefulness."

Bethmann-Hollweg, who succeeded Bülow in the chancellorship, came of a wealthy family of Prussian landlords and, trained in law, had made his career in the Prussian civil service. He

[1] See below, pp. 313–317, 353.

maintained his predecessor's foreign and domestic policies essentially intact, though for legislative assistance he relied chiefly on a coalition of Conservatives and Centrists. Under him, World War I broke; and it was an amazingly strong and united Germany which entered that war.

### 3. THE DUAL MONARCHY OF AUSTRIA-HUNGARY

As an outcome of its defeat by Prussia, the Habsburg Empire was transformed in 1867 into a Dual Monarchy. Henceforth its sovereign was Emperor of Austria and King of Hungary.[1] Between the two parts of the realm economic differences existed and political disputes occurred.

The Austrian part experienced a progressive industrialization, especially in and around Vienna and in Bohemia, with the result that manufacturing, commercial, and banking interests, and an urban industrial proletariat, became important and vied with agricultural interests and a rural peasantry in influencing Austrian policy. Hungary, on the other hand, remained overwhelmingly agricultural, and hence relatively backward in accumulating industrial capital and in developing either a strong middle class or a numerous proletariat; the masses consisted chiefly of a dependent peasantry, and opposition to the predominance of the landed aristocracy came from the professional classes.

*Austro-Hungarian Relations*

In view of the economic disparity between the two parts of the Habsburg Empire, there was recurrent haggling between them over the proportional contribution which each should make to the joint governmental expenses. Moreover, the adoption of military reforms in 1868, based on universal conscription, led to many additional bickerings between the two governments when they had to agree, from time to time, on the size of the contingent to be provided by each and on the regulations which should govern the common army.

Notwithstanding periodic disputes, the governments of both Austria and Hungary perceived advantages in the intimate alliance between them in the Dual Monarchy. In combination they could count for more in the world, materially and in prestige, than either could count separately. Their joint fiscal arrangements served to keep an extensive area in east-central Europe

[1] See *Modern Europe to 1870*, pp. 753–756.

free from internal tariff barriers and at the same time, by means of a common external tariff, to provide privileged markets for Austrian industry in Hungary and for Hungarian agriculture in Austria. Furthermore, their joint military forces served to maintain the Habsburg domain as a great power, and to double the resistance which Austria or Hungary might offer to rebellion of subject nationalities at home or to aggression by Russia from abroad.

The partners in the Dual Monarchy were especially fearful of Russian influence and intent upon counteracting it, in Ottoman and Balkan lands, as well as among the Slavic minorities in their own lands. Wherefore they cooperated in supporting a big military establishment, in building a strong navy in the Adriatic, in forming defensive alliances with the German Empire, Italy, and Rumania, and in attempting to curb the expansionist ambitions of the Yugoslav state of Serbia. In 1878, in temporary league with Great Britain, they managed to deprive Russia of some of the fruits of its victory over the Turks [1] and simultaneously to obtain the assent of the European great powers to Austria-Hungary's "occupation" of three provinces of the Ottoman Empire, the Yugoslav provinces of Bosnia, Herzegovina, and Novibazar. Then, thirty years later, taking advantage of a revolution within the Ottoman Empire and of serious troubles within the Russian Empire, Austria-Hungary formally annexed Bosnia-Herzegovina (1908), while returning Novibazar to Turkish rule. This forceful and spectacular annexation of two populous Yugoslav provinces, which Serbia coveted, was of immediate advantage to the prestige of the Dual Monarchy but eventually led to world war.

In the meantime, the internal politics of the Austrian part of the Dual Monarchy, as distinct from the Hungarian part, were undergoing noteworthy transformation. Alongside the old aristocracy and professional bureaucracy appeared **Austria** rapidly increasing numbers of business men and proletarians, successively clamoring for participation in government. The industrial and financial bourgeoisie, as well as members of the learned professions, had been enfranchised in 1867, and during the 1870's, through the Liberal party to which most of them adhered, they exerted no little influence on Austrian legislation. They promoted policies favorable to big business and high finance,

[1] See below, pp. 160–162.

and in the "liberal" tradition of the Continent they displayed equal anxiety to establish public schools and to banish ecclesiastical influence. They were "enlightened" and "anti-clerical," and, recruited mainly from the German and Jewish elements in Austria, they were inclined to emphasize the German character of the state and the desirability of Germanizing its dissident and "inferior" populations.

In the 1880's the influence of the bourgeois Liberals was weakened by the rise of the Christian Socialist party. This was a Catholic party, organized by Karl Lueger, a Viennese lawyer of lower-class origins who by impassioned attacks on "Jewish capitalism" and earnest pleas for political democracy, social legislation, and justice to Austria's subject nationalities, attracted a large following among the lower middle class of the cities and among the peasantry of the countryside and also won allies among Catholic Poles and Czechs. One significant result was the enactment of several measures designed to better the lot of workmen. Thus, in 1884–1885, factories and mines were regulated; Sunday labor was forbidden; and the employment of women and children in industry was limited. In 1887–1888, trade unions were legalized and safeguarded, and a system of insuring workers against accidents and sickness, similar to Germany's, was adopted. Karl Lueger himself presently became mayor of Vienna and for ten years utilized his position and popularity to make the capital city a leading exemplar of the municipal ownership and operation of public utilities.

Another significant result was the passing of the "liberal" state, with its narrowly restricted franchise, and the coming of **Democracy** the "democratic" state. A law of 1896 more than **and** tripled the number of parliamentary electors in Austria, **Disruptive** **Nation-** and an act of 1907 adopted universal manhood suffrage **alism** and rendered its exercise compulsory. By this time, however, the Christian Socialist party was waning, relatively if not absolutely, not so much because of any marked revival of bourgeois liberalism as because of rapid conversion of young intellectuals and urban workmen to the tenets of Marxian socialism and the newly formed Social Democratic party. In the general election of 1907—the first really democratic election in Austria—the Social Democrats increased their representation in the lower chamber of parliament from 11 to 87. And more ominous in the long run than this evidence of Socialist strength was the evidence which the election of 1907 afforded of the extent of nationalist dissent within Austria.

Here was the cardinal difficulty with which Austria was persistently confronted, complicating the "liberal" experiments of the 1870's, and still more, after 1907, the operation of democratic government. It was the difficulty of reconciling an imperial state with the nationalism of its several peoples. For during the latter part of the nineteenth century and the first decade of the twentieth, nationalism was being progressively propagated among Austria's non-German subjects, not only by local intellectuals, publicists, and political leaders, but by zealous spokesmen of their kinsmen in Russia, Serbia, Rumania, or Italy.

Of all Austria's subject peoples, only the Poles seemed fairly content. There was no free Poland to which they might gravitate, and they were better treated than were the Poles in Russia or in Prussia. On the other hand, Rumanian nationalists dreamed of incorporating the Austrian province of Bukovina in independent Rumania; Slovene nationalists, of uniting the Croats and Serbs to recreate a dimly remembered Yugoslav empire; and Italian nationalists, of completing the political unification of the kingdom of Italy by annexing to it the Italian-speaking districts of Austria —Trent, Trieste, and Istria. Czech patriots were especially aggrieved because the Austrian government had not conferred on the once independent "kingdom of Bohemia" a full autonomy and admitted it to equality with the kingdom of Hungary and the empire of Austria. Czechs constituted, indeed, the forefront and spearhead of all the dissident nationalist opposition to the existing Austrian regime, and on occasion they did not hesitate to avow a lively friendship for foreign foes of Austria, particularly for Russia.

At first only a very small number of the most fanatically minded among the subject peoples worked consciously to disrupt the Empire. What the large majority of them long demanded was cultural freedom and some degree of political autonomy within the Empire. The Austrian government, in fact, did make concessions to them, especially during the 1880's and 1890's, in respect of cultural nationalism, permitting them the free use of their respective languages, splitting the University of Prague into two—a German university and a Czech university—and allowing

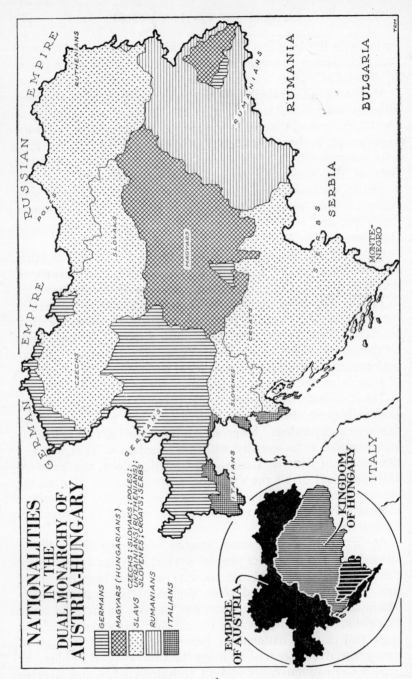

NATIONALITIES
IN THE
DUAL MONARCHY OF
AUSTRIA-HUNGARY

GERMANS

MAGYARS (HUNGARIANS)

SLAVS { CZECHS; SLOVAKS; POLES;
UKRAINIANS (RUTHENIANS);
SLOVENES; CROATS; SERBS }

RUMANIANS

ITALIANS

EMPIRE OF AUSTRIA

KINGDOM OF HUNGARY

GERMAN EMPIRE

RUSSIAN EMPIRE

RUMANIA

BULGARIA

SERBIA

MONTE-NEGRO

ITALY

RUTHENIANS

POLES

SLOVAKS

CZECHS

MAGYARS

RUMANIANS

SERBS

CROATS

SLOVENES

ITALIANS

the local administration of such cities as Cracow, Prague, and Trieste to be conducted respectively by native Poles, Czechs, and Italians. But against demands of political nationalism the Austrian government was adamant. There were too many influential Germans in Bohemia to be arbitrarily subjected to a Czech government there; too many in the Slovene province of Carniola to be put under Yugoslav rule. To the staid and unadventurous mind of the Emperor Francis Joseph, the idea of sub-dividing Austria further was fantastic.

So, conflict between the Austrian government and its subject peoples became ever sharper, on an ever widening front. The more the former tended toward democracy, the greater was the opportunity for the latter to voice their grievances and their demands. Repeatedly, the parliamentary institutions of Austria were paralyzed by fights, both verbal and fistic, in the House of Representatives. For years at a stretch the Emperor and his ministers felt obliged to impose taxes and carry on the administration without express parliamentary sanction. Thus after 1907, while appearing to be a constitutional state with universal manhood suffrage, Austria remained essentially absolutist. Political democracy proved inoperative in a country of such diverse populations.

The internal politics of the Hungarian part of the Dual Monarchy were not so complicated, for the simple reason that the Magyar aristocracy made no pretense of sharing the management of Hungary with the masses of their **Hungary** own people, to say nothing of sharing it with any subject nationality. They preserved their hold on large landed estates throughout the realm. They forced the use of their own language in the public schools of the whole kingdom. They did their best to Magyarize the Slovak peasantry in their northern provinces and the Serb population in the south. They abolished all traces of local autonomy in the large Rumanian-speaking province of Transylvania, in the east. In the west, they put more and more restrictions on the partial autonomy which they had granted in 1868 to Croatia. They kept the Hungarian parliament and the ministry at Budapest under their own domination. They persistently refused to extend the suffrage for parliamentary elections; and so high were the property qualifications for its exercise and so intricate were the electoral laws that in 1910, out of a total population of over twenty million in the Hungarian kingdom, fewer than one million were voters, and, though the total population was about evenly divided between Magyars and non-Magyars, almost all the seats in the parliament were occupied by Magyars.

The subject nationalities in Hungary were thus even more discontented than those in Austria, although their wholesale exclusion from the Hungarian parliament at Budapest deprived them of a central place, such as the parliament at Vienna provided for dissident Austrian nationalists, where they might collaborate against the existing regime and advertise to the world their complaints and demands.

The poorer classes of Magyars as well as the subject peoples suffered from the aristocratic character of the Hungarian government. Though much was done by the Hungarian parliament to foster popular education, and though some of the worst grievances of the peasants against their landlords were redressed, the remarkable agricultural development which Hungary experienced between 1867 and 1914 redounded chiefly to the financial advantage of the great landowners and governmental oligarchy. This fact was evidenced by a startling emigration from the country, amounting to over a million for the years from 1896 to 1910, and by a widespread popular agitation for electoral reform, an agitation which in the first decade of the twentieth century brought the kingdom to the verge of civil war.

Among the governing classes of Hungary, as of Austria, and also among very large sections of the masses in both parts of the **Emperor-King Francis Joseph** Dual Monarchy existed still a deep-seated veneration for the Emperor-King Francis Joseph, whose long reign since 1848 had been replete with historic significance—the wars of 1849, 1859, and 1866; the special arrangement between Austria and Hungary; the economic and political transformation of the Habsburg Empire. Francis Joseph bridged the years between Metternich and World War I. He witnessed the rise and fall of Napoleon III, the coming and going of Disraeli and Gladstone, the beginning and the end of the exploits of Bismarck. With something like awe for the seeming changelessness of the Habsburg monarch in the midst of an otherwise swiftly changing world was mingled a very real sympathy for him in the succession of domestic tragedies which attended his reign: the execution of his brother Maximilian, Emperor of Mexico, in 1867; the suicide of his only son Rudolf in 1889; the assassination of his wife by an anarchist in 1897; and the murder of his nephew and heir, the Archduke Francis Ferdinand, in 1914. Close upon this last domestic tragedy came to the Emperor-King, then in his eighty-fifth year, the war which was to be the ultimate catastrophe of his long reign.

### 4. THE RUSSIAN EMPIRE

The Russian Empire had long been aggressive and expansionist. In the nineteenth century it was the largest state in Europe and, next to the British Empire, the largest in the world. At the end of the century it embraced a sixth of the land surface and a twelfth of the population of the earth. Unlike the British Empire, it was a solid block of contiguous territory, almost as much Asiatic as European.

The Russian Empire, under its Tsars, was also a despotic state. It lagged behind the countries of western and central Europe in the nineteenth-century movements of industrialization, liberalism, and constitutional government. For a brief time in the early 1860's the Tsar Alexander II (1855–1881) had followed a "Westernizing" policy and effected some "liberal" reforms, such as freeing the serfs, authorizing elective *zemstvos* to exercise certain powers of local self-government, and modernizing the Empire's judicial system.[1] But he soon lost his reforming zeal and returned to the traditional practices of repressing dissent at home and promoting expansion abroad. In 1871 he took advantage of the defeat of France by Germany, and of Bismarck's benevolent attitude, to get rid of the limitations which the outcome of the Crimean War had imposed upon Russia and to re-establish its naval power in the Black Sea. He was preparing for another attack upon the Ottoman Empire.

It was easy for the Tsar to find justification for such an attack. Turkish suppression of popular uprisings in the Serb provinces of Bosnia and Herzegovina and likewise in the Bulgarian provinces was accomplished in 1875–1876 with such cruelty as to arouse general indignation throughout Europe as well as among the Christian peoples of the Balkans. English statesmen denounced the "Bulgarian

**Russo-Turkish War of 1877–8**

---

[1] On these reforms, see *Modern Europe to 1870*, pp. 769–771.

atrocities" of the Moslem Turks; and the principality of Serbia
in concert with the diminutive principality of Montenegro went
to war with the Ottoman Empire in behalf of their fellow Serbs
in Bosnia. Simultaneously, the Ottoman government at Constantinople appeared to be drifting rapidly toward impotence and
ruin. It seemed unable to maintain order in the Empire or to
command the loyalty of its provincial governors and soldiery. Its
treasury was bankrupt and its administration paralyzed. A palace
revolution in 1876 brought Abdul Hamid II to the throne.

Abdul Hamid II was essentially a cruel and cunning despot,
but, in order to curry favor with the Western powers, he inaugurated his reign by promulgating (1876) a liberal constitution for the whole Ottoman Empire. In this, the Sultan was quite
insincere, and the constitution remained a purely paper document.
In his purpose of employing any means to restore order in his
dominions and stave off foreign intervention, however, the Sultan
was thoroughly sincere. And he did restore a semblance of internal
order, and thereby only hastened Russian intervention. In April
1877, the Tsar Alexander II, formally espousing the cause of
"oppressed nationalities" within the Ottoman Empire, declared
war against the Sultan.

A Russian army invaded the Ottoman Empire from the north,
traversing Rumania and crossing the Danube in June 1877. To
its surprise, it encountered fierce resistance from Turkish troops
ensconced in the stronghold of Plevna, in Bulgaria, just south
of the Danube. Twice in July, and again in September, the Russian infantry was hurled back by Plevna's Turkish garrison.
Presently, however, after the Russians settled down to besiege the
fortress, its Turkish commander, Osman Pasha, seeing his men
slowly starving to death, attempted a desperate sortie. The attempt failed and Osman surrendered with 40,000 men. In January
1878 the advancing Russians won a second victory and compelled
the surrender of another Turkish army. By this time, Serbian and
Montenegrin troops were clearing the Turks out of the western
part of the Balkan peninsula; Bulgarians were volunteering for
service in the Russian army; and Rumanian troops had already
given invaluable aid to the Russians. The Turkish soldiers fought
stubbornly, but they were outnumbered and outmaneuvered and
apparently incapable of staying the triumphant advance of the
Russians and their Balkan allies. Adrianople fell and a Rus-

sian army marched on Constantinople. The Sultan Abdul Hamid sued for peace.

The immediate outcome was the treaty of San Stefano, March 1878, between Tsar and Sultan. The Sultan was to recognize the sovereign independence of Serbia, Montenegro, and Rumania; he was to sanction the creation of a Bulgarian national state, which should embrace not only Bulgaria proper but most of Macedonia from the Ægean to Albania, and which, though still belonging nominally to the Ottoman Empire and paying annual tribute to it, should possess a prince of its own and enjoy complete autonomy; and he was to carry out sweeping reforms in Bosnia and Herzegovina. Besides, he was to open the Dardanelles and the Bosphorus to the free commerce of all nations. These engagements of the Sultan were to the advantage of the Balkan nations as well as Russia, and the Tsar insisted upon them in the expectation that Bulgarians and Serbs and Rumanians would be the grateful debtors of their Russian "big brother." Directly for the Russian Empire, the Tsar was to receive part of Armenia, a large war indemnity (whose probable non-payment would give him an excuse for renewed interference in Turkey), and a strip of Dobruja (which he planned to exchange with Rumania for the portion of Bessarabia which he had lost in 1856).

*Treaty of San Stefano*

The satisfaction with which the Tsar Alexander II and the Russian Slavophiles regarded the terms of San Stefano was equaled by the criticism and opposition which they evoked from Great Britain and Austria-Hungary. At the head of the British government of the time was the Tory patriot, Benjamin Disraeli, Earl of Beaconsfield, who believed that Britain's national and imperial interests were gravely menaced by such Russian hegemony in the Near East as the treaty of San Stefano implied. Quite as emphatic against the treaty was the Habsburg Emperor, Francis Joseph. He feared that an unchecked triumph of Slavic nationalism in both Russia and the Balkans would intensify the disruptive nationalism of Slavic peoples in his own dominions, and he knew that the entrenchment of Russia in southeastern Europe would prevent Austria-Hungary from obtaining in that direction any future compensation for its past losses in Italy and Germany.

Wherefore Francis Joseph demanded that the treaty of San

Stefano should be revised by a Congress of the European powers which had assumed responsibility for the Ottoman Empire at Paris in 1856—not only the Tsar and the Sultan, but also Great Britain, France, Italy, Germany, and Austria-Hungary. Lord Beaconsfield, on behalf of Britain, promptly seconded the demand; and Bismarck, assuring both Francis Joseph and Alexander II that Germany was disinterested and would be an "honest broker" between them, invited the powers to hold the contemplated congress at Berlin. The Tsar was disappointed and angry, knowing full well that such a congress would be likely to deprive Russia of some of the spoils and prestige of its recent victory, and it required a threat of war from Britain and a demonstration by the British fleet in Turkish waters to induce Alexander II to participate.

*Austro-British Intervention and Berlin Peace-Settlement*

The Congress of Berlin met in the summer of 1878 and negotiated what was termed a "final" settlement of Near Eastern questions. The treaty of San Stefano was superseded by the treaty of Berlin (July 1878), to which all the European great powers (and the Ottoman Empire) were signatory, and in accordance with which less attention was given to satisfying the national aspirations of Balkan peoples and more to bolstering up the Ottoman Empire and effecting a compromise among rival ambitions of Russia, Austria-Hungary, and Great Britain.

Russia was permitted to regain the strip of Bessarabia, north of the Danube delta and east of the Pruth, which it had lost in 1856, and to retain the Armenian districts at the eastern extremity of the Black Sea which the treaty of San Stefano had promised. To offset Russia's gains, however, Austria-Hungary was accorded the right to occupy and administer the Ottoman provinces of Bosnia and Herzegovina and to garrison the province of Novibazar (southwest of Serbia), and it obtained special commercial privileges in Serbia and Montenegro.

Great Britain's "compensation" was provided for in a separate Anglo-Turkish Convention (June 1878), which practically formed a part of the Berlin agreement. In return for a pledge from Britain that it would defend the integrity of the Ottoman Empire, the Sultan handed over the island of Cyprus and promised to reform his government.

The treaty of Berlin embodied the provision of the treaty of

# OTTOMAN EMPIRE
## AND
# BALKAN NATIONS,
## 1878

200 MILES

NOTE: HEAVY BLACK LINES INDIC-
ATE BOUNDARIES SETTLED BY
THE CONGRESS OF BERLIN

OTTOMAN EMPIRE, 1878

"GREATER BULGARIA" AS
PLANNED BY RUSSIA IN THE
TREATY OF SAN STEFANO

TRM

San Stefano recognizing Rumania, Serbia, and Montenegro as independent principalities. But it saddled them with portions of the Sultan's debts, and outraged national feeling in them. Rumania lost all of Bessarabia (peopled largely by Rumanians) to Russia and received in return a part of Dobruja (peopled chiefly by Turks and Bulgarians). Serbia, which was already aspiring to play the role which Sardinia had recently played in Italy, and to unify the whole Serbian nationality, found itself at the close of a victorious war restricted to almost the same narrow territories which it had had before the war, and hemmed in, north, west, and south, by the Habsburg Empire.

Even worse fared the national ambitions of the Bulgarians. The "big Bulgaria," for which the Tsar had stipulated in the negotiations at San Stefano, was divided by the Berlin treaty into three separate parts. The northern part alone was recognized as the autonomous principality of Bulgaria, paying annual tribute to the Ottoman Empire. The southeastern part (exclusive of the province of Adrianople) was formally dubbed "Eastern Rumelia" and left "under the direct military and political control of His Imperial Majesty the Sultan," with special provision that its governor should be a Christian and enjoy some "administrative autonomy." The third part, comprising most of Macedonia and the province of Adrianople, was restored without restriction to the direct rule of the Sultan and his agents. Such treatment of Bulgarian aspirations was dictated by Austrian and British belief that Bulgaria was only a stalking-horse for Russia and that, the bigger Bulgaria was, the stronger would be the Russian Empire in southeastern Europe. The main result was an intense quickening of Bulgarian nationalism.

Greece alone of the Balkan nations profited by the revision of the treaty of San Stefano. By that treaty, Greece had been promised nothing, but as a result of the Congress of Berlin it obtained a considerable extension of territory on the mainland toward the north. The new boundary was not definitely fixed until 1881, when Thessaly was formally annexed to the Greek kingdom.

The general outcome of the Russo-Turkish War of 1877–1878, despite the intervention of the great powers in the peace settlement, was distinctly favorable to the Russian Empire. Russia had avenged its defeat in the Crimean War and enhanced its military prestige. It had annexed Bessarabia and part of Armenia.

It had set up Bulgaria as a satellite state in the center of the Balkans and close to Constantinople.

The Tsar Alexander II did not long survive his victory over the Ottoman Empire. In 1881 he fell victim to an assassin's bomb, and was succeeded by his son, Alexander III (1881–1894).

The new Tsar, rough-hewn in physique, was devoted to reactionary and Slavophile principles.[1] His first official acts were to inflict summary vengeance upon his father's assassins and to proclaim to the world that "the voice of God orders Us to stand firm at the helm of government with faith in the strength and truth of the autocratic power, which We are called to consolidate and to preserve for the good of the people from every kind of encroachment." In carrying out this program, Alexander III had the special assistance of two energetic men of like purpose with himself, Plehve and Pobêdonostsev. The former, a lawyer of Lithuanian stock, was entrusted with the direction of the state police; and so vigorously did he employ it to enforce obedience to the Tsar's will that the reign of Alexander III was marked by a seeming lull in revolutionary propaganda.

The practical work of Plehve was supplemented by the counsels of Pobêdonostsev, an older man, who had been professor of law in the University of Moscow and court tutor to Alexander III, and who was now appointed "Procurator of the Holy Synod," lay chairman of the governing body of the Russian Orthodox Church. From this post he ordered the life and thought of Orthodox clergymen all over the Empire in accordance with the doctrines which he expounded in speech and publication and which endeared him to the Tsar. To him, parliaments were nothing but breeding-places of the most selfish and sordid ambitions; freedom of the press meant license to disseminate falsehood; limited monarchy was a "vain fancy," and trial by jury "an invitation to the arts of casuistry."

Centralization of administration, with repression of liberal dissent, was one of the policies systematically pursued by Alexander III and his chief ministers. He placed the previously autonomous government of the peasant communities, or *mirs,* under the supervision of landed proprietors designated by the imperial ministry. He abridged the authority granted by his father to the provincial

[1] On "Slavophilism," see *Modern Europe to 1870,* pp. 765–766.

*zemstvos* and municipal *dumas*. He frowned upon popular education;[1] over what elementary schooling there was he fortified the control of the state church; and over the curriculum and teaching staff of the universities his agents exercised rigorous supervision. He reinforced, likewise, the governmental censorship of publications and even private correspondence. And for infractions of any of these repressive measures, the police under Plehve were empowered to make arbitrary arrests and mete out arbitrary penalties, while waste spaces of Siberia were made to share with insanitary fortress-prisons of European Russia as detention camps for thousands of "political offenders," some "convicted" and others merely "suspected."

"Russification" was another of the policies pursued by Alexander III and his ministers. It represented an attempt to realize the cultural ideal of Slavophile Russian patriots, and **"Russification"** it involved repressive measures against any language other than the Great Russian and any religion other than Russian Orthodoxy. It was aimed primarily, of course, at the subject peoples in the Russian Empire, who were perforce to abandon their distinctive national traditions and to become "good Russians," obeying the Tsar, employing his speech, and adhering to his faith. A virtual persecution was directed against both the Catholic Church in Poland and the Lutheran Church in the Baltic provinces, and also against the Russian sectarians who dissented from the Orthodox Church and the "uniates" in Ukrainia and White Russia whose ancestors had been converted from Orthodoxy to Catholicism. In Poland the harsh edicts of Alexander II, following the suppression of the revolt of 1863, were confirmed and rendered more harsh. Poles were excluded from public office, and from 1865 to 1897 no Poles were permitted to sell land to a non-Russian. In Ukrainia the Little Russian language was pronounced a "dialect," and its use in printing or singing was prohibited. In the Baltic provinces, Russian was prescribed as the official tongue in 1885; and presently the use of German was forbidden in university lectures and even in private-school instruction, and German place-names were changed to Russian.

---

[1] At the end of the reign of Alexander III in 1894, the percentage of illiterates throughout the Russian Empire was from 50 to 90 in rural communities and from 40 to 65 in urban centers—a higher average than in any other country of Europe.

Persecution of the Jews was a phase of "Russification." The Russian Empire had some five million Jewish inhabitants, settled mainly in cities of Poland, Lithuania, Ukrainia, and Bessarabia. They were disliked because of their clannishness and their somewhat paradoxical reputation for making financial profits and engaging in revolutionary agitation; and Alexander III, backed undoubtedly by popular approval, instituted a series of repressive measures against them. In 1882 he forbade Jews to acquire land. To keep them out of the liberal professions, he restricted the admission of Jews to secondary schools and universities. In 1890 he promulgated a sweeping decree against them; all Jews who lived in the interior of Russia were obliged to emigrate to the western provinces unless they should obtain individual licenses from the government; and in the districts where they were henceforth segregated—the so-called Jewish Pale—they were forbidden to own or lease land and were kept in towns under governmental surveillance. What was still worse for the Jews, many governmental officials, taking their cue from the attitude of the Tsar and his chief ministers, gave free rein to popular anti-Jewish prejudices and tolerated, if they did not incite, more or less organized anti-Jewish riots—*pogroms*—attended by plundering and burning and in some instances by massacre. From *pogroms,* as well as from repressive legislation, the Jews suffered greatly; and, despite the efforts of the Tsar's government to make them stay within the Empire, some 300,000 emigrated from it in the single year 1891. Here was the beginning of large Jewish immigration into the United States.

Alexander III was not so absorbed in combating liberalism and forwarding "Russification" within his Empire as to neglect any opportunity to extend its territorial boundaries or to heighten its international influence. He pushed forward the conquest of Turkestan and its border states to the south. He laid the foundations for Russian supremacy in Persia. While preserving formal peace with his European neighbors, he was ever alert to advance Russian influence among the Slavic peoples in the Balkans.

Territorial Expansion and the French Alliance

In the early 1890's Alexander III entered into an alliance with France. In his opinion, and in that of the majority of Russian patriots, cooperation between the chief Slavic nation and the chief Latin nation would have the triple advantage of curbing Teutonic pretentions in Europe, strengthening Russia in its duel with Great Britain for predominace in Asia, and opening up the money market of Paris for loans needful to the internal development of the Russian Empire and to the maintenance of its heavy armaments.

The death of Alexander III in 1894 did not change matters. His son and successor, Nicholas II (1894–1917), was a weak man, inclined to fatalism and mysticism, but with a streak of petty obstinacy characteristic of weak men. He showed a special deference to his wife, a neurotic woman, who, though a granddaughter of Queen Victoria and quite English in upbringing, displayed in Russia an almost insane devotion to autocracy and the Orthodox Church. Nicholas II let it be known from the outset that he considered any lessening of the Tsar's authority a "senseless dream." He reposed the utmost confidence in Pobêdonostsev and retained him as procurator of the Holy Synod. He kept Plehve in office and promoted him in 1902 to the post of minister of the interior with almost dictatorial powers.

*Tsar Nicholas II*

For eleven years—from 1894 to 1905—Nicholas II persevered in the policies which his father had developed. He maintained the same repression of liberal dissent, the same foreign policies, the same "Russification." In this last respect, he eased, it is true, the persecution of religious dissenters and softened the application of the laws against the Catholic and Protestant Churches. Yet under his auspices the Armenian Church in the Caucasus was interfered with and despoiled; the legislation against the Jews was rigorously enforced, accompanied by *pogroms* such as that at Kishinev in 1903 in which several thousand Jews were massacred; and to the grandduchy of Finland, whose separate constitution and nationality even Alexander III had respected, Russification was now applied. In 1899 Nicholas II substituted Russians for Finns and Swedes in the civil administration of the grandduchy. He introduced a Russian police. He conformed the Finnish army with the Russian. He prescribed that all Finnish legislation should be drafted by Russian ministers in conjunction with the secretary of state for Finland, and to this post he presently appointed the redoubtable Plehve.

Nicholas II liked to think of himself, in a mystical way, both as an avenger of the Slavs throughout the world and as a promoter of the world's peace. He convoked at The Hague in 1899 an international congress for the limitation of armaments and the assurance of peace among all nations.[1] Also, in pursuit of aggressive policies in the Far East, he allowed the Russian Empire to break the peace and to drift into a bloody and fateful war with Japan. The Russo-Japanese War of 1904–1905 proved to be of unimagined significance for the Russian Empire and we shall say more about it in a later chapter.[2]

Meanwhile we must note a very important industrial development which had been going on in European Russia during the reigns of Alexander III and Nicholas II, at first unobtrusively, but by 1904 very clearly. Not only in Poland, where there was already a good deal of industrialization, but also in other parts of European Russia, industrial and commercial activity quickened. Coal fields and iron mines began to be extensively worked in Ukrainia and in the Urals. Oil wells began to be exploited in the Caucasus and about the Black and Caspian Seas. Factories became numerous in Kiev, in St. Petersburg, in Moscow. Shipping rapidly increased in the ports of Riga and Odessa and likewise in those of Vladivostok and Archangel. Between 1881 and 1904 the annual output of pig iron was quadrupled, reaching a total of three million tons and putting Russia in fourth place (after Great Britain, the United States, and Germany) among iron-producing nations. During the same period the annual output of coal multiplied sixfold, from three million tons to eighteen million. The number of factory operatives in the larger industries doubled, and the value of machine-made goods more than tripled.

*Industrialization*

This notable growth of Russian industry toward the close of the nineteenth century was due in part to a cheap and plentiful labor supply provided by the influx of ex-serfs into the cities and in part to the loans of capital by foreign investors, especially French. With the aid of foreign capital and native labor, railway construction was rapidly prosecuted in Russia, and railways stimulated trade and industry.

The Russian Empire as a whole, we must remember, remained predominantly agricultural. In 1914 six-sevenths of its total population were engaged, directly or indirectly, in agriculture;

[1] See below, pp. 309–310.
[2] See below, pp. 340–344.

and its industrial production was overshadowed by its production
of wheat and cattle. Nevertheless, the percentage of urban population had risen from a tenth in 1874 to a seventh in 1914;[1] and
a seventh of the total population of 130 million was not a small
number. By this time the Empire had as many town dwellers as
France and many more factory towns than Italy.

The development of Russian industry served to increase the
size of the middle classes and still more of the urban proletariat,
and hence to add to the difficulties of the autocratic government.
Plehve did what he could to oppose the industrial development,
contending that it would create an urban society inimical alike to
the autocracy and to the rural classes upon which the autocracy
ultimately rested. But Plehve and his many Slavophile partisans
were unable to check the newer economic and social tendencies;
and in another Russian statesman of the time, Count Serge Witte,
Russian industrialists, as well as Russian patriots, found a friend
and champion.

Witte was a native of Tiflis in the Caucasus, where his father
(of Dutch extraction) was an imperial administrator. Educated
at the University of Odessa, he was identified for a
**Count Witte** time with railway construction and finance in southern
Russia. Thus, while remaining a political conservative,
he became an interested advocate of "Western" commercial and
industrial development. Appointed head of the department of
railways in the imperial ministry of finance by Alexander III, he
was promoted to be minister of communications in 1892 and
minister of finance in 1893. For ten years he retained this post
under Nicholas II and used his official and personal influence with
the Tsar to promote policies favorable to big business in Russia,
policies of economic nationalism analogous to those which Bismarck had adopted in Germany. He sought to develop home industries by means of tariff protection and financial reforms. He
strengthened the state banks, rapidly extended the state system
of railways, and, in keeping with the newer economic imperialism,
fostered Russian expansion, commercial and capitalist as well as
military and political, in Persia and Manchuria. At the same time
Witte was anxious to increase the "efficiency" of Russian labor,
and with this end in view he undertook to reduce drunkenness
and promote temperance by making the liquor business a state

[1] A third of the population of Russian Poland was urban at this time.

monopoly. He also provided for government mediation in labor disputes and for state regulation of mines and factories.

Witte's policies elicited much criticism from reactionaries of the type of Plehve and Pobêdonostsev. There was widespread complaint that he was sacrificing agricultural to industrial interests and that his tariff protection was costly to peasants and workmen. Besides, there was the obvious fact that the industrialization which Witte encouraged was being attended, just as Plehve had prophesied, by the growth of urban movements menacing to the traditional autocracy—liberalism among the bourgeoisie, and socialism among the proletariat.

In the circumstances, opposition to the Tsar's government, which, under the watchful eye and vigorous repression of Plehve and the state police, had lain dormant since the days of Alexander II, notably revived and spread in the first years of the twentieth century. One of its most curious features was the participation of many otherwise ultra-conservative landowners and peasants. These had no thought of revolution, nor were they lacking in personal loyalty to the Tsar, but they were annoyed and angered by what they deemed the disproportionate emphasis which Nicholas II permitted Witte to put upon industry and commerce. To appease them Witte in 1902–1903 invited committees of the *zemstvos*, in which they were heavily represented, to recommend what reforms, particularly what agricultural reforms, should be undertaken by the Tsar. The result was that, of the seven hundred reports which were accordingly submitted, four hundred found fault with Witte's economic policies and with the political system which had sanctioned them. It was the blame heaped by Plehve and Pobêdonostsev upon Witte for the hostility to autocracy implied in these reports that caused Nicholas II in 1903 to retire his distinguished minister of finance. The landed classes were glad to see Witte go, but the liberal element among them was strengthened by the Tsar's apparent determination to retain most of Witte's policies.

Nor were the bourgeoisie content with the merely economic measures which an autocratic government had taken in their behalf but which it might rescind as arbitrarily as it dispensed with Witte. The growing class of merchants, factory-owners, and bankers came to believe that their security depended upon the limitation of autocracy and the establishment of a constitutional government in which they should have direct say, and hence they swelled the numbers and enhanced the influence of liberal, "Westernizing" intellectuals. A group of these intellectuals organized in 1904 a liberal party, the "Union of Liberators."

To complaints from the conservative land-owning class and to demands of the liberal bourgeoisie were added an unrest among peasants and a development of extreme revolutionary movements among urban proletarians. Revolutionary anarchism was stealthily propagated in Russia and had no little influence on the formation of secret societies of extremely radical (and frequently unbalanced) intellectuals, workers, and peasants who had a penchant for conspiring against the government, assassinating its officials, and suffering martyrdom.

More significant, however, was the penetration of the gospel of Karl Marx into Russia and its effect on the rise of two distinct revolutionary movements. One of these was repre-

**Marxism in Russia**

sented by the Social Democratic party, formed in 1898, adhering to the precepts of Marxian socialism in all their "Western" rigidity, and securing disciples from among doctrinaires and urban workmen. The other was the Socialist Revolutionary party, founded about 1900, which tried to adapt Marxian socialism to the traditional communal life of the mass of Russian peasants; it advocated socialization of the land and its distribution among those who actually tilled it. The Socialist Revolutionaries gained a large following of peasants and soon vied with middle-class Liberals and aristocratic Constitutionalists for leadership in political and social reform. At first, the Social Democrats were not as numerous or as influential, and in 1903 they split on a question of tactics into a left-wing majority party (Bolshevik), and a right-wing minority party (Menshevik).

Still another fruitful source of opposition to the existing regime in Russia was the reaction which the process of "Russification"

**Subject Peoples**

aroused among its victims—Poles, Jews, Finns, and other subject peoples. These, anxious not to be Russified, were prepared to cooperate with any Russian group that promised respite or relief from persecution.

Altogether, there were many signs, at the opening of the twentieth century, not only of a renewal of foreign aggression by Russia but also of a revolutionary outbreak within Russia.

## 5. THE OTTOMAN EMPIRE AND THE BALKAN NATIONS

In spite of territorial losses to which it was subjected in 1878, the Ottoman Empire was still, at this latter date, a truly imperial domain. In Europe it stretched across the Balkan peninsula from the Adriatic to the Black Sea, including **The Empire in 1878** Albania, Macedonia, Thrace, and, of course, the ancient capital of Constantinople. In Asia, it reached from the Ægean Sea to the Persian Gulf and from the Black to the Red Sea. Between Europe and Asia it owned most of the Ægean islands, including Crete, and in northern Africa the provinces of Tripoli and Barca (Cyrenaica). In addition to these outright possessions the Ottoman Empire still preserved a nominal suzerainty over Bosnia, Herzegovina, and Novibazar (now administered by the Habsburg Empire), over Bulgaria (now under a prince of its own), over Cyprus (now governed by Great Britain), and over Egypt (since 1866 under a practically independent ruler).

Yet this Empire extending into three Continents was no longer the menacing great power which it had been back in the sixteenth and seventeenth centuries. For more than a hundred years it had been declining in strength and prestige, until it was quite outranked by at least six European states (Britain, Germany, France, Italy, Russia, and Austria-Hungary), and fear of what it might do to Europe was lost in the prospect of what Europe could do to it.

In an age when mechanical industry was profoundly affecting most other European countries, increasing the size and taxable wealth of their populations, promoting the consolidation and democratizing of their governments, and enabling them to strengthen their armaments, the Ottoman Empire remained exceptionally backward in economics and politics and material force. Relative to its territorial extent, or to the population of most other European Powers, the population of the Ottoman Empire was sparse and practically stationary, hardly exceeding twenty-five million between 1878 and 1914 and depending almost wholly on primitive agriculture. It was utterly unable to furnish the increment of financial resources requisite to keep the country in step with the political and military progress of industrial nations.

Then, too, in an age when most of the great powers of Europe were national states, commanding the enthusiastic loyalty of their dominant peoples, the Ottoman Empire still harbored the anomalous religio-military imperialism of a much earlier period. Its Emperor—the Sultan—was not merely a secular autocrat like the Russian Tsar. He was also both a Turkish overlord and the "caliph," a kind of honorary chief, for all orthodox (Sunnite) Moslems throughout the world. Moreover, the Ottoman Turks, who constituted a compact and fairly homogeneous population in Anatolia (Asia Minor) and who supplied the Sultan with the majority of his officials and, what was of prime importance, with the backbone of his army, were only a minority of the inhabitants of the Empire, and they were slow to develop the nationalism which became characteristic of Europe in the nineteenth century.

Such a backward and anomalous regime was bound to experience extraordinary difficulties, internal and external, in attempting to survive alongside the industrial nationalist Europe of the **Sultan** nineteenth and twentieth centuries. The Sultan Abdul **Abdul** Hamid II (1876–1909) began his reign by making a **Hamid II** pretense at "modernizing" the Ottoman Empire; he promulgated a liberal constitution of the current Western type. But so vociferous was the opposition of ardent Moslems to any such novel substitute for the venerable traditions of the Empire, and so temperamentally despotic was the Sultan himself, that the constitution of 1876 was promptly "suspended," and for more than thirty years it remained a dead letter. Then, too, far more seriously, Abdul Hamid early in his reign failed to put down insurrections of Bosnians and Bulgarians within the Empire and to halt Russian aggression from without; and the resulting Russo-Turkish War of 1877–1878 only brought into lurid light the strength and the many-sided character of the forces operating against the Ottoman Empire.

First was the vaulting desire of European great powers to profit politically and financially from the weakness of the Ottoman **Empire** Empire. Russia took territory from the Empire in 1878, **and Great** and the only way by which the Sultan could keep **Powers** Russia from taking more was to invoke the outside aid of Great Britain and Austria-Hungary and to pay a price to each: Cyprus to the former, Bosnia-Herzegovina and Novibazar to the latter. Furthermore, the Sultan had to agree, by the peace treaty of 1878, to collaborate with the great powers on a program of "reforms," whose execution would be almost certain to arouse the hostility of his own Turkish subjects and yet the failure of whose execution would afford foreigners a chronic excuse for interference. Besides, the public finances of the Ottoman Empire, already in confusion, were so completely disordered by the Russo-Turkish War that in 1881 the Sultan was obliged to place them under the direction of a commission of foreign bankers. This in turn mortgaged heavily the income of the Turkish treasury and added greatly to the taxation and unrest within the country. It also put foreign capitalists, particularly those of Britain, France, and Germany, in a strategic position to obtain profitable concessions for themselves and to clinch the stranglehold of their several governments on the Empire.

A second disrupting force was nationalism among the Balkan peoples of the Ottoman Empire. This had already eventuated in the establishment of a national Greek state in 1832, **Empire and** and in 1878 in the enforced recognition by the Sultan **Subject** of the complete independence of Rumania, Serbia, and **Peoples** Montenegro, the full autonomy of Bulgaria, and the partial autonomy of Eastern Rumelia. None of these states was satisfied with the settlement of 1878, and what each had gained only heightened its ambition to draw to itself fellow nationals who were left under Ottoman rule. Hence from each proceeded an increasingly inflammatory propaganda of publications, armed bands, and secret societies.

Such nationalist incitement could not be confined to the Christian Balkan peoples. It proved contagious, and was presently communicated to Armenians, to Albanians, and even to Arabs. Nor were the Turks wholly immune. Some of their intellectuals, attending the universities in France or Germany, or otherwise coming into contact with Western civilization, were thereby infected with nationalism, but most Turks caught it while attempting to suppress subject peoples feverish with it. The more the Greeks and Serbs and Armenians insisted that they were equal or superior to the Turks, the more the Turks sought to put them in their proper inferior place. The more violent the former grew, the more vindictive became the latter. Massacres, which had been infrequent and sporadic while the Ottoman Empire embraced Moslems and Christians, became commonplace when the Empire comprised a variety of self-conscious and self-seeking nationalities.

The Sultan Abdul Hamid II, with no little skill, managed to

stave off the seemingly inevitable dissolution of the Ottoman Empire. He played off one great power against another, and one Balkan state against another. At first he relied mainly upon Great Britain to check Russian aggression. Eventually he came to regard Germany as the most dependable prop; it seemed to be comparatively disinterested, at least politically and territorially, and it was strong enough to serve as a counterpoise to either Russia or Britain. So the Sultan employed German army officers to reorganize his army and German financial experts to advise him on matters affecting the treasury. He welcomed somewhat theatrical visits of the German Emperor William II to Constantinople in 1889 and 1899. He granted to German bankers important economic concessions, including the construction of a railway across Asiatic Turkey from the Bosphorus to Bagdad and the Persian Gulf (1899).

In internal affairs Abdul Hamid employed espionage and terrorism to uphold his absolute power. And when Christian peoples grew too restive and threatened revolt, he permitted fanatic Moslem tribesmen, Kurdish or Albanian, to fall upon them and engage in massacre.

Yet the disintegration of the Ottoman Empire proceeded apace. In 1882 Great Britain, already in occupation of Cyprus, effected a **Disinte-** military occupation of Egypt and established a virtual **gration of** protectorate over that nominal dependency of the Otto-**Empire** man Empire. In 1885 the Bulgarians in Eastern Rumelia drove out their Turkish governor and secured the incorporation of their partially autonomous province with the fully autonomous principality of Bulgaria, which thereby was almost doubled in size and likewise in potential menace to the Empire.

In 1896 the Greeks in Crete revolted, and the next year in their behalf the kingdom of Greece went to war with the Ottoman Empire. This time, the Sultan's army put up a stiff fight: it overwhelmed the Greek army on the mainland and advanced on Athens. Whereupon the "protecting Powers" of Greece—Russia, Britain, France, and Italy—intervened and ended the Græco-Turkish War. Greece had to pay a war indemnity and consent to a "rectification" of its northern frontier advantageous to the Ottoman Empire. Yet though Greece was not permitted to annex Crete, the Ottoman Empire practically lost it; it was to enjoy autonomy under the protection of the four great powers, and these named a son of the Greek King as its governor.

The Armenians, too, rebelled in 1894. The rebellion was ruthlessly suppressed, and Kurds and other furious Moslems slaughtered at least 100,000, and perhaps 200,000, Christian Armenians. The great powers expostulated with the Sultan, but obtained only one of his facile promises that "reforms" would be instituted.

In the first years of the twentieth century, domestic criticism of the Sultan's government affected Moslems as well as Christians, Asiatic provinces as well as European, and created a widespread revolutionary unrest. In part it was a sign of the nationalistic spirit which was beginning to take possession of the Turks. In part it was a reaction against a government which permitted foreigners to exploit the country and put intolerable financial burdens on its own subjects, and yet which could not preserve order at home or prevent the loss of territory and prestige abroad. In part, also, it was an outcome of the closer contacts which railway construction—one of the most notable achievements of Abdul Hamid's reign—enabled the peoples of the Ottoman Empire to develop with one another and with western Europe. Whereas the total railway mileage of the Empire in 1885 was only 1,250, most of it being in the European provinces, it amounted in 1908 to 4,400, of which almost three-fourths were in Asia, serving to carry Western ideas as well as commodities to Ankara and Bagdad, Damascus and Mecca.

In 1908, as we shall see in a later chapter,[1] began a series of domestic revolutions and foreign wars which proved to be the death throes of the Ottoman Empire.

Meanwhile, we may note the development of those nationalistic Balkan states which won full or partial independence from the Ottoman Empire in the course of the nineteenth century. The first of these was Greece, which formally began its national career in 1832, and which in the 1860's, obtained a new King and a new democratic constitution.[2] Under **Greece** George I (1863–1913), despite many political and financial difficulties, the country made noteworthy progress, intellectually and materially.

The kingdom of Greece, as it existed from 1832 to 1913, embraced but a minority of the Greek nationality. The majority

[1] See pp. 345–350.
[2] See *Modern Europe to 1870*, pp. 762, 778.

were still under Ottoman rule—in Macedonia, Thrace, at Constantinople, in Smyrna and other towns along the seacoast of Asia Minor, in the Ægean islands and Crete. In 1897, as we know, Greece made an effort to wrest Crete from the Empire. The effort failed of its immediate purpose, but it brought to the fore an outstanding Greek leader, Eleutherios Venizelos. Venizelos, a Cretan by birth, had headed the revolutionary movement for the union of Crete with Greece, and was largely responsible for the management of the island's autonomous government which issued from the war of 1897. By 1910 his popularity was so great in the kingdom of Greece that King George I, against his own personal wishes, was impelled to invite Venizelos to the mainland and to entrust him with the premiership of Greece. Venizelos reformed the Greek government, effected a reorganization of its army and navy, and negotiated with Serbia and Bulgaria a Balkan League against the Ottoman Empire. He thus prepared Greece, internally and externally, just as Cavour had prepared Sardinia, or Bismarck had prepared Prussia, for wars of national unification.

The Rumanian provinces of Moldavia and Wallachia had been accorded autonomy in 1856 and permitted in 1862 to form the united principality of Rumania.[1] In 1866, its native **Rumania** prince was deposed and in his place a member of the German family of Hohenzollern-Sigmaringen was installed as Prince Carol I. Then in 1878, as an outcome of the Russo-Turkish War, the principality was recognized as an independent state, and in 1881 it was designated a "kingdom," Prince Carol I becoming King Carol I and crowning himself with a steel crown wrought from Turkish cannon captured at Plevna.

This Rumanian kingdom, like the Greek, was ambitious to extend its sway over the large portion of its own nationality that dwelt outside its restricted frontiers. Unlike the Greeks, however, the "unredeemed" Rumanians were not confined to the Ottoman Empire. Villages of them were scattered here and there throughout Macedonia, but far more numerous were the Rumanian populations of the Russian province of Bessarabia, the Hungarian principality of Transylvania, and the Austrian crown-land of Bukovina. In other words, the problem of national unification confronting Rumania was much more complex than that facing Greece; the latter would have to reckon with the Ottoman Em-

[1] See *Modern Europe to 1870*, pp. 718–719.

pire, the former with both Russian and Habsburg Empires. Immediately after 1878, anti-Russian sentiment prevailed, and in 1883 Rumania concluded a secret alliance with Austria-Hungary and thus became a satellite of the Triple Alliance of Austria-Hungary, Germany, and Italy. For the next thirty years German influence was dominant in Rumania. The political institutions of the country were modeled after Prussia's, with a parliament elected by a class system of voting which assured to the well-to-do upper classes a complete control.

During the reign of Carol I (1881–1914), Rumania made noteworthy economic progress. Agricultural production was stimulated by the introduction of farm machinery and the development of accessible foreign markets in industrialized Austria and Germany. Simultaneously, through investment of foreign capital, began the profitable exploitation of the country's rich mineral resources, its coal and especially its petroleum. The mass of Rumanian peasantry did not share proportionately, however, in the wealth which accrued to foreign investors or to domestic landlords and middlemen. Rumania was a country chiefly of large landed estates, whose owners were reluctant to countenance any reform which might endanger their economic interests and prone to deflect peasant criticism from themselves to the considerable number of Jews who dwelt in the towns of Rumania and constituted a large part of its trading and money-lending class. This economic situation, in combination with religious intolerance, resulted in the virulent anti-Semitism which characterized Rumanian society and politics during the era.[1] But anti-Semitism was only one symptom of poverty and unrest among the Rumanian peasantry. Emigration was another, and periodic rioting was still another.

Between the Rumanians at the north and the Greeks at the south, the central Balkan territories were inhabited by Slavic-speaking peoples. All these might be termed Yugoslavs—that is, "Southern Slavs"—in contradistinction to the "Eastern Slavs" (Russians) or "Western Slavs" (Poles and Czechs). Conven-

---

[1] Rumania agreed by the treaty of Berlin (1878), as a condition of its national independence, to grant full religious toleration and to admit Jews to civil and political equality with other inhabitants. Subsequently, however, the Rumanian government, backed undoubtedly by public opinion, practically nullified the agreement. Only a very few of the quarter million Rumanian Jews were granted citizenship or permitted to vote or hold office.

tionally, however, the term "Yugoslav" was confined to the Southern Slavs in the western half of the Balkan peninsula: Serbs in Serbia and Montenegro, in the Banat of Hungary, and in the western Macedonian provinces of the Ottoman Empire; Croats in the Hungarian crown-land of Croatia; and Slovenes in the Austrian provinces of Carniola, Carinthia, and Istria. The remaining Southern Slavs, in the eastern half of the Balkan peninsula, were customarily styled "Bulgarians" rather than "Yugoslavs."

In the case of the Serbs, two independent states were erected: Montenegro and Serbia. Montenegro, or "Black Mountain," near the Adriatic, was a very diminutive state, which had **Serbia and Montenegro** long been governed in a patriarchal fashion by native princes and whose full independence of the Ottoman Empire was finally acknowledged by the treaty of Berlin in 1878. The Prince of Montenegro at the time was Nicholas I (1860–1918), a rude but often benevolent despot of the fighting type and something of a poet withal. He was a warm admirer of Russia and a firm friend of the Tsar. In 1905 he granted a democratic constitution, and in 1910 assumed the title of King in place of Prince.

Serbia, the larger and more important of the two Serb states, had been autonomous since 1830 and became an independent principality in 1878. It was a country of peasants, backward and even primitive; and it was long a prey to the rivalry of opposing claimants to its throne and to the interference of jealous foreign powers in its internal affairs. The rivalry was between partisans of the family of Karageorge, the original peasant leader of Serbian rebellion against the Ottoman Empire, and partisans of the family of Miloš Obrenović, the soldier who had secured autonomy for Serbia. The latter were in power from 1859 to 1903, though the relatively long sway of the Obrenović dynasty was punctuated by occasional insurrections of the Karageorge faction and by brutal assassinations. This dynastic feud not only kept Serbia in a disorderly condition but also tended to make it a kind of football in the game of international intrigue between Russia and Austria-Hungary.

The Prince of Serbia during the Russo-Turkish War of 1877–1878 was Milan Obrenović, a man of some natural talents and of notoriously scandalous life. Pro-Austrian by inclination, he was angered by Russia's greater solicitude for Bulgaria than for

Serbia in the peace settlement of 1878, and in 1881 he formed a close secret alliance with Austria-Hungary. In 1882, with Austrian backing, he transformed his state from a principality into a kingdom; and in 1885 he utilized Bulgaria's annexation of Eastern Rumelia as the pretext for going to war with his Slavic neighbor. The Serbo-Bulgarian War of 1885 was a series of victories for Bulgarian arms, and Serbia would have been utterly crushed had not Austria-Hungary intervened and stopped the war. The result was that Serbia passed under the tutelage of the Habsburg Empire, and King Milan lost whatever popularity he had commanded in Serbia. To defray the expenses of his war against Bulgaria, he had to impose burdensome taxes; and in a last effort to regain popular approval he promulgated in 1889 a democratic constitution. Two months later he abdicated in favor of his young son, Alexander I (1889–1903).

Alexander's reign was even more troublous than Milan's had been. The new King set aside the constitution and ruled through favorites. He alienated the extreme nationalist party by adhering to the alliance with Austria-Hungary, and when, toward the close of his reign, he suddenly expressed pro-Russian sentiments, he was deemed insincere. Then, too, he outraged a large part of the nation by his marriage with an ambitious woman of unsavory reputation, and by the favors he showered upon her relatives. A group of army officers, members of a secret society known as the "Black Hand," conspired with the Karageorge faction to overthrow the Obrenović dynasty. In 1903 the conspiracy eventuated in the murder of King Alexander and some fifty of his ministers and attendants, and in the accession of the grandson of Karageorge, Peter I, to the blood-stained throne of Serbia.

King Peter's accession marked a turning-point in Serbian history. It definitely ended the Obrenović dynasty and hence the feud which had impaired the internal unity of the nation. It likewise ended the subservience of Serbia to Austria-Hungary and thus gave free rein to the development of a Serbian nationalism in harmony with Russian desires and zealous to make the kingdom of Serbia the core of a Yugoslavia which should embrace not only all Serbs still under Ottoman rule but all Serbs, Croats, and Slovenes in the Habsburg Empire. King Peter was very much of a soldier-patriot, and also something of a democrat. He restored the constitution of 1889 and chose his ministers from the majority party—the ultra-patriotic Radical party—in the parliament. The leader of this party was Nicholas Pašič, an engineer who had been educated in Switzerland, an ardent patriot, able and unscrupulous. While the King devoted his chief energies to army reform, Pašič reorganized the national finances at home and encouraged nationalist propaganda abroad. The Austro-Hungarian annexation of the Serb-speaking provinces of Bosnia-Herzegovina in 1908, which Serbia was then unable to prevent, served only to intensify anti-Austrian feeling among the Serbs and to quicken the determination of the Serbian government to seek territorial compensation, as soon as possible, wherever it might be found.

The Bulgarians, who comprised the Slavic population in the eastern half of the Balkan peninsula—and the majority of the Slavic population throughout Macedonia—had been promised a comprehensive national state of their own by the treaty of San Stefano between Russia and Turkey in 1878, but the ensuing Congress of Berlin, fearful lest the projected Bulgaria should be a mere satellite of the Russian Empire, reduced its territory and split what was left into two states: the autonomous "principality of Bulgaria," and the semi-autonomous "province of Eastern Rumelia." The sop to Russia was that a nephew of the Tsar Alexander II, Alexander of Battenburg, was chosen to preside over the principality. For a time, this Prince Alexander was obediently pro-Russian. In accordance with his uncle's dictation, he suspended the democratic constitution which Bulgarians had devised, and appointed Russians to high office in his army and civil administration. Presently, however, he tired of Russian tutelage and decided to put himself at the head of those Bulgarian patriots who resented foreign interference. In 1883, consequently, he defied the Tsar by dismissing Russian advisors and establishing constitutional government. Then in 1885 a revolt of Bulgarians against the Ottoman government in Eastern Rumelia enabled him to incorporate this province with his principality; and when Serbia attempted to seek "compensation" from him, his Bulgarian army roundly trounced the Serbian army.

Unfortunately for Prince Alexander, there was delay in getting the Ottoman Sultan and the Russian Tsar to agree to Bulgaria's annexation of Eastern Rumelia, and when Alexander abjectly appealed to the Tsar for assistance, a group of impatient Bulgarian nationalists forced him to abdicate (1886). In selecting as his successor Ferdinand of Saxe-Coburg, a clever German prince, related to the reigning families in Great Britain and Belgium, the Bulgarian parliament angered the Russian Tsar still more. For several years the Tsar treated Ferdinand as a usurper and connived at military conspiracies against him. Nevertheless, Ferdinand clung to his throne, and with the aid of a resolute prime minister, Stefan Stambolov, he gradually strengthened his position both inside and outside Bulgaria. Eventually Stambolov became so dictatorial that he was forced out of office and assassinated (1895), but by this time Ferdinand was so firmly entrenched in power that the Russian Tsar finally recognized him as rightful ruler of Bulgaria.

In 1908, Ferdinand proclaimed the severance of the nominal bonds between Bulgaria and the Ottoman Empire and his own elevation from the status of an autonomous Prince to that of an independent King. Four years later he was a prime mover in organizing with Greece and Serbia a Balkan League to fight the Turks.

# PART II

## BACKGROUND OF TWENTIETH-CENTURY WORLD WARS

# CHAPTER V

## A NEW AGE OF MATERIALISM

 UR present twentieth century differs from the nineteenth century in several respects. One is the passing of the stellar role in society and politics from aristocracy and middle class to the masses. Another is the supplanting of the liberal state by the "welfare" or "socialistic" state, and the rise of a new type of plebeian dictatorship. A third is the speeding up of mechanical invention, and its widespread application to novel means of travel, entertainment, propaganda, and fighting. Still another, most alarming, is the waging of totalitarian world war, at once nationalistic and imperialistic, with unprecedented destructiveness.

Distinctive Features of 20th Century

But perhaps the central feature of the latest age in the history of European and Western civilization is popular absorption in material things and materialist ideas. Among the masses there is heightened faith that machinery and social politics will provide the best sort of life and a veritable heaven on earth. And among intellectuals and would-be intellectuals, nineteenth-century fashions of romanticism and idealism have been outmoded by twentieth-century realism and materialism.

All these characteristic trends of our time are traceable, in their origins, to developments in the nineteenth century and even earlier. It is only their extension and coalescence and cumulative effects which render the twentieth century a new era. The chief developments in back of them are two: (1) the large-scale mechanizing of work and life, the so-called "industrial revolution"; and (2) the marvelous advance and influence of experimental and applied science. The former of these we have already discussed in an earlier chapter.[1] It remains here to discuss the latter and then to indicate certain applications of it to philosophy and social doctrine.

[1] See above, pp. 3–39.

## I. BASIS IN NATURAL SCIENCE

Natural science had been steadily developing since the "Enlightenment" of the seventeenth and eighteenth centuries. At that time, fundamental work had been done in mathematics, physics, and astronomy, and in the latter part of the eighteenth century the painstaking study of "natural history" had begun to yield significant data for chemistry, geology, zoology, botany, and medicine.[1] More recently, science had become a practical and essential adjunct of industrial progress, and by the latter part of the nineteenth century its record was imposing. Industrial corporations were employing a staff of "experts" in engineering or chemistry. Large-scale farmers were being advised by "authorities" on soils, crops, fertilizers, and stock breeding. Governments were calling for ever larger numbers of scientific practitioners in public works, public sanitation, and military and naval armaments. To meet the demand for scientists, new polytechnic schools were being established, while older universities were founding laboratories and faculties of applied science and institutes of industrial and agricultural research.

**Science and Industry**

No longer was science an avocation of the upper and middle classes. It was now a most honorable, and fairly profitable, vocation for any person of talent; and the masses, as well as the classes, were coming under its spell. Everybody hailed each new device, each additional creature-comfort, as still another triumph of "modern science." And, as the pursuit of natural science quickened, it not only enriched the content of physics and chemistry, geology and biology, but also stimulated a like development of "social" studies—sociology and anthropology, economics and statistics, geography and history—which were now formally labeled, imitatively and a little ostentatiously, "social sciences." Incidentally, it inspired some scientists and a goodly number of other persons to philosophize about "science" and to construct systems of thought which had even wider and more profound consequences than the metaphysics which had attended the scientific advance in the seventeenth and eighteenth centuries.

Basic to the newer "scientific philosophy" and "social science" is the development of experimental natural science during the nineteenth century. While physical science remained "Newtonian"

[1] See *Modern Europe to 1870*, pp. 369–375.

in its generalizations about the mechanical and material nature of the universe, it became more specialized and utilitarian, thanks largely to the concurrent industrialization from which it profited and to which it contributed. As the century proceeded, physicists devoted themselves more and more to practical industrial problems, to research in thermodynamics, in optics, in magnetism and electricity.

Thermodynamics, the physical science derived from the study of the motive power of heat, was essentially a nineteenth-century product, an accompaniment of the use of steam-engines. Most earlier physicists had entertained the idea that **Thermodynamics** heat was a subtle imponderable fluid (called "caloric"), and it was not until the eve of the nineteenth century that the idea of heat as a mode of motion, rather than as a substance, was given an experimental basis. This was done by an interesting American, Benjamin Thompson, who as a "loyalist" had quitted his native land in 1776, and, after serving the British government, had held high office in Bavaria and there received the title of Count Rumford, by which he is commonly known. In 1798 he presented to the Royal Society at London the findings of his *Enquiry concerning the Source of Heat which is excited by Friction*. Rumford's contention was ably supported by Sir Humphry Davy, and became the accepted premise of thermodynamics.

Important researches in this field were made by two Britons, James Joule and William Thomson, and by a German, Helmholtz. Joule, a wealthy brewer of Manchester and a master of experimentation, demonstrated the invariable equivalance of heat and of chemical, electrical, and electromagnetic energies as measured in terms of their specifically appropriate units. He gave his name —joule—to the practical unit of energy. Helmholtz, professor at various German universities, generalized Joule's results and established the "law" of the "conservation of energy," that the quantity of force which can be brought into action in the whole of nature is unchangeable, that it can be neither increased nor diminished. William Thomson, best known by his later title of Lord Kelvin, professor for many years at the University of Glasgow, generalized the "law" of the "dissipation of energy," that, while the sum-total of energy is constant, the amount of available energy diminishes by a continual degeneration into non-available or "dissipated" heat.

As a further contribution to thermodynamics, Joule revived in 1857 the kinetic theory of gases, that they consist of minute particles which move in straight lines with high average velocity, constantly encountering one another, and hence continually changing their individual velocities and directions. This theory was substantiated by ingenious experiments conducted by James Maxwell.

Contemporaneously, physicists were studying the phenomena of light and advancing the science of optics. In 1850 a Frenchman, Jean Foucault, established the wave-theory of light.[1] He showed that light travels more slowly in water than in air and that its velocity in different media varies inversely as the refractive indices of the media.

The perfecting of lenses was an outstanding achievement of the 1840's and 1850's. To it, the development of photography contributed in no small measure. And from it came not only greatly improved cameras but telescopes and microscopes and other optical instruments of inestimable service to chemistry and biology, physics and astronomy.

Of all the developments of physical science in the nineteenth century, perhaps the most noteworthy, and certainly the most original, had to do with electricity. Electrical science **Elec-** had begun in the second half of the eighteenth century **tricity** with the work of Franklin, Galvani, and Volta. It was forwarded in the first half of the nineteenth century by the researches, both theoretical and practical, of Ampère and Ohm and especially of Michael Faraday. Then, with the rapid exploitation of electricity for industrial purposes, there was correspondingly increased stimulus to scientific researches into its nature and properties. About 1855 James Maxwell turned from his fruitful study of the kinetic theory of gases to an equally fruitful study of electromagnetic phenomena. He conceived and gradually elucidated an epoch-making theory of electromagnetism, relating optics to electricity and holding that light-waves are the same in kind as those by which electromagnetic oscillations are propagated through the ether.

In the 1880's, Heinrich Hertz, a pupil of Helmholtz, finally established Maxwell's electromagnetic theory of light on an experimental foundation and derived from it the principles which

---

[1] This theory had been proposed by Huygens in the seventeenth century.

were utilized by Marconi in his invention of wireless telegraphy. In the 1890's, Joseph Thomson, in his celebrated research laboratory at the University of Cambridge, was investigating the conduction of electricity through gases and sharing with a Dutch physicist, Hendrik Lorentz, the fame of formulating the "electron theory." Concerning "electrons," and also concerning "atoms" and "molecules"—those basic concepts of nineteenth-century physics—we shall presently say more in connection with chemistry.

Quite as significantly, certain curious forms of radiation were discovered toward the close of the nineteenth century. Wilhelm von Röntgen, director of the physical institute at Würzburg (in Germany), discovered the highly useful "X-rays" (or "Röntgen rays") in 1895. In 1898 Pierre Curie, professor of physics at Paris, working in conjunction with his equally famous Polish wife, managed to extract radium from pitchblende, and thereafter both the Curies did much to make the world marvel at this newly found chemical element and at the essentially new science of radio activity. It was to be put to practical use by physicians and subsequently by makers of the atom bomb.

In chemistry, significant work had been done by Robert Boyle in the second half of the seventeenth century, and in the eighteenth century by Cavendish, Priestley, and especially Lavoisier. In the nineteenth century, however, chemical **Chemistry** science, like electrical science, was powerfully stimulated by industrial developments.

Basic to nineteenth-century chemistry (and physics also) was the hypothesis, convincingly tested at the very beginning of the century, of the atomic and molecular constitution of matter. Since the time of the ancient Greeks, various philosophers and scientists had toyed with an idea of the "atom" as one of the minute indivisible particles of which the whole universe might be composed, but it was not until the first years of the nineteenth century that the idea was clearly defined and firmly fixed in scientific usage. At this time, John Dalton, an English Quaker schoolmaster of Manchester, argued from known facts of chemical composition that every bit of matter consists of "atoms" and that the atoms of one chemical element are distinguished from those of another by different relative weights. Almost simultaneously Count Amadeo Avogadro, an Italian nobleman and professor of physics at the University of Turin, demonstrated that gases consist of comparably minute particles, which he termed "molecules," and set forth "Avogadro's law," that "equal volumes of all gases, under the same conditions of temperature and pressure, contain the same number of smallest molecules."

For a time there was confusion, in chemical nomenclature, between the "atoms" of Dalton and the "molecules" of Avogadro. Gradually, however, the confusion was dispelled by using the word "atom" to define the ultimate particles of simple elements, and the word "molecule" to denote gas particles and the ultimate particles of chemical compounds. Gradually, too, Dalton's conception of atomic weights bore fruit.

In 1869–1871 Mendeléyev, a Russian chemist and professor in the University of St. Petersburg, enunciated his "periodic law," in effect that there is a periodic sequence in the properties of elements arranged in the order of their atomic weights and that gaps in the sequence point to the existence of hitherto unknown elements. In accordance with this law, rare and hitherto unknown elements were soon discovered—for example, gallium in 1871 and scandium in 1879.

Toward the close of the nineteenth century, the advance of electrical science served to complicate and modify prevailing ideas about atoms and molecules. As far back as 1756 Benjamin Franklin had spoken casually of "electric particles," and in the 1830's Michael Faraday had based some interesting experiments on an "atomic" theory of electricity, but the significance of this was long unperceived. Only in the 1890's did the "electron" appear as the ultimate particle of electricity, and then, through the researches of Lorentz and Joseph Thomson, arose the "electron theory," that atoms are not simple indivisible entities, but that they contain electrons. But not until the twentieth century, after 1910, was the "electron theory" fully worked out with revolutionary consequences.[1]

A major achievement of nineteenth-century chemistry was the discovery of ways of making organic substances synthetically. This involved, of course, a repudiation of the conventional distinctions which had long obtained between inorganic and organic bodies, between minerals on the one hand and animals and plants on the other. Such a repudiation was clearly implied in the re-

[1] See below, pp. 520–521.

markable achievement of Friedrich Wöhler, physician and professor of chemistry in the University of Göttingen, who in 1828 demonstrated that urea, a substance hitherto thought of as purely animal, could be artificially produced by synthesis from the chemical elements of which it was composed. Wöhler collaborated with Liebig in many of the investigations preparatory to the latter's celebrated contributions to the science of soils and fertilizers; [1] and their work was fundamental to the subsequent expanding production of synthetic dyes, synthetic drugs, synthetic rubber, and synthetic goods of all sorts. Moreover, the chemical laboratory which Liebig founded at Giessen in 1826 was the prototype of a host of chemical laboratories which governments and universities, industrial corporations and private foundations, soon put up all over Europe and America, and in which practical as well as theoretical chemistry was stressed.

Chemistry, let us emphasize, was intimately associated throughout the nineteenth century with manifold progress in the industrial arts. It contributed a vast deal to the efficiency of all forms of motive power, to the bleaching and dyeing of textiles, to the utilization of cellulose, to agriculture and food preservation, to the refining of petroleum and the production of rubber goods, to the instrumentalities for waging modern war; and all these arts, in turn, stimulated the growth of chemical science. "Chemical engineering" gradually became an important branch of general engineering, and along with "physical chemists" and "electrochemists" emerged "biochemists." For chemistry in the nineteenth century was an ally, not alone of physics, but of biology, physiology, medicine, surgery, and sanitation.

Back in the eighteenth century, it had been usual to lump together all such natural sciences as were not strictly mathematical and physical (or chemical) and to label them "natural history." In the second half of that century, there had **"Natural History"** been some specialization in botany and zoology, geology, and mineralogy, but it was not apt to be the very detailed specialization which is nowadays common, and its exponents continued, well into the nineteenth century, to think of themselves as dealing with "natural history." Such was the case with certain famous scientists of the first part of the nineteenth century, who summarized and interpreted, and sometimes added to, the pre-

[1] On Liebig and his contributions, see above, p. 11.

viously acquired knowledge of animals and plants and earth. Of these "naturalists," two are particularly noteworthy—Lamarck and Humboldt.

Jean Baptiste de Lamarck was a French nobleman who studied medicine at Paris, became interested in meteorology and chem-

**Lamarck** istry, and eventually devoted his talents to botany and zoology. The researches and observations of a lifetime he embodied in his *Natural History of Invertebrate Animals* (1815–1822), a work celebrated for its detailed scientific information and for the general evolutionary theory underlying it, a theory of developmental relationship among all forms of life, a theory which was to exercise an ever greater fascination for nineteenth-century biological science and to distinguish it markedly from that of earlier times. The doctrine of evolution as set forth by Lamarck comprised four "laws": (1) Life by its very nature tends continually to increase the size of every body possessing it up to a limit which life itself sets. (2) A new need continually making itself felt in a body tends to produce a new organ in that body. (3) The development of organs is in constant ratio to their use. (4) Whatever has been acquired or changed in the organization of a living body is conserved by generation and thus transmitted to its descendants.[1]

Alexander von Humboldt, Prussian nobleman and brother of the statesman Wilhelm von Humboldt,[2] was at once a product of eighteenth-century philosophical "enlightenment" and a fore-

**Humboldt** runner of the nineteenth-century organizers and conductors of "scientific expeditions" in quest of "specimens" for botanical and zoological gardens. He made scientific trips to England and through Switzerland and Italy. He pursued scientific investigations for many years at Paris and for many other years at Berlin. He led a famous scientific expedition in 1799–1804 all over South America, observing and collecting data about volcanoes, climate, manners and customs of the people, appearance and habits of birds, fishes, and reptiles, trees and shrubs. Humboldt was a father of the science of climatology, and the idea of "isothermal lines" in geography was his. But he was

---

[1] It should be noted that these "laws" of Lamarck are much vaguer and more general than the later evolutionary doctrine of Darwin, and that the fourth—the hereditary transmission of acquired characterisics—is extremely questionable.

[2] See *Modern Europe to 1870*, p. 586.

no narrow specialist, and the breadth of his knowledge, as well as the charm of his personality and the liberality of his purse, made him, next to Napoleon Bonaparte, the most famous European of his day. When he was an old man, between the ages of 76 and 90, he wrote and published a remarkable work, *Cosmos,* summarizing the scientific knowledge of the time and undertaking to demonstrate the existence of a supreme unity amid the complex details of natural phenomena.

By 1870 "natural history" was being differentiated into a number of specialized sciences. One of these was geology which was immensely forwarded by Sir Charles Lyell, whose classic *Principles of Geology, an attempt to explain the* Lyell and *former changes of the Earth's surface by reference to* Geology *causes now in operation,* appeared in successive editions between 1830 and 1872. The central thesis of this work was not essentially different from that of James Hutton's book (published back in 1785), but it was expressed more entertainingly and supported by a much greater wealth of convincing data. Altogether, Lyell succeeded in persuading his scientific contemporaries that the continuous operation of observable geological processes—volcanoes pouring out vast masses of molten rock, rivers wearing away their banks and depositing strata which could naturally be transformed into sandstone, earthquake shocks producing faults in the rocks, vegetation preparing future coalbeds, land almost everywhere either rising or sinking—would suffice, over a very long period of time, to explain how the surface of the earth had assumed its present physical appearance.

To Lyell's basic contributions to geological science was soon added a good deal of information about fossil remains and their relationship to the rock or silt in which they were found. Thus arose a specialized branch of palæontology, and it became possible to reconstruct in rough outline the story of "prehistoric" geological ages in which now extinct species of animals and plants had flourished, or still extant species had occupied wider habitats.

Evidence also came to light that man himself had existed in "prehistoric" geological ages. In 1846 a French customs officer, Boucher de Perthes, who devoted his leisure to somewhat amateurish geological investigations, announced that he had found, in the gravels of the Somme valley, along with fossil remains of elephant and rhinoceros, certain flints bearing marks

**Discovery of "Prehistoric" Man** of human handiwork. In 1857 the actual remains of a "prehistoric" man—what Boucher de Perthes termed "antediluvian man"—were unearthed in the Neander valley near Düsseldorf (in Germany). In 1868, four skeletons of a different kind of "prehistoric" man—taller and with larger skulls—were discovered in a cave at Cromagnon (in southwestern France). Subsequent research demonstrated that both "Neander-thal" and "Cromagnon" races had been fairly widely distributed at different early ages throughout Europe. It should be borne in mind that all these discoveries and all this research stimulated a remarkable development of anthropology and at the same time strengthened the credibility of current evolutionary teachings of biology.

The word "biology" was introduced into scientific nomenclature by Gottfried Treviranus, a German physician and naturalist, and for many years professor of mathematics at

**Biology** Bremen, who published in 1802–1805 a work with the title *Biology, or Philosophy of Living Nature.* In this work the author maintained that simple forms, which he termed "zoophytes," were "the primitive types from which all the organisms of the higher orders had arisen by gradual development," and he laid down as a fundamental principle "that all living forms are the result of physical influences which are still in operation, and vary only in degree and direction." In an effort to substantiate his theories, Treviranus assembled a mass of anatomical and physiological data and published them in 1831 as *Appearances and Laws of Organic Life.*

Succeeding biologists were greatly aided by the notable improvement which physicists effected in the 1830's in the compound microscope. Just as the earlier invention of the telescope had enabled astronomers to explore the "infinitely great" in distant mysterious space, so the development of the microscope enabled biologists to behold the "infinitely little" in near-by commonplace things. And the more these were studied, the less commonplace did they appear.

One of the outstanding scientists whose use of the new microscopy proved epochal was Theodor Schwann, a native of Rhenish Prussia, and for many years professor of anatomy at the universities of Louvain and Liége (in Belgium). He discovered the organic nature of yeast in 1837 and formulated in 1839 the significant "cell theory," that all living things originate and grow in very small structural units, or "cells." Further investigation by other physiologists confirmed the theory, but added to it, in the 1840's and 1850's, the conception of "cells" as not being ultimate entities in themselves but as containing vital entities—to the matter of which the suggestive name of "protoplasm" was conventionally accorded.

In the latter part of the nineteenth century, microscopy and its attendant quickening of biological research had extraordinary consequences for the practice of medicine and surgery. Before taking up these matters, however, let us consider another kind of epochal contribution which mid-century biology (including zoology and botany) made to subsequent scientific thought—a contribution conveniently designated as "Darwinism," and originating in the independent labors of two eminent "naturalists," Alfred Russel Wallace and Charles Darwin.

Darwin, born at Shrewsbury (in England) of middle-class stock [1] and sent to Edinburgh to study medicine and thence transferred to Cambridge for training as a clergyman of the Anglican Church, displayed in his youth but one ambition—to become a scientist. In his twenty-third year, with the reluctant consent of his family, he abandoned the clerical calling and embarked as a "naturalist" on a surveying vessel, the *Beagle*. He was gone for five years (1831–1836) on a voyage through the South Sea islands and along the South American coasts, observing and gathering "specimens." His observations led him to ponder upon the possibility of attributing variations of species to differences of environment and of natural needs. For several years after his return to England, Darwin was engaged in detailed study along the numerous lines of scientific enquiry suggested by the expedition of the *Beagle*. He was particularly struck by Lyell's *Principles of Geology,* which was already spreading the idea that vast changes could be brought about by natural processes and was thus paving the way for a natural explanation of biological evolution. He was also struck by Malthus's *Essay on Population,* which had argued that the increase

*Darwin and Doctrine of Evolution*

[1] His paternal grandfather was Dr. Erasmus Darwin, an eighteenth-century poet and botanist, and his maternal grandfather was Josiah Wedgwood, the well-known porcelain manufacturer.

(or decrease) of population is related to a struggle for existence among mankind. Why, thought Darwin, could not the principle of Malthus be extended to the whole organic creation and utilized to explain the variation of species?

Wallace, a considerably younger Englishman, began his career as a land surveyor and architect and then, becoming interested in plants and beetles, had served as "naturalist" on scientific expeditions to the Amazon (1848–1850) and through the East Indies (1854–1862). In 1858, while he was lying ill with fever in the Moluccas, he too began to think of Malthus's *Essay on Population* (which he had read several years previously); and the idea of the survival of the fittest flashed over him. In two hours he "thought out almost the whole of the theory," and in three evenings he embodied it in an essay, which he promptly mailed to Darwin as the best known naturalist of the day.

Darwin, upon receiving the manuscript, presented it, together with an essay of his own, before a learned society in London, and the so-called Darwinian hypothesis of evolution was launched. Darwin's ideas were explained at length in his chief book, published in 1859, *On the Origin of Species by Means of Natural Selection, or the Preservation of Favored Races in the Struggle for Life,* and were subsequently elaborated in certain particulars in his *Descent of Man* (1871). The central idea of Darwin—his doctrine of "evolution"—was that animal and vegetable species, in their present very diverse forms and aspects, are not immutably fixed as results of separate special acts of creation but are different and changing natural outcomes of a common original source. Darwin's ideas as to how such change and differentiation took place were threefold: 1) "natural selection," 2) "sexual selection," and 3) "inheritance of acquired characteristics."

Of these, the first—"natural selection"—was most stressed, and may briefly be summarized as follows. The pressure of the struggle for life favors those individuals in each species which possess particular variations from the normal type that are of direct advantage to them in their surroundings. Such individuals tend to survive at the expense of their fellows and to produce offspring. The new generation shows variation also, and, once more, those individuals which depart from the ordinary in the most useful way have a better chance of survival than the others. Thus, gradually, after the lapse of long periods of time, differences so far accumulate in the descendants of each one of the original type that new types, or species, may be formed.

As for "sexual selection," Darwin explained the development of colors and structures peculiar to one sex as the result of its natural selection by the preferences of the other sex. And, to strengthen his whole argument for evolution, he took over from Lamarck the notion that "acquired characteristics" are transmitted hereditarily.

We must here notice certain limitations to the novelty or accuracy of "Darwinism." The general idea of "evolution" was not new. No one could fail to perceive that there were resemblances among all forms of life; and that these resemblances might be traced to some form of evolutionary development had been urged, before Darwin or Wallace, by Lamarck at the beginning of the nineteenth century, and, for the matter of that, had been suggested very much earlier, for example, by St. Augustine in the fourth century A.D., and by Anaximander in the sixth century B.C. Moreover, Darwin's doctrine of the hereditary transmission of acquired characteristics, which he borrowed from Lamarck, has been seriously questioned by later biologists, and his theory of "sexual selection" has been dismissed as unimportant. Even his hypothesis of "natural selection" has had to be refined and modified in the light of more recent studies.

Yet we must point out that "Darwinism," unlike earlier concepts of evolution, was extraordinarily influential. It was put forth in a "scientific" and "materialist" age, when the way to its reception had been prepared by a host of naturalists. It was sponsored by a most respected scientist and backed by his painstaking researches. It not only assumed an evolution in nature but offered a plausible explanation of how such evolution takes place.

Darwin's work was soon supplemented by publications of Wallace—*Contributions to the Theory of Natural Selection* (1871), *Geographical Distribution of Animals* (1876), and *Darwinism* (1889) [1]—and was reinforced by the researches and convictions of several contemporary scientists. Sir Charles Lyell, the geologist, accepted "Darwinism" in his *Antiquity of Man* (1863); and among particularly spirited apostles of "Darwinism" were the Englishman Thomas Huxley and the German Ernst Haeckel.

[1] Against Darwin, Wallace contended that the origin of man, unlike that of other animals, cannot fully be explained by "natural selection."

Huxley, after a training in medicine and surgery, earned a notable scientific reputation by accompanying an expedition of naturalists in 1846–1850 and making a careful study of the surface life of the tropical seas. Subsequently, he served as official naturalist to the English Geological Survey and carried on important original research in palæontology. With a good deal of sound knowledge about biology, Huxley combined an aggressive personality and a signal literary talent—all of which he utilized in defense of "Darwinism." He was "Darwin's bulldog," he said; and in *Man's Place in Nature* (1863) he emphasized, with square-jawed pugnacity, that aspect of the new evolutionary teaching which pointed to the purely natural development of man himself from lower forms of life.

Haeckel, trained also in medicine, and professor of zoology at the Prussian University of Jena, was the first outstanding scientist on the Continent of Europe to adhere fully to Darwin's doctrine of organic evolution. His *General Morphology* (1866) represented a suggestive attempt to work out and apply the doctrine in detail, and for many years afterwards his studies, his lectures, and his fast-flying pen alike contributed to the popularizing of "Darwinism." Haeckel presented to the international zoological congress at Cambridge in 1898 a "genealogical tree" of the relationship between the various orders of animals, tracing the descent of the human race in twenty-six stages from simple bits of protoplasm through the chimpanzees and the "pithecanthropus erectus" [1] to "primitive man." Haeckel was quite dogmatic about his "tree," but other scientists have been more dubious.

By the end of the nineteenth century, the best-known biologists, botanists, and zoologists—and, indeed, the majority of scientists —were proceeding on general Darwinian assumptions. But already two lines of research were raising serious questions. One line was that pursued by August Weismann, professor of zoology at Freiburg (in southern Germany), who reached the conclusion, set forth in his *Essays upon Heredity and Kindred Biological Problems,* that heredity consists of the

**Amendments to Darwinism**

---

[1] "Pithecanthropus erectus" was the name given to a creature, then supposed to be the "missing link" between man and the anthropoid apes, which was imaginatively reconstructed in the 1890's from a thighbone, two teeth, and a skull-cap which were dug up in the East Indian island of Java by a medical officer in the Dutch army. No one knows whether the disinterred remains belonged to one and the same skeleton.

transmission of pure germ plasm in germ cells which have nothing to do with acquired characteristics. Weismann's germ theory, with its attendant denial of the hereditary transmission of acquired characteristics, was hotly contested by Haeckel and other strict "Darwinians," but the more it was investigated, the more it was accepted, so that gradually, and especially after 1900, it brought about widespread scientific dissent from that part of Darwin's evolutionary doctrine which he had derived from Lamarck.

The other modifying line of research was inaugurated earlier, and only a little time after the appearance of "Darwinism," by Gregor Mendel, a native of Austrian Silesia, an Augustinian monk, and eventually abbot of the monastery at Brünn (in present-day Czechoslovakia). Mendel, not **Mendel's Work** satisfied that Darwin's view of natural selection was sufficient to explain the formation of new species, undertook a series of experiments in the garden of his monastery on the cross-breeding of peas. He published his results in the volumes of a local scientific society, where they lay buried for more than thirty years. Their rediscovery in 1900 by a distinguished Dutch botanist and professor in the University of Amsterdam, Hugo de Vries, and their confirmation and extension by him and by other scientists, had revolutionary consequences. "Mendelianism" was established as a practical aid to scientific breeding of plants and animals and also as a very important amendment of evolutionary theory. For the essence of Mendelianism is that in heredity certain characters may be treated as indivisible and apparently unalterable units, thus introducing into biology what may perhaps be termed an atomic conception [1] and greatly complicating the problem as to how an organic evolution of different species actually occurs.

Second only to the development of the evolutionary aspects of biology, in nineteenth-century popular interest, was the parallel (and increasingly connected) progress of physiology and medical science. The founder of the newer scientific physiology was Johannes Müller, professor of **Physiology and Medical Science** anatomy and physiology at the University of Berlin and an inspiring teacher. His *Handbook* (1833–1840) was a classic: it treated of the whole field of human physiology in a highly scientific spirit and with due attention to the latest discoveries in related fields; and it broke fresh ground in its detailed

[1] Related to that of the "chromosomes," on which see below, pp. 522–523.

tracing of the nervous system and the functioning of the senses. Another eminent physiologist was Claude Bernard, a Frenchman, who gave up the writing of dramas to study medicine and became professor at the Sorbonne and director of the laboratory at the Botanical Gardens in Paris. He discovered the vaso-motor system and also opened up the subject of glands and internal secretions.

A prime service to medical and surgical science (and dentistry) was rendered by the development of anesthetics. The anesthetic qualities of nitrous oxide (so-called "laughing gas") were discovered by Sir Humphry Davy in 1800, and those of ether by Michael Faraday in 1818. These discoveries remained scientific curiosities, however, until 1842, when an American physician, Crawford Long, privately performed an operation under ether at a town in Georgia. In 1847 a Scottish physician announced his discovery of the anesthetic properties of choloroform. The use of all these anesthetics spread speedily in Europe and America, and was later supplemented by the employment of cocaine for local anesthesia.

One of the greatest surgeons of the century was Joseph Lister, the founder of aseptic surgery. The son of an English scientist who improved the compound microscope, he studied physiology at the University of London and began the practice of surgery at Edinburgh in 1853. Then, becoming professor of surgery at Glasgow, he proceeded in 1865 to experiment with carbolic acid as a safeguard against the infections which had usually attended surgical operations. His experiments were strikingly successful, and in 1867 he published an account of them in a paper *On a New Method of Treating Compound Fracture, Abscess, etc*. Lister also introduced the use of carbolized catgut for surgical sewings and conducted important researches in bacteriology. He occupied the chair of clinical surgery at Edinburgh from 1869 and at London from 1877; in 1891 he helped to establish the celebrated Lister Institute of Preventive Medicine. A grateful British government honored him with a baronetcy and a peerage.

At the very time when Lister was experimenting with carbolic acid and laying the foundations for aseptic surgery, the French scientist Louis Pasteur was proving that the yeast plant is the agent of alcoholic fermentation and that other small organisms are the agents of other familiar fermentations. Thence Pasteur was led to study abnormal and "diseased" fermentations, and thereby to discover microbes as the cause of disease and to inaugurate a veritable revolution in medical science. Pasteur's work in bacteriology was supplemented, in the field of preventive medicine, by the contemporaneous achievements of a distinguished German pathologist and politician Rudolf Virchow.[1] Professor of pathological anatomy and director of research in the Pathological Institute at Berlin, Virchow in his *Cellular Pathology* (1858) established what Lister described as the "true and fertile doctrine that every morbid structure consists of cells which have been derived from preexisting cells as a progeny." Subsequently, he contributed much to our knowledge of particular diseases and took an active part in assuring to Berlin an excellent drainage system, scientific sewage disposal, and a pure water supply.

*Bacteriology*

Some of the most startling triumphs of modern medical science were secured through the researches of Robert Koch, a German physician, at first a medical army officer and afterwards a professor at Berlin. Koch found means of immunizing human beings against certain dread diseases. One brilliant step in this direction had already been taken by an English physician, Edward Jenner, who had discovered, at the close of the eighteenth century, that the scourge of smallpox could be gotten rid of by "vaccination," that is, by inoculating persons with the vaccine of cow-pox. On the sounder bacteriological basis provided by Pasteur, Koch was able to go much further. In 1876 he obtained a pure culture of the bacillus of anthrax and in 1883 announced a method of preventive inoculation against it.

The work of Koch stimulated widespread interest and much scientific practical progress in bacteriology. Within a comparatively short time, bacilli were detected of lockjaw, diphtheria, the bubonic plague, malaria, and sleeping-sickness, and methods were devised for inoculating persons against several such diseases. By the end of the nineteenth century, thanks to the development of bacteriology and aseptic surgery, medical science was concentrating upon the prevention even more than upon the cure of disease. Certain results were already obvious; a marked lessening of the scope and virulence of "plagues"; a sharp decline in

---

[1] Virchow was a vigorous proponent of liberalism and a leading spirit in the Progressive party formed in Prussia in 1862 to defend political liberalism against the King and Bismarck.

infant mortality; and a considerable lengthening of the average span of human life.

All this advance in physiology and medical science, together with the rise of evolutionary conceptions in biology and the absorption of eminent naturalists in the behavior as well as in the structure of animals and plants, gave impetus to novel attempts **Experi-** to render human psychology a strictly physical science. **mental** The leading figure in these attempts was Wilhelm **Psychology** Wundt, a trained physician and physiologist, and professor of philosophy successively at Heidelberg and at Leipzig. Wundt contended that the soul is not a separate entity or agent but a particular class of bodily actions of a mechanical sort; and in his chief work, *Foundations of Physiological Psychology* (1872), he expounded at length the physical basis of thought and behavior, the affinity of human minds to those of the lower animals, and the experimental laboratory methods which should be pursued. These methods he exemplified in the psychological laboratory which he opened at Leipzig in 1875, and before long they were commonplaces of the "science" of psychology in Europe and America.

Toward the end of the nineteenth century the pervasive supposition that man's mind is biological and evolutionary was being industriously applied to animal psychology, to child psychology, to social psychology, and especially to the testing of "intelligence" and the treatment of criminals and madmen. The pioneer of "intelligence tests" was Alfred Binet, who became director of the psychological laboratory of the Paris Sorbonne in 1894 and was called upon by the French government to devise tests for the investigation which it authorized in 1904 of the condition of mentally defective children in the public schools.

Among psychologists—or "psychiatrists"—who concerned themselves with criminology, the most conspicuous was Cesare Lombroso, professor at the University of Turin. He referred all mental phenomena to biological causes, and held that the so-called "criminal" was not morally responsible for his acts, inasmuch as he was a special being whom processes of degeneration and atavism placed midway between the lunatic and the savage. Though Lombroso's work has since been discredited, it gave marked impetus at the time to the extensive development of "psychiatry" and its practical application to problems of crime and insanity.

## 2. MATERIALIST PHILOSOPHY

"Materialism" may conveniently be used to designate the general nature of a main stream of thought which flowed from nineteenth-century science and industry. In a broad sense, many persons may be accounted "materialist" who were not at all philosophically minded but who were absorbed in "practical matters" of making money, directing banks, organizing industrial corporations, devising machinery, or otherwise "applying" science. Such persons had little time or inclination to think about the ultimates of human life and destiny. They did not necessarily deny the spiritual, but they tended to ignore it or to subordinate it to the physical and the material.

Many an intellectual, speculating about the remarkable scientific achievements of the nineteenth century, went further and deduced from them a purely materialist philosophy. *Science* They seemed to confirm the eighteenth-century con- *and* ception of the universe as a huge machine function- *"Matter"* ing in accordance with immutable "natural laws"—laws at once mathematical and physical. Likewise, it now appeared that earth, sun, moon, and stars not only, but animals, vegetables, and minerals, light, heat, and electricity—all the phenomena of nature—were material things, composed of simple "elements" organized in atoms, molecules, or other particles, and operating in a regular way. With telescope, microscope, and spectroscope, the "matter" of the whole universe might be observed and its mechanical constitution demonstrated.

Support for a peculiarly radical type of materialism was drawn from nineteenth-century "natural history." So long as "scientific" philosophy centered in Newtonian physics, as it had done during the "Enlightenment" of the eighteenth century, its apostles and disciples could marvel at the Deity who had been the Creator and Supreme Lawgiver of the universe and at the peculiar mental endowment of man which enabled him, alone among all God's creatures, to apply his "reason" to discovery of universal natural law. They could be "deists" and "rationalists." But now, in the nineteenth century, evolutionary biology (and geology) shared with Newtonian physics the center of the intellectual stage and contributed to the rise of a materialist philosophy which spurned deism and questioned rationalism.

It cannot be too emphatically stated that conceptions of historical growth and development, of "evolution," held a preeminent, and novel, position in nineteenth-century thought. Contribution of Evolutionary Doctrine This was exemplified by the historical writings with which the century teemed. It was exemplified, yet more tellingly, by the formulation of a series of evolutionary hypotheses. Laplace in his nebular hypothesis (1796) held that the solar system had been gradually evolved from a primeval hot nebula which, as it whirled in space, cast off parts that slowly cooled and shrank into the planets and moons, the sun remaining as a remnant of the original nebula. Lyell maintained (1830) that the physical features of the earth had been formed by natural evolutionary processes and presented convincing proofs of the great antiquity of these processes and of man's existence on earth. Lamarck set forth (1815) an evolutionary doctrine of the common origin and gradual differentiation of all living things on the earth, and Darwin proposed (1859) "natural selection" as the major explanation of how such evolution had taken place, including man's. As these and similar theories gained acceptance, the *tout ensemble* was highly favorable to materialistic philosophizing about man and the universe. So, too, was the "scientific" psychology of the period, which posited man's "animal mind" and toppled "pure reason" from the throne which it had occupied in eighteenth-century philosophy.

Among leading exponents of materialism, three may here be mentioned—Huxley, Haeckel, and Spencer. Huxley was a scientist of no slight ability or achievement, but he was also Huxley and Haeckel a literary artist and much inclined to philosophize on the general significance of the "Darwinism" which as a scientist he forwarded. And he was particularly irked by what he deemed the "obscurantism" of theologians who opposed Darwin's idea of evolution. Huxley was a caustic critic of theism and theology. He did not absolutely deny the possibility of a divine "First Cause," but he insisted that "doubt is a beneficent demon" and declared that "there is no evidence of the existence of such a being as the God of the theologians." To Huxley, moreover, there was no freedom of the human will, only a kind of "scientific Calvinism" according to which everyone must behave as one's physiological processes and the laws of evolution direct.

Haeckel was more uncompromising in his materialism. He

spent many years in expounding the philosophical implications of an extreme and dogmatic "Darwinism," and when he was sixty-five he summarized his convictions in a famous book, *The Riddle of the Universe* (1899). According to him, what purports to be spiritual is really physical. Organic nature is essentially one with inorganic nature, and "life" has sprung naturally from an arrangement of chemical elements. Man's mind as well as his body, together with all animal and vegetable species, has been evolved from protoplasm which arises from nitrogenous carbon compounds by spontaneous generation.

The most comprehensive philosophy of evolutionary materialism was set forth by Herbert Spencer, an Englishman and one of the most typical figures of the late nineteenth century. Spencer was neither an experimental scientist nor a university man. Born of a family of school-teaching Quakers and Meth- Herbert Spencer odists, he was largely self-educated and "self-made." In the early days of English railroading, he was an engineer on the London and Birmingham railway; and for several years after 1848, when economic liberalism was in the ascendant, he was an editor of the London *Economist* and an energetic advocate of individualism. Gradually he turned his attention to theorizing; and in 1857 he maintained, in *Progress, Its Law and Cause,* that all development—of the individual as well as of the solar system—proceeds "from the homogeneous to the heterogeneous." Spencer applauded Darwin's *Origin of Species* and enriched its doctrine with the phrase, "survival of the fittest." And in 1860—the year following the appearance of Darwin's book—Spencer issued the prospectus of his *Synthetic Philosophy,* an enormous work in ten volumes, upon which he was engaged for the next thirty-six years.

The central feature of Spencer's philosophy was that everything organic and inorganic has been naturally evolved, through a "struggle for existence" and the "survival of the fittest," "from the homogeneous to the heterogeneous." Back of this evolution, Spencer reasoned, must be a Power or Cause, but it should be defined as the Unknowable and quite neglected in speculations about matter and motion which alone are "knowable." In his *Principles of Psychology,* Spencer explained the phenomena of adult human mind by reference to its infant and animal ancestry. In his *Principles of Sociology,* he treated of society as an evolving organism, and utilized "Darwinism" to support the industrial competition and capitalism of the age and, indeed, to buttress the whole creed of political and economic liberalism. In his *Principles of Ethics*, he relied upon evolutionary conceptions and concluded most optimistically that, as evolution proceeds, the moral sense must increase and lead on to a state of social harmony so complete as to wipe out the antagonism between altruism and egoism and render duty a pleasure.

The evolutionary materialism of Spencer, Haeckel, and Huxley might, and did, conduce to an optimistic view of human progress, especially when its disciples thought mainly of the continuity of evolution. If matter had evolved so inevitably from protoplasm to present-day man, then man's future evolution into a superman was bound to be quite as inevitable and (it was imagined) even more rapid.

But when thought was concentrated on man's animal and cave-man ancestry and on the earthy nature of his "reason" and "in-

Materialism and Pessimism telligence," pessimism might result. Man had so much of the beast in him and was misled by his imaginings into such gross superstition and such insane "idealism" that there was little chance of improving him—at least within a calculable period or by usual means. It should not surprise us, therefore, that after 1870 a pessimistic, as well as an optimistic, philosophy found favor with a considerable number of persons who were excited by the reputed lessons of science. Nor should it surprise us that, whereas the optimists relied upon the fated "progress" of the human race for the realization of a kind of utopia in the not too distant future, pessimists invoked the arbitrary individual "will" of exceptionally gifted persons as the only possible escape from the prison of matter and unreason.

The philosophy of the "will" had been expounded before the rise of "Darwinism" by a German, Arthur Schopenhauer, in *The World as Will and Idea*, a work originally published in 1818 and subsequently revised and issued in two volumes in 1844. It was a protest at once against the rationalism of the eighteenth century and against the romantic idealism of the first part of the nineteenth century. It maintained that there is no intelligence save what is exhibited by animals. What sways animals (including man) is sheer vital "will" of each individual, acting not from any idealism but from a "realism" based on appetite and passion.

This kind of "realism" was furthered by another German,

Friedrich Nietzsche. He came of a Saxon family of Protestant pastors and was expected to become a clergyman himself, but the reading of Schopenhauer and a special delight in the music of Wagner actuated him to abandon the pursuit **Nietzsche** of theological studies and the profession of Christianity. After obtaining a doctorate in philosophy at the University of Leipzig, Nietzsche taught at Basel from 1869 to 1879, when he resigned on account of ill health and took up his residence in northern Italy and on the French Riviera. In 1889 he broke down completely, mentally as well as physically, and during his last mad years he was tended by members of his family at Weimar.

Nietzsche wrote much during the 1870's and 1880's. At first, he essayed the role of classical scholar and critic. Then, passing from mild criticism of democracy to furious criticism of romanticism, he penned several polemics against contemporary "illusions" of art, religion, and philosophy. At the last, in 1888, he brought out a series of savage attacks on Christianity and its Founder and on "Judæo-Christian" morality. In the meantime, in 1883–1885, he published his philosophical masterpiece, in the form of apothegms put in the mouth of a Persian sage, *Thus Spake Zarathustra, a Book for All and None*. Life, according to the author, has been retarded for thousands of years by an illusory worship of "the good, the true, and the beautiful." There are no such instincts as these in man, nor is there any foundation in nature for ideals of sacrifice, generosity, or gentleness. What does exist is another instinct, another basis for human excellence—the will to power, the will to a stronger and hence a higher life. If this instinct is obeyed, if the weak are ruthlessly trampled upon by the strong, supermen will arise and possess the earth.

The gospel of pessimistic realism had no such popular support as that which optimistic materialism obtained. Schopenhauer had almost no following during his lifetime, and Nietzsche's doctrine made its chief appeal to a coterie of young intellectuals who wanted to be "revolutionary" or were enamored by the literary form of *Thus Spake Zarathustra* as much as by its philosophical content. Yet we must not underestimate the significance of the Schopenhauer-Nietzsche development. Being compatible with a particular view of "science," it could be utilized to explain, even to excuse and extol, the behavior of "supermen" among nationalist statesmen and industrial capitalists, and to justify assaults on supernatural religion and conventional morality. And it was so utilized by an increasing number of persons, especially after 1900. It became a factor in the "realism" which helped to pave the way to world war and dictatorship.

### 3. POSITIVISM AND SOCIAL SCIENCE

Sociology, or "social science," came to the fore in the latter part of the nineteenth century. It represented an attempt to apply the methods of natural science to the study of human relationships, and it was greatly influenced by the "positivism" which had been preached earlier in the century by Auguste Comte.

Comte received a scientific training at the Polytechnic in Paris and earned a precarious living by teaching mathematics, but his chief interest was in the field of social philosophy. Here **Auguste Comte** his innate abilities and methodical habits enabled him, between 1830 and his death in 1857, to produce a large number of heavy, yet meaty, tomes which won him the titles of "father of sociology" and "founder of positivism."

In keeping with other evolutionary conceptions of the time, Comte's basic idea was that man has passed successively through three historical phases: (1) the theological, or fictitious; (2) the metaphysical, or abstract; and (3) the scientific, or positive. In the first phase, man believed that all phenomena are the result of supernatural powers. In the second—a transitional phase—man turned from capricious "spirits" to abstract forces and tried to find the causes of phenomena in "nature" and "reason." In the third and positivist phase, man no longer seeks for causes, whether natural or supernatural, but is content with observable facts.

In divorcing the "facts" of human relationships from abstractions, Comte insisted that he was erecting a new "social science," or, as he styled it, "social physics." Its goal would be the reorganization of the moral, religious, and political systems of mankind in accordance with the dictates of positivism, that is, of "fact."

Comte associated with his positivist philosophy certain ideas of considerable subsequent influence. One was his criticism of the eighteenth-century doctrine of "natural rights": he deemed it "metaphysical," and prophesied that positivists would presently discover a scientific substitute for it. Another was his distrust of the masses, whom he thought too credulous, and his belief that society and government should be directed by landowners, industrialists, and engineers, in accordance with the advice of "scientific experts." Comte also glorified force as the "scientific" cornerstone of the modern state. Force, he held, answers in sociology to tissue in biology; it is the cement of the social organism.

Finally, Comte sought to invest his positivism with religious garb. In place of a supernatural deity he would raise up humanity not only to be studied scientifically but also to be worshipped. The positivist "church" of Comte did not materialize as its founder hoped. True, it was duly inaugurated at Paris, and branches were established in England and Germany. It secured, however, no really popular following, and the number of "intellectuals" who constituted its membership was very slight in comparison with the number who deemed any formal religion quite superfluous.

Nevertheless, the positivist philosophy proved very attractive. Many scientists, and likewise many engineers and industrialists, including some who did not read Comte or know much about the refinements of his teaching, were essentially positivist in that they concentrated on fact-finding and confined their philosophizing about science to an optimistic faith in its all-sufficient utility for human progress.

One of the foremost "liberal" positivists was John Stuart Mill. He began as a devoted disciple of Bentham and a brilliant exponent of economic liberalism, but gradually his interests broadened into the fields of natural science, psychology, and sociology, and he developed a marked sympathy for certain aspects of Comte's teaching. He was too independent a thinker to become a mere follower of Comte, but it was in line with Comte's positivism that Mill in his later life changed the basis of his liberal philosophy (and ethics) from *a priori* reasoning to scientific observation and embodied in his practical program not only an earnest plea for individual liberty but also sweeping demands for sociological, even "socialist," reforms—the emancipation of women, the nationalization of land, the amelioration of the conditions of the working classes. John Stuart Mill was the herald of the "new liberalism"—the positivist liberalism—which after 1880 was intimately associated with "science," with industrial and material "progress," and with a gradual evolution toward "state socialism." **Liberal Positivism**

Another and later apostle of "liberal" positivism (in the form of "pragmatism") was William James, an American trained in

medicine in Germany, who passed in 1875 from the chair of physiology at Harvard to that of psychology. James rebelled against
the mechanical assumptions of contemporary scientists and yet
distrusted reason and felt scant sympathy for earlier "idealism"
or any system of absolutes. He viewed the human scene as one of
change and chance, variety and novelty. Every human trait, he
held, operates as an instrument in the individual's struggle to
live, and its value is relative to its effect upon the struggle. This
pragmatism nicely supplemented the teachings of Comte and Mill.
It enabled one to banish formal logic and metaphysical speculation, and at the same time to expect continuing liberal progress
through a process of trial and error. There was, of course, no
absolute morality; but what "worked" was good and what didn't
was bad. The proof of the pudding was in the eating.

Over against the "liberal" positivism and pragmatism of a Mill
or a James (and their numerous disciples), it should be remembered that positivism was susceptible of quite illiberal interpretation and use. Comte's own criticism of principles underlying the
revolutions of the eighteenth century, and his praise of forcefulness, could be utilized to justify the "realism" of our present age,
its imperialism and wars and dictatorships.

Meanwhile, there can be no doubt that the rise of positivism
gave marked impetus to sociological studies. These took two
chief forms. One was the synthesizing of data of history, economics, and politics with data of natural science and of the new
social sciences of psychology and anthropology into
generalized statements of the "laws" and "trends"
which presumably govern the behavior and evolution
of human society. This was the form of sociology initiated by
Comte and immensely forwarded by Herbert Spencer.

The other was the analysis, through detailed "field" investigation, of the life and labor of particular social classes or groups.
This second form of sociology was suggested by Comte, but its
leading exponent was another Frenchman, Frédéric Le Play, a
graduate (like Comte) of the Paris Polytechnic, who spent five or
six months every year for a score of years in first-hand study
of "typical" families, their income and expenditure, their mode
of life, the problems confronting them and how they met them.
Among numerous similar "social surveys" was a monumental
inquest into the "life and labor of the people of London," directed

Positivism
and Social
Science

and financed by Charles Booth, a British capitalist and philanthropist, and reported by his staff of "experts" in ten huge volumes (1889–1903).

Sociological studies multiplied after 1880 and exerted an ever greater influence on the thought and action of the period. Not only did sociology become a recognized subject of research and instruction in many universities, but its aims and methods were increasingly adopted by disciples of the other and older "social sciences." Historians, for example, concerned themselves less with individual biography and political narrative, and more with general social movements, with the "evolution" of social forces and social institutions. Political scientists, likewise, were moved to stress the practical, rather than the theoretical, aspects of government and to deal not so much with its structure and its relationship to the individual as with its functioning in and on society.

Economists, too, betrayed a sympathy for current sociology. Such a distinguished economist as John Stuart Mill was led by sociological interests to supply "classical" economy (and economic liberalism) with a new social orientation. Moreover, the emergence of a new "statistical" or "value" school of political economy nicely synchronized with the spread of the Le Play type of sociology and was affected by it. Of this "school" of economics, William Stanley Jevons was one of the leaders. He maintained that value depends upon utility, and that the degree of utility of a commodity is some continuous mathematical function of the quantity of the commodity available. This theory he applied, with the aid of elaborate statistical calculations, to special studies of particular industrial and financial phenomena. Jevons thought he could demonstrate mathematically a connection between commercial crises and sun-spots.

Statistics, both as a "science" in itself and as a method for all the social sciences, assumed a special importance. Beginning with sociologists, and following speedily with economists, presently with political scientists, and eventually with social historians, the statistical method was exalted as the "exact" method of "social science," and as such it partially eclipsed the "genetic" or "historical" method which had been most prominent in the earlier part of the nineteenth century.

Sociological and statistical studies were no mere academic exercises. They were patronized by municipalities and national governments as well as by universities and research foundations, and were utilized increasingly after 1880 by legislators and a wide variety of social reformers. They helped to shift popular and political interest from the individual to society. For if the first part of the nineteenth century was characterized by a trend toward individualism and *laissez-faire,* the closing part of the century was distinguished by a socializing tendency.

#### 4. MARXIAN SOCIALISM

Socialism, in one form or another, had been repeatedly advocated throughout the course of European history, and some degree of it had long been practiced. In the nineteenth century, the prevalance of individualism, and especially of economic liberalism, which attended the industrial revolution and was presumably responsible for contemporary misery of the working classes, evoked the appearance of a variety of protesting socialist movements. There were "Utopian Socialists," "Christian Socialists," "Anarchist Socialists," "State Socialists."

Toward the close of the nineteenth century, these varieties of socialism were overshadowed by a very special kind of socialism (or communism), which, being thoroughly materialistic and claiming to be "scientific," attracted an increasing number of followers in an age of science and materialism. Its founder was Karl Marx, **Karl Marx** a native of Rhenish Prussia and the son of an ambitious Jewish lawyer, who, when Karl was six years old, had the family baptized in the Protestant Church and the family name changed from "Mordecai" to "Marx." Karl was sent in due course to the universities of Bonn and Berlin to study law, but to his father's disgust he preferred philosophy and history and eventually took a doctorate at Jena. Unable to obtain an academic position, he embarked upon a journalistic career—of many vicissitudes. From 1849 to his death in 1883 he resided in England, eking out a meager living for himself and his devoted family by translating books and serving as special correspondent for the *New York Tribune.* Marx's career was not externally brilliant, and, though he proclaimed the essential doctrine of "scientific socialism" in the revolutionary year of 1848, it was not until thirty or forty years afterwards that it acquired widespread fame and influence.

Marx derived his ideas from several sources. For his dialectic method and for a vision of historical evolution, he was indebted to Hegel, the master of "idealist" philosophy. Under the influence of the "Younger Hegelians," with whom he studied at Berlin, he developed a strong sympathy for liberal and democratic political ideals.

Presently Marx's interest was aroused in economics; and at Paris this interest was intensified and made fruitful by his personal observations of the new factory system and industrial proletariat about him, by his discussions and debates with Louis Blanc, the "state socialist," and with Proudhon, the "anarchist socialist," by his own critical reading of the "classical" economists and, most significant of all, by his contact with Friedrich Engels.

Engels was a German from Rhenish Prussia (like Marx himself), who, after coming under the spell of Hegelian philosophy, had been sent by his father, a wealthy cotton-spinner, to England to take charge of a branch factory near Manchester and had there been so shocked by what he saw of the condition of the working class that he joined the radical "socialist" element in the Chartist movement. In 1844, on a brief visit to Paris, Engels met Marx, and from this meeting dated the intimate friendship and uninterrupted collaboration which lasted during their lives. It should be emphasized that both Engels and Marx were much influenced by contemporary industrialism and also by the growing materialism, positivism, and "scientific spirit" of the age in which they formulated their economic doctrines.

In 1848 Marx and Engels jointly issued a little pamphlet, the *Communist Manifesto.* It opened with caustic criticism alike of "bourgeois liberalism" and of "utopian socialism," and Communist went on to expound a "scientific communism" of the Manifesto following general tenor. The current economic conflict of 1848 between capitalists and proletarians is but a phase of the age-long economic struggle between social classes. History is simply the record of how one class has gained wealth and then secured political power only to be overthrown and succeeded in wealth and power by another class. Recently the class struggle has been between aristocratic landlords and middle-class capitalists. Now, the factory system is magnifying the wealth and political power of the capitalists at the expense of the landlords, but simultaneously it is creating a proletarian class by whom the capitalist class are to be fought and eventually destroyed. For, through factory exploitation of labor, capitalism will become concentrated, as time goes on, in fewer hands, while the proletariat will absorb the masses of the population and grow more "class-conscious." The day must come when the many will be able to dispossess the few and usher in a solidly proletarian society and government under which the economic means of production and exchange will be owned and operated not privately but socially. On that day will disappear the essentially "bourgeois" institutions and mentality which dominate present society. In the meantime, it is the business of "scientific communists" to prepare the proletarians for their inevitable victory, to inculcate "class consciousness" in them, and to urge them to the "class struggle" which they must wage with capitalists. The *Manifesto* concluded with a revolutionary and international flourish: "The proletarians have nothing to lose but their chains. They have a world to win. Workingmen of all countries, unite!"

The *Communist Manifesto* attracted little attention in 1848, and awoke no immediate response even on the part of proletarians. Nevertheless, Marx continued to devote his major energies (usually in collaboration with Engels) to fortifying the doctrines of the *Manifesto* and trying to induce workmen to organize themselves in support of its philosophy and program. For many years he toiled at a monumental study of economics with a view to showing how the industrial worker was "exploited" by the industrial capitalists; the results were embodied in a bulky treatise, *Capital*, of which the first volume was published by Marx in 1867 and others by Engels after Marx's death.

Fundamental to Marx's mature work and to the movement which he inaugurated, was a philosophy of "economic determin-

**"Economic Determinism"** ism." This may be stated in three postulates: (1) that the distinctive civilization—culture, religion, morality, and art—of each age is determined by its material and economic conditions; (2) that the course of history is determined by a succession of class struggles for material supremacy; and (3) that present-day bourgeois capitalistic society will inevitably be transformed into another society, proletarian and collectivist.

Such an approach to socialism eventually proved "timely." It was advertised as "scientific." It was frankly materialist. It enshrined concepts of evolution and struggle. It appealed in a "realistic" age to a growing number of persons who perceived an affinity of "Marxism" in sociology to "Darwinism" in biology. All of which helps to explain why Marxian doctrines, unheeded in 1848, secured a large following after 1890.

The particular organization which Marx founded and directed was not very strong or influential. Formally established in 1864 as the "International Workingmen's Association," and usually referred to as the "First International," it comprised small groups of workers in various countries of Europe (and in the United States) and held several international congresses. It did spread a knowledge of "Marxism" and it did alarm the governments of the time. Its membership, however, was slight and poor; and, despite the strenuous efforts of Marx and Engels, it suffered from the passions attendant upon the Franco-Prussian War, from the disillusionment following the suppression of the Paris Commune in 1871,[1] and from internal dissensions arising from the expulsion of anarchist members who criticized Marx. The last real congress of the Association was held at Geneva in 1873, and its dissolution was decreed by a few of the faithful assembled at Philadelphia in 1876.

*The First International*

Nevertheless, the failure of the "First International" meant by no means the end of Marxian Socialism. Some of the national groups of which the International had been composed continued to function. In particular, the German group forged ahead, partly because the industrial and intellectual circumstances were favorable and partly because it annexed in 1875 a rival socialist organization which had been founded in 1863 by Ferdinand Lassalle. Lassalle, a well-educated, well-to-do bourgeois, famed both as a man of fashion and as a "messiah of the poor," was less doctrinaire and more "practical" than Marx. His organizing genius was a legacy, along with the gospel of Marx, to the united "Social Democratic" party which emerged in 1875. Thenceforth, until 1914, this party, committed to political democracy and Marxian socialism, grew steadily in Germany.

The Social Democratic party of Germany became the model for similar political organizations of Marxian socialists in other countries. By the end of the 1880's there were such parties in almost every country of Europe (and in the United States), commanding the loyalty of many workmen and a considerable number of intellectuals, and supported by affiliated trade unions

[1] See above, pp. 84–85.

and newspapers. In 1889 delegates of the several "national" parties met at Paris and formed an international federation—the so-called "Second International"—which maintained a central office and held a series of congresses until the World War of 1914. So impressive was the growth of Marxism from 1890 to 1910 that it dwarfed all other types of socialism, and the word "communism" which Marx and Engels had employed to differentiate their "scientific socialism" from "utopian" or "Christian" socialism fell into disuse. In popular parlance and in the usage of Marxians themselves, "socialism" now connoted the economic and political movement associated with the teachings of Karl Marx.

The Second International

Marxian socialism represented a significant intellectual tendency of the new era, and, though it was denounced and combated by the majority of the upper, middle, and agricultural classes, by leading statesmen and zealous patriots as well as by capitalists and ecclesiastics, though its disciples remained a minority in every country, it made no mean contribution to the era's "socializing" achievements. It elicited from its adversaries both enmity and emulation. To wean the industrial proletarians from it, and to inoculate the masses against it, governments enacted socialistic legislation—nationalizing railways and other public utilities, protecting trade unions and cooperative societies, and ameliorating the conditions of labor.

In the 1890's, a decade after the death of Karl Marx, the movement which he had inaugurated was obviously advancing, but it was already threatened with internal disruption. Marx himself had been dogmatic and intolerant; and his chief followers continually disputed among themselves about tactics and doctrinal details. Such disputes were now embittered by divergent criticism of Marx's prophecies. He had foretold that, through the inevitable evolution of capitalism, the bulk of the middle classes would fall into the category of proletarians and that the class-conscious proletariat, thus becoming a numerical majority, would be enabled by sheer weight of numbers to abolish private property and erect the new collectivist society. But it was now pointed out, with array of statistics, that while the management of capital was being concentrated in fewer hands, its ownership was being extended, that accompanying the descent of middle-class persons into the proletariat was a disconcerting

Divergent Marxian Doctrine

ascent of proletarians into the middle class, and that there was no immediate prospect of a class-conscious proletariat's having the numerical strength of itself to capture any government.

If the critics were right, some revision or amendment of Marxian doctrines and tactics appeared necessary. But in what direction? Eduard Bernstein, a prominent figure in the Social Democratic party of Germany and a trenchant critic of orthodox Marxism, argued that Socialists should move toward the "Right." Instead of pursuing tactics in strict keeping with the philosophy of economic determinism, they should collaborate with democratically minded persons, even bourgeois political parties, in any action which would strengthen popular government and advance the socialization of industry. The right-wing Socialists who followed Bernstein were known as "revisionists" or "reformists." They were fairly numerous in trade unions (the "aristocracy" of labor) and among middle-class converts to socialism. Some of them formed "independent" socialist groups, as in France and England, but most of them remained within the regular Socialist parties, as in Germany, and exerted a gradually growing influence upon them.

Other critics of orthodox Marxism urged a movement in the opposite direction—toward the "Left." According to them, Socialists, lacking a numerical majority, should intensify the class struggle, precipitate a violent revolution, and set up a dictatorship of the proletariat. Such counsels appealed particularly to unskilled workers in southern Europe, who had a deep-seated distaste for parliamentary government, and to radical extremists in an absolutist and industrially backward country like Russia. In this way, a "syndicalist" or "direct-action" movement emerged in France, Italy, and various other countries in the late 1890's. It eschewed politics, and devoted itself to "economic" and "moral" preparation of the proletariat for a "general strike" and a social revolution, preparation involving the development of "industrial unions" of unskilled as well as skilled workers and frequent resort to strikes and sabotage.

The chief philosopher of "syndicalism" was George Sorel, a French engineer and littérateur and a curious compound of positivist and mystic. Sorel called himself a "Neo-Marxist." In numerous writings, including his famous *Reflexions on Violence* (1906), he accepted Marx's ideas of the class conflict and the destiny of the proletariat, but he tinged them with pessimism and criticized Marx's concessions to political democracy and his faith in merely material progress.

Until the World War of 1914, all but one of the regular Social Democratic parties were influenced less by "syndicalist" and left-wing agitation than by right-wing "reformism." While continuing to profess orthodox Marxism, they tended in practice to subordinate its revolutionary features to evolutionary political action. The one exception was the underground Social Democratic party of Russia, which consisted chiefly of exiles and which, at a congress held abroad in 1903, split into two hostile factions. The minority (Mensheviks) adhered to the pattern of other Social Democratic parties. But the majority (Bolsheviks) endorsed the left-wing doctrines of proletarian violence and dictatorship which were tirelessly urged by a person far more influential, in the long run, than Sorel or even Marx. This was Vladimir Ulyanov, a middle-class Russian revolutionary, who had spent several years as a prisoner in Siberia and had subsequently taken refuge in Switzerland and adopted the pen-name of N. Lenin.

# CHAPTER VI

## "MODERNISM" IN ART AND RELIGION

OTH the classicism which stemmed from the renaissance of the late middle ages and the romanticism which flourished in the first half of the nineteenth century [1] have had important continuing influence on European art. But to these was added, in the latter part of the nineteenth century, a powerful new influence, that of "modernism." It was a cultural accompaniment of latest developments in natural science, in sociology, and in psychology, and it had significant effects on traditional religion as well as art.

### I. REALIST AND SYMBOLIST LITERATURE

In literature, much of the earlier romanticism of both subject and style survived, and was exemplified, especially in English literature, by several "popular" writers. Thus, romantic adventure was the central concern of that engaging Scottish writer, Robert Louis Stevenson, in the series of delightful volumes which he published in the 1880's. Then, too, a romantic idealism characterized the whole outlook and output of that other engaging Scottish author, James Barrie, the touching humor and pathos of his novels and the fairy-like whimsicality of his plays. Romantic also was Rudyard Kipling, in his jungle tales, his stirring sea stories, and his poetical praise of the newer imperialism, the "white man's burden."

Indeed, the contemporary interest in imperialism and the ever heightening interest in nationalism were reflected in a good deal of romantic literature of the era after 1870, in French and German, Russian and Italian, as well as in English. It was quite obvious that such writers as Maurice Barrès in France and Gabriele D'Annunzio in Italy were literary heirs of the roman-

[1] See *Modern Europe to 1870,* pp. 686–691.

ticism which had reveled in folk manners and folk lore, in national scenery and national "souls."

But in literature, while romanticism still flourished, a "realistic" modernism cropped up fresh and more abundant. It treated usually of one or both of two general subjects: (1) psychological analysis of the individual, with special reference to his "fated" response to his domestic and social milieu and to traditional institutions and ethics; and (2) sociological study of family, class, or social problems, with particular implications of the need for radical social reform—uplifting the laboring classes, emancipating women, exposing social ills, ending war, and redistributing wealth. It treated of its subjects preferably in prose and with a wealth of petty detail, factual and ostensibly scientific.

**"Realism"**

In atmosphere and style, realist literature displayed divergent tendencies. If it was social, it was apt to be optimistic and journalistic. If, on the other hand, it was psychological, it was likely to be pessimistic and to be most meticulously expressed. Some of the foremost psychological realists, especially those in France, were quite classicist in the painstaking care they took to find just the right phrase, just the right proportion, to convey their meaning.

Of such realists, Gustave Flaubert was a forerunner. An extremely neurotic son of a French physician, he refused to practice law in which he was trained and sought escape from chronic melancholy by applying himself to literary labor. His first novel, *Madame Bovary* (1857), was a coolly analytical story of the marital infidelity of a country physician's wife; and his last work, in the 1870's, was a half-finished literary assault on optimism. Flaubert's fame was much greater after his death than during his lifetime. *Madame Bovary*, when it first appeared, was generally regarded as salacious and scandalous, and its author was prosecuted for immorality. After 1880, it was hailed as the highest art.

**In France**

The witty impressionistic narration of "realistic" love-affairs was a specialty of Alphonse Daudet, who, in quite another vein, could specialize in romantic adventures of his *Tartarin of Tarascon*. On occasion, indeed, Daudet was as romantic as Dickens; on other occasions he was as realistic as Flaubert. Somewhat similar to Daudet in style, though always realist in subject-matter and in the sardonic quality of his humor, was Guy de Maupassant, a supreme master of the short story.

Far less of an artist but far more serious in his realism was Émile Zola. The son of an engineer, he was intensely interested in the newer developments of natural science and quite obsessed with the "laws" of heredity; and, brought up in poverty, he was an ardent agitator for social reform. He was a social realist, half novelist and half journalist. In the years following 1871 he turned out some twenty somber volumes on various situations and problems confronting several generations of an imaginary family, and in other novels he wrote about population, about work, about alcoholism. Zola was a radical republican, and toward the end of his life he played no slight role in French politics.[1]

Surpassing all these French writers in contemporary vogue was Jacques Thibault, best known by his pen-name of Anatole France. For thirty years, from 1885 to 1915, French literature, and indeed European literature, was dominated by his fame. No reputation since Voltaire's was comparable with his. He was the son of a Parisian bookseller and began his literary career by writing verse for self-amusement. His first novel, *The Crime of Sylvestre Bonnard* (1881), was a brilliant success, and thenceforth for forty years he poured out a series of witty, mocking, and captivating works of varied content: pungent and mischievous short stories; philosophical and critical books; novels like *The Rotisserie of Queen Pedauque, Thaïs,* and *The Gods Thirst;* a sceptical biography of Joan of Arc; a number of satires on politics and religion, including *Penguin Island* (1908) and *The Revolt of the Angels* (1914).

Anatole France was essentially what Voltaire would have been if he had lived at the end of the nineteenth century instead of in the eighteenth. He had all of Voltaire's cleverness and lucidity and all his pitiless scepticism about the stupidity and silliness of mankind, but the philosophy which he derived from the natural science of his day was more disillusioning and pessimistic. Whereas Voltaire had believed in Deism and in rational human progress, Anatole France until at least 1900 gave no evidence of a belief in anything, either better or worse. He was the perfect sceptic and ostentatiously indifferent to everything except "art." After 1900 he did take some interest in political and social mat-

[1] See above, p. 105.

ters, allying himself at first with radicals and then with social revolutionaries.

Among English novelists who were esteemed as realists toward the close of the nineteenth century were Meredith and Hardy. George Meredith inaugurated his series of psychological novels as early as 1859 with the *Ordeal of Richard Feverel,* but it was not until much later, with the publication of *The Egoist* (1879) and *Diana of the Crossways* (1885), that he became famous for his realistic analysis of character and for his clipped epigrammatic style. Thomas Hardy devoted his talents mainly to studies of the fateful workings of the "struggle for existence" in village and peasant life in the English countryside. His principal novels, such as *The Mayor of Casterbridge* (1886) and *Tess of the D'Urbervilles* (1891), are concerned not with civilization or manners but with animal aspects of human life; and his poetry, which is now esteemed more highly than his prose, shows like concern.

English drama, like the English novel, responded to the scientific realism of the age, less emphatically perhaps along the lines of individual psychology than in the domain of sociology. The outstanding dramatist of the age, with an international vogue and influence scarcely inferior to Anatole France's, was George Bernard Shaw. He was born at Dublin of an Anglo-Irish Protestant family and was schooled at a non-conformist college in his native city. His chief early interests were in music and painting, and in 1876 he betook himself to London and engaged in journalistic art-criticism.

In the early 1880's a special interest in economic radicalism was awakened in Shaw by Henry George,[1] and presently he became a Socialist. With an enthusiasm for Marxism, he combined a faith in the beneficent role of science, mechanical progress, and materialist philosophy, and a caustic witty manner of viewing the obstacles in the way and preaching their removal. He wrote clever novels, brilliant essays, shrewd letters; but his forte was as a playwright. To the "realistic" drama he was impelled by his admiration for the Norwegian dramatist, Ibsen, and beginning in 1893 he produced an amazing number of plays, treating of a variety of social problems—prostitution, militarism, imperialism, socialism, the Nietzschean superman, the Salvation Army, etc.—

[1] See below, p. 319.

all very didactic and entertaining. Shaw had a genius for self-advertisement, and a multitude who were not always sure whether he was making fun of them or not, swarmed to his plays and applauded his sallies. He was the bludgeoning British counterpart to the more rapier-like Anatole France.

A similar vogue attended the literary efforts of H. G. Wells for rather different reasons. Wells came from the lower middle class, the son of a professional cricketer, and from the beginning he was devoted to science. He obtained a scientific degree from London University and for several years as schoolmaster and private coach he taught science. Then, at a time when everybody was talking about the marvels of science, he took the world by storm with a series of "scientific romances"—*The Time Machine, The Stolen Bacillus, The War of the Worlds*—making the most romantic improbabilities seem real and assured. In the meantime he became a convert to socialism, and soon he was fusing his mechanical, "scientific" utopias with social utopias in which machines would work and men would play and from which would be eternally banished religious superstition and everything else inimical to the evolution and reign of superman. This "utopian realism" Wells set forth in a swift succession of vivid writings from *A Modern Utopia* (1905) to *The Research Magnificent* (1915).

Norwegian literature was notably influential in the new age of realism, thanks largely to the international repute of Ibsen. Henrik Ibsen was an unhappy person, and his early dramas, intensely patriotic and quite romantic, were not well received. Forsaking Norway in the 1860's, *In Scandinavia and Germany* first for Italy and then for Germany, he became "realist" and internationally famous. His *Brand* and *Peer Gynt* (1867) were poetical satires on Norwegian life and religion; and in a series of grim dramas during the 1870's and 1880's—*A Doll's House, Ghosts, An Enemy of the People,* etc.—he mercilessly diagnosed various diseases of modern society, especially the disease of hypocrisy. Then, in the 1890's his dramas grew increasingly symbolic and mystical until no clear content but only an esoteric "art" remained.

Ibsen exerted no little influence on younger men throughout Europe. We have already noted his influence on Shaw. It was also apparent in German literature of the era, particularly in the social novels and dramas of Hermann Sudermann and in the peasant-life plays of Gerhart Hauptmann. We may add that Hauptmann in his later years turned from "realism" to "dream poems" and dramatic fairy tales.

Outside the main stream of the new "realism," yet paralleling it, was the important work of an eminent Russian reformer and novelist, Count Leo Tolstoi. He belonged to the Russian aristocracy, and during the Crimean War he served in the Tsar's army. Suddenly, however, he evinced a lively interest in the peasants and in their betterment. He freed the serfs on his own estate before the Tsar Alexander II issued the general edict of emancipation. He conducted several educational experiments among the lower classes. In the 1860's he began his literary career by publishing *War and Peace,* a powerful pacifist novel. Afterwards he grew ever more philosophical and revolutionary, renouncing all private property and extolling a kind of communist and anarchist Christianity. His later novels, such as *The Kreutzer Sonata* (1890) and *Resurrection* (1900), curiously combined a "realism" in presenting current problems of life with a profound mysticism in suggesting solutions.

**Russian Writers**

Two other Russian writers acquired European fame during the period—Chekhov and Gorky. Anton Chekhov, the grandson of a serf, was trained as a physician at the University of Moscow but deserted the profession of medicine for that of letters. His early tales, very popular in Russia, were humorous sketches of peasant life. Subsequently he adopted a pessimistic, psychological "realism" in plays, such as *The Seagull* (1896) and *The Cherry Orchard* (1904), and in a series of extraordinary stories. Chekhov had a genius for portraying moods and states of mind and a deep-seated aversion for the strong and the efficient. He usually ended on a minor key "not with a bang but a whimper."

Maxim Gorky was the pen-name of Alexis Peshkov, a self-educated product of the urban working class, who became a provincial journalist. In the 1890's he wrote the short stories about tramps and social outcasts which made him famous. After 1900 he wrote longer and more ambitious novels and plays, dealing with Russian life in general and with social problems in particular, discursive and increasingly revolutionary. In 1914 Gorky was a pacifist, and in 1917 a Communist.

It is noteworthy that the majority of the writers whom we have been mentioning, especially those devoted to psychological anal-

ysis, associated with their realism a peculiar æstheticism. This
took the form, perhaps most typically, as with Flaubert, Daudet,
Anatole France, Meredith, and Chekhov, of a meticulous use of
words and the studied creation of an "impressionistic" atmosphere, frequently tinged with irony. Occasionally, as with Shaw,
the style, though exceedingly direct, was startlingly paradoxical.
Sometimes there was a marked straining for unusual expression,
and an achievement of mysterious vagueness. In several
cases, as with Ibsen particularly, realism was supple-     "Sym-
mented, especially from the 1890's onward, by mysti-       bolism"
cism in content and a kind of "symbolism" in form. "Not sharp
colors, but pastel shades, not a literal exactness but a suggestive
use of words," was the way in which one symbolist indicated
the ideal of the new æsthetics. "Art for art's sake" was the popular interpretation.

Such symbolism went naturally enough with mysticism, but the
relevance of mysticism and symbolism to the age of machinery,
big business, and scientific realism is not so clear. The mysticism
was vague and varied, it is true, and not at all orthodox, and the
symbolism which attended it was no simple phenomenon. Perhaps the new literary movement owed more to previous romanticism than its devotees would confess. Perhaps it was a reaction
against the certitudes of science. Perhaps, on the other hand, it
was a logical corollary to the latest propositions of science, a
formulation of the notion that the only thing left for man to do,
now that he was demonstrably a very minor cog in a universal
machine of physics and chemistry, was to seek sensations and to
express himself in an art which should have no other object than
"art" itself. At any rate, by the 1890's, the most significant poetry
in an essentially prosaic age was characterized, along with a
growing amount of the prose, by "symbolism" and similar esoteric
qualities, implying that form is more than content, sound is more
than sense, and that the highest goal of human endeavor is "pure
æsthetics."

In France, symbolism was established as a theory and applied
to poetry by Stephane Mallarmé, a mild-mannered professor of
English literature in a Parisian college. Mallarmé taught that
beauty is sensuous and can best be felt through words suggestive
of color, sound, taste, and touch. He was very fond of Edgar
Allan Poe's poetry, which he translated into French, and he held

that the most perfect phrase in all literature was Poe's line about "the viol, the violet, and the vine." His own poetry, beginning with the celebrated *Après-midi d'un faune* (1876), he invested with a strangely jewelled magnificence and a haunting vagueness. As he grew older he grew more obscure and eventually abandoned punctuation.

Mallarmé for years presided every Tuesday evening over a salon to which young writers flocked and at which he held forth on æsthetic feeling and appreciation. It was very effective in forming a generation of symbolists. By the late 1880's and throughout the 1890's a swarm of young men were vowed to "pure æsthetics," and extremists among them were assuming "stained-glass attitudes," caressing Japanese prints and medieval tapestries, carrying lilies and sunflowers, indulging in absinthe and hashish and in the most singular amours. These were the "æsthetes" of the "fin de siècle"; the "decadents" they were called by their critics.

Of all the French decadents, the outstanding literary genius was Paul Verlaine. Born at Metz, the son of a Napoleonic army officer, he was initiated into impressionism while he was a student and clerk at Paris. Then, in the early 1870's, he traveled around with a precocious youth, Arthur Rimbaud, quarreled with him, and for firing a pistol at him was imprisoned for two years in Belgium.[1] While he was in jail, Verlaine was converted from paganism to Catholicism, and some of his finest poetry, published after his release, was sincerely religious in subject-matter while impressionist in form.

In England, a similar trend toward "pure æstheticism" was fostered by Walter Pater, whose position as an Oxford don enabled him to exert an influence on young English writers comparable with that which Mallarmé was contemporaneously exercising on young French writers. Pater was quite pagan in his admiration for the culture of ancient Greece and Rome and in his cult of sensuous enjoyment as opposed to asceticism. He had a

[1] Rimbaud, a vagabond from childhood, wrote in his teens some amazing "symbolist" verse. After his break with Verlaine he disappeared from view, and it was not generally known until after his death that, following the most varied adventures throughout Europe and the Dutch East Indies, he had settled in Ethiopia and become a wealthy merchant and powerful chieftain. Verlaine's publication in 1886 of the verse of Rimbaud (whom he thought dead) did much to forward the symbolist movement.

fondness for beauty of word and phrase, and to select circles he communicated it in his *Marius the Epicurean* (1885).

Pater expressed the new æstheticism in sonorous prose rather than in poetry. The Englishman who contributed to its vogue in poetry was Algernon Swinburne, an aristocrat and neurotic. In form, he was symbolist, but in subject-matter he showed, as time went on, an ever closer adherence to the tradition of Byron and Shelley, the tradition of intellectual revolt against the conventions and restraints of politics, religion, and morality. This tradition he reinforced by his acceptance of an extreme Darwinism and especially by his sympathy with Nietzsche's virulence against Christianity. In his *Songs before Sunrise* (1871), in his second series of *Poems and Ballads* (1878), and in his later poetical dramas, he put a bitter hatred of priests and kings and traditional morality into a framework of alliterative rhetoric, peculiarly alluring to youth.

In Britain æstheticism of the "decadence" reached its zenith in Oscar Wilde, with his affectation of "art for art's sake," with his sparkling plays and coruscating essays and fairy tales, with his bohemianism and fateful imprisonment and what he described as "dying beyond his means." Wilde was only one devotee, albeit the most notorious, of a literary fashion of the fag-end of the nineteenth century. It seemed then as though Europe specialized in minor poets and that these were all symbolist.

Related to the æstheticism of the symbolist movement, and largely inspired by it, was a new concern with finding or inventing symbolic features in folk literature. Ibsen ransacked collections of Norse sagas to find symbols of basic Nor- **National "Souls"** wegian character, and the mysticism of his last period echoed an æsthetic appreciation of pre-Christian mythology. Lesser literary artists in other countries adopted similar methods and moods, evoking as beautiful and aboriginal (and always shadowy) the "soul" of Slav or Celt. A twilight of mystical nationalism seemed to descend upon Europe. Upon Ireland, for example, a peculiarly "Celtic" afterglow was shed in the 1890's by a group of youthful æsthetes, including William Butler Yeats, Lady Gregory, and George Russell (writing under the initials "AE"), who accompanied their mystic poems and plays with erudite footnotes on the symbolism of legendary Gaelic beasts and gods.

Stylistic symbolism was employed not only by a new generation of nationalists, but also by such a "psychological" writer as
Maurice Maeterlinck. Maeterlinck was a Belgian of Flemish
extraction, who, after graduating from the University of Ghent,
lived several years in Paris, becoming acquainted with Mallarmé
and other members of the "symbolist" group, and, under their
influence, beginning to write poetical plays in French. In 1892
appeared his *Pelléas and Mélisande,* and his reputation was made.
During the next twenty years he sustained it with a succession of
dramas and lyrics, treating of the "souls" of orphan princesses,
blind persons, or pale Arthurian knights, who, in shadowy bodies
out of time and space, mysteriously stir about and vaguely sigh
according to the dictates of some inscrutable but thwarting fate.

### 2. MODERNIST ART

There was a quantitative increase of pictorial art during the
latter part of the nineteenth century. Ever so many rising industrialists, or their wives, with more money than taste, acquired a
reputation for culture by collecting pictures, usually through art
dealers, who flourished as never before, and who, if there were
not enough first-rate pictures to go around, could profitably
dispose of second-rate pictures if their style was in fashion or
the artists had fame. The private demand for portraits, landscapes, still-life scenes, human-interest episodes, was unparalleled.
Besides, in an era of mounting national resources and intensifying
national spirit, all the new public buildings—government offices,
town halls, libraries, universities—had to be adorned with historical or allegorical murals.

At Paris, which was the recognized capital of European art
throughout the era, a modernist type of painting known as
"impressionism" was evolved in the second half of the
century. It was certainly not classical, and, though indebted for its dreamy poetical tendency to preceding
romantics (notably Corot), it was not so concerned with pure
naturalism, and not so forceful or vivid, as most romantic painting
had been. Its sources were partly in romanticism but more specifically in the revived appreciation of Spanish painting of early
modern times, particularly the subtle composition and coloring
of Velasquez's canvases and the queer effect of distortion in El
Greco's, and also in a sudden new enthusiasm for the suggestive-

*Impres-
sionism*

ness, the decorum, and the decorativeness of Japanese art. Japan, it should be borne in mind, was opened up anew to Europeans in the late 1850's, and very shortly afterwards its art was influencing European art even more than the Chinese had influenced it back in the eighteenth century.[1]

Impressionism in painting was akin to symbolism in literature, and each reacted on the other. As Mallarmé and Pater were apostles of the new movement in poetry and prose, so Manet was its pioneer in the pictorial arts. Edouard Manet, after completing his academic course in Paris, spent three years in South America and was so enamored by the old Spanish masters whose works he saw there that on his return he made a careful study of the examples of Spanish art in the Louvre and then proceeded to paint, in impressionistic style, a number of engaging pictures, including *A Spaniard Playing the Guitar, Olympia*, and *The Music Lesson*. Like Mallarmé, Manet was attracted to Edgar Allan Poe, and in his illustrations of Poe's *Raven* some Japanese influence was manifest.

Manet's impressionism soon inspired a notable group of French artists. Camille Pissaro began as a student of Corot but presently threw in his lot with Manet. Curious effects of sunlight became almost an obsession with him, and his chief pictures—of boulevards and bridges of Paris and Rouen—he invested with peculiar atmosphere. Edgar Degas painted dancers and ballets, workwomen and jockeys, portraits of criminals, and several likenesses of Manet, all in wistful and vaguely haunting moods. Claude Monet in his paintings subtly suggested, rather than definitely depicted, cathedral towers in varying lights, and rocky cliffs along the seacoast, and architectural piles in Paris and London.

With these French "impressionists" should be classed the son of an American army officer, James McNeill Whistler, who studied with Manet at Paris in the 1850's and afterwards resided in England, with frequent trips to France. Whistler was fascinated by Japanese prints; and his own etchings and lithographs, as well as his "nocturnes" and "tone paintings," were eloquent alike of a sense of harmonious beauty original with him and of a considerable borrowing from Japanese sources. Whistler was a good deal

---

[1] On the influence of Chinese art at that time, see *Modern Europe to 1870*, p. 384. On the "closing" and "reopening" of Japan to Europeans, see below, pp. 285–287.

of a poseur and dandy, and a faulty draftsman, but he was as influential as he was provocative, and in his *Gentle Art of Making Enemies* (1890) he proved that he was a master of prose.

One of the most original of "modernist" painters was Paul Cézanne. He was a schoolmate and lifelong friend of Zola; and, coming to Paris in 1863 to study art, he joined the group about Manet and for a time painted in a thoroughly impressionistic manner. Under the guidance of Pissaro, the best draftsman of the group, he gradually improved his technique; and then, gradually, he outgrew impressionism. He wished to emphasize the "realistic" aspects of his art, and he felt that, to produce the needful psychological effects, he must give more solidity to pictures than the impressionists gave. Secluded in his native Aix (in southern France), he did his most distinctive work in the 1890's; with thick layers of paint he made simple, vivid, and slightly distorted portraits, landscapes, and pictures of card-games. At the very end of his career, we may remark, he reverted to a kind of extreme romanticism. Cézanne's painting was not particularly popular in his own day, but it was subsequently recognized as the starting-point of "post-impressionism." [1]

**Post-Impressionism**

Modernism was also exemplified by two "revolutionary" painters—Gauguin and Van Gogh. Paul Gauguin, half French and half Peruvian, learned the impressionist technique from Pissaro, but exaggerated and transformed it by adopting an extraordinary subjectivity and employing the most startling colors. As one of his disciples said, "Gauguin freed us from all restraints which the idea of copying placed on our painter's instinct. . . . Henceforth we aspired to express our own personality. . . . If at any moment a tree looked reddish to us, we might paint it in vermilion; if a girl's shoulder struck us just right, we might stress its curve even to the point of deformation." Gauguin escaped not only from the canons of conventional art but from the haunts of traditional civilization. The last decade of his life he passed in squalor and semi-insanity on South Sea islands.

Vincent Van Gogh, a Netherlander and the son of a Calvinist pastor, left the business of selling art objects at The Hague, Paris, and London to study theology; he left the seminary at Amsterdam to preach Christian communism and anarchism to Dutch work-

[1] See below, pp. 531-533.

men; and he left Protestant radicalism to become a radical painter. He intermittently studied art at Brussels, Antwerp, and Paris, and for a short time collaborated with Gauguin—until he scared the latter off by trying to kill him and by mutilating himself. At the last, he was quite mad and he died by his own hand. Van Gogh painted blossoming fruit trees, sunlit fields, sunflowers, his own portrait, his simple room, his rustic chair; and whatever he painted he marked with Japanese-like decoration, with the most intense emotion, and with the wildest color.

Both as man and painter Van Gogh was deemed bizarre and of no account by his contemporaries. By them, too, Gauguin was adjudged a "wild man," though they grudgingly admitted that he was contributing something worth while to the art of colored posters. It remained for a later generation to extol Gauguin and Van Gogh as founders of "modern art."

Impressionism flourished and post-impressionism arose in France. Indeed, the most significant painting of all "schools" of the era from 1870 to 1914, whether "radical" or "conservative," was done by Frenchmen or by persons who studied in France. Among the latter, the most memorable, in addition to Whistler, were two Spaniards (Sorolla and Zuloaga) and an Anglo-American (Sargent).

Joaquin Sorolla, a native of Valencia, was half romantic and half impressionistic. His first striking success was *Another Margaret* and one of his best-known pictures is *The Fishermen's Return*. He was popular as a portrait painter and a mural decorator. Ignacio Zuloaga, a native of the Basque region, was considerably affected, while a youthful student at Paris, by Gauguin, and much more, on his return to Spain, by El Greco and Goya. Zuloaga's specialty was colorful depiction of bull-fighters.

Portrait painting, which had been exemplified in England by a distinguished line of artists, was best represented there in the new age by John Sargent, who was born in Italy of American parents and made his headquarters at Paris until 1885 and afterwards at London. Sargent displayed, in the spirit of the age, a remarkable control of light and shade and a tendency to accentuate the less pleasing qualities of his sitters. "I chronicle, I do not judge," he said. His portraits are "psychological" and at the same time decorative. Between 1890 and 1916 Sargent executed a series of huge murals on the *History of Religion* for the Boston Public Library.

More pronouncedly than in painting, the new realism was set forth in the art of caricature, which was highly developed and especially popular during the era. A large number of caricaturists found outlet for their work in the multiplying comic journals of the time; and, on the whole, their pictures were apt to be better drawn and to deal more directly with the realities of social and political life than the pictures of contemporary painters. Of the caricaturists and illustrators of the era, four may here be mentioned.

**Caricature**

Perhaps the greatest of the caricaturists was a Frenchman, Jean Louis Forain, who in his drawings for various Parisian journals (usually of a conservative trend) mercilessly exposed the weaknesses of republican politicians and the capitalistic bourgeoisie. He derived the scathing bitterness of his satire from Daumier,[1] and his pictorial style from Manet and Degas (though his draftsmanship was superior to any of the impressionists). A close second to Forain was an Englishman, John Tenniel, associated with the London *Punch* for over fifty years. Tenniel's work was characterized by an accuracy of drawing almost equal to Forain's, and by a greater geniality of satire.

The designing of "posters" was done with distinction by Henri de Toulouse-Lautrec, an admirer of Degas and of Japanese woodcuts, who, as something of a symbolist and "decadent," provided illustrations of Parisian night-life, specializing in types of Montmartre and in circus-scenes. Another kind of illustrating—the drawing of fantastic decorative figures in black and white—was done to perfection by a short-lived English "decadent," Aubrey Beardsley.

In music, such outstanding composers of the mid-nineteenth century as Gounod, Wagner, and Verdi[2] lived considerably beyond the year 1870 and exerted a strongly romantic influence on the succeeding generation. The tradition of a national French opera, firmly established by Gounod, was continued by Camille Saint-Saëns, with his *Samson and Delila,* first produced in 1877, and by Jules Massenet, with his *Manon, Thaïs,* and *Jongleur de Notre Dame.* The tradition of distinctively German music, fathered by Wagner, was continued by Richard Strauss. Strauss composed songs in the romantic manner of Liszt

**Music**

---

[1] On Daumier, see *Modern Europe to 1870,* p. 689.
[2] See *Modern Europe to 1870,* pp. 690–691.

and Mendelssohn and some early operas and orchestral pieces in that of Wagner. Then, aspiring to be modernist and coming under the double influence of Nietzsche and the symbolists, he produced the somewhat bizarre *Hero's Life* and the sensational operas of *Salome* (1905) and *Elektra* (1910). In Italy, the romantic Verdi was supplemented and succeeded by Puccini, whose *La Bohème* (1896), *Tosca* (1900), and *Madame Butterfly* (1904, with its "Japanese" flavor) enjoyed an immense popularity.

Indeed, the prevailing inspiration and mood of musical art, unlike literature and painting, continued down to 1914 to be national and romantic. Such was the case with Johannes Brahms, an eminent German musician, long resident in Vienna, who wrote a *Song of Triumph* in celebration of German military victories in 1870–1871 and who in his later *Hungarian Dances* and his many other compositions displayed a lively appreciation of Hungarian and German nationalism. Such, too, was the case with a group of notable composers who, by utilizing and elaborating folk-melodies, sought to create a distinctive national music for several lesser peoples in Europe: for example, Anton Dvorák for the Czechs, and Edward Grieg for the Norwegians. Such, also, was the case both with Johann Strauss "the Younger" whose sparkling waltzes, such as the *Blue Danube,* and popular operettas, such as *Die Fledermaus,* were peculiarly "Viennese" and quite romantic, and with Arthur Sullivan, whose songs were finely sentimental and whose well-known light operas were as "English" and as genially satirical as the drawings of Tenniel.

Such, finally, was the case with the more sober "school" of music which arose in Russia. Peter Tschaikovsky based his opera of *Eugen Onegin* on a folk story by Pushkin and composed his famous descriptive *1812 Overture* in commemoration of his country's successful conflict with Napoleon; while his "symphonic poems," and particularly his celebrated "sixth symphony" —the *Pathétique*—betrayed his romantic heart. Modeste Moussorgsky inaugurated the peculiarly "Russian opera" with his forceful, fateful *Boris Godunov* in 1874, and Nicholas Rimsky-Korsakov not only continued and developed it in *Sadko* and *Coq d'Or* but displayed a genius for enshrining Russian folk-music in orchestral suites of modernist conception and effect.

Some reaction against romanticism, some response to newer tendencies in literature and painting, was evidenced by a few first-rate musical composers prior to 1914. At least in form, if not always in subject, both Rimsky-Korsakov and Richard Strauss were increasingly "modern" and "realist." The outstanding innovator in musical art, however, was Claude Debussy, a Frenchman who studied under Massenet and began in the 1880's to experiment with unusual scales and "mystical" dissonances calculated to appeal to the sophisticated imagination rather than to the simpler emotions. The new style seemed quite in keeping with the impressionism of contemporary painting and with the symbolism of current literature, and Debussy employed it in musical settings for poems of Verlaine, for the *Après-midi d'un faune* of Mallarmé, and most fully, for the *Pelléas and Mélisande* of Maeterlinck. Debussy's work was significant and influential in the transition from the music of the nineteenth century to that of the twentieth.

In architecture, both classical and romantic styles continued to be utilized and adapted. The romantic "Gothic revival" slackened; few of the newer public buildings or private Architecture dwellings were dominated by it.[1] Yet it by no means went entirely out of fashion. It was evidenced in a number of ecclesiastical and collegiate edifices, especially in Britain and the United States.

Classicism was, indeed, the prevailing mode in architecture after 1870, but it was an "eclectic classicism"—a decorative baroque classicism, varying from country to country in accordance with historic and national circumstance, and not disdaining to make use of novel materials, such as steel and concrete, and curious bits of embellishment suggestive less of purely Greek and Roman models than of Egyptian or Hindu or Japanese or even Gothic. This eclecticism was symptomatic of the rapidly broadening interests with which the rampant imperialism of the time was endowing Europe. Some of its best-known examples are the grandiose court theater in Vienna, the heavy Reichstag building at Berlin, the colossal national memorial at Rome to King Victor Emmanuel II, and the lighter and more graceful "Little Palace of the Fine Arts" put up at Paris in connection with the international exposition of 1900. The "Little Palace" was the

[1] Notable among the exceptional public buildings which were erected in the Gothic style were the parliament buildings at Budapest in Hungary and at Ottawa in Canada.

perfect flower of "official" French architecture and, by reason of the commanding position of French art in general, it was extremely influential at the beginning of the twentieth century as an inspiration for the designing, all over Europe and America, of art galleries and libraries and of mansions for industrial capitalists.

Two variants of classicism during the period should be mentioned. One was the revival of a Byzantine style, illustrated most monumentally in the Church of the Sacred Heart, reared atop Montmartre in Paris as "an act of national expiation" following the Franco-Prussian War, and in the great Catholic cathedral of Westminster, in London.

The other variant was a new type of domestic architecture, based on classical models but aiming at "picturesquesness" in appearance and "livableness" in interior appointments. In France and Germany it was exemplified by suburban dwellings which betrayed the influence of the châlets of Switzerland, and in England (and the United States) by the "Queen Anne" house.

Thus, in greater or less degree, traditional classicism (and romanticism) entered into the prevailing "eclectic" architecture of the new age. But the age witnessed the beginning of quite a different movement in architecture—one which was not "eclectic" and which spurned tradition whether romantic or classical. This movement, to which the name of "functionalism" is sometimes given, was associated in spirit as well as in **Functionalism** time with the spread and intensification of machine industry, with the vogue of natural science and materialist philosophy, and with the rise of impressionist painting and realist literature. Especially from Darwinian biology it took its cardinal principle that form must be rigorously adapted to environment and function. Its exponents, chief among whom was a German, Otto Wagner, contended that the new age required a brand-new architecture which would conform the appearance of buildings to their actual use and purpose and at the same time give expression to contemporary culture.

Before the emergence of full-fledged functionalism, there had had been a good deal of experimentation with new building materials: with iron, as in the reading-room of the National Library at Paris (1855–1861); with glass and iron, as in the Crystal Palace in England (1851) and in the buildings of the Paris Exposition of 1878; and with "reinforced concrete," as popularized in France in the 1870's. Then, when functionalism did appear as a definite movement in the late 1880's and in the 1890's, it took over the new materials and utilized them as integral parts of its schemes for modernist architecture.

Functionalism bore fruit in the Eiffel Tower at Paris (1889), and, most significantly, in a variety of structures in Germany and Austria, such as the stations of the urban railway in Vienna (designed by Otto Wagner) and the Wertheim department-store in Berlin (1896–1904). It also exercised an ever widening influence on the construction of bridges, factories, and shops. Eventually, after 1910, it would reach gargantuan proportions.[1]

Sculpture was plentiful during the new age, and the best examples of it reflected either the eclectic tendencies in architecture **Sculpture** or the naturalist trends in literature and painting. An outstanding representative of the French eclectic was Jules Dalou, such an ardent radical republican that he participated in the Paris Commune of 1871 and had to live in exile in England during the next eight years while royalists were dominant in his own country. Dalou consciously patterned his sculpture after the paintings of Rubens,[2] striving for a similar richness of content, vivacity of effect, and "realism" of anatomy and flesh. His first and most renowned achievement of this kind was the monument called *The Triumph of the Republic* in the Place de la Nation at Paris. Subsequently he executed a number of memorials, to Delacroix for example, in which the effigy was surrounded, usually at a lower level, by large related figures allegorical or historical—a type of memorial which became very common. In his last days Dalou forsook the pompousness of classical allegory, and, under the influence of Marxian socialism, projected a great "naturalist" monument to Labor.

Some elaborate and frequently "pretty" form of baroque was utilized by numerous sculptors for a multitude of patriotic memorials which were erected after 1870 in Italy, England, and Germany, as well as in France. They fitted in with the grandiose eclectic architecture of new public buildings. In Germany, particularly, there was a pronounced revival of baroque sculpture, not so much "pretty" as exuberant and forceful, whose loud

[1] See below, pp. 534–535.
[2] On Rubens, see *Modern Europe to 1870*, pp. 226, 382.

strains were evoked to celebrate Teutonic pride in recent triumph
of German arms and creation of the German Empire. The "official" German sculptor of the new era was Reinhold Begas. His
monument to the Emperor William I at Berlin was a baroque
outburst; and the female figures which which he decorated many
of his other monuments surpassed in sensuousness anything which
the French school had done.

Of all the sculptors of the era, the most influential were undoubtedly the Frenchman Rodin and the Belgian Meunier.
Auguste Rodin showed a modernist repugnance to classical form.
He was interested in psychological analysis, animal passion, and
the Nietzschean "will to power," and expressed his interests,
somewhat mystically and symbolically, in the blurred outlines of
impressionistic painting but with a greater ruggedness and
strength. His *Man with a Broken Nose* is dreadfully realistic.
His *Thinker* suggests the evolution of man from the lower animals. His uncompleted masterpiece, *The Gate of Hell,* inspired
by Dante's Inferno, is an impressionistic, heavily tragic setting
forth of "modern sufferings, doubts, and discontents."

Constantin Meunier, after acquiring some fame as a painter
of religious themes, turned his attention in 1880 to the sculptural
representation of the Industrial Revolution, especially the role of
labor in it. He discerned better than any other sculptor the
æsthetic values of the workman's body as molded, muscularized,
made lithe, and hardened by toil, and by his own genius he did
much to emphasize the dignity and idealism of labor. Among his
distinguished figures were *The Puddler, The Hammerer, The
Sower, The Mower, The Smith, The Miner.*

### 3. NEW QUESTIONINGS OF SUPERNATURAL RELIGION

For centuries prior to our own twentieth century, European
civilization had been characterized less by common material concerns than by common faith in a particular supernatural religion.
Christianity had been a basic feature of the civilization as a whole,
and the mass of Europeans had belonged to some Christian
Church—Catholic, Orthodox, or Protestant.

On the eve of the twentieth century, however, developments
in science and industry, in philosophy and psychology, in literature and art, conspired to raise serious doubts about supernatural
religion and to wean away from Christianity a relatively large

number of Europeans, among the masses as among the intellectual
class. The notion spread that the past Christian civili-

**Factors
Militating
against
Religion**

zation of Europe must sooner or later give way to a
"modern civilization," material and scientific in nature
and world-wide in extent. To the weakening and decline
of older religious conviction and practice, several factors contributed.

(1) Intensifying *industrialism* promoted indifference if not hostility to the claims of religion. It held out the prospect of a
mechanized Europe (and world) in which human comfort and
happiness could be assured without recourse to creed or prayer.
Likewise, in stimulating extensive migration, from field to factory,
from one town to another, from one country to another, it tended
to loosen the hold of the masses upon ancestral traditions, including the practice of religion.

(2) *Radical Liberalism* tended to minimize religion and to
foster "anti-clericalism." Holding that religion is not at all a public concern, but a purely private matter, it opposed governmental
support of any particular religion or church, and insisted that the
state should be strictly "neutral" and progressively "lay." Religious instruction should have no place in public education; and
the influence of clergymen over the lives of the laity or on the
politics of the state should be limited.

(3) Nationalism in the abstract was not necessarily inimical
to historic Christianity. Indeed, the Protestant and Orthodox
Churches had always been markedly national, and the Catholic
Church had recognized the principle of nationality and had frequently made concessions to it; and many nineteenth-century
patriots were devout Christians. Nevertheless, the *rampant nationalism* of the latest age was subversive of Christian teaching
and tradition. It was becoming a kind of religion itself, a natural
tribal religion in actual, if not theoretical, competition with supernatural, universal Christianity. Its chief concern was not with
Christendom but with the nation, not with Christian ideals and
civilization but with national ideals and culture.

(4) If radical liberalism and rampant nationalism were "un-
Christian" in their general tendencies, *Marxian Socialism* was
definitely anti-Christian. Its philosophy was dogmatically materialist and determinist; it repudiated the freedom of the individual
will and denied the efficacy if not the existence of any "spiritual"

powers. Its goal was a strictly earthly paradise; and its declared method of reaching its goal was not through social cooperation but through class conflict. Moreover, militant Marxists were prone to assail traditional society and the traditional family, as well as the institution of private property, and actively to abet "anti-clericalism."

(5) Most conducive to agnosticism about supernatural religion, and underlying all the other factors in the weakening of Christianity, was the dazzling *scientific progress* of the nineteenth century. One feature of this, and the one which appealed most to the masses, was the practical application of science to the current mechanizing of man's ways of working, traveling, and living. Though it had no direct or logical bearing upon Christian faith or dogma, it undoubtedly promoted popular indifference to Christian ideals and practices by concentrating attention upon the "marvels" of human achievement, by exalting engineers over preachers or priests, and by stimulating a greater ambition for creature-comforts than for personal holiness.

Experimental science, of itself, did not necessarily involve any conflict with Christian theology. The physicist or chemist might be enlarging human knowledge about a material, finite world without subtracting anything from the beliefs of man about a spiritual, infinite universe. In fact, there was a considerable number of practicing Christians among the outstanding scientists of the era. But with many intellectuals and would-be intellectuals, science was now not merely a matter of experiment or of practical utility, but the only method of arriving at any substantial truth; and as it dealt only with natural phenomena, the supernatural must be either unknowable or non-existent.

Besides, in more concrete respects, the biological and social sciences were now yielding discoveries and observations which seemed quite at variance with historic Christian belief. They clearly implied that the Biblical account of creation was erroneous, that man had not been created by special act of God a few thousand years ago but had been evolved from lower forms of life by entirely natural processes over a very long period of time. Parallel interpretations of research in psychology and anthropology carried the even more revolutionary implications that man had no soul or moral responsibility, that his "sins" were attributable to physical disease or biological atavism, and that all his religions were so many evolutionary expressions of primitive myths and fears. And by way of confirming this last implication, certain students of "comparative religion" and "higher criticism" argued that Christianity was a bundle of superstitions borrowed from various older religions and philosophies, that the New Testament as we have it had been written (like the Hebrew Scriptures) long after the events it purported to relate and was hopelessly corrupt, and that Jesus had been an obscure mystic or deluded fanatic.

By the last decades of the nineteenth century, moreover, all these novel conceptions were associated with some system of philosophy quite anti-Christian or un-Christian: the optimistic materialism of Haeckel; the pessimistic will-to-power of Nietzsche; the positivism of the followers of Comte; and the struggle-for-existence and survival-of-the-fittest philosophy of Spencer. To one or another of these philosophies numerous European and American intellectuals (scientists, professors, engineers, physicians, lawyers, publicists, etc.) were drawn; and, the same philosophies actuated, in greater or less degree, the majority of outstanding European men of letters during the period—Anatole France and Zola, Hardy and Swinburne, Shaw and Wells.

In face of all these startling developments, many Europeans and Americans repudiated or profoundly modified their traditional **Different** Christian beliefs and practices. An extreme group— **Christian** chiefly of intellectuals and proletarians—broke away **Reactions** altogether from the Churches and rejected Christianity entirely. These went to swell the minority of agnostics and "infidels" (or "pagans") who had been continuously in evidence in Europe and America since the "Enlightenment" and French Revolution of the eighteenth century and who, now becoming numerous in many countries, put new energy into anti-clerical and anti-religious campaigns.

Another and less extreme group, particularly of the bourgeoisie, while accepting with only minor qualifications the general trends of "modern civilization" and the special teachings of "modern science," remained nominally within the Churches and continued to profess Christianity, though seeking to supplant its traditionally fixed "deposit" of faith and morals with up-to-date evolutionary conceptions which would bring the historic Churches abreast of "modern progress" and preserve them as carriers of the modern "scientific spirit." Such persons, advocates of a "progressive" Christianity without definite dogmas and with morals derived from experience rather than from revelation, came to be known as "Modernists."

On the other hand, a sizable number of persons who remained within the Churches, resisted "modernism" and clung to historic Christianity. The most extreme defenders of traditional religion, including many clergymen and members of the lower middle and agricultural classes, especially of "evangelical" antecedents, assumed a rigidly uncompromising position, affirming that the Bible was the literally inspired "Word of God," denouncing the "higher critics" of it, insisting that men could not be "descended from apes," and denying the whole doctrine of evolution. The designation most appropriate to these extremists is the term originally applied to them in the United States—"fundamentalists."

Less extreme in opposition to assumptions of "science," but no less desirous of preserving historic dogmatic Christianity, were numerous clergymen and laymen who viewed the newer intellectual difficulties somewhat like this: That current discoveries about the material universe did not and could not disprove the existence of a greater and more enduring spiritual universe; that "Darwinism" was only an hypothesis which was being confessedly weakened in certain details, and which, if true, could explain only the evolution of man's material body, not the creation and life of immortal spirits; that there could be no "conflict" between science rightly understood and theology divinely inspired; that current "higher criticism" of the Bible and the Church was "destructive" and displayed too much bias, but that, if pursued in dispassionate scholarly fashion, it would but confirm the essential uniqueness and truth of Christianity; and that the Bible, anyway, was not a textbook in science, and that parts of it, as foremost fathers of the Church had recognized, were susceptible of allegorical, as well as literal, interpretation.

It should be borne in mind that militant defenders of dogmatic Christianity and direct assailants of it constituted minority groups, and that the majority of Europeans and Americans went their usual way, evincing more and more interest in science, in nationalism, and in liberalism or socialism, but continuing to adhere formally to the religion of their ancestors. In the latter part of the nineteenth century, church attendance, especially on the part of men, gradually lessened in certain countries, for example, in Britain, France, Italy, and Scandinavia. The urban proletariat became increasingly unchurched, and the universities more "godless." Yet Christianity was so vital a part of European tradition and experience—it was so intertwined with the history, institutions, and culture of every "Western" nation—that it could not suddenly be shorn of a widespread popular following, even in an age of materialism. At least in the crises of life, the masses still went to church, to be baptized, to be married, to attend funerals. Sundays and church holidays were still almost universally observed, and no little social prestige still attached to church-members and church-goers. Moreover, the number of "practicing" Christians was still relatively large all over Europe and America, and there was a noteworthy growth of Christian missionary enterprise overseas and of Christian "social work."

So far, we have spoken in general terms of Christianity in the latter part of the nineteenth century—its continuing vitality, and its accumulating difficulties. Christianity, however, was no unit. It was represented, in the nineteenth century as in the sixteenth, by the Catholic Church, by the Orthodox Church, and by a variety of Protestant Churches and sects. Each of the major divisions of Christianity had distinctive traditions of its own, and therefore felt the effect of contemporary social, political, and intellectual movements in peculiar ways and responded to them somewhat differently. It accordingly behooves us, if we would understand the religious situation in developing industrial society, to pass from general discussion of Christianity to specific consideration of its Churches and then to say something of non-Christian minority groups (Moslem and Jewish) which survived in traditionally Christian lands.

### 4. IMPACT ON THE CHURCHES

Against the Catholic Church, as the largest body of Christians and the one most intransigent in its devotion to tradition and most authoritarian in its manner of speaking,[1] the **Catholic Church** opposition was emphatic and many-sided. And against "the errors of modern society and thought," the Popes of the period—Pius IX (1846–1878), Leo XIII (1878–1903),

---

[1] On the organization and doctrine of the Catholic Church, see *Modern Europe to 1870*, pp. 129–132.

and Pius X (1903–1914)—directed a vigorous counter-offensive.

Pius IX began his pontificate with a reputation for friendliness to liberalism and nationalism, but the reputation was short-lived. After 1849 he issued against liberalism a series of documents, culminating in a famous encyclical, *Quanta Cura,* and an accompanying *Syllabus of Errors* (1864). In the encyclical, Pius IX condemned the modern liberal ideas of extreme individualism and of the supremacy of the secular state over the Church and lauded the earlier ideal of the "Christian state" in which the Church, though independent of secular authority, was supported by it. The *Syllabus* "of the principal errors of our time" reproduced in abbreviated form the specific doctrines, political as well as philosophical and religious, which had latterly received papal condemnation. The listed "errors" were of several different groups: "freethinkers" and "agnostics," who denied or doubted the divine origin and mission of the Church; "materialists" and "naturalists," who repudiated the spiritual or subordinated it to the physical; "anti-clericals," who aimed at restricting the freedom of the Church, exalting the secular lay state, and overthrowing the temporal dominion (and hence weakening the spiritual independence) of the papacy; "liberals" and Freemasons and "indifferent" persons, who imagined that one religion was as good (or as bad) as another, who sought to reduce the Church to the condition of a private association, or who thought that the Pope should reconcile himself with "modern society" and "modern civilization."

*Pius IX and Syllabus of Errors*

The *Syllabus* was not issued as dogma, and several leading Catholics, including Newman, took pains to explain that it was in the nature of counsel against peculiar developments of the time in Italy and against the "abuses" of modern liberalism. Nevertheless it strengthened the impression in many minds that the papacy was conducting a crusade against modern civilization, and it evoked storms of criticism from liberals and protests from prominent statesmen.

In 1869, while discussion of the *Syllabus* was still heated, Pius IX convened at the Vatican a general council of the Catholic Church, the first such council since that of Trent three centuries previously. The Vatican Council, attended by nearly eight hundred prelates from all over the world, elaborated the

traditional teaching of the Church on the relationship between faith and reason, but its most sensational achievement was the
Vatican
Council
definition, despite earnest preliminary opposition from a minority of its members, of the dogma of papal infallibility. It solemnly proclaimed as "a dogma divinely revealed, that the Roman pontiff, when he speaks *ex cathedra*— that is, when in discharge of the office of pastor and doctor of all Christians, he defines, by virtue of his supreme apostolic authority, a doctrine regarding faith or morals to be held by the universal church—is possessed, by the divine assistance promised him in Blessed Peter, of that infallibility with which the Divine Redeemer willed that His Church should be endowed for defining faith or morals."

While the Vatican Council was still in session, the Franco-Prussian War broke out. The French garrison which had been protecting the temporal sovereignty of the Pope was withdrawn from Rome, and in September 1870 Italian troops of King Victor Emmanuel II seized the city by main force and transformed it from the age-long supra-national city state of the Popes to the new national capital of united Italy. Pius IX protested, immured himself as a "prisoner" in the Vatican, and in October 1870 prorogued the general council on the plea that it could no longer deliberate in requisite freedom.

Opponents of the Catholic Church were elated by the overthrow of the Pope's temporal power but pained by the simultaneous definition of papal infallibility which, they feared, would give him a dangerous new weapon against liberalism and nationalism. Over the doctrine of papal infallibility, therefore, the storm which had been brewing since the *Syllabus of Errors* raged with unusual violence. The majority of Catholic intellectuals, to be sure, defended the doctrine and the mass of Catholics adhered to it. All the bishops accepted it, and only a small minority of professors and other laymen, chiefly in Germany and Switzerland, actually left the Church and formed a dissident "Old Catholic" sect. On the other hand, the doctrine was widely assailed by Protestants and agnostics, liberals and patriots, and by leading statesmen. In Prussia, and eventually throughout Germany, Bismarck waged a *Kulturkampf*—a "struggle for civilization"—with the Catholic Church. In England, Gladstone published a pamphlet in support of the thesis that Catholics could not be "good citizens." [1] In France, Gambetta arrayed the republican party under the banner of "anti-clericalism." In Spain, the revolutionary government of the day nullified the existing agreement with the papacy. In Italy, the liberal regime of Victor Emmanuel II took "defensive" measures against the Church. In Austria, a liberal ministry of the time prevailed upon the Emperor Francis Joseph to repudiate his concordat with Pius IX.

When Pius IX died in 1878, the Catholic Church appeared to be at losing feud with almost every European government. And the succeeding pontificate of Leo XIII (1878–1903) was the very period in which the rising philosophies of materialism and the widening researches in anthropology and comparative religion bade fair to undermine historic Christianity.

Yet the period proved not so disastrous for the Catholic Church as was anticipated. Leo XIII was a scholar and a sincere sympathizer with democratic and social-reform movements. Moreover, he was not content to denounce the "errors" **Leo XIII** of the time. He perceived "good" as well as "evil" in modern civilization, and he fostered a constructive program of Catholic action.

In the intellectual domain, Leo XIII stood by the historic dogmas of Catholic Christianity, and not only renewed his predecessor's condemnations of the "vagaries" of modern philosophy, but also revived, as a special corrective, the medieval philosophy of Thomas Aquinas. At the same time he encouraged the study of church history and opened to scholars the valuable archives of the Vatican. He procured an eminent scientific staff and the best scientific instruments for the astronomical observatory at the Vatican.

Of the political principles of Pius IX, Leo XIII professed not to change a jot. He expressed in a series of encyclicals the same ideal of the "Christian state" and similar condemnations of certain features of liberalism and "anti-clericalism." He insisted that the Church was a "perfect society" in itself, whose authority in its own spiritual realm was, by divine institution, independent of, and superior to, the authority of any temporal state or sovereignty. He reasserted the right of the Church to a privileged position in the state, and especially its right to maintain schools and carry on

---

[1] The most interesting—and important—reply to Gladstone's pamphlet was Newman's *Letter to the Duke of Norfolk.*

its mission without let or hindrance from the state. Yet Leo XIII was no partisan of any particular form of government. He was not a "reactionary" in the earlier sense, and he was as willing to negotiate with governments nominally "liberal" as with those nominally "conservative."

Indeed, Leo XIII was inclined to sympathize with the democratic trend of the time. He thought it compatible with Christian philosophy and tradition and imagined that it might serve to enlist popular support for the Church. He looked with favor upon the development of Catholic political parties, popular and democratic, in Germany, in Austria, and in Belgium. He counseled French Catholics to accept and cooperate with the republican government of their country. He expressed admiration for the constitution and political institutions of the United States.

Leo XIII was fully aware of the social problems attending contemporary industrialization. He commended the efforts of **Catholic** clergymen and laymen to build up a Catholic social **Social** movement which, combating economic liberalism on the **Movement** one hand and Marxian socialism on the other, would aim at the Christianizing of modern industrial society. Such a movement gathered headway in the 1870's and 1880's, and in 1891 the Pope gave it a guiding charter in his encyclical, *Rerum Novarum*. Against Marxian socialism, this document defended private property as a natural right, emphasized the importance of the family, protested against the exalting of the state, condemned the doctrine of economic determinism, and declared that "class is not naturally hostile to class." On the other hand, against economic liberalism, it held that "labor is not a commodity," that "it is shameful to treat men like chattels to make money by," that the state should prevent the exploitation of labor, encourage collective bargaining, and enact social legislation. The encyclical specifically urged a wider distribution of private property, a fostering of industrial trade unions and agricultural cooperative undertakings, a restriction of the hours of employment, especially of women and children, and the assurance of a "living family wage."

The encyclical *Rerum Novarum* inspired the formation of Christian trade unions, which in certain countries, for example in Germany, Belgium, and France, eventually counted a following second only to that of the Socialist trade unions.

Catholic Christianity held its own during the pontificate of Leo XIII. In several traditionally Catholic countries, it is true, the Church seemed weaker in 1903 than in 1878. In Italy, there was no settlement of the "Roman question" between King and Pope, and only increasingly embittered relations between state and church. In France, where the most ardent Cath- *Catholic* olics were apt to be anti-republican, there was a marked *Political* growth of "anti-clerical" agitation and legislation. In *Activity* Spain and Portugal, and in countries of Latin America, there were sporadic, and sometimes tempestuous, attacks on ecclesiastical property, schools, and monasteries. On the other hand, Catholics put a stop to the *Kulturkampf* in Germany, regained an ascendancy in Austria, and obtained control of the Belgian government. Moreover, they notably increased their numbers and influence in Switzerland, in the Dutch Netherlands, and, most strikingly, in English-speaking countries.

Here the increase was attributable in some part to conversion but in chief part to nineteenth-century migration of European Catholics, particularly of the Irish, to England, Scotland, the United States, Canada, Australia, etc. In all these countries, by the end of the nineteenth century, Catholicism was represented by firmly established hierarchies, by fairly large numbers of both "secular" and "regular" clergy, by schools, and by an augmenting minority of the lay population.

During the pontificate of Pius X (1903–1914) the Catholic Church was troubled by several acute conflicts with national governments and also by the rise of "modernism" *Pius X and* within its own ranks. In Italy, to be sure, there was *Condem-* a slight easing of the strain between church and state. *nation of* Pius X, though continuing to regard himself as a *"Modern-* "prisoner of the Vatican" and to demand the restoration of the *ism"* temporal sovereignty of the papacy at Rome, withdrew the prohibition which his predecessors had put on the participation of Italian Catholics in the politics of the Italian kingdom and encouraged the formation of a Catholic "popular party" to safeguard their economic, as well as ecclesiastical, interests. In France, however, a bitter conflict led to the abrogation of the concordat which had regulated the relations of church and state since the time of Napoleon Bonaparte and to the enactment of especially drastic "anti-clerical" legislation. Almost simultaneously, legislation hardly less drastic was enacted in Portugal, Spain, and Mexico.[1]

Complicating the political difficulties, moreover, was the persuasive contention on the part of a considerable number of Catholic priests and laymen—themselves obviously influenced by "Darwinism" and by the "higher criticism" of the Bible—that the Church must "modernize" its teachings and discipline if it would recover its popular prestige and stop the leakage of intellectuals. Although these "Modernists" differed among themselves about many details, they generally held that dogma is not immutable but evolutionary, that the basic apology for the Church is less its divine origin than its human utility, that ecclesiastical authority should be reformed and restrained, and that "science" should be independent of the Church and the findings of the former superior to the dictates of the latter.

Against the Modernists, Pius X was adamant. He had the "Holy Office" publish a *Syllabus* of their "errors" (1907), and concurrently he issued an encyclical, *Pascendi,* denouncing Modernism as a "summation of heresies." He excommunicated some of its leaders and put their writings on the Index; and he obliged all Catholic priests throughout the world to take a special oath against it. The Catholic Church was thus purged, and its traditional beliefs and papal authority reasserted. There was some loss to the Church of individual priests and laymen, but there was no mass secession in any country.[2] "Modernism" ceased to be an important movement within Catholic Christianity, at the very time when it was becoming influential within Protestant Christianity.

Protestantism displayed throughout the nineteenth century—and increasingly in the first decade of the twentieth—two divergent tendencies. The one involved a notable decline of dogmatic teaching about faith and morals (a tendency diametrically opposed to that of contemporary Catholicism). The other involved a development of "good works" and "ritualism" and, in extreme instances, of a movement which may be described as "neo-Catholicism."

---

[1] On such legislation, see below, pp. 278–279, 330–333, 337, 339.

[2] In Bohemia and Austria, a so-called "Los von Rom" ("Away from Rome") movement reached large proportions early in the twentieth century, but it was motivated by nationalism more than by modernism.

In certain respects, Protestantism seemed more adaptable than Catholicism to "modern civilization." Machine industry began in overwhelmingly Protestant Britain and spread most spectacularly in predominantly Protestant Germany and America. Protestant apologists delighted in identifying the ideal of material "progress" and "capitalistic prosperity" with the "rugged individualism" and "sober thrift" of traditional Protestant ethics. Then, too, the major Protestant churches· had always been national churches—the Anglican in England, the Presbyterian in Scotland, the Dutch Reformed in Holland, the Lutheran in Scandinavia, etc.—subservient to secular governments and responsive to patriotic emotions. They could accept and forward the nationalism of the nineteenth century more naturally than could the international, supra-national Catholic Church. Most important of all, Protestants could invoke the "right of private judgment" to justify themselves in putting their own interpretations on the relationship between religion and science and in still remaining "Christian" while rejecting the creed of any Church.

*Protestantism and "Modern" Civilization*

Wherefore, Protestanism was not seriously disturbed by conflicts between state and church; and "anti-clericalism," common in traditionally Catholic countries, was exceptional in countries traditionally Protestant. What did disturb Protestantism very seriously—far more so than Catholicism—was the questioning of its distinctive historic principle of religious authority. For Protestantism, in rejecting the papacy as the divinely inspired custodian of religious tradition, interpreter of the Bible, and supreme ecclesiastical authority, had insisted that the Bible itself was the sole rule of faith for Christians and their sole guide of conduct. But now, "Darwinism" and "higher criticism" were casting most serious doubts upon the authenticity of the Bible. These doubts, troublesome enough to "modernist" Catholics, shook Protestantism to its foundations.

The outcome was the emergence, by the end of the nineteenth century, of three different trends among Protestants. (1) A minority of nominal Protestants, including a relatively large proportion of "intellectuals," were moving toward an *agnostic* position. Unable to square the Bible with "science," they threw over the former, and, unable to accept Catholicism, they repudiated historic Christianity altogether. Some of

*Different Protestant Trends*

them sought refuge in positivism (the "religion of humanity") or in "ethical culture."

(2) At the opposite extreme, considerable numbers of Protestants—relatively more numerous among the masses than among the classes—were impelled to take a *fundamentalist* position, holding to the Bible as the literally inspired "Word of God" and denouncing any "scientific" explanation which contradicted or questioned their own traditional interpretation of the Bible. "Fundamentalists" were to be found among Lutherans and Calvinists and in the so-called "low" or "evangelical" section of the Anglican Church, but they were especially influential in English-speaking countries and in such evangelistic sects as the Methodist and Baptist.[1]

(3) While some Protestants became frankly agnostic and left their respective churches, and while others fortified their abiding faith with "fundamentalism," a gradually growing number became

**Protestant Modernism**

*modernist.* That is, they remained "Protestant Christians" in name and in actual church membership but they subordinated church creeds and the Bible itself to the latest fashions in scientific speculation and "higher criticism." They tended to stress the "beauty" rather than the "truth" of religion, to prize the Holy Scriptures not as the inspired "Word of God" but as "great literature," and the Founder of Christianity not as God but as a moral teacher or poetical idealist or social reformer. Indeed, they were disposed to admit that the Bible was a collection of human and hence fallible stories and sermons, and that historic Christianity was but one, though probably the best, of evolving, uplifting world religions. Modernists of this sort had their most natural home in a Protestant sect like the Unitarian, but they gradually made fruitful homes for themselves in leading theological schools, whether Lutheran, Calvinist, Anglican, or "Evangelical." And as there was no central authority in any of the Protestant Churches capable of combating "modernism"—as the papacy combated it in the Catholic Church—it

---

[1] The Christian Science Church, which was founded by Mary Baker Eddy at Boston in 1879, and which subsequently secured a considerable following in America and Europe, was nearer to "fundamentalism" than to "modernism." Though "scientific" in name and "modern" in its practical solicitude for physical health, it was quite "evangelical" in origin and, in its faith healing and in its central doctrine of the reality of mind and the unreality of matter, quite antithetical to "Darwinism" and all other materialist science.

was fairly rapidly communicated from Protestant professors to the rising generation of Protestant clergymen and thence to Protestant laymen. By the twentieth century, a "modernist" change was being wrought in Protestantism far more revolutionary than the religious upheaval of the sixteenth century.

Innumerable, of course, were the gradations and shades of Modernism within the Protestant Churches. What distinguished it as a whole was its evolutionary attitude toward religion in general and Christianity in particular. It involved a sharp reversal of the Protestant habit of seeking "pure religion" in a venerable volume and identifying "ecclesiastical reform" with a return to primitive Christianity.

It also involved a curious shift of emphasis from "faith" to "good works." To a rapidly growing number of Protestants, "dogmatic" and "theological" became words of reproach, connoting ideas as repulsive as the word "superstitious." But these same Protestants, as they ceased to dwell upon particular dogmas, evinced a special regard for such "good works" as social uplift, popular education, public health, organized recreation, and campaigns against alcoholism and juvenile delinquency.

Altogether, Modernism was providing a lowest common denominator for numerous Europeans and Americans who were Protestant in background and name, who still "felt" religious, and yet who were hostile or indifferent to the theology in which they had been reared. No matter to what denomination they belonged, they could stand together against "outworn dogmas" and, a little more vaguely, in support of "the good life." Standing together— cooperation—became indeed a characteristic and essentially novel ideal of the Protestantism of the twentieth century.

To the realization of such an ideal the Modernist movement certainly contributed; and to it contributed also the synchronous development of several comprehensive organizations half religious and half social. One of these was the "Young Men's Christian Association," founded in England in 1844 for the union of youthful "evangelical Christians" in social and religious comradeship. Another was the "Salvation Army," established in England in 1880 by William Booth for "saving" slum-dwellers.

Mention should here be made, too, of Freemasonry. It had taken root in the eighteenth century,[1] but in the latter part of the

[1] See *Modern Europe to 1870*, pp. 400–401.

nineteenth century it flourished as never before. Its lodges were more widespread, and its membership more numerous. It was primarily a social and benevolent organization, though it had no slight religious significance. Inasmuch as it had been condemned by a succession of Popes, its membership was now practically restricted to non-Catholics; and among these—Protestants, Jews, and agnostics—it was peculiarly influential. On the continent of Europe, particularly in traditionally Catholic countries, Freemasonry provided a common platform and program for various opponents of Catholic Christianity. Here it was markedly anti-clerical, potent in Radical politics, and strongly inclined toward materialistic atheism. In English-speaking countries, on the other hand, it was more conservative, less directly political, not professedly anti-religious or anti-Christian, and hence notably effective as a solvent of sectarianism. In these countries, moreover, Freemasonry was imitated by a variety of associations which helped to popularize the idea that Christians should be vague in what they believe and progressive in what they do.

It must not be gathered from what we have said that there was any decline in activity or membership of the several Protestant Churches. On the contrary, just as many persons in Europe and America were affiliated with Protestantism in 1914 as in 1870 or at any earlier date; and most of the Protestant Churches were far more active in social work and missionary enterprise than ever before. What we have been pointing out is that within these Protestant Churches a revolution was taking place. Their creeds were being blurred or cast aside, and, despite the resistance of "fundamentalists," an increasing proportion of their members were adopting a "modernism" at variance with historic Protestant ideas of the Bible and of dogmatic and moral theology.

The outstanding development in nineteenth-century Protestantism was undoubtedly the Modernist revolution. But there **High-** was another noteworthy development—a "Catholic" **Church** counter-revolution. For in the nineteenth century some **Movement** Protestants took to "protesting" against Protestantism and trying to "re-Catholicize" it. The impetus to such a counter-revolution was furnished in first instance by romanticism—particularly the emotional sympathy it engendered for the middle ages and the resulting appreciation of the historic character and services of the Catholic Church—and eventually by the intellectual conviction that Protestantism, by departing too far from Catholic tradition and authority, was ceasing to be a bulwark against agnosticism. What was sought was a *via media*, a middle road, between Rome and the Reformation.

This "Catholicizing" trend within modern Protestantism was evidenced most clearly and fully in the Anglican Church. But it was evidenced to some extent also by contemporary "high-church" developments in the Lutheran Churches of Scandinavia and Germany, and, more strangely perhaps, by a new vogue of ritualism among many Protestants who were not at all "high church" in belief. "Evangelical" Protestants evinced a gradually lessening repugnance to the ceremonial aspects of historic Christianity, and Modernist clergymen discovered that religious rites could provide a strong attraction for persons whose religious dogmas were nebulous or non-existent. There was a widening observance of ecclesiastical holy days and seasons such as Christmas, Good Friday, and Lent. There was a marked tendency to adorn church edifices with crosses, stained glass, and statues of saints, to elevate the "communion table" into an "altar" and embellish it with flowers and candles, and to enrich church services with vested choirs and set forms of prayer and praise.

To what we have been saying about Protestantism and Catholicism a few words should be added concerning the other great historic division of Christianity—the Orthodox communion of eastern Europe. This was not a single ecclesiastical organization like the Catholic Church, nor was it a merely nominal bond like Protestantism for discordant beliefs and practices. Rather it was a federation of Churches in close communion one with another. Originally, of course, it had been a single ecclesiastical organization headed by the Greek Patriarch of Constantinople, but the nationalizing of the part of it in Russia [1] served as a model during the nineteenth century for the nationalizing of other parts of it in countries which became politically independent of the Ottoman Empire. In this way, so-called "autocephalous" Orthodox Churches were established, usually with the reluctant consent of the Patriarch of Constantinople, for Greece in 1850, and in the 1870's for Serbia, Rumania, and Bulgaria.

One distinguishing feature of Orthodox Christianity, then, was

[1] See *Modern Europe to 1870*, pp. 308–309.

its organization on strictly national lines and in frank subservi-
ency to secular governments. Another distinguishing feature was
its doctrinal unity and conservatism. The several Churches which
composed it vied with one another in the ardor with which they
clung to the historic creeds, ritual, and observances of the mother-
church at Constantinople. They frowned on the Catholic Church,
but they held aloof from the Protestant Churches.

Orthodox Christianity was less obviously troubled by nineteenth-century developments than Catholicism or Protestantism.
The countries in which it was the prevailing religion were relatively "backward." The great mass of its adherents were still agricultural and illiterate, accustomed not to question but to con-
serve their ancestral cult. Nor was there any serious conflict in
these countries between church and state, between Christianity
and nationalism. Practically, each Orthodox Church was a national institution and an agency of a particular state, controlled
by it and helping to forward its ends and to protect it against
revolution. Naturally, the sovereigns and leading patriots of the
state were especially intent upon maintaining and fostering the
church.

Beneath the surface, however, lurked dangers for Orthodox
Christianity. There was danger in the steady indigenous growth
of dissenting sects in the Russian Empire, and much graver
danger in the gradual importation, from the West, of machine
industry and its novel intellectual attendants—liberalism, materialism, "higher criticism," Marxian socialism. These novelties did
not immediately affect the mass of peasantry, but they did contribute to the spread of religious indifference among the middle
classes and to more or less open hostility to the Orthodox Church
on the part of "intellectuals" and urban workmen.

At the opening of the twentieth century, Europe still harbored two religious minorities of considerable importance—the
Jewish and the Moslem. The Moslem minority was concentrated
in southeastern Europe and comprised the governing
**Islam**  classes (and a portion of the masses) in what remained
of the Ottoman Empire and smaller and less influential groups
in adjacent (and predominantly Christian) countries which had
latterly been freed from Turkish dominion. It had dwindled as
the military fortunes of the Ottoman Turks ebbed, but it was still
an important minority, and was backed up by the much larger,

and still expanding and aggressive, Islam outside Europe—in Asia, Africa, and the East Indies. Moreover, all Islam was treated with increasing tenderness and circumspection by so-called Christian powers of Europe (notably Great Britain, France, and Russia) as these, in pursuit of the "new imperialism," enlarged their extra-European territories and acquired more and more Moslem subjects. Not until the World Wars did the impact of "modern civilization" on the Moslem world produce significant consequences.

The Jewish minority was dispersed all over Europe, and in America, northern Africa, and western Asia. In eastern Europe, where the Jews were most numerous, they still maintained a community life of their own, social and cultural as well as religious; and here they continued to suffer (espe- Judaism cially in Russia and Rumania) from restrictions on their personal freedom of occupation and education, from spasmodic persecution, and from occasional mob violence. On the other hand, the Jews of central and western Europe had undergone, since the "Enlightenment" of the eighteenth century and in harmony with the liberalism of the nineteenth century, a gradual "emancipation" from restrictive legislation and had adapted themselves to "modern civilization." [1] Particularly in western and southern Europe (in Great Britain, the Netherlands, France, Italy, etc.), and only a little less so in Germany and Austria, they had come by 1870 to enjoy full rights of citizenship and to be hardly distinguishable from their fellow citizens except that they were still called "Jews" and were still attached, at least sentimentally, to the Jewish religion. These Jews exerted an influence from 1870 to 1914 out of all proportion to their actual numbers. Many of them were conspicuous in business—in capitalistic industry, trade, and banking; others, in science, in the arts, in journalism, or in patriotic or humanitarian undertakings; others, in Freemasonry and "radical" politics. Some took an active part in Marxian socialism.

In the novel circumstances of the nineteenth century, traditional Judaism was greatly troubled, and its followers divided into three camps. (1) Some, chiefly in eastern Europe, remained rigidly "orthodox," resisting "higher criticism" and holding to

[1] On the beginnings of Jewish emancipation in the era of the Enlightenment, see *Modern Europe to 1870*, pp. 402–404.

the "tribal" Jewish laws and observances. (2) Some, including the majority in central and western Europe and in America, became "reformed," which was another name for "modernist." In various ways, these rationalized and universalized their religion, lessening its ceremonial observances, softening or neglecting its special laws, and approximating it to the contemporary Unitarian and "Ethical Culture" movements in Protestant Christianity. (3) A small but perceptibly growing number in almost every country, while still thinking of themselves as Jews in "race," drifted away from the Jewish religion whether orthodox or reformed, severed any connection with the synagogue, and became frankly agnostic or enthusiastically Marxian.

Complicating the Jewish situation still more was the external development, in the latter part of the nineteenth century, of nationalistic anti-Semitism. European liberalism had been favorable to Jewish "emancipation" and "absorption"; and so long as European nationalism was preponderantly "liberal," fairly rapid progress was made, at least in central and western Europe, in breaking down political and cultural barriers between Jews and non-Jews and in accustoming both to submerge religious and "racial" differences in a common patriotism. But gradually, nationalism was intensified and liberalism waned or was modified. By the 1880's an extreme and essentially illiberal nationalism was inspiring popular agitation within each state against any minority of its citizens who were presumed, by reason of racial or social peculiarities or international affiliations, to be lacking in devotion to the national institutions and ideals of the majority. In the circumstances, it was but natural, for example, that German nationalists who waged a *Kulturkampf* against the Catholic Church and campaigned against Marxian socialism should also react against Jews. Such reaction was by no means confined to Germany. It was evident, simultaneously, in Russia, in Rumania, in Austria, in France, and it was echoed elsewhere.

Anti-Semitism did not profess to oppose the Jewish religion as such. Rather, its concern was with the Jewish "race." With much parading of "scientific" theory about biology and eugenics, it preached the doctrine that the "Semitic" inheritance of Jews endows them with physical and mental traits different from, and repugnant to, the traits inherent in Aryans or "true Europeans," and hence renders them a permanently "alien" and potentially corrupting body in the several European nations. However unfounded and preposterous this "racialism" was, it was accepted as true not only by unbalanced agitators but by some "intellectuals" and by sizable groups among the masses; and the attendant propaganda quickened anti-Jewish prejudice in the minds of many persons who were not expressly anti-Semitic.

The rise of anti-Semitism in the 1880's did not immediately lead to any legal discrimination against Jews, except in Russia and Rumania. Yet it complicated the domestic politics of other (and more democratic) countries, and it had significant consequences for the Jews themselves. Suffering from imputations against their "racial" character, they became acutely "race-conscious" and thereby were attached to an idea of ethnic unity transcending religious and cultural differences. Suffering, too, from governmental oppression in eastern Europe, numerous Jews emigrated thence to regions where at least there were no legal handicaps, to Germany for example, and, in largest numbers, to the United States. Suffering, moreover, from nationalist taunts that Jews everywhere were "aliens," some of them—the so-called Zionists—formulated a nationalism of their own.

The leading apostle of Zionism was Theodore Herzl, who urged that the Jews were a distinct nationality and that an independent national state should be erected for them in Palestine. **Zionism** Zionism was political and cultural rather than religious; by seeking to draw together Orthodox and Reformed Jews and Jews who were such only by "race," it clearly subordinated religion to nationalism. And it proved to be still another source of dissension to Judaism. For most Jews had no thought of settling in Palestine, and many of them were hostile to Zionism elsewhere, either on principle or on the tactical ground that espousal of it might compromise their existing citizenship. On the whole, nevertheless, if nineteenth-century developments were emphasizing Jewish differences in religion, politics, and economics, they were bringing Jews into new prominence and were reuniting them in sentimental bonds of race and nationality.

## 5. RENEWED MISSIONARY ENTERPRISE

Of importance to the religious aspect of Western civilization were the multiplying contacts in the latter part of the nineteenth century between Europe and the other Continents. These stimulated a remarkable extension of Christian missions outside Europe, while awakening within Europe a curious sympathy for Oriental philosophy and religion.

Christianity had always been conspicuously expansive, and successive waves of proselyting zeal had expanded its professed following ever more widely: throughout the Mediterranean world in the first five centuries, into England in the sixth century, into central Europe in the seventh and eighth centuries, into northern Europe in the tenth, eleventh, and twelfth, throughout the American continents and into the Philippines and India (and temporarily into China and Japan) in the sixteenth and seventeenth centuries. The nineteenth century, however much or little it may have weakened Christianity in Europe, witnessed a new wave of Christian expansion outside Europe—in Asia, Africa, and Australasia.

The Catholic Church, under whose auspices and in whose behalf the greater part of earlier missionary work had been done, played a leading part in nineteenth-century missions. **Catholic Missions** Under the continuing direction of the papal Congregation of the Propaganda, which had been established at Rome in 1622, and with more liberal financial aids from the laity, an increasing number of Catholic missionaries went out from Europe to convert the "heathen." By 1914 Catholic missionaries in Africa, Asia, and Oceania numbered about 41,000, comprising (in round figures) 8,000 European priests, 6,000 native priests, and 27,000 sisters and lay brothers.

This new wave of Catholic missionary endeavor produced results. At the beginning of the nineteenth century, the Philippine Islands were the only part of the world outside Europe and America where the Catholic Church was established firmly and with as large a native following as it had ever had. Japan and China had been closed to it. The number of Catholics in India had shrunk to barely 350,000. There were no Catholics in Indo-China or Oceania and hardly any in Africa. In the course of the nineteenth century, however, a remarkable change occurred. Catholic missionaries reentered China in 1842 and Japan in 1861; they settled in Korea, Indo-China, Oceania, and Africa; and they redoubled their efforts in India. Catholic hierarchies were created for China in 1875, for India in 1886, and for Japan in 1891. When the century closed, Catholics numbered about two and a quarter million in India, slightly over a million in China, some sixty thousand in Japan, close to sixty thousand in Korea, and two and a half million in Africa.

Protestant Christians had evinced, prior to the nineteenth century, comparatively little interest in foreign missions. Just on the eve of the century, however, an awakening of interest was indicated and stimulated among English-speaking Prot- **Protestant** estants by the organization of Baptist, Presbyterian, **Missions** and Anglican missionary societies. Other Protestant Churches and sects, in Britain and the United States and also on the continent of Europe, soon caught the contagion, and by the middle of the century dozens of Protestant societies were competing with one another and with Catholic missionaries in efforts to Christianize the peoples of the non-European world. By 1914 the number of active Protestant missionaries totaled over 18,000, comprising 13,000 Europeans and Americans (5,700 clergymen, 2,800 laymen, and 4,500 unmarried women) and 5,000 native clergymen. And by this time Protestantism in one form or another was the religion of one and a half million persons in India, a quarter of a million in China, eighty thousand in Japan, and two and a half million in Africa.

Since the sixteenth century the Orthodox Church of Russia had been steadily expanding over northern Asia, in measure as Russian emigrants settled in Siberia and Russian Tsars extended their political sway and ecclesiastical patronage. In the nineteenth century, it became more zealously proselyting. It sponsored missions among the natives of eastern Siberia and Alaska, and also in China and Japan. By 1914, Orthodox Christianity had fifteen million followers in Asia.

Altogether, in the first decade of the twentieth century, Christianity was professed outside the traditionally European or Western world by some forty-one million persons, of whom **Missionary** the majority were the fruit of nineteenth-century mis- **Fruits** sionary activity. But there were other, and more incalculable, fruits. For, while the number of actual converts to Christianity constituted a very small proportion of the populations of India, China, Japan, and even Africa, it should be remembered that Christian missionaries were an effective agency, along with traders and governmental agents, for spreading at least the externals of Western civilization among a large part of those populations and thus contributing to the Europeanization of the world. Especially through the numerous schools and hospitals which missionaries established, many natives who did not become Christian acquired at any rate a taste for the education, the science, the machinery, the clothing, and the sports of contemporary Europe.

Besides, many natives who retained an attachment to the religion of their ancestors—to Hinduism, Buddhism, Taoism, or Shintoism, as the case might be—tended, under the influence of Christian teaching and example, to interpret their own religion in "modern" terms and to invest it with ethical principles borrowed more or less consciously from Christianity. It would be going too far to assert that Hinduism or Buddhism was transformed; these historic religions remained for the mass of their disciples what they had previously been. But for "intellectuals," the impact of Christianity and Western civilization on the East gradually wrought a veritable revolution. A few accepted Christianity; a larger number became agnostic; and some turned to "reform movements," seeking to reconcile their traditional faith with modern developments.

On the other hand, there was a heightening interest of "intellectuals" of the West in the civilizations of the East. This was evidenced by European artists—by painters like the French impressionists and Whistler who tried to be "Japanese," or by a "modernist" painter like Gauguin who preferred primitive Tahiti to sophisticated Paris. It was evidenced, too, by European scholars who produced learned tomes, ever bigger and more abundant, about the languages and customs, religions and antiquities of the Orient, and who, through extensive translation, made available to Western readers the classics of India and China and the Moslem world. It was evidenced likewise by a novel vogue in Europe and America of oriental philosophies and religions.

In the West, there was little or no organized propaganda by Moslems, Buddhists, or Hindus, such as Christians were conducting in the East. Yet many Westerners, as they grew sceptical or Modernist about Christianity, developed a high appreciation, perhaps more romantic than realist, of the "spirituality" and "profundity" of traditional Oriental thought and an enthusiasm for the "beauty" and "nobility" of the ancient sacred books and cults of the East. By the beginning of the twentieth century, most metropolitan centers of Europe and America had groups who curiously combined with a devotion to science and material ease and "social uplift" a penchant for religious novelties—for Theosophy or Baháism, for spiritualistic séances with mediums, for personal attachment to mysterious mahatmas and yogis, or for more nebulous worship of what was termed "New Thought."

Simultaneously, in ethical-culture societies which were arising and in "radical" Protestant circles which were becoming ultramodernist, respect was being inculcated for all the "great prophets" of the human race—for Confucius, Gautama Buddha, Laotse, and Mohammed, no less than for Jesus—and their collective moral teachings, divorced from their several "dogmas," were being drawn upon to provide a spiritual and ethical setting for contemporary material progress. "Progressive" people were apt to perceive in these urban religious novelties, as well as in the advance of science and machine industry, sure signs of the passing of narrowly Christian European civilization into a broadly humanitarian world civilization.

# CHAPTER VII

## EUROPEAN DOMINANCE OF THE WORLD

### 1. NATIONAL ARMAMENTS AND NATIONAL IMPERIALISM

 REATER progress was made in European domination of the world during the brief era of forty years from 1870 to 1910 than during the long span of four previous centuries. This extraordinary development is primarily attributable to the fact that in the new era Europe was highly advanced industrially and nationally. It had material wealth and armaments and nationalistic ambitions vastly superior to what the rest of the world possessed.

Some degree of "militarism" had long been an earmark of the European state-system, and most European states of the seventeenth and eighteenth centuries had spent the main part of their public revenues on the upkeep of professional armies. On occasion, certain states had even attempted to make all their able-bodied men liable to military service: Sweden under Gustavus Adolphus; Prussia under Frederick the Great and again during the "War of Liberation" in 1813–1814; and, most notably, France under the First Republic and the First Napoleonic Empire.[1] It was not until the 1860's, however, that the principle of the volunteer professional army commenced to be supplanted effectively and permanently by that of the conscript popular army, **National Conscript Armies** and not until then that national governments were in a position greatly to increase their military expenditure. This was rendered practicable in Europe by contemporary industrialization. In measure as a nation was industrialized, its ma-

[1] It may be added that Russia employed a form of conscription from the time of Peter the Great and that the Russian army throughout the nineteenth century was—on paper—the largest in Europe.

chinery could relieve men from ordinary work, its factories could produce clothing and arms and military supplies of all sorts, its mechanized farms and foreign shipping could yield surplus food-stuffs, its railways (and later its motor cars) could carry soldiers *en masse* quickly and widely, and its industrial wealth could be utilized to provide necessary funds for increasing the size and efficiency of its military establishment—officers and men, fortresses and firearms, artillery and engineering works, transportation and supply.

At least for the European great powers, the bigger and better armies, which were made possible by industrial progress, proved their worth in a series of explosive, nationalist wars during the score of years from 1859 to 1878—The Franco-Austrian, the Danish-German, the Austro-Prussian, the Franco-German, the Russo-Turkish. The very suddenness of these wars, the speed with which they were conducted, and the decisiveness with which they seemed to effect radical changes, were amazing novelties to Europeans and had profound consequences. Particularly did the Franco-German War of 1870–1871 indicate that a militarily "prepared" nation could make short shift of an "unprepared" nation and that therefore every nation, for its own security, should be in constant state of military "preparedness," in peace-time as well as in war-time. The lesson was taken to heart by European statesmen, and likewise by the most influential classes and a large part of the masses in Europe.

For the wars which ushered in the new era were popular wars, and so too were the armies which won them. Previously, military establishments had been the concern of monarchs and a professional class, and whenever conscription had been resorted to by a Russian Tsar or a Prussian King, it had been met by their subjects with sullenness and sometimes with hostility. But the new age was one of popular enthusiasm for nationalism and democracy, and the masses could now be counted upon to second, or at any rate to accede to, the military policies of their several national governments. If a nation, such as Germany or Italy, had recently won its freedom and unity by force of arms, then all its patriotic citizens, regardless of class, felt a responsibility for continuing an armed "preparedness" which would preserve the nation's unity and freedom. If a nation, such as France, had recently lost territory and prestige through military defeat, then its patriotic citizens felt obliged to support a "preparedness" which would prevent further losses and eventually avenge defeat.

In the circumstances it is not surprising that the majority of the Prussian parliament, who had bitterly opposed the extension of compulsory military training in their country in 1862, endorsed it with enthusiasm after it had proved its worth in the war against Austria in 1866.[1] Nor is it surprising that the Prussian military "reforms"—based upon the principle of "the nation in arms"— were speedily adopted by the other German states, becoming a permanent feature of the new German Empire, and were imitated by Austria-Hungary in 1868, by France in 1872, by Russia in 1874, and by Italy in 1875. Almost every country aspiring to be a great power now armed itself as it had never been armed before, and the lesser powers on the Continent of Europe increased their armaments, made them more efficient, and spent larger sums of money on them. Great Britain, alone among the great powers of Europe, retained a relatively small, professional army,[2] although the expenditure on it rose steadily.

Big armies and big military budgets thus became the order of the day in Europe from 1870 onwards. They were represented by statesmen and publicists, and accepted by the majority of people, as making for peace—as assuring "national defense." Peace actually did prevail among the major powers of Europe from 1878 to 1914, but it was an "armed peace." And there was not peace for "backward" peoples outside of Europe. These, lagging behind in industrial development and hence in military strength, fell easy prey after 1870 to the expansive ambitions and armed might of European powers.

Naval armaments were especially effective in securing Europe's dominance of the world. To back up a merchant marine, to ensure the import of raw materials and foodstuffs and the export of manufactures, to protect traders and investors (and missionaries) in "backward" lands, to obtain and enlarge distant "spheres of influence," to advertise the goods and promote the prestige of a "progressive" people, it seemed highly

**Naval Armaments**

---

[1] See *Modern Europe to 1870*, pp. 743–746, 750–751.

[2] The United States also, after the Civil War (1861–1865), reverted to the policy of maintaining a relatively small professional army. It should be borne in mind that, alike in the case of Great Britain and in that of the United States, geographical location was an important factor in lessening popular feeling of need for big land armaments.

desirable to the governments of industrialized countries, and to influential and interested patriots among their citizens, that the latest technological developments should be utilized for warships. In the 1880's France set out to modernize its navy, and at the end of the decade Great Britain, long the foremost maritime power, acted upon the advice of a committee of "experts" that "no time should be lost in placing the British navy beyond comparison with that of any two powers." Germany and the United States, and also Japan, took to building large navies in the 1890's, and by the opening of the twentieth century all the great powers had important fleets of warships.

The use or threatened use of superior naval and military power was the means by which Europe obtained and exercised its world dominance after 1870. The incentives to it were fundamentally economic and nationalistic.

Prior to 1870 there had been, under liberal auspices, a notable loosening of colonial empires, an abatement of colonial wars, and a good deal of criticism of overseas imperialism. France, it is true, had acquired Algeria in the 1830's and 1840's, though in a hesitant manner and without any great popular enthusiasm, and then, under Napoleon III, had given several signs of renewed imperial pretensions in other parts of the world. On the other hand, the British Empire had apparently been weakened by the grant of self-government to many of its overseas areas; the Spanish colonial empire had obviously been all but destroyed; Dutchmen and Portuguese had had no thought of adding to their colonial possessions; and certainly it had not occurred to Germans or Italians or Belgians or Americans that they should rule over distant alien peoples.

In the new era, particularly after 1880, there was a strong reaction. By this time, in industrialized countries, there was need of a greatly augmented supply of raw materials and foodstuffs from "backward" areas, and, under the developing system of economic nationalism, it was argued that such a supply could be obtained more cheaply and would be more stable if a "progressive" nation owned or controlled a large extent of "backward" lands. *Economic Incentives to Imperialism*

Again, there was need of ever larger markets for surplus products of machine manufacture, and as "progressive" nations put up tariff barriers against each other their merchants sought compensatory markets in "backward" countries, and it was argued that sales could be speeded up if the "backward" countries were "colonies" or "protectorates." Unfavorable tariffs and other economic handicaps could then be gotten rid of in those areas, and the demand for European goods and the ability to pay for them could be enhanced. And requisite internal peace and trade prestige could be afforded by friendly officials of one's own nationality better than by natives.

Furthermore, there was now a growing tendency to export surplus capital from "progressive" countries and to invest it in "backward" countries where rates of interest were usually higher than at home. Prior to 1870, the "progressive" country par excellence had been Great Britain, and the "backward" countries in which it had made its foreign investments (amounting in 1870 to about five billion dollars) were principally the United States and the Continental states of Europe. After 1870, however, as these states underwent rapid industrialization, they in turn became "progressive," ceasing to depend on British capital and beginning to export capital of their own. It thus transpired that, during the era which we are now considering, Germany and France and Belgium and the United States joined Great Britain as significant investors in "backward" countries, and that the "backward" countries in which foreign capital was invested were not so much in Europe and North America as in Latin America, Asia, and Africa. Such investments were apt to involve considerable risk to capitalists, and these, in order to diminish the risk, found it convenient to appeal to their respective national governments for protection of their property abroad and sometimes for the political annexation of regions in which they had valuable "concessions."

Besides, "progressive" nations toward the close of the nineteenth century, thanks to the rapid perfecting of means of communication and instruments of warfare, were in a vastly better position than nations had been in any earlier period to appropriate far-off "backward" areas and to police and administer them. And the simultaneous intensification of nationalism among the masses provided popular support for imperialist undertakings of traders, investors, and governments.

Indeed, the advocates of national imperialism were inclined to put less stress on strictly economic arguments than on broadly patriotic pleas. They talked about the defense of "national rights," the promotion of "national interests," and the avenging of "national honor." They talked about the signal genius which their own nationality had displayed in securing political unity and becoming an industrialized great power and which therefore qualified it as a "progressive" nation to control "backward" peoples. They talked, moreover, of the inevitability, the blind necessity, of imperialism; some of them labeled it "manifest destiny." They talked, too, about the problem of "surplus population," arguing that part of the "surplus" could be supported at home if the industry of the mother-country were allowed freely to expand in colonial territory, and that the rest of the "surplus" could then emigrate, not to foreign countries, but to colonies wherein they would retain their national language and loyalty. They talked, also, about the "higher civilization," the duty incumbent upon a great and civilized nation to instruct and prepare a less favored people for full participation eventually, perhaps remotely, in the blessings of the machine age, possibly to "Christianize" it, and certainly to endow it with mechanical devices, with sanitation and schools, with order and security. The duty was described in prose as "trusteeship" and in poetry as "the white man's burden."

*Nationalistic Incentives*

To the pleas of patriots and the desires of investors and traders, the statesmen of the leading industrial countries responded. In Great Britain, Benjamin Disraeli did a good deal during his Conservative ministry from 1874 to 1880 to favor and foster the revival of imperial ambitions and to acquire new additions to the British colonial empire. In France, a similar development took place under the leadership of a conspicuous "liberal" republican, Jules Ferry, in the early 1880's. In the later 1880's, Germany, with the sanction of the conservative Bismarck, acquired a considerable overseas dominion, and Italy, under the "radical" statesman Crispi, started to acquire one. In the 1890's and early 1900's, the United States, guided officially by William McKinley and Theodore Roosevelt, launched an overseas empire. And by this time, Belgium and Japan were likewise becoming imperialist powers, Spain was endeavoring to recoup losses in America by gains in Africa, and the already huge Russian Empire was expanding still farther in Asia.

*Response of Statesmen*

Between 1870 and 1914, European imperialism overspread the

globe. Almost the entire African continent was partitioned among European powers. The vast continent of Asia and the numerous islands of the Pacific were largely parceled out into political dependencies, or economic "spheres of influence," of European powers. Arctic and Antarctic regions were explored and much of their frozen expanse was claimed by Europeans. The American continents were fastened ever more firmly to Europe, not by political bonds, but by economic and cultural links. The fullness of the Earth seemed incontestably to be Europe's, and European shipping covered the seven seas. Everywhere, the customs and manners, the science and art, and, most of all, the mechanical contrivances of industrial Europe and America were becoming the central features of what promised to be a novel and essentially material world civilization.

### 2. EUROPEANIZED AMERICA: THE ATLANTIC COMMUNITY

The dominance which Europe acquired after 1870 was over Asia and Africa. It was not over North and South America. These continents had been Europeanized long before, and so thoroughly that they should be considered as possessing in modern times the "Atlantic Community" same basic civilization as Europe and as constituting with it an Atlantic Community.[1] Indeed, the Atlantic Ocean since the sixteenth and seventeenth centuries has been not a boundary but the very center of European, or "Western," civilization.

The American countries on the west side of the Atlantic have been for a long time as much a part of "Europe" as countries on the east side—Britain or Spain, France or Germany. Their languages are European. So are their religious beliefs, their social customs, their cultural traditions. Their population is mainly European in blood. Their histories are inextricably interwoven with Europe's. They have thought similar thoughts, cherished similar ideals, followed similar fashions, experienced similar vicissitudes. The United States of America, for example, has certainly been as "progressive" with machine industry and political democracy, with nationalism and imperial expansion, as any country on the Continent of Europe. The dominance of "Europe" since 1870 has been really a dominance of the Atlantic Community.

[1] The only comparably Europeanized areas outside the Atlantic Community are Australasia and the Philippines.

In 1914 the population of the American continents was little short of 200 million, half that of Europe. Of the total, a little more than fifty per cent were English-speaking, while the remaining 94 million were "Latin Americans"—speaking Spanish, Portuguese, or French.

Of self-governing Canada and Newfoundland, we have spoken elsewhere.[1] Here we merely remark the essentially European character of their society, politics, and culture. Of the United States, we shall speak only of outstanding developments which were strikingly similar to Europe's. The United States grew rapidly in population during the nineteenth century, partly because of natural increase of the European stock that had come to it as colonists in the seventeenth and eighteenth centuries, partly because of a similar increase of the African stock that had been imported as slaves, partly because of a swelling stream of new immigrants from Europe.[2]

United States

Like Europe, the United States was nationalistic. It sought, with noteworthy success, to "Americanize" all its inhabitants— immigrants and Negroes as well as original white stock—which meant that they were Europeanized in a particular English fashion and with special devotion to their own national government and history. English was the unifying language, and English were the common literary traditions, though at the same time the political and social developments were regarded as peculiarly "American." Like western Europe, moreover, the United States evolved and applied on a gigantic scale a system of free public schools, by means of which illiteracy was almost completely done away with and patriotism promoted. And from western Europe the United States derived its religion: the majority of its inhabitants were traditionally Protestant, and a growing minority were Catholic.

Like Europe, too, the United States became ever more democratic in the form and operation of its political institutions. Qualifications of religion and property were gradually abolished, and

[1] See above, pp. 61–62.

[2] The number of European immigrants, amounting to 400,000 for the forty years from 1790 to 1830, totaled almost 20 million for the forty years from 1870 to 1910. The original stock, and most of the early immigration, was British. Beginning in the 1840's, large numbers came from Germany and Ireland, and, in the latter part of the century, from Scandinavia, Italy, Hungary, and the Slavic countries. In 1914, fifteen per cent of the total population of the United States were foreign born, and ten per cent were Negroes.

universal manhood suffrage was introduced about the same time as in France. Two major political parties alternated in the conduct of the national government, just as in England, though the United States was more sluggish than England in giving rise to a third, "Labor," party. And the United States, like Germany and Italy, was doomed to fight, at about the same time, a war of national unification—the Civil War, or "War between the States," of 1861–1865.

Industrial development of the United States kept pace with that of western Europe. By the opening of the twentieth century America was forging ahead of Germany and even Great Britain in the production of coal and iron, electric power and light, and a wide variety of mechanical appliances. It was a foremost agricultural as well as industrial country, and the standard of living of its people was relatively high.

The United States felt the same intellectual currents as did Europe, and almost if not quite at the same periods. First, it shared in the mid-century vogue of liberalism and romanticism, under whose twin influence it inaugurated a distinctively "American" literature, realized the ideal of "free churches in a free state," elaborated the freedom of education, and waged a crusade against Negro slavery. Subsequently, in the latter part of the nineteenth century, it participated in the European drift toward "realism" and economic nationalism, adopting high tariff protection, enacting some labor legislation, going in for the newer navalism and overseas imperialism, and in its literature beginning to indulge in "muck-raking," in sociology and psychology.

Following the example of other great powers—Britain, France, Germany, and Italy—the United States at the end of the nineteenth century embarked on definitely imperialist policies. Hawaii was appropriated in 1898. In 1899–1900 the Samoan Islands were partitioned with Germany and Britain. In 1898 was brought on the Spanish-American War, eventuating in the annexation of Puerto Rico and the Philippines and in a virtual protectorate over Cuba. In 1900, in cooperation with European powers, a military expedition was sent into China. In 1901 a native revolt in the Philippines was suppressed by force. In 1903, the separation of Panama from Colombia was effected, and across the isthmus a "zone" was acquired in which the Panama Canal was promptly built.

The Latin-American nations were essentially European too, though their cultural ties were with another part of Europe from that with which the United States was most intimately connected. In one respect they were less European than **Latin America** the United States; that was in blood. Whereas the vast majority of the inhabitants of the United States (and Canada) were of European stock, a large proportion of the inhabitants of most Latin American countries had aboriginal Indian or Negro blood in their veins. There had not been in Latin America the wholesale extinction of Indians or the strong feeling against racial intermixture which characterized "Anglo-Saxon" America. In the West Indies and along the coasts of the Caribbean, Negro blood predominated, while in Mexico, Central America, and a large part of South America most of the "common people" were Indians or cross-breeds. Only the well-to-do upper and middle classes were apt to be "pure" Spanish or Portuguese.

Yet, though many Indians preserved their tribal speech and customs, the prevailing civilization all over Latin America was unmistakably European and Latin. The language of officialdom, of schools, armies, courts, newspapers, and of polite society, was Spanish or Portuguese, and the only publicly professed religion of any importance was Catholic Christianity. Like Latin Europe, Latin America was predominantly agricultural, and in politics it presented marked resemblances to Spain and Portugal. There was a similar indifference of the masses to ordinary political action, a similar supremacy of particular classes and professional politicians, similar cliques of "liberals" and "anti-clericals," or of "conservatives" and "clericals," a similar preponderant influence of army officers, and similar tendencies toward dictatorship and sudden revolution. All the Latin-American governments were republican in form, but presidents were usually superior to constitutions and rifles more decisive than ballots.

The Latin tradition was sustained and reinforced, moreover, by a steady immigration from Latin Europe, especially from Portugal, Spain, and Italy, and also by an habitual sending of the sons of the upper classes to institutions of higher learning in Spain or France. This meant a strengthening of cultural ties between Latin Europe and Latin America, and more particularly a familiarity of the governing groups in most Latin-American countries with the latest Parisian ideas and fashions.

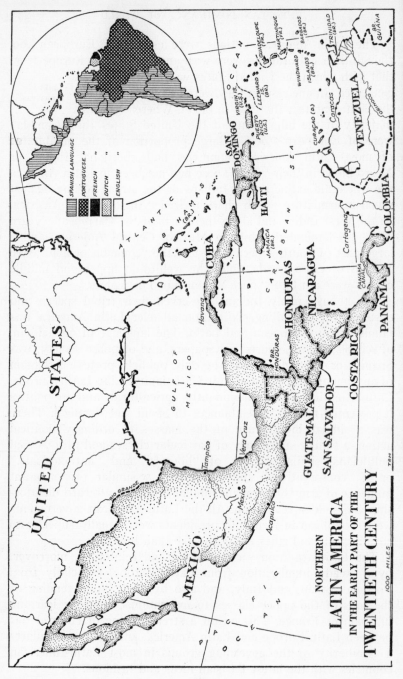

NORTHERN
LATIN AMERICA
IN THE EARLY PART OF THE
TWENTIETH CENTURY

1000 MILES

SPANISH LANGUAGE
PORTUGUESE "
FRENCH "
DUTCH "
ENGLISH "

UNITED STATES

MEXICO

GUATEMALA
SAN SALVADOR
HONDURAS
NICARAGUA
COSTA RICA
PANAMA

CUBA
HAITI
SAN DOMINGO
JAMAICA (BR.)
BAHAMAS (BR.)

COLOMBIA
VENEZUELA

BR. HONDURAS

PUERTO RICO (U.S.)
VIRGIN IS.

LEEWARD IS. (BR.)
GUADELOUPE (FR.)
MARTINIQUE (FR.)
WINDWARD ISLANDS (BR.)
BARBADOS (BR.)
TRINIDAD (BR.)
BR. GUIANA

CURAÇAO (D.)
CARACAS

ATLANTIC OCEAN

GULF OF MEXICO

CARIBBEAN SEA

PACIFIC OCEAN

Havana
Tampico
Vera Cruz
Mexico
Acapulco
Rio Grande
Cartagena
Panama Canal
Orinoco R.

274

SOUTHERN
LATIN AMERICA
IN THE EARLY PART OF THE
TWENTIETH
CENTURY

1000 MILES

CARIBBEAN SEA
PANAMA CANAL — Cartagena
WINDWARD ISLANDS (BR.)
CURAÇAO (D.)
MARTINIQUE (FR.)
BARBADOS (BR.)
TRINIDAD (BR.)
ORINOCO R.
Caracas
VENEZUELA
Bogotá
COLOMBIA
GUIANA (BR.) (D.) (FR.)
Quito
ECUADOR
Guayaquil
EQUATOR
Belém
ORINOCO R.
RIO NEGRO
AMAZON R.
MADEIRA R.
B R A Z I L
Natal
Pernambuco
PERU
Lima
Cuzco
SÃO FRANCISCO R.
Bahia
Arica
BOLIVIA
Sucre
Potosí
GRAN CHACO
PARANÁ R.
PARAGUAY
Asunción
São Paulo
Rio de Janeiro
PACIFIC OCEAN
PARANÁ R.
URUGUAY R.
ATLANTIC OCEAN
Valparaíso Santiago
Buenos Aires
CHILE
URUGUAY
Montevideo
RIO DE LA PLATA
ARGENTINA
P A T A G O N I A
FALKLAND ISLANDS (BR.)
STRAITS OF MAGELLAN
Punta Arenas
CAPE HORN

SPANISH LANGUAGE
PORTUGUESE "
FRENCH "
DUTCH "
ENGLISH "

TRM

275

Then, too, Latin America was increasingly dependent on Europe—and the United States—in the economic sphere. It remained overwhelmingly agricultural at a time when most of the Atlantic Community was undergoing intensive industrialization. It grew surpluses of coffee, wheat, cattle, sugar, tropical fruit, etc., the markets for which were in North America and Europe; and for the development of its agriculture, for the exploitation of its natural resources—notably its mines and oil-wells—and for the development of its armies and public works, it sought loans in Paris, London or New York and granted "concessions" to European or North American corporations.

Nationalism played a somewhat different role in Latin America —at least in Spanish America—from what it played in the United States or in Latin Europe. Instead of uniting a linguistic nationality in a single national state, it confirmed the political separatism of an earlier day and fostered rivalry among **Separate States** a gradually increasing number of proudly sovereign states. The Portuguese-speaking people of South America managed to hold together and to emphasize their unity in the federal state of Brazil, but the Spanish-speaking population of the New World had begun their independent political career as eight distinct nations, and within a century the number swelled to eighteen. The eight which emerged from the Wars of Independence of 1810–1825 were: Mexico, Central America, Colombia, Peru, Bolivia, Paraguay, Argentina, and Chile. In 1828 Uruguay revolted against Argentina, and, after resisting Brazilian aggression, established its independence in 1830. From Colombia seceded Venezuela in 1829, Ecuador in 1830, and Panama, much later, in 1903. In the 1840's Central America broke up into the five separate republics of Guatemala, Honduras, Nicaragua, Salvador, and Costa Rica, while Santo Domingo became a state distinct from Haiti. Cuba, after repeated revolts and the intervention of the United States, gained general recognition as an independent republic in 1899. Each of the eighteen Spanish republics, thus established, had a distinctive nationalism of its own, and likewise the Portuguese republic of Brazil and the French Negro republic of Haiti.

The largest and in many ways the most important of the Latin-American nations was Portuguese-speaking Brazil. Its area exceeded that of continental United States (exclusive of

Alaska), and its population rose from 4 million in 1830 to over 30 million in 1910. Its economic resources and development were remarkable. By 1914 it was furnishing almost **Brazil** three-fourths of the world's coffee, exporting large amounts of timber and minerals and meat, and producing manufactured goods of an annual value of half a billion dollars.

The political foundations for this economic progress had been laid by a monarchical regime, which had been established by a branch of the Portuguese royal family in 1822,[1] and which lasted, as the Empire of Brazil, from that date to 1889. Especially helpful was the long reign of the Emperor Pedro II (1831–1889), an enlightened prince and inveterate reformer. The slave trade was abolished in 1853, and Negro slavery, abated in 1871, was ended, without civil war, in 1888. In 1889, however, the Empire of Pedro II was abruptly overthrown. Influential landlords resented the loss of their slaves, and army officers chafed at the subordinate position in which the Emperor kept them. The latter therefore supported the Republic which one of their number, Marshal Deodoro da Fonseca, proclaimed in November 1889, and the former offered no resistance. Pedro and his family were exiled. State and church were separated. A republican constitution, modeled closely after that of the United States, was adopted in 1891.

Fonseca might profess liberalism and democracy, but actually his government was a military dictatorship and one of scandalous corruption. In 1891 he was overthrown by another army chieftain, Marshal Floriano Peixoto, who in turn had to deal in 1893 with a stubborn insurrection of still other military and naval officers. Following the retirement of Peixoto in 1894, the republic passed into civilian hands and gradually gained stability and respect.

Of the Spanish-American states, the foremost, in one way or another, were Argentina, Chile, and Mexico. Argentina, during the first half of the nineteenth century, was a prey to **Argentina** civil war and military dictatorship, but from 1862, under a more orderly republican government, it significantly gained in population and in material well-being. It became a great grain-growing and meat-producing country, and its capital city of Buenos Aires became the metropolis of the southern

[1] On the establishment of the Brazilian Empire by Pedro I in 1822, see *Modern Europe to 1870*, p. 633.

hemisphere and one of the most beautiful and cultured urban centers in the world. In military and naval strength, Argentina ranked with its neighbors, Brazil and Chile, forming with them the so-called group of A-B-C powers.

Chile, occupying the long narrow strip of territory along the Pacific west of Argentina and the Andes, achieved fairly early a kind of political stability. The civil government, **Chile** republican in form, was conducted most of the time by the conservative upper classes in harmony with the military. Education was fostered, agriculture and commerce promoted, art cultivated, and the cities of Santiago and Valparaiso developed. As an outcome of a war with Bolivia and Peru in 1879–1883, Chilean rule was extended northward over the provinces of Tacna and Arica, with their rich nitrate deposits.

Mexico was the most populous of all the Spanish-American states; though exceeded in area by Argentina, it had twice as many inhabitants. Yet Mexico was relatively "back-**Mexico** ward," exemplifying in an extreme form the traditional social cleavage which to some extent characterized all Latin America. Most of the country's basic agriculture was conducted on extensive plantations, which were owned and exploited by an upper class of cultured well-to-do persons, Spanish in descent and tradition and influential in state and church, and on which lived and toiled a lower class of ignorant, poverty-stricken peasants—or "peons," as they were called—largely Indian in blood and servile in condition. Among the upper class emerged the usual divisions of conservative and liberal, clerical and anti-clerical, but such divisions ordinarily meant little to the lower class. In the 1850's and 1860's, it is true, Benito Juarez, a full-blooded Indian and a declared champion of the lower class, led a revolutionary movement and succeeded in overcoming French interference and putting the intruded Emperor Maximilian to death (1867). Jaurez, nevertheless, displayed more energy in fighting "reactionaries" and promulgating decrees against the Catholic Church than in improving the lot of the peons. And his successor, Porfirio Diaz, who was virtual dictator of the country from 1877 to 1911, though less hostile to the Church, was not much concerned with social reform.

In certain respects Mexico made progress under Diaz. Foreign capital was employed for the construction of railways and the development of the country's mineral and oil resources. Fiscal reforms were instituted and general administration improved. Some Mexicans waxed wealthy, and likewise a considerable number of American, British, and other foreign investors. But in measure as Mexico was brought into contact with the outside world and as Diaz aged and became more despotic, Mexican "liberals" multiplied and the Indian masses grew restless. At length in 1910, a wealthy landowner, Francisco Madero, raised the standard of constitutionalism and agrarian reform and, with several disaffected army officers, took the field against Diaz. Diaz resigned and fled to Europe, and Madero was made president— without accomplishing any agrarian reform, however. Then a counter-revolutionary movement ensued; General Victoriano Huerta overcame Madero and had him put to death in 1914. Next, revolutionary satellites of Madero, with the support of the United States, overthrew Huerta (1915), and, after much quarreling and fighting among themselves and an armed intervention by the United States, one of them, Venustiano Carranza, got the upper hand, and under his auspices a new constitution was adopted in 1917 and drastic anti-clerical legislation enacted. But not until later, when the "Mexican Revolution" took on a more radical complexion, was social reform seriously attempted.[1]

Conditions similar to those in Mexico existed in most of the lesser Latin-American states. But their economic backwardness and political revolutions must not be allowed to overshadow the very real European civilization which obtained throughout Latin America.

### 3. TUTELAGE OF ASIA

In Asia, the largest and most populous of all the world's continents, some European influence had been continuously exerted since the sixteenth century, but in only two parts of Asia did it produce any such Europeanization in language and culture as was simultaneously produced in America. One part was the northern plain—the vast expanse of Siberia—into which Russian colonists trickled during the sixteenth and seventeenth centuries and poured during the eighteenth and nineteenth, bringing with them Russian speech, Russian customs, Russian Christianity, and the rule of the Russian Tsars. In the

Prior to 1850

[1] See below, pp. 508–511.

frozen "far north" of Siberia and in the desert regions to the south, primitive tribes remained; but by the latter part of the nineteenth century most of Siberia was quite Russian.

The other Europeanized part of Asia was the Philippine archipelago, which, subject to Spanish rule from 1565 to 1898, experienced a development similar to Spanish America's. There was much racial intermixture, and the emerging "Filipino" nationality, though predominantly Malayan in blood, was Spanish in speech, Catholic in religion, and Latin European in culture. Some Moslem and some pagan tribesmen remained, it is true, in out-of-the-way islands of the archipelago, and its conquest by the United States introduced a new and alien rule. Yet neither of these circumstances could alter the basic fact that on the whole the Philippines were as European as, say, Mexico or Peru.

The vast region of India and the East Indian Islands of Sumatra, Java, and Celebes had been in contact with European powers—Portugal, the Netherlands, France, or England—for as long a time as the Philippines had been subject to Spain, or Siberia to Russia. Until the latter part of the nineteenth century, however, the contact was primarily commercial, and secondarily political. With the exception of a few places on the Malabar coast of India, whither Portuguese colonists and missionaries came in the sixteenth century, familiarizing natives with the Portuguese language and converting them to Catholic Christianity, there was no real Europeanization of a cultural sort. The population of India was altogether too numerous and too deeply rooted in its own complex culture to be much affected in this respect by the presence of European merchants or "governors" in a few coastal cities.

In the nineteenth century, European influence was enormously extended and quickened in India, and also in other parts of **After 1850** Asia. With the rapidly increasing eagerness of the industrialized nations of Europe to secure raw materials, to sell manufactured commodities, and to invest surplus capital, and with their greatly improved means of establishing and exercising overseas imperial sway, European merchants were no longer content with limited coast traffic in Asia or with cumbersome dealings of chartered commercial companies with native princes and potentates. They must penetrate inland, building railways, stringing telegraph wires, accustoming natives to machine-made goods and machine-age civilization; and all these things they could accomplish more satisfactorily if their particular national state in Europe acquired supremacy throughout the economically backward area. Industrialized European nations now had naval and military establishments and financial resources adequate to bring Asiatic rulers to terms.

Thus, in the second half of the nineteenth century, a new European imperialism was inspired and expedited in India and indeed over the greater part of the huge Asiatic continent and its adjacent large islands. It involved, in many areas, an expansion and intensification of direct European rule, and, on a wider front and even more significantly, it served to spread European material civilization and European political ideas on top of the abiding linguistic, religious, and social cultures of the several Asiatic peoples. In a word, there was now a material European tutelage of Asia.

How the British constructed and ruled the Empire of India has elsewhere been explained.[1] Here we shall merely catalogue the acquisitions of Asiatic territory by European powers and then pass on to a summary consideration of their influence on Japan and China, with a few supplementary words about Siam and the Moslem regions of the "Middle East."

Great Britain added to its Indian Empire in the 1880's Burma and Baluchistan. In southeastern Asia it bordered Singapore and Malacca with the Federated Malay States (1874, 1909) and across the sea to the east appropriated a third of the island of Borneo (1881–1888). In southwestern Asia, it acquired between 1839 and 1901 a series of protectorates from Aden at the foot of the Red Sea to Kuwait at the head of the Persian Gulf, and by agreement with Russia in 1907 a "sphere of influence" in southern Persia. From China, Britain wrested Hongkong in 1842, leased Wei-hai-wei in 1898, and shortly afterwards obtained a privileged position in Tibet and the Yangtze valley. At the opening of the twentieth century, Britain governed a third of the whole population of Asia.

*European Dominion*

France, besides continuing to hold a few trading posts on the coast of India, built up an empire of Indo-China. In 1896 it delimited with Great Britain "spheres of influence" in Siam, and in 1899 it leased Kwangchow from China and obtained a privileged

[1] See above, pp. 71–76.

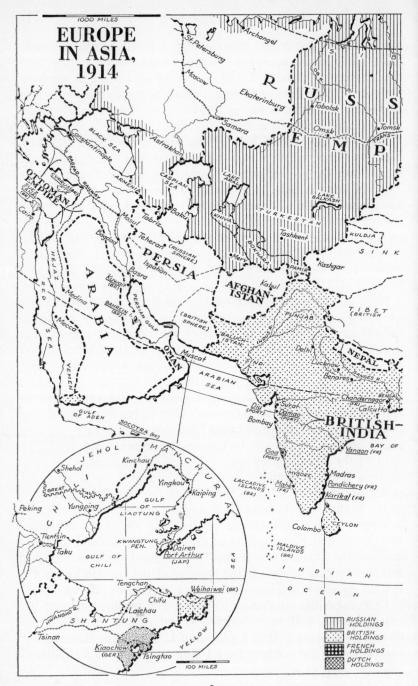

# EUROPE
## IN ASIA,
## 1914

1000 MILES

Archangel

St. Petersburg

Moscow

Ekaterinburg

R U S S

Tobolsk

Samara

Omsk

Tomsk

Astrakhan

E M P

Black Sea

Constantinople

OTTOMAN EMPIRE

BAGDAD RAILWAY

ARMENIA

CASPIAN SEA

Baku

TURKESTAN

Tashkent

KULDJA

S I N K

Cairo

Mosul

Tabriz

Teheran

(RUSSIAN SPHERE)

Merv

BOKHARA

Kashgar

HEJAZ

Bagdad

PERSIA

Isfahan

PAMIR

Kabul

AFGHANISTAN

T I B E T
(BRITISH)

Kuwait (BR)

Basra

PERSIAN GULF

BAHREIN (BR)

(BRITISH SPHERE)

BALUCHISTAN

SIND

INDUS

PUNJAB

Delhi

Lucknow

Benares

GANGES R.

NEPAL

Medina

ARABIA

OMAN

Muscat

Mecca

RED SEA

YEMEN

ARABIAN SEA

Chandernagor (FR)

BENGAL

Calcutta

Diu (PORT)

Surat

Damao (PORT)

Bombay

BRITISH-INDIA

Goa (PORT)

Yanaon (FR)

BAY OF

GULF OF ADEN

SOCOTRA (BR)

MYSORE

Madras

Pondichery (FR)

LACCADIVE ISLANDS (BR)

Mahé (FR)

Karikal (FR)

Colombo

CEYLON

MALDIVE ISLANDS (BR)

I N D I A N

O C E A N

### Inset map (Manchuria / China):

JEHOL

MANCHURIA

Shehol

Kinchau

Yingkou

GREAT WALL

Yunping

GULF OF LIAOTUNG

Kaiping

Peking

Tientsin

Taku

KWANGTUNG PEN.

Dairen

Port Arthur (JAP)

GULF OF CHILI

Tengchan

Chifu

Weihaiwei (BR)

Laichau

SHANTUNG

SEA

Tsinan

HWANGHO R.

Kiaochow (GER)

Tsingtao

YELLOW

100 MILES

### Legend

| | |
|---|---|
| ▥ | RUSSIAN HOLDINGS |
| ⋯ | BRITISH HOLDINGS |
| ▦ | FRENCH HOLDINGS |
| ▨ | DUTCH HOLDINGS |

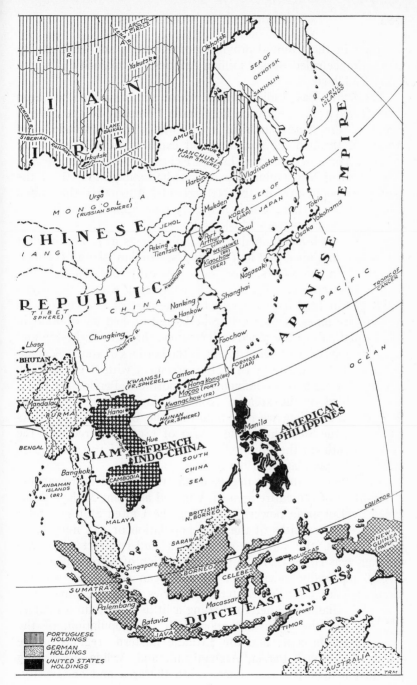

position in the Chinese provinces of Kwangsi and Hainan. By 1914 France ruled twenty million Asiatics, the majority of whom were Buddhists.

The Dutch East Indian empire, whose administration had been transferred from the Dutch East India Company to the government of the Netherlands in 1798, was greatly extended and solidified through the conquest and exploitation of the interior of the islands of Sumatra, Java, Celebes, two-thirds of Borneo, and a half of New Guinea. Java alone had almost four times the area and population of the Netherlands. Altogether the Dutch Netherlands in 1914 dominated fifty-four million Asiatics, the majority of whom were Moslems.

Portugal still maintained a few trading posts in India, the port of Macao in China, and half of the East Indian island of Timor. Germany in the 1880's took possession of 70,000 square miles of northeastern New Guinea, rechristening it Kaiser Wilhelmsland, and in 1898 leased from China the port of Kiaochow, with 200 square miles. Russia held Siberia and pushed its frontier, in the second half of the nineteenth century, through Turkestan and other regions of west-central Asia to the borders of India, Afghanistan, and Persia, and in 1907, by agreement with Great Britain, obtained a "sphere of influence" in northern Persia. By 1910, over a third of the area of Asia was immediately subject to Russia. In addition, we may note that the United States, by its victory in the Spanish-American War of 1898, acquired near the Asiatic continent the Philippines, with an area of 100,000 square miles and a population of ten million.

Altogether, in the first decade of the twentieth century, almost three-fifths of the entire area of Asia and adjacent Malaysia was ruled by European powers (including the United States), and a little over four-ninths of the total population of 925 million. In other words, the number of Asiatics under direct European tutelage was larger than the total population of Europe itself.

Still nominally independent of European rule were two sections of Asia: the "Far Eastern" countries of China, Japan, and Siam, together comprising a little more than a quarter of the area, and about half the population, of the Continent; and the "Middle Eastern" regions of the Ottoman Empire, Persia, Afghanistan, and Arabia, embracing together a little less than one-seventh the area and one-twenty-

**The Far East**

third the population of the continent. But all these lands were now being influenced by European material civilization as they had never been before. Japan, in particular, was already a great power in the European sense, more strikingly Europeanized in government, industry, and armaments than any Asiatic country actually administered by Europeans.

There had been some European commercial and missionary penetration of Japan back in the sixteenth century. Portuguese traders had "discovered" Japan in 1542, and St. Fran- Japan cis Xavier had inaugurated Catholic missions there in 1549. By the end of that century Japanese converts to Christianity numbered 300,000; and Spaniards and Dutchmen were competing with Portuguese for Japanese trade. Shortly afterwards, however, the major native princes and the leading exponents of native religion (Buddhism or Shinto) became alarmed lest their influence should be undermined, and their power destroyed, by the ambition and intrigue of Europeans. In 1587 foreign priests were ordered to leave the country on penalty of death, and in 1614 Christianity was definitely banned. In 1624 Spanish merchants, as well as missionaries, were excluded, and in 1638 Portuguese. Thousands of native Christian converts were put to death, and commercial intercourse with the outside world was rigidly restricted to one closely supervised station to which a few Dutch ships might come. Otherwise no foreigner might enter Japan, while no native might go abroad and no ocean-going ships might be constructed. For over two centuries, from 1638 to 1853, Japan was practically cut off from Europe, and Europe from Japan.

The "reopening" of Japan to European influence was an outcome of a naval expedition, under Commodore Matthew Perry, which the United States dispatched to the Far East Reopening in 1853 with instructions to secure from the Japanese of Japan government a pledge of protection for American trade. and The Japanese were duly impressed by the spectacle of National Revolution Perry's four warships steaming into Uraga Bay near Yokohama, still more impressed by the sewing machines and other devices which he exhibited as samples of Western industrial civilization, and most impressed by the sight and sound of the big grim cannon which his ships carried as the final proof of Western superiority. So vastly impressed, indeed, was the Japanese governing prince that in 1854 he signed with Perry a treaty, by which Japan promised to allow American merchantmen to visit two ports. Very shortly, Great Britain, the Netherlands, and Russia obtained similar privileges. Then, in 1859, another envoy from the United States, Townsend Harris, negotiated a new treaty whereby the port of Yokohama was opened to American commerce. And, again, similar treaty rights were soon accorded to European merchants.

The prince who signed these commercial treaties in behalf of Japan was not the sovereign of the country, but only the hereditary chief official (or "Shogun") of the Emperor (or "Mikado"). The Emperors belonged to a "divine" family which was supposed to have sprung from a sun-goddess and to have reigned in Japan continuously since the seventh century B.C.[1] Being so very sacred, they had long since taken to living in ceremonial seclusion in the "holy city" of Kyoto and leaving the exercise of regal authority to one or another of the feudal princes —or "daimios"—of the realm, who thus was styled the Shogun. Since the end of the sixteenth century the daimio of the Tokugawa clan had been the Shogun, and to keep himself in power he had waged war repeatedly with other daimios.

The Shogun's action in "opening" Japan to foreigners in the 1850's was resented by other daimios and by the Emperor as a sacrilegious reversal of traditional policy and was utilized by them to undermine the Shogun's authority and to reassert the Emperor's. But even the anti-foreign sentiment of daimios and Emperor was altered when, in 1863–1864, bombardments of Japanese ports proved the effectiveness of Western gunnery and the inability of Japan to defend itself unless it possessed the Western type of cannon. Hence daimios who had recently been most vehement in reviling "European barbarians" now suddenly changed their tune and began to insist that Japan should freely admit the Westerners, learn from them, and excel them in their own arts. At the same time they retained their hostility to the Shogun and demanded that the powers which he had been exercising should be restored to the Emperor.

The ensuing agitation against the Shogun thus involved a demand for an assimilation of Western civilization and likewise a

[1] There is solid historical evidence that it has reigned since at least the fifth century A.D.

mounting enthusiasm for national unification under the Emperor and for the national religion of Shinto of which he was at once the sacred representative and the chief object of worship. It eventuated in the Japanese Revolution of 1867–1868. The last of the Shoguns was compelled to abdicate and to retire into private life, and the youthful but able Emperor, Mutsuhito, was made actual as well as titular monarch of Japan. By a remarkable act of patriotism, the chief daimios surrendered to him their respective feudal rights and possessions, and the lesser nobles followed their example. Then in 1871 feudalism was formally abolished by imperial decree. The ex-daimios and certain other leaders in the revolution were rewarded with new titles of nobility borrowed from European usage and with high offices and ample salaries under the new centralized government. The peasants were freed from servile dues and made owners of the land they tilled and immediate subjects of the Empire.

Under Mutsuhito (1867–1912) Japan was rapidly "Europeanized," militarily, politically, and educationally. Young Japanese were sent to Europe or America to observe and study. Europeans and Americans were welcomed to Japan. Christian missions were tolerated. Foreign trade **"European-izing" Japan** was encouraged. European counsel was eagerly sought, and European models closely followed, in modernizing the political, economic, and military institutions of the country. The Japanese army was reorganized in the 1870's on the German pattern, and a navy was constructed in accordance with British advice. Codes of civil and criminal law were fashioned after those of France and Germany. A public-school system of the "Western" type was established, and universities were set up at Tokyo and Kyoto. In 1889 the Emperor promulgated a constitution, vesting legislative power in a bicameral parliament, the upper chamber being aristocratic and the lower "liberal," that is, elected by the propertied classes.

Simultaneously the material civilization of Europe and America was making swift progress in Japan. The first railway, steeling the eighteen miles from Tokyo to Yokohama, was opened in 1872. By 1914 Japan had 6,000 miles of railway, almost all of which were owned by the state. Moreover, within fifteen years of the repeal of the old law prohibiting the construction of seagoing ships, Japan had 138 such vessels, and by 1914 its merchant marine exceeded the French in tonnage and was plying to Europe, America, Australia, and India. The cotton industry, which was non-existent in Japan prior to 1880, grew so fast that in 1914 Japanese cotton factories contained two and a half million spindles, which turned out 550 million pounds of yarn.

The foregoing figures testify that in the last quarter of the nineteenth century and the first decade of the twentieth, Japan experienced an industrialization comparable with that of Europe and the United States. And with it emerged trade unions and serious labor problems as well as business corporations and high finance. Industrial bourgeoisie combined with agricultural aristocracy to direct governmental policies, and workmen became infected with imported principles of political democracy and even of Marxian socialism.

In part because Japan was imitating so many other features of European development, in part because its industrialists were anxious to extend their operations and add to their profits, and in part because its population was cramped and uneasy and its army officers ambitious and ultra-patriotic, the Japanese government was not content merely to "Europeanize" the homeland. It
**Japanese Imperialism** must engage in imperialistic enterprise and extend its military and political sway. Early in the 1890's, Japan began seriously to meddle in Chinese affairs, and in the resulting Chino-Japanese War of 1894–1895, it detached Korea from the Chinese Empire and acquired the island of Formosa. It would likewise have acquired Port Arthur and the Liaotung peninsula had not Russia, with the backing of France and Germany, intervened and stopped it.

It soon became clear that Russia had designs of its own on Port Arthur and also on Manchuria and Korea; and at length in 1904 Japan went to war with Russia. For this, its first struggle with a European power, Japan was well prepared. It had the advantage, moreover, of being relatively near to the scene of hostilities and of commanding the united loyalty and intense patriotism of its whole population. The story of the Russo-Japanese War of 1904–1905 will be sketched later.[1] Here it suffices to note that, by the treaty of Portsmouth terminating the war, Japan took over from Russia the lease of Port Arthur and the Liaotung peninsula, reacquired the southern part of the island

[1] See below, p. 340.

of Sakhalin which had been ceded to Russia back in 1875, and obtained from Russia a pledge of political disinterestedness in Korea and Manchuria.

With Russia out of the way and with the support of Great Britain (which made an alliance with Japan in 1902 [1]), Japanese officials and financiers proceeded with a "peaceful penetration" of Korea, until in 1910 its native ruler was deposed and it was formally incorporated, under the name of "Chosen," with the Japanese Empire. The territory thus annexed, about twice as large as the American state of Ohio and thrice as populous, was valuable as a granary for Japan, a market for Japanese goods, and a field of investment for Japanese capitalists.

The Chinese Empire, though opened to European trade and influence somewhat earlier than Japan, was much more sluggish in undergoing "Europeanization." In considerable part this was attributable to the size of the Empire and to **Chinese Empire** the peculiar nature of its civilization. In area and in population it was approximately equal to the entire continent of Europe. The large majority of its 375 million inhabitants dwelt along the river valleys of the Huang (or Yellow), the Yangtze, and the Si, and were included within the eighteen provinces of China proper, which territorially constituted about a third of the Empire as a whole. China proper was the core of the Empire. But there were numerous outlying provinces:

(1) Manchuria, to the north, had been united with China in the seventeenth century when an ambitious Manchu warrior had supplanted the native dynasty of Chinese Emperors. Since then, a Manchu dynasty had ruled the whole Empire. (2) The Amur coastal district, north of Korea, was a relatively undeveloped dependency. (3) Mongolia, to the northwest of China proper, was a vast territory almost seven times the size of France but with fewer people than Paris and these chiefly nomadic. "Inner Mongolia" adjoining Manchuria, was under the immediate rule of the Manchu Emperors of China, but "Outer Mongolia" was too remote and too unruly, and, although a Chinese agent was maintained at Urga, the hereditary khans were practically independent. (4) Sinkiang, in the far west of the Empire, embraced the regions of Eastern Turkestan and Kuldja. (5) Tibet, south of Sinkiang and west of China proper, was another vast and

[1] See below, pp. 311–312.

sparsely settled region. At its capital of Lhasa resided the Buddhist "pope," the Dalai Lama, whom the Tibetans regarded as
their religious head and ultimate authority. The Empire was
represented by a few Chinese officials and some Chinese soldiers.

Altogether, the Chinese Empire was vast, yet notably persistent. If any European analogy is sought, it may be found in
the ancient Roman Empire rather than in any modern state.

There had been some intercourse of Europe with the Chinese
Empire in the sixteenth and seventeenth centuries. It had been
primarily commercial and secondarily religious. Europeans had
met Chinese Emperors and officials, had traded in Chinese seaports, and had converted some Chinese to Christianity. But these
achievements had been spasmodic and relatively unimportant.
They had not affected the mass of the Chinese people or appreciably altered the traditional course or content of Chinese civilization. In the seventeenth century, China, like Japan, had banned
Christian missionaries and all but banned European merchants.

In the nineteenth century, however, China was forcefully
"opened" and kept open by the newly industrialized great powers
of Europe. The process began in 1840 with the so-called Opium
War waged by Great Britain against the Chinese Em-
**European**
**Aggression**      pire. It grew out of a quarrel between the Chinese government, which had forbidden the importation of
opium, and British traders at Canton, who persisted in bringing
opium from India into China. It was marked by British bombardment and capture of several Chinese cities on the coast and
was terminated by the treaty of Nanking (1842) in accordance
with which the four ports of Amoy, Ningpo, Foochow, and
Shanghai, in addition to Canton, were opened to British traders,
the island and city of Hongkong were ceded outright to Britain,
and China had to pay a war indemnity. The fruits of British victory were soon shared with other Western nations—American,
French, Belgian, Prussian, Dutch, and Portuguese—for the governments of these nations during the next decade obtained similar
treaty privileges for their citizens.

In 1856 both France and Great Britain made war on China,
the former to avenge the murder of a missionary and the latter
on the ground that the crew of a ship sailing under the British
flag had been arrested and jailed as pirates by a Chinese official.
The British again occupied Canton, while a combined Franco-

British military expedition captured the defences of Tientsin and advanced toward Peking, the Emperor's capital. Only after protracted negotiations and the arrival of the expedition at the very gates of Peking was the Second Chinese War ended by the treaties of Tientsin (1860). China agreed to open six additional ports (including Tientsin) to foreign trade, to legalize the opium traffic, to receive foreign ministers at Peking, to tolerate and protect Christian missionaries, and to guarantee the safety of Europeans traveling in the interior.

In 1860, the very year of the Emperor's yielding to Britain and France, Russia extorted from him the Amur coastal district in the far northeast. There Russia founded Vladivostok and used it as a point for radiating influence in Manchuria.

More steps toward the dismemberment of the Chinese Empire were taken in the 1890's. They were inaugurated by the Chino-Japanese War of 1894–1895, already referred to, as an outcome of which the Empire was compelled to cede Formosa and the Liaotung peninsula (within striking distance of the capital city of Peking) to Japan and to renounce suzerainty over Korea. Russia at once stepped in, as we know, with the support of Germany and France, and prevented Japan from taking the strategically important peninsula of Liaotung. But this action signified no tender regard on the part of European powers for the integrity of the Chinese Empire. Only three years later (1898), Russia wrung from the Emperor a "leasehold" of Liaotung, including Port Arthur, and with it numerous economic concessions in Manchuria. In the same year, Germany, on the pretext of indemnifying itself for the murder of two missionaries of German nationality, acquired a similar ninety-nine–year lease of Kiaochow and similar economic concessions in the Chinese province of Shantung. Also, in the same year, France demanded and obtained a like lease of Kwangchow and like economic rights in the island of Hainan and the mainland provinces of Kwangsi and Yünnan. Great Britain, not to be left behind by its imperialist rivals of Continental Europe, made due representations at Peking, eventuating in a lease of the port of Weihaiwei, opposite Port Arthur, "for as long a period as Port Arthur shall remain in the possession of Russia," in an additional ninety-nine–year lease of the Kowloon peninsula, opposite Hongkong, and in the recognition of Britain's "privileged position" in the Yangtze valley.

Subsequently, in 1904–1905, Russia and Japan warred over their respective shares in the "dismemberment" of the Chinese Empire. Russia was forced to surrender the Liaotung peninsula to Japan and to give Japan a free hand in Korea. Shortly afterwards, however, Japan and Russia were agreeably delimiting "spheres of influence" between themselves throughout the northern area of the Empire. Japan annexed Korea in 1910 and acquired railway concessions in Manchuria. Russia in 1913 obtained a virtual protectorate over Outer Mongolia.

In the meantime, between 1842 and 1912, and more especially from the 1890's, European influence was progressively affecting the Chinese Empire in different ways and by various means. The opening of China proper to foreign trade, missionary enterprise, and financial investment, as well as the transfer of outlying provinces to foreign rule and the lease of seaports to foreign powers, brought into the country a steadily augmenting number of Europeans (and Japanese), with Western customs and ideas. From the "treaty ports," in which Europeans had their own settlements and law courts, from the Catholic and Protestant missions, which gradually dotted the interior as well as the coast and with which were associated schools, hospitals, and orphanages, and from the official representatives of Western nations, radiated ever more widely a knowledge of European industry, European politics, European "progress," and a desire to emulate the West in all these respects. The peasant masses were least touched—there was such a multitude of them! and they were so habituated to old customs! But in the cities were "Western" stirrings, and ambitious young natives began to go abroad, observing and studying the West in its universities and commercial centers, and to return imbued with patriotism and a conviction that China, like Japan, to save itself, must be "Westernized."

*European Influence*

In the economic sphere some Westernization was obviously going forward. The value of Chinese foreign trade grew from 215 million dollars in 1875 to 608 million in 1914,[1] and by the latter date some 6,000 miles of railway were in operation within the Empire and 2,300 miles more under construction.

---

[1] Most of the tonnage of foreign shipping was distributed in 1913 as follows: Great Britain, 38,120,000; Japan, 23,422,000; Germany, 6,320,000; France, 1,233,-000; the United States, 900,000; and Norway, 740,000.

In other respects, nevertheless, the Westernization of China was seriously impeded by the enormous size of the country and the bitterness of the popular reaction against chronic interference and aggression of the European great powers and Japan, and by the unwillingness or inability of the Chinese government to adopt and pursue any such revolutionary program as enabled Japan to become politically and militarily "European." The Chinese Empire was presided over by the Manchu dynasty, originally alien to the real Chinese and now seemingly decadent. The Emperor Kuang Hsü (1875–1908) was a small boy when he ascended the throne and, though he was hailed as "the son of Heaven" and surrounded with due pomp, he remained a weakling, dependent upon the conservative advice of court mandarins, upon the uncertain support of a corrupt group of military chieftains and civil governors, and upon the vigorous but capricious promptings of his aunt, the Empress Dowager, Tz'ŭ Hsi, who had been regent during his minority. Had it not been for this remarkable old lady, the Manchu dynasty would not have lasted as long as it did, and she was the personification of hostility to "Europe" and the "West."

*Chinese Reaction and "Reform"*

Following the Chino-Japanese War and just when all the European great powers seemed most intent on dismembering his Empire (1898), Kuang Hsü surprised everyone by issuing a series of reforming decrees. The imperial bureaucracy was to be reorganized along European lines. An imperial university and a system of schools were to be established for the study of modern European science as well as ancient Chinese classics. A central cabinet of ministers of the European type was to be instituted, and corresponding changes were to be wrought in the high command of the army. These decrees aroused a storm of opposition from officials, civil and military, who by conviction or interest were wedded to the old order and also from some moderate reformers who thought the action of the Emperor too precipitate. The Empress Dowager Tz'ŭ Hsi put herself at the head of the opposition and cooperated with a prominent army general, Yüan Shih-kai, to effect a palace revolution in September 1898. Kuang Hsü was practically imprisoned, and obliged to assent to the restoration of a regency under Tz'ŭ Hsi. For the next ten years the crafty forceful Dowager Empress was the ruler of China, and the nominal Emperor a shadowy figure in the seclusion of the palace.

Tz'ŭ Hsi promptly annulled the reform decrees, put several reformers to death, and announced her intention of combating all foreign influences. Encouraged by her attitude, reactionaries throughout the Empire gave vent to their hatred of foreigners, and the more violent among them formed a body known **The "Boxers"** as "Righteous Patriotic Fists," or "Boxers," who attacked the property of aliens and massacred Christian missionaries and their Chinese converts. In the spring of 1900 Boxer outrages occurred in all the major cities and reached a climax at Peking, where the German minister was killed and the foreign residents were closely besieged and threatened with extermination. Whereupon an international military expedition, comprising soldiers or marines of Russia, Great Britain, the United States, France, Italy, Germany, and Japan, hastily assembled at Tientsin, fought its way to Peking, and put the Chinese troops to rout and the imperial court to flight. In 1901 Tz'ŭ Hsi reluctantly accepted the Allied terms of peace: China would pay to the several Powers indemnities totaling 333 million dollars, would safeguard foreigners and foreign interests within her territories, and, as a precautionary measure, would permit foreign powers to maintain armed forces for self-protection at Peking and Tientsin.

The reactionary policy of Tz'ŭ Hsi thus proved worse than a failure, and henceforth the somewhat chastened Empress Dowager tried to make amends by restraining anti-foreign agitation and introducing some reforms. The traditional classical education of Chinese officials was modified and some attention given in the schools to natural science, political economy, and modern languages. A commission was sent abroad to investigate the political institutions of the West, and Chinese students were encouraged to attend universities in Europe and America.

These reforms were not radical enough to satisfy the growing party of "Westernizers" among the younger generation of Chinese intellectuals, many of whom by this time had studied abroad and **Sun Yat-sen and Chinese Revolution of 1911–1912** all of whom were coming to believe that Chinese regeneration depended upon getting rid of the Manchu dynasty and its conservative bureaucracy. The leader of the party was Sun Yat-sen, a man of humble origin who had been trained in medicine and had become a Christian and who, though compelled to live in exile, exerted a tremendous influence on the formulation and propagation of a revolutionary program of nationalism, republicanism, and political and social democracy. In 1908 the almost simultaneous deaths of the Dowager Empress Tz'ŭ Hsi and the puppet Emperor Kuang Hsü served to quicken the revolutionary agitation of Sun Yat-sen and his radical following, for the succeeding Emperor, Hsüan T'ung, was only an infant.

In vain the conservative regime at Peking made concessions to the radicals, sanctioning provincial assemblies in 1909 and convoking a National Assembly in 1910. The followers of Sun Yat-sen refused to compromise with the existing government and in October 1911 rose in arms against it. Ambitious military chieftains, including the powerful Yüan Shih-kai, refused or delayed to obey the orders of the court to suppress the rebellion, and very soon the revolutionaries were in possession of several important cities and provinces. In December 1911 a provisional republican government was established at Nanking, with Sun Yat-sen as President, and in the following February the boy-Emperor Hsüan T'ung [1] abdicated and the Manchu dynasty ceased to rule.

To consolidate the new Chinese Republic, Sun Yat-sen turned over the presidency to General Yüan Shih-kai; and to render it "liberal," a constitution was adopted at Nanking in March 1912 providing for a popularly elected parliament to which the President and his ministers should be responsible. All of which was hailed by optimists in Europe and America as indicating the triumph of their "progressive" principles.

In fact, however, the Chinese Revolution of 1911–1912 was but an episode in the long and very painful process of "Europeanizing" the Chinese Empire, and for sometime afterwards China's internal affairs went from bad to worse. The failure and overthrow of the imperial government destroyed the prestige and ended the orderly functioning of the traditional civil and military bureaucracy; and the Republic was too novel and too weak to provide a substantial substitute. Its informed and sincere supporters were only a small fraction of the Chinese nation, intellectuals of the stamp of Sun Yat-sen, inexperienced in prac-

[1] This was his ceremonial name. After his abdication he was known as Henry Pu-yi. For a time he continued to live in the palace at Peking and to receive a pension from the Chinese Republic. Subsequently he made his escape and became a pensioner of Japan, through whose interested offices he was installed in 1932 as Emperor of Manchuria (Manchukuo). See below, p. 607.

tical politics and inclined to be doctrinaire. Between these, constituting a majority in the parliament and forming a political group known as the Kuomintang, and a self-seeking President with an army in back of him, an unequal conflict soon raged. Parliament enacted laws, and the President ignored or violated them. Then, in 1913, when the Kuomintang inspired a revolt, Yüan Shih-kai easily suppressed it and followed up his success by exiling Sun Yat-sen and destroying the parliament. In 1915, by virtue of a "referendum" which he carefully directed, Yüan proclaimed the restoration of the monarchy with himself as Emperor. Resistance was again offered by the Kuomintang and this time also by jealous generals, and only death from disease in 1916 saved Yüan Shih-kai from death by violence.

Siam was a third country of the Far East which came under some degree of European tutelage during the latter part of the **Siam** nineteenth century without losing its identity or sovereignty. True, it was pressed in upon by France from the east and by Great Britain from the west. Both of these European powers deprived it of border provinces, and in 1896 they agreed upon a division of the whole country into "spheres of influence" for themselves. Nevertheless, thanks to an adaptable and patriotic King, Chulalongkorn (1868–1910), the greater part of Siam remained intact and won respect for the orderly progress it made. Chulalongkorn abolished slavery, erected schools and hospitals, modernized the army, remodeled the civil administration, and introduced scientific and mechanical features of Western civilization. He established a standard coinage, postal and telegraph services, and a department of public health. He built a thousand miles of railway. He lighted his capital city of Bangkok with electric lights. He had several of his sons educated in England. At the same time he promoted Siamese nationalism and retained the traditionally autocratic form of government, believing that Siam would then make greater progress than under democratic forms borrowed from Europe.

The Moslem "Near East" and "Middle East" felt the impact of Western European civilization simultaneously with the non-Moslem "Far East," although the relative poverty of the Moslem world as a whole, together with the traditional tribalism and religious fanaticism of its peoples, tended to make it less alluring and less amenable to European imperialism.

In other places we describe the delayed "Europeanization" of the Asiatic provinces of the Ottoman Empire—the introduction of railways, the scramble of European powers for eco- **Moslem** nomic concessions and political preeminence, the re- **Near and** sulting development at the beginning of the twentieth **Middle** century of a sentiment of nationalism and a demand for **East** reform among Turks and Arabs.[1] The Arabs undergoing some "Europeanization" were those of Mesopotamia (Iraq), Syria, and the narrow settled coasts of Arabia. Much of the greater part of the Arabian peninsula was desert, peopled by nomadic warlike tribes who were left usually to their own devices.

The Moslem population of Turkestan, too, was mainly nomadic, though, being better off economically and less bellicose, it was gradually absorbed into the Russian Empire and brought under Russian influence.

Afghanistan, a region considerably larger than France and almost as large as the whole Japanese Empire, was so mountainous and unproductive, and its population, though numbering fewer than six million, was so adept at fighting, that it successfully resisted encroachments of Russia from the northwest and Great Britain from the southeast and preserved both its independence and its "backwardness."

Persia (or Iran), the seat of an ancient empire and civilization, had been for centuries an independent Moslem state, presided over by a "king of kings," or "Shah," and character- **Persia** ized, like most Moslem countries, by religious fanaticism, economic primitiveness, some delightful domestic art, and chronic warfare between ambitious chieftains. In the latter part of the nineteenth century, Persia's internal affairs were immensely complicated by rivalry between Russia and Great Britain for control of the country's resources and government. If Russia supported and influenced one faction, Great Britain supported and dominated an opposing faction. If Russia obtained a concession, Great Britain must be compensated by securing another. At least this was the situation until 1907, when the two Powers agreed to recognize each other's "sphere of influence" in Persia—Russia's in the north and Britain's in the southeast and along the Persian Gulf—and to cooperate in exploitation. Which was better for them but worse for the Persians.

[1] See above, p. 175, and below, p. 347.

In resisting foreign imperialism and effecting needed internal reform, no real leadership was provided by the Persian sovereigns. One Shah after another traveled repeatedly in Europe, but what they chiefly derived therefrom was a taste for European pleasures and an extravagance in satisfying it. To get all the money they could, they imposed burdensome taxes, abetted the official corruption which ate like a canker throughout the government, and mortgaged themselves and their country ever more heavily to Russia and Britain. In vain a party of Nationalists arose and forced the grant of a constitution in 1906 and the deposition of a Shah in 1908. Russian troops, on the pretense of "preserving order," invaded and occupied the northern part of the country, and the Nationalists fell to quarreling among themselves. For a time in 1911 an improvement of Persian conditions was promised by the appointment of disinterested Swedish officers to modernize the native army and of a resourceful young American, Morgan Shuster, to reform the national finances. Within a year, however, Russia obliged the Persian government to dismiss Shuster, who had declared with more truth than prudence that the selfish policies pursued by the Russians and British were largely responsible for the misgovernment and anarchy prevalent in "weakened, war-cursed Persia."

#### 4. CONQUEST OF AFRICA

Northern Africa, like western Asia, had long been overwhelmingly Moslem. Here, since the seventh century, the indigenous Egyptians and Berbers had been largely fused with conquering Arabs and subjected to a succession of essentially oriental despotisms—Arab or Turkish—characterized by common Moslem culture and by incessant strife within and depredations from without. Gradually, too, Moslem religion and Arab customs had been communicated to Negro tribesmen along the eastern coast of Africa and across the Sahara desert into the Sudan. Timbuctu had become a Moslem commercial center in the sixteenth century, and by the second half of the nineteenth century the whole interior of the vast African continent bade fair to become Moslem like the North. By this time, however, the partition and conquest of Africa by European great powers was more startling and impressive than the conversion of primitive Negroes to the tenets of Islam.

*Moslem North Africa*

The northern coastland along the Mediterranean, which had always been in contact, friendly or hostile, with Europe, was loosed from the Ottoman Empire and appropriated piecemeal by various European powers: Algeria by France between 1830 and 1870; Tunis by France in 1881; Egypt by Great Britain in 1882; Tripoli and Cyrenaica by Italy in 1911–1912. Morocco alone had had no nominal connection with the Ottoman Empire, but its native Sultan in the nineteenth century had as many troubles at home and abroad as the Khedive of Egypt, and though like the Ottoman Sultan he profited for some time from the rivalry of European powers he eventually in 1912 had to submit to a division of his country into a major French protectorate and a minor Spanish protectorate.

Prior to 1880, Europeans knew relatively little of Africa as a whole. They had usually referred to it as the "Dark Continent," and had no interest in it beyond the northern shore and a few coastal stations which Portuguese and Dutch, French and British had established here and there as stopping-places on the way to India or for traffic in "gold dust" or, much more lucratively, in Negro slaves. The Portuguese had been most persistent and tenacious in occupying territories on the east and west coasts (Mozambique and Angola, respectively), and the Dutch and British in promoting some colonization in a limited area of South Africa. But the net result, in respect of any Europeanizing of Africa, was slight, and with the abolition of the slave trade in the first half of the nineteenth century it promised to become even less.

*A "Dark Continent"*

In fact, the abolition of the slave trade proved the prelude to a swift partition of almost all Africa among European powers and a rapidly ensuing extension of European conquest and influence from the coastal regions into the far interior. For the abolition of the slave trade was inspired by humanitarian zeal and the new industrialism, and both these phenomena continued to function. Humanitarians were not content to abolish traffic of British or other European slave dealers on the coasts of Africa. They must interfere with the slave-dealing of Arabs and Negroes, and bring light to all benighted humanity; they must push inland and uplift potential slaves and acquaint them with Christianity and European civilization. Moreover, the new industrialism demanded rubber and other raw

*Exploration and Partition*

materials which tropical Africa could supply, and at the same time stimulated the hope that a Europeanized Africa would provide a profitable field for European salesmanship and investment and, through the achievements of modern sanitation, for European colonization.

European penetration of the "Dark Continent" was inaugurated just after the middle of the nineteenth century by a number of intrepid explorers and adventurers, of whom four merit special mention. David Livingstone, a Scottish physician, went to Africa in 1840 as a Protestant missionary, but he won fame less as an evangelist than as an explorer. For thirty years he headed expeditions into the wild jungles of south-central Africa and published accounts which fascinated scientists and aroused a lively interest throughout Europe and America. Toward the close of his life Livingstone seemed to have been lost in the jungle, and a New York newspaper proprietor capitalized the widespread curiosity concerning Livingstone's fate by dispatching a clever and adventurous Anglo-American journalist, Henry Stanley, to find him. Stanley "found" Livingstone in 1871, and then engaged in important explorations of his own, circumnavigating the great lakes of Tanganyika and Victoria and tracing the course of the Congo River. The thrillingly told tale of his trip *Through the Dark Continent* went through countless editions, while Stanley himself interested King Leopold II of Belgium in the commercial possibilities of the Congo region and became the chief "promoter" of that greedy monarch's "Congo Free State." [1]

Another famous European adventurer in Africa was Karl Peters, a German student of British colonial activities and the organizer and chief propagandist of a German colonial society. In 1884 with a few companions he landed on the east coast of Africa, and, by plying native chieftains with grog and presenting them with an assortment of toys, he obtained from them within ten days as many as a dozen "treaties" ceding to his company about 60,000 square miles of territory. The next year he prevailed upon Bismarck to take the company and its land under the formal protection of the German government, and within the next five years, by methods similar to Peters', German East Africa was expanded into a domain of 200,000 square miles.

Even more celebrated as an African "empire builder" was the

[1] On Leopold II and the Congo Free State, see above, p. 109.

Englishman Cecil Rhodes. The son of an Anglican clergyman, he was intended for the church, but being sickly in his youth he was sent off in 1870 to "rough it" in Natal, in South Africa, and soon found wealth as well as health in the newly discovered diamond fields at Kimberley. Then, after returning to England and studying at Oxford, he went back to South Africa and became its outstanding "promotor," financier, and statesman. He acquired an enormous fortune from mining and commercial activities. In 1889 he organized the British South Africa Company, which obtained title, in manner resembling Karl Peters's, to the vast area known later as Rhodesia.

From 1890 to 1896, as prime minister of Cape Colony, Rhodes actively advanced plans for incorporating the Dutch republics of Transvaal and Orange Free State with British South Africa and extending the sway of the British Empire the whole length of Africa northward from the Cape of Good Hope to Alexandria on the Mediterranean. At his death in 1902 he left a part of his fortune as an endowment to provide for the education of select young men from "Anglo-Saxon" countries—the British colonies, the United States, and Germany—as "Rhodes Scholars" at Oxford, the intellectual center of the British Empire.

Under pressure from such active propagandists as Rhodes, Peters, and Stanley, and from a host of explorers, traders, prospectors, and missionaries, who roamed over Africa in the 1870's and 1880's, and in accordance, furthermore, with the evident wishes of industrialists and journalists and zealous patriots at home, various European governments were soon parceling out almost the whole of the African continent among themselves. A claim to a region was asserted, a flag raised, "treaties" negotiated with native chieftains, a police force landed, and a protectorate or "colony" established.

When rival claims to the same region were asserted, the respective European governments involved would negotiate a special "deal," whereby one would be left in possession of the disputed area and the other receive compensation elsewhere, usually at the expense of native tribes. In the incredibly brief span of twenty-seven years—from 1885, when an international congress at Berlin approved and authorized the erection of King Leopold II's Congo Free State and laid down certain simple rules which the powers should observe in acquiring African territory, to

1912, when Morocco passed finally under Franco-Spanish "protection"—the entire continent, with the exception of two very minor countries (Ethiopia and Liberia), was conquered and partitioned by European nations.

The partition occasioned a good deal of friction in international relations, but it was eventually accomplished without direct or immediate recourse to armed conflict among the European powers. The aspiration of Portugal to link up Mozambique on the east coast with Angola on the west, and the desire of the Dutch Boers to retain their independence, alike ran counter to the ambition of Britain to extend its African empire northward from Cape Colony; the Portuguese aspiration was sacrificed by a treaty of 1891 and the Dutch desire by the Boer War of 1899–1902.[1]

**International Rivalry**

Still farther north, the project of a continuous stretch of British dominion from the Cape to Cairo was threatened by the extension of German East Africa inland to the frontiers of the Congo Free State, and by the ambition of France to join Algeria and Tunis not only with its holdings in Senegal and on the Congo but also with its foothold on the Somali coast of the Red Sea in a huge imperial domain that would cover northern Africa from west to east. Britain thought fit to compromise the German claim in a treaty of 1890 and thereby to concede a temporary severance of its projected north-and-south empire. But toward France, Britain was less yielding.

In 1898 a French expedition headed by an army officer, a certain Captain Marchand, proceeded all the way from the mouth of the Congo (on the west coast) to the upper valley of the Nile (in eastern Africa), and here in the Egyptian Sudan, at a little village called Fashoda, the captain hoisted a French flag and asserted French claims to the surrounding country. But the British insisted that the Egyptian Sudan was a part of Egypt and that Egypt was in their own "sphere of influence," and against the French Captain Marchand at Fashoda advanced from Khartum the British General Kitchener with a larger expedition and bigger guns.[2] Under pro-

**Fashoda Crisis**

---

[1] On the Boer War, see above, pp. 66–67.

[2] Kitchener had just won the decisive victory of Omdurman (near Khartum) over the Sudanese natives and had thus fortified the "rights" of Great Britain in the Egyptian Sudan. See above, p. 71.

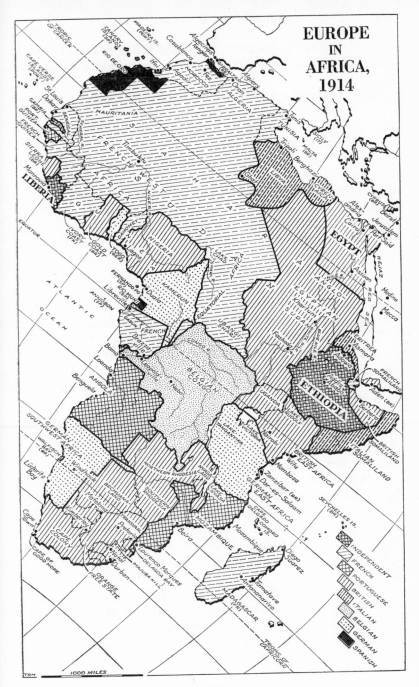

EUROPE
IN
AFRICA,
1914

INDEPENDENT
FRENCH
PORTUGUESE
BRITISH
ITALIAN
BELGIAN
GERMAN
SPANISH

1000 MILES

test and with great reluctance, Marchand withdrew from Fashoda; and by treaty of 1899 France yielded to Britain the Egyptian Sudan.

This treaty of 1899 proved to be the forerunner of a close *entente* concluded between France and Britain in 1904, whereby the latter was entrenched in Egypt and the former assured of a privileged position in Morocco.

The last phase of international negotiations concerning Africa, prior to 1914, had to do chiefly with the effort of Germany to thwart the French in Morocco and, failing in this, to secure "compensation" for Germany at the expense of French Equatorial Africa. A settlement was eventually arrived at in 1911–1912,[1] but the accompanying exacerbation of Franco-German ill-will helped to prepare the way for world war.

By 1914 Europe owned almost all of Africa. Of the eleven and a half million square miles of territory in the continent, almost

**Fruits of European Conquest** four million were French, three and three-quarters million were British, nine hundred thousand were German and about the same number Belgian, eight hundred thousand were Portuguese, six hundred and fifty thousand Italian, and a hundred thousand Spanish, while only the remaining four hundred thousand (barely a thirtieth part of the whole) belonged to independent native states.

Included in the area reckoned as owned by Europe were certain countries which retained native sovereigns, but so long as the Khedive of Egypt had to follow advice of a British "Resident," and the Bey of Tunis or the Sultan of Morocco had to obey instructions of French "High Commissioners," such countries could hardly be termed independent.

Included within European Africa, moreover, were gigantic tracts either quite unfit for European habitation, such as French Equatorial Africa, Belgian Congo, and British Nigeria, or quite unprofitable for European exploitation, such as the great Sahara Desert.

Yet none could doubt that toward the end of the nineteenth century and at the beginning of the twentieth, enormous strides were taken toward Europeanizing Africa. It was not merely that European powers held political sway or that European immi-

---

[1] See below, pp. 315–316.

grants were coming into South Africa from the British Isles and into North Africa from Italy and France. The Negro tribesmen of tropical Africa were being taught by European missionaries and school teachers, were learning European languages and ways, were more or less docilely working for European capitalists and serving under European army officers. Even the Arabs of desert Africa were becoming accustomed to the profits of European trade and the penalties of European police. Optimists, with whom the first decade of the twentieth century abounded, were eloquent in voicing the expectation that within another generation or two the formerly "Dark Continent" would bask in the full sunshine of modern material civilization—with railways and telegraph wires radiating everywhere, with modern science bringing salubrity to the tropical jungles and fertility to the desert sands, and with the twin spirits of "progress" and "prosperity" duly communicated from white men to black and tan.

Two African countries were still independent—and correspondingly "backward." The larger of the two was Ethiopia (or Abyssinia), a landlocked Negro state wedged in the mountainous country between Somaliland and the Egyptian Sudan. Its dominant tribes had been Christian of a primitive sort since the fourth century, and in the latter part of the nineteenth century its "King of Kings," the Emperor Menelek II (1889–1913), who claimed descent from King Solomon and the Queen of Sheba, succeeded in fighting off Italian invaders and winning from Italy, and other European powers, a recognition of Ethiopia's independence.[1] Even the Emperor Menelek, however, was not averse to Europeanizing his army and permitting French capitalists to construct a railway from his capital to the coast.

*Ethiopia*

The smaller of the two independent African states was Liberia, which had been established on the west coast in 1847 by emancipated Negro slaves from the United States. Its civilized English-speaking inhabitants were greatly outnumbered and given a good deal of trouble by barbarous natives in the hinterland, and gradually its area was hemmed in and reduced by encroachments of the British from the west and of the French from the east and north. In the first decade of the twentieth century it was a small, poor country, and the main question was whether it would be Europeanized and rendered "progressive"

*Liberia*

[1] See above, pp. 128–129.

through its own efforts or through the forceful intervention of France or Britain or perhaps the United States.

By 1914 Africa, along with Asia, was being subjected to a process of Europeanization which promised to produce in the near future, out of the distinctively Western civilization of Europe, America, and Australia, a common material civilization for the whole world. And by this time, the world as a whole was known as it had never been known before. In 1909 an indefatigable Arctic explorer, Robert Peary, reached the North Pole and in the ice which covered the ocean depths below planted an American flag. In 1911 a Norwegian explorer, Roald Amundsen, perilously making his way over the big, ice-encased, and mountainous continent of Antarctica, reached the South Pole.

### 5. PEACE EFFORTS AND THREATENING CRISES

At the beginning of the twentieth century, there was popular optimism about the chances of maintaining peace and increasing cooperation among the advanced and powerful nations of Europe and America. These nations still waged wars, it was recognized, against "backward" peoples and in "uncivilized" parts of the world, but it was obvious that among themselves there had been no violent conflict since 1871. Whence it seemed reasonable to suppose that before long their world dominance would enable them to enforce a world peace.

*International Co-operation*

Certainly the great powers were furnishing numerous examples of pacific cooperation. By joint action at the Congress of Berlin of 1878, they prevented the Russo-Turkish War from precipitating a much vaster struggle wherein Great Britain and Austria-Hungary might easily have become involved with Russia.[1] At another Congress of Berlin in 1884–1885, they agreed upon a set of rules which helped to preserve peace among them in their conquest and partition of Africa. In 1885 Austria, with the consent of the other great powers, stopped a war between Bulgaria and Serbia.

In 1897 Russia, Great Britain, France, and Italy cooperated to end an armed conflict between Greece and the Ottoman Empire. In 1900, all the European great powers, together with Japan and the United States, intervened in China to suppress the Boxer insurrection; and with politeness if not perfect sincerity

[1] See above, pp. 159–162.

they endorsed the American proposal that China's territorial integrity should be maintained and its trade doors kept open to all.

Meanwhile, a special effort was being made to insure international peace on the American continents. In 1881 the United States invited the several countries of Latin America to participate in a Pan-American Conference "for the purpose of considering and discussing the methods of preventing war between the nations of America." The first such conference was held at Washington in 1889, a second at Mexico City in 1901, a third at Rio de Janeiro in 1906, and a fourth at Buenos Aires in 1910.

For other specific purposes, there emerged a multiplicity of international organizations. All the "civilized" nations of the world joined the Red Cross society, which had been founded in 1864. Thirty formed a Universal Telegraph Union (1875). Twenty-three agreed to make common use of the metric system of weights and measures (1875). Sixty adhered to a Universal Postal Union, created in 1878, with headquarters at Berne, in Switzerland. Nineteen ratified a convention of 1883 for the standardization of patent laws. Fifteen signed another convention of 1887 providing for practically uniform copyright laws.

The judicial settlement of international disputes was gaining favor likewise. Great Britain and the United States developed a habit of submitting their disputes to arbitration—the *Alabama* claims in 1871–1872, a controversy over Bering Sea in 1892, a dispute over the boundary between Alaska and Canada in 1903—and with such success that the possibility of war between the two major English-speaking countries seemed more and more remote and well-nigh unthinkable.

In 1886 Pope Leo XIII arbitrated a colonial dispute between Germany and Spain. In 1902 King Edward VII of Great Britain arbitrated a boundary dispute between Chile and Argentina. In 1909 France and Germany submitted a Moroccan dispute to international arbitration.

It should be borne in mind that all the governmental arbitrations and conventions and all the cooperative efforts of Pan-American Conferences and European Congresses betokened and strengthened popular interest in international solidarity. In the latter part of the nineteenth century, as industrialization progressed and the most diverse localities and nationalities were knit together by railways, steamships, telegraphs, and cables, the number and importance of common concerns rapidly increased. There was a prodigious stimulation of trade and travel from one country to another.

The international character of industrial and commercial capitalism was emphasized by banks and corporations which outgrew the country where they originated and became world-wide in their ramification and functioning. The international character of the problems of industrial workers was stressed by international congresses of Socialists and by international federations of cooperative societies and trade unions. An international agricultural institute was founded at Rome in 1905. Similarly, in the political sphere, earnest advocates of parliamentary government organized an international Parliamentary Union (1889), and proponents of woman suffrage and feminism took to holding international congresses.

Religion, too, felt the same general impulse. Protestant Christians of a hundred divergent creeds met in world congresses, and Catholic Christians, more mindful than ever of the universal traditions of their faith, instituted in 1881 a series of Eucharistic Congresses, which drew large numbers of clergymen and laymen from many climes now to Paris, now to London, now to Jerusalem, now to Montreal. For the advancement of science and learning, moreover, there were periodical world congresses of distinguished physicists, chemists, biologists, historians, and economists, and exchange of professors and students between the universities of different countries. There was developing around the globe a community of intellectual interests, the product of what was termed "the international mind."

Pacifist agitation was growing. Especially after 1878, associations of professed pacifists multiplied throughout the Western world, and their international congresses became regular annual events after 1889. The movement was patronized, moreover, by outstanding industrialists. Alfred Nobel, a Swedish scientist and capitalist, devoted the major part of the princely fortune which he had amassed from the manufacture of high explosives to the cause of international peace. Andrew Carnegie, a Scottish-American business man, drew liberally upon the wealth that he had accumulated in the steel industry to endow pacifist propaganda and to build a "temple of peace" at The Hague and a Pan-American "palace" at Washington.

*Pacifist Movement*

To the generation of pacifists that flourished in the first decade of the twentieth century, war, at least among great civilized nations, seemed anachronistic and therefore fated to disappear in the near future. The capitalists of every progressive country had too many foreign investments or were too involved in foreign trade to welcome war, and they were too influential to be ignored by their several governments. The industrial workers had too much to lose from a state of war in the way of employment and wages, and, besides, many of them were so actively identified with international Socialism as to threaten a revolutionary overturn of any government which might engage in foreign war. The intellectual classes were too "enlightened" and by this time too internationally minded not to perceive the fallacies in all arguments and pretexts for war. The Christian churches were traditionally committed to support of peace.

Pacifists were somewhat troubled by the obvious fact that since 1860 military and naval armaments had been increasing in almost every country. To be sure, most advocates of heavy national armament, themselves influenced wittingly or unwittingly by the pacifist spirit of the age, insisted that all such armament was strictly defensive, that it constituted mere preparedness against dreadful but possible eventualities and was the surest pledge of enduring peace. Nevertheless, foremost pacifists scented danger in military and naval preparedness, and many other persons who were not professionally pacifist complained of the growing burdens of taxation which that kind of "peace insurance" entailed. It was argued that competitive national armaments would lead more or less inevitably to international war, which, in the contemporary machine age, would be on so gigantic a scale and so costly as to be utterly ruinous to Europe and all western civilization. Hence, a conspicuous and attractive plank in the pacifist platform was the demand for a limitation of armaments by international agreement, coupled usually with a plea for the establishment of an international court of arbitration.

For the express purpose of meeting this demand, the Tsar Nicholas II of Russia, with the concurrence of Queen **Hague** Wilhelmina of the Netherlands, convoked an inter- **Peace Con-** national peace conference at The Hague in 1899. **ferences** "The preservation of peace," the Tsar said, "has become an object of international policy." At the conference the sovereign states of

Europe and Asia and likewise the United States and Mexico were represented—twenty-six nations in all. No agreement could be reached on any general limitation of armaments, but steps were taken to restrict the use of certain weapons in the event of war, to codify international law, and to establish a court of arbitration.

In 1907, with the prompting of President Theodore Roosevelt of the United States and on the formal invitation of the Tsar, a second international peace conference was held at The Hague, representing this time forty-four governments, including nineteen in America. Again the much-mooted question of general limitation of armaments was left unanswered, but certain humane amendments were made to the laws of maritime and land war, an international prize court was provided for, and conventions were adopted requiring a formal declaration of war before the opening of hostilities and restricting the employment of force for the collection of foreign debts. Finally, the holding of similar conferences at regular intervals in the future was recommended.

Here, optimistic pacifists imagined, was the real beginning of an organized international community, with its capital at The Hague, with its periodic congresses, with its statutes and codes, with its court of arbitration. If the German Empire, the United States, and Switzerland could be organized and function successfully as federal states without internal strife, why should not external war be banished through an International Federation of the World? In fact, the international court of arbitration was duly instituted, and by it several international disputes were pacifically settled between 1901 and 1914. A third Hague conference was projected for 1915; it might take a big step forward on the road of international cooperation and peace.

Before 1915, however, the prospect of a peaceful twentieth century was obliterated by world war. The pacifist ideal was not to be easily realized. In truth, as we now look back upon the first years of the twentieth century, we can all see that they held an even greater promise of war than of peace and that the pacifists of the time, like most of their contemporaries, looked so intently on evidences of material and scientific progress as to neglect the more fateful evidences of impending disaster.

Actually, international cooperation was less substantial than international competition. This was accentuated by a rampant nationalism, which had already inspired the series of wars for the unification of Italy and of Germany, and which became progressively more forceful and intolerant after 1870. It gave popular support and impetus to competition of one nation with another in armaments, tariffs, imperialistic enterprise, and prestige. Within Europe, it constantly embittered relations between France and Germany, and by the opening of the twentieth century it was gravely menacing the integrity and very existence not only of the Ottoman Empire but also of the Dual Monarchy of Austria-Hungary.

*International Competition*

The imperialism of the age, it must be borne in mind, was nationalistic even more than economic, and as such it tended to increase the jealousy and friction among European nations engaging in it. Though it occasioned no outright war between European great powers, it motivated the Spanish-American War of 1898, the Boer War of 1899–1902, and the Russo-Japanese War of 1904–1905. It also intensified the rivalry of the great powers for control of weaker powers, both inside and outside of Europe. The big stakes after 1900 were the Chinese and Ottoman Empires, and possibly the oversea dominions of the lesser European powers of Portugal, the Netherlands, and Belgium.

Aggravating the nationalist and imperialist rivalry was the disturbed state of the European "balance of power," particularly after 1900. Previously, there had been a Triple Alliance of Germany, Austria-Hungary, and Italy, and a Dual Alliance of France and Russia, with Great Britain in "splendid isolation." [1] On the eve of the twentieth century, however, a considerable amount of anti-British cooperation between the two Continental alliances, especially in China and during the Boer War, alarmed Great Britain and caused it to depart from its traditional isolationist policy and to seek special friends abroad. To obtain them on the Continent was at first very difficult. On the one hand, an intense naval and commercial rivalry was developing with Germany; and on the other hand, imperialistic rivalry was acute with France in Africa and with Russia in the Far East.

*Britain's Search for Security*

In the belief at first that it would be easier and more rewarding to obtain the friendly cooperation of Germany than that of the Dual Alliance of France and Russia, the British government

[1] See above, pp. 77, 80, 136–137, 167–168.

sounded out the German government in 1901 regarding a special understanding between the two countries. Germany insisted, however, that Britain should join the Triple Alliance, and the British were unwilling to assume the definite and far-reaching commitments of that alliance.[1] So the Anglo-German negotiations broke down, and Great Britain looked elsewhere for friends.

**Overtures to Germany**

In 1902, in order to check Russian advance in Asia, Britain entered into an alliance with Japan. This provided that if either Japan or Britain should become involved in war with two powers over China or Korea the other would give military assistance. In 1905 the Anglo-Japanese alliance was renewed for ten years, with the added stipulation that both nations would fight if either should be attacked by a single power in India as well as in the Far East.

**Alliance with Japan**

Fortified by the Japanese alliance in Asia, Great Britain next sought to safeguard its position in Africa through a friendly understanding with France. The British overtures were favorably received by the French foreign minister, Théophile Delcassé, who was inveterately anti-German and perceived in them an opportunity to secure for France another friend against Germany. Consequently in 1904 were signed several Franco-British treaty conventions which not only gave Great Britain free rein in Egypt, and France in Morocco, but paved the way for the development of cordial cooperation between the peoples and governments of France and Britain—the so-called *Entente Cordiale*.

**Entente Cordiale with France**

Meanwhile, Delcassé, in his anti-German policy, was courting Italy and inducing it to terminate its long feud with France,[2] even at the expense of its loyalty to the Triple Alliance. By a convention of 1900, Italy recognized the French protectorate over Tunis and French claims to Morocco, and France accorded Italy a free hand in Tripoli and Cyrenaica. By a second secret convention, in 1902, Italy and France mutually pledged themselves to remain neutral if either should be attacked by a third power or if either, "as the result of a direct provocation, should find itself obliged, in defence of its honor or security, to take the initiative of a declaration of war." This

**Franco-Italian Agreements**

---

[1] See above, pp. 136–137.
[2] See above, pp. 128, 136.

arrangement was cemented by a visit of the French President to the Italian King in 1904.

To counter these maneuvers, the German Emperor William II encouraged Russia to go to war with Japan in 1904, and then, in July 1905, when Russian troops had been decisively defeated in Manchuria, he met the Russian Tsar at Bjorkö and persuaded him to agree to a Russo-German alliance, directed actually, though not expressly, against Great Britain and open to French adherence. France declined to adhere to it, and the advisers of the two Emperors, deeming it quixotic, practically nullified it.

Indeed, the Russo-Japanese War of 1904–1905 had highly important effects on the balance of power in Europe. The war in its early stages endangered the recently formed Anglo-French Entente by pitting Russia, the ally of France, against Japan, the ally of Great Britain. British sentiment was then strongly anti-Russian, and the impressionable Russian Tsar seemed to be pro-German.

But with the final defeat of Russia, and the collapse of the project for a Russo-German alliance, the situation changed radically. Russia reacted sharply against German influence, which was blamed, rather unjustly, for the disastrous outcome. On the other hand, Great Britain lost its fear of Russia and began to perceive advantages in coming to terms with France's ally. Consequently, in 1907, the British and Russian governments managed to arrive at a mutual understanding concerning disputed spheres of influence in *Triple Entente, including Russia* Persia, Afghanistan, and China, and to sign conventions which paralleled the Entente between Great Britain and France with a second Entente between Great Britain and Russia. Japan, also, was brought into harmonious relations with the new Entente, through a Russo-Japanese convention of 1910 and through the renewal of the Anglo-Japanese alliance in 1911.

In Germany, meanwhile, many publicists and the government itself were viewing with alarm what was termed a "hostile encirclement." Italy was suspected, correctly as we now know, of disloyalty to Germany and Austria. Russia was allied with France. Great Britain was in ententes with France and Russia. Japan was allied with Britain. *German Reaction vs. Entente Powers* Austria, alone of the great powers, stood by Germany.

From 1905 to 1914 German diplomacy sought in divers ways

to break up the Ententes, to bolster Austria and increase its prestige, to win the Ottoman Empire as an ally, and to strengthen Germany's position as a great world power. The new German effort did not break up the Ententes, but it produced periodic crises in the relations between the Entente Powers (Great Britain, France, and Russia) and the Central Powers (Germany and Austria-Hungary)—crises which grew ever more menacing to the preservation of peace and more symptomatic of an impending war of huge dimensions. These crises had to do alternately with Morocco and with the Near East.

In the case of Morocco, a crisis was precipitated at the end of March 1905. By this time, the French foreign minister, Delcassé, had plans well advanced for the establishment of a French protectorate over the greater part of the country. He had obtained the assent of Italy in 1900 and of Great Britain in 1904; and he had just reached an agreement with Spain whereby it would obtain a protectorate over the part not appropriated by France. To be sure, the independence of Morocco had been affirmed by an international congress at Madrid in 1880. But Morocco was a backward and brigand-ridden country, bordering on the French empire in Africa and on Spanish posts on the Medi-
**Moroccan Crises** terranean; and its fate seemed to Delcassé to be a practical concern of only France and Spain. The German Chancellor, Bülow, thought otherwise. He was anxious to assert Germany's interest in Morocco and to utilize the occasion to check Delcassé and to weaken the Entente between France and Great Britain.

Bülow picked a favorable opportunity—exactly three weeks after the decisive defeat of the Russians by the Japanese in the battle of Mukden—when he knew that Russia could give no support to France. On that date he had the Emperor William II disembark at Tangier and declare in a vigorous speech that he came to visit the Sultan of Morocco as an independent sovereign in whose lands all foreign powers were to hold the same footing and enjoy the same rights.

There followed a brief moment of awful suspense. Then Delcassé resigned, and his colleagues in the French ministry agreed to submit the whole Moroccan question to an international congress. The Congress, meeting at Algeciras in Spain in 1906, did not reveal the cleavage between France and Great Britain which

Bülow had hoped for. On the contrary, Britain consistently backed the French position, and so did Italy. The agreement finally reached at Algeciras, while paying lip service to the territorial integrity of Morocco and the sovereignty of its Sultan and pledging the "open door" to merchants and investors of all the powers, authorized France and Spain to instruct and officer a native police force and to oversee the execution of "reforms." To all intents and purposes, it was a French victory.

Civil war in Morocco and outrages against foreigners, especially Frenchmen, afforded the French government an excuse to land marines at Casablanca in 1907. Germany repeatedly expostulated against the continued presence of French troops in Morocco; and in 1908 an attempt on the part of the German consul at Casablanca to protect from arrest a number of deserters from the French foreign legion precipitated a second crisis, which was successfully passed in 1909 by reference of the questions at stake to the Hague Tribunal. The simultaneous negotiation of a special Franco-German convention in 1909 seemed to preclude further misunderstandings. Germany put on record that its interests in Morocco were "only economic" and pledged itself, so long as "economic equality" was safeguarded, to recognize the political preponderance of France.

But the Franco-German agreement of 1909 was not observed. The French discriminated against German trade and investment in Morocco, and the Germans protested against the tightening of French political and military control. A new and severe crisis was precipitated in 1911 by the action of France in sending an army to Fez, the Moroccan capital, "to restore order." Germany then dispatched a warship to the Moroccan port of Agadir, ostensibly to safeguard German mining property, but with a significant hint that the warship would be withdrawn as soon as conditions were sufficiently settled to admit of French withdrawal from Fez. The gravity of the international situation was felt throughout Europe, and as neither Germany nor France showed signs of yielding, the prospect of war between them loomed large.

Nevertheless, the French had to recognize that without the active military support of their Russian ally they stood little chance of waging successful war against Germany, and such support they could hardly expect in view of Russia's still weakened condition. France would have to make some concessions to

Germany. On the other hand, Germany had no serious intention of fighting for Morocco; rather, it was utilizing the occasion to compel France to grant it "compensation" elsewhere. Diplomatic negotiations were therefore undertaken between the two powers; and they were expedited by a public warning from Great Britain that it would not tolerate excessive German demands on France.

The outcome was a second Franco-German convention, whereby Germany promised not to oppose the establishment of a French protectorate over Morocco, and France agreed to maintain the "open door" there and to cede two strips of French Equatorial Africa to Germany. Although France was thus enabled in 1912 to settle the political question of Morocco satisfactorily to itself (and incidentally also to Spain), the Agadir crisis in 1911 served to quicken anti-German sentiment in France, and at the same time to consolidate the friendship between France and Great Britain. On the other hand, Germans felt that their legitimate interests in Morocco had been prejudiced and their position as a world power jeopardized by the joint machinations of the French and the British.

Still more disquieting than the Moroccan crises were the crises in the Near East, where Russia and Austria-Hungary, instead of **Austro-** France and Germany, were the protagonists. But while **German** in the case of Morocco, Russia, on account of its weak-**Ambitions** ened military position, was able to give but little effec-**in Near** tive support to its French ally, in the case of the Near **East** Eastern crises Germany had economic motives and powerful military means for backing Austria-Hungary.

From the opening of the twentieth century the Austro-Hungarian government favored the political and economic expansion of the Dual Monarchy in a southerly direction through Bosnia and Macedonia to Salonica on the Ægean, and many influential Germans cherished the idea of "Germanizing" the Balkan states and the Ottoman Empire. So Germany and Austria-Hungary, acting in harmony, gradually extended their political and economic influence in southeastern Europe. In 1899 the Emperor William II ostentatiously visited the Ottoman Sultan Abdul Hamid II, and in 1903 a German company obtained a concession for the construction of a railway across Asia Minor, Armenia, and the fertile valleys of the Tigris and Euphrates, to Bagdad and the head of the Persian Gulf. Austrian influence was paramount at the Serbian court from the Congress of Berlin (1878) to the assassination of King Alexander in 1903; and Prince Ferdinand of Bulgaria, a German by birth, was long estranged from Russia and dependent upon Austria-Hungary. The King of Rumania was a kinsman and ally of the German Emperor, and the wife of the future King Constantine of Greece was a sister of William II. In a word, the Teutonic powers stood in the way of the Russian ambition of ousting the Turks from Europe and ruling at Constantinople; they began to buttress the Turk, to train his army, to exploit his country, and to seek to minimize both Russian and British influence throughout southeastern Europe.

In 1903 the Balkan policy of Germany and Austria-Hungary received a check. A palace revolution at Belgrade put an end to the rule of the pro-Austrian dynasty in Serbia and brought to the throne a King who was ardently in sympathy with the nationalist propaganda of the Serbs and openly dependent on Russia.

Balkan crises ensued in 1908, and again, most ominously, in 1912–1913. As they were precursors of a third crisis which in 1914 precipitated World War I, we defer their story to the next chapter.

# CHAPTER VIII

## POLITICAL AND MILITARY DISTURBANCES, 1901–1913

### 1. BRITISH DISPUTES ON SOCIAL REFORM AND IRISH HOME RULE

 LECTION of 1906 in Great Britain was in the nature of a peaceful political revolution. It closed a period of Conservative preponderance which had lasted since 1874 and put the Liberal party in power with overwhelming popular support.[1]

But, what was most significant about it, the victorious Liberals of 1906 were quite different in outlook and purpose from those who had followed Gladstone back in the 1870's. They represented a younger generation intent upon a thorough democratizing of government and upon radical social—even "socialistic"—reform.[2] This was, of course, a basic departure from the middle-class and *laissez-faire* liberalism of the nineteenth century. It reflected a remarkable change which several developments had gradually brought about.

**Ascendancy of Socializing Liberals**

One was the undermining with Liberals, as with the public at large, of the older faith in "classical" economics, in individual competition and governmental *laissez-faire,* and the substitution for it of an interest in sociology, in collective undertakings and democratic control. John Stuart Mill gave a new slant to "liberal" political economy by distinguishing between the production of wealth, governed by "natural laws," and the distribution of wealth, susceptible of regulation by state law. Other economists and

---

[1] The Liberals took office in 1905; the election of 1906 confirmed them in office. See above, p. 54.

[2] The British "revolution" of 1906, it may be noted, was comparable with what happened in the United States in 1933 when "Liberal" Democrats took office and ushered in the "New Deal."

political scientists praised what foreign or colonial countries—
such as Germany or Australia—were doing to ameliorate the condition of workmen and dwelt upon the "backwardness" of Britain
in this respect.

Second, there was much discussion and criticism of "landlordism" in Britain—the monopoly of agricultural land by titled
nobles and country gentlemen, and the ownership of urban land
and congested urban tenements by a relatively small number of
wealthy aristocrats. Discussion of the problem, with denunciation
of the evil effects of landlordism on the working classes in town
and countryside, was stimulated by lectures of an American reformer, Henry George, and by his cogent and eloquent book,
*Progress and Poverty*. A young Welsh Liberal, David Lloyd
George, was especially impressed by Henry George.

Third, and most effective, there was extraordinary agitation,
political as well as economic, on the part of urban workmen.
Among these, particularly among skilled factory operatives and
miners, trade unions had been steadily developing. For some time,
the leaders and the rank-and-file were under the spell of Liberals
like John Bright; "liberal" in philosophy and mainly so in political affiliation, they sought amelioration of their lot less through
state action than through direct bargaining with employers. At
the end of the 1880's and at the beginning of the 1890's, however,
British trade unionism was influenced by two novel movements.
One was an unprecedented activity among "unskilled" workers
—dock laborers, etc.—who, under young "radical" leaders, participated in a series of strikes involving much violence, repeated
defiance of the government, and no little criticism of the conservative tactics of earlier trade unionism. The other was an
advance of Marxian socialism in Britain.

In 1881 a group of intellectuals, including William Morris,
the artist, and Henry Hyndman, a scholar and man of fashion,
formed the "Social Democratic Federation" for the propagation
of revolutionary Marxian socialism among the masses. In 1883
the "Fabian Society" came into being, and presently, enlisting the
talents of such persons as George Bernard Shaw and Sidney Webb
(a government employee and the historian of British trade unionism), and without adhering strictly to "Marxism," it conducted
a brilliant literary campaign in behalf of the socialization of industry, land, and government. In 1893, Keir Hardie, a Scottish

miner, founded the "Independent Labor party," which adopted a program in harmony with "revisionist" Marxism and put up candidates of its own for election to Parliament in opposition to those of the Liberal and Conservative parties.

Professed Socialists were only a small minority among British trade unionists, but they were very active and increasingly influential with the majority. And trade unionists, as they became more "radical" and more politically minded, grew in numbers and resources. The number of major English unions mounted in 1890 to 490, with a membership of 650,000 and an annual income of £1,000,000; and in 1906 to 675, with a membership of 1,720,000 and an annual income of £2,700,000. In the meantime, an event of first-rate importance brought the whole trade-union movement into active politics. For, in 1901 the House of Lords, in its capacity as the supreme law court of the realm, decided that a trade union was legally liable for damages resulting from any strike conducted by its members. This judicial decision—the so-called Taff Vale decision—imperiled not only the "right to strike" but the whole trade-union organization and its financial resources. Almost immediately, trade-union leaders effected a political coali-

**Rise of Labor Party** tion with the Independent Labor party, the Social Democratic Federation, and the Fabian Society. The coalition became known as the "Labor Party." It was semi-Socialist and semi-trade unionist. While declaring its willingness to cooperate with any other political party which would forward labor legislation, it strove to be a distinct working-class party. In the general election of 1906, it elected twenty-nine workmen to seats in Parliament.[1]

The rise of the Labor party was important in itself, and also for its effects on the other parties. It gave impetus to the conversion of the Liberal party from *laissez-faire* to the championship of social legislation, and it contributed to the defeat of the Conservative party in the election of 1906. The Conservative leaders were too divided over tariff protection and

**Liberal Leaders** too compromised by the Taff Vale decision to keep their hold on the British masses. On the other hand, the Liberal leaders could now win a broad popular

---

[1] In addition, eleven workmen were elected by the Miners' Federation, which was not formally affiliated with the Labor party until 1908, and thirteen workmen were elected as candidates of the Liberal party.

following. A "radical" group among them, including David Lloyd George [1] and Winston Churchill, [2] vied with Laborites in espousing social reform and attacking "landlordism," while an "imperialist" group, embracing Herbert Asquith [3] and Sir Edward Grey, [4] promised that in the pursuit of domestic reform a Liberal government would not neglect British interests abroad. And binding the two groups together was the common advocacy of free trade. This still remained a vital tradition of British Liberals—and the British public—at the very time when nationalism and imperialism and "socialism" were transforming all the other tenets of historic liberalism.

For ten years, from 1905 to 1915, the Liberals were in office. At first the "radical" Campbell-Bannerman was Prime Minister, with the "imperial" Asquith as Chancellor of the Exchequer and chief assistant. Then, in 1908, when Campbell-Bannerman fell sick and died, Asquith became Prime Minister, with the "radical"

[1] David Lloyd George, a Welsh lawyer of the lower middle class, Baptist in religion, had come into prominence in the 1890's as a flaming antagonist of the landed aristocracy, the Anglican Church, and the imperialism of Joseph Chamberlain. A zealous Welsh nationalist, he was ardently pacifist during the Boer War; and coming from the "common people," he thought of himself as their special spokesman. By reason of his popular following and his gifts as a debater in the House of Commons, he was given a place in the Liberal government. Before long, he was its most influential member.

[2] Winston Churchill, son of Lord Randolph Churchill and his American wife, was a natural heir to "Tory democracy"; and with great intellectual talents he combined a forceful impetuosity. After experiences in the army and in journalism (he was a press correspondent during the Boer War), he entered Parliament in 1900 as a Conservative, but his enthusiasm for free trade and social reform soon caused him to break with his party and join the Liberals.

[3] Herbert Asquith, the son of a manufacturer, liberal and non-conformist, had entered Parliament in 1886 and, following the lead of Lord Rosebery, had become an apologist for the "new imperialism." At the same time, however, he clung to the traditional free-trade tenets of the Liberal party, and bore the brunt of the fight against Chamberlain's tariff proposals. In 1905, as first lieutenant to Sir Henry Campbell-Bannerman, he became Chancellor of the Exchequer; and in 1908 he succeeded his chief as Prime Minister. Much later he was raised to the peerage as Earl of Oxford and Asquith, by which title he is now known.

[4] Sir Edward Grey belonged to a famous family of Whig aristocrats, one of whose members had sponsored the Reform Act of 1832 (see *Modern Europe to 1870*, pp. 645–646). He was a country gentleman whose very respectability gave him a position in Liberal politics which his actual achievements in Parliament from 1885 to 1905 hardly warranted. He was recognized as an "imperialist" disciple of Lord Rosebery, sympathetic with the Boer War and with the foreign policies of the Conservative government; and as such he was named foreign minister in Campbell-Bannerman's Liberal cabinet. This post he continued to occupy during the momentous years from 1905 to 1916, when he was honorably retired and elevated to the peerage as Viscount Grey of Fallodon.

Lloyd George as Chancellor of the Exchequer and chief assistant. While free trade was maintained, the central feature of the period was social legislation. In this the Liberals were consistently backed and pushed on by the new Labor party; and until 1909 the Conservative party usually acquiesced. Indeed, until then the British nation seemed a unit in support of democratic social reform. From 1909 to 1914, however, as the Liberal program assumed an ever more socialistic complexion and became entangled with the question of home rule for Ireland, bitter disputes arose in Parliament and in the nation at large, and Conservative opposition was vociferously voiced.

Favors were accorded to trade-union activity, both economic and political. A "trade disputes act" in 1906 practically reversed the Taff Vale decision by protecting the funds of trade unions against suits for damages and expressly allowed trade-union pickets to employ "peaceful persuasion" in strikes. In 1911, in order that trade unionists might better afford to sit in the House of Commons, Parliament authorized the payment of regular salaries to its members. In 1913 it legalized the use of trade-union funds for electoral and other political purposes.

**Favors to Trade Unionism**

Meanwhile, a series of enactments extended the scope of state intervention in industry and of state help to workmen. A "workmen's compensation act" of 1906 applied the principle of employers' liability on a much larger scale than the act which Joseph Chamberlain had sponsored in 1897.[1] It required almost every employer to insure his workmen against accidents and against certain industrial diseases. A "labor exchange act" of 1909 set up a system of free public employment bureaus to inform the unemployed where work might be had and, if necessary, to pay for their transportation thither. A "trade boards act" of 1909 established special boards, composed of representatives of employers and employees in equal numbers, to fix a "minimum wage" which should be paid to workers in "sweated industries." In 1912 minimum-wage legislation was enacted for the benefit of coal miners.

**Welfare Legislation**

Special responsibility was assumed by the state for children, for old people, and for the employment and health of the whole nation. A comprehensive "children's act" of 1908 sought to regu-

[1] See above, p. 52.

late in considerable detail many phases of child life, providing free medical attendance at childbirth and free medical examination and care of infants and young children, prescribing exceptional treatment of juvenile offenders, facilitating the removal of children from homes where they were abused to public institutions where they would be cared for, and enlarging the opportunities of young persons for recreation and for part-time schooling. At the other extreme of human life, an "old-age pensions act" of the same year obligated the state to pay a subsidy to every needy old person; by 1913 a million elderly Britishers were receiving old-age pensions from the public treasury. To improve the living conditions of the urban masses, a "housing and town planning act" of 1909 authorized public authorities to condemn and tear down unsanitary tenements and replace them with parks and "model dwellings." And capping the whole series of social enactments was the "national insurance act" of 1912. This compelled employers and employees to contribute to funds, to which the state made a special contribution, for the insurance of almost all industrial workers "against loss of health and for the prevention and cure of sickness" and, simultaneously, for the insurance of certain specified categories of workmen against unemployment.

To most of this social legislation, there was comparatively little opposition. The Laborites complained that it did not go far enough, and a handful of individualistic Liberals (survivors of an earlier day) denounced it as going much too far. The Conservative minority in the House of Commons was apt to be critical in debate—not so much of the measures themselves as of the Liberal ministers who sponsored them—and then to concur in voting them, though in a few instances the Conservative majority in the House of Lords imposed amendments which weakened the measures and rendered them less "radical." In general, however, strenuous partisanship was not manifest until David Lloyd George brought forward, as Chancellor of the Exchequer, his budget proposals of 1909 for meeting the greatly increased public expenditure necessitated in part by the new social legislation and in part by the costs of military and naval armaments.

Lloyd George was faced with the problem not only of getting more money but of getting it by direct taxation, for the free-trade principles of the Liberal party, and also the Labor party,

precluded him from resorting to indirect taxes in the form of tariff
duties as Joseph Chamberlain and a section of the Conservative
**Lloyd** party urged. The solution which Lloyd George offered
**George** was sensational; and to aristocrats and the well-to-do,
**Budget** to the leading lights of the Conservative party, it was
**and Party** shocking. He frankly proposed, in his budget of 1909,
**Strife**
to put the financial burden of social reform on the shoulders of
the rich and to make the taxation of landlords a means of effecting still more radical social reform. Specifically, he asked Parliament to levy, in addition to customary stamp taxes and excise
taxes, a steeply graduated income tax (with a seemingly con-
fiscatory "super-tax" on very large fortunes), a heavy inheritance
tax, and special taxes on motor cars, on undeveloped land, and on
the "unearned increment" of land values. He would force the
landlords, he said, to disgorge their "ill-gotten gains," and he
would expedite a more equitable distribution of national wealth.
The Laborites and "radical" Liberals acclaimed the budget and
the motives in back of it, and most of the other Liberals acquiesced in it for the sake of party unity, though without enthusiasm.
On the other hand, the Conservatives, almost to a man, denounced
it as revolutionary and unjust.

The famous Lloyd George budget passed the House of Commons by a strict party vote in 1909, and then by a strict party vote
it was defeated in the House of Lords. This action of the Lords
was almost as startling as the budget itself, inasmuch as it had
long been customary for the upper house of the British Parliament
to give perfunctory assent to finance bills adopted by the House
of Commons. The Conservatives defended the Lords on the
ground that the budget of 1909 was not an ordinary finance bill,
but an extraordinary "socialist" measure on which the whole nation should be consulted through a general election. The Liberal
government responded with the declaration that the Lords had
"violated the British Constitution," and with an appeal to the
country to rebuke the Lords.

New elections were held in January 1910 amid popular excitement and passionate oratory. The Liberals lost a considerable
number of seats, so that in the new House of Commons they were
almost exactly balanced by the Conservatives. Nevertheless, the
Liberal ministry of Asquith was enabled by Labor and Irish Nationalist support to remain in office and to put the Lloyd George

budget anew through the House of Commons. This time the Lords confined their opposition to speech-making, and the budget became law. It did yield the promised revenue, but it exacerbated the feelings between political parties and between social classes. From 1910 to 1914, along with multiplying social legislation, went a rising tide of partisanship. Some there were who saw Britain headed straight toward civil war.

Close on the heels of the fight over the budget, followed a constitutional conflict over the House of Lords. Liberals were annoyed by the fact that however strong they might be in the House of Commons, all their legislation had to be reviewed and could be amended or emasculated by an upper house where, thanks to its hereditary character, the Conservative party was always dominant, and they were particularly nettled by the latest action of the Lords in throwing out a finance bill and precipitating a general election. Moreover, "radical" Liberals and all the Laborites regarded the House of Lords as an aristocratic anachronism in an age of democracy,[1] while Irish Nationalists knew very well that however difficult it might be to pass a home-rule bill through the House of Commons, it would be impossible to get one through the House of Lords. The entire coalition of Liberals, Laborites, and Irish Nationalists pressed Asquith's government to rebuke the House of Lords and deprive it of its power.

In 1910, therefore, the Liberal government submitted a "parliament bill," with three main provisions: (1) finance bills passed by the Commons would automatically become law whether the Lords approved them or not; (2) other public bills might become law, despite repeated rejection by the Lords, if they were passed by the House of Commons in three successive sessions and if at least two years elapsed between the first and third passage; (3) a general election of members of the House of Commons would have to be held at least every fifth year, instead of every seventh year as had previously been the rule. The Conservatives could not pre-

---

[1] The membership of the House of Lords in 1910 totaled more than 600, and comprised: (1) hereditary English peers (dukes, marquesses, earls, viscounts, and barons), (2) 16 elected representatives of the Scottish nobility, (3) 28 elected representatives of the Irish nobility, (4) 26 prelates of the Anglican Church, (5) 4 "law lords," ranking as barons and appointed for life to exercise the judicial functions of the House of Lords. Ordinarily, only a small percentage of the Lords attended the meetings of their House.

vent the parliament bill from passing the House of Commons, but in the House of Lords they could—and did—reject it. Whereupon, the Liberal government had the King dissolve Parliament and call for a second general election in the year 1910, this time on the constitutional fate of the House of Lords.

The election of December 1910 produced much the same political results as that of the previous January. Again, the Liberals and the Conservatives obtained about the same number of seats in the House of Commons; and again, the balance of power was held by Laborites and Irish Nationalists, both intent upon enacting the parliament bill into law. As soon as the new Parliament met, in 1911, Asquith, the Prime Minister, put the bill again through the Commons and then announced that unless the Lords accepted it without further ado the King would name a sufficient number of Liberal peers to outvote the existing membership of the aristocratic House.

A great hubbub ensued. Conservatives protested against the Prime Minister's "threat" and tried to arouse popular feeling against the Liberal government by accusing it of "dragging the crown in the mire." They declared that the parliament bill hastened the death, in 1910, of King Edward VII and that his inexperienced son and successor, George V, was forced to begin his reign by taking sides in a constitutional conflict against his true friends and his best judgment. A large number of Conservative peers—the so-called "die-hards"—insisted that, come what might, they would oppose the bill to the bitter end. The Liberal government, however, was adamant, and the country at large was more amused than alarmed by the attitude of noble "die-hards." Eventually, the Conservative leaders decided that acceptance of the Liberal bill by the existing House of Lords would be a lesser evil than flooding the House with hundreds of new peers. Consequently, in April 1911, enough Conservative nobles absented themselves from the House of Lords to enable the Liberal peers to outvote the remaining "die-hards" and thus finally to assure the bill's enactment. The Parliament Act of 1911 was almost, if not quite, as epochal in British constitutional history as the Reform Act of 1832.[1]

Political acrimony which attended the controversies over the Lloyd George budget and the Parliament Act was intensified by

[1] See *Modern Europe to 1870*, pp. 646–647.

the attempts which the Liberal government of Asquith and Lloyd George made immediately after 1911 to pay off its debt to Laborites and Irish Nationalists and other "radicals" for **Other** the support which these were giving it in the House of **Disputed** Commons. (1) To please the Laborites, and advanced **Measures** democrats generally, the government introduced into the Commons in 1912 a bill to abolish "plural voting," that is, the right of a man's exercising the parliamentary franchise wherever he could satisfy certain property qualifications and which permitted a landlord or other person of wealth to cast several ballots in a general election while a workman could cast only one. (2) To satisfy the demands of religious non-conformists, who constituted a large and influential section of the Liberal party, and particularly to humor David Lloyd George, the government also introduced into the Commons in 1912 a bill to disestablish and disendow the Anglican Church in Wales.[1] (3) Simultaneously to reward the Irish Nationalists, the government prepared and presented to Parliament a new "home-rule bill" for Ireland.

These three bills—for Irish home rule, for Welsh disestablishment, and for strictly democratic voting—were strenuously opposed by the Conservatives, and, though passed by the Commons, were rejected by the Lords. Taking advantage of the Parliament Act, the government reintroduced all three bills early in 1914; again they were passed by the Commons, and again they were rejected by the Lords. One more passing of them by the Commons would automatically make them laws, without further consultation of the House of Lords. And in 1913—in the midst of extremely angry debates over these measures—David Lloyd George and Winston Churchill launched a provocative campaign against "landlordism." The whole land system of the realm must be reformed, they said; the state must actively intervene between the owners and the users of the land, protecting the latter and gradually dispossessing the former. Lloyd George's land campaign, on top of his famous budget, added fuel to the fire of Conservative indignation.

The indignation was at fever heat by 1914. While landlords were being warned by the Chancellor of the Exchequer that "the chariots of retribution are drawing nigh," Conservative leaders

---

[1] Only a relatively small minority of Welshmen were Anglicans. The large majority were non-conformists (Methodists, Baptists, or Congregationalists).

were ready to seize any opportunity which promised embarrassment for the Chancellor and a distancing of his "chariots." An opportunity presented itself in connection with Irish "home rule."

The Irish Nationalist party, led by John Redmond [1] and representing the large majority of the population of Ireland, was not altogether content with the home-rule bill which the British Liberals conceded to them in 1912,[2] but they accepted it as the best obtainable at the time. Against it, however, were arrayed two minority groups of Irishmen. One was a recently founded group of extreme nationalists, the Sinn Fein,[3] who denounced the bill as a sorry compromise of Irish freedom. The other was the minority of "Unionists," composed chiefly of Protestants in the province of Ulster, who assailed the bill as a treasonable attempt to destroy the unity of the British Empire and put "progressive" Protestant Ulster under the yoke of "backward" Catholic Ireland. The Sinn Feiners were as yet not numerous enough to make serious trouble, but it was otherwise with the Ulster Unionists. These found a militant and eloquent leader in Edward Carson; and with the sympathy and backing of British Conservatives, they held imposing mass-meetings, bound themselves by a "solemn covenant" never to submit to an Irish parliament, and raised a volunteer army of some 100,000 men.

By the spring of 1914, the Liberal government was faced with the prospect of open armed rebellion in "loyal" Ulster. It would be, moreover, a rebellion which most Englishmen, by reason of their own nationalism and their religious sympathies, would be likely to condone and even to assist. While Irish Nationalists were recruiting an army to oppose the "Ulster volunteers," British army officers in Ireland were actively cooperating with the latter, and prominent British Conservatives were egging them on.

The prospect of rebellion and civil war was suddenly and dramatically dispelled, in the midsummer of 1914, by the outbreak of world war, in which Great Britain was speedily engulfed.

*Crisis over Irish Home Rule*

---

[1] Redmond was a successor of Parnell, the original organizer of the Party. See above, pp. 54–56.

[2] This bill, similar to those sponsored by Gladstone in 1886 and 1893, provided for the establishment of a democratic parliament at Dublin, with jurisdiction over local affairs throughout Ireland but subordinate to the British Parliament at Westminster in military, financial, and certain other matters.

[3] For a fuller account of Sinn Fein, see below, pp. 459–461.

Confronted by foreign foes, domestic disputes were pushed into the background. Conservatives and Unionists immediately pledged their support to Asquith and his Liberal cabinet in waging the war; and the Irish leader, Redmond, evoked applause from the whole British House of Commons by declaring that against the common enemy his Nationalist followers would gladly join arms with the Irish Unionists. Redmond was rewarded by the final enactment of the home-rule bill in September 1914. But Carson and his Ulstermen were rewarded, too, by the enactment at the same time of a "suspensory bill," whereby the home-rule law would not be put into effect until after the war. And other "debatable" legislation was similarly postponed.

We must bear in mind that the furtherance of British nationalism and imperialism was no monopoly of Conservatives. Indeed, from 1905 to 1914, during the very years when "radical" Liberals and Laborites were seemingly engrossed in social legislation and democratic reform, "imperialist" Liberals were manning important offices in the government and pursuing foreign, colonial, and military policies hardly distinguishable from those which a Disraeli or a Salisbury might have pursued and yet which now evoked little criticism. The foreign minister throughout the period was Sir Edward Grey, and he was no "little Englander." He strengthened the entente which his Conservative predecessor had made with France in 1904, and he supplemented it in 1907 with an entente with Russia.

The foreign policies of Sir Edward Grey were supplemented by the activities of the Liberal war minister, Richard Haldane. While keeping the British army on a professional rather than a popular basis, Haldane rendered it more efficient by creating a general staff and more expansive by establishing "officers' training corps" in connection with schools and universities and by building up a trained reserve. He also did much to relate, in practical ways, the latest advances in science to the art of warfare, and to forward plans for military cooperation, in the event of war, between Britain and its overseas Empire, and between Britain and its "friends" on the Continent, France and Russia.

There was also a steady strengthening of the British navy. This was motivated, in general, by a popular conviction, in which Liberals fully shared, that naval supremacy was essential to the protection of the far-flung British Empire and to the assurance of vital overseas trade on which industrial Britain depended for raw materials, foodstuffs, and markets. And it was specifically motivated by the obvious fact that Germany was becoming a first-class naval power and a potential rival of Britain for naval supremacy. In the circumstances, the Liberal government of Asquith showed itself quite as anxious as any Conservative government could have been to maintain Britain's lead in the race of naval armaments with Germany. British expenditure for social reform rose fast between 1905 and 1914, but expenditure on the British navy rose faster.

## 2. STATE-CHURCH QUARRELS IN FRANCE AND SPAIN AND OVERTHROW OF MONARCHY IN PORTUGAL

In France, the first decade of the twentieth century was marked by an embittered conflict between "Left" and "Right"—between Radicals and Socialists on the one hand, and Conservatives and Royalists on the other. It was an outgrowth of the famous Dreyfus affair of the 1890's and the accompanying division between Leftist "Dreyfusards" and Rightist "anti-Dreyfusards." [1] The former eventually got the upper hand; they formed the *Bloc* ministry of Waldeck-Rousseau in 1899 and elevated Émile Loubet to the presidency.

The Leftist Republican *Bloc* was not content with rehabilitating Dreyfus and discrediting his detractors. With passionate earnestness, it took advantage of popular reaction against the evident bad faith or bad judgment of the anti-Dreyfusards to penalize the two institutions in which Royalists and Conservatives were most influential—the army and the church. As for the army, its higher offices were transferred from Royalists to Republicans, from Conservatives to Radicals; it was strictly subordinated to the civilian ministry; a spirit of pacifism was encouraged, and in 1905 the term of service in the army was reduced from three years to two.

In respect of the Catholic Church, an especially drastic policy was pursued. In 1901 the ministry of Waldeck-Rousseau put through parliament an Associations Act, providing that every religious order or congregation which wished to continue its work in France must obtain specific authorization from the government and submit to continuous governmental regulation. Loud was the

[1] See above, pp. 103-105.

protest from the religious orders, from zealous laymen, and from the Pope. Nevertheless, the popular majority which the Leftist *Bloc* obtained in the general election of 1901 only intensified its campaign against the Church. The relatively moderate Waldeck-Rousseau was succeeded in the premiership by Émile Combes, a very active Freemason and doctrinaire Radical. Under his rigorous enforcement of the Associations Act almost all the religious orders, excepting only those engaged in hospital work or in the training of foreign missionaries, were denied governmental authorization and formally dissolved, thousands of their members leaving France and seeking refuge in Spain, Belgium, Great Britain, or the United States.

*Anti-Clerical Legislation in France*

This action against the religious orders imposed special hardships on church schools in France. There was an alarming shortage of lay teachers who could take the place of the religious; time was required to train such lay teachers as might be secured, and greater financial support was needed for them. The result was, as Combes expected, a steady growth of the non-religious (frequently anti-religious) state schools at the expense of the religious "free" schools, so that by 1913–1914 four and a half million French children were attending the former and only one million the latter.

But meanwhile, Combes was inducing the *Bloc* in parliament to give serious attention to an even more startling proposal—the abrogation of the concordat which had regulated the relations of France with the Catholic Church ever since its original negotiation by Napoleon I and Pope Pius VII in 1801,[1] and the adoption by the French Republic of a substitute scheme for the "separation of the churches from the state." To clear the way for favorable action on the proposal, Combes had President Loubet pay an official visit to the King of Italy at Rome in April 1904, in full knowledge that such a visit must offend the Pope, who since the seizure of Rome by Italian troops in 1870 had refused to accord recognition to the King and had requested Catholic sovereigns not to visit him. Pius X, who had recently been elected Pope, duly protested. Whereupon Jean Jaurès, the leader of the Socialists in the French parliament, speaking in behalf of the majority of the *Bloc,* de-

*"Separation" of Church and State*

[1] On the Concordat of 1801, see *Modern Europe to 1870,* p. 538.

manded "reprisals" for what he termed foreign interference in
the political affairs of France; and Théophile Delcassé, the foreign minister in the cabinet of Combes, recalled the French ambassador from the Vatican.

Already another Socialist, Aristide Briand, had been at work
with a parliamentary commission drafting a bill "for the separation of the churches [Protestant and Jewish, as well as Catholic]
from the state." Now that diplomatic relations with the papacy
were ruptured, the time appeared ripe to bring the bill into parliament and have it enacted by the nation's representatives without seeking the consent of the Pope. There was somewhat more
opposition to the bill than had been anticipated, and debate on it
was bitter and protracted. But, despite the fact that the stubborn
Combes was forced out of the premiership while the bill was in
its early stages, the Radicals and Socialists were strong and
determined enough to retain control of the ministry and eventually, late in 1905, to enact the Separation Law.

Under this law, the concordat of 1801 was formally denounced.
State support of bishops and priests of the Catholic Church, and
of Protestant pastors and Jewish rabbis, was ended, except that
pensions might temporarily be paid to aged clergymen. Title to
all property of the churches was vested in the state, though associations of laymen were authorized to make arrangements with
state officials for the use of church edifices for public worship.
And, of course, the state would no longer nominate bishops as it
had done under the concordat.

The Protestants and the Jews accepted the Separation Law
more or less cheerfully; they were traditionally allied with the
Radical political groups in opposition to the Catholic Church,
and they now formed the prescribed associations of laymen and
otherwise conformed with the provisions of the law. To the Pope
and to leading French Catholics, however, the law appeared very
objectionable. In its preparation the ecclesiastical authorities had
not been consulted. It was contrary to canon law in that it entrusted the management of ecclesiastical affairs to laymen. It was
unjust in that it confiscated church property, and, by withdrawing state financial support from the Church, it virtually repudiated a debt which the state owed the Church for the wholesale
secularization of ecclesiastical property in the days of the French
Revolution. For these reasons, Pope Piux X condemned the law

and forbade its observance; and French Catholics formed no associations for public worship.

Two years of chaos ensued in ecclesiastical affairs. Extremists in the Leftist *Bloc* urged that Catholic buildings should be closed and Catholic worship stopped, while zealous Catholics proclaimed their anxiety to die on the thresholds of the churches as martyrs in defense of Christianity and religious liberty. At length, in 1907, through the tactful efforts of Briand, who the year before had been read out of the Socialist party for accepting membership in the ministry, the French parliament made a concession, permitting clergymen to use church edifices for public worship even if the previously authorized associations of laymen were not formed.

Despite this concession, the ecclesiastical legislation from 1901 to 1907 remained a serious bone of contention between "Left" and "Right." True, the Right as a whole was no longer a menace to the democratic Third Republic. While some bishops and priests remained royalist in sentiment, a growing number of the clergy, as well as of laymen, loyally accepted the Republic, and turned their attention to a strictly religious and moral apostolate among workmen and intellectuals. Yet the whole Catholic "Right" continued to protest against what it regarded as Leftist persecution of the Church. And the issue was seized upon by Charles Maurras, himself a disbeliever in Christianity, to draw some Catholics, especially among the nobility and among the youths, into a militantly nationalist and royalist movement which he launched in 1906 under the name of Action Française.

By 1907 the Leftist *Bloc* was disintegrating. In vain its leader of the time, Georges Clemenceau, prime minister from 1906 to 1909, tried to hold it together by advocating still more drastic measures "to protect the Republic against the priests." Most of the Radicals seconded the counsels of Clemenceau, but its more moderate members were becoming sceptical about any further danger to the Republic from priests and less fearful of Conservatives on the Right than of Socialists on the extreme Left.

Socialist growth was phenomenal. In 1905 hitherto separate groups of Marxians managed to surmount their differences and to establish a unified Socialist party, under the joint **Growth of** leadership of Jean Jaurès and Jules Guesde; and so **French** effective among the French electorate was the campaign **Socialism** of the party that its representation in the Chamber of Deputies

mounted to 54 in 1906, to 76 in 1910, and to 101 in 1914. Simultaneously, a movement of "revolutionary syndicalists" gathered
headway still farther to the Left; by 1914 half a million workmen adhered to its program of "direct action" by labor unions
to bring about a "dictatorship of the proletariat."

Against the rising tide of social unrest, Clemenceau unrelentingly set his face, and in this he was supported by Moderates
and Conservatives and by a majority of the Radicals. But neither
Conservatives nor Moderates liked his ecclesiastical policy, and
when his finance minister, Joseph Caillaux, proposed the imposition of a progressive income tax, they united with the advocates
of social legislation to throw Clemenceau out of the premiership
(1909) and to bring Briand in. Briand put through parliament
one significant piece of social legislation, establishing a system of
old-age pensions for the mass of wage-earners, but in the country
he had to cope with disturbances inspired by revolutionary syndicalists and culminating in a general strike of railway men. It was
ironical that Briand, by utilizing the army to suppress the strike,
should become the hero alike of the Right and of Clemenceau's
Radicals and the villain of the extreme Left. The republican *Bloc*
was clearly a thing of the past, and as it receded, ministerial instability reappeared in an aggravated form. In the three years
1911–1914, just before the outbreak of world war, nine ministries
succeeded one another.

The *Bloc* during its heyday from 1899 to 1905 had been so
absorbed, we know, in safeguarding the republican form of government within France, in waging war with French clergymen,
and in weeding royalists out of the French army that it had had
little time or inclination to concern itself with foreign affairs. Indeed, a large part of it seemed to forget about Alsace-Lorraine
and to content itself with decrying "militarism," deprecating the
alliance with Tsarist Russia, and espousing a vague but optimistic
"internationalism." It was doubtless the very indifference of the
governing majority to foreign affairs which enabled the
nationalistic Théophile Delcassé to remain the foreign
minister of France continuously from 1898 to 1905. As
such he sedulously cultivated the alliance with Russia,
and adroitly supplemented it with agreements with Italy and
Great Britain.[1]

Delcassé
and French
Foreign
Policy

[1] See above, pp. 312–315.

Delcassé's plan to establish a French protectorate over Morocco brought on, in 1905, a grave crisis in Franco-German relations. Germany demanded that its own rights in Morocco be respected and that the unfriendly French foreign minister be removed from office. To France was left the choice of complying with these demands or of fighting. Delcassé himself inclined to the latter alternative. But his Radical colleagues in the cabinet, awakening suddenly to the terrifying possibilities of their Foreign Minister's policies, decided to sacrifice him and to seek a peaceful settlement with Germany.

The international crisis of 1905 served to arouse French concern about foreign affairs and gradually to develop differences of opinion in parliament and within the *Bloc* itself on foreign policy. One opinion, voiced by Caillaux and shared by the Socialists and by many Radicals, was that France should effect a *rapprochement* with Germany to ensure the peace of Europe and to lighten the French military burden. Another opinion, held by more nationalistically minded members, including not only those of the Right but also Clemenceau and his personal following of Radicals on the Left, was that German aggressiveness constituted a standing threat against French security and could be met only by French "preparedness."

For a time the rival tendencies appeared to be so nicely balanced as to neutralize each other. In 1911, however, occurred a second crisis in Franco-German relations over the fate of Morocco,[1] and Caillaux, who was premier and foreign minister at the moment, and quite conciliatory, had to purchase the Moroccan protectorate for France by agreeing to cede to Germany a large slice of French Equatorial Africa. This tipped the balance against the "pacifists" and in favor of the advocates of "preparedness." Caillaux was forced out of office and was succeeded in the premiership and ministry of foreign affairs by Raymond Poincaré, a native of Lorraine, lawyer and scholar, a man of substance and intense patriotism. Under Poincaré's leadership, anticlericalism and socialism became matters of relatively less importance to parliament and to the country at large than matters of national defense.

Spain was notably troubled as the twentieth century opened. Partly it was the result of growing pains of industrialization;

[1] See above, pp. 315–316.

partly, of losses suffered in the war of 1898 with the United States; and partly, of renewed conflict between extremes of "Right" and "Left," of reaction and revolution, which had characterized so much of Spanish history in the nineteenth century.[1] Between these extremes it proved difficult for Alphonso XIII and his constitutional government of moderate Liberals and Conservatives to steer a middle course.

*Spain and Partisan Strife*

On the extreme Left were Republicans, Socialists, Syndicalists, and Anarchists. The first of these groups increased its following in the universities, in the Masonic lodges, and in parliament; it insistently assailed the monarchy and the church. Marxian Socialists and Trade Unionists (Syndicalists) came to the fore in industrial centers, combating employers on the one hand and the government on the other, and staging strikes and political demonstrations. Anarchists, aiming at the destruction of all authority, whether of state or of church, exerted no little influence among the peasantry of southern Spain as well as in the industrial city of Barcelona; on occasion they resorted to violence and assassination. In 1906, for example, an attempt was made to assassinate the King on the occasion of his marriage with a granddaughter of Queen Victoria, and several bystanders were killed.

Against these extremists of the Left were arrayed, on the extreme Right, the Carlists and their reactionary sympathizers, especially in Navarre and among the Basques, who refused to acknowledge Alphonso as the legitimate sovereign and assailed the whole liberal regime. And in more or less close contact with the Carlists, and fully sharing their antipathy to contemporary liberalism, were prominent churchmen, many members of religious orders, and high-ranking army officers. Some of the last were chronically disposed to regard military dictatorship as the one effective means of repressing unruly elements in the nation and restoring its unity and prestige.

Complicating the situation was the intensification of nationalism among Basques and Catalans. Leaders of both these peoples raised their voices in criticism of the centralization of the Spanish monarchy and in demands for cultural freedom and political autonomy. Yet the Basque and Catalan nationalists, or "regionalists," were divided among themselves. Some were allies of the

[1] See above, pp. 118–121, and also *Modern Europe to 1870*, pp. 611–615, 643–644, 730–732.

reactionary Carlists. Others were allies of the revolutionary Left. The latter, in conjunction with Socialists and Syndicalists, actually provoked at Barcelona in 1909 a Catalan rebellion which was put down by the army with some effort and much vindictiveness.

Amid all these conflicting elements, the royal constitutional government carried on with increasing difficulty. Some social legislation was enacted, regulating factories, authorizing the formation of cooperative societies, legalizing trade unions, and establishing employers' liability. An educational law of 1902 provided for state supervision and direction of elementary schools, and another of 1909 prescribed attendance at them for all children.

In 1910, following the suppression of the rebellion at Barcelona, José Canalejas, a scholar and engineer and the leader of the Liberal party in parliament, became prime minister. Anxious to appease the Republicans and Socialists and to draw them into alliance with the constitutional Liberals, he adopted a policy of anti-clericalism patterned after that of the Republican *Bloc* in France, and one to which all groups of the Left might agree. He put through parliament a so-called "padlock law," prohibiting the establishment of any more Catholic religious houses without governmental sanction. He next broke off diplomatic relations with the Pope, apparently preparatory to a separation of church and state like that in France. But while these measures evoked applause from the Left, they encountered bitter antagonism on the part of the Right. And the Right was less divided within itself than the Left, and through the Church and the army its propaganda was more effectual with the country at large.

*Anti-Clerical Legislation in Spain*

The assassination of Canalejas in 1912, and an attempt on the life of the King shortly afterwards, halted the anti-clerical campaign and led to the resumption of diplomatic relations with the papacy. But the net result was sharpened cleavage between Right and Left. Reactionaries were outraged that an attack on the Church had been begun. Revolutionaries were angry that it had been stopped. And supporters of the constitutional monarchy, compelled to take one side or the other, indulged in mutual recriminations.

Meanwhile, to distract attention from troubles at home and to obtain compensation for colonial losses overseas, Alphonso XIII and his ministers persevered in an imperialist policy in Africa. By agreements with France and Great Britain, Spain was accorded **Imperialist Policy in Africa** a definitive protectorate over the northern coast of Morocco and outright ownership of an extensive though not very valuable tract of territory—Rio de Oro—on the western coast of Africa south of Morocco.[1] But in order to possess and administer its portion of Morocco, Spain was obliged to maintain large military forces there and to employ them in an exceedingly trying kind of warfare against native tribesmen. The King was resolute, but a growing number of Spaniards were critical. And, as a portent of what might eventually happen in Spain, a republican revolution occurred in neighboring Portugal in 1910.

Domestic troubles in Portugal had long resembled those in Spain,[2] and in certain respects were more acute at the beginning of the twentieth century. The Portuguese monarchy was particularly discredited by the extravagance and immorality **Portugal and Republican Revolution of 1910** of King Charles I (1889–1908) and by the scandalous corruption of the politicians who occupied the ministries and manipulated the parliament and who bankrupted the state without bettering the lot of the masses. Chief opposition to the regime came from middle-class intellectuals, from Freemasons, and from within the armed forces, and was crystalized in a radical Republican movement. In vain the King in 1907 entrusted dictatorial powers to a reforming minister, João Franco. The next year Charles and the Crown Prince were assassinated while driving through the streets of Lisbon, and Franco fled into exile.

Manuel II, the inexperienced youth who succeeded Charles on the damaged Portuguese throne, was utterly unable to cope with the situation. Matters went from bad to worse.

The murder of a prominent Republican physician in October 1910 was the signal for revolution. Soldiers in Lisbon, cooperating with armed civilians and with sailors from warships in the Tagus, put an end to the monarchy and proclaimed the Portuguese Republic. King Manuel escaped to Gibraltar and thence to England.

---

[1] In 1900 Spain secured title to another and smaller colony, Rio Muni, on the central west coast between German Kamerun and French Equatorial Africa. Altogether the Spanish colonies in 1912 were confined to Africa and comprised an area of 140,000 square miles and a population of less than a million.

[2] See above, pp. 615–616, 644–645, 730.

A provisional government was formed at Lisbon under the presidency of Dr. Teófilo Braga.

A constitution was adopted by a democratically elected Assembly in 1911. It was modeled rather closely after that of the Third French Republic, and under it, Manuel Arriaga was chosen first President of the Portuguese Republic. The new regime was different in name from the old and was manned by a quite different set of politicians. And in the one matter of religion it pursued a different policy. It was vehemently and vigorously "anti-clerical," and one of its leaders, Afonso Costa, boasted that it would blot Catholicism out of Portugal within two generations. Religious orders of men and women were expelled from the country and their property confiscated. The Church was separated from the state in the French manner. Religious instruction was banished from all the schools. Under the guise of safeguarding the secular Republic, most of the bishops were imprisoned or exiled and many churches were closed.

The Republic proved very unstable. Its supporters divided into quarrelsome factions. Royalists and reactionaries provoked insurrections. Socialists and radical revolutionaries inspired riots. Groups of military or naval officers employed their men with increasing frequency to force out of office a minister whom they disliked or to put themselves in office.

Within the four years from 1911 to 1915 there were eleven different ministries. The Republic could achieve no lasting constructive reforms and could hardly preserve order. Public finances were in utmost confusion. And worse was to come with Portugal's entry into world war in 1916.

### 3. RUSSO-JAPANESE WAR AND REVOLUTIONARY OUTBREAK IN RUSSIA

In the early years of the twentieth century, as we have seen, there were several significant and perhaps ominous happenings in western Europe: the partisan strife in Great Britain and the threat of civil war in Ireland; the domestic dissensions in France and Spain; the overthrow of monarchy in Portugal; the separation of Norway from Sweden.[1] These were overshadowed, nevertheless, by a series of international wars and revolutionary outbreaks profoundly affecting the Russian and Ottoman Empires of eastern Europe.

[1] See above, pp. 115–116.

The series of international wars began with an imperialistic struggle between Russia and Japan for supremacy in the Far East, particularly in Manchuria and Korea. Japan, we may recall, had warred on the Chinese Empire in 1894–1895 and deprived it of Korea, Formosa, and the Liaotung peninsula in southern Manchuria, including the strategic base of Port Arthur.[1] But Russia, in conjunction with France and Germany, had then intervened and prevented Japan from annexing either Korea or the Liaotung peninsula. And this was soon followed by Russia's appropriation of Port Arthur and penetration into Manchuria and Korea.

Wounded in its national pride, anxious to reassert itself in the Far East, and assured by its British alliance of 1902 [2] that it

**Russo-Japanese War**

would not have to face a combination of great powers, Japan went to war with Russia in February 1904. Japan had the advantage of naval superiority, rapidity of mobilization, and relative proximity to the scene of hostilities. It also had the advantage of popular enthusiasm for the war. To the consternation of the Russian government and the surprise of the world at large, the Japanese won victory after victory. In May 1904 they drove Russian armies from the Korean border and north of Port Arthur. In July they destroyed Russian fleets venturing out from Port Arthur and Vladivostok. In September they forced the main Russian army back into Manchuria. In January 1905 they brought the long siege of Port Arthur to a successful issue. In February and March they won the protracted but eventually decisive battle of Mukden. In May 1905 they annihilated the last Russian warships, which had made a despairing voyage all the way from the Baltic to the Sea of Japan. By the treaty of Portsmouth (in New Hampshire, U.S.A.), in September 1905, which was signed for the Tsar by Count Witte, Russia acknowledged its reverses by surrendering Port Arthur, the peninsula of Liaotung, and the southern half of the island of Sakhalin to Japan, and by agreeing to leave Korea to Japan and Manchuria to China.

Contributing immeasurably to the outcome of the Russo-Japanese War was the inability of the Russian government, on the one hand, to marshal all its forces against far-away Japan while revolution was threatening it at home, and, on the other

[1] See above, p. 288.
[2] See above, pp. 289, 312.

hand, to silence its domestic critics while it was losing battle after battle in foreign war. As one telegram followed another from the distant fighting front in Manchuria, admitting a succession of Russian defeats, it was borne in upon the Russian people as never before that the Tsarist autocracy must be responsible. Under it, officials were corrupt, generals incompetent, common soldiers needlessly sacrificed, national wealth wasted, and national honor stained. This feeling of national humiliation manifested itself in popular mutterings and disorder. In July 1904 Plehve, **Russian** the most conspicuous symbol and most energetic agent **Revolu-** of the autocratic regime,[1] was blown to pieces by a **tionary** bomb. In November an informal assembly of prominent **Movement, 1904–1905** members of local *zemstvos* and municipal *dumas* petitioned the Tsar to reform the political system by guaranteeing individual liberties, extending local self-government, and instituting a national parliament.

Nicholas II ignored the petition and appointed General Trepov, a man of the same mould as Plehve, to head the police. But Trepov soon had his hands full. Middle-class Liberals held political banquets and delivered provocative speeches. Workmen staged political strikes at Moscow, Vilna, and other industrial centers. At St. Petersburg a procession of strikers, headed by an Orthodox priest, Gapon by name, was fired upon by troops on its way to present a petition to the Tsar, the "Little Father"; and the resulting bloodshed earned for the day (January 22, 1905) the title of "Red Sunday." In rural districts, bands of peasants wandered about under Socialist Revolutionary leaders, pillaging and burning the mansions of noble landlords and country gentlemen. The Tsar's uncle, the Grand Duke Serge, was assassinated at Moscow in February 1905; and numerous other political murders ensued.

Faced with growing disorder, the Tsar falteringly made concessions. Hoping to appease the subject peoples, he promised religious toleration, licensed the use of Polish in private schools, and relaxed the enforcement of anti-Jewish legislation. Hoping to quiet the peasants, he remitted the arrears owed by them for their shares in the communal lands. Pressed by Liberals, he consented to work out a plan for constitutional government. Then, after further hesitation, and after further rioting in the country, he announced in August 1905 that he would constitute a parlia-

[1] See above, pp. 165–166, 168.

ment—an imperial Duma—to counsel with the government in the making of laws. This he followed up, continually under pressure, by dismissing Pobêdonostsev, Trepov, and other reactionary ministers, by summoning Count Witte to be premier, and by issuing in October 1905 a kind of constitution in the form of a "manifesto." The October Manifesto guaranteed personal liberties, established a moderately popular franchise for the election of the Duma, and stated that no law should be valid without the Duma's consent. Two months later, Nicholas II was prevailed upon to concede practically universal manhood suffrage for Duma elections.

Meanwhile, in November 1905, the Tsar was moved by a general strike in Finland to restore the autonomy of that grandduchy. The Finnish Estates General accordingly met at Helsingfors in December 1905—for the first time since 1899—and drafted a "modern" constitution for Finland, substituting for the medieval Estates General a single-chamber parliament chosen by universal suffrage, female as well as male, with provision for proportional representation. This democratic constitution Nicholas II ratified in 1906 in his capacity as Grand Duke of Finland.

In Russia, however, the revolutionary wave of 1905 soon spent its force and in 1906 began slowly but surely to recede. The conclusion of peace with Japan put an end to the series of disgraceful defeats abroad and enabled the government to utilize the army for the restoration of order at home. Then, too, after nearly two years of foreign war and domestic rioting, many Russians began to long for peace and quiet and for the economic advantages which public order would bring. Moreover, the revolutionary elements commenced to disintegrate and to waste their strength in factional quarrels. Bolshevik Communists quarreled with Menshevik Communists, and both with Socialist Revolutionaries. Socialist Revolutionaries were distrusted by Liberals, and Liberals—professional men and *zemstvo* members—soon split into rival parties.

A radical group of Liberals, forming the Constitutional Democrats, popularly known as the "Cadets," under the leadership of a professor of history, Paul Miliukóv, refused to recognize the finality of the Tsar's decrees and demanded that the first Duma should act as a constitutional convention and devise a form of government in which the Tsar should be a mere figurehead and the whole administration should be entrusted to a ministry responsible to parliament. Another group, the "Octobrists," comprising more conservative Liberals, especially the *zemstvo* men, were content to accept as definitive the Tsar's "October Manifesto," with its provision for a Duma as a check upon, but not as a complete substitute for, the traditional autocracy.

In measure as the revolutionary elements in Russia disintegrated and fell to quarreling, the reactionary elements plucked up courage, closed their ranks, and prepared to do battle for the preservation of the autocracy, the large landed **Reaction in Russia** estates, and all the traditional practices and policies of the old regime. Such elements, made up of great nobles and landlords, courtiers and bureaucrats, army officers, Orthodox clergymen, and Slavophile patriots, organized a "Union of the Russian People," which early in 1906 inaugurated a counter-revolutionary movement. "Black bands," or "black hundreds," as the agents of the Union were popularly styled, engaged in reactionary terrorism, committing outrages against radical sympathizers and especially inciting mob violence against Jews. Leaders of the Union also exerted pressure on the Tsar to withdraw the concessions he had made, and Nicholas II showed himself more amenable to pressure from this quarter than from the other. By decree of March 1906, he expressly excluded from parliamentary discussion the constitutional laws of the state, asserted the Tsar's unrestricted control of army, navy, and foreign affairs, authorized the imperial ministers to promulgate laws when the Duma was not in session, and provided that, if the parliament should not approve the budget in any year, the government might continue in force the budget of the preceding year. Then Nicholas II dismissed Count Witte from the premiership, and put an energetic conservative, Peter Stolýpin, in the ministry of the interior.

Stolýpin repressed revolutionary agitation with a severity that resembled Plehve's and treated quite cavalierly the Duma, which had been elected and assembled at St. Petersburg in May 1906. When it proposed reforms, he brusquely dissolved it and ordered new elections. In vain, some two hundred Cadet members of the Duma drew up, at Viborg in Finland, a solemn protest. They were penalized, and the few attempts at insurrection were suppressed.

The opponents of autocracy, despite governmental interference at the polls, obtained a majority in the second Duma, which met in March 1907. Again there was an *impasse*. Again the government dissolved the Duma. This time, however, Nicholas II issued **"Constitutional Monarchy under Autocratic Tsar"** a new "constitutional law," clearly intended to assure the election of future Dumas which would not oppose the government. The suffrage was elaborately restricted, and by means of a class system of voting, akin to Prussia's, greater weight was given to landlords than to other classes in Russia.

The new electoral arrangements operated as Nicholas II and Stolýpin intended. The third Duma, chosen in October 1907, was composed mainly of landlords with a sprinkling of bourgeois capitalists and intellectuals. The overwhelming majority, made up of Conservatives and Octobrists, were quite resigned to the maintenance of the Duma as a purely consultative body; and even the Cadet minority were willing to abandon obstructionist tactics and to play the role of polite critics. Outside the Duma, Socialist Revolutionaries and Social Democrats and the disaffected subject nationalities persevered in opposition, but they no longer terrified the government as they had recently done nor swerved it from its purpose. The revolutionary upheaval of 1905 had subsided, and the only apparent outcome, aside from the democratic reform in Finland, was a slightly altered form of imperial government, appropriately described as "a constitutional monarchy under an autocratic Tsar."

From 1907 to 1914 the Russian government and administration seemed to slip back into the old grooves. The Duma, it is true, was suffered to remain, and in some notable instances its advice was accepted. Certain moderate land reforms were effected. A scheme of workmen's insurance was adopted. Elementary education was extended under the supervision of the Orthodox Church. But in general the government led and the Duma followed. Indeed, Stolýpin was as really free of parliamentary dictation and as determined to maintain the system of reaction as Plehve had been. He repressed revolutionaries, and imprisoned or banished suspects. He enforced the laws against the Jews and sponsored new legislation against the Poles. The dagger thrust of a Jewish lawyer in a theater at Kiev removed Stolýpin in September 1911, but not the regime which he represented and faithfully served.

Meanwhile the Tsar was growing ever more mystical, ever more responsive to his wife's fancies. The emotional Tsarina, in turn, sought providential guidance from a strange assortment of religious fanatics and charlatans, the most notorious and sinister of whom was Rasputin. This untutored Siberian peasant, with powerful physique and magnetic person- **Emergence** ality, and with a dubious reputation for saintliness, was **of Rasputin** presented at court in 1907 and soon contrived, through faith-cure treatments of the Tsar's sickly son and heir, to obtain a psychical domination over the Tsarina. She came to regard him as a loved friend and divine counselor and to insure that no important governmental appointment should be made without his approval. In the direction of policy Rasputin was usually but a tool of extreme reactionaries, although the most unexpected persons were named to the highest offices through his favor.

The best efforts of the reactionary statesmen of Russia were expended on restoring the Empire's international prestige which was so badly damaged by the Russo-Japanese War. In 1907 was negotiated the friendly understanding with Great Britain, which had the effect of supplementing the Franco-Russian Dual Alliance with a Triple Entente. Then under the guidance of Stolýpin's brother-in-law, Serge Sazonov, who became foreign minister in 1910, a vigorous policy was resumed in the Balkans. Meanwhile, the government undertook a needful reorganization of the Russian army, planned an additional network of strategic railways to be completed in 1917, and started construction of a new navy.

### 4. THE YOUNG TURK REVOLUTION AND ITALIAN AND BALKAN WARS

The revolutionary outbreak in Russia in 1905–1906 was soon followed by a nationalistic revolution in the Ottoman Empire. One of the most respected of Turkish statesmen, Kiamil Pasha,[1] had long recognized the need of reform within the Ottoman Empire, and as chief minister ("grand vizier") in the 1890's he had counseled the Sultan Abdul Hamid II to put into effect the liberal constitution which had been drawn up in 1876. Though the Sultan rejected his advice and dismissed him from office in 1896, Kiamil gathered about him a sizable party of liberal-minded Turks.

More radical and more nationalistic was a group of compara-

---

[1] An Egyptian by birth and a soldier by training, he had been taken into Ottoman government service in 1861. For an account of the Ottoman Empire in the latter part of the nineteenth century, see above, pp. 173–177.

tively young men, the "Young Turks" as they were popularly
styled, who formed secret societies and spread clandestine propaganda, especially within the Turkish army, preparatory
to a revolution which should transform the Ottoman
Empire into a national state whose whole population
would be infused with a common patriotism and a common desire
for "modern progress." One of the most active "Young Turks"
was Enver Bey, an army lieutenant stationed at Salonica, who
with fellow officers organized the revolutionary "Committee of
Union and Progress."

"Young Turk" Revolution

In July 1908 this Committee executed a military *coup* at
Salonica. It proclaimed in force the long-suspended constitution
of 1876 and threatened the Sultan with deposition if he should
offer resistance. Abdul Hamid II, thoroughly frightened, made
haste to accept the new order. He endorsed the "restoration" of
the constitution. He decreed abolition of censorship and espionage.
He called the liberal Kiamil Pasha to be the first grand vizier
of the constitutional regime. Only a few persons attempted open
opposition, and they were speedily dispatched. In December
1908 a duly elected parliament met at Constantinople and began
to debate proposals of general reform.

By this time, however, the Empire was in tumult. Kurdish
troops in Asia revolted against the liberal government and committed fresh depredations against the Armenians. Mutinies occurred in Arabia and Mesopotamia. In Albania and Macedonia
conditions were anarchical. A sharp cleavage appeared, moreover,
between the liberal Grand Vizier and the nationalist Enver Bey;
and, to cap the climax, Austria-Hungary and Bulgaria took
advantage of the internal difficulties of the Ottoman
Empire to detach territories from its suzerainty and
to impair still more its external prestige. In October
1908 Austria-Hungary proclaimed the end of Ottoman sovereignty over Bosnia and Herzegovina and the incorporation of
these provinces with the Dual Monarchy.[1] Simultaneously the
autonomous Prince of Bulgaria declared the complete independence of his country, including Eastern Rumelia, and assumed
the title of King. Helplessly though haltingly the Turkish govern-

Foreign Aggression

---

[1] As a sop to Turkish pride, Austria-Hungary handed back to the Ottoman Empire the other province of Novibazar which it had been occupying since 1878. See
above, p. 162.

ment acquiesced in what it could not prevent and for comparatively small financial indemnities surrendered Bulgaria and Bosnia-Herzegovina without a struggle.

Affairs were obviously going from bad to worse, and at length in April 1909 Enver and the Committee of Union and Progress, with the support of the army, executed a second *coup*. **Deposition** This time Abdul Hamid II was deposed and imprisoned, **of Abdul** his mild elderly brother was made nominal Sultan with **Hamid II** the title of Mohammed V, the liberal cabinet of Kiamil Pasha was supplanted by a Young Turk ministry, and the parliament became a National Assembly.

From 1909 to 1918 the Ottoman Empire was practically under a military dictatorship of the Young Turk Committee of Union and Progress, in which Enver Bey (soon promoted to the dignity of Enver Pasha) was the most vigorous and influential figure. The central purpose of the Young Turks was to regenerate the Empire by nationalizing it, and to nationalize it they believed they had to make it Turkish. So they prescribed Turkish as the official language of the Empire, planned a system of **"Turkifi-** Turkish national schools, and proclaimed that hence- **cation"** forth the Turkish army would be based on the principle of compulsory service for all citizens—Arabs equally with Turks, and Christians equally with Moslems. They had the existing army in back of them and used it to enforce their will, not only on disaffected minorities, but also on the National Assembly.

The attempt to "Turkify" the Ottoman Empire proved disastrous. There were altogether too many non-Turks to be "Turkified," and the non-Turks were now too nationalistic themselves. Moslem Arabs in Asia as well as Christian peoples in the Balkans resented and resisted the Young Turk regime. In the case of the Balkan peoples, resistance was ever more actively abetted by kinsmen in the adjacent states of Greece, Serbia, Montenegro, and Bulgaria. And the more resistance the Turkish government encountered, the more interference it invited from abroad.

In September 1911, Italy suddenly announced its intention of appropriating the Ottoman provinces of Tripoli and Cyrenaica in northern Africa. The Young Turk government re- **Italian** plied with a resolute declaration of war and dispatched **Attack** Enver Pasha to defend the provinces. But the ensuing hostilities involved a double loss for the Empire. Not enough

Turkish forces could be supplied to prevent Italy from despoiling the Empire in Africa, and yet enough were sent across the Mediterranean to encourage the Balkan nations to attempt a spoliation of the Ottoman Empire in Europe.

King Ferdinand of Bulgaria was the prime mover in bringing the Balkan nations together for common action against the Turks. Satisfying himself that Austria-Hungary would not oppose him, he tactfully employed the good offices of Russia to persuade King Peter of Serbia to form an alliance with Bulgaria in March 1912, and shortly afterwards he negotiated with the Greek prime minister, Venizelos, a similar Graeco-Bulgarian alliance. Thus concerted action against the Ottoman Empire was arranged for by Bulgaria, Serbia, and Greece, with Montenegro acceding, and between Bulgaria and Serbia a tentative division of the spoils was outlined. Northern Albania and the extreme western part of Macedonia would go to Serbia; the rest of Macedonia and Thrace would pass to Bulgaria; and the Russian Tsar would be invited to arbitrate any differences that might arise. Feverish military preparations ensued throughout the Balkans, the Albanians rose in revolt, and in October 1912 a declaration of war by tiny Montenegro was the signal for joint attack of all the Balkan allies on the Ottoman Empire.

*Balkan Coalition and War*

The Empire made heroic efforts to overawe and overcome the allies. Kiamil Pasha, reinstalled as grand vizier, obtained an express pledge from the great powers that they "would not permit any modification of the territorial *status quo* in European Turkey." The Turkish army was mobilized, and Enver Pasha and other officers were summoned from Tripoli to Thrace. And, to concentrate all its energies in the Balkans, the Ottoman government terminated the Italian war by signing the peace treaty of Lausanne (October 1912), formally ceding Tripoli and Cyrenaica to Italy and allowing Italy to occupy and administer twelve of the Ægean islands, the so-called Dodecanese.[1]

---

[1] The Turco-Italian War of 1911–1912 had been confined to irregular but fierce fighting in Africa between an Italian military expedition on the one side and the Turkish garrisons and native tribesmen under the leadership of Enver Pasha on the other, and to an Italian naval expedition in the Ægean. Italy, after obtaining title to Tripoli and Cyrenaica (Barca) by the treaty of Lausanne, gave them the collective title of "Libya."

Despite frantic endeavors, the Turks proved unequal to the emergency. To the surprise of the great powers, and even of the Balkan allies, Ottoman resistance all but collapsed. While Serb and Greek armies were capturing Salonica and Monastir and overrunning Macedonia almost at will, the Bulgarians were investing Adrianople and hammering the main Turkish army back through Thrace to within a few miles of Constantinople. In December 1912, less than two months after the beginning of the war, the Ottoman government sued for peace, and negotiations were opened at London.

The negotiations were interrupted in January 1913 by a frenzied revolution at Constantinople which overthrew the pacific Kiamil Pasha and put the bellicose Enver Pasha in the saddle. But the resumption of hostilities brought no consolation to the Turks. In March Adrianople capitulated to the Bulgarians, and in April Scutari, the last Turkish stronghold on the Adriatic, surrendered to the Serbs. Finally, in May 1913, even Enver Pasha consented to accept the peace terms of the Balkan allies as amended by the great powers and incorporated in the treaty of London. The Ottoman Empire thereby formally yielded all its European territory except Constantinople and a narrow strip along the Dardanelles.

It was one thing to despoil the Ottoman Empire, and quite another to divide the booty. Here, the greed and mutual jealousy of the Balkan allies came into full play, and were enhanced by conflicting policies and ambitions of the great powers. The triumph of the Balkan allies against the Turks was generally interpreted as a gain for the prestige of Russia and correspondingly as a blow to the prestige of Austria-Hungary and Germany. An enlarged pro-Russian Serbia would be menacing to the continuing integrity of the Habsburg Empire with its large Yugoslav population in Bosnia and Croatia. Consequently Austria-Hungary was determined to prevent Serbia from reaping the fruits it expected from its victory over the Turks. For a time it seemed likely that a vast world war would immediately issue from the Balkan War, but a compromise was reached. Serbia was allowed to expand southward, but it was barred from the Adriatic by the erection of an independent state of Albania, over which a German prince would rule and in which Italy would have a privileged position.

But thereby, if world war was staved off, another Balkan

war was precipitated. For Serbia, deprived of the portion of Albania promised to it in its treaty of alliance with Bulgaria, demanded "compensation" in that part of Macedonia which had been tentatively allotted to Bulgaria. This demand King Ferdinand was encouraged by Austria-Hungary and pressed by his own army chiefs to refuse. In vain the Russian Tsar attempted to arbitrate between Bulgaria and Serbia. Both were unbending, and, complicating their feud, a bitter quarrel developed between Bulgaria and Greece over the disposition of Thrace. In June fighting began between Bulgaria on the one side, and Serbia and Greece on the other; and soon the latter were joined by Rumania and the Ottoman Empire. Rumania, fearful of being overshadowed by a Greater Bulgaria, wanted to expand its own territory if the other Balkan states were expanding theirs, while the Turks perceived an opportunity to regain at least a portion of what they had lost.

*Second Balkan War*

This second Balkan War was as brief as it was sorry. Within the single month of July 1913 the Turks recaptured Adrianople, while armies from Rumania, Greece, and Serbia invaded Bulgaria and closed in upon Sofia. Unable to elicit any assistance from the great powers, who could not agree among themselves as to what should be done, King Ferdinand bowed to the inevitable and early in August concluded with the other Balkan states the treaty of Bucharest. Thereby the spoils of the previous war were distributed. To Serbia was assigned the greater part of Macedonia. To Greece were allotted Crete, southern Macedonia (including Salonica), and western Thrace. To Bulgaria was left a bit of Macedonia and central Thrace down to the Ægean, though it had to cede Dobruja to Rumania and subsequently to relinquish Adrianople to the Ottoman Empire.

The Balkan Wars served to intensify the nationalism and stimulate the predatory ambitions of the several peoples and governments involved. The Bulgarians, embittered by the knowledge that they had contributed most to the defeat of the Turks and yet had gotten least from it, were doubly eager to avail themselves of any opportunity to take revenge on Serbia and to appropriate Macedonia for themselves. The Turks, too, became rapidly more nationalist. Enver Pasha tightened his dictatorship, speeded up the process of "Turkification," and cemented a military and economic alliance with Germany.

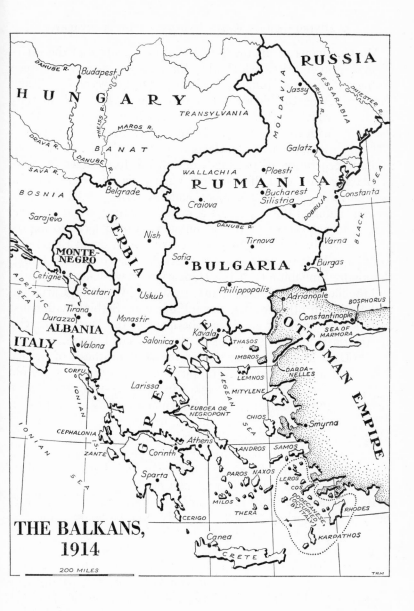

THE BALKANS,
1914

200 MILES

## 5. AUSTRO-SERBIAN CRISES AND GREAT-POWER RIVALRY

Most ominous of all the Balkan developments was the series of ever graver crises which they brought on directly between Serbia and Austria-Hungary, and indirectly between Russia and Germany. After the bloody palace revolution at Belgrade in 1903 which supplanted the pro-Austrian King Alexander with the pro-Russian King Peter,[1] Serbian nationalism became intensely Slavophile and bellicose. A new and militant generation of patriots came to the fore, eager to make Serbia the core of a big, united Yugoslavia of Serbs, Croats, and Slovenes, just as Piedmont had been the motive force in creating a united Italy, or Prussia, in building the German Empire. Serbia, to achieve its "national mission," would have to appropriate not only Serb-speaking districts of the Ottoman Empire. It would also have to incorporate the Serbs of the Hungarian Banat, the kindred inhabitants of the Hungarian crown-land of Croatia, and the Slovenes of the Austrian provinces of Carniola, Carinthia, and Istria. In other words, the fulfilment of Serbian nationalist ambition would involve a dismemberment of the Dual Monarchy of Austria-Hungary as well as of the Ottoman Empire.

**Serb Nationalism**

The Dual Monarchy represented the very antithesis of Serbia. It was not a new national state, but rather a survival of the old Habsburg Empire, embracing a hodge-podge of diverse nationalities; and its government, with the support of army and church and of its dominant German and Magyar peoples, was determined to keep it intact and to ward off any such threat to its territorial integrity as Serbia held out. The immediate issue was between a defensive Habsburg imperialism and an aggressive Yugoslav nationalism.

**Threat to Austria-Hungary**

But there were more far-reaching issues. The Habsburg Empire, despite earlier setbacks in Italy and Germany, was still entitled, by its size and wealth and by its military strength, to rank as a great power. It had, moreover, the firm alliance and interested backing of the powerful German Empire. For Germany, scarcely less than Austria-Hungary, was now vitally concerned with the Balkans. It was obtaining economic, political, and military ascendancy within the Ottoman Empire; and rulers

[1] See above, pp. 180–182

of Rumania, Bulgaria, and Greece were closely related to German princely families. Serbia alone, after 1903, was outside of Germany's "sphere of influence," and its hostility to Austria-Hungary was hostility to Germany's most dependable ally.

On the other hand, Russia was now the interested backer of Serbia. Between them was the sentimental tie of Panslavism, and they had a common interest in weakening both the Ottoman and the Habsburg Empires. Especially after 1907, when its entente with Great Britain removed sources of conflict with that power in Asia, Russia, under Stolýpin and Sazonov, redoubled its efforts to check Austrian and German influence throughout southeastern Europe.

A serious crisis in Austro-Serbian and hence in German-Russian relations occurred in 1908. The Habsburg Empire, as a safeguard against Serbian aggressiveness, took advantage of the contemporaneous Young Turk revolution formally to **Crisis of 1908** annex Bosnia and Herzegovina, the two Serb-speaking Ottoman provinces which previously it had merely administered under an international mandate,[1] and which lay as buffers between Serbia and Croatia. Serbia, swept by a wave of popular indignation at this Austrian "aggression," immediately assumed a warlike attitude, and in this it was encouraged by Russia which began mobilizing its army. Whereupon Germany intervened with a peremptory ultimatum to Russia that it cancel its mobilization and stand aside or else accept war with the combined forces of the Austrian and German Empires.

Russia was not ready to risk war of such dimensions. Too little time had elapsed since the disastrous Russo-Japanese War, and the revolutionary outbreak at home. So Russia gave way to Germany; and Serbia, left alone to face the overwhelming might of the Central great powers, felt compelled to accede to their demands. Serbia gave a solemn promise that in the future it would not abet any anti-Austrian propaganda but would live on "good neighborly terms" with the Dual Monarchy. The crisis of 1908 was thus surmounted and peace preserved. But Russia and Serbia did not forget the humiliation they had suffered. They drew closer together, awaiting a favorable opportunity for revenge.

For a time, Serbian attention was deflected from the Austrian to the Ottoman Empire and was riveted on the formation of the

[1] Of the Congress of Berlin of 1878. See above, pp. 161–165.

Balkan League and the waging of the two Balkan Wars of 1912–
1913. But these wars brought on more crises. Though all the
European great powers managed to keep up a semblance of harmony through a continuous "conference of ambassadors" at
London, differences between them, and particularly between
Russia on the one hand and Germany and Austria-Hungary on
the other, were chronic and frequently acute.

While Russia favored the Balkan allies against the Turks in
the first Balkan War, and Serbia against Bulgaria in the second,
both Germany and Austria-Hungary were distinctly pro-Turkish
in the first and anti-Serbian in the two wars. Indeed, it was
threats by the latter great powers which obliged Serbia to relinquish various Adriatic ports it conquered from the Turks and
thus to forego any outlet to the sea. And this was what brought
on the conflict between Serbia and Bulgaria in Macedonia and
the second Balkan War.

Altogether, the Balkan Wars exacerbated both nationalism and
international rivalry. Serbia, elated by its successive victories
over Turks and Bulgarians, was the more determined
**Crisis
of 1913** to avenge itself on Austria-Hungary for depriving it of
some of the fruits of victory; as its prime minister,
Nicholas Pašič, remarked, "the first round is won, now we must
prepare for the second, against Austria." To cope with the renewed menace, Austria decided in 1913 to attack and crush Serbia
and put an end to its independence; and only the objection of
Germany and Italy to the taking of such drastic action caused
its postponement. Germany and Austria-Hungary did take precautionary measures against Serbia by forming military alliances
with the Ottoman Empire and with Bulgaria. On the other side,
Serbia received new assurances and encouragement from Russia.

Rivalry in the Balkans combined with accumulating rivalries
elsewhere to make the international situation in 1913 extremely
perilous. Recurrent crises in Morocco, as well as in the Near East,
were costing every great power some measure of prestige. Ger-
**Stakes of
Great
Powers** many had been outplayed in the Moroccan crises by
France and Great Britain. Yet France had been forced
to cede African territory to Germany, and Great
Britain to yield predominance in the Ottoman Empire. Russia
had been outplayed in the successive Near Eastern crises by
Austria-Hungary and Germany. Yet Austria-Hungary had been

flouted by Serbia and held in leash by Italy, and Germany had to face the fact that instead of exercising a hegemony in Europe, as it had done in the days of Bismarck, it was now "encircled" by a ring of potentially hostile powers.

But the more a great power was threatened with the loss of prestige, the less yielding and conciliatory it was likely to be. By the end of 1913 Austria-Hungary was determined not to submit to any further diplomatic restraints or military threats, and so was Russia. So, too, were Germany and France.

In an atmosphere less conciliatory, the current winds were more gale-like than ever. Naval rivalry was in full swing between Great Britain and Germany, and attempts to halt it by mutual agreement had been unsuccessful [1] and had now ceased altogether. Imperialistic rivalry, if assuaged as between Great Britain and France and Russia, was intensified for all these powers by recent achievements of Italy and new thrusts of Germany. Nationalism, in an aggravated form, was everywhere rampant; it was dictating to governments an emotional, rather than a reasoned, behavior; and, quite triumphant now in the Balkans, it threatened speedily to become so throughout east-central Europe. It immediately menaced the Habsburg Empire.

The threat against Austria-Hungary had no terror for Russia, and Russia sympathized with Serbian ambitions. It did have a terror, however, for Germany; Austria-Hungary was Germany's one dependable ally. France had no immediate stakes either in Serbia or in Austria-Hungary, but as the ally of Russia it might readily become embroiled in a general war. Great Britain's position was less certain, and so likewise was Italy's. Great Britain was in an *entente* with France and Russia, and was concerting military and naval plans with them, but it was not bound by a formal alliance and it was notoriously prone "to consult its own interests." Italy was in formal alliance with Germany and Austria-Hungary but it simultaneously had a foot in the rival camp and what one of its leading statesmen described as a "sacred egotism." In the uncertainty as to what Italy and Great Britain might do in a conflict between Russia and Austria-Hungary, there was special peril. There was a temptation to gamble.

[1] Lord Haldane, on behalf of the British government, made such an attempt through direct negotiations at Berlin early in 1912. The German government insisted that Britain should pledge neutrality in the case of war, a pledge which the British government would not give.

Meanwhile, during the year 1913, the powers vied with one another in making preparations against possible attack. Germany **Armament Race** increased its standing army from 656,000 men to 870,000 and appropriated almost a billion marks for "extraordinary" military purposes. France lengthened the term of compulsory service from two years to three. Russia adopted a new program of army expansion. Great Britain added considerably to its already huge naval expenditure.

No responsible statesman really desired war, and "enlightened" and "progressive" people still assumed that a general European war would not and could not occur. In the spring of 1914 the German Emperor and the Russian Tsar were still exchanging letters couched in endearing terms, and Germany and Great Britain were arranging with each other, secretly but quite amicably, for cooperation in immediate financing of the Bagdad railway and in future partition of the Portuguese colonies.

Nevertheless, despite appearances and optimistic longings to the contrary, rivalry among the great powers had now reached a stage in which world peace was at the mercy of an accident. Indeed, the powder magazines throughout Europe were so well stocked, and nationalist feeling so strong and the pursuit of prestige so eager, that any untoward event was likely to produce a world-shaking explosion.

# PART III

## THE "FIRST" WORLD WAR AND ITS PROMISING AFTERMATH, 1914–1929

# CHAPTER IX

## WORLD WAR I, 1914–1918

### 1. PRECIPITATION

URDER precipitated world war. On June 28, 1914, the Archduke Francis Ferdinand, nephew of the Emperor-King Francis Joseph **Murder of** and heir to the Habsburg Empire, was **Austrian** assassinated, together with his wife, at **Archduke** Sarajevo, the chief town of Bosnia, by a band of fanatically nationalist Serbs. The assassination sent a thrill of horror all over Europe and evoked a storm of indignation in Austria and Germany.

Here was a favorable opportunity as well as an obvious obligation, reasoned the Austrian Foreign Minister, Count Leopold Berchtold, to have a final reckoning between Imperial Austria and that center of subversive Yugoslav nationalism, the independent state of Serbia. Berchtold had harried and repeatedly thwarted Serbia during the Balkan Wars of 1912–1913, but he had been restrained by Germany and Italy from attacking it. Now he would chastise Serbia so severely that it would be unable to endanger the integrity of the Habsburg Empire.

We now know that the assassins of the Archduke, though natives of Bosnia and subjects therefore of the Habsburg Empire, were members of the Serbian secret society of the "Black Hand," [1] that they obtained their weapons and training in Serbia, and that they planned and executed their crime with the assistance of several high officers in the Serbian army. Also, we now have grounds for believing that Nicholas Pašič, the prime minister of Serbia, had foreknowledge of the conspiracy and yet gave the Austrian government no adequate warning. In other words, the Serbian government had a real share of responsibility.

[1] See above, p. 181.

At the time, however, Berchtold lacked proof of Serbia's complicity. Indeed, his own official investigator reported that there was "nothing to prove or even to cause suspicion of the Serbian government's cognizance of the steps leading to the crime." Nevertheless, Berchtold was resolved to act, and he accordingly pretended to have evidence against Serbia which actually he did not possess.

Before venturing to take drastic action, Berchtold sought the consent of his own government and the sanction of Austria's ally, **Austria** Germany. The Hungarian premier, Count Stephen **Supported** Tisza, had qualms, however; he thought the policy too **by Germany** adventurous and counseled the Emperor Francis Joseph not to assent to an armed attack upon Serbia. The aged Emperor hesitated, and it required all of Berchtold's powers of persuasion to get him to sign the communication which the Foreign Minister had prepared for secret dispatch to the German Emperor William II. "The crime against my nephew," the communication read, "is the direct consequence of the agitation carried on by Russian and Serbian Pan-Slavists, whose sole aim is to weaken the Triple Alliance and shatter my Empire. . . . Though it may be impossible to prove the complicity of the Serbian government, there can be no doubt that its policy of uniting all Yugoslavs under the Serbian flag promotes such crimes, and that a continuation of this situation endangers my dynasty and my territories. The aim of my government must henceforth be to isolate and diminish Serbia."

On July 5-6 the Austrian ambassador to Germany and a special emissary of Count Berchtold bearing the communication from the Emperor Francis Joseph conferred secretly with the Emperor William II at Potsdam. How fully the Austrians revealed Berchtold's plan we do not know. We do know that William II definitely pledged Germany's unqualified support of Austria in any action it might take against Serbia, even if such action involved war with Russia. He was doubtless influenced by the emotion he felt over the murder of his friend, the Austrian Archduke, and he must have been impressed by the urgency of the situation and by the fear that Germany might alienate its one dependable ally. William II neither wished nor expected to precipitate a world war. He imagined that Austria could make quick work of Serbia and that German threats would suffice in 1914, as they had sufficed in 1909,[1] to deter Russia from intervening. He considered, of course, the possibility of Russia's not being deterred this time, but William II was willing to gamble, and his Chancellor, Beth-mann-Hollweg, an honest but weak man, was meekly acquiescent. So Germany presented a "blank cheque" to Austria-Hungary and underwrote Berchtold's venture.

Thus fortified, Count Berchtold had no serious difficulty in persuading all the members of the Austro-Hungarian government, including Count Tisza, that drastic action should be taken forth-with against Serbia. Then, while the Austrian Chief of Staff was planning the military campaign, Berchtold drafted an ultimatum which Serbia would be almost certain to reject. The ultimatum was presented to Serbia on July 23. It declared that Serbia, by failing to suppress anti-Austrian conspiracies, had violated its promise of 1909 to "live on good neighborly terms" with Austria-Hungary and had therefore compelled the government of the Dual Monarchy to abandon its attitude of "forbearance" and to insist on guarantees of good behavior by the Serbian government. Spe-cifically, Serbia was called upon to ban anti-Austrian publications and societies, to oust any official whom the Austrian government should accuse of subversive propaganda, to discard anti-Austrian textbooks from the Serbian schools, "to accept the collaboration in Serbia of representatives of the Austro-Hungarian government for the suppression of the revolutionary movement directed against the territorial integrity of the Dual Monarchy," and to signify unconditional acceptance of the whole ultimatum within forty-eight hours.

On July 25 the Serbian government replied, promising com-pliance with such demands as "would not impair the country's independence and sovereignty" and offering to refer all disputed points to the international tribunal at The Hague or to a con-ference of the great powers. Simultaneously Serbia ordered the mobilization of its army. Whereupon the Austro-Hungarian gov-ernment pronounced the reply evasive and unsatisfactory, broke off diplomatic relations with Serbia, and likewise ordered mobi-lization. War was clearly impending between Austria-Hungary and Serbia.

But a much vaster and more terrible war was also impending. The Russian government felt that if it stood aside from what

[1] See above, p. 353.

promised to be a supreme test between Austria-Hungary and
Serbia, Russian prestige would suffer irreparable harm. It had
French
Support
of Russia suffered enough through Russia's standing aside in
1909; it must now be maintained at any cost. In
the present emergency, moreover, national sentiment
among the Russian people, and among other Slavic peoples also,
could be counted upon to back energetic action by the Russian
government—and by the Russian army if necessary. Consequently, on July 18—five days before the presentation of the Austrian ultimatum to Serbia—the Russian foreign minister, Serge
Sazonov, warned the Austrian ambassador at St. Petersburg that
"Russia would not be indifferent to any attempt to humiliate
Serbia; Russia could not permit Austria to use menacing language
or military measures against Serbia."

Besides, Russia soon received assurances of French support,
for Raymond Poincaré, the President of the French Republic,
Serbia
Supported
by Russia paying a state visit to St. Petersburg on July 20–23,
declared to the French ambassador that "Sazonov must
be firm, and we will support him." Neither Sazonov nor
his sovereign, the Tsar Nicholas II, wished war—any more than
did the German Emperor and his Chancellor. But the Russian
foreign minister was confident that Austria-Hungary could be
checked by a firm stand just as Russia had been checked in 1908–
1909, and the Tsar, in an exalted mood, hoped for the best. As
for the French government, it too had no eagerness for war,
though it had a morbid fear lest France should lose an ally and
the alliance should lose its prestige; and if, peradventure, general
war should come, it might have the advantage of enabling France
to undo the defeat of 1870.

On July 26, Sir Edward Grey, the British foreign minister,
urged that diplomatic representatives of Italy, France, Germany,
and Great Britain "meet in conference immediately for the pur-
Failure
of Nego-
tiation pose of discovering an issue which would prevent complications" and that "all active military operations be
suspended pending results of conference." The Italian
and French governments responded favorably, but the German
government, fearful lest such a conference, like the one at Algeciras in 1906,[1] would put Germany in a minority and lower
the prestige of the Central Empires, replied that the basic dispute

[1] See above, pp. 314–315.

concerned Austria-Hungary and Serbia alone and that the efforts of other powers should be concentrated on "localizing" it. With this evidence of Germany's firm stand, Austria-Hungary on July 28 declared war against Serbia, in order, as Berchtold informed the German ambassador at Vienna, "to cut the ground from any attempt at intervention."

Thenceforth events marched fast. Amidst frantic endeavors of diplomats to discover some means of preserving peace without losing prestige, military preparations went feverishly forward. Already, on July 26, Winston Churchill, First Lord of the Admiralty in the British cabinet, had given orders on his own responsibility that the British fleet, then mobilized for annual maneuvers, should not disperse but should hold itself in readiness for war. Then, on July 29, when news of the Austrian declaration of war reached St. Petersburg, the Tsar was prevailed upon to sanction a general mobilization of the armed forces of Russia.

For a few hours that same night and the next morning the prospect of a peaceful outcome seemed to brighten. William II and Bethmann-Hollweg, who had rashly given a "blank cheque" to Berchtold and blindly allowed him to use it as he would, were suddenly shocked by the realization of the enormous payment in money and men which Germany was almost certain to be called upon to make in honoring the "cheque." They had imagined that they could "localize" the Austro-Serbian conflict; the determined attitude of Russia now filled them with consternation. So, somewhat tardily, Bethmann-Hollweg pressed Austria to negotiate directly with Russia; and when he got no immediate response, he testily wired the German ambassador at Vienna: "As an ally we must refuse to be drawn into a world conflagration because Austria does not respect our advice. Tell Berchtold with all emphasis and great seriousness." And just as the Tsar was ordering Russian mobilization, William II frantically wired him imploring him to avoid military measures which "would precipitate a calamity we both wish to avoid."

The change of front at Berlin had little effect on Count Berchtold, who refused to believe that Germany would really go back on the original promise it had made to Austria-Hungary. It did have some effect, however, on the impressionable Tsar Nicholas II, who, on receipt of the telegram from William II, promptly countermanded the order for general mobilization of the Russian army, which had not yet been published, and decreed instead a partial mobilization, "as a precautionary measure," along the Austrian (but not the German) frontier.

What thus began auspiciously, though tardily, ended speedily and direfully. The Tsar's shift of orders threw the Russian military authorities into a panic. They had a detailed plan for general mobilization but not for such a partial mobilization as the Tsar now contemplated, and they begged the foreign minister, Sazonov, unless he would disorganize the Russian army and do without it in his negotiations, to bring about another shift in the Tsar's mind. Sazonov saw the point and on July 30 entreated Nicholas II to renew the order for general mobilization. Nicholas hesitated: "Think of the responsibility you are advising me to take! Think of the thousands and thousands of men who will be sent to their death!" Sazonov persisted, and presently the Tsar yielded. Sazonov rushed to the telephone and informed the Chief of Staff that he was authorized to proceed with general mobilization. "Now you can smash the telephone," Sazonov added; "give your orders, General, and then disappear for the rest of the day."

Russian mobilization transformed the Austro-Serbian war into a Russo-German war. For the German Chief of Staff had no difficulty in convincing William II and Bethmann-Hollweg that the Russians meant business and that any delay in counter-mobilization would spell disaster for Germany. On July 31 Germany presented a twelve-hour ultimatum to Russia, demanding immediate demobilization. Russia did not comply. Germany declared war.

**Germany and Russia at War**

Germany knew that war with Russia was practically certain to involve France. Accordingly, on the very day of delivering the ultimatum to Russia, Germany presented an ultimatum to France, demanding a declaration of neutrality within eighteen hours. If perchance such a declaration should be forthcoming, Germany was prepared to make the further demand that France permit German troops to occupy the fortresses of Toul and Verdun until general peace should be restored. In fact, the declaration was not made. France merely stated, on August 1, that it "would consult its interests," and at once began mobilization. On August 3, 1914, Germany declared war on France.

**Involvement of France, Belgium, Britain**

Thus, within a week of the declaration of hostilities by Austria-

Hungary against Serbia, four great powers were in a state of war —Germany and Austria-Hungary opposed to Russia and France. Italy and Rumania, nominal allies of the Central Powers, promptly proclaimed their neutrality, on the ground that the war was not defensive on the part of Austria-Hungary and Germany, but offensive, and that therefore they were not bound to give assistance to their allies. Thereby Italy kept its secret agreement of 1902 with France; and before long Italy, and Rumania likewise, was pressing Austria-Hungary for "compensations" in accordance with provisions of the Triple Alliance.

Great Britain, on the other hand, almost immediately entered the war. The British people, on the whole, had by this time greater sympathy for France than for Germany, and Sir Edward Grey had already informed Germany that he could not bind Great Britain to observe neutrality. On August 2 he went further and announced that Great Britain would not tolerate German naval attacks on French coasts or shipping. There was still considerable pacifist sentiment in the British cabinet, and a minority in it were critical of the Foreign Minister's manifest partiality for France. On August 4 occurred an event, however, which enabled Sir Edward Grey and the other pro-war members of the cabinet to force out the pacifists and to unite the overwhelming majority of the British parliament and British nation in enthusiastic support of Great Britain's entrance into the war on the side of fellow members of the Entente—France and Russia.

German troops had been set in motion toward the French frontier, not only against the French border fortresses of Verdun, Toul, and Belfort, but toward the neutral countries of Luxemburg and Belgium, which lay between Germany and less well-defended districts of northern France. Both Germany and France had signed treaties to respect the neutrality of these "buffer states," and France had already announced its intention of adhering to the treaty engagements. But on August 2 German troops occupied Luxemburg, despite protests from the Grand-Duchess; and on the same day the German government presented a twelve-hour ultimatum to Belgium, demanding that German troops be permitted to cross into France, promising, if permission were granted, that Belgium would be indemnified, and threatening, if resistance was encountered, that the decision of arms would determine the future relations of Belgium to Germany. The Belgian government characterized the ultimatum as a gross violation of international law, refused to grant the German request, and appealed for British help in upholding the neutrality of Belgium.

The neutrality of Belgium had long been an important point in the foreign policy of Great Britain. The British had fought against Napoleon I in part because of the annexation of Belgium by France, and they had been hostile to the ambition of Napoleon III in respect of Belgium. They were not likely to view with pleasure Belgium's incorporation with the German Empire. On August 4, therefore, when news was received in London that German troops had actually crossed the border into Belgium, Sir Edward Grey dispatched an ultimatum to Germany, requiring assurances by midnight that Germany would respect Belgian neutrality. Germany refused, on the ground of military necessity, and Bethmann-Hollweg, the German Chancellor, terribly tired and disappointed, berated the British ambassador: "Just for a word 'neutrality,' a word which in war time has so often been disregarded—just for a scrap of paper—Great Britain was going to make war on a kindred nation who desired nothing better than to be friends with her." At midnight Great Britain declared war on Germany.

On August 7, Montenegro joined its fellow Yugoslav state of Serbia against Austria-Hungary. Then Japan became a party to the war, partially to fulfill its treaty obligations to Great Britain and partially to avenge itself on Germany, for the Japanese had not forgotten the German Emperor's slighting references to them in the past, nor the part Germany had played in preventing Japan from retaining Port Arthur in 1895 after the Chino-Japanese War. Accordingly, on August 17 Japan presented an ultimatum to Germany, demanding that it immediately withdraw all its warships from Chinese and Japanese waters and deliver up the leased territory of Kiaochow before September 15, "with a view to the eventual restoration of the same to China." Upon the refusal of the German government to comply with the ultimatum, Japan declared war (August 23, 1914).

*Involvement of Japan and Ottoman Empire*

Against the combination of so many foes, Germany and Austria-Hungary obtained support from the Ottoman Empire. Many patriotic Turks had come to believe that the integrity of their Empire was menaced far more by the Entente powers than by Germany and Austria-Hungary. On August 1, the very day that

Germany declared war against Russia, the Ottoman government, dominated by Enver Pasha, signed a secret treaty with Germany, promising aid against Russia. For a time the Ottoman Empire pretended to be neutral, but at length on October 29, 1914, when military preparations seemed sufficiently advanced, Turkish warships bombarded Russian ports on the Black Sea. Russia responded with a declaration of war, and, on November 5, France and Great Britain declared war on the Ottoman Empire.

Thus, in the three months from July 28 to October 29, 1914, a conflict between Serbia and Austria broadened into a world war in which Germany, Austria-Hungary, and the Ottoman Empire were arrayed against Russia, France, Great Britain (with Canada, Australia, New Zealand, and South Africa), Japan, Belgium, Serbia, and Montenegro. Six of the eight great powers were immediately involved, and five of the six continents.

No nation willed the war, and statesmen blundered into it rather than sought it. Nor is there any scientific way of apportioning blame for it among the various sovereigns and diplomats and chiefs of staff whom we have referred to in the preceding pages. Some of them were cunning, some were cowardly, and some of them were merely stupid. They would have been quite unable to precipitate a world war, had they not been, equally with millions of common people, the more or less willing agents of immense forces which for a generation had been predisposing the civilized world to mortal combat.

### 2. FROM MOBILIZATION TO TRENCH WARFARE, 1914

For an instant, the popular reaction to the outbreak of worldwide war was one of shock, but this soon gave place to a strange sense of resignation. The masses, no more than the governments, had wished war, and yet war was now a grim reality.

Once the die was cast, there was little opportunity or inclination to "reason why." For from declaration of war to mobilization of troops the passage in every belligerent country was immediate and inexorable. By the system of conscription **Mobilization** and mobilization which Prussia had developed by 1866 and which other Continental nations had adopted during the generation following 1870, the strength of the peace-time army was doubled or trebled by calling back to the colors reservists who had already received military training; and the regiments thus raised to war footing were entrained for the frontier according to prearranged plans. Within a fortnight from the ordering of mobilization, therefore, five million men or more throughout Europe were suddenly drawn from their ordinary occupations, clothed and equipped for war, gathered into military units, and transported to the frontiers. Mobilization with such rapidity and on such a scale involved a quasi-paralysis of the economic life of Europe, an upsetting of the normal affairs of practically every family in the belligerent countries.

Mobilization was likewise attended in every country by an almost instantaneous merging of partisan differences in national solidarity. Opposition parties lined up behind the several governments. All elements and all strata of society reacted similarly. The specifically "disaffected" groups—revolutionary or antimilitarist—behaved like the rest. In the supreme crisis, pacifism collapsed, and no effective protest was forthcoming from any international society or movement—from the Christian churches, from Marxian socialism, from scholars, business men, or financiers.

Each warring government published its own account of the diplomatic negotiations preceding the war, suppressing whatever appeared unfavorable to its own cause, exaggerating whatever seemed unfavorable to the cause of enemy countries, **National Solidarity** and on occasion deliberately falsifying the account. These official apologies of the several governments were soon supplemented by patriotic propaganda; and the pious mythologies, thus built up, and protected by military censorship, became veritable creeds for entire nations, promoting and sustaining the collective morale of each.

To the winning of the war was directed all this nationalist propaganda. To the same end was directed a radical reorganization of economic life within each belligerent nation. Industry, transportation, agriculture, commerce, and finance were progressively subjected to drastic regulation and control by the several governments, to such a degree as eventually to introduce *de facto* a war-time "state socialism" and to engage all the economic resources as well as the whole man-power of a nation in support of the war.

Thus the economic as well as strictly military effort of the warring governments fused all elements of each nation into an unprecedented unity of purpose—the limited purpose of seeing the war through. Party alignments were wiped out in each country; class divisions and religious quarrels were put aside. National solidarity was exalted as never before, and this fact made it possible alike for the masses and for the classes to endure the protracted hardships and suffering which the war entailed. From the standpoint of social history, this temporary fusion, or unity, is perhaps the outstanding fact of the World War.

At the outset, there was anxious hope that the war might be brief and end in a "knockout blow." The wars of 1859, 1866, and 1870–1871 had each centered in a single campaign and been decided by a single battle. The Russo-Japanese War of 1904–1905 had been over within a year, and the Balkan Wars of 1912–1913 within a few months. With all the latest mechanical inventions, the present war might conceivably set a record for speed and decisiveness. Otherwise, the prospect would be too dreadful to contemplate.

The common system of mobilization on the Continent made it certain that big armies would be ready to move against each other in little more than a fortnight from the declaration of war. Each of the general staffs had carefully elaborated a scheme for the opening operations with a view to taking the **Strategic Plans** offensive and winning a decisive battle within the shortest possible time. In general, the French and Russians planned to strike Germany simultaneously from two sides. While the French would attempt a general advance along the Franco-German frontier from Charleroi to Nancy and a more concentrated attack in Lorraine, the Russians would hold off the Austrians and invade East Prussia in force. On the other hand, the Germans planned to cope with their hostile neighbors in turn: to overwhelm the French with superior numbers and then to turn against the Russians.

To overwhelm the French and any British army which might come to their assistance, the German staff, under its chief, General von Moltke,[1] gathered a decisive superiority of forces on the northern and western wing of the armies facing Belgium and France. Belgium, when summoned to let the Germans pass, courageously refused and made a stand against overwhelming

---

[1] A nephew of the Moltke who had commanded in the Franco-Prussian War of 1870.

odds. The gallant defense of the Liége forts allowed the Belgian army to mobilize, but the last fort at Liége fell by the time the German right-wing armies were ready to move forward.

**Early German Success in West**

These scattered the Belgian army, crossed the country,[1] and reached the French border according to plan; and here with a decisive superiority they met the northern wing of the French army (and a supporting "expeditionary force" from Britain). Not only here, but in the whole series of opening engagements known as the Battles of the Frontier, the French armies were defeated. The French offensive from Charleroi to Nancy was halted in its tracks, and the French advance into Lorraine was turned back. All the German armies were ordered forward in pursuit, and on August 25 Moltke wired to William II that "in six weeks the whole story will be concluded."

This prediction proved erroneous. The German plan had assembled a superiority of forces at the critical point and had defeated the enemy at the time and place anticipated. But the defeat was less severe than at first appeared, and in the next conflicts the French troops proved far steadier. Above all, Joffre, the French commander-in-chief, held his retiring armies under firm control, transferred troops from right to left, and continued an orderly retreat until he could redispose his forces and stand to fight along a more favorable position. Just south of the Marne, he halted the retreat; and on September 6 his forces turned to deliver battle.

All the armies between Paris and Verdun were engaged in this new conflict. The Battle of the Marne, as it came to be known,

**Battle of the Marne**

comprised five or six more or less distinct battles along a 150-mile front, lasting four days. These actions were fought by troops not yet hardened to war, who had been marching or fighting for three weeks in the hottest of midsummer weather. Along most of the battle front, the actions were indecisive; but the German advance was definitely halted, and in the western sector the British army pushed forward through a gap between the German armies of Kluck and Below. By the

---

[1] Acts of retaliation which German troops inflicted on Belgium for its resistance—such as the burning of the library of the University of Louvain—provided some substantiation for a host of "atrocity stories" which were utilized to confirm the morale of Allied peoples and to arouse anti-German sentiment in neutral countries. By the latter part of August 1914, most of Belgium was under military occupation by Germany, and a German governor was installed at Brussels. King Albert of Belgium with a remnant of his army was with the French and British.

morning of September 9 the British had crossed the Marne; Kluck and Below were completely separated; and to prevent disaster the German right wing retreated from the Marne to the Aisne. The armies farther east followed suit, and by September 14 the Germans were on the defensive.

The French in turn had to face the disappointment of not being able to force the defensive position of the Germans, and thus the third phase of the opening engagements in the West ended in a stalemate. But though tactically indecisive, the Marne campaign marked the complete failure of the strategy of a speedy German victory over France. Moltke, the German commander, realized only too clearly the full meaning of the failure of his offensive. On September 9, the day his armies began their retreat, he wrote his wife: "It goes badly—The first hopes have been utterly belied. . . . Bitter disillusionment is already upon us." Moltke himself collapsed from the blow, and a new German Chief of Staff, Erich von Falkenhayn, had to be appointed in the midst of the crisis.

The stalemate along the Aisne left the opposing armies pinned to the ground with their western flanks uncovered and with vital railway communications unprotected. From common necessity both Falkenhayn and Joffre set to work to prolong their lines in this quarter and, if possible, to outflank each other. Falkenhayn, with spirited energy, ordered a new attack in the West in order to cut off Paris from the Channel ports (through which British reinforcements were arriving) and from all northern France. Joffre checked the attack and turned the line northward, but try as he would during the next month he could not outflank the Germans. The net result was a new entrenched front reaching from the Aisne northward to the western tip of Belgium. In the last phase of this "race to the sea," Falkenhayn gathered all available troops and a new army corps of fresh troops raised since the beginning of hostilities, and made a fierce attempt to break through to the Channel ports. The British army, centering at Ypres, had to bear the brunt of the assault, which continued without let-up for three weeks. The Battle of Ypres was in fact the longest and most hard-fought battle up to this time. It left both armies ex-  **Entrenched** hausted; and with the commencement of winter the **Western** Western Front stabilized in entrenched lines running **Front** from Nieuport and Ypres (in southwestern Belgium) southward to the Aisne River, thence eastward to Verdun, and thence southward again to Belfort and the Swiss frontier—a total distance of about six hundred miles.

This long Western Front left in German hands most of the industrial area of Belgium and northern France, which was a serious handicap to the Allies throughout the war. The Allies, however, maintained securely their hold on the Channel ports, which assured effective lines of communication between France and England and made it easier for the Allies to blockade the German coasts. With their existing supplies, the Allies had little prospect of breaking through the entrenched German position across France. But, on the other hand, the existence of this "impregnable front" committed the German army to the very thing the General Staff had sought to avoid: an interminable siege warfare which might drain away Germany's resources while permitting France and Britain to draw freely upon the outside world.

In the East, meanwhile, the war had reached a similar result. The war plans of Russia, Austria, and Germany alike had ended in frustration, and the failure of the German offensive in the West was paralleled by a deadlock along an entrenched Eastern Front.

Originally the Russian war plan had contemplated offensives against both Germany and Austria, but some years before 1914 the Russian military authorities had promised the French that in case the main German attack was launched against France, the major part of the Russian forces would be directed at the outset against Germany. This promise was not carried out. When war actually came, the Russians yielded to the temptation to direct their chief effort against the "favorite enemy"—Austria. They were rewarded by a striking victory along the whole Austrian front in Galicia. But between the diversion of forces thereby entailed and an extraordinarily faulty execution of the long-

**Early German Success in East: Battle of Tannenberg** planned invasion of East Prussia, the Russian offensive against Germany ended in sensational disaster. The Russian armies which advanced into East Prussia were together numerically superior to the German army, but while the Russian generals dismally failed to cooperate, the Germans, under the central command of General Paul von Hindenburg, with General Erich Ludendorff as his chief of staff, acted as a unit and managed to deal with the Russians piecemeal. It thus transpired that in each of the three battles fought in East

Prussia in August 1914, the Germans brought into action more battalions than the Russians. And at the culminating Battle of Tannenberg (August 26–29) one of the Russian armies was routed with a loss of 125,000 prisoners, while another broke to pieces in attempting a sudden retreat and lost an equal number of men.

By this disaster the Russians lost the strategical opportunity to overrun East Prussia, which was of critical importance to their general war plan. Moreover, it prevented them from fully harvesting their victory on the Austrian front in Galicia. And the loss of 300,000 trained officers and men, with corresponding quantities of war material, was irreparable.

The Austrian misfortunes arose from cross-purposes at the outset of the war. Throughout the diplomatic crisis of July the government at Vienna held to the plan of a war on Serbia alone, on the premise that clear-cut diplomatic **Austrian Defeats** support from Germany would keep Russia from actual conflict. When Russia suddenly ordered mobilization and Germany declared war, an Austrian army was already on its way to Serbia; and the government decided to carry through the Serbian campaign as planned. Through shocking mismanagement, this campaign ended in utter defeat, and the Austrian invaders had to retire behind their own frontiers. The troops used for the vain effort could not take their place in the line of battle in Galicia, where the Russian advance had to be met immediately afterwards. With a substantial superiority of numbers, the Russians hammered back the whole Austrian line to western Galicia, and here the exhausted and sadly weakened Austrian army made a stand behind the Dunajetz River. Desperately the Austrian commander called up the German General Staff for the reinforcements due at this stage—six weeks after the outbreak of war. He called in vain. The Austrian defeat in Galicia took place almost simultaneously with the Battle of the Marne, and the Western Front held in ever firmer grip the main strength of the German army.

By the end of 1914 the lines in the East settled down in a more or less entrenched front extending from the borders of East Prussia through western Russian Poland and across Galicia to the Carpathian Mountains—a distance of some nine hundred miles. In the East, as in the West, the war had reached a seeming deadlock. On both fronts, and by both sides, the opportunity for a strategic decision and a "knockout blow" was lost. The prospect now was a dreadful one of prolonged trench warfare.

### 3. GROWING MAGNITUDE AND INDECISIVENESS, 1915–1916

By the winter of 1914–1915 the war was assuming unprecedented magnitude. Millions of men were under arms, and "trench warfare" was taking the place of field operations. Each of the contending armies was ensconced in a system of trenches, running two or three deep in zigzag parallels, connected with one another by laterals, and connected also with underground "dugouts" in which soldiers rested and supplies were kept. Between the opposing systems was "no man's land," a waste space obstructed with mounds of dirt and tangles of barbed wire, through which infantry must advance if they would capture the enemy's trenches.

Trench and Machine Warfare

On the Western Front, as we have pointed out, such trench systems of the Germans and of the French and British (and Belgians) now faced each other in a line six hundred miles long. On the Eastern Front, the opposing trench systems of the Russians and of the Germans and Austrians were less elaborate but more extensive, covering a distance of some nine hundred miles.

Trench warfare was supplemented by the latest mechanical devices. Cavalry, in the circumstances, could be employed very little, but artillery was used on a scale hitherto undreamed of. Machine guns were utilized in prodigious numbers, and big cannon were installed all along the trenches to mow down the obstructions in "no man's land," to destroy the enemy's positions, and to screen the charges of infantry. Chemical inventions and appliances were increasingly made use of, so that to shell and shot were added explosive bombs and exploding mines, and considerably later in the war poisonous gases were discharged with deadly effect. Later in the war, too, the Allies built "tanks," cars encased in iron and driven by gasoline engines, which crawled over hills and gullies on caterpillar treads and spat out bullets. Gasoline engines proved, in fact, a most important auxiliary of the new warfare. They were employed not only eventually in "tanks," but immediately in the myriads of motor lorries which supplied troops at the front with ammunition and food and conveyed prisoners and the disabled to the rear, and also in the host of airplanes which darted above the trenches, spying out the

WESTERN AND EASTERN
BATTLEFRONTS
IN EUROPE
AT THE END OF 1914

〰〰〰〰〰 BATTLEFRONTS

movements of the enemy, fighting off hostile planes, and dropping explosives.

With these new methods of warfare, and with millions of men directly involved on each side, the winning of decisive battles appeared almost impossible. To "carry" trenches required a vast concerted effort of artillery and infantry and an enormous expenditure of shot and shell and of human life. And to provide the millions of soldiers at the front with needful supplies necessitated the persistent and united cooperation of the whole civilian population of every belligerent nation. The financial expenditure was gigantic. Heavy taxes were levied and huge sums were borrowed.

Nevertheless, in the late winter and early spring of 1915, despite German success in East Prussia and outright conquests in Belgium, northern France, and western Russian Poland, the Allied nations of France, Russia, and Great Britain **Allied** were sanguine of ultimate triumph. In population, in **Prospects** wealth, and in natural resources they collectively excelled the Central Empires of Germany and Austria-Hungary. They made much of the fact that the latter constituted a "beleaguered fortress," against which the Russians would exert increasing pressure from the east, while the French and British (now being rapidly reinforced by volunteers from the British Isles and by armies from Canada, Australia, and New Zealand) would push hard from the west. They confidently predicted that their superior numbers and resources would prove decisive and that even without "knock-out blows" they could exhaust the Central Empires and bring them to terms. British sea power was already destroying Germany's oceanic trade, detaching its colonies, and threatening to deprive it of needful supplies.

In such an optimistic frame of mind the Allied governments arranged a division of the spoils which would accrue to them from their eventual triumph. Back in September 1914, they had solemnly promised one another, by the Pact of London, not to make peace separately but to hold together until they had achieved a common victory. Then, in March 1915, they secretly agreed among themselves that in the future peace settlement Russia should appropriate Constantinople and all of Poland, France should regain Alsace-Lorraine and dominate the left bank of the Rhine, and Great Britain should take most of the German colonies.

But the Germans hoped for ultimate victory too. They were superbly united and resolute. The military endeavors of Austria-Hungary had been disappointing, but the Dual Monarchy had not been shaken by any actual revolt of its **German Prospects** subject peoples—as the Allies had hoped—and some of the most influential Polish leaders, for example, were so anxious to prevent Poland from being Russianized that their continuing loyalty to the Habsburg Empire could be depended upon. Under German leadership, the armies of Austria-Hungary, and of the Ottoman Empire also, could be made efficient and very useful.

Germany and Austria-Hungary admittedly constituted a "beleaguered fortress," but this had some advantages. It meant that the armies of the Central Empires could operate on interior rather than exterior lines, and that reinforcements could be transferred with relative ease and dispatch from one front to another, wherever they might count the most. Besides, the whole military strategy of the Central Empires could be directed by a single authority, the German General Staff, which, by coordinating the efforts of the Austrians, Hungarians, and Turks with those of the Germans, could strike telling blows first in one direction and then in another. In this respect the situation within the "beleaguered fortress" was in marked contrast to that of the besieging hosts, who were subject to the orders of several separate and jealous general staffs—Russian, French, British, and Serbian. Unity of command was as advantageous to the Central Empires as disunity was costly to the Allies.

For the new type of entrenched warfare, the Central Empires at the beginning of 1915 had advantages in equipment and trained soldiery. Germany, no more than the enemy powers, had originally accumulated stocks of munitions sufficient to outlast the opening campaigns, but with methodical foresight the war ministry at Berlin had planned the inevitable expansion of war industry. It had made surveys of German industrial plants, determined what work each could do, and prepared specifications for a rapid change to production of war material. As a result, munitions contracted for after the declaration of war were being delivered in huge quantities to the German field armies early in 1915, just when the Allies were facing a serious shortage of munitions—when France was deprived of its major industrial centers, when Britain was only beginning to transform peace industries into war industries, and when Russia was literally starving for guns and munitions.

At this time, also, Germany could put reserves of man-power more promptly in the field. Joffre, the French commander, had far fewer of such reserves upon which to draw; and Lord Kitchener, the British war minister, having started with only a relatively small professional army, had to take time to recruit and train wholly new units. Falkenhayn, on the other hand, by a skillful mixing of fresh young conscripts and trained personnel, put a group of new army corps into the field in November 1914; and by the close of the year, in addition to supplying losses in the existing ranks, he had ready another body of fresh troops as large as the entire British army in France.

In the circumstances Falkenhayn sought a military decision without delay. He would attempt a smashing attack upon the British sector of the Western Front before Kitchener's new British army could arrive. Such an attack might well have been decisive. Beyond doubt the general condition of the Western Front at the time offered a better opportunity than was ever to occur again for the Germans to smash through and overwhelm France and Britain.

But the Austrian failures of 1914 in the East now embarrassed the German Command. The Russian armies seemed on the point of breaking through the Carpathian Mountains and deluging the Hungarian plain. A second disastrous attempt to invade Serbia had weakened still further the Austrian army and left it divided on two far distant fronts. Moreover, both the diplomatic and the military authorities in Germany observed that Italy and Rumania were preparing to enter the war on the side of the Allies and against the Central Empires. If they should enter the war, they might overwhelm Austria.

To avert such a catastrophe, Falkenhayn compelled the Austrian foreign minister to offer Italy territorial "compensations" as a price for its continuing neutrality. Italy, in accordance with the terms of the Triple Alliance, had been demanding "compensations" ever since the beginning of the war, but the Austrian government had been quite unheedful until pressed by Germany, and even now it had no faith that Italy could be satisfied. Public sentiment in Italy was by this time predominantly anti-Austrian and pro-Ally; and, after all, the Allies could promise

Italy more territory at Austria's expense than Austria could be expected to do. So Italy, while continuing to negotiate with Austria, signed at London in April 1915 a secret treaty with the Allies. Thereby it obtained from them a pledge that if it helped them in the war it might annex the southern half of the Tyrol (including Trent), Trieste, Istria, and part of the Dalmatian coast, and, in addition, it might enlarge its African colonies and share in the partition of the Ottoman Empire. "This," the British statesman, Lord Balfour, later explained, "is the sort of thing you have to do when you are engaged in war."

*Bargaining of Italy and Rumania*

In Rumania were divided counsels. The Hohenzollern King Ferdinand and a number of the country's "elder statesmen" wished to be loyal to the Triple Alliance and perceived in taking sides with the Central Empires an opportunity to obtain from the Russian Empire the Rumanian-speaking province of Bessarabia. On the other hand, a majority of the "younger statesmen" were inclined to throw over the Triple Alliance entirely, to unite with the Allies, and to participate in a partition of Austria-Hungary, whence Rumania might secure provinces larger and more valuable than Bessarabia. The Allies offered the main part of Transylvania but they were precluded by Russian and Serbian objections from offering as much as the King and his advisers deemed necessary to overcome their scruples. Consequently the Rumanian government wavered back and forth and awaited the time when its services would command a higher price.

While Falkenhayn was doing his best to keep Italy and Rumania neutral, Hindenburg, the "hero" of the Battle of Tannenberg and now the military idol of the whole German nation, came forward boldly with promises of swift annihilating victory over Russia. The German Chancellor, Bethmann-Hollweg, and likewise Admiral von Tirpitz backed Hindenburg; and finally, in view of Austria's critical position, Falkenhayn acquiesced.

*German Offensive in East*

Wherefore Falkenhayn reluctantly abandoned the prospect of victory in the West and turned East for the campaign of 1915. "With a heavy heart" he sent off to Hindenburg his reserve of fresh troops, "including the best that Germany possessed in the war." These troops were used up at once in battles fought in a midwinter blizzard—without perceptibly diminishing the pressure of the Russian army against Austria. After this fiasco, Falkenhayn took the relief offensive into his own hands. The French and British were already commencing to hammer at the Western Front, and it was impossible to transfer another whole army eastward. But by draining men from each of the divisions in the West, Falkenhayn was able to assemble twelve new divisions in time to save the Austrian front. They were grouped with picked Austrian divisions, under a good General, August von Mackensen, and one of the best German staff officers, Hans von Seeckt, whose careful arrangements produced for the first time the grand-style artillery preparation which thereafter became a characteristic feature of the war. The result was a triumph of Austro-German operations: the Austrian divisions did as well as the German; the Russian line was broken through at Gorlice; and in a fortnight (in May 1915) Falkenhayn's "relief-offensive" advanced ninety-five miles. The whole Russian front in Galicia began crumbling, and the general balance of the war in the East was suddenly reversed.

Rumania dropped at once all idea of intervening against the Central Empires, but even in the full tide of Austro-German suc-**Allies Joined by Italy** cess Italy declared war on Austria-Hungary. This was a disappointment to Falkenhayn's hopes, although the defeat of the Russians permitted Austria to reinforce it troops on the Italian border. For Austria the crisis had passed, and the mountainous Italian frontier was easily organized for defensive warfare. For over a year, in fact, it stood secure against Italian offensives.

In Poland, meanwhile, the Austro-German advance relentlessly continued, and it presently became clear that the Russian armies **German Conquest of Poland** were woefully short of munitions. Up to the last minute the war ministry at Petrograd [1] sought to escape blame by concealing and then by denying the fact. It was then too late to supply the shortage; and all that the Russian commander-in-chief, the Grand-Duke Nicholas, could do was to avoid battle and keep retreating. It was thus possible for Falkenhayn to extend his advance in the East without drawing more reinforcements from the Western Front. By September 1915 all Poland, together with the greater part of Lithuania, was in military possession of the Central Empires.

[1] The name of the Russian capital had recently been changed from the German "St. Petersburg" to the Slavic "Petrograd."

Russian losses in the summer of 1915 were not confined to territory. Half a million soldiers were killed, a million wounded, and another million captured. The remaining Russian armies, at least temporarily, were demoralized by defeat and retreat. And it boded ill for the future that the Tsar Nicholas II, now more than ever under the spell of his hysterical wife and her strange bewitcher, the "monk" Rasputin,[1] dismissed the Grand-Duke Nicholas and took nominal command himself of the Russian armies. The Tsar insisted that the war should go on, but he was too irresolute to prevent confusion from becoming worse confounded.

Having badly battered Russia, Falkenhayn hurried West with some detachments to meet an expected French attack in Champagne. It was in the nick of time. Joffre was launching the most powerful offensive yet seen on any front. The German line was on the point of yielding, and Falkenhayn arrived just in time to cancel an order for retreat which would have broken the entrenched front in France.

This crisis passed, Falkenhayn next switched a group of divisions from Poland to the Serbian front and prepared with due care the invasion twice bungled in Austrian hands. As a by-product of the Austro-German victory over Russia, Bulgaria definitely allied itself with the Central Empires (September 1915), accepting their offers of territorial aggrandizement and promising to cooperate with them in the attack on Serbia. **Central Powers Joined by Bulgaria** In October, therefore, Serbia was assailed simultaneously from the east by Bulgarian armies and from the north by an Austro-German army under Marshal von Mackensen. Against the double invasion Serbia could not stand, and an expeditionary force which the Allies managed to organize "for the relief of Serbia" and to land at Salonica (in Greek territory[2]) was too small to do aught but prevent King Constantine from bringing Greece into the war on the side of the Central Empires. Within two months, Serbia was over-**Conquest of Serbia** run by the Austro-Germans and Bulgarians, and its royal family and the remnants of its army were refugees. The same fate befell Montenegro, and Albania was occupied.

[1] See above, pp. 344–345.

[2] This involved, of course, an Allied violation of Greek neutrality, but it was excused on the ground of "military necessity," as Germany had excused the earlier violation of Belgian neutrality, and of assent by the Greek minister Venizelos, who was notoriously hostile to his sovereign.

At the outset of 1915 Germany had been viewed, and had viewed itself, as a beleaguered fortress. By the end of the year Falkenhayn had extended the fortress to include all Poland, most of the Balkan peninsula, and the Ottoman Empire in Europe and Asia Minor. A new ally in Bulgaria, with a strong army, counterbalanced Italy's turning to the opposite side; and the conquests in the Balkans redoubled the value of Turkey as an ally.

Already, in the winter of 1914–1915, when Russia was in dire need of munitions, Winston Churchill, the head of the British Admiralty, had counseled the Allies to force open the Turkish **Allied** Straits connecting the Mediterranean with the Black **Failure at** Sea, so that commerce between Russia and Britain **Dar-** might be expedited. But Joffre, the French commander-**danelles** in-chief, afraid of weakening the Western Front and convinced that the war must ultimately be decided there, was opposed to a military diversion at the Straits; and the British had more ships than men to spare. As a compromise, it had been agreed that a naval attack should be made on the Straits, and accordingly, in February and March 1915, a powerful Franco-British fleet essayed to silence and destroy the Turkish land forts lining both sides of the Dardanelles. The attempt failed. Several battleships were sunk, and the others had to be withdrawn.

Much wrangling ensued in Allied headquarters as to whether a military expedition should and could be sent to do what the naval expedition had failed to do. By the time another compromise was reached and an expeditionary force of Britishers, Australians, and New Zealanders, with a sprinkling of colonial French troops, was ready to disembark at the tip of the Gallipoli peninsula (bordering the Dardanelles), the Turks, under a German commander, Marshal Liman von Sanders, had had ample time to perfect their defenses and render the peninsula well-nigh impregnable. The expeditionary force fought gallantly, but it could make little headway, and its commander, Sir Ian Hamilton, was denied necessary reinforcements. It struggled intermittently for several months, and always unsuccessfully. In December 1915, it was finally withdrawn.

Not only were the Turks enabled, through German advice and supplies, to defeat the Allies at the Dardanelles but also to hold in check an attempted Russian advance through the Caucasus into Armenia, and at the same time to threaten the Suez Canal and to capture an Anglo-Indian expeditionary force which had been landed in Mesopotamia. Simultaneously the Bulgarians, likewise buttressed by Germany, were holding the Balkans and keeping an Allied force pinned to defensive positions at Salonica.

Against the brilliant German record of 1915, the Allies could offer merely a drab background of failure. On the Western Front, they had felt obliged to maintain almost constant attacks in order to prevent a greater shifting of German divisions to the Russian front. These attacks had begun before a proper reinforcement of guns and munitions was at hand, and some had been badly bungled. They had perhaps saved the Russian army from annihilation, but they brought no victories—terrible wastage.

By the end of 1915, however, the British and French were at last amply provided with munitions. Falkenhayn, knowing this, concluded that Germany could no longer expect to win a "military decision" against them. But to stand indefinitely on the defensive would mean the certain exhaustion of the Central Empires. The war could not go on forever as a stalemate. It must be ended, and this could be brought about only by proving to France that a military victory over Germany was impossible. To wear down French morale, therefore, he proposed a sustained offensive against a favorable point on the Western Front.

The German government endorsed Falkenhayn's proposal, and without waiting for the end of winter the offensive was opened against Verdun in February 1916. But the opening **German** attack did not succeed as planned. The spirit of the **Failure at** French army, under General Pétain, stiffened to meet **Verdun** so direct a challenge, and the wearing-out battle dragged on in more and more hopeless effort from February to July. Both armies suffered frightful losses and both were exhausted, but Verdun remained in French hands. And at the end the test of strength lowered the morale of the German nation at large more than the French.

Moreover, the Allies by now were far stronger than in 1915. A much larger British army was provided for by the imposition of universal conscription in January 1916. Both French and British armies were better supplied with guns and munitions, and even the Russian forces were now being rearmed. Besides, the Allies arranged to coordinate their military effort; and at a conference presided over by Joffre in the spring of 1916, France,

Britain, Russia, and Italy agreed to concentrate their energies each on a single vigorous offensive. These attacks on various fronts were to be delivered simultaneously in July.

The drain of Verdun diminished radically the French share in the joint effort, but in the East the Austrian commander, Conrad, played directly into the Allied plans. Yielding to the temptation of a decisive victory over Italy, he transferred a large part of his best troops and heaviest artillery from the Russian Front and opened a drive from the Tyrol. The Italians soon brought this to a halt, and a Russian army, under General Brusilov, then struck the sector whence the Austrian troops and guns had been withdrawn. The Austrian line collapsed quite as brusquely as the Russian line early in 1915. The Russians reoccupied eastern Galicia and took numerous prisoners.

By shifting divisions from other fronts, Falkenhayn was able to stay the Russian advance and reestablish new lines in Galicia. But on the heels of Brusilov's attack, the British and French drove hard at the German front in the West in the region of the Somme. The first assaults failed to break the German position, and slow progress could only be made with heavy loss. But from the German perspective, the general situation of the war was again reversed. Verdun, then at its extreme point of danger, was relieved of serious pressure, and the German forces in the West were thrown on a desperate defensive.

Soon afterwards, at the command of General Cadorna, the Italian army opened an energetic offensive in Istria on the Isonzo front. It profited from Austrian concern with Brusilov and his Russians and began with brilliant promise. Gorizia, a key point, was promptly captured; and once again Austria appeared on the verge of collapse.

Meanwhile, in March 1916, Great Britain had persuaded Portugal to seize German vessels in its harbors and to follow up Germany's resulting declaration of war by sending a Portuguese army to join the Allies on the Western Front. Now, in August, these favorable events elicited a declaration of war from Rumania against the Central Empires, and on the same day Italy declared war on Germany.[1] The failure of the long German effort in the West, at Verdun,

*Allies Joined by Portugal, and Rumania*

---

[1] Italy, in declaring war against Austria back in May 1915, had then refrained from declaring war against Germany.

and the obvious weakening of the Austrian army convinced the Rumanian leaders that their country's intervention would bring about the immediate debâcle of the Habsburg Empire. As a first impression, this opinion was held unquestioningly by the public at large, not only in Allied nations, but more poignantly in Germany and Austria.

In point of fact, the Rumanians had waited just too long— partly in driving a hard bargain with the Allies.[1] At the crisis of Brusilov's offensive in Galicia, in June, Rumanian intervention might well have been decisive. But by the end of August the Galician front had been patched up, and Falkenhayn, fully warned, was prepared against Rumania's action. He had been able, even in the thunderstorm of enemy offensives on every front, to gather a new army along the Transylvanian border. This army struck promptly; and soon the whole Rumanian plain north of the Danube was another Austro-German con- quest. Instead of destroying the Habsburg Empire, the net result of Rumania's entry into the war was that all the Balkan states, except Greece, were now controlled by the Central Empires.

German Conquest of Rumania

But within Germany, meanwhile, Rumania's declaration of war had produced an immediate crisis. The Emperor William II was thoroughly broken by the news, and to his intimates he declared that the war was lost and that peace must be made without delay. On the country at large the effect was much the same, for the fearfully wearing struggle at Verdun, followed by a storm of enemy offensives at every point, had strained all nerves to the breaking point. In this general mood, Bethmann-Hollweg, the Chancellor, with other high officials, prevailed upon William II to dismiss Falkenhayn and to summon Hindenburg and Ludendorff to the supreme command (August 1916).

William II had resisted this step for a year and a half. Ever since 1913 there had been sharp personal enmity between him and Ludendorff; and since the beginning of the war Luden- dorff had industriously built up Hindenburg's popu- larity and prestige in opposition to the Emperor and to Falkenhayn. William II understood clearly that, in summoning Hindenburg and Ludendorff, he was in effect abdicating his "ultimate" authority in the state to a masterful and domineer-

Ludendorff and Hindenburg

---

[1] The secret treaty, as finally signed in August 1916 by Rumania with the Allies, pledged it, as the price of its military support, not only Transylvania and Bukovina but also the Serbian Banat and the plain of Hungary as far as the Theiss River.

ing rival, and he yielded only because the pressure upon him was too great.

The appointment of Hindenburg as commander-in-chief, with Ludendorff as quartermaster-general (and virtual dictator), amounted to a political revolution in Germany, and produced no less radical a change in the character and scope of the war. Falkenhayn's policy of "possibilities," as regards strategy and war aims, gave place by degrees to an unlimited program of conquest and an arraying of almost the whole world against the Central Empires.

Hindenburg's first act after assuming command was to inspect the Western Front, which he and Ludendorff now saw for the first time. The two were appalled by the character of the Somme offensive, still under way; and without delay they ordered the building of the "Hindenburg Line," a heavily fortified line in the rear, whither the German divisions could take refuge from the untenable positions into which they had been forced. In addition, Hindenburg and Ludendorff reported certain conclusions: (1) that against such military resources as the Allied Powers were now bringing into the field, there was no possibility of Germany's winning the war by land offensives; (2) that even by holding to the defensive, the troops could not stand the strain of another continuous battle such as the Somme; and (3) that the only hope was for Germany to turn to unrestricted submarine warfare. Through the submarine Britain might be compelled within the first six months of 1917 to cease effective cooperation with its allies and thereby to leave them with no choice but to make peace with Germany.

In the minds of the new German Command, Britain held the key position. Allied fortunes had waxed in 1916 with increasing British success on the seas. They would wane rapidly if Britain suffered sea disaster in 1917.

#### 4. BRITISH MARITIME SUCCESS, 1914–1916

Great Britain's naval superiority had been utilized from 1914 to 1916 in many ways advantageous to the Allied cause. First, it was employed to clear the high seas of enemy warships. One British squadron, it is true, was defeated by a German fleet off the coast of Chile near Coronel in November 1914; but another British squadron was promptly sent out, and in the next month near the Falkland Islands it encountered and destroyed that German fleet. In general, German warships which were at sea when war was declared put hurriedly into neutral ports and were duly interned, and the main battle fleet and some of the finest cruisers of Germany, which happened to be in home waters, stuck close to the German harbors where floating mines and land batteries could protect them against British attack. Occasionally, German cruisers made stealthy trips across the North Sea and bombarded English coast towns. Occasionally, too, German "raiders" took to the high seas and preyed upon Allied merchantmen, but their careers were usually brief and always ended either in capture or in internment in neutral ports. *Britain's Naval Superiority*

The British kept their major battle fleet "in reserve," that is, stationed in the waters north of Scotland, carefully guarded against surprise attacks by German submarines or bombers and yet ready to engage the German fleet if it should issue from its havens. In this way the British may be said to have exercised their naval power more by frightening the enemy than by actually fighting him. On one occasion—at the end of May 1916, almost two years after the beginning of hostilities—the German battle fleet did emerge into the North Sea and *Battle of Jutland* oblige the British armada to fight. The British lost more lives and ships than the Germans in the battle of Jutland, as the contest was called, but they could afford to lose more, and they were victorious in that the surviving German warships returned to their home harbors and did not again venture out on the high seas.

With German (and Austrian) warships driven from the high seas, Great Britain and France could freely transport troops and munitions to and from oversea areas. French colonial troops from Algeria, Senegal, and Indo-China were thus transported in safety to France to reinforce the Allied Western Front. To France, moreover, for the same purpose, armies were brought not only from Great Britain but also from Canada, Australia, New Zealand, and India. Thereby, the number of British troops in France grew steadily until, with the imposition of conscription by the British parliament in January 1916, it equaled the number of French troops. There was opposition to conscription in Ireland, and a group of extremists of the Sinn Fein and Labor parties rose in revolt at Dublin in Easter week of 1916 and proclaimed an "Irish Republic." The majority of the Irish people, however, remained quiet, and, thanks again to British sea power, troops which were dispatched from England suppressed the revolt quickly—and vindictively.[1]

The uninterrupted stream of men and munitions which the British poured into France during 1915 and 1916 explains, along with the fighting ability and good generalship of the French, why the Germans in those years could make no such headway in western Europe as they made in the east. But western Europe was not the only field of military operations where British naval supremacy counted heavily. With Germany deprived of the means of aiding its overseas colonies, these were invaded and conquered by Allied forces. The British navy was, indeed, the chief factor in expanding the European war into a real World War.

In August 1914 the German colony of Togoland in Africa was captured. Then, expeditionary forces penetrated into the larger **Conquest of German Colonies** and more important German colony of Kamerun, gradually overcoming the resistance of its weak garrison and compelling its surrender at the beginning of 1915. Against German Southwest Africa, General Louis Botha [2] inaugurated a campaign with a South African army in September 1914, but anti-British sentiment among a portion of the Dutch-speaking Boers produced within the Union of South Africa a serious revolt. Halting the campaign against German Southwest Africa, therefore, General Botha, with the cooperation of General Smuts, crushed the revolt in the Union. As soon as this was accomplished, early in 1915, Botha and Smuts renewed the attack on German Southwest Africa and completed its conquest in July.

The conquest of German East Africa proved more difficult. Although British warships seized the port of Dar-es-Salaam in August 1914, the German governor of the colony, General von Lettow-Vorbeck, was so resourceful in commanding the loyalty of the natives and in conducting military operations that he kept the British on the defensive throughout 1915 and actually carried

---

[1] Only about 2,000 Irishmen actively engaged in the insurrection of 1916. About a hundred British soldiers were killed in putting down the "revolt." Afterwards, fifteen "rebels" were executed, and many others, including "suspects," were imprisoned. On the long-range effects, see below, pp. 459–461.

[2] See above, pp. 66–67.

the war into British East Africa. In 1916 General Smuts managed to conquer the greater part of German East Africa, but
the surrender of Lettow-Vorbeck was not effected until November 1918.

In the southern Pacific, a contingent of New Zealanders captured German Samoa in August 1914, and shortly afterwards
Australian expeditions seized New Guinea, Kaiser Wilhelmsland,
and the Bismarck Archipelago. In the northern Pacific, and in
the Far East generally, Japan as the ally of Great Britain was
enabled to make short work of German concessions and colonies.
Japanese warships seized the Ladrones and Caroline Islands
and convoyed to China a military expedition which captured
Kiaochow in October 1914.

In the Near East, Great Britain employed its naval superiority to penalize the Ottoman Empire for siding with Germany.
At the beginning of Turkish hostilities, in October 1914, Britain
formally freed both Cyprus and Egypt from nominal **Assaults**
vassalage to the Ottoman Empire. Cyprus was trans- **on Ottoman**
formed into an outright British colony, and Egypt **Empire**
into a full-fledged British protectorate. Then, while an Anglo-
Egyptian army warded off Turkish attacks against the Suez
Canal, an Anglo-Indian army was landed at the head of the
Persian Gulf and undertook the conquest of Mesopotamia.

In 1915 the Turco-British phase of the World War was disap-
pointing to Great Britain and the other Allies. The Anglo-Egyptian
army was on the defensive and barely able to hold the Suez Canal.
Half of the Anglo-Indian army, after advancing 180 miles up the
Tigris, was surrounded by superior Turkish forces at Kut-al-
Amara and compelled to surrender in April 1915. And, as we have
previously pointed out, the prolonged efforts of the British at the
Dardanelles, first by sea and next by land, ended in sorry failure.

In 1916, however, the tide turned and Great Britain gained
several advantages in the Ottoman Empire. First, the peninsula of
Sinai, between Egypt and Palestine, was conquered by an Anglo-
Egyptian army reinforced by Australians and New Zealanders
who had been transported from Gallipoli. Second, the town of
Kut-al-Amara on the Tigris was retaken by an Anglo-Indian
army; in March Bagdad was captured, and by the end of the year
the greater part of Mesopotamia was in British hands. Last, but
not least, a remarkable and adventurous young Britisher, known

as Colonel Lawrence, won Arab respect and support. He ingrati-
ated himself with the Arab ruler of Mecca, Hussein, and with his
fighting son, Feisal, and persuaded them to head a general Arab
revolt against the Turks. Hussein proclaimed the independence of
Hejaz in June 1916; and presently Feisal, with Lawrence as the
liaison officer between him and the British, was making raids
against the Turks and spreading nationalist propaganda among
the Arabs northward in Palestine and Syria.

Back of these growing threats against the Asiatic provinces of
the Ottoman Empire, as back of the overthrow of Germany's
colonial empire in Africa and the Pacific, was British naval supremacy. And less showy but more fundamentally important were
the commercial effects of Great Britain's naval superiority. German merchantmen, as well as German warships, were
driven from the seas; and the British navy enforced,
with growing stringency, a virtual blockade of German
seaports and interfered more and more with neutral trade with
Germany. Germany, of course, continued to import and export
goods across the Netherlands or the Scandinavian countries, but
vessels to or from these countries were subjected to search by
the British, and commodities clearly German in origin or desti-
nation were usually confiscated. Germany was thus deprived of
profitable foreign markets for manufactures and likewise of a
copious supply of needful raw materials.

Britain's industry was correspondingly stimulated. It profited
from the slowing down of non-military production in Allied countries, from enemy occupation of the chief industrial centers of
France, and especially from the disappearance of German competition. With the stimulation of industry and commerce went a
relatively great accumulation of "war profits," so that Britain,
retaining its position as workshop and banker of the world, was
enabled to lend money to its allies, as well as to furnish them
with more munitions.

Even Britain would have cracked under the strain of financing
and supplying all its far-flung naval and military forces—and
acting as banker and munitions-maker for its numerous allies—
had it not been in a position to avail itself of the trade with
neutrals which it denied to Germany. With the United States,
particularly, Great Britain traded freely and permitted its allies
to trade, just as it practically prevented American trade with

Germany. This meant that, thanks to British supremacy on the high seas, the mills and factories of industrialized America were at the service of the Allies rather than of the Central Empires and that many manufacturers and bankers in neutral America were themselves amassing "war profits" from the sale of munitions and the loan of money to Great Britain, France, Italy, etc. Furthermore, it meant that the United States was more open to Allied propaganda than to that of Germany. The majority of American citizens were naturally disposed to sympathize with the Allies rather than with the Central Empires.

Still another commercial advantage of great importance Great Britain had over Germany, and that was in respect of foodstuffs. At the beginning of the war, Germany with Austria-Hungary was almost if not quite self-sufficing in grain, meat, and most other agricultural staples, while Britain was dependent for most of its foodstuffs on foreign imports. As the war went on, Britain's mastery of the seas assured to itself and its Allies a sufficient importation of foodstuffs from the United States, Canada, Argentina, and Australia, but there was increasing hardship for the Central Empires, and especially for Germany. Germany had to put more farm-hands in its armies or in its munition plants, with consequent loss of agricultural self-sufficiency; and the British "blockade" steadily lessened the chance of Germany's supplying the deficiency from abroad. By the end of 1916 hunger threatened to undermine German morale.

In the submarine—or "U-boat," as they called it—the Germans had one weapon which, if fully developed and freely used, might nullify the advantages accruing to the Allies **Germany's** from British supremacy on the seas. It might be em- **Submarine** ployed to destroy enemy warships, to interfere with the **Weapon** transportation of men and munitions from England to the Continent, and perhaps to starve out Great Britain. Some enemy warships and transports were actually destroyed by German submarines in the early stages of the war, and in June 1916 the cruiser on which Lord Kitchener, the British War Minister, was traveling to Russia for a conference with the Tsar, was sunk by a mine which had been planted by a German submarine. By 1917 it seemed as though a large-scale submarine campaign against British shipping was the one chance—and a good chance—which Germany had of overcoming Great Britain.

So the Germans reasoned. Unfortunately, a large-scale submarine campaign was fraught with danger for Germany as well as for Britain. The ultimate success of such a campaign would depend upon the destruction of many merchant vessels bound to or from England, some of which might be flying neutral flags and carrying neutral passengers. Neutral nations would be apt to protest emphatically against the torpedoing of their ships and the killing of their citizens, and, if Germany were to persevere in the campaign, this or that neutral nation would be almost certain to abandon its neutrality and to enlarge the already big circle of active enemies.

The United States, of all the neutrals, had most at stake. American citizens were always traveling to England, frequently on British ships; quantities of American munitions and foodstuffs were being sold in Britain; and the United States was the only great power which was not yet identified with one or the other of the belligerent coalitions.

In May 1915 a German submarine torpedoed and sank, off the coast of Ireland, one of the largest of British merchant vessels, the *Lusitania,* which was carrying from the United States to Britain a cargo of arms and some 1,200 passengers, including a hundred American citizens. The United States government had previously protested against British interference with American property on the high seas. Now, backed by strongly pro-Allied sympathy at home, it protested with greater vigor against German destruction of American lives on the high seas. For a year diplomatic notes were exchanged between Germany and the United States, interrupted now and then by new submarine attacks and by acute crises, until in May 1916 Germany acceded to American demands and promised that thereafter, unless it gave due notice to the contrary, no merchant vessel would be sunk without warning and without provision for the safety of passengers.

It thus transpired that the United States called a halt on Germany's using to the full the one weapon which might directly and seriously cripple Great Britain. In the meantime Great Britain clinched its hold on the seas and on lands overseas; and, by pressing its "blockade" of Germany's home ports, it intensified the threat of starving out the German people and nullifying their military successes on the Continent.

## 5. THE CRISIS OF THE WAR, 1917–1918

Despite the brilliant successes of the Central Empires against Russia and Serbia in 1915 and against Rumania in 1916, despite the drain of man-power which Germany had latterly exacted from its enemies on the Western Front, hopes of the Allies ran high in the winter of 1916–1917. The course of events seemed as auspicious for the Allies as it was critical for the Central Empires. Germany was suffering from the British "blockade," and its armies could apparently make no headway against France; they had been repulsed at Verdun, and farther west they had been obliged to retire to the "Hindenburg Line." In Austria-Hungary, the death of the venerable Emperor-King Francis Joseph in November 1916 gave impetus to disruptive agita- **Austrian** tion among subject peoples, and his conciliatory grand- **Peace** nephew who succeeded him as Charles I soon initiated **Proposals** secret negotiations with the Allies looking toward the Dual Monarchy's withdrawal from the war.

The Emperor Charles indicated his willingness to let France regain Alsace-Lorraine, Russia take Constantinople, Serbia gain an outlet to the sea and a portion of Albania, and Italy annex Trent. The negotiations, begun in January 1917, broke down in May because of stubborn opposition from both Italy and Germany. Charles sadly confessed that his realm could not fight another year without internal revolution.

The main reason why Germany opposed the Austrian peace proposals was the prospect of winning the war by resort to un- restricted submarine warfare. Hindenburg and Luden- **Submarine** dorff advised it. The German Admiralty pronounced it **Warfare** feasible and predicted that it would starve out England **and In-** in six months. The Chancellor and the Reichstag ap- **of United** proved, and public opinion was favorable. Both the **States** military and the diplomatic authorities recognized that in reply the United States would probably go to war, but they thought that American intervention could not thwart the prompt success of the U-boat campaign. The possibility of an American army being sent to Europe was also taken into account, but it was reckoned—quite accurately—that no large force could be organized and transported until long after the six-month period counted upon for the submarines to achieve their aim.

Preparations for the new German effort were matured by January 1917, just when the Habsburg Emperor was making his peace overtures to the Allies. On the last day of the month Germany notified the United States and other neutral powers that it was withdrawing the pledges previously given and that thenceforth all sea traffic within specified areas adjoining the British Isles, France, and Italy would, "without further notice, be prevented by all weapons." In other words, German submarines would sink at sight all merchantmen, regardless of the flag they flew and the passengers they carried. The United States, under the leadership of its President, Woodrow Wilson, at once broke off diplomatic relations with Germany, and, after debating a project for "armed neutrality," at length on April 6 declared war on Germany.

The American declaration of war was but a logical outcome of the position which Wilson had taken about unrestricted submarine warfare a year previously. It was naturally hailed with popular applause in the Allied countries. It justified their cause anew and temporarily reassured them. Yet, as the Germans anticipated, America could be of hardly more practical help to the Allies immediately after the declaration of war than it had been previously. Whether American intervention was of significance or not would depend in last analysis upon the success or failure of the German U-boats in 1917.

Almost simultaneously with the intervention of the United States, Russia underwent an internal revolution which also, at the **Russian Revolution of March 1917** moment, was popularly acclaimed in Allied countries, though actually it was of very dubious value to the Allied cause. Ever since the terrifying military reverses of 1915, affairs in Russia had been going from bad to worse. The temporary comeback which General Brusilov staged in eastern Galicia in the summer of 1916 was more than offset by the increasing incompetence of the Tsarist regime. The Tsar himself was quite unequal to the role of commander-in-chief, and the Tsarina, left in charge of the government at Petrograd, blindly followed the whims of Rasputin in filling offices and determining policies, and stubbornly refused to heed the gathering storm of criticism and opposition. In December 1916 a group of noblemen, headed by a relative of the Tsar, hatched a plot against Rasputin as the evil genius of the regime and made doubly sure of getting rid of him by poisoning him and then stabbing him. Not even this assassination brought the Tsarina to reason, for the dead Rasputin exercised upon her disordered mind, and through her upon the Tsar's mind, an even greater influence than had the living Rasputin.

During the winter of 1916–1917 popular disaffection overspread Russia. Patriots complained that the government was hampering the prosecution of the war and hinted that it was conducting treasonable negotiations with the enemy. The subject nationalities grew restless. The middle classes grumbled. There were riots of peasants and strikes of urban workmen.

Revolution was precipitated by decrees of the autocratic government, on March 11, 1917, that Petrograd strikers should return to work and that the recently reassembled Duma should again go home. The strikers refused to obey and won over to their side the soldiers whom the government relied upon to suppress them; they then formed a revolutionary "soviet (or council) of soldiers and workmen." The Duma likewise refused to obey, and its president dispatched a telegram to the Tsar, imploring him to name a new and liberal ministry. On March 15, a deputation from the Duma waited on the Tsar at Pskov and convinced him that he must abdicate. Abdicate he forthwith did in favor of his brother, the Grand-Duke Michael. But already it was too late for any member of the imperial Romanov family to command the revolutionaries, and Michael declined to assume the crown.

By agreement between the Duma and the Petrograd Soviet, a provisional government was established under the chairmanship of Prince George Lvov, a liberal landlord, head of the Union of Zemstvos, and member of the Constitutional Democratic party. It at once proclaimed freedom of association, of the press, and of religion. It liberated thousands of political prisoners and removed the ban on political exiles. It restored full autonomy to Finland and promised to extend it to Poland. It announced that a National Constituent Assembly would shortly be elected by universal manhood suffrage to determine the permanent form of Russia's future government. Simultaneously it labored to infuse new energy into Russia's conduct of the war.

There was rejoicing in the countries allied with Russia and in the United States. Russia, it was popularly believed, would fight harder and more effectively now that it was overthrowing autocracy and becoming democratic. The struggle against the Central Empires would henceforth be, as President Wilson declared, "a war to make the world safe for democracy."

In March, when the Russian Revolution occurred, the British administered a stinging defeat to the Turks in Mesopotamia and captured the important city of Bagdad. In April, when Allied Offensives the United States entered the war, General Robert Nivelle, who had succeeded General Joffre as commander-in-chief of the French armies, opened a fierce offensive against the German trenches on the Western Front along the Aisne River. Simultaneously, elaborate preparations were made for an offensive in the Balkans on the part of the Allied army at Salonica, now commanded by General Sarrail and comprising 600,000 men. To insure that the pro-German King of Greece would not embarrass this offensive, an Anglo-French naval expedition was dispatched to Athens; in June it obliged Constantine to abdicate and quit the country and installed the pro-Ally Venizelos as Greek Premier under the purely nominal rule of Constantine's youthful second son, Alexander I. In the meantime, the United States persuaded Panama and Cuba to declare war on Germany (April 1917). Siam followed suit in July, and Liberia and China in August. The whole world seemed to be arraying itself on the side of the Allies.

With American intervention and the Russian Revolution to the fore, and with the German army on the defensive, awaiting the outcome of the submarine campaign, it was not surprising that a wave of popular pacifism—or "defeatism"—swept Defeatism in Germany over Germany. Early in 1916 the German Social Democrats had split into two factions, the majority, under Friedrich Ebert and Philip Scheidemann, continuing to support the government in the prosecution of the war, and the minority, under Hugo Haase and Eduard Bernstein, refusing to approve of further military expenditure.[1] Now early in 1917, the majority joined the minority in counseling peace and urging democratic reform within Germany, and to the pacifist agitation of the Socialists was added that of the Catholic Center party. Against this

---

[1] A third and small group of German Socialists, led by Karl Liebknecht and Rosa Luxemburg, were even more radical. Known as "Spartacans," they denounced the war and advocated the establishment of "a dictatorship of the proletariat." Their leaders were jailed by the German government.

agitation Hindenburg and Ludendorff were adamant. They countered it by promising German victory in the submarine warfare and eventually on the Western Front; and in July they forced the Emperor William II to dismiss the Chancellor, Bethmann-Hollweg, whom they accused of being too conciliatory to the Socialists and Centrists, and to appoint in his place a conservative bureaucrat who would be a mere agent of the army chiefs. But even with the backing of Hindenburg and Ludendorff, the new Chancellor could not prevent the Centrists and Socialists from putting through the Reichstag in July 1917 a resolution requesting the government to make peace on the basis of "no annexations, no indemnities."

Nor was the internal situation in the Habsburg Empire reassuring. Already, mutinies were occurring in Czech, Croatian, and Polish regiments of the Austro-Hungarian armies, and presently some of their soldiers deserted to the Allies, while "provisional governments" of the several disaffected nationalities were set up at Paris or London. In July 1917, on the Greek island of Corfu, representatives of the Austro-Hungarian Yugoslavs (Croats, Slovenes, and Serbs) signed with Nicholas Pašič, the premier of Serbia, a formal declaration of their joint purpose to create at the close of the war a unified democratic state with King Peter of Serbia as their common sovereign.

In the circumstances, seemingly auspicious for a general peace settlement, Pope Benedict XV on August 1, 1917, called upon the warring countries to end "the fratricidal conflict" and to negotiate "a just and durable" peace. He proposed the substitution in international affairs of the "moral force of right" for the "material force of arms," the restoration of all conquered territories, and the mutual cancellation of claims to indemnity, a guarantee of the freedom of the seas, provision for the future adjustment of international disputes by arbitration, a decrease in armaments, and a conciliatory settlement, involving plebiscites if necessary, of rival claims to such territories as Alsace-Lorraine, Poland, and Trentino.

*Papal Peace Proposals*

By August 1917, however, neither group of belligerents was willing to listen to papal admonitions. The war was at a crisis. German hope of victory was rising anew with the progress of the U-boat campaign and with the firm and reassuring attitude of Hindenburg and Ludendorff. And the Allies were more than ever reluctant to negotiate with Germany, now dominated by a High Command which was committed to territorial annexations. President Wilson replied to the Pope, in behalf of "the allied and associated powers," that peace could not be made with such a regime as Germany's.

The Allies faced a critical situation. Back in April, the French offensive on the Aisne had broken down with terrible losses, and the luckless General Nivelle was supplanted as commander-in-chief of the French armies by General Pétain, with General Foch as his chief of staff. The Allies were barely holding their own on the Western Front. Nor was the elaborately prepared offensive in the Balkans, under General Sarrail, any more successful.

While the Central Empires were holding their military conquests on the Continent, Germany was prosecuting its submarine campaign with considerable success. From January to June 1917, German submarines sank nearly four million tons of Allied shipping. If this amount could be doubled during the second half of 1917, Germany, it was recognized, would be enabled to starve out England and also to prevent the transportation of American troops to France.

America did its utmost, after declaring war on Germany, to aid the Allies. It increased taxes and floated "liberty loans," from the proceeds of which it made liberal financial grants to the Allies. It speeded up its production of munitions and other war supplies. It conscripted four million young men and prepared them for active service. It joined its naval forces to those of Great Britain, and constructed hundreds of new transports for conveying soldiers and supplies to Europe. But the doing of all these things took time. It was estimated that at least a year must elapse before the full weight of America's participation in the World War could be felt. In the meantime the German submarine warfare threatened to nullify it completely.

In the situation, pacifism, or "defeatism," passed from the Central Empires to some of the Allied countries. In France, several bankers and politicians worked to bring about an early peace with Germany on the basis of mutual concessions, and, paralleling their conferences and intrigues, pacifist agitation spread among the French populace and produced serious mutinies in the French army. In Italy, a similar defeatist movement gathered even greater head-

**Defeatism in France, Italy, Russia**

way during the summer of 1917 and threatened to undermine the morale of the Italian army.

In Russia, defeatism grew rapidly and most alarmingly. As the event proved, the high expectation popularly entertained in France, Britain, and America of the help which the Russian Revolution of March 1917 would be to them was quite unjustified. Most Russian soldiers were much more concerned with getting something for themselves from the provisional government at home than with waging a foreign war; and the provisional government, though anxious to continue the war, was unable to agree upon a generally acceptable program of internal reforms or to resist the importunities of the rapidly spreading "soviets of soldiers, workers, and peasants." In May the conservative Prince Lvov resigned, and was succeeded by a radical, Alexander Kerensky.

This change in the personnel of the Russian government did not silence the destructive criticism or halt the subversive activity of the extreme Socialists, the "Bolsheviks" or "Communists." [1] These, astutely led by Lenin, who had returned from exile in Switzerland under safe conduct from the German government, and by Leon Trotsky, who had returned similarly from America, preached the doctrine that the Revolution should make no compromise with capitalism and the bourgeoisie, that a dictatorship of the proletariat must be established by the Bolsheviks alone, and that the cessation of foreign war was a necessary condition for accomplishing any real domestic reforms. Lenin and Trotsky gradually acquired great influence over the Petrograd Soviet and over other soviets. A large part of the industrial proletariat was soon converted to enthusiastic support of the Bolshevik program, and a multitude of peasants in the armies at the front, if a bit hazy about the economic philosophy of the Communists, were ready to acclaim any group which promised to take them out of the trenches and let them go home. Such readiness on the part of Russian soldiers was quickened, moreover, by propaganda which German agents spread along the Eastern Front.

*Russian Communist Revolution of November 1917*

In vain Kerensky begged the Allies to consent to a general peace "without annexations or indemnities." In vain he labored to combat both Bolshevik and German propaganda and to restore

[1] On the various groups of "Socialists" in Russia, see above, pp. 172, 342.

the discipline of the faltering Russian armies. In vain he launched a desperate offensive, in July 1917, against the Austrians and Germans. Russian troops mutinied. The Austrians recovered all of Galicia. The Germans captured Riga and penetrated into Estonia. In vain, Kerensky turned to the "Right" and schemed for the establishment of a military dictatorship; he and the army chiefs could not agree upon the dictator, and none of them was sufficiently daring to strike. In vain he turned to the "Left" and promised speedy reforms within Russia. Kerensky was a weak and wordy man, but a much stronger man would have had difficulty in counteracting Bolshevik agitation and in making the Russian masses fight when they would not fight. In November 1917 a second revolution occurred in Russia. Kerensky's "provisional government" was overthrown, and Lenin at the head of the Communists took charge of affairs.[1]

One of the first acts of the Communist dictatorship was to agree to a truce with the Central Empires; and in March 1918, after **Surrender of Russia and Rumania** protracted wrangling and practically at the point of the victor's bayonet, a peace treaty was signed at Brest-Litovsk by Russia on one side, and by Germany, Austria-Hungary, Bulgaria, and the Ottoman Empire on the other. Poland, Lithuania, and the Latvian province of Courland were ceded outright to Germany (and Austria). Bessarabia was entrusted to the Central Empires for transference to Rumania, and Armenian districts south of the Caucasus were surrendered to the Ottoman Empire. Finland, Estonia, the Latvian province of Livonia, and the Ukraine ("Little Russia") were detached from Russia and recognized as "independent" states.

Rumania, completely isolated by the collapse and defection of Russia, felt obliged to sue for peace and to agree to a treaty which the Central Empires imposed at Bucharest in the same month of March 1918. Thereby Rumania yielded Dobruja to Bulgaria and certain mountain passes on the Hungarian frontier to the Dual Monarchy; and, in return for its promise of cooperation with Germany and Austria, it was promised Bessarabia.

With the surrender of Russia and Rumania, German might was unquestionably paramount throughout central and eastern Europe. The areas appropriated from Russia were administered as

[1] On the Russian Revolution of November 1917 and its domestic consequences, see below, pp. 553–569.

dependencies of Germany, which was thus relieved of the necessity of maintaining an eastern battle front and enabled to devote undivided efforts to the task of crushing resistance of Italians, French, and British in the West. Defeatism ceased to disturb the German government. The German people as a whole seemed to forget the slogan of "no annexations and no indemnities" and to rally behind Generals Hindenburg and Ludendorff with renewed enthusiasm for "victory and conquest first, peace afterwards."

In October 1917 Austro-Hungarian armies, taking advantage of the prostration of Russia and the development of defeatism among the enemy, undertook to put Italy out of the war. They overwhelmed a demoralized Italian army at Caporetto and compelled the rapid retirement of all the Italian forces from Austrian soil back into Italy as far as the Piave River, close to Venice. Only Austrian inability to bring up arms and supplies necessary for pursuit and the prompt cooperation of France and Great Britain permitted the Italians to reform their lines and cling to the Piave.

Throughout the winter of 1917–1918, while German diplomats were negotiating peace with Russia and Rumania, General Ludendorff was making gigantic preparations for a supreme German military effort against the Allied armies in France. All available troops were concentrated on the Western Front. All available machine-guns and ammunition were brought hither. The biggest cannon, the so-called "Big Berthas," were put in place to shell Paris at a distance of sixty miles. All was made ready for a series of assaults surpassing any that the world had ever known.

*Supreme German Effort in West*

In March 1918 the Germans smote the British trenches in the valley of the Somme, near St. Quentin, and ploughed a path through to Amiens. In April, they hit the British west of Lille and advanced some fifteen miles. In May, they assailed the French along the Aisne and fought their way southward across the intervening hills to the Marne River, reaching Château-Thierry, only about forty miles from Paris. These furious drives and sledge-hammer blows netted Germany considerable territory and much booty of prisoners and guns and served to restore the Western Front approximately as it had been in 1914 on the eve of the battle of the Marne. Nevertheless, they were supremely

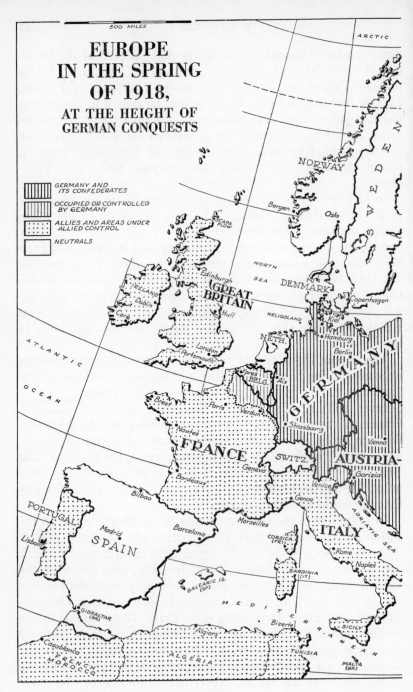

EUROPE
IN THE SPRING
OF 1918,
AT THE HEIGHT OF
GERMAN CONQUESTS

GERMANY AND
ITS CONFEDERATES

OCCUPIED OR CONTROLLED
BY GERMANY

ALLIES AND AREAS UNDER
ALLIED CONTROL

NEUTRALS

500 MILES

ARCTIC

NORWAY

Bergen

Oslo

SWEDEN

SCAPA
FLOW

Edinburgh

GREAT
BRITAIN

Hull

DENMARK

Copenhagen

Kiel

NORTH
SEA

HELIGOLAND

IRELAND

Dublin

Cork

London

Portsmouth

NETH.

pres.
BELG.

Aix

Hamburg

Berlin

GERMANY

ATLANTIC

OCEAN

Brest

Paris

Verdun

Strasbourg

Vienna

Nantes

FRANCE

SWITZ.

AUSTRIA-

Gorizia

Bilbao

Bordeaux

Geneva

Venice

ADRIATIC
SEA

Genoa

PORTUGAL

Lisbon

Madrid

SPAIN

Barcelona

Marseilles

CORSICA
(FR.)

ITALY

Rome

Naples

BALEARIC IS.
(SP)

SARDINIA
(IT)

GIBRALTAR
(BR)

MEDITERRANEAN

Algiers

Bizerte

SICILY

Casablanca

FRENCH
MOROCCO

ALGERIA

TUNISIA

MALTA
(BR)

expensive, for they were attended by awful devastation and by a frightful loss of life.

In June 1918 the Austrians made a desperate attempt to supplement the German drives in France by assailing the Italian front along the Piave. They crossed the river at several points, and at one place advanced five miles. But the Italians rallied and dislodged them with heavy losses. This Austrian failure on the Piave marked the turn of the tide. Military successes of the Central Empires ceased, and the final triumph of the Allies began.

### 6. VICTORY OF THE ALLIES, 1918

Despite the collapse of Russia, the submission of Rumania, and the forced retirement of the Italians to the Piave and of the French to the Marne, the Central Empires were not winning the World War. Allied resistance was stiffening in Italy, in France, and on the high seas. The governments of the allied great powers were displaying a greater energy than ever before, and their peoples were evincing anew a firm determination to achieve "peace through victory." What was most decisive, the German submarine warfare was proving ineffectual.

Previously there had been much bungling by cabinet ministers in Allied countries and notorious lack of cooperation on the part of Allied generals. As early as December 1916 the British government had been reformed and put into the competent hands of David Lloyd George. Then, in November 1917, after the disaster at Caporetto, the Italian ministry was reorganized, with Vittorio Orlando as premier and practical dictator. Simultaneously, the French government passed into the active hands of Georges Clemenceau, the veteran politician of the Radical "Left" and a very determined person. And in Woodrow Wilson the United States had a President distinguished equally for his vigor in pressing the war and for his eloquence in sustaining popular morale.

In November 1917 a Supreme Allied War Council was created to coordinate the military efforts of France, Great Britain, Italy, and the United States; and in March 1918, in the midst of the furious German drives on the Western Front, the allied great powers at last agreed to entrust to one man the central direction of their military operations in France. For this responsible post, Marshal Ferdinand Foch, a short, grizzled, deep-eyed Frenchman of sixty-five, the foremost military genius of the time, was selected. To Foch were subordinated the French armies under Marshal Pétain and the British under Sir Douglas Haig. Thus in the fourth year of the war the Allies finally achieved a real coordination of command.

There can be little doubt that popular morale in Allied countries was heightened, as that in the Central Empires was gradually lowered, by the idealistic utterances of Woodrow Wil- **Wilson's** son. In one of his most famous speeches, in January **Fourteen** 1918, he appealed to world sentiment to back the Allied **Points** war aims, which, he declared, consisted of "fourteen points": (1) open covenants of peace, openly arrived at, and in the future no secret diplomacy; (2) absolute freedom of navigation upon the seas, outside territorial waters, alike in peace and in war, except when the seas are closed by general international agreement; (3) removal, as far as possible, of all economic barriers to international trade; (4) reduction of national armaments; (5) impartial adjustment of all colonial claims, with the interests of the subject populations receiving equal weight with the government seeking title; (6) evacuation of Russian territory, with full opportunity for Russia to determine its own future development; (7) evacuation and restoration of Belgium; (8) evacuation and restoration of French territory, and righting of the wrong done in 1871 in the matter of Alsace-Lorraine; (9) readjustment of Italian frontiers along clearly recognizable lines of nationality; (10) autonomous development for the peoples of Austria-Hungary; (11) evacuation and restoration of Serbia, Montenegro, and Rumania, with an outlet to the sea for Serbia and with interrelations of the several Balkan states according to historically established lines of allegiance and nationality; (12) secure sovereignty for the Turkish portions of the Ottoman Empire, with autonomy for other portions and with freedom of shipping through the Straits; (13) establishment of an independent Poland, including all territories inhabited by indisputably Polish populations, and having access to the sea; (14) formation of a general association of nations under specific covenants for the purpose of affording mutual guarantees of political independence and territorial integrity to great and small states alike. These "fourteen points," though vague in general and ambiguous in detail, elicited the hearty approval and stimulated the hopes of multitudes, not only in America, Britain, France, and Italy, but also among the "subject nationalities" of the Austrian and Ottoman Empires. Even in the German Empire, a growing number of people read into Wilson's words a promise that if only they would democratize their country it would be let off easily.

Most significant, the submarine campaign was not bringing Germany the speedy victory which Hindenburg and Ludendorff **Waning of** had predicted. By virtue of the vigilance of the British **Submarine** and American navies and the convoy and patrol sys- **Menace** tems which they jointly developed, the destruction of Allied shipping by German submarines gradually declined. The tonnage destroyed in the first half of 1917 was four million; in the second half of 1917, two and a quarter million; and in the first half of 1918, less than two million. Meanwhile, shipbuilding was being pushed so rapidly that in 1918 newly launched merchant vessels far exceeded in tonnage old ones destroyed. England, therefore, was not starved out by Germany, nor were the oceanic communications of the Allies seriously interfered with. On the other hand, Great Britain, with the active cooperation of the United States, drastically tightened the blockade of German ports and starved Germany to a degree never felt or anticipated before the submarine effort. Meanwhile the United States was contributing men and money to the Allies and was persuading still other nations to make common cause with them. Brazil declared war on Germany in October 1917; Guatemala, in April 1918; Nicaragua, in May; and Haiti and Honduras, in July. By the summer of 1918 the four states of the Mid-European Confederacy were confronted with a hostile coalition of twenty-five independent nations [1] and five "dominions," [2] representing every continent and most of the islands of the world.

In June 1918 military successes of the Central Empires on the Continent of Europe ceased. Austria-Hungary was exhausted by **Passing of** its desperate drive against the Italians on the Piave. **Offensive** Germany was halted by the British on the Somme and **to Allies** by the French at the Marne, and no reserves of manpower were left to withstand the hundreds of thousands of Amer-

[1] Four of these—Bolivia, Ecuador, Peru, and Uruguay—broke off diplomatic relations with Germany in 1917 but did not participate actively in the War.

[2] Canada, Australia, New Zealand, South Africa, and India.

ican soldiers who were beginning to reinforce the Allied armies in France.

In July, when the Germans attempted to cross the Marne, Marshal Foch called fresh American troops to the assistance of his French and British veterans and gave battle. The resulting "second battle of the Marne" was a deadly two weeks' combat and an Allied triumph. Not only was the German advance definitively stopped, but the French drove the enemy back northward across the Aisne River. To the Germans the second battle of the Marne, in 1918, was far more disastrous than the first battle of the Marne in 1914. In 1914 the Germans, with superior artillery and greater stores of ammunition, could entrench themselves on the heights of the Aisne and successfully resist the counter-attacks of the French. In 1918, however, they had no such advantage. They were unable to repair the damage done, and they were helplessly inferior to the Allies in numbers and equipment.

The Allies, flushed with victory and guided by the master-hand of Marshal Foch, did not fail to follow up their success at the Marne. Relentlessly they hammered at the German trenches everywhere in France. While Franco-British armies recaptured Cambrai and Lille, Franco-American armies drove the Germans from St. Mihiel, south of Verdun, and cleared the ground northward in the Argonne along the Meuse River. By the end of October 1918 the Germans were crowded almost completely out of France and compelled to evacuate a large part of Belgium.

Allied military success was not confined to the Western Front. Already in October 1917 the British army which had previously advanced from Egypt and defeated the Turks in the Sinai peninsula, penetrated victoriously into Palestine under the command of General Edmund Allenby and in cooperation with the Arab forces of Feisal and Captain Lawrence. Turkish resistance, organized and conducted by the German General von Falkenhayn, was stubborn but ineffectual. Jaffa fell to the British in November, and Jerusalem in December.

The British and Arabs then overran all Palestine, secured the country east of the Jordan, and advanced into Syria. At the beginning of October 1918 they captured Damascus, and by the end of the month they were in possession of Aleppo and prepared to effect a juncture at Mosul with the Anglo-Indian (and Arab) army in Mesopotamia.

Meanwhile, in September 1918, the composite Allied army at Salonica, newly reinforced and put under the command of General Franchet d'Espérey, struck out northward into the Balkan peninsula against the Bulgarians. The Bulgarian army no longer had the support of Austrian and German divisions, and its protracted inaction in Macedonia had lowered its morale. Consequently the vigorous Allied offensive from Salonica produced sudden and decisive results. Within two weeks, Macedonia and Serbia were recovered, and the Allies were ready to subjugate Bulgaria.

Almost simultaneously, the Dual Monarchy of Austria-Hungary collapsed. Encouraged by Allied victories in the Balkans and by

**Collapse of Austria-Hungary**
German defeats in the West, the Czech and Yugoslav deputies in the Austrian parliament publicly proclaimed on October 1, 1918, the right of their respective peoples to national self-determination. On October 18 the formal declaration of the independence of the "Czechoslovak Republic" was issued by a "provisional government" headed by Thomas Masaryk, an outstanding Czech scholar and patriot. Eleven days later the Croatian Diet voted to break its ties with Hungary and to join Serbia in creating a national union of all the Yugoslavs. Nor were the Austro-Hungarian armies in any position to oppose such revolts in Croatia and Bohemia. The victorious Allied army of General Franchet D'Espérey threatened Hungary from the south. The Rumanians, tearing up the humiliating treaty of Bucharest which they had signed with the Central Empires in March, resumed hostilities and invaded Hungary from the east. The Italians, under General Diaz, drove the Austrians in disorder from the Piave and pursued them into Istria.

The confederacy of the Central Empires, which had stood like a granite fortress for four years, was finally crumbling. Its armies were defeated and demoralized. Its monarchs and statesmen were panic-stricken. Its peoples were clamoring for peace. Bulgaria, the last to join the confederacy, was the first to quit it. Bulgaria surrendered unconditionally to the Allies on September 30, 1918; and, a month later, so did the Ottoman Empire and the Dual Monarchy of Austria-Hungary. Germany was left to end the World War as best it could.

Already, in August 1918, General Ludendorff had told William II that the war was lost, and at the end of September, prostrated by the news of Bulgaria's surrender, he besought the Emperor to make peace immediately. The Emperor responded by appointing a new and liberal Chancellor, Prince Maximilian of Baden, and instructing him to negotiate with the Allies. Prince Maximilian appealed to the President of the United States to mediate, and Wilson, reiterating his contention that the imperial regime in Germany could not be trusted, practically called for an internal revolution. Ludendorff, outraged by the prospect of revolution more than by that of carnage at the battle front, then begged William II to dismiss Prince Maximilian and go on with the war. But the Emperor knew that to go on would mean certain revolution, and when he gave no heed to the General's impassioned pleas, Ludendorff angrily resigned and retired to Sweden. For once, Hindenburg, the nominal commander of the German armies, refused to follow his mentor, and remained at the front.

After a month's interchange of notes between Prince Maximilian and President Wilson, the Allies agreed to make peace on the basis of the "fourteen points," subject to reservations on the freedom of seas and the fate of Austria-Hungary and to an explicit pledge of German reparation "for all damage done to the civilian population of the Allies." On this basis an armistice was signed on November 11, 1918, between Germany and the Allies, but by this time revolutionary agitation and naval and military mutinies within Germany had brought the downfall of the imperial government of William II and Prince Maximilian and the succession of a Republican and Socialist government. It was consequently this latter government which signed the armistice of November 11.

*Armistice of November 1918*

In accordance with the armistice, the Allies occupied the left bank of the Rhine, the French establishing themselves in Alsace-Lorraine and at Mainz, the Americans at Coblenz, and the British and Belgians at Cologne. To the Allies, furthermore, Germany surrendered all its battleships and submarines and great numbers of guns, locomotives, motor lorries, and railway cars. The Mid-European Confederacy was broken and disarmed. Germany, Austria-Hungary, Bulgaria, and the Ottoman Empire lay prostrate at the feet of the triumphant Allies.

The armistice of November 11, 1918, brought an immediate sense of relief and exhilaration to the whole world. The horrible blood-letting of four years and more, with all its attendant havoc, suffering, and misery, was at last halted. Peace might now be made.

The war, thus closing, was indeed a World War. It was waged by thirty nations, including every one of the so-called great powers. Sixty-five million men bore arms in it. Eight and a half million men were killed. Twenty-nine million men were wounded, captured, or "missing." Every family in eastern and central Europe, every family in Italy, France, and the huge British Empire, and many families in America suffered loss of near relatives or close friends. The direct financial cost of the war has been estimated at over two hundred billion dollars; its indirect cost, at over a hundred and fifty billion dollars more; and these figures do not include the additional billions in interest payments, veterans' care and pensions, and similar expenses with which the world was saddled after the war. Never before had there been a struggle so gigantic, so deadly and costly.

# CHAPTER X

## THE PARIS PEACE SETTLEMENT, 1919–1920

HE military disaster which befell the Mid-European Confederacy in the autumn of 1918 was the signal for immediate political revolutions within its members. The revolutions, though precipitated in several instances by Socialists, proved to be uniformly mild and more conducive to democratic nationalism than to any basic social change.

In Germany, Prince Maximilian, the Chancellor on whom the Emperor William II imposed the unpleasant task of opening peace negotiations with the Allies, sought to allay domestic **Germany** unrest by promising in October a number of constitutional reforms. But the more he promised in the way of reform, the louder grew the demands for an overturn of the whole monarchical regime, and to such demands the counsel of the American President, Woodrow Wilson, gave point and cogency. On October 28 a naval mutiny occurred at Kiel, and on the next day the Emperor hurried from Berlin to military headquarters at Spa, imagining that the army would safeguard alike his person and his throne.

Within a week, almost every city in the German Empire witnessed Socialist rioting and the formation of revolutionary "workers' councils." On November 8, amid disorders at Munich, Bavaria was proclaimed a "democratic and socialist republic," with Kurt Eisner, a left-wing Socialist, as president. In vain Chancellor Maximilian begged William II to save the Hohenzollern dynasty by abdicating in favor of his infant grandson. The Emperor, relying on the army, was deaf to the Chancellor, and by the time the high military officers, including Hindenburg, reluctantly informed him that even the army was seething with sedition and could not be relied upon, there was no longer a friendly Chancellor to advise him. In the night of November 9–10 **Flight of** William II ingloriously took flight across the frontier **William II** into the Netherlands. The history of the German Em**and** **Succeeding** pire of the Hohenzollerns was thus almost exclusively **Republic** the history of two reigns—that of William the First (1871–1888), under whom the Empire had been reared in might, and that of William the Last (1888–1918), under whom it fell with a fearful crash.

Already, on November 9, 1918, Prince Maximilian of Baden had felt obliged to turn over the chancellorship to a Socialist, Friedrich Ebert, and presently, under the latter's guidance, a "Council of People's Commissars" was installed at Berlin in imitation of the contemporary revolutionary administration in Russia. But though Ebert and his fellow Socialists in Germany were willing to borrow nomenclature from the Russian Bolsheviks, they had no serious thought of adopting their policies. Only a small group of German Socialists—the so-called "Spartacans"— were in full sympathy with the Russian Communists and eager to emulate them in a violent exercise of proletarian dictatorship. The major groups, on the other hand—those that shared in the provisional government—were too anxious for national regeneration to countenance civil war and too devoted to democracy to favor any dictatorship, even of themselves.

The "moderation" of the Socialists was supported by the Catholic Center party, led by Matthias Erzberger, and also by the Progressives and left-wing National Liberals, newly fused into a Democratic party. It thus transpired that the three political organizations—Progressive, Centrist, and Social Democratic— which had repeatedly united in opposition to illiberal policies of the Hohenzollern Empire,[1] now joined anew to supplant the Empire with a liberal democratic Republic. Against this Republican *bloc* were arrayed a Royalist "Right" and a Communist "Left." The "Right" comprised the former Conservative and Free Conservative parties, now reorganized as the Nationalist party and intent upon the restoration of monarchy, and the more moderate group of right-wing National Liberals who, under the leadership of Gustav Stresemann, a wealthy industrialist, assumed the title

[1] See above, pp. 141–142, 151, 396–397.

of "German People's party" and, while preferring monarchy, expressed a willingness to collaborate with Republicans. The "Left" was composed of Liebknecht's Spartacans, who refused to participate with the "bourgeoisie" in the election of a Constituent Assembly and preached popular insurrection.

In January 1919, on the eve of the elections, the Spartacans staged a revolutionary demonstration at Berlin, but their leaders were more adept at talking than at acting, and the attempted insurrection was sternly suppressed. In the following month the assassination of Kurt Eisner, the radical Socialist president of Bavaria, gave rise to fresh disorders, which, however, were firmly dealt with by the central government.

Meanwhile a Constituent Assembly was elected by secret ballot of all Germans over twenty years of age, men and women alike; and on February 6 it met at Weimar. Its overwhelming **Weimar** majority was composed of Socialists, Centrists, and **Constitution** Democrats, and these jointly directed its constructive **tution** work—its ratification of the peace treaty with the Allies in June 1919, and its adoption of a constitution at the end of July for the future government of the country.[1] Ebert was elected first constitutional President of the Republic, and another Socialist, Scheidemann, was appointed its first Chancellor.

By August 1919 it seemed as if the German revolution was successfully accomplished. The Hohenzollern Empire was ended and a democratic Republic inaugurated with comparatively little bloodshed and with the backing of a large majority of the popular electorate. There were many differences of aim and policy among the groups composing the victorious coalition. But for the time being, at any rate, liberal and democratic republicanism functioned in Germany.

In the imperial Dual Monarchy of Austria-Hungary, the revolution of 1918–1919 was not only democratic but disruptive. In vain the Emperor-King Charles I published a concili- **Break-up** atory manifesto on October 16, 1918, promising to **of** reorganize the monarchy on a federal basis so that each **Austria-** of its nationalities would possess democratic autonomy. **Hungary** By this time it was too late for compromise. Leaders of the subject nationalities were resolved on achieving a separation from the Habsburg Empire, and the collapse of the Austro-Hungarian

[1] On the Weimar Constitution of 1919, see below, pp. 463–464.

armies removed the one means which Charles might have employed to enforce obedience.

On October 18, a group of Czech patriots, including Thomas Masaryk and Eduard Beneš, proclaimed at Paris the deposition of Charles of Habsburg as King of Bohemia and the independence of the "Czechoslovakian Republic." Ten days later, a self-constituted Czech "national council" took over the government at Prague, and the next day a similar "national council" in the Slovak provinces of Hungary voted for a union of the Slovaks with the Czechs in a new "Czechoslovakia." A national assembly was speedily convened at Prague. In November it ratified what had been done and chose Masaryk as President of the Republic, with Beneš as foreign minister, and eventually in February 1920, after protracted debates, it adopted a democratic constitution.

*Czecho-slovak Republic*

The southern Slavs of Austria-Hungary revolted simultaneously with the Czechs and Slovaks in the north. On October 29, 1918, the Croatian Diet proclaimed the deposition of Charles of Habsburg and the separation of the "kingdom of Croatia and Dalmatia" from Hungary. Authority was then transferred to a revolutionary Yugoslav Congress, to which representatives were admitted from Bosnia-Herzegovina and likewise from the Slovene province of Carniola; and on November 23, in accordance with the earlier Declaration of Corfu,[1] the Congress voted to incorporate all the Yugoslav territories of Austria-Hungary with the independent state of Serbia in a "Kingdom of Serbs, Croats, and Slovenes." Of the new kingdom—really a Greater Serbia—King Peter of Serbia assumed the kingship in December, with his son Alexander as Regent and with a ministry headed by the veteran Serbian politician, Nicholas Pašič. Against the Yugoslav union, Austria-Hungary was powerless. Only King Nicholas of Montenegro attempted to oppose it. But his little country was quickly occupied by Serbian troops and subjected to the new regime.

*Yugoslav Kingdom*

The Poles of Austrian Galicia likewise seceded from the Habsburg Empire and joined the Poles of Prussia and Russia in establishing a national state. In this they were unexpectedly aided by the military reverses of all their "oppressors," not only Austria and Germany but also Russia. In the early stages of the World

[1] See above, p. 397.

War, Polish patriots had been divided on the question of tactics. One group, represented by the celebrated musician Ignace Paderewski, hoped for an Allied victory, imagining that the defeat of Austria and Germany would force them **Polish Republic** to surrender their respective Polish provinces and that victorious France and Britain would persuade their Russian ally to grant autonomy if not complete independence to reunited Poland. Another and larger group, taking their cue from a soldier and "radical," Joseph Pilsudski, were not so sanguine of Allied victory or of Russian altruism or Franco-British benevolence. Mindful that Austria had treated its Polish subjects better than Russia, they thought that their immediate task was to assist the Central Powers in conquering Russian Poland and uniting it with Austrian Poland. Consequently, while Paderewski was issuing pro-Allied propaganda and currying favor with French and British statesmen, General Pilsudski had organized a Polish legion and fought on the side of the Central Powers.

Fortunately for the Polish nation, the conflicting efforts of Pilsudski and Paderewski were both crowned with success. Pilsudski had the satisfaction of witnessing the Russian military débâcle of 1915–1916 and securing from the Austrian and German Emperors a joint pledge, on November 5, 1916, that they would create an "independent" kingdom of Poland, "a national state with an hereditary monarch and a constitutional government," in "intimate relations" with their own realms. Whereupon, a "regency" was set up at Warsaw, and by the treaty of Brest-Litovsk, in March 1918, Russia formally renounced all claim to Poland.

By this time, however, Pilsudski was becoming disillusioned about the magnanimity of the Central Powers. For it was quite clear that in their hour of triumph over Russia they had no intention of bestowing real independence on Russian Poland or of joining their Polish provinces to it. So Pilsudski turned against the Germans and was duly imprisoned by them, while Paderewski had the satisfaction of knowing that at last his own pro-Allied efforts would command the united support of the whole Polish people. During 1918 Austrian Galicia, as well as Prussian Posen, was rife with Polish sedition, and Polish volunteers joined the Allied armies in increasing numbers. With the triumph of the Allies and the pledges of Woodrow Wilson, Poland's deliverance was at hand.

The deliverance came in the midst of the revolution throughout central Europe. When the Dual Monarchy collapsed, Galicia naturally gravitated toward "independent" Poland; and when Germany surrendered, the Poles of Posen, West Prussia, and Upper Silesia moved in the same direction. Pilsudski, released from his German jail, arrived in Warsaw in November 1918 and took over from the Austro-German Regency the provisional government of the country. Then, in January 1919, with himself as President and Paderewski as premier and minister of foreign affairs, a Constituent Assembly was elected by universal suffrage.

The revolutionary emergence of a united and independent Poland thus synchronized with the attainment of political unity and freedom by Czechoslovakia and by Yugoslavia, and also with Rumania's forceful appropriation of Bessarabia from Russia, Transylvania from Hungary, and Bukovina from Austria. The national unification of the Rumanian-speaking peoples was an important phase of the general revolutionary movement and of the attendant disintegration of the Habsburg Empire.

Simultaneously the two cores of the Dual Monarchy—Magyar Hungary and German Austria—were revolutionized. In Hungary, **Hungarian Republic** Count Michael Károlyi, who, despite aristocratic ancestry and great wealth, was a chronic critic of the existing illiberal and monarchist regime, put himself at the head of a "provisional government" on October 24–25, 1918. Two weeks later he proclaimed Hungary an independent Republic, with himself as Governor, pledged to democratize the country and to redress the grievances of its subject nationalities. Károlyi's government soon encountered extraordinary difficulties. The subject nationalities would not recognize it, and it was unable to prevent the secession of the Croats and Slovaks or to resist the occupation of Transylvania by a Rumanian army.

In March 1919, when it became clear that the Allies meant to back the aggrandizement of Rumania, Yugoslavia, and Czechoslovakia at Hungary's expense, Károlyi resigned the government into the hands of a left-wing Socialist and Jewish journalist, Béla Kun by name, who had recently returned from Russia where, as a prisoner of war, he had acquired a fanatical enthusiasm for Communism. Béla Kun at once proclaimed a "dictatorship of the proletariat" in Hungary and feverishly proceeded to rain Communist decrees upon the Magyars and at the same time to employ force against the revolting nationalities. He organized a "red army" and dispatched it in turn against the Slovaks and against the Rumanians. Against the former, he obtained a temporary success. But against the Rumanian army, the ragged and ill-equipped forces of Communist Hungary could not stand. As the Rumanians advanced on Budapest and domestic plots thickened against him, Béla Kun in terror fled on August 1, 1919, into Austria, where he found refuge in a madhouse. Budapest was occupied by Rumanian troops throughout the autumn of 1919, while control of the internal affairs of Hungary passed to a group of aristocrats, including Admiral Nicholas Horthy and Count Stephen Bethlen. Following the withdrawal of the Rumanian army, a general election was held in Hungary in January 1920, with results favorable to the reactionaries. Admiral Horthy was immediately made "Regent," and in April 1921 Count Bethlen began what proved to be a ten-year term as premier and practical dictator.

Meanwhile, Vienna was the scene of a revolution. Here, on October 30, 1918, in the midst of military collapse and governmental paralysis, and at the very time when the disinte- German gration of the Empire was reducing "Austria" to its Austrian original German provinces, mobs of workmen and Republic students inaugurated a series of demonstrations which rapidly grew in size and in determination to have done with the Habsburgs. The Emperor Charles knew that he was powerless to stem the tide. He was ruined by the World War which he had not made and by circumstances over which he had little control. Young, well-intentioned, and amiable, his respectable personal qualities were no proof against the vast elemental forces which took his ancestral realm from him and left him the unenviable fame of being the last of the Habsburg Emperors. On November 11, 1918, Charles abdicated.[1]

The "provisional government" of the "national German state of Austria" was already constituted by mutual agreement among the leaders of the Social Democratic, Christian Socialist, and Nationalist parties, and on November 12 it proclaimed Austria

[1] In March 1919 he took up his abode in Switzerland. Subsequently, when professed royalists had obtained the upper hand in Hungary, he made two unsuccessful attempts to regain the Hungarian crown—in March and in October 1921. After the second attempt, the Allies practically exiled him to Madeira, where he died in April 1922, leaving his claims to his young son, the Archduke Otto.

a Republic. In the following February a Constituent Assembly was elected by universal suffrage, and eventually it adopted a democratic constitution similar to the one prepared at Weimar for Germany.

The World War had begun in July 1914 with the attack of the Dual Monarchy of Austria-Hungary, then rated as a great power, upon the little Slav state of Serbia. Five years later, thanks to military fortunes and revolutionary upheavals, Serbia was free and amply revenged. Within the former confines of the Dual Monarchy were now the three independent states of Czechoslovakia, Hungary, and German Austria, while large portions of its erstwhile territories were appropriated by Serbia, Rumania, Poland, and Italy.

Moreover, all those powers which had taken their stand with the Dual Monarchy in the World War were undergoing revolution. Germany, as we have already indicated, was supplanting the Hohenzollern Empire with a democratic Republic and relinquishing some of its territory to resurrected Poland. And political revolutions were simultaneously occurring in Bulgaria and the Ottoman Empire.

In Bulgaria, the dynasty and the form of monarchy remained, thanks largely to the circumstances that King Ferdinand was **Change of Monarch in Bulgaria** canny enough to abdicate the crown and leave the country in October 1918 and that his youthful son and successor, Boris III, entrusted practically dictatorial power to a forceful and popular statesman, Alexander Stambulinsky. Stambulinsky, a peasant by birth and the leader of the Agrarian party in Bulgaria, had spent three years in jail for opposing King Ferdinand's juncture with the Central Empires in the World War. He could not be held responsible, therefore, for the resulting misfortunes, and his vigorous insistence upon internal reforms which would be beneficial to the peasantry tended during the critical post-war period to allay the outraged patriotic sentiment and to brighten the economic prospects of the Bulgarian masses.

In the Ottoman Empire, Sultan Mohammed V had died in July 1918, and in the ensuing October, when Allied armies and Arab forces were overrunning Palestine, Syria, and Mesopotamia, his successor, Mohammed VI, accepted the resignation of Enver Pasha and the other "Young Turk" ministers whose alliance with

Germany had brought the Turkish power to the brink of ruin. Against the pusillanimous conduct of the Sultan during the winter of 1918–1919, as well as against the seeming determination of the Allies to partition what was left of the Empire, patriotic Turks found a capable and resourceful leader in Mustafa Kemal, who belonged to the left wing of the Young Turk movement and had been notably critical of Enver Pasha's policies in the World War. While the Sultan Mohammed VI maintained only the form of an imperial Ottoman government at Constantinople, Mustafa Kemal began in the late spring of 1919 to establish a separate and strongly nationalist Turkish government in Anatolia. Gradually, through military prowess as well as organizing ability, Mustafa Kemal secured the unity and independence of the Turkish provinces of the Empire, until by 1923 he was able to appropriate Constantinople, depose Mohammed VI, and finally transform the Ottoman Empire into the national Republic of Turkey, with its capital at Ankara.

*Turkish Republic*

### 2. CONGRESS OF PARIS AND TREATY OF VERSAILLES WITH GERMANY

The revolutions in central Europe and the prompt establishment of democratic Republics in Germany, Austria, and Hungary aroused popular hope in the defeated and disarmed countries that the victorious Allies in dictating the peace settlement would be exceptionally considerate. The President of the United States had declared that chastisement by the Allies would be directed not against peoples but against autocratic governments, and it was on the basis of his "fourteen points" that Germany agreed on November 11, 1918, to lay down its arms and make peace.

*Peace Hopes and War Psychology*

The hope of the defeated peoples simply did not square with realities in the victorious countries. Allied statesmen had paid lip service to the "fourteen points," which at best were vague and susceptible of various interpretations, but they were much more definitely committed to the series of "secret treaties" which they had negotiated with one another during the war and which promised to this or that country, as the price for its services on the Allied side, specific aggrandizement at the expense of Germany or its confederates. Even if Allied statesmen had been minded to interpret the "fourteen points" in a conciliatory sense and to revise the secret treaties accordingly, they could hardly have commanded the support of their respective nations, now fired with a fierce hatred of the "enemy."

For four years and more, the popular psychology in Allied countries, especially in France, Great Britain, and Italy, had been keyed up to fever pitch, we must remember, by war propaganda and by personal experience of the horrors of death and destruction. The vast majority of people in every Allied country held Germany guilty of the war and responsible for its havoc. They were mindful, too, of the imperialist peace which Germany, as recently as March 1918, had dictated to Russia and Rumania, and they believed that if its armies on the Western Front had been successful in the summer of 1918, it would have shown no mercy to them. Now that their own armies were triumphant, why should they show mercy to Germany?

Clemenceau of France and Orlando of Italy, backed by their nations, demanded the dire punishment of the Central Empires. In Great Britain a general election of December 1918 registered a thumping majority for Lloyd George's slogan of "Hang the Kaiser and Make Germany Pay." In the United States, two ex-Presidents of the Republican party, Theodore Roosevelt and William Taft, issued a joint pronouncement against any "parleying" by Wilson which might concede to Germany "a peace around a council-table instead of a sentence from a court," and the Republican party carried the congressional elections of November 1918.

It had been decided to exclude the enemy states from the Peace Congress until the Allies should have agreed among themselves upon the terms of peace. It had also been decided that the negotiations should be conducted at Paris, the very center of Allied hostility to Germany. Just as January 18 had been the date in 1871 when a Hohenzollern King of Prussia, in the midst of a successful war against France, and surrounded by his triumphant generals and statesmen, had stood in the Hall of Mirrors

**Allied Peace Congress at Paris** in the palace at Versailles and been proclaimed German Emperor, so now, precisely forty-eight years later, at the close of an overwhelmingly victorious war against Germany, statesmen and generals of the Allies assembled in the same hall to undo the work of Bismarck and the Hohenzollerns. On January 18, 1919, the Peace Congress held its inaugural session.

It was a brilliant assemblage of the foremost men of the Allied countries—except Russia. The Russian Empire of the Romanov Tsars, which had played a stellar role in bringing on the World War, had disappeared from the stage before the war was over, and the succeeding Russia of the revolutionary Communists was as much a pariah among the Allies as Germany or any other enemy state. The remaining "allied and associated" powers—there were thirty-two of them [1]—were eminently represented. There was Clemenceau, the old "tiger" of French politics, premier of his country and honorary president of the congress. There was Marshal Foch, the organizer and winner of military victory. There was President Wilson, who in coming to Europe for the congress had established a wholly new precedent for American executives. There was Lloyd George, who from being the most resolute social reformer in Great Britain had become the most conspicuous patriot in all the dominions of King George V. There was Orlando, the Italian premier; Marquis Saionji, twice prime minister of Japan; Venizelos, the chief statesman of Greece; Arthur Balfour, British foreign secretary, who had attended the Congress of Berlin in 1878; Generals Botha and Smuts, erstwhile Boer warriors against Great Britain, now stalwart champions of the British Union of South Africa; the prime ministers of Australia, New Zealand, Canada, and Newfoundland; princes from India and Arabia; the president-elect of Brazil; the premiers of Belgium, Portugal, and Rumania, and likewise of the new states of Yugoslavia, Poland, and Czechoslovakia. Attending these celebrities were a host of more obscure "experts"—geographers, historians, economists, lawyers, and secretaries—a host as necessary to the making of peace as privates had been to the waging of war. And waiting upon them, and seeking to influence them, were numerous "agents" from a variety of national, racial, and religious groups—Irishmen, Koreans, Jews, Egyptians, Ethiopians, etc.

The Peace Congress, after its formal inauguration on January 18, 1919, met rarely, and then in manner ceremonious and perfunctory. The real work of the Congress was done by special

[1] The thirty-two did not include Russia, or Montenegro (which was now incorporated with Serbia), but they did include, in addition to the other twenty-four powers which had broken with Germany, the three newly formed states of Czechoslovakia, Poland, and Hejaz, and the five British Dominions of Canada, Australia, New Zealand, South Africa, and India.

committees of diplomats and "experts" selected as needs arose,
and it was done in privacy, only such reports being
passed on to the whole Congress as met the approval
of the spokesmen of the Allied great powers. For several months the principal decisions were made by the "Big Four"
—Clemenceau, Lloyd George, Orlando, and Wilson.

It was no easy task to reconcile differences of opinion and
policy among the thirty-two delegations and to preserve a
united front on the part of all the "allied and associated" governments. Woodrow Wilson, who had set his heart upon fashioning a permanent League of Nations, felt obliged to make repeated concessions to his fellow negotiators in order to enlist
their support for his pet project. The tragedy of the American
President's position at Paris was that for the assurance of the
"fourteenth point" of his peace program he had to surrender or
compromise many of the other thirteen points. For example,
Point One (open covenants openly arrived at) quickly evaporated in the atmosphere of the Congress. Also, Point Two
(freedom of the seas), of which the President talked much
before he went to Europe, was sacrificed to British susceptibilities. It was likewise a concession to British demands that
Point Five was so interpreted as to admit of the transfer of the
bulk of German colonies, under a so-called "mandatory" system,
to the British Empire. Wilson, with the backing of Lloyd George,
did resist a French demand for the whole left bank of the Rhine,
and he also held out so stubbornly against an Italian demand for
the Adriatic port of Fiume that the Italian delegates temporarily
withdrew from the Congress. Eventually, however, Italy got
Fiume.

It was very difficult to satisfy the territorial demands of
the lesser powers—Poland, Czechoslovakia, Rumania, Yugoslavia, and Greece—without doing injustice to the principle of
nationality. Nationalities were too intermingled in east-central
and southeastern Europe to permit any hard-and-fast segregation
of them within national frontiers. If, for example, all Poles
were included in Poland, a considerable number of Germans
would be included too; or, if all Czechs and Slovaks were
incorporated in Czechoslovakia, a large number of Germans and
Magyars would likewise be incorporated. In general, wherever
the Allied diplomats had to choose between being unjust to

enemy states and being unjust to pro-Ally states, they made the former choice. But in many instances, bitter boundary disputes raged between pro-Ally states themselves. Only the weariness of the several peoples concerned and the dictatorial attitude of the representatives of the great powers enabled the Peace Congress to conclude its labors.

The draft of the proposed peace treaty with Germany, containing about 80,000 words, was agreed to by the "Big Four" and endorsed by the Congress in plenary session on May 6, 1919.[1] On the following day the German plenipotentiaries were admitted to the Congress and presented with the draft. They protested that it was intolerably severe and obviously contradictory of the "fourteen points," on the basis of which they had consented to the armistice. They pleaded for its radical amendment.

*Peace Dictated by Victorious Powers*

To German entreaties, the Allied statesmen were deaf. Then, after demonstrations of protest throughout Germany, after threats of compulsion on the part of the Allies, after the resignation of the Scheidemann ministry at Berlin, after several days of awful suspense, the German Constituent Assembly at Weimar on June 23, 1919, the last day of grace, finally voted to accept unconditionally the Allied terms of peace.

On June 28, in the Hall of Mirrors in the stately old palace of Louis XIV, the treaty of Versailles was signed by representatives of Germany and of thirty-one nations leagued against Germany.[2] The scene was that in which in 1871 the Hohenzollern Empire had been proclaimed, and the date was that on which in 1914 the Archduke Francis Ferdinand of Austria-Hungary had been assassinated. The World War was thus formally ended on the fifth anniversary of the immediate occasion of its beginning.

*Treaty of Versailles with Germany*

By the terms of the treaty, Germany ceded Alsace-Lorraine to France, the towns of Eupen and Malmédy to Belgium, the

---

[1] This plenary session was secret, and the treaty draft was endorsed without its details being fully known. Only a 10,000-word digest was submitted to the session. Several powers—Portugal, France, China, and Italy—agreed to it "with reservations."

[2] One of the thirty-two delegations on the Allied side—China—refused to sign the treaty of Versailles, because of concessions to Japan. General Smuts, in attaching his signature on behalf of South Africa, protested against what he conceived to be the illiberality of the victors to the vanquished.

city of Memel to Lithuania,[1] and the province of Posen and a strip through West Prussia (the so-called "corridor") to Poland.[2] Furthermore, plebiscites would be held, under international auspices, to determine whether Upper Silesia and the southern part of East Prussia should be annexed to Poland, and Schleswig to Denmark.[3] Besides, Germany surrendered outright the important Baltic port of Danzig, which became an internationalized "free city," and for a period of fifteen years the valuable coal region of the Saar, which passed under the administration of the League of Nations and the economic control of France. In the case of the Saar, a plebiscite would determine at the end of fifteen years whether it should remain permanently under international government or revert to Germany or be annexed by France.[4]

In addition to territorial cessions in Europe, Germany parted with all its overseas imperial domain. Its lease of Kiaochow and privileged position in the Chinese province of Shantung, as well as its Pacific islands north of the equator, were transferred to Japan; its portion of Samoa, to New Zealand; its other Pacific possessions south of the equator, to Australia; German Southwest Africa, to the British Union of South Africa; German East Africa, to Great Britain, except a small section in the northwest, which went to Belgium; and Kamerun and Togoland were divided between Great Britain and France. In most cases the powers receiving German colonies did so not as absolute sovereigns but as "mandatories" of the League of Nations, to which they promised to give periodic accounts of their stewardship.

Germany recognized, moreover, the independence of Belgium, and likewise of Poland, Czechoslovakia, and German Austria. It specifically renounced the treaties of Brest-Litovsk and Bucharest, which it had signed in March 1918 with Russia and

---

[1] The treaty merely provided for the cession of Memel to the Allies. Memel was "appropriated" by Lithuania in 1923 and retaken by Germany in 1939.

[2] The "corridor," which cut off East Prussia from the rest of Germany, had belonged to Poland until 1772.

[3] As the outcome of these plebiscites, in 1919, the northern third of Schleswig joined Denmark, and all East Prussia remained with Germany. In Upper Silesia, the plebiscite was delayed and interfered with by nationalistic fighting and disorder; when it was held, in 1921, it was generally favorable to Germany, though certain districts gave Polish majorities; and in 1922 the League of Nations arbitrarily partitioned Upper Silesia between Germany and Poland.

[4] The plebiscite, held in 1935, was favorable to Germany. See below, p. 610.

Rumania respectively, and gave the Allies *carte blanche* to settle as they would the affairs of eastern Europe.

Militarily, Germany promised to reduce its army to 100,000 men; to abolish conscription; to raze all fortifications between its western frontier and a line drawn fifty kilometers east of the Rhine; to stop all importation, exportation, and nearly all production of war material; to reduce its navy to six battleships, six light cruisers, and twelve torpedo boats, without submarines; and to abandon military and naval aviation. Germany also agreed to demolish fortifications at Heligoland, to open the Kiel Canal to all nations, to refrain from building forts on the Baltic, and to surrender its transoceanic cables. It expressly consented to the trial, by an international tribunal, of the Emperor William II for "supreme offense against international morality." [1]

Germany was forced to acknowledge responsibility for the World War and to promise that it would make financial reparation "for all damage done to the civilian population of the Allies and their property." It was to make an initial payment of five billion dollars and such subsequent payments, up to "the utmost of its ability," as a special Reparations Commission of the Allies should direct. In the meantime Germany was to pay shipping damage on a ton-for-ton basis by cession of most of its existing merchant marine and by new construction; to devote its economic resources to the rebuilding of devastated areas in France; to supply France, Belgium, and Italy with coal; to return works of art taken from Belgium and France, and to deliver to Belgium manuscripts and books of equivalent value to those destroyed at Louvain.

Until the treaty of Versailles was fully executed, Allied armies should continue to occupy the left bank of the Rhine and the bridgeheads on the right bank of Cologne, Coblenz, and Mainz, with Germany footing the bills. The one concession was that if Germany should be duly fulfilling its obligations,

---

[1] In accordance with this provision, Great Britain, France, and Italy, in 1920, requested the Netherlands to hand over William II for trial. Queen Wilhelmina's advisors declined on the ground that no existing international court possessed legal jurisdiction and that the Dutch people "could not betray the faith of anyone who has confided himself to their free institutions." Upon the promise of the Dutch government to take necessary precautions to prevent the ex-Emperor from endangering the world's peace, the Allies dropped the project of trying William II.

Cologne would be evacuated by the Allies at the end of five years, Coblenz at the end of ten years, and Mainz at the end of fifteen years.

Harsh, indeed, were the terms of the treaty of Versailles. Germany lost considerable territory and population in Europe and its whole overseas empire. It was disarmed and heavily mortgaged. For a long time, seemingly, it would be under the tutelage and dominance of its conquerors.

### 3. OTHER PEACE TREATIES

The treaty of Versailles was only one, albeit the most striking, of the series of treaties which constituted the general peace settlement of Paris. After making peace with Germany in June 1919, it remained for the Allies to make peace with Germany's wartime confederates—Austria, Hungary, Bulgaria, and the Ottoman Empire—and to provide for the new or enlarged states which were already emerging in east-central Europe, such as Poland, Czechoslovakia, Yugoslavia, Rumania, etc. All this was done by Allied diplomats at Paris in the year 1919–1920. And just as representatives of Germany had been called upon to accept Allied terms at Versailles, so, in turn, representatives of Germany's confederates were summoned for like purpose to other suburbs of Paris. Peace treaties were thus signed at St. Germain with Austria on September 10, 1919; at Neuilly with Bulgaria on November 27, 1919; at the Trianon with Hungary on June 4, 1920; and at Sèvres with the Ottoman Empire on August 10, 1920.

Austria, by the treaty of St. Germain, was required to recognize the independence of Hungary, Czechoslovakia, Poland, and Yugoslavia, and to cede to them, and to Italy and

**Treaty of St. Germain with Austria** Rumania, the bulk of the realm which previously, in union with itself, had composed the Dual Monarchy of Austria-Hungary. Austria was left, thereby, a small independent German state, with an area and a population smaller than Portugal's. Part even of the German-speaking Tyrol was detached and added to Italy, and Austria had to promise that it would not unite in the future with Germany. It was deprived of seaports; its army was restricted to 30,000 men; and it was obligated, like Germany, to pay such indemnity as the Reparations Commission should determine.

From Bulgaria were taken, by the treaty of Neuilly, most of the land it had acquired in the Balkan War of 1912–1913 and all its conquests in the World War. Dobruja went to Rumania; the greater part of Macedonia, to Yugoslavia; and the Thracian coast, to Greece. Bulgaria promised to pay an indemnity of almost half a billion dollars and to reduce its army to 33,000 men. Treaty of Neuilly with Bulgaria

Hungary, by the treaty of the Trianon, was stripped of non-Magyar subjects as completely as Austria had been shorn of non-Germans. The Slovak provinces went to Czechoslovakia. Transylvania and a strip of land to the west of it were ceded to Rumania. Croatia was yielded to Yugoslavia. The Banat was divided between Yugoslavia and Rumania. Hungary thus shrank from an imperial and maritime domain of 125,000 square miles, with twenty-two million inhabitants, into a landlocked Magyar state of 36,000 square miles with a population of eight million and with an army limited to 35,000 men. Treaty of the Trianon with Hungary

Determination of the fate of the Ottoman Empire was delayed by the persistence of acute differences among the Allies—especially between France and Great Britain, and between Italy and Greece—about the distribution of the spoils, and also by the existence of rival Turkish governments, that of the Sultan at Constantinople and that of Mustafa Kemal at Ankara. An agreement was eventually reached among the Allies; and by the resulting treaty of Sèvres with the Sultan's government, the Arab state of Hejaz, embracing the strip of territory east of the Red Sea, would be independent; Armenia would be a free Christian republic under international guarantees; Palestine, Mesopotamia (Iraq), the trans-Jordan area, and Syria would be detached from the Empire and the first three made "mandatories" of Great Britain, and the fourth, of France; Cilicia would be a "sphere of influence" for France, and southern Anatolia, including the port of Adalia, a "sphere of influence" for Italy; Smyrna and adjacent territory on the coast of Asia Minor, together with Thrace, Adrianople, the peninsula of Gallipoli, and the remaining Ægean islands would be surrendered to Greece. The Dardanelles and the Bosphorus would be internationalized, and the once mighty Ottoman Empire would be contracted into a petty Turkish state retaining only the Abortive Treaty of Sèvres with Ottoman Empire city of Constantinople and the interior of Asia Minor and subjected to crushing debts and to foreign control of its finances.

The government of the Sultan Mohammed VI at Constantinople agreed to the treaty of Sèvres, but the Turkish National Assembly at Ankara, under the leadership of Mustafa Kemal, refused to ratify it. Taking advantage of the demobilization of the Allied armies and of the war weariness of the Allied peoples, Mustafa Kemal, with his Turkish forces, obliterated the Armenian republic and obliged Italian troops to quit southern Anatolia and the French to desist from occupying Cilicia. The governments of France and Italy, thus discomfited by the Turkish military revival and already critical of the advantages conferred by the treaty of Sèvres on Great Britain and Greece, were favorable to a revision of the treaty. At the same time, at Moscow, the Communist government of Russia signed a treaty with the Turkish Nationalists, condemning the treaty of Sèvres, disavowing Russian ambitions in the Ottoman Empire, re-ceding Kars and Ardahan to Turkey, and proclaiming "the solidarity which unites Turkey and Russia in the struggle against imperialism."

In the meantime the British government, which had most to lose by the revival of Turkish power, was abetting the proposals of Venizelos and of the recently restored King Constantine that Greece should undertake the suppression of the militant Turkish Nationalists and the enforcement of the treaty of Sèvres.[1] Accordingly, in July 1921 a large Greek army, under Constantine, advanced from Smyrna against Mustafa Kemal. At first the Greeks gained some ground, but presently they were turned back and eventually overwhelmed and driven from Smyrna. They received no substantial aid from the British, who distrusted King Constantine and who had had enough fighting for the present, while, on the other hand, the Turks were supplied with arms and munitions by the French and the Italians. In triumph, therefore, the troops of Mustafa Kemal possessed themselves of the

---

[1] Both Venizelos and Constantine favored war with Mustafa Kemal, but no love was lost between the two Greeks or between the republican and royalist factions which they respectively headed. Following the death of King Alexander I of Greece in 1920, Venizelos and his republicans were defeated in a general election by the royalists; Venizelos accordingly withdrew from the government, and Constantine was restored (November 1920). In September 1922, following the disastrous rout of his armies in Asia Minor, King Constantine again abdicated, this time in favor of his son, George II, and removed himself finally from Greece.

whole of Asia Minor and in November 1922 occupied Constantinople.

The victories of Mustafa Kemal and his Turkish Nationalists scrapped the treaty of Sèvres and called for a new peace settlement in the Near East. After another series of difficult and delicate negotiations, peace was finally concluded between Turkey and the Allies at Lausanne, in Switzerland, on July 24, 1923. By the terms of the new treaty, Turkey definitely resigned all claims to Hejaz, Palestine, Trans-Jordania, Iraq, and Syria, but it retained the whole of Anatolia and likewise Cilicia, Adalia, Smyrna, Constantinople, and eastern Thrace. It consented to the freedom of the Straits and their demilitarization, but it escaped any foreign control of its internal affairs.

*Treaty of Lausanne with Turkey*

The heaviest loser by the treaty of Lausanne was Greece. It was compelled not only to surrender Smyrna, Gallipoli, and eastern Thrace to Turkey, but also to resign to Italy the Greek-speaking Ægean islands known as the Dodecanese. By a remarkable special arrangement between Greece and Turkey, the Christian Greek inhabitants of Asia Minor were transplanted to Greece and the Moslem Turkish residents of Greece were removed to Turkey.

The Peace of Paris of 1919–1920 included not only the Turkish treaty of Sèvres (as subsequently revised by the treaty of Lausanne), the Hungarian treaty of the Trianon, the Bulgarian treaty of Neuilly, the Austrian treaty of St. Germain, and the German treaty of Versailles, but numerous supplementary conventions and agreements among the Allies.

To delimit the boundary between Italy and Yugoslavia proved especially troublesome. Italy insistently demanded not only Istria, the Adriatic islands, and that part of Dalmatia promised by the secret treaties of wartime, but the important port of Fiume also. But counter-claims of Yugoslavia, particularly to Fiume, were stubbornly backed by President Woodrow Wilson and hardly less so by the French. In September 1919, Fiume was forcibly seized by a free-lance Italian expedition under the ultra-patriotic Gabriele D'Annunzio, now turned soldier-adventurer. Eventually a settlement was reached by the treaty of Rapallo (November 1920): Fiume became a free neutralized city; a strip of Dalmatian coast extending southward from Istria as far

*Treaties among Allies*

as Fiume, and also the town of Zara, passed to Italy, and the remainder of Dalmatia to Yugoslavia. Still later, in accordance with the supplementary treaty of Rome (January 1924), the main part of Fiume was annexed by Italy, and its chief suburb by Yugoslavia.

Meanwhile a series of treaties was concluded by the Allied great powers with national states which had recently been created or much enlarged—Yugoslavia, Poland, Czechoslovakia, Rumania, etc. These treaties related to boundaries, to the assumption of the public debts of annexed regions, and to commercial affairs. In most instances, moreover, they guaranteed certain rights and privileges to national, racial, or religious minorities within the several states.

The chief proponents of these provisions for "minority rights" were Jews, who were fearful of losing their identity or being discriminated against in the strongly nationalistic countries of east-central Europe, and they gained the interested support of the British and American governments. The British government had already committed itself, in 1917, to Zionist demands for a "Jewish home land" in Palestine.[1] National minorities, other than Jewish, were to share in the new treaty rights, partly because the Jews did not wish to be singled out by name and partly because the Allies felt apologetic about incorporating large numbers of Germans or Magyars with Poland, Czechoslovakia, Yugoslavia, and Rumania.

In the Peace of Paris and its manifold negotiations and treaties, Russia had no direct part. Indeed, at the very time when the Allies were making peace with Germany, they were encouraging military revolts against the Communist government in Russia.[2] **Peace Treaties of Communist Russia** Nevertheless, the Russian Communists gradually got the upper hand in their own country, and the series of separate treaties which they concluded in 1920–1921 with the non-Russian states that had emerged out of the old Russian Empire belonged, logically and chronologically, to the general peace settlement.

From its advent to power in November 1917 the Communist dictatorship of Russia had proclaimed its intention of abandoning the imperial policies of previous Russian governments and re-

[1] See below, p. 494.
[2] See below, pp. 556–558.

specting the doctrine of national self-determination, and to this intention it adhered after Germany had been compelled by the Allies to renounce the treaty of Brest-Litovsk and after the peoples in the former western provinces of the Russian Empire had set up provisional governments of their own. Consequently, Russia negotiated treaties in 1920 with Finland, with Estonia, with Latvia (comprising the Letts of Livonia and Courland), and with Lithuania, recognizing the independence of each.

For a time, hostilities were carried on between Russia and Poland. Both aspired to dominate Byelorussia (White Russia) and the Ukraine, and neither would accept the compromise boundary—the so-called "Curzon line"—proposed by the British Foreign Minister, Lord Curzon. The first successes of the Polish army in 1919–1920 were followed by reverses, and Russian forces fought their way to the gates of Warsaw. But here, with French assistance, the Poles under Pilsudski rallied and drove back the Russians. Peace negotiations were then opened; and on March 18, 1921, was signed the treaty of Riga. Russia recognized the independence of Poland; Poland obtained strips of Byelorussia and the Ukraine east of the "Curzon line"; and each of the parties pledged itself not to participate in military activities against the other and not to interfere in any way in the internal affairs of the other.

There still remained a serious dispute between Poland and Lithuania over the city of Vilna, which the former had taken by force in October 1920. Otherwise, however, the territorial settlement appeared satisfactory both to Russia and to the new national states which separated themselves from it along the Baltic. At a congress of their representatives at Warsaw in March 1922, Russia agreed with Poland, Latvia, Estonia, and Finland to confirm the existing treaties with one another and in future to arbitrate all disputes.

#### 4. THE COVENANT OF THE LEAGUE OF NATIONS

Into the major treaties of the Paris peace settlement was incorporated a special "Covenant," providing for the establishment and functioning of a League of Nations and an affiliated Court of International Justice. And by a supplementary "convention," an International Labor Organization was provided for.

Back of the Covenant and the Labor Convention was a wide-

EUROPE AFTER THE
PARIS PEACE
SETTLEMENT
OF 1919-1920

spread popular desire to prevent the recurrence of war and to organize the world for peace. The Hague Peace Conferences of 1899 and 1907 [1] had aroused the desire, and the World War greatly quickened it. If most of the nations of the world could pool their resources of men and money and cooperate as allies in a protracted war, it was argued, they should find it as possible as it was desirable to form an enduring league in the common cause of peace; if there had been such a league in 1914, the World War might have been prevented.

To such arguments and to obvious popular desire, statesmen paid respectful attention, and the President of the United States appended to his famous peace program of January 1918, as its fourteenth and final point: "A general association of nations must be formed under specific covenants for the purpose of affording guarantees of political independence and territorial integrity."

In Woodrow Wilson's program this point might be last but it was not least. It would be, he reiterated, "the most essential part of the peace settlement." He insisted upon its unqualified acceptance by the Allies and by Germany as a condition of the armistice, and in the peace negotiations at Paris he labored most assiduously for a league of nations.

Concerning just what the league should be there were wide differences of opinion, ranging from the hope of Lansing, the American Secretary of State, that it should be no more than an improved Hague Court for international arbitration, to the desire of Clemenceau, the French premier, that it should be a military alliance for the enforcement of peace. The Covenant, as eventually agreed to at Paris, embodied a compromise.

Under the Covenant, a League of Nations would be instituted and provided with two main agencies: (1) an Assembly, consisting of delegates from the several nation-members of
**Covenant Provisions** the League, with each member having one vote and not more than three delegates, and meeting at Geneva in neutral Switzerland; and (2) a Council, a smaller body, holding more frequent sessions and composed of representatives of permanently designated great powers and of a few lesser powers selected from time to time by the Assembly. In addition, the Covenant provided for a Secretariat, responsible to the Assembly and Council, and served by a staff of officials with headquarters

[1] See above, pp. 310–311.

at Geneva.[1] In close association with the League, furthermore, provision was made for a permanent Court of International Justice and for an International Labor Office.

The purposes of the League, as stated or implied in the Covenant, were four: to prevent war, to organize peace, to discharge certain special duties imposed by the peace treaties of 1919–1920, and to promote international cooperation in that undefined field where the interests of nations are common or subject to amicable adjustment. Of these purposes, the main one, at least the one uppermost in the minds of the framers of the Covenant, was the first—to prevent war.

Article 10 obligated members of the League "to respect and preserve as against external aggression the territorial integrity and existing political independence" of one another. Article 11 empowered the League to "take action that may be deemed wise and effectual to safeguard the peace of nations" and authorized any member to bring to the attention of either Council or Assembly "any circumstance whatever affecting international relations which threatens to disturb international peace." Article 12 required the members to submit disputes either to arbitration or to inquiry by the Council and "in no case to resort to war until three months after the award by the arbitrators or the report by the Council." Article 13 bound the members to "carry out in good faith" any arbitral award and not to resort to war against "any member of the League that complies therewith." Article 15 prescribed that any dispute which could not be settled by arbitration must be submitted to the Council, and it prohibited any resort to war in contravention of a unanimous decision of the Council exclusive of the parties to the dispute. Article 16 ordained, in summary, that a member which should resort to war in disregard of these provisions of the Covenant, should "*ipso facto* be deemed to have committed an act of war against all members of the League." Finally, in respect of any dispute between a member and a non-member, Article 17 declared that if the non-member "refuses to accept the obligations of membership in the League for the purposes of such dispute and shall resort to war against a

---

[1] At first, the permanent seats on the Council were assigned to Great Britain, France, Italy, Japan, and the United States, and the temporary seats to Belgium, Brazil, Spain, and Greece. Subsequently Germany and Russia were given permanent seats, and the number of temporary seats was raised.

member of the League, the provisions of Article 16 shall be applicable as against the state taking such action."

War was not altogether forbidden by the Covenant. Armed rebellion and civil war were plainly excluded from the League's jurisdiction by a stipulation in Article 15. Even international war might legally be waged if the parties to it had previously submitted their dispute to mediation and the Council had failed to reach a unanimous decision. Even to prevent "illegal" war, the League, having no armed force of its own, could rely only upon the "moral obligations" which its members assumed.

The Covenant did specify "sanctions" to be taken by the League against recalcitrant members and non-members. If any state resorted to war in disregard of the Covenant, Article 16 required the other members of the League "immediately to subject it to the severance of all trade or financial relations," to prohibit "all intercourse between their nations and the nations of the covenant-breaking state," and to prevent "all financial, commercial, or personal intercourse between the nationals of the covenant-breaking state and the nationals of any state, whether a member of the League or not." In such a case, furthermore, it would become the duty of the Council to recommend "what effective military, naval, or air force" the members of the League should severally use to uphold the Covenant.

In such fashion the League of Nations would attempt to prevent international war. But the League was not to confine itself to a merely negative role of prohibiting war and recommending "sanctions" against nations which engaged in it. The League was expected to do more—to act positively and constructively to uproot underlying causes of war and to organize peace. The central agencies of the League—Secretariat, Council, and Assembly— were designed for this long-range purpose as well as for the immediate purpose of preventing war, and so was the permanent Court of International Justice, which, authorized by the Covenant, was duly founded in 1921. This Court was similar in certain respects to The Hague Tribunal which had been established by the Peace Conference of 1899; it had its seat at The Hague, rather than at Geneva, and it was a judicial rather than a diplomatic or political body. But whereas The Hague Tribunal was not a permanent organic institution but only a panel of judges from which arbitrators might be selected for a particular dispute, the

Court of International Justice was a continuously functioning bench of fifteen judges, appointed for a term of nine years by joint action of the League's Council and Assembly, and empowered "to hear and determine any dispute of an international character which the parties thereto submit to it" and to "give an advisory opinion upon any dispute or question referred to it by the Council or by the Assembly."

In the belief that secret treaties had contributed to bringing on the World War, the framers of the Covenant sought to outlaw them. Provision was accordingly made that treaties should be published and that none should be binding unless registered with the Secretariat. Besides, a pledge was exacted from every League member that it would abrogate all existing "obligations or understandings" inconsistent with the terms of the Covenant and would not enter into any new ones, though a special proviso was inserted—at American request—that "nothing in the Covenant shall be deemed to affect the validity of international engagements, such as treaties of arbitration or regional understandings like the Monroe Doctrine, for securing the maintenance of peace."

The Covenant recognized, moreover, the peril, in a changing world, of too rigid insistence on a *status quo* consecrated by treaties of the past. It expressly enabled the Assembly to "advise the reconsideration, by members of the League, of treaties which have become inapplicable and the consideration of international conditions whose continuance might endanger the peace of the world."

Furthermore, the Covenant aimed at doing away with big competitive armaments, which were generally regarded as a major cause of past war. It therefore obliged the members of the League to "recognize that the maintenance of peace requires the reduction of national armaments to the lowest point consistent with national safety" and also that "the manufacture by private enterprise of munitions and implements of war is open to grave objections," and it instructed the Council to formulate definite plans alike for the limitation of armaments and for the prevention of "the evil effects" attendant upon their private manufacture.

In addition to preventing war and organizing peace, the League of Nations was to perform certain tasks bequeathed to it by the peace treaties of 1919–1920. It was to supervise the plebiscites in Schleswig, East Prussia, and Upper Silesia. It was to administer the Free City of Danzig. It was to govern the Saar for fifteen years and then hold a plebiscite to determine whether the district should revert to Germany or pass to France or remain under the League. It was to oversee the enforcement of the special treaty provisions concerning "minority rights." Besides, the League of Nations was to possess at least a nominal suzerainty over the former German colonies and Ottoman territories which were "mandated" to other powers, and the League Council was to receive annual reports from the mandatories and to seek the advice of a permanent commission of the League "on all matters relating to the observance of the mandates."

Finally, the League was charged with promoting cooperation in matters of general humanitarian concern. To this end, all previously established international bureaus and commissions were placed under the League's supervision, and to it were entrusted the making and oversight of international agreements to secure "fair and humane conditions of labor for men, women, and children," "just treatment of native inhabitants" of colonies belonging to members of the League, "freedom of communication and of transit and equitable treatment for the commerce of all members of the League," and regulation of "the traffic in women and children," "the traffic in opium and other dangerous drugs," and "the trade in arms and ammunition with the countries in which the control of this traffic is necessary in the common interest." To the same end, the League was "to take steps in matters of international concern for the prevention and control of disease" and "to encourage and promote the establishment and cooperation of duly authorized voluntary national Red Cross organizations" for "the mitigation of suffering throughout the world."

In intimate association with the League, and serving as its instrument in the labor field, was a special international organization, separately provided for by the "Labor Convention" adopted at Paris in 1919 and, like the Covenant of the League of Nations, incorporated in the several peace treaties. The Labor Convention recognized "relations between capital and labor" to be "matters of international concern," and for their regulation created an International Labor Conference and an International Labor Office.

International Labor Office

From what we have now said, it must be obvious that, under

the Covenant, the League was expected to be the cornerstone of a new world-order of pacific collaboration and general security. It must also be obvious that, if the League was to fulfill this expectation, its membership should embrace almost if not quite all of the sovereign states of the world. The Covenant, in fact, invited all the Allies and almost all neutral nations to accede to it "immediately" and "without reservation," and thus to become initial members of the League. Further, it provided for the subsequent admission of any "fully self-governing state, dominion, or colony" by two-thirds vote of the Assembly, and, membership being voluntary, for the withdrawal of any member on two years' notice.

In January 1920, pursuant to the call of President Wilson of the United States, the League of Nations was formally inaugurated at Paris with an initial meeting of the Council, and the first Assembly convened at Geneva in the following November. By this time all the Allies in the **Start of the League** World War save one and nearly all the invited neutrals had ratified the Covenant and joined the League—a total of forty-two members.[1] In time, the former enemy states and the Russian Soviet Union joined it, and by 1935 the number of countries which had adhered to the League reached the impressive total of sixty-two—twenty-eight in Europe, twenty-one in America, eight in Asia, three in Africa, and two in Australasia.

From the outset, a serious handicap to the League of Nations was the abstention of the United States. It meant the withholding of the moral support and active cooperation of a great power which had taken a decisive part in the World War and whose President had been chiefly responsible for creating the League. How the United States came to adopt an attitude of such grave import to post-war international relations calls for special explanation.

While fighting went on, most Americans had been proud of the

---

[1] The "allied and associated" powers which promptly joined the League numbered twenty-nine: Great Britain and the five "Dominions" of Canada, Australia, New Zealand, South Africa, and India, France, Italy, Japan, Belgium, Portugal, Poland, Czechoslovakia, Rumania, Yugoslavia, Greece, China, Siam, Liberia, Brazil, Cuba, Panama, Haiti, Guatemala, Nicaragua, Honduras, Peru, Bolivia, and Uruguay. Thirteen neutral powers similarly adhered: Spain, the Netherlands, Switzerland, Denmark, Sweden, Norway, Persia, Argentina, Chile, Colombia, Venezuela, Paraguay, and Salvador.

diplomatic leadership which the Allies accorded to the President
of the United States, and few raised serious or sustained protest
against President Wilson's statement of war aims or his championship of a league of nations. But with the defeat of Germany,
acute political partisanship was resumed in the United States, and
Wilson as the leader of the Democratic party became the target
of the rival Republican party, which carried the congressional
elections of November 1918 and obtained a majority in the Senate,
whose consent was necessary for the ratification of treaties. Then
the President, hoping no doubt that the peace settlement would
redound to the political advantage of himself and his party,
widened the breach with the Senate majority by taking Democrats
but no prominent Republican with him to the Peace Congress at
Paris. In the circumstances the Republican party sought especially to discredit him and his work. At first he was
assailed because he seemed too conciliatory toward
Germany. Later, when the terms of the peace settlement were disclosed, he was accused of fatally compromising his
own principles, of agreeing to a peace of vengeance rather than
of justice, of sacrificing American interests, and of ensnaring the
United States in European quarrels.

**Abstention of United States**

When President Wilson returned to America in July 1919 and
sought the necessary ratification of the League Covenant and the
treaty of Versailles, he encountered widespread popular opposition and stubborn hostility from the Senate majority. Among his
adversaries were those who objected to the League of Nations as
tending to impair American sovereignty and to vitiate certain
constitutional powers of the American Congress, or as tending, in
disregard of the admonitions of George Washington, to entangle
the United States still more in the meshes of Old World diplomacy. There were others who objected to the treaty of Versailles:
idealists who contrasted it with the "Fourteen Points"; patriots
who denounced its concessions to Japan and Great Britain; German Americans who resented the degradation of the Fatherland;
Italian Americans who thought it unfair to Italy; Irish Americans
who thought it too fair to Great Britain. All these insisted that
the United States should not underwrite such a peace.

For almost two years a deadlock ensued between President
Wilson and the Senate majority, the latter stubbornly refusing
to ratify the League Covenant except with "reservations" which

the President quite as stubbornly declined to accept. In September 1919 Wilson undertook a tour of the country in order to reenlist popular support, but he was stricken with a paralysis from which he never fully recovered. Henceforth a broken and almost helpless man, he faced death and, what undoubtedly seemed worse to him, the defection of his own country from that League of Nations upon which he had set his mind and heart. The longer the deadlock continued, the higher mounted the wave of Senatorial hostility to the President's peace program. In November 1919 and again in March 1920 the Senate adopted by majority vote some fourteen drastic reservations to the League Covenant, but the minority, faithful to the President's injunctions, blocked ratification with these reservations.

The dispute was settled and the deadlock broken by the verdict of the American people in the presidential election of November 1920. At that time the candidate of the Democratic party, a supporter of the policies of President Wilson, was overwhelmingly defeated, and Warren Harding, a Republican Senator, was elected to the presidency. The new President, addressing the Congress shortly after his inauguration, in March 1921, declared that "in the existing League of Nations, world governing with its superpowers, this Republic will have no part."

After concluding separate peace treaties in 1922 with Germany, Austria, and Hungary, the United States persistently held aloof from the League of Nations. Eventually, some partial and halting cooperation was achieved through the presence of American "observers" at Geneva, through American representation on certain League commissions, through American participation in special conferences called by the League, such as those on disarmament, and, in 1934, through America's acceptance of membership in the League's Labor Organization.

The abstention and critical attitude of the United States undoubtedly injured the League of Nations. But there were other and hardly less grave gaps in the League's membership. Only belatedly was Germany admitted; and for fourteen years Russia was not a member, partly because its Communist dictatorship regarded the League as an international agency for preserving capitalism, and partly because most members of the League were hostile to the Russian dictatorship and sceptical of its willingness or ability to cooperate with them.

### 5. IMPLEMENTING THE PEACE SETTLEMENT

In view of the length and magnitude of the World War and the complexity of its results, it is especially noteworthy that a general peace settlement was made within a year and that the Paris peace treaties were put into effect with promptness and a fair degree of success. The prescribed plebiscites were duly held, and most of the new political boundaries were drawn in orderly fashion. Only in two instances were there serious armed clashes, one between Poland and Russia and the other between Greece and Turkey; but, as we have already mentioned, the former of these minor wars was liquidated in 1921 and the latter in 1923. Politically, the product was a new Europe in which old empires were replaced by national, democratic, and mainly republican states.[1]

There was now, also, the League of Nations, which, despite the abstention of the United States and the temporary exclusion of Germany and Russia, began to function, in a promising way, in 1920. Its Secretariat gathered and published much useful data about world conditions, political, economic, social, and cultural. Through its agencies, it did much to check the spread of typhus and the international traffic in opium. Through its associated Labor Office and Labor Conferences, it prompted a good deal of international collaboration in dealing with problems of industrial labor. Through its Court of International Justice, a considerable number of controversial matters were successfully adjudicated; and through special committees which it sponsored, a start was made toward a codification of international law.

*Operation of League of Nations*

In the adjustment of international disputes, the League was helpful with its convenient agencies, with its painstaking investigations and reports, and with its less tangible but still important contributions to the formation of pacific public opinion. And at least in disputes between lesser powers, it mediated with considerable success. For example, a dispute between Finland and Sweden in 1920 over the ownership of the Aland Islands in the Baltic was referred to the League, and the Council, after investigation by a special commission, awarded the islands to Finland. Again, a dispute between Poland and Germany over the boundary

---

[1] On the democracy and the national self-determination which seemingly triumphed as an accompaniment of the Paris peace settlement, see the next chapter.

line which should be drawn in Upper Silesia following the confused plebiscite there, was referred to the League in 1921, and the Council adjusted it by a compromise. Then, too, in 1925 a Greek attack upon Bulgaria in retaliation for frontier incidents was stopped by remonstrances of the League Council and the threat of an economic boycott against Greece.

League mediation was not so successful in disputes to which great powers were party. In a dispute of 1923 between Poland (backed by France) and Lithuania over the city of Vilna, attempted League mediation was pushed aside and Poland's armed seizure of Vilna was upheld by an independent accord between France and the other great powers of Britain and Italy. In another dispute of the same year between Italy and Greece, arising from the murder, presumably by Greek bandits, of several Italian members of an Albanian boundary commission, Italy without recourse to the League demanded of Greece an apology and heavy indemnities and, to enforce quick compliance with its demands, it bombarded and occupied the Greek island of Corfu. In vain Greece appealed to the League. Italy would accept no League dictation. Asserting its national dignity and sovereign rights, it only consented to evacuate Corfu through the friendly mediation of its "equals"—Britain and France—and on terms necessitating Greek acceptance of its major demands.

In 1926, the good offices of the League were, indeed, utilized to settle a protracted dispute over the ownership of the rich oil fields of Mosul between Great Britain as mandatory for Iraq on the one side and the weaker state of Turkey on the other, but this case was not a conclusive test of the League's strength. For, inasmuch as the settlement was favorable to Great Britain (and Iraq), the great power gladly accepted it, and the lesser power was induced, by minor British concessions, to acquiesce.

Full implementing of the Paris peace settlement, especially of its Covenant for the League of Nations, was handicapped by postwar differences and rivalry among the three victorious great powers in Europe—France, Great Britain, and Italy. France, in particular, was extremely fearful of Germany, more so **French** than either Britain or Italy. Germany, in spite of mili- **Search for** tary defeat and territorial losses, was still a potentially **Security** great power, superior to France in population, natural resources, and industrial strength. To delay German recovery and ward off

any German war of revenge, France zealously pursued a variety
of plans after 1918, and, in doing so, encountered no little opposition from other great powers.

At first, while the Paris Peace Congress was in progress, the
French government and Marshal Foch pleaded earnestly that the
future security of their country, and therefore the peace of
Europe, depended upon the severance of the whole left bank of
the Rhine from Germany. Then, when President Wilson pressed
for a League of Nations, the French negotiators urged that the
League be furnished with "teeth," that it be provided with a
strong international army to enforce strict observance of the
treaties of peace. Neither President Wilson nor Lloyd George
would assent to the League's being made a hard-and-fast military
alliance or to the extension of French frontiers to the Rhine, and
eventually France agreed, though reluctantly, to an alternative
plan for its special security. This was to be a defensive triple
alliance by the terms of which the United States and Great Britain
would jointly guarantee the territorial integrity of France and
would come to its military assistance if it should be attacked by
Germany. The treaties of alliance were duly signed at Paris, and
on the strength of them France abandoned its claims to German
lands (except Alsace-Lorraine) and accepted a relatively innocu-
ous League of Nations. But the refusal of America to act on President Wilson's advice and ratify the Franco-American treaty rendered the alliance inoperative for Great Britain as well as for the
United States, and left France to seek security by still other
means.

One obvious means was to tie in defensive alliance with France
the lesser states of Europe which had a common interest in supporting the peace settlement and opposing treaty revision, and
this means was exploited to the full. France contracted a military
alliance with Belgium in 1920, with Poland in 1921, and with
Czechoslovakia in 1924. The last-named country had already
formed, in 1920–1921, a "Little Entente" with Rumania and
Yugoslavia to safeguard territories which they had severally
appropriated from Hungary, and this arrangement helped France
to draw into its own circle of alliance Rumania in 1926 and
Yugoslavia in 1927.

There were drawbacks about these French alliances. They were
expensive, because they had to be buttressed by fairly frequent

loans. They were none too reliable, because the parties to them, other than France, were minor powers, widely scattered, whose fighting abilities, if not patently slight, were unproved. Besides, the alliances involved France in all the controversies of eastern, as well as western, Europe, and they especially aroused the distrust of Italy. Indeed, Italy, in furtherance of its own ambitions and as a counterpoise to the French alliances, wooed Hungary, Austria, and Bulgaria, and encouraged them to hope for treaty revision.

Wherefore, France sought anew a strengthening of the Covenant of the League of Nations. From the French point of view, there were two fatal weaknesses in the Covenant: (1) it did not define "aggression"; and (2) it did not specify with sufficient exactitude the action to be taken against an "aggressor." To remedy these weaknesses, France sponsored the drafting by an international commission, in 1923, of a "treaty of mutual assistance," which, as revised in 1924 under the title of "Geneva Protocol," was submitted to the members of the League for ratification. It prescribed the settlement of every international dispute by arbitration or by conciliation. A state which refused to accept the award, or which in any way prejudiced the peaceful solution of a dispute, was *ipso facto* the "aggressor." Against such an aggressor, each signatory of the Protocol would undertake to act "in the degree which its geographical situation, and its particular situation as regards armaments, allows." 

*"Geneva Protocol" and Differences between France and Britain*

Practically, what France wanted from the Protocol was a more effectual underwriting of the peace settlement by the whole League, and particularly by Great Britain as its most puissant member. Britain was very chary of the Protocol, however. In general, Britain disliked the idea of obligating itself either to obey or to enforce each and every decision of an international body in which France and the Continental satellites of France would probably have a preponderant voice. And, backed by public opinion at home and in the self-governing Dominions, the British advanced two specific objections to the Protocol. First, it might involve them in war with the United States, which, being outside the League and spurning its agencies of arbitration and conciliation, might be deemed an "aggressor" in any serious dispute with a League member. Second, it would almost certainly require Great Britain to serve as a kind of police officer all over the world, including regions, such as eastern Europe, where it was not directly interested. The first objection France could have overcome by exempting American cases from the scope of the Protocol, but the second was insurmountable. So Britain withheld ratification, and the Protocol of Geneva collapsed.

Immensely aggravating the post-war difficulties were the related problems of inter-Allied debts and German reparations.

**Inter-Allied Debts and German Reparations** The debts included large loans which Great Britain made to its Continental allies during the first three years of the World War and still larger loans which the United States made to Great Britain, France, and Italy (and lesser countries) during the last year of the war and just after the armistice. The American loans totaled over eleven billion dollars.

France was not only the chief debtor to the United States and Great Britain, but it suffered during the war a destructive enemy invasion which neither Britain nor America—nor Germany—experienced. Consequently, to rehabilitate itself and to repair the ravages wrought on its soil, as well as to enable it to pay its heavy share of the inter-Allied debts, France was particularly anxious to exact ample reparations from Germany and the other vanquished nations. Provision for such reparations was inserted, as we know, in the major Paris peace treaties.

But it was one thing for the vanquished to be compelled to promise to pay, and quite another thing for them to keep their promises. Little in the way of reparations was actually forthcoming from Austria, Hungary, or Bulgaria. These states were so reduced in area and resources, and so hemmed in by tariff barriers which their neighbors erected against them, that, if they were to escape internal bankruptcy, they would have to receive, rather than give, financial assistance. Bulgaria was a very poor country anyway, and Austria and Hungary were no longer the hubs of an extensive and fairly prosperous imperial domain. Hungary was now a petty agricultural country without ports or markets, while Austria lacked means of sustaining its overgrown urban population at Vienna. Very soon the finances of both Austria and Hungary were so wrecked by inflation that the League of Nations felt obliged to arrange for foreign loans to them.

In the case of Germany, from which France and other creditor nations naturally expected most, the payment of reparations involved manifold difficulties. The German people were not minded to pay reparations at all. They felt that the promise to pay had been extorted from them under duress and they resented its coupling with the allegation that they were "guilty" of the war. They and their government would pay only what they were compelled to pay. And in compelling Germany to pay, the Reparations Commission which represented the several creditor nations had its hands full.

The Allies—and the Reparations Commission—took the stand immediately after the war that Germany must be made to pay the most that it could pay, and yet nobody knew just how much that might be; the estimates of economists were far more modest than those of statesmen, especially of French statesmen. No precise amount had been fixed by the treaty of Versailles, and the resulting uncertainty was troublesome and exasperating. It sharpened the rivalry among the Allies for preferential treatment of their respective claims, and at the same time it retarded Germany's economic recovery and lessened its ability to pay. In 1920, after much haggling, the Allies agreed, at an international conference at Spa, upon a percentage division of whatever reparation payments Germany could be compelled to make.[1] Then, in 1921, after more haggling, the Reparations Commission fixed the total German indemnity at thirty-two billion dollars.

There remained no little doubt as to whether Germany really could pay this sum, and no little perplexity as to how it would pay it if it could. It was argued at first that Germany would pay a considerable part in kind, that is, by giving its creditors coal, locomotives, textile machinery, and other products of its mines and factories; and in fact it did make some payments in kind. The more it thus paid, however, the louder grew the complaints in Allied countries that they were being deprived of markets for their own goods; and presently the Allied governments called a halt on payments in kind from Germany.

Money payments were supposed to constitute the major part of the indemnity, but they could be made by Germany only if it enjoyed a favorable balance of trade, that is, if its exports exceeded its imports. But this condition was very difficult of attainment. Russia, which had formerly provided a valuable market

[1] According to the agreement at Spa, France would have 52 per cent, Great Britain 22, Italy 10, Belgium 8, and the others 8.

for German manufactures, was now in chaos and virtually closed to economic penetration from the outside world. Germany no longer possessed overseas colonies or "spheres of influence" where its goods might receive preferential treatment. Moreover, neighboring Poland was entering into economic competition with Germany, levying high tariffs against German imports and diverting its own exports from customary German routes to a newly established route across the Polish "corridor." For a brief time, such handicaps to German enterprise were partially offset by currency inflation, which artificially stimulated Germany's production and enabled it to undersell its chief competitors—Britain, France, and the United States—even in their home markets. But these countries soon heightened their tariff walls against the flood of "cheap" German goods, while within Germany inflation reached such a stage that the currency became practically worthless.

In the latter part of 1922 Germany declared its inability to meet its financial obligations to the Allies and requested a two-year moratorium. The British government, anxious to expedite the resumption of normal commercial relationships, gave favorable ear to the request, but the French government, then presided over by Raymond Poincaré, resolved to apply force.

**French Seizure of Ruhr** Wherefore, in January 1923, a French army crossed the Rhine and took possession of the rich mining region of the Ruhr, the very nerve-center of Germany's industrial life. The event proved sorry for all concerned. The Germans, outraged by the hostile incursion and yet unable to oppose it by force of arms, were welded together in patriotic fervor and in stubborn determination to pursue a policy of passive resistance to French demands, even if such a policy meant the economic ruin of their country. The French, on the other hand, were scandalized by the general strike which almost completely paralyzed industry in the Ruhr and indicated Germany's purpose to prevent the collection of reparations, and they were still more scandalized by the eventual discovery that their expedition into the Ruhr cost them more money than they got out of it. By the autumn of 1923, it was obvious, even to the French, that Germany's economic life was in dissolution and that the reparation arrangements would have to be revised.

In 1924, therefore, as a result of international negotiations and of deliberations by a commission of economic experts headed by an American banker, Charles Dawes, new arrangements were agreed to by the Allies on one side and by Germany on the other. There was no change in the total amount of the Ger- **"Dawes** man indemnity, but it was made payable over a long **Plan"** period of time in annual installments and in accordance with special regulations to be administered by a neutral "agent-general for reparation payments." Simultaneously Germany cancelled its inflated currency and, at great cost to a large part of its population, restored the pre-war mark and instituted new taxes, while France withdrew its armed forces from the Ruhr and awaited the flow of money from Germany.

In 1925 Franco-German relations underwent some improvement, thanks to the temporarily successful operation of the Dawes Plan, and thanks also to the mutually conciliatory attitude of the foreign ministers of the two countries, Aristide Briand in France and Gustav Stresemann in Germany. Both of these statesmen had come to believe that they could promote the security of their respective nations by direct agreements, and as this belief was consonant with British interests, Britain's Foreign Minister, Austen Chamberlain, encouraged the negotiations and persuaded the Italian government to do likewise.

The outcome was a group of treaties, drafted in October 1925 in idyllic surroundings at the Swiss health resort of Locarno on Lake Maggiore and collectively styled the Pact of **Pact of** Locarno. Germany would enter the League of Nations **Locarno** and receive a permanent place, as a great power, on its **Kellogg-** Council. Simultaneously, Germany would definitely de- **Briand** sist from seeking treaty revision by force of arms and **Pact** would settle by arbitration or conciliation every dispute which might arise with France, Belgium, Czechoslovakia, or Poland. Germany would reserve the right to seek a peaceful modification of its eastern frontiers but it would expressly recognize the permanence of the new western borders. Wherefore, as the most significant feature of the Pact, Germany and France and Belgium would forever respect their mutual frontiers and refrain from war with each other except in self-defense or in accordance with the stipulations of the League Covenant; and Great Britain and Italy would guarantee this feature of the Pact by giving armed assistance to any of the three powers if it should be faced with a violation of the Pact by any other of the three.

The Pact of Locarno, though assailed by extremists in both Germany and France, was generally hailed at the time as an epochal event: as marking a final reconciliation between victors and vanquished and constituting a big step forward toward world peace. In the afterglow of optimism thus engendered, the American Secretary of State, Frank Kellogg, acting on a suggestion of Briand, proposed to all the nations of the world that they pledge themselves by a solemn pact "to outlaw war," that is, "to renounce the use of war as an instrument of national policy." Briand was not completely satisfied with the form which Kellogg gave to his suggestion. The American Secretary was insistent, however, that the pact should embody only a principle and that its enforcement should rest solely upon the "good faith" of the several signatories. Perhaps a little cynically, Briand acquiesced in this interpretation; and the Kellogg-Briand Pact was signed at Paris in August 1928. Being but a pious declaration, it was speedily adhered to by almost every nation.

Not the Kellogg-Briand Pact and not even the Locarno Pact actually solved the problem of security. On the Locarno Pact, France and Germany put different interpretations. France imagined it meant full German acceptance of the treaty of Versailles. Germany expected that it would be followed by a revision of the treaty of Versailles. Both were mistaken. Germany pressed the harder for annulment or amendment of those clauses in the treaty charging it with war-guilt, imposing heavy financial burdens on it, limiting its armaments, and contracting its historic eastern borders.

Against such pressure, France was adamant. It would make no further concessions; and now that it was promised British and Italian assistance in preserving the territorial arrangements of the treaty of Versailles concerning the West, it felt all the freer to oppose any alteration of those affecting the East. Consequently, France renewed and strengthened its military alliances with Poland and Czchoslovakia; and in the spring of 1931, in concert with Italy, it estopped Germany from forming a close tariff-union (Zollverein) with Austria.

In the meantime, the "Dawes Plan" for Germany's payment of reparations was meeting with obstacles. The plan had been admittedly only a temporary expedient; and the Germans soon became impatient with its close regulation of their domestic affairs by foreigners, a regulation which threatened to be interminable. They argued that the total amount of thirty-two billion dollars, which they were expected eventually to pay, was beyond all reason and must be pared down. With this argument, there was considerable sympathy in Great Britain and the United States, but all the other Allies and particularly France were anxious to couple with any reduction of German reparations a corresponding reduction of the inter-Allied debts. In the United States, however, the government and the weight of public opinion opposed any cancellation of the inter-Allied debts and supported a tariff protection which further handicapped France and other debtor nations.

In 1929, in response to German protests, a second commission of economic experts, under the chairmanship of another American financier, Owen Young, met at Paris and recommended a radical revision of the "Dawes Plan" of reparation payments. The total amount of such payments would be reduced by three-fourths—from thirty-two billion dollars to eight billion—and the payments would be made by Germany during a term of fifty-eight years without direct foreign supervision. These recommendations, together with a provision for complete and immediate Allied evacuation of the Rhineland, were embodied in an international agreement signed at The Hague early in 1930. *Revision and Collapse of Reparations*

By this time, however, a world-wide economic depression of the most serious kind was setting in, and German national sentiment was solidly inimical to further payment of reparations. In 1931, the creditors of Germany felt obliged to grant a moratorium, and in 1932, through an international conference at Lausanne, they finally expressed their willingness to fix the remaining German indemnity at the modest figure of 700 million dollars if the United States would agree to a corresponding slashing of the inter-Allied debts. The United States would not agree, but in the industrial paralysis of the time the Allies ceased paying anything to the United States [1] or receiving anything from Germany. Practically, both reparations and inter-Allied debts were thus wiped off the slate of international accounting, but only after they had grievously impaired the economic stability of the world and the Paris peace settlement.

[1] Finland was the single exception.

The hopes for a general disarmament which were entertained
by President Wilson at the Paris Peace Congress, and which were
**Problem of** expressed in the Covenant of the League of Nations,
**Disar-** proved illusory. No general disarmament was achieved.
**mament**
France, it is true, cut its standing army in half by reducing the term of service from three years to eighteen months;
Italy called fewer men to the colors; and, in accordance with the
peace treaties, the armies of Germany, Austria, Hungary, and
Bulgaria were drastically curtailed. Yet the principle of universal
military service was in effect not only in most countries which
had adopted it prior to 1914 but also in all the newly created or
newly unified states. Russia, too, gradually built up a larger, and
eventually more efficient, army than it had had before the war.
Moreover, while the British navy was smaller than it had previously been, it was still a superior fighting force; and the navies
of the United States and Japan were considerably stronger than
they had been. Altogether there was a vast deal of continuing
"preparedness." It was costly. It consumed a large part of the
financial resources of the several governments and gravely embarrassed their post-war efforts at economic reconstruction. It
was dangerous. It kept up and even exaggerated the rivalry, the
sudden alarms, and the chronic sense of danger, which had attended the "armed truce" of Europe from 1871 to 1914.

Yet each nation wanted some other nation to take the initiative
in general disarmament, and no nation would take it. Every
state was convinced that the armaments of other states, but not
its own, were inconsistent with "national safety." The United
States and Great Britain continually found fault with France and
Poland for not reducing their armies and applying the sums of
money thus saved to the discharge of their foreign debts. But
France and Poland both retorted that they would reduce their
armies if they could count on assistance from the United States
and Great Britain in protecting them against possible German
aggression and that in the meantime the English-speaking powers
should evidence their sincerity by reducing their navies.

The basic difficulty, indeed, was one of security. National armaments might be dangerous in the future, just as they had been
before the World War, but to get rid of them would be still more
dangerous. If France and Poland, for example, should reduce
theirs to a level with Germany's, what would prevent Germany

from tearing up the treaty of Versailles and renewing the World War? But if France and Poland would not reduce their armaments, why should Germany be expected to keep its armaments reduced at the sacrifice of national security?

With every nation in quest of security through armaments, it proved quite impossible to bring about general disarmament. All that was practically possible was to try to keep down the armaments of those nations which had been vanquished in the World War, and among other powers to arrange such balancing of existing armaments as would temporarily serve to uphold the *status quo* and prevent the increase of national armies and navies from becoming madly competitive.

An international conference on the limitation of naval armaments was held at Washington in 1921–1922 and attended by representatives of all the naval powers, not only the United States, Great Britain, and Japan, but France and Italy.[1] The outcome was an agreement to retain for ten years approximately the existing ratio among battleship tonnages of the several powers: Great Britain 5, the United States 5, Japan 3, France 1.67, Italy 1.67. In vain the United States sought to include a limitation of light cruisers; Great Britain successfully opposed it. In vain Great Britain sought to include a prohibition on any use of submarines in war; France refused to agree to it. The Washington Conference did halt—for ten years— the highly provocative and expensive building of so-called "capital ships." But its failure to agree upon a similar check for other naval craft meant that in this respect naval rivalry continued, and the sense of security, instead of growing, actually lessened. Britain complained about the submarines which France proceeded to build, and the United States, about Britain's excess of cruisers.

Another conference was held at Geneva in 1927, but no agreement could be reached about cruisers. In 1930 still another conference was held at London. This was hardly more successful than the earlier ones in effecting a general limitation of naval armaments. Assent was given, it is true, to a prolongation of the Washington agreement; and the United States and Great Britain man-

*Naval Conferences*

---

[1] The Washington Conference, being called to consider general international questions in the Pacific and the Far East as well as the specific question of naval armaments, included representatives also of China, the Netherlands, Portugal, and Belgium. On the resulting agreements which dealt with matters other than naval limitation, see below, pp. 604–605.

aged to supplement it with an arrangement between themselves whereby Britain would be allowed a superiority in light cruisers and America a corresponding superiority in large cruisers. In this arrangement Japan acquiesced, though very reluctantly and only on condition that it be accorded parity with the others in the matter of submarines and some increase of its ratio for cruisers. But neither France nor Italy would adhere to it. Consequently the London agreement bound only three of the five naval powers, and its binding of the three was weakened by a provision (the "escalator clause") that any of them was free to exceed the specified tonnage totals if it should deem its "national security" to be "materially affected" by naval increases of another power.

Attempts to negotiate a general limitation of land armaments were even less successful. In 1925 the League of Nations created a special commission to study the problem and draft recommendations preparatory to the calling of a "disarmament conference." The commission soon discovered that both technically and politically the problem was well-nigh insoluble. Technically, the chief difficulty was in distinguishing between what was strictly and immediately military and therefore to be limited and what was only incidentally military and hardly susceptible of limitation. An actual standing army and its actual arms and equipment could be recognized and perhaps dealt with, but what about a potential army and its potential resources? What about army reserves, militias, and police forces? What about ordinary mail and passenger airplanes which could easily be converted into military planes? What about a nation's wealth and man-power and industrial production, employed in peaceful pursuits today but employable for military purposes tomorrow? If answers could be found to these and similar technical questions, a supreme political question would remain. How to reconcile the military needs of a nation intent upon preserving the *status quo* with the military demands of a nation zealous to change it?

For five years the Commission toiled at the problem, and eventually, like the proverbial mountain, it brought forth a mouse. It took the form of a "draft treaty," providing for a limitation, "in principle," of the number of men in active service in land, naval, and air forces, of governmental expenditure on army material, and of military (but not commercial) aircraft; a con-

> **Negotiations for Army Reductions**

demnation of the use of poisonous gases and "all bacteriological methods of warfare"; and a permanent commission to collect information and report periodically on the progress of "disarmament." As if to prove that the "draft treaty" should not be taken too seriously, it contained a special "escape clause," proposed by the United States and providing that if a "change of circumstances constitutes, in the opinion of any high contracting party, a menace to its national security, such high contracting party may suspend temporarily, in so far as concerns itself, any provision or provisions of the present convention other than those expressly designed to apply in the event of war."

Despite these and other failures fully to implement the Paris peace settlement of 1919–1920, popular hopes ran high throughout Europe and America until at least 1929 that the peace settlement would endure and usher in a better and more orderly era of the world's history.

# CHAPTER XI

## SEEMING TRIUMPH OF DEMOCRACY AND NATIONAL SELF-DETERMINATION

### I. EMERGENCE OF NEW NATIONAL STATES IN EUROPE

ATIONALISM was greatly forwarded by the World War and its aftermath. The doctrine of national self-determination, the doctrine that people who speak a common language and cherish common historic traditions should live under a polity of their own making, was invoked during the World War by Tsarist Russia against the Ottoman and Habsburg Empires, by Germany against Russia, by the Allies against the Mid-European Confederacy, and, most enthusiastically of all, by President Wilson. Aroused national sentiment proved a most efficacious stimulant of popular morale in waging the war, and hope of achieving national independence spurred on the various subject peoples in the Empires of central and eastern Europe.

**Intensified Nationalism**

Back in 1815 the Congress of Vienna, in its territorial settlement of Europe, had spurned the principle of nationality.[1] The principle was then too novel and too closely identified with the vanquished France of the Revolution. By 1919, however, the principle could not be spurned. It had become enshrined in the historic "unifications" of Italy and Germany; and during the second half of the nineteenth century and the first decade of the twentieth it had been gaining devotees in an ever widening area. The World War began as a despairing effort of the imperial domain of Austria-Hungary to stay the disruptive process which the principle of nationality, as represented by Serbia, was fostering. Indeed, the World War, however much economic imperialism

[1] See *Modern Europe to 1870,* pp. 588–593.

was associated with some of its participants, was basically and strikingly a nationalistic war. It was an extension, on a colossal scale, of the series of nationalistic wars of the third quarter of the nineteenth century. It was an herculean effort to complete or restore the national unifications of France, Germany, and Italy, and to follow them up with national unifications of Rumanians, Greeks, and the several Slavic and Baltic peoples. In this respect the World War was eminently successful. The Congress of Paris of 1919–1920 recognized the principle of nationality and wrote it into the public law of Europe. At last, the political map of the Continent was radically revised and re-drawn. Big imperial domains and fragmentary nations were wiped out, and in their place appeared an emphatically nationalistic—and novel—state-system.

Four great imperial domains were dismembered—the Dual Monarchy of Austria-Hungary, the Ottoman Empire, the Russian Empire, the German Empire. Moreover, certain small states or provinces whose inhabitants comprised but a part of a given nationality lost their historic identity—for example, Montenegro, Croatia, Bohemia, Transylvania, Galicia, Livonia, Courland, Schleswig. From the welding together of disjointed members of the same linguistic nationality and from the partition of multi-national empires, six national states were newly created—Poland, Czechoslovakia, Lithuania, Latvia, Estonia, and Finland; six existing national states were enlarged and consolidated—Serbia (Yugoslavia), Rumania, Greece, Italy, France (by recovering Alsace-Lorraine), and Denmark (by obtaining northern Schleswig); and five states which had previously been imperial were compressed within national limits—Germany, Austria, Hungary, Turkey, and Russia. Altogether, where there had been twenty-one sovereign states in 1914, there were twenty-seven in 1920, and almost all the twenty-seven were national.

The Communists in Russia seemed as ready to recognize the principle of nationality as was the Peace Congress at Paris. Not only did they consent to the break-up of the historic Russian Empire and the secession of Finland, Estonia, Latvia, Lithuania, and Poland, but they acquiesced in the incorporation of Bessarabia with Rumania and they reorganized what remained of the Empire on a federal basis. Much the greater part of it—the part peopled by Great Russians—became the "Russian Soviet Socialist

Republic," with its capital at Moscow. But federated with this Great Russian state, and accorded some degree of cultural nationalism, were "Soviet Socialist Republics" for Ukrainians, Byelorussians, etc.[1]

To re-cast the political map of eastern and central Europe on a strictly national basis was extraordinarily difficult. To bring together all Poles, for example, in a single Polish state, **Problem of** involved the inclusion of a considerable number of **National** Germans, as well as Jews. In general, as we know, the **Minorities** new boundaries were drawn by the peacemakers at Paris in such a way as to reward the nations which had favored the Allies in the World War and to penalize those which had opposed them. Thus it befell that whereas the Italians gained all of "Italia irredenta," new "irredentas" were created for Hungary, Bulgaria, and Germany. Sizable German minorities passed under the sway of Czechoslovakia (where they were known as Sudetens), Poland, and Italy; Magyar minorities, under the rule of Czechoslovakia, Rumania, and Yugoslavia; and Bulgarian minorities, under the dominion of Yugoslavia, Rumania, and Greece. And, contrary to the principle of nationality, German Austria was prohibited from uniting with Germany. Besides, the arbitrariness with which frontiers were delimited between some of the Allied national states—for example, between Italy and Yugoslavia, and between Poland and Lithuania—tended to accentuate, rather than to allay, nationalistic rivalry. To the same end operated the compulsion which the Allies exerted on newly founded or enlarged states, such as Poland and Rumania, to get them to accord special rights to national minorities within their respective territories.

Nationalism could not be so aroused in belligerent countries during the World War or so applied to the post-war territorial settlement in eastern and central Europe, without affecting the whole world. In Belgium, the Flemish- or Netherlandish-speaking population grew embittered against their French-speaking countrymen, some going so far as to demand political autonomy or even independence; and after the war, the Belgian government felt obliged to make several significant concessions to the Flemish national movement, such as emphasizing the equality of the Flemish language with French and transforming the University

[1] See below, pp. 559–560.

of Ghent into a purely Flemish institution. In Spain, simultaneously, there was a marked recrudescence of autonomous agitation among Catalans and Basques. In Iceland, nationalism reached such a threatening stage that Denmark agreed in 1918 to recognize its ancient colony as a sovereign state; henceforth the only bond between Iceland and Denmark was a common King.

In Ireland, too, separatist nationalism produced a veritable revolution. At the beginning of the World War the Irish masses (outside Ulster) had seemed content to follow John Redmond and his parliamentary Nationalist party. But the Home Rule Bill, already passed,[1] was not applied, while, on the other hand, the British government inflicted the direst punishment on the handful of Irishmen who participated in the Easter rebellion of 1916 at Dublin [2] and likewise proposed to enforce military conscription on all Irishmen. In the circumstances, the relatively mild home-rule nationalism of John Redmond lost popular support in Ireland, and the more uncompromising nationalism of the Sinn Fein party gained ground.

The foremost advocate of the new Irish nationalism, and the founder of the Sinn Fein party, was Arthur Griffith, a native of Dublin and a printer by trade. He began his political career as a fervent disciple of Parnell, but the factional quarrels among Irish Nationalist members of Parliament following Parnell's downfall led Griffith to despair of achieving "home rule" or any other reform for Ireland by parliamentary means. His goal was a united Irish nation, with a constitution of its own making, and with a government entirely independent of Great Britain's except possibly for a "personal union" (like Austria and Hungary after the Ausgleich of 1867 [3]) under a common sovereign. The means which he urged of realizing the goal should be neither parliamentary pressure on Britain nor forceful insurrection in Ireland but rather such "passive resistance" on the part of Irishmen as Hungarians had successfully employed in 1866–1867. The Irish people should not participate in the British government; they should refuse to serve in its army or pay taxes to it; and their elected members of Parliament should absent themselves from Westminster and con-

*Sinn Fein Nationalism in Ireland*

[1] See above, pp. 327–329.
[2] See above, pp. 387–388.
[3] See *Modern Europe to 1870*, pp. 755–756.

stitute a governing council at Dublin. In a word, national self-reliance should be the means and the end of Irish politics.

Griffith launched his new political party in 1906 under the name of "Sinn Fein"—Gaelic for "we ourselves." At first it was small, and, although it attracted a number of youthful intellectuals and secured allies in the radical element of the urban working class, its electoral successes prior to the World War were limited to placing some of its members on the local governing bodies of Dublin and a few other towns. The golden opportunity for Sinn Fein came with the World War and its aftermath.

By this time, Griffith shared the leadership of Sinn Fein with two younger men, Eamon De Valera and Michael Collins. De Valera, born in New York in 1882 of a Spanish father and an Irish mother, had been educated at Dublin and had developed into a strenuous advocate of national independence for Ireland; he participated in the armed insurrection of 1916, and escaping from a British prison in 1919 he toured the United States and collected funds for the Sinn Fein organization. Collins, born of a peasant family near Cork in 1890, resigned a position in the British civil service at London to join the "Irish Volunteers" and engage in the 1916 rebellion; managing to get out of jail and thereafter to elude arrest, he soon became a guiding spirit of the Sinn Fein movement.

In the general elections to the British Parliament in December 1918, three-fourths of all the Irish constituencies—which formerly had elected Nationalists of the Redmond party—returned Sinn Fein candidates. As many of these as were not in jail, acting on the principles enunciated by Griffith, promptly met at Dublin (instead of taking seats in the British Parliament at Westminster), and proclaimed themselves the legal Parliament (or Dail) of the "Irish Republic," with De Valera as President and Griffith as Vice-President.

A desperate struggle ensued between the nationalist "Irish Republic," on one hand, and the British government and Ulster Unionists, on the other. There were frequent skirmishes between Republican riflemen and British troops, many assassinations, and much destruction of property. For three years matters went steadily from bad to worse.

In 1920 David Lloyd George, the British prime minister, with Unionist support, attempted to solve the problem by putting through the British Parliament a new Home Rule Act, providing for two separate and partially autonomous governments in Ireland, one for the six counties in Ulster and the other for the twenty-six counties in the rest of the country. The Unionists in Ulster accepted the Act as a satisfactory compromise and accordingly instituted at Belfast a local government of their own, the government of "Northern Ireland." But the Act was bitterly opposed by the Republicans of the south, as sanctioning the division of Ireland and as conferring little power on the proposed Irish Parliament at Dublin.

Finally, when no other solution seemed possible, Lloyd George invited the "Irish Republic" to send delegates to London to negotiate terms of peace with Great Britain. The outcome was a treaty of London, signed in December 1921, which provided for the establishment of an "Irish Free State" **Irish Free State** as a self-governing Dominion within the British Empire, similar in status to Canada; Ulster could join the Free State if it so determined by plebiscite, or it might continue under the separate government provided by the Home Rule Act of 1920. The treaty was speedily ratified by the British Parliament, and, despite the impassioned opposition of De Valera, by the Irish Dail also. Of the new Irish Free State, Griffith became provisional President and Collins prime minister.

The Irish Free State began its career in most difficult circumstances. Ulster voted to stay out. Republican followers of De Valera terrorized southern Ireland. Griffith soon died, and Collins was assassinated. Nevertheless, the "provisional government," guided by Collins's successor, William Cosgrave, slowly but surely gained strength and stability. The British military forces evacuated Ireland. A working agreement was reached between the Free State and the government of Northern Ireland. A democratic constitution was adopted by the Dail and ratified by the British Parliament. The greater part of Ireland, under the inspiration of Sinn Fein nationalism, thus joined Canada, Australia, New Zealand, and South Africa as a self-governing Dominion. Before long it would go farther and become an independent Republic.[1]

The triumph of nationalism in Ireland synchronized with special manifestations of nationalism in other parts of the British

[1] See below, pp. 699-700.

Empire. Each of the self-governing Dominions—Canada, Australia, New Zealand, and South Africa—experienced special pride in its military exploits during the World War, faith in its increasing importance in the future, and determination to have its voice **British** heard in the counsels of the world, not indirectly **Dominions** through London, but directly from its own national **and** **Statute of** capital. Each of these Dominions signed the peace **West-** treaties of Paris as a sovereign power, and each was **minster** admitted to separate membership in the League of Nations. Three of them—South Africa, Australia, and New Zealand —acquired individual "mandates" for German colonies.

The nationalism implicit in these developments was affirmed as a principle in the so-called "Balfour Report," which was adopted by an Imperial Conference of the statesmen of Great Britain and the self-governing Dominions in 1926. "They [Great Britain and the several Dominions] are autonomous communities within the British Empire, equal in status, in no way subordinate one to another in any aspect of their domestic or external affairs, though united by a common allegiance to the Crown, and freely associated as members of the British Commonwealth of Nations." It remained to have this principle enacted into imperial law, and this was accomplished in December 1931, with the passage of the "Statute of Westminster" by the British Parliament.

The Statute recognized the legal equality of the Dominions with the mother-country and their practical independence of one another. It provided that no law of the British Parliament might be applied to any Dominion without the latter's express consent, that no law of a Dominion parliament might be "disallowed" by the British government, and that no alteration in the laws concerning the royal succession or titles might be made without the assent of all the Dominion parliaments as well as the British. Implicitly, at least, each Dominion was to be free to direct its foreign affairs as it would. Thereby an important part of the British Empire—Canada, Australia, New Zealand, South Africa, and likewise the Irish Free State—was legally transformed into a merely sentimental alliance of independent states, officially styled the "British Commonwealth of Nations."

Rising nationalism was indeed a characteristic and almost universal phenomenon of the post-war years. It manifested itself among all the European powers and in the self-governing Dominions of the British Empire. Nor was it henceforth a primarily European (and American) phenomenon. As we shall presently see, it overspread Asia and penetrated into Africa.[1]

## 2. VOGUE OF DEMOCRATIC REPUBLICANISM

The immediate aftermath of the World War seemed to confirm Woodrow Wilson's contention that it was waged "to make the world safe for democracy." For, with the exception of Russia, where the Tsarist regime was supplanted by a Communist dictatorship,[2] all the great powers and most of the lesser ones adopted or elaborated democratic forms of government. And with the extension of democracy was associated a vogue of republicanism.

In 1914, six of the great powers were monarchical. In 1919, only three remained such, and these three—Great Britain, Italy, and Japan—had reconsecrated their political institutions by military victory. The three most famous European dynas- Vogue of ties—the Habsburg, the Romanov, and the Hohen- Republi- zollern—had ceased to reign, and lesser princely canism families had been expelled from the several German states. All the newly created states of central Europe were republics—Poland and Czechoslovakia, Lithuania and Latvia, Estonia and Finland. Not only were the American continents almost wholly republican, but Europe was now predominantly so, and even in Asia the vast and populous country of China was at least nominally republican, while from the ruins of the Ottoman Empire was rising a Turkish Republic.

Moreover, democracy seemed triumphant. Thoroughly democratic constitutions were evolved by popularly elected assemblies in the revolutionized Central Empires and in the newly Democratic founded or newly unified states of central and eastern Consti- Europe. The German constitution, adopted by the tutions Weimar Assembly in 1919, retained the federal organization of the German Empire while lessening the powers of the several states and broadening those of the central government. For the exercise of the latter, it entrusted authority jointly to a Reichstag, representing the people, and to a Reichsrat, representing the states, and executive authority to a President, elected by the people for seven years, and to a Chancellor and his associate ministers,

[1] See below, pp. 487–503.
[2] See above, pp. 394–396, 399–400, 704–711, and below, pp. 553–569.

responsible to the Reichstag. The suffrage was accorded to all German citizens, male and female, over twenty years of age; a detailed bill of rights was included; and provision was made for the initiative, referendum, and recall, and for proportional and professional representation. Contemporaneous changes in the state constitutions of Prussia, Bavaria, Württemberg, Saxony, and all the others guaranteed the democratic character of the whole German Republic.

The Austrian constitution of 1920 established a federal republic of eight diminutive states, with a legislature similar to Germany's, and an executive like the French—a titular President elected by the legislature (for four years instead of seven, however) and a directing ministry responsible to the legislature. The Czechoslovak constitution of 1920 and the Polish constitution of 1921 were alike modeled on that of the French Republic. Each provided for a bicameral parliament—a senate and a chamber of deputies—which should choose the President, enact the laws, and control the ministry. Both constitutions—and the Austrian likewise—were more democratic than the French, in that they enfranchised women as well as men.

Yugoslavia and Rumania retained the institution of monarchy, but adopted constitutions, the one in 1921 and the other in 1923, which resembled the democratic constitution of the Italian kingdom. Both guaranteed individual liberties, parliamentary government, and ministerial responsibility. Both, despite provincial opposition, affirmed the unitary, rather than the federal, character of the state, and provided for local administration under prefects appointed by the central government. Both granted universal manhood suffrage.

Simultaneously, Finland, Estonia, Latvia, and Lithuania adopted constitutions at once republican and democratic. Sweden, Denmark, and Iceland, though remaining nominally monarchical, removed all property qualifications for the exercise of the suffrage and enfranchised women.

In Great Britain, the earlier electoral reforms of 1832, 1867, and 1884–1885 [1] were consolidated and supplemented by an important democratic Act of 1918, enfranchising all men who were over twenty years of age and had maintained a residence or place of business for six months, and all women who were over twenty-

[1] See above, p. 48.

nine years of age and had owned or tenanted premises for six months or were married to men who owned or tenanted premises. Voting in a general election would take place on one and the same day. No person could vote in more than two constituencies. Parliamentary seats were redistributed so that each would represent approximately 70,000 of the population. Subsequently, in 1928, the British Parliament took an additional step toward the democratic goal and granted the suffrage to women as freely as to men.

Meanwhile, the constitution of Northern Ireland, embodied in an act of the British Parliament of 1920, conformed in democratic tenor with the British reform of 1918, while the constitution of the Irish Free State, as adopted in 1923, went further. It enfranchised all citizens over twenty years of age and elaborated a system of proportional representation.

In Belgium, an electoral reform of 1919 abolished the existing system of plural voting and substituted for it the system of one-man-one-vote, and a further reform of 1921 partially enfranchised women. In the Dutch Netherlands, democratic government was attained in 1917 by the extension of the suffrage to all men and women and the establishment of proportional representation.

In general it may be said of all the newer constitutions and electoral reforms of the years from 1917 to 1923 that special emphasis was put on representative, democratic government, on ministerial responsibility, and on guarantees of individual liberty. In most of the changes, the enfranchisement of women stood out conspicuously; it seemed an appropriate recognition of the significant role which women had played in the World War and were playing in industrialized society, as well as a logical application of the principle of political democracy. Full suffrage was accorded to women, on the same basis as to men, in Germany, Austria, Czechoslovakia, Poland, the Baltic and Scandinavian states, the Netherlands, Luxemburg, Great Britain, and the Irish Free State. In the United States, moreover, a constitutional amendment providing for universal woman suffrage was approved by the Congress, ratified by the federated states, and formally proclaimed in 1920. Japan, too, felt the surge of the democratic movement in Europe and America; it did not enfranchise women, but in 1925 it put an end to property qualifications and extended the parliamentary suffrage equally to all adult male citizens.

All this radical democratizing of political institutions was hailed as a world-wide fruition of the seed which had been planted in France and the United States in the eighteenth century, which had germinated and sprouted in western and central Europe in the second half of the nineteenth century, which in the first decade of the twentieth, on the eve of the World War, had pushed its shoots upward through the unpromising soil of the Russian, Ottoman, and Chinese Empires, and which now, in the aftermath of the World War, seemed unmistakably to assure to the whole world a common type of political aspiration and achievement. The world, it was boasted, was at last safe for democracy, and political democracy would amply justify itself in its rapid amelioration of social conditions and international relations. There was still, during the immediate aftermath of the World War, a remarkable note of optimism in European thought and word.

Yet the seemingly all-but-universal triumph of democracy came at the moment when international relations were embittered by the World War and the Peace of Paris, when the gravest problems of economic reconstruction were confronting statesmen and peoples, and when nationalism, rather than democracy, was commanding the deepest affections of the masses of mankind. In the circumstances, the triumph of democracy, at least of the traditionally liberal type, was more apparent than real. It proved a passing phase of the immediate aftermath of the war. Already, in fact, it was menaced by the rise of Communist dictatorship in Russia and by vigorous widespread agitation for like dictatorship elsewhere.[1]

### 3. DEMOCRATIC STRENGTH IN WESTERN EUROPE

Democracy was more deeply rooted and met fewer obstacles in western Europe than in eastern or central Europe. Personal liberty and parliamentary government were traditions of long standing and great weight in Britain, and hardly less so in France, Belgium, and Switzerland; and for a century prior to the World War they had been a constant goal of political aspiration in the Netherlands, Scandinavia, Spain, and Portugal. Moreover, none of these countries was faced after the war with such complex problems of territorial reconstruction and internal consolidation

[1] On the Russian dictatorship, and also on the post-war political developments in Italy and east-central Europe. see Chapter XIII, below.

as confronted the newly created or drastically altered countries of east-central Europe.

True, the post-war economic and financial conditions within France, Britain, Belgium, and Portugal were grave and troublesome, but they were certainly less so than in Russia or Poland, Germany or Italy. Only in western Europe had there been neutral nations during the war, and these—Switzerland, the Netherlands, Scandinavia, and Spain—at least temporarily improved their financial position. And the belligerent peoples of western Europe, the British, the French, and the Belgian, were naturally more wedded to a democratic regime which had "won the war" and dictated a peace satisfying to national prestige than were the Russians or Germans who had suffered crushing defeat or the Italians who were keenly disappointed with the peace.

In Great Britain, the outstanding problems of the post-war years were economic. The difficulty of resuming normal peacetime production in the face of increasing foreign competition and diminishing foreign markets jeopardized Britain's century-old position as "the banker and workshop of the world." Its production of coal and iron, of cotton goods and certain other basic commodities, was still impressive, but it showed a decline from pre-war standards both in absolute amount and in relation to the production of other industrial nations, most notably the United States and France. Hence, there was a shortage of jobs in mines and factories for the masses of British industrial workers, and unemployment promised to become chronic and acutely troublesome. The number of registered adult workers who could not obtain work was over two million in 1921 (out of a total of about twelve million); and around that figure it subsequently hovered.

*Great Britain*

This standing army of unemployed persons and the still larger host of their dependent families had to be provided for in some way. But the national debt had been so enormously increased by the war that the interest charges alone amounted to 360 million pounds sterling in 1921–1922 as over against 22 million ten years previously. To meet these charges, and at the same time to defray current expenses of army, navy, and civil administration and extraordinary expenses of unemployment relief, meant national taxation so heavy as to threaten the capitalistic system on which Britain's industrial supremacy had been·built.

The British government which first had to face these economic problems was the coalition of Liberals and Conservatives, headed by Lloyd George, which had been formed in 1916 and which had received a thumping vote of confidence from the country at large in the "khaki election" of December 1918.[1] It negotiated the peace treaties of 1919–1920, and effected the peaceful demobilization of the conscript war armies. It opposed the republican movement in Ireland, but finally, though reluctantly, agreed to the treaty of 1921 establishing the Irish Free State. It extended the insurance of workmen against illness and unemployment and greatly increased the governmental subsidies (or "doles," as they were called) to the unemployed. It also managed, by introducing many economies and by imposing heavy income taxes, to balance the budget. In 1921, with the purpose of arresting the industrial decline, it departed from the long-established policy of free trade and imposed tariff duties on the importation of certain foreign manufactures which were underselling British key industries in the home market.

Following a repudiation of the coalition government by a Conservative caucus in October 1922, Lloyd George resigned, and King George V entrusted the premiership to Andrew Bonar Law, the nominal leader of the Conservative party. The ensuing general election returned a clear Conservative majority, though the Laborites, under the guidance of Ramsay MacDonald,[2] secured a larger representation than they had ever had before and in excess of the Liberal party's. It was obvious that liberalism of the pre-war kind was being ground between the upper and nether millstones of conservatism and labor.

The Conservative victory proved abortive. Bonar Law, on

[1] On the pre-war career of Lloyd George, see above, pp. 321–327; on the formation of his Coalition ministry in 1916 and his war activities, see above, p. 404; and on the parliamentary election of 1918, see above, p. 420.

[2] Ramsay MacDonald, the son of a Scottish workman and largely self-taught, had been conspicuous in the Labor party from its origin, serving as secretary until 1912 and then as leader until 1914. He professed a kind of right-wing Socialism, and for his pacifism during the World War he suffered political ostracism and temporary imprisonment. His marriage in 1896 to a niece of Lord Kelvin, the famous scientist, (see above, p. 189), had brought him considerable wealth and strengthened his desire to ally intellectuals and "respectable" middle-class reformers, as well as trade unionists, with the Labor party. Such a desire he largely realized after the war, and this, along with popular reaction against the horrors of war and the sorry economic conditions of the time, helps to explain why the Labor party expanded rapidly after 1918.

account of illness, soon retired from the premiership in favor of Stanley Baldwin, a business man who had occupied several important financial offices since 1917. Baldwin's announcement that tariff protection was the remedy for the country's economic ills evoked dissension among Conservatives as well as strenuous opposition from Laborites and Liberals.

Alternating Conservative and Labor Governments

On the tariff issue, Parliament was dissolved and new elections held in December 1923. This time the Conservatives were reduced to a minority, while both the Laborites and the Liberals gained ground. Early in 1924 the new parliamentary majority voted Baldwin out of office and permitted Ramsay MacDonald to form a Labor government.

But the Labor government was short-lived, too. It could last only as long as the Liberals were willing to support it, and the "moderation" which they insisted upon was likely to alienate the extremist element among the Laborites. Before coming into office, MacDonald had advocated a capital levy and other drastic socialist measures for dealing with the domestic situation. Once in office, however, he dropped all such proposals and contented himself with obtaining from Parliament the repeal of some of the existing tariff duties and an authorization for the construction of workers' dwellings. Presently, while a section of his own party grumbled at his "moderation," the Liberals took alarm at his "extravagance" and the mounting cost of unemployment relief; and when he finally decided to recognize the Communist dictatorship in Russia, the Liberals repudiated him. In vain he appealed to the British electorate in October 1924. Though the popular vote for Labor candidates went up by a million, the Conservative party, on a platform of opposition to the "red peril," secured an overwhelming majority in the House of Commons. MacDonald's Labor ministry was succeeded by a Conservative ministry under Baldwin.

The second Baldwin ministry lasted almost five years, from November 1924 to May 1929. It sponsored several important measures. One was the definitive adoption of tariff protection. Another was the enfranchisement of women on the same basis as men. A "general strike" of British workmen in May 1926, the climax of protracted and bitter labor troubles in the coal mines, created grave apprehension and led to the enactment of a "trades dispute bill," outlawing general strikes and imposing restrictions on trade union activity.

At the regular general election in 1929, the Conservatives met defeat. The Labor party obtained a plurality of seats in the House of Commons, and though still dependent for an absolute majority upon the remnant of Liberals headed by Lloyd George, there was no question about its assuming the conduct of government. Accordingly, Baldwin resigned and Ramsay MacDonald formed his second Labor cabinet, including for the first time in English history a woman member—Margaret Bondfield as Minister of Labor.

At the outset of his second ministry MacDonald appeared to be less "compromising" than he had been during his first ministry, but fundamentally he was more intent upon a pacific foreign policy than upon domestic social reform and temperamentally he was more susceptible to the appeals of persons of birth and substance than to the urgings of lower-class extremists in his own party. As economic conditions grew rapidly worse in Britain, reflecting in an acute form the world-wide depression which set in seriously in 1930,[1] MacDonald abandoned any idea which he may previously have had of resorting to radical socialistic expedients. In 1931, against the counsel of the majority of his cabinet, he endorsed the proposals of his Chancellor of the Exchequer, Philip Snowden, to reduce governmental expenses and to effect drastic economies in unemployment relief. This split the Labor party. A minority stuck by MacDonald and Snowden and took the title of "National Laborites." The majority repudiated the Prime Minister.

Whereupon MacDonald invited the Conservatives and the Liberals to unite with him in backing a "national" government. **National Government of 1931** The Conservatives responded with alacrity, and so did a fraction of the Liberals, with the result that the new ministry, as formed in August 1931 under MacDonald's titular headship, comprised two or three "National Laborites," two or three "National Liberals," and a majority of Conservatives (including Baldwin and Neville Chamberlain). In the ensuing elections, the coalition won eight-ninths of all the seats in the House. To be sure, the opposing Labor party polled a popular vote of six and a half million and elected four times as many members as did the National Labor party of MacDonald; but the

---

[1] On the economic crisis of 1929–1930, see below, pp. 546–547, 580.

parliamentary representation of the Laborites as a whole was sharply cut, and against 68 National Liberals who supported the coalition, only Lloyd George and three other Liberals remained in opposition.

Thus the British government was essentially conservative and nationalist during the crisis of economic depression from 1931 to 1939, as it had been in the crisis of peace-making and post-war readjustment from 1918 to 1922. In name, it was a coalition government. In fact, it was a government of the Conservative party; and just as formerly the Conservatives had taken Lloyd George, a radical Liberal, in tow, so now they had captured Mac-Donald, the Labor leader. Under MacDonald until 1935, under Baldwin until 1937, and then under Neville Chamberlain, the government pursued policies at once conservative and patriotic. Tariff protection was elaborated by an act of 1932, and certain features of the old Corn Laws were revived.[1] British imperialism was given a new slant by the Statute of Westminster (1931), in accordance with which the self-governing Dominions were recognized as "nations" and grouped together as a "Commonwealth." National appropriations for army and navy were maintained at a relatively high level (averaging 115 million pounds sterling annually during the decade from 1925 to 1935 as compared with 64 million in 1910). At the same time, national expenditure for unemployment-relief remained large; and only by withholding debt payments to the United States and abandoning the gold standard did the government appreciably lighten its grievous financial load.

During most of the post-war period, and in its most critical years, the Conservative party was dominant in Great Britain. The Liberals, who had been in power for almost ten years immediately preceding the World War, were now rent by internal dissension and deprived of any large popular following. Principal opposition to the Conservative party had definitely passed from the Liberals to the Laborites, and, though the latter suffered a setback through the secession of Ramsay MacDonald and his fellow "National Laborites" in 1931, there was evidence aplenty that the setback was only temporary and that a new political (and social) alignment was becoming ever more sharply

[1] On the Corn Laws, see *Modern Europe to 1870,* pp. 459–460, 650–651, and above, pp. 53–54.

defined between Conservatism and Labor. This did not signify, however, that Britain was headed toward revolution or dictatorship.

It is true that there was an unusual amount of criticism of parliamentary government in post-war Britain. At one extreme, some workmen and a few intellectuals espoused Communism of the Russian variety. At the other extreme, Sir Oswald Mosley, a volatile aristocrat, who had been in turn a Conservative and a Radical Laborite and was always something of a poseur, underwent a sudden conversion to Fascism of the Italian (and German) kind and began to inveigh against Parliament and the Jews and to organize a band of "black-shirts." Nevertheless, the confessed Communists in Britain, though noisy, were not numerous, and Sir Oswald's Fascists were an object of popular scorn and derision.

The vast majority of the British people continued to support the parliamentary party of the Conservatives or that of the Laborites, and both parties were seemingly as desirous as the dwindling Liberal party to retain the characteristic political institutions of modern England. The strength of monarchical tradition was vividly illustrated by the popular enthusiasm which greeted the accession of Edward VIII on the death of his father, George V, in 1936; and less than a year later, when the new King abdicated rather than give up a divorced woman with whom he was infatuated, by the even greater enthusiasm attending the succession of his more prosaic brother, George VI.

Two democratic governments were maintained in Ireland from 1922 onwards. One was the government of Northern Ireland,

**Ireland Divided**

which functioned at Belfast under the premiership of Sir James Craig (Viscount Craigavon), with a parliamentary majority of Unionists and in subordination to the British government at Westminster.[1] The other was the government of the Irish Free State, which exercised sway at Dublin over the greater part of Ireland in accordance with the written constitution which it adopted (with the sanction of Great Britain)

---

[1] Northern Ireland, though accorded a local parliament of its own in 1921 (see above, p. 461), continued to be represented in the British Parliament. It is interesting to note that the title of "United Kingdom of Great Britain and Ireland," which had been the official designation of the British monarchy since the Union of 1801, was changed, after the creation of the Irish Free State, to "United Kingdom of Great Britain and Northern Ireland."

in 1922. This government was directed for ten years, from 1922 to 1932, by William Cosgrave with the backing of moderate Sinn Feiners. Internal order was restored, religious and other individual liberties were respected, the Irish (Gaelic) language was given an equal legal status with English, and much was done to promote Irish agriculture, industry, and public works. Following the electoral success of extreme Sinn Feiners in 1932, Eamon De Valera became premier, and under his guidance a more intensely nationalist policy was pursued. The oath of allegiance to the King was abolished. Appeals to British courts were forbidden. By a new constitution of 1938, the state was re-named "Eire," and the British Governor was replaced by a "President."[1] In the same year a favorable trade agreement was negotiated with Great Britain.

All the self-governing Dominions of the British Empire stuck to political democracy.[2] In Canada, the government was directed from 1917 to 1921 by a coalition of Conservatives and Liberals, then almost continuously for nine years by a Liberal ministry headed by Mackenzie King, then for five years by a Conservative ministry under Richard Bennett, and from 1935 by another Liberal ministry under King. In Australia, the government was in the hands of a patriotic coalition during the war and throughout the post-war period, except for two years (1929–1931) when the Labor party was in power. In New Zealand, the ministry of William Massey, which had originally been formed in 1912, lasted until his death in 1925, and the same moderate and conservative elements which had supported him retained control of the government until 1935, when the more radical Labor party won the general election and formed a ministry. *Self-governing Dominions*

In South Africa, General Smuts, with the joint backing of moderate Boer nationalists and British unionists, was prime minister from the death of General Botha in 1919 until 1924, when he was succeeded by General Hertzog, who had the support of extreme Boer nationalists and also of labor. Hertzog was a democrat as well as a nationalist, and under his leadership the franchise was extended to all men and women of white extraction, while immigration was restricted to persons coming from "Nordic"

---

[1] The first President of "Eire" was Douglas Hyde (see above, p. 57).
[2] On the previous history of these Dominions, see above, pp. 60–68.

nations. In the elections of 1933, Smuts joined forces with Hertzog, and the coalition triumphed.

In all the English-speaking countries (including the United States), there was more concern with radical movements after the war than previously, more talk about Socialism and Communism, and at the same time more manifest nationalism. But in all of them, democratic traditions were cherished and democratic usages observed.

It was likewise in France. Here, the democratic and parliamentary institutions of the Third Republic continued to function **France** in much the same way as they had functioned before the war. True, extremes of "Left" and "Right" were more vocal with subversive propaganda and more active with hostile demonstrations. On the one hand, a Communist party arose and flourished, denouncing the "bourgeois" Republic and demanding a "dictatorship of the proletariat." On the other hand, the royalist and ultra-patriotic Action Française,[1] intensifying its campaign against the Republic, gained the allegiance of many youths, especially at Paris, and contributed to the growth of a Fascist movement. Yet the agitation of one extreme tended to counteract the other's, and between the two extremes stood the large majority of Frenchmen.

From 1919 to 1924 the French government was controlled by a "National Bloc," in which the conservative and very patriotic groups of the Center and Right were particularly influential, though Socialist Radicals of the Left continued to man the strategic departments of education and the interior. Clemenceau, prime minister during the latter part of the war and during the peace negotiations, retired from office in 1920, following his defeat for the presidency of the Republic in succession to Poincaré. Alexandre Millerand, once a Socialist and now a conservative and nationalist, became prime minister and shortly afterwards was elevated to the presidency.[2]

The successive Bloc ministries labored with remarkable success to reconstruct the war-devastated areas of northern France and to restore economic prosperity. Factories were rebuilt and equipped with up-to-date machinery. The output of mines and foundries

---

[1] See above, p. 333.

[2] Poincaré had been succeeded as President in 1920 by Paul Deschanel, but later in the year Deschanel resigned and was succeeded by Millerand.

was greatly increased, and hydroelectric power was highly developed. Indeed, French machine industries—both textile and metal—advanced, rather suddenly, into a class with those of Germany and Britain. This industrial advance, coupled with the maintenance of normal agricultural production and the persistence of peasant proprietorship, helps to explain why there was no such pressing problem of unemployment in France as in Great Britain, and why there was no such social disturbance or political revolution as in central or eastern Europe. To be sure, the public debt of France was prodigiously swelled by the war and by post-war reconstruction, and the Bloc ministries, counting upon reparation payments from Germany, failed to balance the budget.

The "National Bloc" was less anti-clerical than the pre-war Radical governments of France had been. It resumed diplomatic relations with the papacy and left the relations of church and state in the recovered provinces of Alsace-Lorraine to be regulated by the concordat of 1801 rather than by the "laic laws." [1] Throughout France, moreover, it eased the enforcement of the Associations Act of 1901 and tolerated the revival of Catholic religious communities.

In the elections of 1924 the Socialist Radicals deserted the "National Bloc" and re-created with the Socialists a "Cartel of the Left," which, profiting from popular disappointment at the failure to make Germany pay, won a majority of seats in the parliament. Whereupon Millerand, who had openly opposed the Cartel in the elections, was forced out of the presidency of the Republic, and under his less assertive successor, Gaston Doumergue, a Radical ministry was installed with Édouard Herriot as premier.

Herriot's Radical ministry lasted barely a year. It withdrew French armed forces from the Ruhr and otherwise evinced a willingness to compromise with Germany. At the same time it undertook an anti-clerical campaign, breaking off diplomatic relations with the papacy and threatening to denounce the concordat in Alsace-Lorraine and to stiffen and enforce the "laic laws" throughout France. The result was an alienation of moderates, and their counter-campaign against the Cartel was seconded by many patriots who thought Herriot too conciliatory toward Germany and not conciliatory enough toward Alsace-Lorraine. But

[1] On the "laic laws," see above, pp. 98–99.

what chiefly brought about Herriot's downfall was the sorry state of public finance, and the differences within the Cartel over the means of remedying it. Inflation and a capital levy, advocated by Socialists and extreme Radicals, were repugnant to moderate Radicals, while the former were most reluctant to seek a balancing of the budget through drastic economies and ordinary taxation, which the latter favored. In 1925, with financial affairs reaching a critical stage and the government seemingly powerless to handle them, Herriot resigned. For a year longer his Radical supporters composed ministries which succeeded one another in kaleidoscopic fashion, until at length in 1926, following an alarming decline of the franc and a riotous demonstration at Paris, Herriot and his Radicals on the Left broke with the Socialists and joined the groups of the Center and Right in constituting a ministry of "national union" under Raymond Poincaré's premiership.

National Ministry of 1926

Poincaré's "national" ministry rehabilitated French finances. It stabilized the currency, with the franc at about a fifth of its pre-war value. It increased taxes and introduced many economies. It gave France a businesslike administration, completed the reconstruction of the country, and fostered production alike of fields and of factories. Simultaneously, it appeased the Catholics by restoring diplomatic relations with the papacy and by reversing the anti-clerical policies of the Herriot ministry. In 1928, for the benefit of workmen, it sponsored the enactment of a comprehensive social-insurance law.

The general election of 1928 was a decisive victory for Poincaré and his ministry of National Union, but he was already in bad health and the next year he felt obliged to retire from public life.[1] His immediate successors, however, relied upon the same backing and pursued similar policies, until 1932, when new elections again brought forward a "Left Cartel" and enabled Herriot to form another Radical cabinet.

The Cartel, this time, was very precarious. The Socialists at the Left were more disposed to fraternize with the Communists at the extreme Left, and the Radicals could not quite make up their minds whether they should go with the Socialists or break with them and join the Center. Besides, a most unedifying scandal came to light concerning a financial promoter by the name of

[1] Poincaré died in 1934. Briand predeceased him in 1932.

Stavinsky and involving a number of republican politicians, especially in the Radical camp. Herriot's ministry, which had been formed in June 1932, was forced to resign in December, and during the next fourteen months five other Radical ministries rose and fell. In February 1934 popular resentment against the Radicals was utilized by extremists, both Royalist and Communist, to precipitate at Paris a series of street riots, in which several persons were killed. Whereupon, to allay the resentment and prevent civil strife, the Radicals united with groups of Center and Right to constitute another "national union." Gaston Doumergue, whose term as President of the Republic had expired the previous year,[1] headed the new coalition ministry. He conducted affairs much as previously, in similar circumstances, Poincaré had conducted them. He was not quite so forceful, and he did not have quite as much personal prestige. And, failing to get Radical support for a constitutional law which would enable the ministry to dissolve the Chamber of Deputies and hold new elections, he resigned in 1935.

In 1936 the Socialists and even the Communists formed with the Socialist Radicals a coalition—the so-called "Popular Front" —on a platform of defending democracy, resisting **Popular** Fascist tendencies, and effecting social reform. Follow- **Front** ing the victory of the coalition at the polls in June, the **of 1936** Socialist leader, Leon Blum, headed a Popular Front ministry which lasted a full year and carried out a large measure of its electoral promises. Fascist organizations were dissolved and a good deal of radical labor legislation was enacted.

By the middle of 1937, however, the Popular Front government was encountering serious dissension within its own ranks as well as embittered criticism from without. On the one hand, the Communists were dissatisfied with its compromising moderation and its failure to intervene actively in a civil war in Spain,[2] while, on the other hand, many Radicals were alarmed by the epidemic of strikes and labor troubles which its policies seemed to invite and by the rapidly growing financial deficit which its prodigal expenditures appeared to entail. For a time after Blum's resignation the coalition troublously continued under a succession of

---

[1] Doumergue's successor in the presidency was Paul Doumer, who was assassinated in 1932. Albert Lebrun was then elected President, and reelected in 1939.

[2] See below, pp. 620–623.

Radical premiers, but eventually in 1938, as public finances went from bad to worse, the Radicals again broke with the extreme Left and, under the leadership of Édouard Daladier, formed a coalition with the Center and Right. To Daladier the parliament at once entrusted limited dictatorial powers in order to introduce needful economies and to restore public confidence.[1]

Democratic institutions were also maintained and respected throughout the post-war period by the peoples of Belgium, the Dutch Netherlands, and Switzerland. In each of these countries there were grave economic and financial problems and in Belgium a special cultural problem arising from differences between Flemings and Walloons,[2] but all such problems were dealt with in orderly democratic fashion and with considerable success. In all three countries, there was a weakening of the middle-class Liberal parties and a corresponding access of strength for the more democratic parties of Socialists and Catholics. Communist groups arose and obtained some representation in the several parliaments, but their popular following was relatively small and unimportant.

*Low Countries and Scandinavia*

In the Scandinavian kingdoms of Denmark, Norway, and Sweden, and likewise in the neighboring republic of Finland, political democracy was firmly established and popularly supported. In the kingdoms, Socialists or Laborites comprised nearly half of the membership of the several parliaments and frequently presided over the responsible ministries, but the large majority of Scandinavian Socialists were democratic social reformers, willing to cooperate with liberals and even with agrarians, and not disposed to champion a social revolution or a political dictatorship. Under Socialist premiers, Denmark banned strikes and lockouts in 1933 and Sweden enacted an unemployment-insurance law in 1934. Finland, under a democratic government of conservative leanings, outlawed Communist propaganda in 1930, suppressed a reactionary movement in 1932, and in 1933 forbade the advocacy of "direct action" and the maintenance of armed forces by any political group.

In the Iberian countries of Spain and Portugal, political democracy was more a theory than a practice. It was provided for by written constitutions, but its actual operation was impeded, and

[1] On Daladier's momentous foreign policy, see below, pp. 629, 632–633.
[2] See above, pp. 107, 458–459.

at times frustrated, by the continuing prevalence of those peculiarities of public life which had characterized Spanish and Portuguese history for a century prior to the World War: a violent partisanship by extremists; a quasi-anarchistic attitude of the masses; a manipulation of elections by professional politicians and local "bosses"; and spasmodic exercise of dictatorial power by army chiefs.

In Portugal, the troubles which had beset the nominally democratic Republic since its revolutionary establishment in 1910,[1] were magnified by its participation in the World War.[2] Loss of Portuguese lives on French battlefields, and added financial burdens for an impoverished country and bankrupt state, brought no compensation in the way of national prestige. During and after the war, while popular unrest increased, the Republic continued to be the plaything of a swift succession of corrupt politicians and ambitious army officers.

*Portugal and Regime of Salazar*

At length in 1926, General Antonio Carmona, by a military *coup*, took control of Portugal and inaugurated a regime of more enduring and constructive character. Under the forms of constitutional and democratic government, he secured his election in 1928 to the office of President for a regular term of four years, and this term was lengthened in 1932 to six years. Then, in accordance with a new constitution which was approved by general plebiscite in 1933, he was confirmed as President for an additional term of seven years. Meanwhile, in 1928, he called to his assistance a remarkable professor of economics at the University of Coimbra, Antonio de Oliveira Salazar, who speedily proved himself so energetic a reformer and so successful a statesman that General Carmona entrusted him with practically dictatorial authority.

Under Salazar's guidance, Portuguese conditions were perceptibly improved. Public administration was bettered at home and throughout the overseas empire. National finances were reorganized, indebtedness reduced, and credit restored. Anti-religious campaigns were stopped, and relations between church and state were harmonized. Strikes and lockouts were prohibited, and provision was made for the compulsory arbitration of labor disputes. Revolutionary agitation was sternly suppressed.

[1] See above, pp. 338–339.
[2] See above, p. 384.

Spain, at the close of the World War, was still a constitutional monarchy, with a parliament elected by universal manhood suffrage and with a ministry appointed by the King but responsible to the parliament. The government momentarily profited in popular esteem from the economic advantages which accrued to Spain as a neutral in the World War, but with the cessation of the war Spain was deprived of exceptional markets for its products, the financial returns to its farming class diminished, unemployment increased among the laboring class, and fault-finding with the existing political and social order became more pronounced. Republicans, Socialists, and Anarchists intensified their subversive propaganda and multiplied their ranks. A Communist party was organized. An epidemic of strikes paralyzed the country's economy and threatened political revolution.

**Spain and Republican Revolution of 1931**

Aggravating the situation were the protracted and apparently disastrous efforts of the royal government to put down native uprisings in the northern part of Morocco which had been allotted to Spain before the World War. For several years the fighting in Morocco had taken a toll of Spanish soldiery and Spanish treasure, without achieving its objective, and in July 1921 it reached a sorry climax in an utter rout and almost complete extinction of a Spanish army. This disaster outraged patriotic sentiment in Spain and turned it against King Alphonso XIII, to whose personal interference with the military command in Morocco the rout was chiefly attributed.

In an attempt to save his throne and silence his critics, Alphonso XIII connived at the forceful establishment, in September 1923, of a military government headed by Primo de Rivera, a nobleman and army officer who had served with distinction in the Spanish-American War and in Morocco. Primo de Rivera suspended the constitution, exercised a censorship of the press, and for seven years (from 1923 to 1930) maintained a dictatorship with the motto, "country, monarchy, religion." He infused new energy into the Moroccan enterprise, and in cooperation with French arms he finally brought it to a successful issue in 1926. Within Spain, he aimed at a "corporate state," directed by a single Nationalist party. To this end, he set up in 1928 a state department of national economy and prescribed the compulsory arbitration of labor disputes, and in the same year he authorized an advisory assembly to draft a new national constitution of an essentially fascist character.

Primo de Rivera was an honest man and not without personal ability. But he had no large following, and he was not forceful (or unscrupulous) enough to overcome opposition. He failed to build up a strong supporting party or to allay popular discontent, which continued to express itself in strikes, riots, and occasional mutinies, and he was handicapped by interference and intrigues of the King. Eventually, disillusioned and broken in health, Primo de Rivera resigned and retired to private life in January 1930 as suddenly and unexpectedly as he had seized power. His successor at once yielded to public clamor and restored the democratic constitution.

In the ensuing local elections of April 1931 the Republicans won an overwhelming victory, and their leader, Niceto Alcalá Zamora, threatened a general insurrection unless the King should immediately abdicate. Alphonso XIII replied by flight, and Zamora put himself at the head of a "provisional government." It was the beginning of eight tempestuous years of the Second Spanish Republic.[1]

### 4. DEMOCRATIC EXPERIMENT IN GERMANY

The German Republic, which had been proclaimed at the time of the collapse of the Hohenzollern Empire in November 1918 and provided with a democratic constitution by the Weimar Assembly in 1919,[2] was gravely handicapped by the post-war requirement of making vast yet indefinite reparation payments to the Allies. This involved currency inflation, cancellation of internal indebtedness, drastic taxation at home and big borrowings abroad.[3]

Yet, bad as were the economic circumstances of post-war Germany, it is doubtful whether they were essentially worse than those of post-war Britain or France. Britain's burden of taxation was considerably heavier, its industrial recovery much slower, and the number of its unemployed much larger. France's war debt was staggering, and, unlike Germany (or Britain), it had to re-

---

[1] See below, pp. 617–623, and on the First Spanish Republic, see above, pp. 118–119.
[2] See above, pp. 463–464.
[3] See above, pp. 446–449.

build an extensive war-devastated area. Nevertheless, in grappling with their economic problems, both the British and the French possessed governments which had been newly consecrated in popular esteem by the seemingly victorious war they had waged, and which therefore were not readily subject to subversion.

The Germans, on the other hand, were undertaking a novel experiment in self-government; and a people who had thought of the Hohenzollern Empire as a great power, occupying a preeminent position in arms and diplomacy, in science and industry, in world prestige, were naturally prone to abuse the Republic which began its career by accepting the treaty of Versailles with all its humiliations for Germany.

Nor could the Republican government obtain from the Allies such timely modification of the treaty of Versailles or of the reparation arrangements as might have served to disarm its critics and strengthen its hold upon the German masses. The concessions which it did obtain—the paring down of reparations and the withdrawal of foreign troops from the Ruhr and the Rhineland—were made haltingly and with poor grace.

Despite all these unfavorable circumstances, the German Republic managed to survive under its democratic constitution for fourteen years—from 1919 to 1933. At first, while popular reaction against the war was still potent, the republican

**Republican Parties** parties of Socialists, Centrists, and Democrats commanded a large majority of the German electorate and hence of the Reichstag, and through close cooperation these parties constituted the ministries and directed the policies of the state.[1] As domestic and foreign difficulties multiplied, there were frequent changes of ministry, but every ministry comprised Centrists and Democrats and everyone was supported, if not directly participated in, by Socialists. From 1923, moreover, when French occupation of the Ruhr called forth a united German resistance, the People's party (formerly the National Liberal party) was induced by its leader, Gustav Stresemann, a prominent industrialist and perhaps the most statesmanlike of all post-war Germans, to abandon its opposition to the republican form of government. Stresemann headed a coalition ministry in 1923, and though he soon resigned the chancellorship he retained the post of For-

[1] On these parties of Socialists, Centrists, and Democrats, and also on the People's party, see above, pp. 412-413.

eign Minister under successive Chancellors until his death in 1929.

From 1923 to 1929, the German Republic seemed to be gathering strength and attaining stability. There was some improvement, through the "Dawes plan" and the "Young plan," in the arrangements about reparation payments. There was a marked revival of business. There was some balm to national pride in certain successes which attended Stresemann's diplomacy: he negotiated the "Locarno Pact" to lessen the danger of another war between France and Germany; and he gained the admission of Germany to the League of Nations and to a place, as a great power, on its Council. At the general elections of 1924, the republican coalition polled eighteen million votes out of a total of twenty-nine million. At the general elections of 1928, it polled almost twenty-three million out of a total of thirty-one million.

The Republic seemed to be more solid than it really was. The governing coalition as a whole might win elections and collaborate in maintaining the democratic constitution, in distributing offices, and in sustaining Stresemann's conduct of foreign relations, but its elements were too diverse to enable it to adopt and pursue any consistent policy in respect of internal reforms, which were popularly demanded, or in respect of the opposition which beset it from the Nationalist Right and the Communist Left.

Communism of the Russian variety had been preached in Germany during the republican revolution of 1918–1919, but its apostles were then few and ineffectual, and the riots which they precipitated were fairly easily put down. *Communist Opposition* Presently a leader emerged in the person of Ernst Thälmann, a mechanic of Hamburg; and a definitely Communist party was organized with local "cells" and regional "soviets" and in intimate relationship with Moscow. Its popular vote increased from half a million in 1920 to nearly six million in 1932, the increase being almost entirely at the expense of the Socialist vote. Thälmann had no great organizing or managing ability; and his lieutenants were second-rate, lacking in personal initiative and repeating the phrases rather than emulating the deeds of the Russian Communist leaders. Yet the growing membership of the Communist party in Germany and its intransigent attitude toward the existing order served to stimulate and intensify extremist counter-propaganda.

Subversive propaganda from the extreme Left was trouble-some enough to the German Republic, but more disturbing and eventually more fateful was subversive activity by the extreme Right. Here, the original core of the opposition was the landed Prussian aristocracy, long identified with the monarchy and with high office in its army and civil service, and now organized in an anti-republican and anti-democratic Nationalist party. At first the popular following of the Nationalist party was not impressively large. In the election of the Weimar Assembly in 1919, the party polled only three million votes out of a total of thirty million, and for some time afterwards it seemed to be powerless, despite constant vehemence and occasional violence,[1] to arrest the democratic movement and restore the old order. In vain one of its leaders, Wolfgang Kapp by name, with the assistance of General von Lüttwitz, executed a *coup d'état* at Berlin in 1920 and put the Republican government to flight. A strike of Socialist workmen promptly turned the tables, so that Kapp and Lüttwitz ran away and the Republican officials returned. In vain an odd team of nationalistic fanatics, the renowned elderly General Ludendorff and a hitherto inconspicuous young man by the name of Adolf Hitler, attempted another *coup* at Munich in 1923; they were arrested and Hitler was jailed.

*Rightist Opposition*

If Nationalists were as yet unable to overthrow the Republic, they at least could rejoice by 1924 that their cause was gaining ground. For the prevalent financial disorder and economic insecurity of the preceding four years, which was swelling the ranks of the revolutionary Communist party, was operating also, along with widespread popular hatred of foreign tutelage and growing impatience at the seeming ineffectualness of the Republican government, to reinforce the reactionary Right. In the regular election of 1924 the Nationalists polled over five and a half million votes.

Early in 1925 the Nationalists, by clever maneuvering, obtained an even more ominous success. The death of Friedrich Ebert, the Socialist who had been President of the Republic since 1919, necessitated the popular election of a successor; and against the

---

[1] Erzberger, a Catholic Centrist leader, was assassinated by fanatical Nationalists in 1921, and Walter Rathenau, a leader of the Democratic party and an outstanding Jewish capitalist, suffered a like fate in 1922.

candidate of the Republican coalition, Wilhelm Marx (a leader of the Center party), the Nationalists put forward Field-Marshal Paul von Hindenburg, Prussian squire and national hero of the battle of Tannenberg.[1] Thanks to Hindenburg's personal fame and thanks to the fact that Thälmann, the Communist leader, entered the campaign as a third candidate, the Nationalists secured a plurality (though not a majority) of the votes cast and thus elected Hindenburg to the presidency. Hindenburg was an old and doubtless overrated man, but he had a venerable appearance and great prestige. It was well known where his basic loyalties were—to Empire, to army, to landed nobility, to the Protestant state-church of Prussia; and it was the hope of reactionary Nationalists, as it was the fear of democratic Republicans, that he would employ his new key-position to forward attempts at restoring the Hohenzollern Empire.

*Hindenburg as President*

Hindenburg did nothing of the sort, however. Instead, throughout the seven years of his full presidential term, from 1925 to 1932, he cooperated with the Republican majority in the Reichstag and with the Republican Chancellors and ministries. It was a source of disappointment to the Nationalists, as it was of satisfaction to the Republicans.

But while the Republican coalition of Socialists, Democrats, and Catholic Centrists was more than holding its own against the conservative and monarchical Nationalists, it had to contend not only with Communists but also with a growing party of militant National Socialists, or "Nazis" as they were popularly styled. This was being built up by Adolf Hitler, the plebeian fanatic who had been jailed in 1923 for an attempted *coup d'état* against the Republic. At that time he was not widely known, and there was little in his previous career to indicate that he would ever emerge from obscure mediocrity.

*Hitler and Rise of Nazi Party*

Hitler had been born in Austria in 1889 of a family of the lower middle class and had grown up with only ordinary schooling and with only frustrated ambitions. As a youth he had failed to gain admission to the Austrian Academy of Painting and had eked out a meager livelihood by working long hours in an architect's office at Vienna and, from 1912, as a free-lance illustrator at Munich, solacing himself meanwhile with enthusiastic apprecia-

[1] See above, pp. 372-377, 385-386.

tion of Wagner's operas, Nietzsche's philosophy of the superman, and the anti-Semitic writing of Stewart Chamberlain.[1] Influenced by these sources, he had already become an ardent German nationalist when the World War broke out. Though still an Austrian citizen, he enlisted in the German army, and in it he served throughout the war. He was awarded an iron cross for valor, but he was never promoted beyond the rank of corporal; and his cup of bitterness was filled to overflowing when the victory of the Allies was followed by the Republican revolution within Germany. "My brow burned with shame," he wrote, "and my hatred against the men who had brought about this crime grew and grew; I decided to become a politician."

In 1919, therefore, Hitler joined with a handful of his youthful army acquaintances in forming a political organization—the National Socialist (or Nazi) party. In 1920 the group adopted an "unalterable program." It was certainly radical. It denounced the entire Peace of Paris and demanded the union of all Germans in a Greater Germany, the restoration of the German colonies, and the full rearming of Germany. It assailed Jews within Germany as "aliens," denied them German citizenship, and threatened them with exile. It proposed to prohibit foreign immigration, to ban all "unpatriotic" newspapers or associations, and to "nationalize" popular education. It called for the adoption of economic reforms in harmony with the principle of national, rather than Marxian, socialism. It condemned the "corrupting parliamentary system" and championed professional representation directed by "a strong central authority."

Almost simultaneously with the adoption of this program, Hitler made the significant discovery that he had oratorical ability, that by "letting himself go" in frenzied exposition of woes and wrongs of Germany and in fierce denunciation of Jews and foreigners he could attract and hold large audiences. To a person who had been thwarted all his life, it was gratifying to know that he had at least one talent which he could put to effective use. So, with zest, Hitler took to spellbinding; and in a country where political oratory was relatively rare and customarily re-

---

[1] See above, on Wagner, p. 234; on Nietzsche, pp. 209–210. Chamberlain, a Teutonized Britisher, was the son-in-law of Richard Wagner and the author of a ponderous tome, *Foundations of the Nineteenth Century*, in support of the thesis that virtue and civilization are the product of the "Aryan race" and are endangered by the "Semitic race."

strained, and where of course the general economic and psychological conditions were especially propitious, Hitler's spellbinding drew circus-crowds.

The attempted *coup* of Hitler in 1923 was premature. As yet he was a local rather than a national figure, and his convinced disciples were few. The ensuing year, however, was helpful to him and to his cause. The notoriety which he gained from his arrest, trial, and imprisonment aroused interest in him and in National Socialism, at the very time when French occupation of the Ruhr was producing financial chaos and an outraged state of mind all over Germany. Furthermore, Hitler utilized the enforced leisure of a year in jail to write *Mein Kampf*, a sensational account of his life and ideas, a kind of Nazi bible, which soon became a "best seller."

During the next four or five years, Hitler and his lieutenants perfected the party organization and staged ever bigger and more theatrical demonstrations against the Republic. The Nazi popular following steadily grew, but not until after 1929 did it reach alarming proportions. Then it would grow by leaps and bounds and eventually destroy the democratic German Republic.

## 5. SPREAD OF DEMOCRATIC NATIONALISM IN ASIA

Nationalism and democracy could not be such loudly proclaimed doctrines and such popular motive forces in Europe during and immediately after the World War without becoming ideals for most other parts of the world. The war was a truly world war, actively involving not only European and American nations but peoples of Near East and Far East (Turks and Arabs and Egyptians, Hindus and Siamese, Japanese and Chinese) and even African tribesmen. As the pre-war years had witnessed a remarkable spread of European imperialism throughout Asia and Africa, accompanied by the introduction into these Continents of material and religious aspects of Western civilization,[1] so now there was widespread adoption or imitation of Western nationalism and democracy.

The Moslem Near East became belligerently nationalist. It had started in this direction before the World War, but the war and its immediate aftermath were decisive in clarifying

[1] On the "Europeanization" of the world during the preceding era, from 1870 to 1914, see above, pp. 264–306.

the goal and hastening its attainment. The traditional religious unity of the "Moslem world" and the age-long political
comprehensiveness of the Ottoman Empire went down

**Moslem Near East**    in ruins together, and in their stead emerged the separate nationalisms of Turk, Arab, Egyptian, and Persian.

It has previously been related how, following the defeat of
the Ottoman Empire in the World War, a forceful and patriotic

**Mustafa Kemal and National- ist Turkey**    Turkish army officer, Mustafa Kemal, established the
national Republic of Turkey, with its capital at Ankara
and with himself as its President, and how, by fighting
and diplomacy, he wrung from Greece and the allied
great powers a revision of the peace settlement (in the treaty of
Lausanne of 1923) assuring to his state possession of all ethnically
Turkish lands—the whole of Anatolia and Asia Minor and the
European district of Constantinople.[1] Turkey, as thus constituted,
was only a portion of the former Ottoman Empire, but it was an
important portion and it was a strictly national state.

Nominally the new Turkey was republican and democratic. A
"fundamental law" of 1921 proclaimed the doctrine of popular
sovereignty and vested supreme authority in a National Assembly; and an elaborated constitution of 1925 provided for the
election of the Assembly by universal suffrage of the Turkish
people every four years and for the choice by the Assembly every
fourth year of a President of the Republic. Actually, however, the
new Turkey was conducted by Mustafa Kemal as a nationalist
dictatorship. This he was enabled to do by reason of the personal
fame which attended his military successes and which earned him
the popular title of "Ghazi" ("The Victorious"), and by reason
likewise of his continuing leadership of the army and the single
well-organized political party in the country, the People's party.
As chief of the People's party, he controlled the Assembly, dictated its policies, and insured his election to the presidency. As
President of the Republic, he appointed the officials. As commander of the army, he enforced obedience to his Assembly, his
agents, and himself.

Under Mustafa Kemal's dictatorship, Turkey was rapidly nationalized. Not only was the old imperial Ottoman tradition

---

[1] See above, pp. 427–429. To emphasize the nationalist character of the new
Turkey, the Greek name of "Constantinople" was supplanted by the Turkish,
"Istanbul."

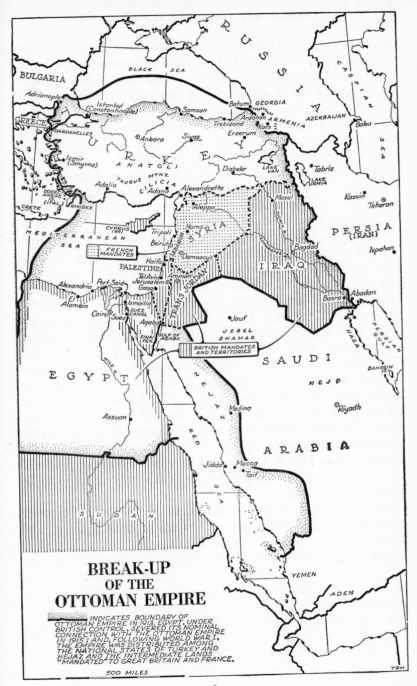

BULGARIA

BLACK SEA

*Adrianople*

Istanbul
(Constantinople)
*Samsun*

RUSSIA

*Batum* GEORGIA

*Ardahan* ARMENIA
*Trebizond* *Kars*

AZERBAIJAN

*Baku*

CASPIAN SEA

GREECE

DARDANELLES

*Ankara*
*Sivas*

T U R K E Y

*Erzerum*

*Diabekr*

LAKE VAN

*Tabriz*

LAKE URMIA

*Kazvin*
*Teheran*

*Izmir*
(Smyrna)

A N A T O L I A

*Adalia*

TAURUS MTNS.

CILICIA

*Adana*

*Alexandretta*

*Mosul*

PERSIA
(IRAN)

*Ispahan*

DODECANESE IS. (ITAL.)

*Aleppo*

*Homs*

SYRIA

TIGRIS R.

*Bagdad*

CRETE

RHODES

CYPRUS (BR.)

*Tripoli*
*Beirut*

LEBANON

*Damascus*

EUPHRATES R.

MEDITERRANEAN SEA

FRENCH
MANDATES

*Haifa*

PALESTINE

*Tel Aviv*
*Jerusalem*
*Gaza*

*Amman*

TRANS-JORDAN

I R A Q

*Basra*
*Abadan*

*Alexandria*
*El
Alamein*

*Port Said*
*Ismailia*

*Cairo*
*Suez*

SUEZ
CANAL

*Aqaba*

SINAI
PEN.

GULF OF
AQABA

*Jauf*

J E B E L
S H A M A R

BRITISH MANDATES
AND TERRITORIES

HASA

PERSIAN GULF

S A U D I

BAHREIN IS.

E G Y P T

NILE R.

H E J A Z

*Assuan*

*Medina*

N E J D

*Riyadh*

A R A B I A

RED SEA

*Jidda*

*Mecca*
*Taif*

S U D A N

YEMEN

ADEN

# BREAK-UP
## OF THE
## OTTOMAN EMPIRE

INDICATES BOUNDARY OF
OTTOMAN EMPIRE IN 1913. EGYPT, UNDER
BRITISH CONTROL, SEVERED ITS NOMINAL
CONNECTION WITH THE OTTOMAN EMPIRE
IN 1915; AND, FOLLOWING WORLD WAR I,
THE EMPIRE WAS DISTRIBUTED AMONG
THE NATIONAL STATES OF TURKEY AND
HEJAZ AND THE INTERMEDIATE LANDS
"MANDATED" TO GREAT BRITAIN AND FRANCE.

500 MILES

TRM

489

destroyed by the overthrow of the Sultanate and the expulsion of Mohammed VI in 1922, but, what was more fundamental, Turkish institutions were pried loose from their historic Moslem setting and endowed with a secular and national character. Mohammed VI and his Ottoman predecessors had been not merely Sultans of an Empire but Caliphs of all orthodox Moslems, and their authority resided as much in the Caliphate as in the Sultanate. With the deposition of Mohammed VI in 1922, his cousin, Abdul Medjid II, was suffered to succeed him as Caliph though not as Sultan. This proved but a makeshift, for Mustafa Kemal soon took steps to destroy the religious as well as the political influence of the imperial family and to undermine the hold of Islam on the country. In 1924 Abdul Medjid II was expelled from Turkish soil and the Caliphate was abolished; and in the same year, governmental appropriations for religion were suppressed and religious schools were transformed into state schools. Then in 1926 the old legal system, which had been based on prescriptions of the Koran and decisions of Moslem judges, was superseded by a modern national system. Polygamy was prohibited, and marriage, to be binding, must be performed by civil rather than religious officials. The Gregorian calendar was substituted for the Moslem, and the Roman alphabet for the Arabic. The metric system of weights and measures was adopted. The fez and turban were outlawed in favor of hats and caps; women were forbidden to wear veils; and the Turkish people were told to take surnames.[1] By government decree, the Moslem holy day was changed from Friday to Sunday. In 1928, by a constitutional amendment, the Turkish Republic was expressly declared to be independent of Islam.

Of course, most Turks continued to be Moslems, but their religion was henceforth a private and not a public concern; and the dictatorship which wrought this astounding change was fully determined not to grant to Christianity or other supernatural religion any favor which it denied to Islam. Christian missions in Turkey were regulated by Mustafa Kemal's government more rigorously than they had been by any Ottoman Sultan.

Many Moslem clergymen were aggrieved by Mustafa Kemal's religious policy, and in 1924–1925 the fanatically Moslem Kurds rose in revolt. At the same time, leaders of the Union and

[1] Kemal took for himself the name of "Ataturk" ("Chief Turk").

Progress party,[1] which had guided Turkish affairs during and just before the World War, reemerged from obscurity and began to form a "Republican Progressive" party in opposition to the new regime. Kemal hit back promptly and with vigor. He put down the Kurdish revolt, and against political adversaries he conducted a reign of terror, exiling some and executing others.

Simultaneously, in order to arouse the patriotism of the Turkish masses and make it a prop for his own party and policies, he inaugurated an extensive program of education and propaganda. He equipped every sizable town with a public school for children and with a reading and radio center for adults. Into all the radio centers was poured a stream of nationalistic speeches and news bulletins from Ankara, and into all the schools were put uniform nationalistic textbooks prepared under Kemal's personal auspices and expounded by teachers of his own selection. Everybody was pressed to become literate, adults as well as children.

One result of these educational endeavors was to reduce Turkish illiteracy, which had long been notoriously high. From 95 per cent in 1920, it was brought down in the next fifteen years to 65 per cent. Another and still more significant result was to enlarge the scope and increase the effectiveness of governmental propaganda. The Turks were learning to read, as well as being accustomed to hear, that they were a pure and superior "race," descended from the highly civilized ancient Hittites, that throughout the ages they had had a "mission," that now, under the benign guidance of the "Ghazi," they were again fulfilling their destiny, and that in the future they would be a truly great people if only they would be intensely loyal to their race and nation.

The nationalist government of Mustafa Kemal gave much attention to Turkey's economic betterment. A twelve-year public works plan was launched in 1929, providing for railway extension, harbor construction, and a large number of irrigation and reclamation projects. In 1933 a five-year industrial plan was adopted, calling for the development of hydroelectric power, the exploitation of coal, copper, and oil deposits, and the erection of state factories in Anatolia. All these undertakings were to be national, with minimum financial borrowing from foreign countries and without onerous concessions to them.

Turkey under Mustafa Kemal was proudly self-reliant. It

[1] See above, pp. 345–347.

would pursue its own interests and tolerate no external interference. By force of its own arms it had torn up the treaty of
Sèvres and imposed on unwilling foreigners the treaty of Lausanne. Thereby it had rid itself of political and economic tutelage
to other powers, and in particular had secured the abolition of the
so-called "capitulations" which in Ottoman days had deprived
the government of jurisdiction over foreign residents in Turkey.
For the retention of these gains it would rely above all on its own
efforts. Mustafa Kemal was a military man, and as such, and as
an ardent nationalist too, he kept the Turkish army strong and
ready for any emergency.

In foreign affairs, once he had secured Turkey's independence
and "national" frontiers, Kemal was generally conciliatory. It
was the best way, he believed, of serving national interests, upholding the *status quo* established by the treaty of Lausanne,
and assuring an uninterrupted development of domestic reform.
With Russia he concluded a treaty of mutual guarantee and
neutrality in 1925. He cultivated friendly relations with Greece
and arranged an entente with the Greek government in 1930.
He brought Turkey into the League of Nations in 1932, and in
1934 he made Turkey a party to a Balkan Pact with Greece,
Rumania, and Yugoslavia. In 1936 he regained for Turkey the
right to fortify the approaches to Constantinople, and in 1938,
by an agreement with France, he was enabled to garrison Alexandretta. Kemal died in 1938, but the Turkish nationalist regime
continued. The second and succeeding President of the Republic
was General Ismet Inonu.

Nationalism was also rife during the post-war period among
the Arabs, though these, unlike the Turks, possessed no comprehensive state and no leader whom they would all follow. Arabs comprised the large majority of the population in all the former Asiatic provinces of the Ottoman
Empire which were not included in the new Turkey, but the peace
settlement of 1919–1920 partitioned them among various sover-
eignties: the nominally independent kingdom of Hejaz; the British mandates of Palestine, Transjordania, and Mesopotamia; and
the French mandate of Syria. This partition and especially its
attendant subjection of the major parts to European powers
served to accentuate and give direction to Arab nationalism. In
all Arab lands, agitation was ceaselessly vocal and sometimes

*Arab*
*Nation-*
*alism*

violent; it would create as much trouble as possible for British or French rule. In other words, Arab patriots were less immediately concerned with building a unified national state than with opposing alien imperialism in the several existing states.

Shortly after assuming its mandates, Great Britain thought to conciliate the Arabs by entrusting Mesopotamia to Prince Faisal, a son of King Hussein of Hejaz, with the title of King of Iraq, and Transjordania to another son, Abdullah by name. The appetite of Arab nationalists was only whetted thereby. Especially in Iraq, the agitation for self-government and complete independence, adroitly guided by King Faisal, gathered strength and momentum. Bit by bit the British High Commissioner gave way, making one concession after another. At length, after protracted negotiations, Great Britain concluded a treaty at Bagdad in 1930, recognizing the independence of Iraq, promising to sponsor its admission to the League of Nations, and agreeing, when this was brought about, to renounce all mandatory rights over the country and within five years to withdraw all troops. In accordance with the treaty of Bagdad, Iraq was admitted to the League in 1932 and the last of the British garrison was evacuated in 1935. Britain retained a defensive alliance with the country and some economic privileges in it. In the meantime, in 1933, King Faisal died and was succeeded by his son Ghazi, who in turn was succeeded in 1939 by his son, Faisal II. Iraq was already a practically independent Arab state, with rich natural resources, a fairly strong army, a form of parliamentary government, and a resolute national spirit.

Transjordania was not so successful in achieving independence. Its population of 300,000, though solidly Arab, was largely nomadic and much more backward than the comparatively settled population of Iraq, and Abdullah was more dependent than his brother Faisal on British financial and military assistance. Hence, while Great Britain agreed in 1928 to a measure of self-government for the region, confirming Abdullah as Emir and authorizing him to create a Council and an elective Assembly for the enactment of local laws, actual British control continued. British armed forces might be sent into the country at any time, and acts of the Emir or of the Assembly might be disallowed by a resident agent of the British High Commissioner of Palestine.

In Palestine, west of the Jordan, the situation was complicated by the promise which the British government had made, in the "Balfour Declaration," [1] to respect the national aspirations of Jews as well as Arabs. Palestine had long been an Arab country—largely Moslem, though in part Christian—but as soon as a British administration was installed after the war a tide of Jewish immigration set in, rapidly increasing the Jewish minority from barely 70,000 in 1920 to over half a million in 1938. The Jewish newcomers, with superior technical skill and with financial subsidies from Zionist organizations in the West, undoubtedly contributed to an economic and industrial renaissance in Palestine, but in doing so they displaced many Arabs in gainful occupations and thus added to Arab grievances and nationalistic agitation.

**Palestine and Jewish-Arab Conflict**

The British administration did its best to soften the conflict between Arabs and Jews. It tried to respect equally the cultural traditions of both groups, religious, linguistic, and educational. While assuming a paternal attitude toward Jewish undertakings and encouraging their colonizing projects, it sought to reassure the Arabs by withholding special political privileges from the Jews and discouraging their indiscriminate immigration. Above all, it endeavored to dispense even-handed justice and to enlist the cooperation of both groups in matters of common interest and advantage—in modernizing Jerusalem, in promoting public health, in improving transportation, in increasing the yield of farm and factory. Yet the nationalism of neither Arab nor Jew was thereby mitigated. The Jews were eager to make Palestine theirs; the Arabs, to keep it theirs. The former wanted immigration to proceed without restriction; the latter demanded that it stop altogether. Neither would agree to schemes for a Palestinian parliament which the British put forward in 1922 and again in 1936, each fearing it would but serve the purposes of the other.

[1] This Declaration was made by Arthur Balfour, British Foreign Minister, in response to pressure from Jewish Zionists (on Zionism, see above, p. 259) in November 1917, while the World War was in a critical stage and just before General Allenby had captured Jerusalem (see above, p. 407). It stated: "His Majesty's Government view with favor the establishment in Palestine of a national home for the Jewish people and will use their best endeavors to facilitate the achievement of that object, it being clearly understood that nothing shall be done which may prejudice the civil and religious rights of existing non-Jewish communities in Palestine, or the rights and political status enjoyed by Jews in any other country."

In the circumstances there was frequent incitement to acts of violence, and repeatedly there were bloody riots at Jerusalem and in the countryside. Serious Arab outbreaks against the Jews occurred in 1929 and 1933, and from 1936 disorders and outrages were chronic. The British government replied by reinforcing its garrison, expelling Arab leaders, and proposing in 1937 a partition of Palestine. To this proposal both Arabs and Jews objected and in 1939 the British tried in vain, through direct conferences at London, to induce the leaders of the two groups to cooperate in creating a single semi-autonomous state with minority rights for the Jews.

It was likewise with the French in Syria. Here the Arab population was large and relatively progressive, and its leaders were as eager for national independence as were those of Iraq. In order to lighten their task, the French, soon **Syria and Lebanon** after assuming the mandate, cut off from Syria the region around Beirut, which was predominantly Christian and seemingly more kindly disposed to a French protectorate, and constituted it the autonomous "Republic of the Lebanon," with a native President and an elective Assembly. The rest of the mandate—the main part of it—was then consolidated into the "State of Syria," with its capital at Damascus and under the direct rule of the French High Commissioner. Despite the fact that most of the occupants of this post were tactful administrators as well as able soldiers and that they did a good deal to develop the country, there was constant protest from Arab nationalists and on occasion serious rioting at Damascus. The worst rioting occurred in 1925, when a new and exceptionally untactful Commissioner appeared in the person of General Sarrail, and it was rendered more serious by a simultaneous revolt of the Druses, a Moslem sect of warlike mountaineers. Sarrail's failure to suppress the Druse revolt and his attempt to stop the rioting at Damascus by subjecting the city to a deadly forty-eight-hour bombardment created the gravest kind of unrest all over Syria and provoked a general insurrection. Hastily Sarrail was recalled to France, and a new High Commissioner was sent out with military reinforcements. He restored order in 1927.

Whereupon the French High Commissioner authorized the popular election of an Assembly to draft a constitution for Syria. The result was a sweeping victory for Arab Nationalists and a consequent impasse between the Assembly, which demanded complete independence, and the French officials, who would admit only a qualified autonomy. In 1930 the High Commissioner dissolved the Assembly and decreed a constitution, providing for a Syrian Republic in subordinate alliance with France, though with a parliament of its own and a native President. The Syrian parliament, however, was as insistently nationalist as the Assembly had been, and after an unsatisfactory attempt to rule without it, France finally gave way and in 1936 signed a treaty with Syria, promising the gradual withdrawal of foreign troops and the eventual admission of Syria, as an independent state, to the League of Nations.

In the Arab state of Hejaz (lying along the coast of the Red Sea and embracing the Moslem "holy cities" of Mecca and Medina), King Hussein aroused patriotic opposition

**Hejaz**

by his subservience to Great Britain and Moslem opposition by his pretentions to the caliphate in succession to the Ottoman Sultans. Both kinds of opposition were exploited by an ambitious Arab chieftain, Abdul Aziz ibn Saud, Sultan of Nejd (a primitive principality in the Arabian desert) and leader of the austere Moslem zealots known as Wahabis. After extending his sway over the nomadic tribes of the desert, Abdul Aziz invaded Hejaz in force in 1925. Hussein abdicated, his son Ali was defeated and expelled, and Mecca was captured. Early in 1926 Abdul Aziz took the title of "King of Hejaz and Nejd," and then subjugated almost all the semi-independent chieftains of the Arabian peninsula. In 1932 he changed the name of his enlarged realm from "Hejaz and Nejd" to "Saudi Arabia." Abdul Aziz ibn Saud gave Arabia a respite from tribal feuds and raids and a novel political unity. He promoted motor transportation throughout the country. He annulled foreign concessions, and in the interest of Arab solidarity he made friendly overtures to the sons of King Hussein whom he had overthrown, and concluded treaties of alliance and arbitration with King Faisal of Iraq and Emir Abdullah of Transjordania.

Egypt was likewise Arab in speech. But its historical traditions, as well as its geographical situation, predisposed it less to any Pan-Arab nationalism than to a separate nation-

**Egypt**

alism of its own. Though most Egyptians welcomed the final extinction of Ottoman suzerainty in 1914 and the accompanying change in the title of their immediate ruler from "Khedive" to "Sultan," many did not take kindly to the continuing and apparently strengthened British protectorate.[1] Especially after the accession of the Sultan Fuad in 1917, the native Nationalist party increased its popular following and its demands for national independence. The leader of this party, Saad Zaghlul, a lawyer of peasant stock, was insistent on Egypt's being represented at the Paris Peace Congress as a sovereign power; and his arrest and deportation to Malta by the British authorities precipitated an insurrection which was put down in 1919 only by the energetic campaigning of General Allenby at the head of a British army of 60,000 men. Lord Milner was then sent out from London to "conciliate" the Egyptians, and in accordance with his recommendations a treaty was signed in 1921 between Great Britain and the Sultan Fuad, whereby Egypt would be nominally independent—the Sultan assuming the title of King—though still subject to "supervision" and "advice" of a British High Commissioner. The treaty was rejected by the Nationalist followers of Zaghlul, and, after more rioting and more military suppression, it was put into force by a unilateral proclamation of the British government in 1922.

In the Egyptian parliament which was created by a constitution of 1923, the Nationalists speedily got the upper hand, so that Zaghlul was recalled from exile to head a native ministry and, following his death in 1927, others of like mind held the premiership until after the death of King Fuad nine years later. Step by step the Nationalist government wrung concessions from Great Britain, which ultimately agreed by a new treaty in 1936 to accept the status of "ally" instead of "protector," to recognize the independence of Egypt, to abolish the office of High Commissioner, and to withdraw all troops except a guard for the Suez Canal. In the next year Egypt was admitted to the League of Nations, and an international conference at Montreux (in Switzerland) consented to the eventual abrogation of foreign law courts and other "extra-territorial rights" in Egypt.

The mass of natives backed and applauded the Nationalist government in its struggle for Egyptian independence and also in its promotion of elementary schooling, but dissatisfaction

---

[1] On these events of 1914, see above, pp. 367, 389. On the previous history of Egypt, see above, pp. 70–71.

developed with its failure to accomplish any important economic or financial reform. In 1938 King Farouk, the youthful son and successor of Fuad, abruptly dismissed the Nationalists from office, and his action received popular endorsement at the polls.

Persia, during the post-war years, underwent a revolution akin to Turkey's. The Persian counterpart to Mustafa Kemal was Riza **Riza Pahlavi and Nationalist Persia** Pahlavi, who, born in 1878 of a poor family near the Caspian Sea, had been a soldier since youth, serving under Russian officers before the World War and rising to chief command in northern Persia with the withdrawal of the Russians during the war. In 1921 Riza suddenly appeared at Teheran, the Persian capital, at the head of a disciplined fighting force, and with its loyal backing he set up a Nationalist government with himself as Minister of War. This post he utilized to reorganize the Persian army and bring it under his personal control, just at the time when Russia and Great Britain were halting their chronic interference in Persian affairs. The result was that Riza could act freely without the risk of foreign intervention and that he could take advantage of the patriotic fervor which overspread the country with the removal of the long-standing threat of its partition by foreign powers. Likewise, he was in a position to dominate, and if necessary to defy, the youthful and capricious weakling, Ahmed, who was nominal Shah of Persia.

Friction soon developed between Ahmed Shah and Riza Pahlavi. In 1923 the latter assumed the premiership, and, availing himself of the former's absence on a pleasure jaunt in Europe, called together the Persian parliament, or Majlis, and induced it to grant him wide powers independent of the Shah. Then in 1925 he caused the Majlis to depose the still absent Shah Ahmed and to convoke a special National Assembly. This Assembly, late in 1925, elected Riza Pahlavi as Shah of Persia, with right of succession to his heirs. He was now titular as well as actual head of the state, and its military dictator.

Riza Shah was a warm admirer, and almost slavish imitator, of Mustafa Kemal. Following the example of the Turkish leader, he abrogated the "capitulations" and banned all alien checks on national sovereignty. Moreover, he introduced into Persia most of the novel laws and decrees which Kemal was issuing in Turkey, especially the laws directed against the influence and privileged status of the Moslem religion and the decrees looking toward a "modern" secularized nation, with European dress, calendar, weights and measures, legal codes, and social usages. Like Mustafa Kemal, too, Riza Shah sought to intensify the national patriotism of the Persian people by teaching them, in army and public school and by aid of all the technical devices of propaganda, to cherish their distinctive language, their history, and their "mission." In line with this purpose, he announced in 1934 that the nation would no longer be officially designated by the corrupt and unnational name of "Persia," but by the ancient and racial name of "Iran." The Persians, he explained, were the true "Iranians," the pure "Aryans." Also, like Mustafa Kemal, Riza Shah evolved schemes for the economic betterment of his country.

National dictatorship was confronted with greater obstacles in Iran than in Turkey. The country was more rugged and less productive. Its people were more primitive and more fanatically Moslem, and they were less disposed to subordinate their customary tribal life and their traditional religious habits to the exigencies of new secular nationalism. There were spasmodic revolts of tribesmen and steady resistance on the part of leading Moslems.

The huge Empire of India seethed with nationalist agitation throughout the post-war period. A governmental reform which the British Parliament enacted in 1919,[1] setting up native provincial councils and giving them some supervision of education, agriculture, and public health, failed to offset the effects of repressive military measures [2] and only stimulated and spread the agitation. In 1920 control of the native "All-India Congress" [3] passed from "moderates" to "extremists," and these elected to its presidency Lajpat Rai, a Hindu lawyer and patriot, who had been deported in 1907 for advocating Dominion status for India, and who, after spending the war years in America, returned home and became editor of an influential nationalist newspaper at Lahore. Through his journalism and through his following in the Congress, Lajpat Rai

*Nationalist India and Gandhi*

---

[1] The "Montagu-Chelmsford Reform," so called from its authors, respectively British Secretary for India and British Viceroy.

[2] These reached a climax in the "massacre of Amritsar," in the spring of 1919, when several hundred natives who had assembled to protest against the government were attacked and killed by British troops under the command of General Dyer.

[3] See above, p. 74.

spread his conviction, especially among Hindu intellectuals and among the masses in the Punjab, that India must have the same national status as that enjoyed by Canada or South Africa. But of greater effectiveness in consolidating Hindu nationalism throughout India was another native lawyer, Mohandas Gandhi.

Gandhi came from a traditionally pro-British and devoutly Hindu family. After studying at the University of London, he had begun the practice of law at Bombay in 1892, but, called to South Africa the next year on professional business, he had remained there for twenty-one years, concerning himself with the sorry plight of lower-class Hindu immigrants and carrying on a tireless struggle in their behalf. On his return to India in 1914 he applied the methods which he had developed in South Africa to the home-rule movement and began to preach resistance to the British by "soul force" and "non-cooperation." From 1919 his counsels grew more urgent and more widely influential. In 1920 he proclaimed a general campaign of "civil disobedience," that is, of "non-violent non-cooperation." As long as British rule continued in India, natives should refrain from supporting or participating in it. They should accept no public office. They should withdraw their children from government schools. They should not appear in law courts. They should not buy foreign commodities. They should boycott British machinery and restore the domestic spinning-wheel. Gandhi was earnest and ascetic, and quite opposed to the use of force, and he soon acquired an immense personal influence over the Hindu masses, who acclaimed him with the honorary title of "Mahatma" or "Great Soul." In 1921 Lajpat Rai joined Gandhi, and the All-India Congress voted to follow unquestioningly the dictates of the latter and of any successor he might designate. Gandhi sought, at first with some success, to make his movement truly All-Indian, to include in it not only the higher-caste Hindus but the lowest caste, the so-called "untouchables," and also the Moslems.

Eventually, however, Gandhi could not overcome Hindu intolerance of Moslems or Moslem contempt and distrust of Hindus. Nor could he restrain hotheads from committing acts of violence which indirectly embarrassed him and directly profited the British. In 1922 the British officials felt solid enough to arrest and jail him for sedition, but they released him early in 1924 when he went on a hunger-strike. Although Gandhi failed to unite

Moslems with Hindus in a common Indian nationalism, he performed a signal and lasting work by giving point and inspiration to the nationalism of the Hindu majority.

For a time the British regime continued to function in India under a succession of able Viceroys. Important labor laws were enacted by the Legislative Council in 1922–1924: a factory act restricting the employment of children, a mines act, and a workmen's compensation act. Agricultural production was increased by extensive irrigation works. Simultaneously, the output of mines and factories, especially cotton factories, forged steadily ahead. Though the number of schools was increased, the government continued to spend much larger sums on army and police than on education, and in 1938 only eight per cent of the 350 million natives could read or write. In 1931 splendid new government buildings were opened with pomp at Delhi, the capital of Britain's Indian Empire.

Meanwhile, Hindu Nationalists were pressing ever harder for self-government. In 1928, when the British cabinet in London sent out a special commission, headed by Sir John Simon, to study the political situation in India and to recommend what if any change should be made in the Act of 1919, the Nationalists held a convention and drafted a set of "minimum demands," according to which India as a whole should enjoy Dominion status within the British Empire and under a written constitution of its own. Such a constitution, the Nationalists proposed, should guarantee individual rights and provide for a federal system of government, with a central parliament at Delhi and with provincial parliaments in the several states, all to be elected by universal suffrage, both male and female, without any favor to minorities. This last proposal antagonized the mass of Indian Moslems and cemented their alliance with other opponents of Hindu "radicalism": Indian princes, who were fearful of democracy and anxious to preserve the *status quo;* "moderate" Hindus who stood to profit from the existing regime; and British who desired, whether for selfish or for altruistic motives, to retain as much political and economic control of India as possible. Gandhi labored tirelessly to counteract these divisive developments and to promote harmony and concord within India, but he was only partially successful.

As an outcome of the recommendations of the Simon Commission and of a series of round-table conferences at London,

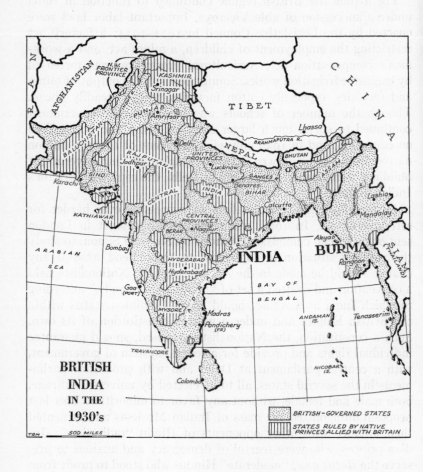

BRITISH
INDIA
IN THE
1930's

500 MILES

BRITISH-GOVERNED STATES

STATES RULED BY NATIVE
PRINCES ALLIED WITH BRITAIN

the British government endorsed in 1933 the project for an Indian constitution submitted by the Marquess of Linlithgow, a Conservative statesman and the official reporter for the round-table conferences. According to the proposed constitution, all India directly under British rule, excepting Burma, would be divided into eleven states,[1] and these would be federated with the states under native princes to form the United States of India. Each state would have a large measure of local autonomy, exercising it through a native prince or an elective native legislature, as the case might be; and for general legislation there would be a federal parliament, comprising appointed representatives of the princely states and elected representatives of the others, with a ministry responsible to it. Elections, both federal and state, would be restricted by qualifications of religion, property, and literacy to about ten per cent of the men and about half of one per cent of the women of India. At the head of the whole Indian government would be a British Governor-General (subject only to the cabinet at London), who would direct foreign relations and military affairs independently of the Indian parliament, and who might similarly employ "emergency powers" in crises involving religion, minorities, currency, and justice to Europeans.

*Constitution for India*

This constitution, after strenuous opposition to it on the part of extreme British imperialists, was enacted by the British Parliament in 1935, and the Marquess of Linlithgow was appointed Viceroy of India and charged with the difficult tasks of obtaining the necessary ratification of it by the various native princes, and overcoming the hostility and securing the cooperation of the Hindu Nationalists.

Japan had become, before the World War, a Europeanized great power. It already ranked with the leading nations of Europe and America in industrial and commercial development and in military strength and prestige, and its position was enhanced by the war and its aftermath. The defeat of Germany, the revolution within Russia, the depression in Britain, the absorption of France in problems of

*Japan and Trend Toward Military Dictatorship*

---

[1] The eleven would be: Bengal, Assam, Bihar, Orissa, Madras, Bombay, the Central Provinces (centering in Nagpur), the United Provinces (centering in Lucknow), Sind, the Punjab, and the Northwest Frontier Province. Burma was to be excluded from the Indian Federation and provided with a separate government.

domestic reconstruction and security, all contributed to freeing Japan from checks upon the extension of its trade and sway in the Pacific and on the Asiatic mainland. And the industriousness and intense patriotism of the Japanese nation amply seconded the determination of its business men and statesmen to take full advantage of the opportunities thus offered.[1]

During and just after the war the Japanese government was controlled by the Conservative party—the Seiyukai. Then, following a terrible earthquake which in 1923 wrecked the cities of Tokyo and Yokohama and united the urban electorate in demands for speedy and businesslike reconstruction, the Liberal party—the Menseito—got the upper hand. It carried the general election of 1924, and, under one of its most eminent leaders, Viscount Kato, a wealthy industrialist who was premier until his death in 1926, it pushed forward the reconstruction of the devastated centers, pursued a conciliatory foreign policy, and in 1925 established universal manhood suffrage. After Kato's death, the Seiyukai contrived to man a ministry from 1927 to 1929, but a sweeping victory of the Menseito in the general election of 1930, the first under universal suffrage, seemed to promise to this party a long period of predominance and to Japan a continuing evolution toward national democracy and international peace.

The promise was soon belied, however. The Menseito was not truly a popular party. It gained its electoral victory by usual methods of political corruption, and the attitude of its leaders toward difficult national problems, which were then becoming acute, aroused the active hostility of large sections of the population. For example, the finance minister and party chairman, Junnosuke Inouye, seeking to overcome the economic depression which beset Japan in common with all other industrial nations, urged a drastic curtailment of governmental expenditure and a general policy of financial deflation (instead of inflation), which was strenuously opposed by governmental officials, both civil and military, by agricultural interests, and by organized labor. Again, the foreign minister, Baron Shidehara, in his desire to promote peace and lighten the burden of armaments, consented to the London naval agreement of 1930[2] and sought an amicable adjust-

---

[1] The "divine" objects of national Japanese patriotism during the period were the Emperors Yoshihito (1912–1926) and Hirohito (1926–    ).

[2] See above, pp. 453–454.

ment of Japan's differences with China, which outraged Japanese nationalists, particularly officers in army and navy. In the circumstances, nationalist propaganda against the government made rapid headway. While a cabal of army officers took it upon themselves to open hostilities against the Chinese in Manchuria, thereby nullifying the peace efforts of Shidehara, Nationalist organizations sprang up in Japan, applauding the strong action of the military, demanding the overthrow of parliamentary government, and insisting that the only cure for domestic economic ills was a forceful extension of the Japanese Empire. Faced with a rising tide of popular conversion to militarist and nationalist propaganda and unable to prevent attendant acts of terrorism, the Menseito ministry resigned in December 1931.

For a time an aged Seiyukai premier, Inukai, attempted to carry on. He dissolved the parliament and so manipulated the ensuing general election as to insure the return of a large popular majority for his party. Yet he soon discovered, when he tried to assert the supremacy of civilian authorities, that the militant groups were no more respectful of a Seiyukai ministry than of a Menseito government. There was a steady increase of insubordination and terrorism in the winter and spring of 1932, beginning with the assassination of Inouye, the leader and ex-minister of the Menseito, and culminating in the murder of Inukai, the Seiyukai premier.

Following this murder, an extra-parliamentary ministry was set up, headed by Viscount Saito, elderly ranking officer of the Japanese navy and for several years strong-arm governor of Korea. Counter-demonstrations were repressed, a rigid censorship enforced, and steps taken to emphasize nationalism at home, in press, schools, and religion, and to promote imperialism abroad.

Japan's swiftly growing power in the Far East was at the expense of China, whose affairs, after the death in 1916 of the nominal President and actual dictator, Yüan Shih-kai, went from bad to worse.[1] A form of republican government continued, but for at least a decade it was the plaything of greedy and unscrupulous provincial governors, who, with the aid of mercenary troops, wrung all the money they could from the people within their jurisdiction and intrigued and fought with one another for supreme control. One such "war-

*Chinese Republic and Its "War-Lords"*

[1] See above, pp. 295–296.

lord" might get the upper hand for a moment and install a "President" who would do his bidding, but he would soon fall prey to other "war-lords" and his puppet president would be replaced by another. The civil government of the Chinese Republic was not only kaleidoscopic but corrupt, and quite unable to command the united loyalty of the nation or to preserve its territorial integrity. Whole provinces and even larger areas were practically detached from any central authority. Then, too, as early as 1917, the central government at Peking was defied by a rival "nationalist" government which Sun Yat-sen established at Canton (in southern China). And while Russian agents were spreading Communist propaganda widely in southern China, Japanese agents were obtaining favors from the government in northern China.

At first the nationalist efforts of Sun Yat-sen seemed as ineffectual as the more conservative regime at Peking. He had in back of him a party of intellectuals, the so-called Kuomintang, who helped him to organize his government at Canton in 1917 and formally conferred upon him in 1921 the title of "President of the Chinese Republic." But he was preacher and visionary rather than organizer, and for several years the Kuomintang lacked competent generals and was torn by internal dissensions. The best that Sun Yat-sen could do was to retain a precarious foothold in the city of Canton and the adjacent province of Kwantung and to welcome overtures from the government at Peking for a conference looking to the reestablishment of national unity. He was participating in such a conference when he died at Peking in 1925.

The Kuo-
mintang

With the death of Sun Yat-sen, he was extolled all over China as a national hero and his ideas became the inspiration for a revival and rapid extension of the Kuomintang. China, the party declared, must possess a democratic government, a higher standard of living for the masses, and an intensity of national feeling that would preserve its historic territory and distinctive culture and tolerate no foreign interference or tutelage; and, pending the achievement of these ultimate goals, China must submit to a dictatorship. Such was the program, and for its execution emerged an extraordinary leader, Chiang Kai-shek.

Born in 1886, Chiang had joined the Kuomintang in his youth and had been entrusted in 1920 with the command of a military training school at Canton. In 1925 he was appointed chief of the

Kuomintang forces; and during the next year, with military ability of his own and with helpful popular propaganda on the part of temporarily cooperating Communist advisers from Russia, he overcame opposition in southern China and Chiang Kai-shek advanced northward to the Yangtze River. In 1927 he occupied Nanking in force and there installed the Nationalist government. In vain the remaining war-lords of the North put themselves under the direction of the governor of Manchuria and attempted to stem the tide. Their armies melted away; the remnant was overwhelmed; and the commander, retreating into Manchuria, was killed. In 1928 the victorious Chiang Kai-shek entered Peking in triumph.

Peking was renamed Peiping ("Northern Peace") and the capital of the Chinese Republic was transferred thence to Nanking. In October 1928, on the seventeenth anniversary of the outbreak of the Revolution,[1] Chiang Kai-shek was inaugurated as President of the Republic. He thus combined the headship of the civil government, the chairmanship of the Kuomintang, and the command of the army. He reaffirmed his devotion to the program of Sun Yat-sen, save for its Communist tendencies, which he now expressly repudiated. He chose his chief advisers and lieutenants from the Kuomintang. He married the sister-in-law of Sun Yat-sen. In 1931 he convoked at Nanking a National Convention, which drafted a "provisional constitution" and elected a civilian as titular head of the government, though it confirmed the existing dictatorship by making the Kuomintang the only legal party in the state and by empowering Chiang Kai-shek to appoint the ministers and to direct military affairs.

The Nationalist dictatorship of Chiang Kai-shek fostered popular patriotic education, multiplying elementary schools and supplying them with textbooks in the simplified ver- National-alist Dictatorship nacular writing which had recently been devised by James Yen, a social worker and a graduate of Yale University. By 1930 millions of farmers and day laborers were learning to read and write, although sixty per cent of the vast Chinese population were still illiterate. Above all, the government was intensifying the nationalism of those who could read. Foreign investors and traders and foreign missionaries were regarded with increasing suspicion and put under closer surveillance. Boycotting

[1] See above, pp. 294–295.

of foreign goods for political reasons was invoked more frequently and obeyed more generally.

Yet the task confronting the Nationalist dictatorship in China was herculean. The country was so big and its population so numerous. Banditry was so usual, corruption so habitual, and the opportunities for ambitious and grasping officials so great and alluring. The government of Chiang Kai-shek did better than its immediate predecessors in grappling with internal difficulties, but it possessed neither the financial resources nor the military strength to overcome all of these and at the same time to withstand, unaided and successfully, the forceful aggression of disciplined foreign powers. It could hardly maintain its authority in China proper. It could not prevent the Moslems in the extensive western territory of Sinkiang from revolting in 1928 and setting up a practically independent government. It could not control the tribesmen in Mongolia and keep those in Outer Mongolia from falling under the domination of Soviet Russia. It could not prevent the spread of subversive Communist propaganda or overcome armed Communist resistance. To cap the climax, it had to suffer Japanese conquest of Manchuria and other northern provinces and ultimately the horrors of a general war with Japan.[1]

### 6. DEMOCRATIC NATIONALISM IN LATIN AMERICA

Post-war political developments among major Latin nations on the American continents reflected prevalent currents in Europe.[2] There was similar popular unrest and a similar intensification of nationalism.

In Mexico, the revolutionary movement, which had begun in 1910, took on a much more radical complexion as its original leaders were supplanted in turn by Alvaro Obregon and Plutarco Elias Calles. Both these men were natives of the northern state of Sonora, the former a planter and the latter a school teacher. Both had become "intellectual radicals" in their youth and voluble advocates of land reform in behalf of the native Indian population. Both had recruited Indian troops and risen to the rank of general in the revolutionary armies which put Madero into the presidency in 1911 and Carranza in 1914. Obregon was at first the more influential of the two. As

*Revolutionary Mexico*

[1] See below, pp. 605–607, 624–625.

[2] For an outline of the pre-war history of these nations, see above, pp. 273–279.

acknowledged leader of the radical wing of Carranza's followers and as commander-in-chief of the army, he forced into the constitution of 1917, against Carranza's wishes, some of its most revolutionary provisions, notably those promising the partition of large landed estates and vesting in the government the ownership of all mineral and petroleum resources.

In 1920 an open break occurred between Carranza and Obregon: the former, seeking reelection in violation of the Constitution, ordered the latter's arrest; and the latter, commanding superior forces, headed a revolt against the former. Carranza was deposed and murdered, and Obregon was elevated to the presidency, with Calles as his Minister of the Interior. Then, on the expiration of his term of office in 1924, he secured the election of Calles as President, with himself as Minister of War. Obregon planned to resume the presidency again in 1928, but after his election and before his inauguration he was assassinated. It was left for Calles to continue and develop the revolutionary government, and this he did through the National Revolutionary party which he organized and led and which dominated the army and the parliament.

Both Obregon and Calles championed an intense Mexican nationalism and directed it against every "alien" influence. They catered to the native Indian element, numerically large but long neglected. They sponsored a considerable amount of land reform and labor legislation. They prompted a campaign of popular education, establishing public schools in rural villages as well as in urban centers, and supplying them with nationalist teachers and textbooks. They extolled and encouraged native Indian art.

They were especially jealous of foreign influence or tutelage. They induced the parliament to impose severe limitations on foreign economic enterprise in Mexico, agricultural, industrial, mining, and commercial. Though they welcomed the recognition which the United States accorded to their revolutionary regime in 1923 and utilized it to strengthen their own position, they were careful not to make any exceptional concessions to the United States, and until 1931 they held aloof from the League of Nations. Moreover, it was to oppose "alien" influences, as well as to weaken the chief traditional prop of "reaction" within Mexico, that Obregon and Calles and their supporters waged war against the Catholic Church.

Controversy between church and state in Mexico was no novelty, but it was greatly embittered by the drastic ecclesiastical restrictions which were written into the Constitution of 1917, and it reached an acute stage during the presidency of Calles. In 1926 Calles had his subservient parliament enact a series of laws, applying and supplementing the constitutional provisions: the church might own no property, maintain no monastic establishment, conduct no school, and carry on no propaganda; the government might permit the use of church buildings for strictly religious purposes, but ecclesiastics would be subject to special regulation and close surveillance; no foreign priest might function or reside in Mexico; native priests must register with the government and assure it of their "good behavior"; and laymen as well as clergymen were forbidden to urge any alteration of these repressive measures. Even further went some of the local state governments, which, at the dictation of fanatical allies of Calles, closed churches altogether. Against all this legislation, and specifically against the requirement of registration, the Mexican clergy, with papal approval, went on "strike"; and for three years bishops and priests conducted no regular religious services in Mexico. In 1929 the government consented to a truce with the Catholic hierarchy, whereby assurances were given that the anti-clerical laws, without being repealed, would be leniently enforced, and religious services were therefore resumed. In 1931, however, a new tide of governmental activity set in against the Church and indeed against all religion. In vain the local clergy and the Pope protested. The papal delegate—a native Mexican— was expelled as a "pernicious foreigner"; and religious persecution became general.

The Mexican government, nominally democratic, was essentially a dictatorship. Only one political party was allowed to exist and engage in propaganda—the National Revolutionary party— and this, through its control of the army and the civil administration, held every seat in the Mexican parliament, every ministerial post, and the presidency of the Republic. The masses were largely indifferent to politics, and dissent or opposition among the classes was ruthlessly suppressed. There were, of course, some differences of opinion and some personal rivalries within the National Revolutionary party. Though solidly nationalist, it represented various degrees of devotion to socialism and to anti-clericalism, and gradually the preeminence of Calles in it was undermined by one of his lieutenants and protégés, General Lazaro Cardenas. Cardenas, belonging to a family part Spanish and part Indian, rose under Calles's auspices to be secretary of the National Revolutionary party and Minister of War, and these strategic positions secured his election to the presidency in 1934 for a six-year term. He was younger and more vigorous than Calles, less concerned with the somewhat stale issue of anti-clericalism, and more eager to forward economic policies of a socialistic character. He threw himself with energy into the prosecution of a "six-year plan" for the "Mexicanizing" of industry, the development of public works, the construction of model dwellings for urban workmen, and the distribution of communal lands among agricultural villages. He also halted the religious persecution and tolerated resumption of church services.

If in Mexico nationalism was stressed by the protracted revolutionary movement and given an anti-religious and eventually socialistic slant, it was emphasized in two major countries of South America—Argentina and Brazil—by a sudden break in the orderly functioning of government which had long prevailed and a forceful seizure of power by conservative groups. In Argentina, the Radical government of Hipolito Irigoyen, who was President from 1916 to 1922 and again from 1928, was overthrown in September 1930 by a *coup d'etat* of General José Uriburu, who assumed a temporary dictatorship and utilized it to assure the election a year later of another Conservative officer as constitutional President of the Republic.

In Brazil, a similar revolt in October 1930, led by Vetulio Vargas and supported by army officers and by popular sentiment against the existing hegemony of the state of São Paulo **Vargas** in national politics, drove the President and President- **Regime** elect into exile and installed Vargas as dictator. Vargas **in Brazil** suppressed a counter-revolt in São Paulo in 1932 and then decreed the election of a National Assembly by universal suffrage, including women. The new constitution which issued from the Assembly in 1934, while retaining the federal character of the Brazilian state, enlarged the powers of the central government; and while prescribing that four-fifths of the Chamber of Deputies should be democratically elected by universal suffrage, it recognized the principle of the "corporate state" by providing that the remaining fifth of the Chamber should be chosen by professional and trade associations. The constitution also granted nationalist demands by limiting foreign immigration and foreign investment. Likewise it favored the Catholic Church by permitting religious instruction in the schools, guaranteeing the freedom of religious congregations, and authorizing the substitution of religious for civil marriage. In 1934 the National Assembly formally elected Vargas as constitutional President, and in 1938 he suppressed a revolt.

The upheavals of 1930 in Brazil and Argentina were attributable in considerable part to the economic depression and financial instability then current throughout the world, and this factor was certainly important in the epidemic of revolutions which affected most other Latin-American countries after 1929.

For several years after the World War, the countries of Haiti, Santo Domingo, and Nicaragua were occupied and governed, directly or indirectly, by armed forces of the United States. **Anti-Imperial Reaction in United States** Gradually, however, the United States reconsidered and revised its imperialist policy, partly because of nationalist pressure from the natives, partly because of waxing hostility to the United States all over Latin America with attendant discrimination against traders and investors from the United States, and partly because of a growing concern of the American people with domestic and narrowly national problems. In 1924 American armed forces were withdrawn from Santo Domingo, and in 1933 they finally quitted Nicaragua. In 1930 the native Haitian parliament was permitted to assemble for the first time in seventeen years and to elect a native President, and in 1934 American troops evacuated the country.

It is also noteworthy, in this connection, that in 1934 the United States Congress, taking account of vigorous nationalist sentiment in the Philippine Islands, enacted a law, which was speedily accepted by the Philippine legislature, providing for the transformation of the dependency into an autonomous Commonwealth, **Philippine Commonwealth** with power to devise its own constitution (subject to approval by the President of the United States), to elect a native Chief Executive and a native Congress, and to make and execute its own laws, and providing further for a gradual withdrawal of American troops and, if the experiment in self-government should prove successful at the end of ten years, for the formal recognition by the United States at that time of the complete independence of the Philippines. The Philippine Commonwealth was inaugurated in 1935.

Meanwhile, a protracted nationalist war began in 1928 between the two South American states of Bolivia and Paraguay. To both, the acquisition of the swamp-land of the Gran Chaco seemed a national interest so vital that they would not negotiate any compromise between themselves or acquiesce in any arbitration by outsiders; they simply had to fight it out. One attempt after another was made to restore peace between the belligerents—by neighboring powers jointly and singly, by the League of Nations, by Pan-American Conferences at Washington in 1928 and at Montevideo in 1934—all in vain. Only utter exhaustion of the two countries halted the fighting and eventually brought about a settlement in 1938 favorable to Paraguay.

**Chaco War between Bolivia and Paraguay**

The Chaco War was a conflict between third-rate powers, but it was symptomatic of the breakdown of international law and order which by 1935 was becoming manifest in many parts of the world and, most menacingly, in the relations among European great powers.

# CHAPTER XII

## CONTEMPORARY CULTURAL CHANGES

### I. INDUSTRIAL AND TECHNOLOGICAL ADVANCE

SOME very significant cultural changes have occurred in the present century, especially since 1910. They have affected the science, art, religion, and philosophy of traditional European, or Western, civilization. And closely associated with these changes, and in large measure conditioning them, has been an intensifying and expanding development of machine industry.

The so-called "Industrial Revolution," which had begun in England and spread to other countries in the nineteenth century,[1] was not halted by the World War. On the contrary, it reached a new stage of achievement in the next thirty years. Not only was the output of previously mechanized industries greatly augmented by technological improvements, but new machine industries sprang up and expanded with astounding suddenness. Not only was industrialization intensified in "capitalistic" countries, but it was sedulously fostered by the Communist regime in Soviet Russia and patronized by dictatorships in such "backward" countries as Turkey and Mexico. Not only was all Europe being swiftly mechanized, the east and south as well as the west and north, but the newest material features of what had been deemed distinctively "western civilization" were becoming common characteristics, or at least aspirations, of what now appeared as "world civilization."

Production of coal and iron—the twin bases of modern industrialization—was almost doubled throughout the world between 1910 and 1940. A slight decline occurred in Great Britain, but it was much more than offset by gains in the United States, and also

[1] See above, pp. 3–39.

in Russia and Japan. By 1940 Russia was mining almost as much coal and iron as Germany, and Japan almost as much as France; and there was now large-scale production of coal in China and India and South Africa.

It was similar with the textile industries. While the world production of cotton gained only slightly, that of wool increased by over a third, that of natural silk more than doubled, and that of artificial silk (or rayon) multiplied four-hundredfold—mounting from 6 million pounds in 1910 to 2,400 million in 1940. This rayon development was **Expansion of Older Mechanized Industries** one of the outstanding accomplishments of contemporary industrialization. It had hardly begun before 1910, and it assumed large proportions only after 1920. From the start, too, it was a thoroughly mechanized industry: the raw material was made by machinery, and its whole manufacture of thread and cloth was by machinery. Furthermore, it became suddenly important all over the world—in almost every European country and in the United States and Argentina, Japan and Australia. The new rayon industry only emphasized the post-war trend of the older textile industries toward ever more automatic mechanizing and toward ever broader diffusion.

Along with the textile industries advanced other well-established industries: leather, pottery and porcelain, paper and printing, typewriters, cutlery, firearms, furniture, tinware, tools, canning and refrigeration, electrical goods. There was an especially marked advance of the electrical industries. Electric power was substituted more and more for steam power. Hydroelectric power plants were multiplied. Electric lighting was immensely bettered through the use of the tungsten filament lamp which had been invented just before World War I.

Undoubtedly the most striking and significant industrial developments had to do with means of communication and transportation. The existing network of railways was much **Communication and Transportation** extended in Asia, Africa, and South America, and rail locomotives, driven by steam or electricity, conveyed prodigious numbers of persons and prodigious quantities of goods. And over the whole earth messages were carried by telegraph and telephone wires. In 1940 the mileage of telegraph wires amounted to eight million; and of the sixty million telephones in operation, almost half were "automatic."

The existing network of steamship lines was similarly expanded, and the total tonnage of the world's merchant shipping rose from 42 million in 1910 to 59 million in 1939. Great Britain retained a larger merchant fleet than any other nation, but the ratio of its tonnage to the world-total decreased from forty-four per cent to thirty. The tonnage of the United States and also of Italy and the Netherlands doubled beween 1910 and 1939 and that of Japan tripled, while the merchant shipping of both France and Norway increased by a half.

To telephone and telegraph, steamship and railway, which had already had revolutionary significance for communication and transportation in the nineteenth century, were now added new twentieth-century devices of automobile, motor truck, airplane, motion picture, and radio. Originating just prior to 1910, all of these were greatly improved during the post-war period, when their production assumed colossal proportions as their operation wrought gigantic changes.

Production of motor cars and trucks developed principally and very rapidly in the United States. Here the annual manufacture of passenger cars rose from 181,000 in 1910 to 4½ million in 1929, while that of trucks mounted from 6,000 in 1910 to 750,000 in 1940.

Outside the United States, moreover, gradually increasing numbers of cars were produced in Great Britain, France, Germany, Spain, and Italy, and also in Canada and Japan; and regardless of where they might be manufactured, their use was ever extending. By 1939 the number of registered motor vehicles throughout the world exceeded forty-three million.

Aviation, just beginning in 1910, was enormously stimulated and developed by World War I and was utilized immediately

**Aviation**     afterwards for commercial carrying of mails, passengers, and express. Regular airplane service was soon inaugurated between Paris and London and between other chief cities in Europe and also in America, and presently it was established from London to Alexandria in Egypt and on to Bagdad and India, from Paris across northern and western Africa to Brazil, and from New York southward to Mexico and Central and South America. For most flying, airplanes were employed, but particularly in and from Germany some airships or "Zeppelins" continued in use for a time. In 1929 a Zeppelin circumnavigated the globe, from Friedrichshafen (in Germany) via Tokyo and Los Angeles and New York back to Friedrichshafen, in twenty days.

Already, in 1927, an American aviator, Charles Lindbergh, won international fame by flying an airplane alone and without a stop from New York to Paris. By airplane an American naval officer, Admiral Richard Byrd, explored the Arctic Ocean and visited the North Pole in 1927, and then in 1929 explored the Antarctic Continent and flew over the South Pole. By 1939 commercial airlines were being operated by every major nation and were carrying mail, merchandise, and passengers over all oceans and all continents.

The fueling of gasoline engines for the rapidly growing number of automobiles, motor trucks, and airplanes gave impetus to the petroleum industry—to the production of the crude oil and to its refining and distribution. Between 1910 and 1939 the world output of petroleum increased over sixfold, from 325 million barrels to 2,000 million.

Another industry, which had been comparatively an infant in 1910 but which was brought to speedy maturity by the needs of the new motor transportation, was the rubber industry. This, like the petroleum industry, consumed multiplying quantities of raw material, rising from 75,000 tons in 1910 to over a million in 1939. Almost all the crude rubber now came, not from "wild" trees, but from cultivated "plantations," principally in the Dutch East Indies, the Malay peninsula, and Ceylon. There was a beginning, too, of the production of synthetic rubber.

Elaboration of motor highways attended the development of motor transport, and was attended in turn by an ever greater and more widespread utilization of "concrete." Concrete roads soon paralleled railways or provided a substitute for them, and, in addition, concrete (reinforced by iron or steel) was increasingly employed for public buildings, industrial plants, garages and hangars, piers, bridges, and even shipbuilding.

Motion pictures were still another universal phenomenon of the post-war period. Though originally invented prior to 1910, they were perfected and popularized during the World War and more especially after 1920. In 1928 "sound" pictures (or "talking movies") were first made, and very shortly afterwards they were being heard, as well as seen,

*Motion Pictures and Radio*

all over the world. The large majority of films displayed in the British Dominions, Latin America, and most countries of Europe, were American-made, although most foreign governments were beginning to censor and limit American imports and to favor domestic production.

Accompanying the rise of motion pictures and excelling them in revolutionary effect was the development of radio. Wireless telegraphy had been in some use since the opening of the twentieth century, but it was not until 1920 that the first permanent radio broadcasting station was put into operation—by an American concern, the Westinghouse Company—and private homes began to be equipped with radio-receiving sets. Thenceforth, progress in the production and use of radios was sensationally rapid. Within fifteen years every nation in the world had broadcasting stations; and everywhere there were enough receiving-sets to enable the vast majority of mankind, whether in town or country, to receive practically simultaneous news of what was happening in Rome or Manchester, Berlin or Moscow, Tokyo or Mexico City, Calcutta or Melbourne, Cape Town or Minneapolis, Jerusalem or Mecca. In the United States alone, fifty-one million radio sets were in use in 1940.

From hearing at a distance, it was only a step to seeing; and this step was initiated in the 1920's by experiments with television carried on more or less independently by several European and American physicists. In 1928 began the successful transmission of pictures across the Atlantic and in color.

Industrial advance of the post-war period was accompanied by an increase in the world output of foodstuffs. For the indus-

**Foodstuffs**  trializing and mechanizing of agriculture continued, and produced an ever larger yield of meat and grain, vegetables and fruits. In respect of grain, for example, the wheat crop of the world steadily enlarged from 3,250 million bushels in 1920 (which was about what it had been in 1900) to 4,600 million bushels in 1938, at the very time when scarcely smaller gains were being made in the world-production of rye, barley, oats, corn, and rice. Apparently the latest phase of industrialization was promising to provide humankind with an ampler supply of food and clothing as well as with more expeditious means of communication and a greater range of creature comforts.

## 2. NEW SCIENTIFIC ACHIEVEMENTS AND DOCTRINES

The progressive industrializing and mechanizing of the world has continued since 1910, as previously, to be intimately associated with accumulating achievements of technology, of engineering and applied science, and, fundamentally, of experimental science. Without intensive and manifold pursuit of the natural science which had developed during the eighteenth and nineteenth centuries,[1] the twentieth century could not be the supreme machine age which it is.

Physics and chemistry have been the twin sciences most esteemed and forwarded. Their practical applications have proved most rewarding. Applied physics has provided man with constantly improving automobiles, airplanes, radios, electric power and lighting, and all sorts of machinery. Applied chemistry has enabled him to multiply the production of field and factory, to make synthetic goods and artificial ice, to preserve foodstuffs, to "take" pictures and show "movies." There is, of course, no sharp cleavage between physics and chemistry. Practical application of the one has always involved some practical application of the other, and progress in the one has contributed to progress in the other. The physicist and the chemist are natural allies. They are joint directors of contemporary technology, and, incidentally, joint inspirers of modern philosophy.

But while the practical applications of physics and chemistry have been continuous and constantly augmenting, certain earlier postulates of physical science have undergone in the twentieth century a startling change—a kind of revolution. Prior to the present century, and from the time of Galileo and Newton, scientific progress had steadily reinforced the idea of the material, mechanical, and deterministic nature of the universe. Now, however, the latest scientific advance has served to upset that idea. It has brought forth new conceptions of Newtonian physics, of matter and motion, of "natural law," even of "cause and effect." *New Concepts of Physical Science*

Three developments in twentieth-century physics inaugurated the change: the quantum theory; the principle of relativity; and the study of atomic structure and activity. The quantum theory was propounded by a German physicist, Max Planck, in 1901.

[1] See above pp. 187–204, and *Modern Europe to 1870*, pp. 369–375.

It held that energy is given off by a vibrating body irregularly in little lumps or packets or units (called quanta), and not steadily or with a wavelike ebb and flow as the older physics had assumed. The theory soon received confirmation and extension from a wide variety of sources. In 1918 Planck was awarded a Nobel prize for his achievement.

Meanwhile, Albert Einstein, a German of Jewish family and the director of the physics institute at Berlin,[1] set forth a "special **Einstein's** theory of relativity" in 1905 and a "general theory" **"Rela-** in 1915. According to these, Newtonian physics had **tivity"** been guilty of a kind of scientific provincialism. It had treated motion in space either as relative to our own solar system or as relative to an imaginary "ether" filling all space. As the existence of any such "ether" had recently been disproved,[2] Einstein worked out ways of stating motion so that the statement would be equally correct for an observer on the Earth or on any star. This involves very elaborate mathematical concepts. It uses the velocity of light as an absolute (the same for all observers) and makes time a fourth dimension (in addition to length, breadth, and thickness). Einstein's relativity did not change ordinary measurements on the Earth, but it did alter astronomical calculations; and it indicated that gravitation is not a force operating mysteriously through space, but rather an even more wonderful distortion of space-time.

The third, and perhaps most striking, novelty has been in the field of atomic research.[3] In 1911 Sir Ernest Rutherford, a native of New Zealand and professor of physics in the **Atomic** English University of Manchester, deduced from pre- **Research** vious and current study of radioactivity and of the spectra of light and X-rays a new theory about atoms. It held that each atom is composed of a nucleus (or proton) charged with positive electricity and of negatively charged particles (or electrons) revolving around the nucleus. In other words, the atom is a miniature of the solar system, with the proton resembling the sun, and the electrons the planets. With this basic explanation

[1] Einstein remained at Berlin until 1931, when the anti-Semitic campaign of the Nazis made him glad to accept a proffered asylum at Oxford University. In 1933 he settled in the United States at Princeton. He had been awarded a Nobel prize in 1921.

[2] Originally by Albert Michelson in 1887 and subsequently by others.

On earlier atomic theory and research, see above, pp. 191–192.

of Rutherford's, a Danish physicist, Niels Bohr, presently combined Planck's quantum theory.

The new atomic conceptions speedily received confirmation from intensive investigations of numerous physicists in Europe and America and gave rise to some astonishing results. Apparently, the atoms of chemical elements, such as radium and uranium, are not immutable but undergo disintegration and change; heat and light arise from energy given off by atoms as they change from one state to another; and "matter" may no longer be thought of as something solid and permanent but rather as a form of motion or energy—"a mere series of events occurring in space-time." And just as the new atomic and quantum theories have forced a radical change of ideas about the character of "matter," so the theory of relativity has led to strange new hypotheses as to the nature of the universe. According to Einstein's physics, space is curved, and, paradoxically enough, the farther one moves out in it the nearer one approaches the place where one started!

Another amazing deduction from the new physics is the "principle of indeterminacy," as described by a German scientist, Heisenberg, in 1927. Observing that the behavior of single electrons in an atom follows no set pattern or "law," and is therefore unpredictable, he concluded that, at least in the realm of the ultra-microscopic, the long-posited axiom of causality must be rejected. The action of such phenomena as electrons cannot be viewed individually as "caused" or "determined," but only *en masse* by the principle of probability, just as an insurance company deals with human beings.

Contemporary physics has certainly revolutionized earlier ideas about the strictly material and mechanical nature of the universe. But quite as sensationally, and far more ominously, it has made practical application of the new theories by production of the atomic bomb. Only time will tell whether atomic energy is to be used for human well-being or for mass destruction.

The revolution in physics (and chemistry) has tended to push into the background the contemporary developments in biology. But though biology now arouses no such popular ex- Contemcitement as it did in the nineteenth century when porary Darwin put forth his famous doctrine of evolution, it Biology has become an increasingly important associate of physics and chemistry. Indeed, it can almost be said to resolve, in the latest age, into biophysics and biochemistry. And like its associated sciences, it has proved increasingly useful, especially in physiology, medicine, and surgery. Painstaking microscopic investigation of animal bodies has disclosed elaborate mechanisms, the existence of which had hardly been suspected previously, and has led to experimental work on them of prime significance to the physical health of human beings. For example, much has latterly been discovered about the hitherto mysterious ductless glands, or secretory organs, in animals and humans. Likewise it is demonstrated that physical health requires in the diet certain "accessory factors," to which the name of vitamins is given, and thanks to researches of biochemists several different kinds of vitamins have been discovered and their respective functions described.

On the Darwinian theory of evolution, twentieth-century biologists amassed much factual data of considerable importance. The more evidence they accumulated, the more it confirmed the basic assumption of Darwin, that the process of life on the earth has been evolutionary. At the same time, however, it made clear that the process was not so simple as Darwin had surmised and certainly not so simple as Huxley or Haeckel had maintained. As a distinguished biologist said in 1922, summarizing contemporary scientific evidence for evolution: "In dim outline evolution is evident enough. From the facts it is a conclusion which inevitably follows. But that particular and essential bit of the theory of evolution which is concerned with the *origin and nature of species* remains utterly mysterious." In other words, the particular explanations which Darwin offered of the origin of species—natural selection, sexual selection, and inheritance of acquired characteristics—do not really explain. The inheritance of acquired characteristics, though still debatable, is extremely doubtful, and a new difficulty has arisen from the seeming dependence of variation on elements being lost and not gained.

Mendel's basic principles of heredity have been confirmed and their application extended. Many deficiencies and abnormalities, such as color-blindness and eye cataract, have been shown to **Chromosomes and Genes** follow Mendelian rules in their descent. Investigation of the cell structure of the fruit-fly by an American biologist, Thomas Morgan, has revealed that within each cell-nucleus is a number of threadlike bodies which have been called "chromosomes," and that there is a numerical correspondence between the number of groups of hereditary qualities and the number of pairs of chromosomes. Additional study has disclosed that there are different numbers of paired chromosomes (or "genes") in different plants and animals; four in the fruit-fly, seven in the garden pea, eight in wheat, probably twenty-four in man. It has further been demonstrated that with twenty "genes" there would be, by permutations and combinations, over a million possible kinds of germ cells, and that with the juncture of two such sets (male and female) there would be a prodigiously greater number of possible combinations. Biology thus offers a scientific explanation as to why no two individuals in a mixed race are identical.

Not only has biology become increasingly practical in combination with chemistry and physics, but earnest efforts have been made to render psychology similarly practical. **Psychology** Following in the footsteps of Wundt, the "father of physiological psychology," a Russian physician, Ivan Pavlov, had begun in the 1890's to make detailed psychological observations of animals and humans, not in terms of supposed internal consciousness, but in those of external physical stimuli and reactions. The outcome was a physiological psychology of "conditioned reflexes," which, as subsequently developed by an American professor at Johns Hopkins University, John Watson, became widely known after the World War as "behaviorism." According to the behaviorist, no one from outside can detect a being's consciousness, sensation, perception, or will, and consequently these concepts must be regarded by the scientific psychologist as unreal or unknowable. It suffices for him to suppose that "we talk and then we think—if indeed we think at all," and to concentrate on the study of stimulus and response.

Whatever may be the doubt about the "whole truth" of behaviorism, there can be no doubt that it was of practical value, especially in the observational and experimental study of child psychology. It also contributed, along with other types of psychological research, to the vogue of "intelligence tests" and "aptitude tests." Such tests have been numerously devised and extensively applied, and although there has been a tendency to claim too much for them, some of them are doubtless useful in indicating, at least roughly, what a person is mentally equipped to undertake.

Side by side with "behaviorism," arose a rival psychology bearing the German name of Gestalt, meaning "shape" or "form." As developed by Max Wertheimer, it combated purely physiological psychology and particularly its tendency to reduce individual behavior to a sequence of conditioned reflexes and thereby to deprive it of any meaning or significance. According to the Gestalt concept, psychology, instead of ignoring everything except physical reactions to physical stimuli, must take into account the entire nature, or "shape," of a perception. Thus, the seeing of a square does not consist in seeing four equal straight lines enclosing four right angles, but is the perception of the square as a whole. In the same way a melody is the totality of a series of tones and not just a succession of separate tones. The whole should be regarded as greater than the sum of its parts.

Another novel and much more influential interpretation of psychology was made by Sigmund Freud, an Austrian Jew, who, **Freud and Psychiatry** after studying medicine at Vienna and Paris, became a clinical neurologist and the foremost practitioner of "psycho-analysis." Freud invested psychology with a strict determinism, explaining everything, from our most trivial mistakes to our most cherished beliefs, as due to the operation of powerful instinctive forces, which mature with the body and which, if checked or distorted, may be the cause of mental ill-health. He particularly stressed (1) the existence of the "unconscious" and its dynamic influence on consciousness, (2) the existence of intra-psychical conflicts between various sets of forces, the chief of which is "repression," (3) the existence and paramount importance of infantile sexuality, and (4) the use of psycho-analysis, that is, of resuscitating buried memories through a process of "free association," as the remedy for mental disorder.

Freudian psychology speedily attracted numerous disciples and practitioners. In 1908 the first international congress of psychoanalysts was held, and in 1910 a permanent international association was formed. Before long, Freudian principles and methods were being applied not only to living individuals but to historic personages and also to nations and to society at large. Many differences of emphasis arose among Freud's disciples, and latterly there has been a marked reaction against his dogmatism and in favor of a considerably modified "psychiatry."

Manifold attempts to apply the methods of the natural sciences to human psychology have been paralleled by similar attempts on the part of students of human affairs—historians, anthropologists, economists, publicists, and sociologists. In the present century these have contended, more strenu- **Social Science** ously than ever before, that their several subjects were "social sciences," susceptible of the same objective treatment and mechanical interpretation as physics or chemistry or biology—involving the same minute observation of phenomena, the same marshaling of facts, the same eventual deduction of "laws." As the natural scientists collaborate in laboratories and research institutes, so the social scientists have taken to cooperating in libraries, research councils, and field work. Vast masses of factual data have been collected and published about man's present and past occupations and activities, about his social life, about his economic life, about his political life, about his cultural life. Never before had there been such an outpouring of doctoral dissertations, such a profusion of "scientific" monographs, such an elaboration of cooperative research and publication, so much teaching of "social science" in the schools. Never before had governments and private corporations availed themselves so much or so consistently of the findings and advice of social scientists.

Yet recently, in face of the contemporary revolution in physical science, there has been much soul-searching among social scientists and doubts have multiplied about their ability to achieve any such scientific objectivity as they have sought or to deduce from the greatest possible mass of data any ultimate laws. In 1916 the Italian philosopher, Benedetto Croce, asserted in dramatic fashion that "scientific history" is nearing its end, that its devotees, who imagine themselves to be concerned only with objective "facts," are constantly revealing their own subjectivity by their selection and organization of facts, and that, in any event, historical "truth" is not absolute but merely relative.

Of sociology, similar disillusioning criticism has been voiced. It has been shown how one sociological "system" after another had been put forth as "scientific"—Comte's and Herbert Spencer's and latterly Pareto's [1]—only to be regarded by succeeding generations as a "dated" commentary on the thought of a particular person or group at a particular time. In the case of

---

[1] Vilfredo Pareto published his *General Sociology* in 1916. It was an imposing pile of fact and conjecture, partially "positivist" and partially critical.

politics and of economics, actual occurrences in the latest era have been even more disillusioning than academic discussion has

**Newer Scientific Doubt**
been critical. Just as "political science" could not predict but only describe the rise of dictatorships, so "scientific economics" could neither prevent nor cure the depression which overspread the world in 1930.

The newer scientific doubt, especially as it affects the social sciences, has been thus epitomized: "Deprived of the certainty which it was once believed science would ultimately deliver, and of the very hope that it can in the nature of things disclose certainty, human beings must now concede their own fallibility and accept the world as a place of trial and error, where only those who dare to assume ethical and æsthetic responsibility, and to exercise intuitive judgment, while seeking the widest possible command of realistic knowledge, can hope to divine the future and mold in some measure the shape of things to come." [1]

The twentieth-century revolution in scientific doctrines, being many-sided, has helped to emphasize and increase a diversity in philosophic thought and speculation. At the close of the nineteenth century the dominant philosophy was materialistic, based on Newtonian physics and fortified by "Darwinism"; its extreme expressions were those of Herbert Spencer and Ernst Haeckel.[2] This type of philosophy was so entrenched that it has continued to be advocated in the latest age, especially by doctrinaire Marx-

**Current Philosophies**
ians and Positivists, even though physicists have raised grave doubts about the "matter" which was the basis of materialism. It should be noted, however, that the latest generation of "materialists" are apt either to soften or to broaden the dogmatism of their predecessors, and that the main body of Socialists—the Communists—put less stress nowadays on Karl Marx's doctrine of a fated and inevitable evolution than upon his preachment of willed and forceful revolution.

In the current reaction against "materialism" and "determinism," several different philosophies have come to the fore. On one hand, the reaction has been utilized to reassert and develop the essentially Christian philosophy of the primacy of the spiritual over the material, and of the dignity and freedom of the individual. This has been most brilliantly expounded by Jacques

[1] C. A. Beard, *The Open Door* (1934), p. 20.
[2] See above, pp. 199–200, 206–208.

Maritain, a French scholar and an interpreter of Thomas Aquinas.

But on the other hand, and to a greater extent, the reaction has found expression in philosophies which are not Christian or "religious" in any traditional sense. For example, the "idealism" which stemmed from Kant and Hegel,[1] and which was repellent to most persons of scientific bent in the second half of the nineteenth century, has attracted anew in the present century an impressive group of apostles throughout Europe. A leading figure among them is Croce, who began in 1902 the systematic exposition of his "philosophy of the spirit," divided into æsthetics, logic, ethics, and history; and by the 1920's he was exercising widespread influence. To him, "spirit" is manifest in the whole content of actual human experience, that is, in history; and the business of history is not merely to amass facts but to give them meaning and significance in terms of purpose and spirit.

A parallel philosophic trend has been toward what is described as "creative evolution"—the idea that human progress depends less upon any fated operation of nature or any ordinary use of reason than upon the will-power of heroic, forceful individuals. The idea had been foreshadowed earlier, in a pessimistic way, by Nietzsche,[2] but without much immediate effect. In the more favorable climate of the twentieth century, however, it was developed and given an optimistic slant by a French Jewish philosopher, Henri Bergson, and was enthusiastically seized upon by a varied coterie of disciples. To Bergson, the *élan vital*—or vital urge—is all important, and instinct and intuition are more significant than reason. There may be final causes, but they do not matter, for immediate causes are molded anew as evolution proceeds. Bergson himself, like his contemporary Croce, was liberally minded; and it is ironical, as well as symptomatic of the latest age, that the philosophies of both men have been exploited by apologists for dictatorship.

One of the outstanding features of contemporary thought has been its belittling or repudiation of the rationalism which was so highly esteemed by the "enlightenment" of the eighteenth century.[3] Curiously enough, the chief defense of human reason has

---

[1] See *Modern Europe to 1870,* pp. 601–602.
[2] See above, pp. 209–210.
[3] See *Modern Europe to 1870,* pp. 377–378.

now passed to such Christian philosophers as Maritain, while
its foremost critics are to be found among agnostics and atheists.

**Anti-Ra-
tionalism**
Some of these critics, intent upon promoting the "good
life," and yet influenced by the newer trends in psychology, by the doubts and uncertainties about social
science, and by the contemporary revolution in physical science
have latterly been drawn to a somewhat vague philosophy championed by a Frenchman, Jean Paul Sartre, and bearing the cum-
brous title of "existentialism." Sartre harks back to a Danish
Protestant theologian of the nineteenth century, Sören Kierke-
gaard, who sharply distinguished between knowledge and faith,
and between thought and life. With this as a starting point, Sartre
maintains that the only certainty is human existence and experience; one may properly be sceptical about knowledge and reason.

Contemporary thought about scientific progress and the new
scientific doctrines—and about almost everything else—is indeed chaotic.

### 3. CHAOS IN THE ARTS

The doubts and confusion which have increasingly characterized the thought of the European world have been reflected in its
art. This has become at once revolutionary and chaotic. For while
contemporary literature, painting, sculpture, and music alike
evince, in greater or less degree, a rebellion against tradition,
each displays an extraordinary variety of inspiration and technique. There is no single dominant fashion in present-day art-
forms, such as "classicism" was in early modern times, or "romanticism" in the nineteenth century, or "realism" at the beginning
of the twentieth. All these moods and modes still persist and are
simultaneously exemplified by works of art in the latest age, but
side by side with them appear strange new tendencies.

There is a novel "primitiveness," an enthusiasm for the simplicity of the antique, even of the barbarous. There is also a
sophisticated "modernism," a cultivation of the abstract rather
than the concrete, accompanied by much experimentation with
geometrical design. There is, too, a related "functionalism,"
an earnest effort to render art peculiarly expressive of the massive-
ness and speed of the machine age and in many instances of the
age's democratic or Marxian trend. There is, moreover, an icono-
clastic "futurism," a wild and willful flight from the past and even

from the present, sometimes as a release for highly charged emotions, and sometimes as a mere stunt. At the opposite extreme, there is a noticeable religious element in contemporary art, representing not so much a revival of the romantic medievalism of the nineteenth century as a novel reinterpretation of traditional religion in terms of the newest art forms.

A particularly radical revolt against all tradition has been urged by an Italian, F. T. Marinetti. In a pioneering manifesto of 1909, he denounced "the cult of the past" as the bane of art, and set forth the goal of "futurist" literature in these words: "We futurists uphold the ideal of a great and strong scientific literature, which, free from all and every classicism and pedantic purism, will magnify the most recent discoveries, the new intoxication of speed, and the celestial life of aviators. Our poetry is poetry essentially and totally rebelling against all used forms. The tracks of verse must be torn up and the bridges of things already said must be blasted and the locomotives of our inspiration must be started toward the coming, toward the boundless fields of the New and the Future! Better a splendid disaster than a monotonous race daily re-run! We have put up too long with the station masters of prosody." Marinetti himself was an unbalanced egotist and hardly a literary genius, but he expressed ideas about literature which have found increasing **Literature** favor in the latest age. And the result, whether it is called "futurist" or not, is the appearance in almost every country of strange new types of prose and verse—of verse that is prose, and of prose that only the author knows what if anything it means.

As to literary content, the sociological and psychological interests of the preceding "age of realism" have remained important, the psychological gradually outweighing the sociological and assuming more and more a Freudian complexion. In English literature, for example, such a sociological "realist" as H. G. Wells, after resigning himself to the World War in his *Mr. Britling Sees It Through* (1916) and becoming almost theological in his *God the Invisible King* (1917), rushed on to outline universal history in pessimistic vein, and in optimistic vein to psycho-analyze himself.

Wells, like Bernard Shaw, had survived from an earlier age, and was probably less representative of the new age than certain other and younger masters of English prose or poetry whom we may mention. Thus, John Galsworthy inaugurated in 1906 the long series of his *Forsyte* novels, nicely articulating the psychological with the sociological in detailed studies of the decay of an upper middle-class family, and presently he was writing plays in terse natural dialogue about disturbing ethical problems of the time. James Joyce, an Irishman who by preference resided abroad, chiefly at Paris, combined æstheticism with a revolutionary frankness about sex in his *Portrait of Artist as a Young Man* (1916) and in his still more sensational *Ulysses* (1922); and his ultimate work, *Finnegan's Wake* (1939), was so chaotic as to be for most people quite unintelligible. Among other writers who in widely different ways have been symptomatic of current revolt, mention may be made of Somerset Maugham and David H. Lawrence, of Ezra Pound and Ernest Hemingway.

The most influential French novelist of the time was Marcel Proust. He came of a gifted Parisian family, his father being a professor of medicine and his mother of Jewish extraction. As a young man he contributed to Socialist publications, translated Ruskin into French, expounded the "creative evolution" of Bergson, and played a conspicuous part in polite society. About 1902, however, failing health induced him to withdraw from active life; and his new-found leisure he employed in penning an elaborate psychological exposé of the society he had known. He planned it as a series of fifteen novels under the general title of *À la Recherche du Temps Perdu:* the first volume was published in 1913; another in 1918; the third and fourth in 1921; and three others after his death. The characters are erotic and abnormal, having little in common with the generality of mankind; they are always in process of development and change, and they are frightfully futile. Proust won some recognition in France during his life, but only after the World War and after his death did his fame spread widely and his influence become profound.

In German literature, the foremost post-war novelist was Thomas Mann. He came of a patrician merchant family of Lübeck, and in his native city he laid the scene of a remarkable character- and period-novel, *Buddenbrooks, the Ruin of a Family,* which he published in 1903 and which established his reputation. In this and in his later work, he has displayed a fondness for lingering among trivial details with considerable irony and cumulative effect, and also a wistful regret at the apparently inevitable swamping of aristocracy in a modern sea of plebeian mediocrity. Mann received the Nobel prize for literature in 1929; and after the advent of the Nazi dictatorship in his native land, he took refuge in the United States.

Against the dominantly pagan trends of the second quarter of the twentieth century, a distinctively Christian reaction was represented by such varied authors as Claudel, Chesterton, Undset, and Eliot. Paul Claudel, long in the consular and diplomatic service of France, was trained in the school of the symbolists and particularly indebted to Rimbaud, but he broke away from them in essential respects and produced lyrics and mystery plays with beauty of form and deeply religious meaning. Gilbert Chesterton, an English journalist who entered the Catholic Church in 1922, was a voluble and paradoxical literary champion of traditional religion against such "materialists" as Shaw and Wells. Essays poured from his pen, and so did ballads, biographies, literary studies, and detective stories. Never was Christian civilization defended in manner so unconventional—or so witty.

Sigrid Undset, the daughter of a Norwegian archæologist and another convert to Catholicism, won local fame by a novel, *Jenny*, in 1912, and then international fame by two series of "realistic" novels of medieval Norway. These were no romantic idealizations, but very "frank" and almost photographic expositions of life and society in the middle ages, and they were presented in an ultramodern style. Thomas S. Eliot, an American who settled in Great Britain and became a high-church Anglican, has written some of the best and most influential English poetry of recent times. His symbolic drama, *Murder in the Cathedral*, appeared in 1935, and his *Cocktail Party* in 1949.

Of the art of painting, Paris has remained the focal point, and here the post-impressionism inaugurated by such artists as Cézanne, Van Gogh, and Gauguin has been developed **Painting** and given new and revolutionary direction, especially by two masters—Matisse and Picasso. Henri Matisse, in full revolt against both classicism and impressionism, began where Cézanne and Gauguin left off. He varied and exaggerated the former's use of distortion and intensified the latter's bright coloring. Gradually he worked out an essentially new technique, rendering form quite unconventional, and treating light, not as the impressionists had done, by means of the juxtaposition of minute touches of color, but by employing pure tones on a large scale and thus producing the effect of modeling and the illusion of space. As he reacted against the traditions of "civilized" painting, he became infatuated with the art of "barbarous" peoples—Polynesians, African Negroes, and Mexican Indians—with its abbreviations and accentuations of form, its bizarre coloring, and its "rhythm."

Pablo Picasso, a Catalan Spaniard and son of an artist and professor at the Academy of Barcelona, settled in Paris in his youth and speedily became a leading post-impressionist and "naturalist." Choosing his subjects from the circus and the morbid side of life in a big city, he drew them with forceful directness and colored them with striking originality and restraint. Then, just before the World War, he took to painting still-life pictures of grouped fruit-bowls, bottles, or musical instruments, in manner more and more abstract and angular. This was a new manner, to which the name of "cubism" has been given: it was an attempt to cover the surface of a canvas with form and at the same time to reduce all form to simple geometric design. Picasso produced some attractive as well as astonishing "cubist" pictures, which enjoyed a notable vogue and were widely imitated. After the war, however, Picasso tired of "cubism" and reverted to his "naturalist" style, applying it to both painting and sculpture. Next to Cézanne's, Picasso's is probably the greatest influence in ultramodern art.

Cubism has gone on without Picasso, and in its wake have issued from Paris a swift succession of other pictorial isms: "futurism," reacting against the static quality of all past painting and striving to portray motion; "lyricism," seeking a close analogy in expression between painting and music; "surrealism," rejecting reasoned technique and depending upon inspiration to depict dreams and states of mind; "popularism," based on the supposition that common people without any technical training produce the most naive and sincere pictures and therefore the best. None of these isms—or of the many others which might be mentioned—has amounted to much in itself. Yet they are symptomatic of the turmoil into which painting has fallen, and suggestive of certain general tendencies among the large majority of contemporary painters the world over. "Naturalness" is eagerly sought after. Content matters less than form, and form must be unconventional, must convey some sense of thickness as well as of length and breadth, must express not merely concrete images but abstract conceptions.

Of course, ultra-modern painting is not just "art for art's sake." It is put to special uses, nationalistic, socialistic, religious. Of these, the nationalistic probably predominate, for ultra-modern forms seem peculiarly appropriate to the glorification of the primitive ancestors of one's nation or to the symbolizing of its abstract mass and might. Striking pictures of the kind, and some good ones, have been produced in Communist Russia and in Nazi Germany, and also by the native Mexican artist Diego Rivera, who, on one huge mural after another, has portrayed the primitive Indian life and labor of his country.

Of course, too, there are many contemporary painters who cling to past traditions. But most of them betray, in greater or less degree, the influence of newer schools. For example, the tradition of British portrait painting has been maintained and handed on from Sargent to such a "modern" as Sir William Orpen. Orpen's early work was marked by the use of quiet harmonies of gray and brown, in the manner of Whistler, but the influence of the French post-impressionists was evident in his later treatment of coloring and light. Orpen was the official British artist of the World War, and he painted the Paris Peace Congress of 1919.

Significant, too, is an American artist, George Bellows, whose painting represented a compromise between "realism" and "post-impressionism." He was a good draughtsman and a master of color. With dignity of composition he combined an intense vitality. Bellows pictured numerous sporting scenes quite realistically. Besides, he produced several religious works; his Crucifixion, for example, was what El Greco might have done if he had lived in the 1920's.

The latest age has given impetus not only to new methods and fashions of painting but also to similar developments in all the pictorial arts. Many "modern" artists have devoted themselves to engraving and etching and have produced works of unconventional but real distinction in these fields. Moreover, the art of posters, beginning in a significant way with Gauguin, has since been stimulated by the propagandist activity of governments, especially during the World War, and by commercial advertising. Then, too, the art of caricature, being particularly prized by a disillusioned public, has commanded the services of some of the best and most original draughtsmen of the latest age. For example, Forain, the most skillful of French cartoonists, found new inspiration for his talents in popular disillusionment about the World War and the League of Nations. And so, in only lesser degree, did the famous English caricaturist, Sir Bernard Partridge.

Architecture, as the most monumental and enduring of the arts, has always been more conservative than the others. It has been so in the latest age. Severely classic models have been

**Architecture** followed, for example, in the post-war Commerce Building and Supreme Court Building in Washington, and in the War Cenotaph in London. Romantic Gothic has provided models for recent ecclesiastical edifices, notably the great Anglican cathedral at Liverpool by Sir Gilbert Scott, and in New York the (Baptist) Riverside Church.

Yet architecture responds to current demands for new models in stricter keeping with contemporary developments, and the result is an accelerating "modernism" in all sorts of construction. Progressive industrialization of the past quarter-century has led to a general adoption of the building technique of industrialism— steel skeleton construction, and the wide use of reinforced concrete. It has also called for new types of office building, factory, garage, hangar. Moreover, growing urbanization of the population of every country has necessitated city planning on a large scale and a revaluation of the aims of domestic as well as public architecture. Furthermore, the expanding cult of applied science has prompted architects to seek some "scientific," or "functional," expression of the new materials, to adapt the appearance of a building to its actual use. Steel and concrete, with glass blocks, suggest the employment of strong vertical lines, wide spans, and slim supports; and, in addition, reinforced concrete lends itself to curving forms. And architects have shared in the widespread feeling engendered by the World War that the old order was passing away, and a new and quite different one was emerging. In view of all these considerations, it is not surprising that in the post-war years architecture has become steadily more "modernist" and "functional."

Among preachers and practitioners of revolutionary architecture, the American Frank Lloyd Wright merits special mention.

Before the war he designed a number of "functional" structures, which were then deemed freakish, and, to secure disciples, he wrote several books and founded a training school. Then, after the war, he won international recognition by building at Tokyo the great Imperial Hotel, an excellent example of the artistic beauty attainable by purely "modernist" methods.

Extreme "modernist" architecture has especially flourished in Germany, Austria, and Scandinavia. Here it appears in newer public buildings and factories, in apartment houses, and in war memorials. It is impressively exemplified in the Socialist housing developments in Vienna, in the Town Hall of Stockholm, and in the Finnish railway station at Helsingfors. The last named, in grandeur, in logic of design, and in decorative richness, is now the finest railway station in Europe.

The new architecture is in evidence in almost every country. It has been employed for new church edifices. It has been widely adapted to the fashioning of "cubicle" family-houses, all of them starkly simple and some of them very ugly. For some structures of marked beauty and dignity, it has been assimilated with traditional forms, for example with the Gothic, as in the Nebraska state capitol. In general, it has served to put a premium on simplicity, on the renouncing of superfluous architectural detail, and to invite a renewed dependence upon harmonious embellishment with sculpture, painting, and mosaics. This dependence has been beautifully achieved, in several French war memorials, in which sculpture and architecture reach a new unity of effect, fresh and unconventional, and in the interiors of certain "modernist" churches, in which mural decoration of paint and mosaic is integrated with architectural material and design.

Sculpture, like painting, has reacted sharply against traditions of the immediate past and exhibited novel and diverse trends. A leading sculptor of the age, and the chief exponent of "primitivism," is the Frenchman Aristide Maillol. Be- **Sculpture** ginning as a painter, he was induced by Gauguin to abandon impressionism, and for several years he worked on tapestry design, made majolica vases, experimented with glazes, and modeled wall fountains. Then, about 1910, becoming fascinated with archaic Greek statuary of the early fifth century B.C., he took to sculpture and thereafter produced a large number of monumental statues and terra-cotta statuettes, all characterized by a naive "primitiveness." Perhaps Maillol's most distinguished statue is the reclining goddess *Fame* which he fashioned for a memorial to Cézanne.

Indeed, much of the newer sculpture is consciously archaic in inspiration and in effect. It is imitative not alone of primitive Greek art but also, in many recent instances, of even more primitive art of ancient Etruscans or modern Negroes, Redmen, and South Sea Islanders. It represents in measure a reversion to paganism and barbarism.

On the other hand, much of the newer sculpture, like much of the newer painting, tends away from the primitive and concrete and toward an ever greater abstraction. This aspect of modern sculpture may be illustrated by reference to Jacob Epstein and Amadeo Modigliani. The former, born in New York in 1880, the son of Polish Jewish parents, studied at Paris and settled in London in 1905. The large sphinx which he carved in 1909 for the monument to Oscar Wilde in the Père Lachaise cemetery, at Paris, established his fame, and presently he extended his abstract experimentation with surer mastery and growing popular appreciation. Eventually, however, his radicalism lessened; and the fine series of bronze portraits which he executed during and after the World War were more traditional in form though still quite "modern" in feeling. Modigliani, a precocious Italian, commenced his artistic career as a "post-impressionist" painter but soon passed from "cubist" painting to a kind of "cubist" sculpture, utilizing such simple geometrical figures as the cube and the sphere as patterns for "abstract" portrait busts. Modigliani and Epstein are only two of a considerable number of gifted artists who have spread the vogue of abstract sculpture.

An outstanding sculptor of the latest age is a Croatian, Ivan Meštrović, who was apprenticed in childhood by his father, a peasant, to a marble-cutter at Spalato. Here he learned the trade so well and displayed such creative talent that his employer sent him to the art school at Vienna, and by 1906 his work attracted the favorable attention of Rodin. Meštrović has been thoroughly "modernist," but instead of following any one of the several modernist trends, he has managed to fuse them in a remarkable originality of his own. He is "primitive," "archaic," and at the same time "abstract," and yet not at all contemptuous of tradition.

In some ways comparable with Meštrović was the Englishman,

Eric Gill, who studied architecture and then sculpture, and, reaching the conclusion that art and religion are inseparable, became a Catholic in 1913. While accepting and developing "modernist" art forms—primitivism, abstraction, and all the rest—he employed them primarily for religious ends. Some of his work was in stone, but he excelled in wood-carving. Notable among his creations are the *Stations of the Cross* in Westminster Cathedral and a war memorial for the University of Leeds.

In music there has been reaction, akin to that in sculpture and painting, against tradition and convention, though more gradual and less complete. "New" music began to make itself **Music** heard prior to 1910, and two composers associated with its origins we have elsewhere discussed, Richard Strauss and Claude Debussy. Debussy died in 1918, but during the post-war years Strauss remained productive and influential. New operas and pantomimes he produced with a mastery of peculiar technique and gorgeous setting. And scores of younger musicians, consciously or unconsciously, have imitated his tricks and patterned their style after his.

Certain younger composers have gone much farther with "new" music. The chief of these is undoubtedly the Russian Igor Stravinsky. A pupil of Rimsky-Korsakov, he created a sensation with his *Firebird* (1910), a ballet motivated by a Russian folktale but treated in quite novel musical diction. The qualities here displayed—freedom from rhythm as well as harmony, brilliant coloring, impetuous violence, and strangely penetrating charm— Stravinsky has developed and accentuated in numerous later ballets. More than anyone else, he has blazed new trails along which the latest generation of "modernist" musicians are proceeding. The general direction is toward "abstract" and "primitive" music—perhaps through chaos to a new cosmos.

#### 4. NEW RELIGIONS FOR OLD?

Until the twentieth century there was little question that the Christian religion was distinctive of, and basic to, European or "Western" civilization. To be sure, ecclesiastical conflicts had long since given rise to divergent interpretations of Christianity by Catholic Church, Eastern Orthodox Churches, and Protestant Churches and sects. Moreover, conflicts over the respective jurisdictions of church and state had been many and chronic. And beginning with the "Enlightenment" of the seventeenth and eighteenth centuries, and accentuated by subsequent intellectual developments, there had been a gradual growth of scepticism and indifference, if not open hostility, toward Christian teaching and practice.

Especially in the latter part of the nineteenth century the drift away from Christian observance and from faith in any supernatural or "other worldly" religion was increasingly evident among intellectuals and also among urban workmen.[1] Nevertheless, the majority of Europeans and Americans still adhered, at least formally, to one or another of the Christian Churches; and while governments generally pursued a policy of secularization—transferring functions of education and charity from church to state—they usually professed respect for Christian principles.

In the present century, a significant change has occurred. The drift away from Christianity has reached large proportions; and **Drift away from Christianity** since World War I it has been actively fostered by a considerable number of governments. The change is attributable in part to popularization of the agnosticism of intellectuals; in part to upsetting economic and cultural conditions of the post-war period; and doubtless in chief part to the rise and energetic propaganda of new and rival pseudo-religions. Apparently, some sort of religion, some sort of "faith in things unseen," is necessary to most persons; and the void created by repudiation of a particular religion is sooner or later filled by adoption of a substitute. Many an intellectual, grown sceptical about Christianity, has made "science" a religion.

But pure "science," in the present age, has no such widespread quasi-religious attraction as Marxian communism or totalitarian **Appeal of New Religions: Communism, Nationalism** nationalism. The former of these, as established in Russia and fanatically preached elsewhere, is not only an economic and political system; it is a veritable religion, a new and proselyting and highly intolerant religion. And so too, in only lesser degree, has been the extreme "integral" or "totalitarian" nationalism which attended the Nazi movement in Germany and has flourished for a time in Italy, Hungary, and Mexico.

Both of these new religions, in marked contrast with Christianity, are essentially atheistic, rejecting or ignoring the super-

[1] See above, pp. 239–244.

natural; and both have this obvious advantage over Christianity that they promise the speedy attainment of a heaven on earth. In an era replete with novelties, they tellingly denounce Christianity as "old-fashioned" and "outworn," and wherever they are established they dictatorially abridge or suppress its exercise. Especially under Communist auspices, whole nations have been largely de-Christianized.

Nor is the current revolt against traditional supernatural religion confined to Christendom. It has appeared in Moslem Turkey and Iran, in Buddhist China and Japan. In some degree, it is world-wide, with the result that everyone of the great historic religions is extraordinarily troubled and its missionary endeavors seriously handicapped.

Yet, despite difficulties, old and new, with which it is confronted in the present age, despite universal progress of secularization and relative decline of ecclesiastical influence on society and on the shaping of public policies, despite dictatorial attempts to suppress it, organized supernatural religion is by no means dead. Its roots are struck deep in human habits, if not in human nature; and apparently it satisfies vital human needs and aspirations.

Of the major Christian bodies, the Catholic Church continues to be the largest and the most intransigent in its opposition to the new pseudo-religions. The World War caused it immediate political embarrassments, and the Pope of the time, Benedict XV (1914–1922), had to employ all his diplomatic talents to preserve his neutrality between the belligerents, while his earnest peace pleas fell on deaf ears.[1] In several ways, however, the war years proved temporarily advantageous to the Church. They witnessed a noteworthy revival of Catholic activity and influence in France and Italy; and the political map of Europe which resulted from the war enhanced the prestige of the Church. Catholics were numerically preponderant in the newly created nations of Poland, Lithuania, Czechoslovakia, and the Irish Free State, and they were numerous in the enlarged states of Yugoslavia and Rumania. For several years after the war Catholic political parties dominated or held a balance of power in the governments of Germany, Austria, Belgium, the

*Catholic Church*

---

[1] On the peace efforts of Benedict XV, see above, p. 397. An outstanding monument of his pontificate was the completion (1917) of the codification of canon law which had been begun under his predecessor, Pius X.

Netherlands, and Hungary. This improved international position of the Catholic Church was made the most of by the able successor of Benedict XV—Pope Pius XI (1922–1939).

Pius XI was both scholar and statesman. He successfully negotiated with the Italian government the Lateran treaty of 1929, settling the "Roman question" and reestablishing, after the lapse of fifty-nine years, an independent temporal sovereignty for the papacy. True, the seat of this sovereignty, "Vatican City," was an extremely small part of Rome, but it sufficed to symbolize to the world that the Pope was no longer a "prisoner" of Italy or subject to Italian law, but that, instead, he was a supra-national figure, guaranteed as such by an international treaty.

With most nations in Christendom, Pius XI maintained or newly established friendly relations, and he concluded concordats with Latvia (1922), Poland (1925), Lithuania (1927), Czechoslovakia (1928), Italy, Portugal, Rumania (1929), and Germany (1933). These concordats assured to the Pope the appointment of bishops within the countries concerned and to the Church the right of imparting religious instruction, and if in some instances they restricted political activity of the clergy they uniformly promised to respect Catholic social action.

On the other hand, there were some very serious setbacks for Catholicism. The Catholic minority in Russia (largely concentrated in Ukrainia and Byelorussia) suffered from the anti-religious policies and actions of the Communist dictatorship; and repeated protests of Pius XI were unheeded. Nor could the Pope stem the anti-clerical and anti-Christian tide in Mexico; the papal delegate was expelled from Mexico City and the National Revolutionary dictatorship of the country made few concessions. In Spain, moreover, the establishment of the Republic precipitated in 1931 an acute conflict between state and church and led to a series of drastic anti-Catholic enactments, and during the ensuing civil war the Spanish clergy suffered direfully. Then, too, not all the new concordats were scrupulously observed by governments which agreed to them, and especially in the case of Germany the Nazi regime flouted the concordat of 1933 and pursued an actively anti-Catholic policy.

Under Pius XI, the missionary activities of the Church were extended farther in Asia and Africa. To meet nationalist objections to "European" missionary enterprise, the Pope increased the number of natives in the hierarchies of China, Japan, and India, for example, and entrusted to them the conduct of the missions within their respective countries. Many European (and American) priests, monks, and nuns still labor in far-away fields, but to a much greater degree than formerly their labors are supplemented by those of native clergymen.

In several important encyclical letters, Pius XI discussed current questions and indicated the attitude which Christians should take toward them. Both "totalitarian" nationalism and atheistic communism were condemned. Limitation of armaments and judicial settlement of international disputes were urged. The principles and program of Catholic social reform as outlined by Leo XIII in 1891 were reaffirmed. Unnatural means of birth-control were denounced. The traditional "rights" of the Church, especially in the education of youth, were reasserted.

On the death of Pius XI in 1939, his experienced Secretary of State, Cardinal Pacelli, was elected to succeed him and took the title of Pius XII. The new Pope, while maintaining his predecessor's general policies, had to face a succession of extraordinary difficulties attending and following World War II. Though he had the satisfaction of witnessing the defeat of totalitarian nationalism and a resurgence of Catholic activity in Italy and western Europe, he could only denounce the spread of Communism and protest against the persecutions it inspired not only in Russia, but in Yugoslavia, Hungary, Rumania, Czechoslovakia, Poland, and also in China.

The Eastern Orthodox Churches, in some respects, have been even harder hit. They had never had any such independence of secular government as the Catholic Church and, with **Eastern** the recent overthrow of governments on which for cen- **Orthodox** turies they relied, they have suffered a notable decline **Church** and shrinkage. The disruption of the Ottoman Empire and the rise of the Turkish dictatorship of Mustafa Kemal served to narrow the jurisdiction of the Orthodox Patriarch of Constantinople and to deprive him of any privileged position and of much of his prestige. Far more serious, and affecting indeed the large majority of the Orthodox communion, was the revolution in Russia, with its destruction of the Tsardom, which had always supported the Church, and its establishment of the Communist dictatorship. Orthodox Christianity continues to exist and be practiced in Russia; but the Church, now again under a Patriarch of Moscow, is barely tolerated and constantly dictated to by the state, and the vast majority of young people are being brought up in ignorance of Christianity and usually in militant opposition to it.

The pattern in vogue in Communist Russia has recently been copied by Communist dictatorships elsewhere and applied to national Orthodox Churches in Rumania and the Balkan states. If these have not suffered the outright persecution which the Catholic Church has suffered, it is only because they subordinate themselves to state dictation.

Protestant Christianity has developed since World War I along lines which had been marked out with some clearness between 1870 and 1910.[1] Probably there are now as many pro-

**Protestant Churches**

fessed Protestants throughout the world as ever before, and perhaps more. But Protestantism is less than ever a single coherent movement. On the one hand, "high-church" Anglicanism—latterly styled Anglo-Catholicism—has been coming to the fore and likewise a similar "high-church" trend in Lutheranism, while ritualistic observances have been growing in most Protestant churches and in some a "fundamentalism" has continued to be preached. On the other hand, the "broad-church" or "modernist" trend has become much more pronounced. With multitudes of professed Protestants, little remains of historic Protestantism, that is, of Protestant faith and practice of the sixteenth century. There is widespread repugnance to anything savoring of dogma, a sharp reaction against "puritanism," and an absorption in "good works" and the "good life."

In the circumstances, Protestant sectarianism has lost most of its earlier distinctiveness, and increasingly successful attempts have been made to federate, if not to unify, various Protestant denominations in particular countries. Thus, in 1922, was created an international council for coordinating Protestant missionary endeavors throughout the world. In 1925 an "ecumenical Christian conference on life and work" at Stockholm was attended by delegates of thirty-one non-Catholic bodies; it naturally refrained from discussing ecclesiastical organization and creed, but it issued a joint report on social and international morality. In 1938 an international federation of all these bodies was established.

[1] See above, pp. 250–255.

Protestant, like Catholic, missionary enterprise has remained impressive in Asia and Africa, though in China, at any rate, all Christian missions have recently been endangered by triumphant Communism. And though there have been too few Protestants in Russia or east-central Europe to feel the heavy hand of irreligious or anti-religious dictatorships to the extent which Orthodox or Catholic Christians have felt it, the Protestant majority in Germany was temporarily afflicted with similar coercion during the Nazi sway.

Judaism has continued to comprise "orthodox" and "reformed" groups, the latter growing at the expense of the former.[1] It has continued, too, to be partly religious and partly national, to foster Zionism and to be plagued by anti-Semitism. **Judaism** It has greviously suffered from a systematic "racial" persecution of the most violent sort in Germany,[2] and from a less violent but more subtle "materialistic" subversion within Russia.

Islam has begun, only since World War I, to encounter head-on the forces of opposition and criticism with which Christianity has long been confronted. But the encounter is as upsetting as it has been sudden. The Moslem caliphate is **Islam** now at an end. The process of secularization is steadily advancing in Turkey and Iran, and clearly beginning in Egypt, Syria, India, and Indonesia. Despite the fact that millions still profess allegiance to Allah and to Mohammed as His prophet, there is as yet no evidence of any profound or widespread revival of Islam. And it is somewhat similar with Hinduism and with Buddhism.

The basic religious question of the twentieth century is not one between "science" and "theology." It is one between atheism and supernaturalism. It is whether in the long run an exclusively "this-worldly" faith such as Marxian Communism can and will provide the masses of mankind with a satisfying substitute for "other-worldly" faith which from time immemorial humanity has cherished.

### 5. ECONOMIC DIFFICULTIES, SOCIAL STRAINS, AND IDEOLOGICAL CONFLICT

Despite the advance of industrialization and considerable popular optimism about the spread of democracy and the attainment of international peace, a remarkable instability characterized

[1] See above, pp. 257–259.
[2] See below, p. 586.

European life after World War I. There were unwonted economic difficulties. The war had been extremely expensive and

**Economic Difficulties**

destructive, and at its conclusion the governments of the several belligerent nations found themselves saddled with huge war debts, and, in addition, with extraordinary obligations for the rehabilitation of wounded men and devastated areas.

Then, too, the demobilization of the big war-time armies, the release of millions of men from trench and camp and their return to rural field or urban factory, tended to glut the labor market just when the special demand of the preceding years for munitions and foodstuffs sharply declined. Furthermore, the scrapping of numerous war industries involved a stoppage of the abnormal profits and wages which had been accruing to employers and workmen respectively; and the prospect of reaping comparable returns from the resumption of ordinary industrial and commercial enterprises was obscured alike by cut-throat international competition and by diminution of the purchasing power of the general public. Complicating the situation was the intensification of nationalism, which, being economic as well as political, led not only to an increase in the number of sovereign states in Europe but also to the adoption by each of protective tariffs that checked international trade and hence domestic production.

Still further complicating the economic situation were the related and troublesome problems of German reparations and inter-Allied debts. As we have pointed out in another connection, these problems plagued Europe for ten years and more after the Paris peace settlement of 1919 and contributed potently to financial instability and international friction.[1] Nor should we overlook the failure to bring about any general disarmament[2] which might have lessened the financial burdens and promoted a greater sense of security and stability. Altogether, every European nation experienced, in greater or lesser degree, alternate waves of inflation and deflation; and the steps taken by the several national governments to meet their economic difficulties had upsetting effects on the traditional classes of European society.

The titled nobility, as a class, were especially hard hit. Throughout eastern Europe, they were shorn of much of their

---

[1] See above, pp. 425, 446–451.
[2] See above, pp. 454–455.

landed wealth and political influence. In Russia they were dispossessed altogether of their property and either put to death or driven into more or less penurious exile. In Germany **Impact on** and Austria they were stripped of privileges and largely **Various** supplanted in public office by commoners. In Rumania, **Classes** Poland, and other states of east-central Europe, they bowed to the threat of popular revolution and acquiesced in a series of landreforms which transferred large portions of the ancestral estates into peasant farms.

The peasantry, speaking generally, profited—at any rate temporarily. The war increased the demand for farm products, and the economic instability succeeding the war proved less disturbing to agriculture than to manufacturing. In particular, the depreciated currency of most European countries enabled peasants to pay off mortgages on their holdings at the very time when in several countries new land legislation was enabling them to add to their holdings. For some years after the war it seemed as though the greater part of continental Europe was undergoing a social transformation in the direction of peasant proprietorship of land and as though the newly emancipated farmers, by means of cooperative enterprise, would make significant contributions to the stability and conservatism of European society and perhaps in the long run to the orderly economic reconstruction of the world. Yet there were many gradations in European "peasantry." Some peasants were mere agricultural laborers without land of their own and utterly dependent on a highly disorganized and uncertain labor market. Others had holdings too small to be of profit to themselves under the most auspicious circumstances. Those who were the best off were handicapped by increasing burdens of taxation, direct or indirect, and by decreasing stability in finance, trade, and industry.

Among the middle classes—or bourgeoisie—a distinction must be made. A group of financiers and investors, together with captains of certain key industries—collectively the *haute bourgeoisie* —amassed handsome personal fortunes, in part from war-time "profiteering" and in part from post-war speculation. On the other hand, the lower middle class—professional men and salaried employees and many shopkeepers—suffered greatly from the general economic instability and especially, just after the war, from depreciated currency and resulting inflation. In Germany, inflation reached such an extreme in 1923 as to render valueless the bonds which had been issued during the war and which were held principally by the middle class. In France, inflation was not quite so drastic in effect, but it sufficed by 1926 to reduce by four-fifths the principal and income of domestic stocks and bonds. And Russia's repudiation of all its foreign indebtedness added to the difficulties. Altogether, throughout the greater part of continental Europe, the lower middle class saw its savings wiped out and its pensions and insurance reduced to zero. The economic instability of this class promoted its political instability and tended to make the class as a whole impatient with democratic government and receptive to demagogic dictatorship.

Post-war developments were beneficial to some of the industrial proletariat and injurious to others. In Russia the entire class was peculiarly favored by the Communist revolution, whose major efforts were directed in its behalf. In Germany, at least for a time, the artificial stimulation of industrial enterprise by reparation payment and inflation assured full employment to urban workers, while Socialist participation in the country's government guaranteed the maintenance of favorable labor-legislation. In France and Belgium, too, the rebuilding of devastated areas provided gainful employment for workmen. On the other hand, the unsettled conditions in commerce and manufacturing reacted unfavorably upon workmen almost everywhere. Feverish activity quickly alternated with depression and unemployment, and increase of wages hardly kept pace with increasing cost of living. In Austria, the peace treaties deprived industrialized Vienna of usual markets, with terrible economic consequences to proletariat as well as to bourgeoisie. In Italy, proletarian distress was evidenced immediately after the war by an epidemic of strikes and a contagion of Communist agitation. In Great Britain, an army of unemployed men, aggregating two million in 1921, was being supported by government doles and public taxation.

For a brief time, between 1924 and 1928, matters seemed to mend, and hope ran high that Europe would surmount its economic difficulties. But then came, with resounding crash, a most fateful depression. It was by no means the first depression in modern times, but it was far more general and much more severe than any previous one. Beginning in 1929, every country was affected in measure as it had been

**Economic Depression of 1929**

industrialized. Stocks and bonds depreciated in value. Factories and mills shut down. Industrial workers lost their jobs and their wages and had to be cared for by private charity or public doles. By 1932 the number of unemployed and destitute workers in western and central Europe, the United States, and Japan—the most highly industrialized portions of the earth—was estimated at 30 million. With these and their families thus deprived of purchasing power, the demand for the products of machine industry, and hence for raw materials and foodstuffs, markedly declined, with further deleterious effects upon industry and commerce and likewise upon agriculture. To the millions of persons who had no income at all were added many more millions whose income was gravely reduced.

Practically, what was done in most industrial nations to cope with the new and critical situation was for government to intervene—to provide subsistence for the enlarging armies of the industrially unemployed either by giving them outright doles or by paying them wages for public works, and to meet the resulting increased expense by imposing heavier taxes upon the wealthy minority or by borrowing huge sums of money from them. It involved some degree of state socialism and corresponding contraction of personal liberty.

The depression of 1929–1930 climaxed the economic difficulties and social strains of the decade after World War I. It also accentuated a twofold ideological conflict. One part of this conflict was between optimism and pessimism. Optimism had been a main feature of European thought ever since the "Enlightenment" of the eighteenth century, and it continued after the World War to inspire many persons with the hopeful belief that rapid progress was being made toward a better and happier Europe and a better and happier world.

But over against this optimism, a novel pessimism appeared. It was an outgrowth of disappointments and disillusionments attending the World War and its aftermath, and was eloquently voiced by a variety of scholars and publicists, including the German Oswald Spengler, the Spaniard José Ortega, and the Englishman Arnold Toynbee, who stressed the decline and decay of civilizations, especially of Western civilization. There was growing scepticism about "progress," and notable questioning of ideals which had previously been prevalent.

By the 1930's some sound basis undoubtedly existed for the newer pessimism and for its reaction against the older optimism. But this reaction was only a part of the ideological conflict of the post-war years. A more disturbing part was the conflict, in the political domain, between what may be called a "New Left" and a "New Right."

"Right" and "Left" were terms which had been employed throughout the nineteenth century respectively to denote "Conservatives" and "Liberals." The differences between these, once wide, had gradually lessened, and by the opening of the twentieth century the bulk of both Conservatives and Liberals (and also Socialists) were supporting personal liberty and political democracy.[1] There remained, of course, in most countries on the European Continent an Extreme Right of "reactionaries," antagonistic to individualistic democracy, and an Extreme Left of "revolutionaries," seeking a violent overthrow of existing government and society. But on the eve of World War I, neither of these extremes commanded any large following or seriously threatened public order.

*Ideological Conflict*

After the war, the situation changed. Economic and financial instability, with its upsetting effects on the traditional social classes of Europe, made for political instability. The democratic governments which emerged almost everywhere in 1919–1920, and were then popularly acclaimed, encountered a rising tide of criticism and opposition as they attempted, with only partial success, to grapple with the complex national and international problems of the next fifteen years. They now had to face large militant groups of an Extreme Left on the one hand, and of an Extreme Right on the other.

The new Extreme Left was an offshoot of Marxian Socialism, which, as a general movement, gained bigger followings in the post-war years than ever before and actually took possession of the extensive Russian Empire. Prior to the war, the large majority of Marxian Socialists had inclined toward "reformist" tactics,[2] accepting political democracy and emphasizing the evolutionary character of social change except for their advocacy of radical social reform they were hardly distinguishable from the older Liberal "Left." Such

*New Extreme "Left": Marxian Communism*

[1] See above, pp. 81–82.
[2] See above, p. 219.

Marxians continued during and after the war to adhere to "regular" Socialist or Social Democratic parties and to collaborate with other democratic parties in the conduct of affairs in central and western Europe. In 1919 they reconstituted the international organization—the so-called "Second International"—which had been founded in 1889 [1] but which the war had temporarily disrupted.

After the war, however, the moderation of the Social Democratic parties and the Second International was no longer characteristic of Marxian Socialism as a whole. A split occurred, and a rival faction came into prominence, preaching "direct-action" tactics,[2] revolutionary seizure of power by industrial workers, and forceful socialization through a proletarian dictatorship. It was this faction which engineered and profited from the Russian Revolution of November 1917, and which assumed the title of "Communist" to distinguish it from the Social Democrats. Presently, many of the latter, impatient with democratic procedure and attracted by the Russian example, formed separate Communist parties in central and western Europe; and in 1919 these were federated at Moscow into a world organization in open competition with the Second International and known therefore as the Third, or Communist, International—the Comintern.

Rival efforts of Communists and Social Democrats to capture the urban proletariat were attended by mutual recriminations. Communists accused Social Democrats of condoning "the exploitation of the masses." Social Democrats accused Communists of sabotaging efforts at reform. After 1920, there was a marked drift, wherever economic instability was most pronounced, toward Communism. And Communism did constitute a new and extreme Left, in outspoken and even violent opposition to liberal democracy and to every government not dominated by Communists.

Violence and dictatorship were essential parts of the ideology of the "New Left." They were likewise essential parts of the ideology of a "New Right." For, as nationalism was **New Extreme "Right": Fascism and Nazism** intensified and the economic lot of certain classes worsened, sizeable groups of patriots and of noblemen and bourgeois came to believe that the surest and best defense against international socialization, and especially against

[1] See above, p. 218.
[2] On the antecedents of this faction, see above, pp. 219–220.

Communism, was not in tolerant democratic parliaments but in forceful nationalist dictators. Beliefs of this kind inspired such movements as Fascism and Nazism, which, like Communism, were thoroughly antithetical to liberal democracy.

By 1930 the post-war prospect of a world-wide triumph of democracy was dimmed. Almost everywhere, democracy was now being assailed, and its operation rendered increasingly difficult, by basic ideological conflict between its supporters and the expanding subversive groups of Extreme Right and Left. On the rise of these groups we shall have more to say in the next chapter. They provide the central theme for the latest stage in the history of Europe—and the world.

# PART IV

## LENGTHENING SHADOWS AND THE "SECOND" WORLD WAR

# CHAPTER XIII

## RISE OF TOTALITARIAN DICTATORSHIPS

I. COMMUNIST DICTATORSHIP IN RUSSIA

PERIMENTALLY, from March to November 1917, Russia was presided over, as we have elsewhere explained,[1] by a revolutionary "provisional government," desirous of establishing political democracy as well as of prosecuting the World War, but unable to agree upon a program of internal social reform. Indeed, by November 1917 this provisional government was so divided in its counsels, so uncertain as to what it should or could do, and so devoid of any large popular support that it was at the mercy of a mere handful of resolute persons well organized and fearlessly led. Which explains why it was then overthrown by the Bolshevik faction of Marxian Socialists.

Marxian Socialists comprised a very small part of the vast Russian population, and of that part the Bolshevik faction was hardly a half.[2] Yet what the Bolsheviks lacked in numbers they compensated for in leadership, in definiteness of purpose, and in tactical resourcefulness.

The leader of the Bolsheviks was Vladimir Ulyanov, generally known by his pen-name of N. Lenin. He belonged to a middle-class family, and as a law student at the University of Kazan he became an ardent disciple of Karl Marx—a discipleship in which he was confirmed by the execution of his older brother for complicity in a plot against the Tsar Alexander

Lenin

---

[1] See above, pp. 394–395, 399–400.

[2] On the two factions of Marxian Socialists in Russia before 1917—the Bolsheviks and the Mensheviks—and on the rival "Social Revolutionaries," see above, pp. 172, 342.

III. In 1894, the year of the accession of the Tsar Nicholas II, young Ulyanov—or Lenin—undertook Marxian propaganda in St. Petersburg, for which he was imprisoned and then exiled for three years to Siberia. This exile he utilized to write a book on Russian capitalism, which subsequently attracted considerable attention in Socialist circles. From 1900 to 1917 Lenin made his headquarters in Switzerland, with the exception of two years (1905–1907) when revolutionary disturbances in Russia invited and enabled him to return home. Wherever he was, he directed a tireless agitation in behalf of Marxian socialism and (after 1903) of its extreme left wing. Lenin was undersized, with a wide forehead and piercing eyes. He had great driving force, and, with an iron will and a fanaticism about the ends he sought, he combined a sense of political expediency. It was this man who returned finally to Russia in April 1917 and, by converting the St. Petersburg "soviet of workers and soldiers" to his views, managed to precipitate the revolution of November 1917 and to inaugurate the Communist dictatorship.

Lenin had several capable lieutenants, of whom two merit special mention. Levi Bronstein (or Leon Trotsky as he called himself) was a flaming person who came of a middle-**Trotsky and Stalin** class Jewish family and was educated at the University of Odessa. Arrested as a revolutionary and exiled to Siberia, he escaped in 1902 to western Europe where he made the acquaintance of Lenin, though he then sympathized more with the Menshevik Socialists than with the Bolsheviks. Trotsky returned to Russia in 1905 and took an active part in the St. Petersburg soviet of that period. Then, after a second arrest and exile to Siberia, he escaped again and led a roving existence. From Paris he was expelled for pacifist agitation in 1916, and from New York, where he briefly found refuge, he sailed in March 1917 for Russia, arriving at St. Petersburg shortly after Lenin. Here, during the ensuing summer, he definitely cast his lot with the Bolsheviks and played a role hardly second to Lenin's in preparing the way for the Communist revolution.

Joseph Stalin, the son of a Georgian peasant shoemaker in the Caucasus, was no such theorist as the middle-class Trotsky or Lenin, but he was a sturdy and persistent propagandist of the latter's doctrines. Dismissed from an Orthodox seminary in 1896, when he was seventeen years of age, for "unreliability and lack of religious vocation," he joined the extremist Socialist group, and thenceforth until 1917 he waged warfare with the Tsarist regime, using strong-arm methods, and being punished by frequent imprisonments and Siberian exiles.

Lenin's party of professed Communists was small when he seized power in November 1917, but his program was calculated to enlist popular support. He proclaimed that his dictatorship was a "dictatorship of the proletariat," including workers, peasants, and soldiers; and upon each **"Proletarian" Dictatorship** of these numerous classes he proposed to confer immediate benefits. In behalf of the industrial workers, he decreed the confiscation of private factories and their transformation into government institutions, with shop committees of workers in control of production, purchase, and sale. In behalf of the peasants, he decreed the expropriation of landlords and the nationalization of the land, with peasant-communities in charge of its partition and use. In behalf of the war-weary soldiers, he took Russia out of the World War and concluded with the Central Powers the treaty of Brest-Litovsk (March 1918).[1] He also issued, in November 1917, a "Declaration of the Rights of Peoples," recognizing the principle of cultural nationalism and promising to accord to subject peoples in Russia a measure of self-determination.

This program appealed to numerous soviets which had been set up throughout Russia during 1917, and through them Lenin extended Communist sway beyond St. Petersburg and Moscow to the country at large. At first there was a good deal of opposition, not merely from habitual supporters of the Tsardom—bureaucrats, army officers, nobles, and Orthodox clergymen—but also from many Constitutional Democrats ("Cadets") among the bourgeoisie and from the radical parties of Social Revolutionaries and Menshevik Socialists. Indeed, anti-Bolsheviks obtained three-fourths of the seats in the democratically elected Constituent Assembly which had been provided for in 1917, prior to Lenin's seizure of power,[2] and which met at Moscow in January 1918. But Lenin denounced the Assembly as an agency of "reaction," and his soldiers broke it up, while Communist soviets throughout the country, representing only a small minority of the population, albeit a determined minority, terrorized the majority.

[1] See above, p. 400.
[2] See above, p. 395.

The Communists were resolved to achieve a thorough social revolution, and against "reaction" of any sort they struck hard. "Direct action" was employed against recalcitrant nobles and capitalists and against army officers and bureaucrats of the old regime; such as could not flee were put to death. Energetic measures were taken, in accordance with a decree of January 1918, to disestablish the Orthodox Church in Russia and to silence all Christian clergymen. In July 1918 the Tsar Nicholas II, his wife, and children, who had been held under guard at Ekaterinburg (near the Urals), were slaughtered by order of the local soviet. And against all dissident political groups, even that of the Menshevik Socialists, Communist soldiers and revolutionary tribunals conducted a veritable reign of terror. A considerable part of the opposition was won over, or at any rate was frightened into passivity, but tens of thousands were killed and other thousands escaped death only by flight abroad.

The terrorism was aggravated by the hostility with which most of the outside world viewed the Communist dictatorship in **Failure of** Russia. During and immediately after the negotiations **Foreign** for the treaty of Brest-Litovsk (March 1918), the **Intervention and** Germans interfered in Russia. Their purpose was to **Domestic** strengthen their own military position and to pre- **Revolt** vent the spread of Communism in central Europe. They extracted from the Bolshevik government a formal promise not to countenance subversive propaganda in the Central Powers. They encouraged leaders of the "liberated" border countries, including Ukrainia, to set up national governments allied with Germany. Not until the final military collapse of the Central Powers in November 1918 were the Russian Communists relieved of the menace of German intervention.

But already the Allies were intervening. Statesmen and leading citizens of France, Great Britain, Japan, and the United States were angered by the actions of Lenin's dictatorship in withdrawing from the war, in making a separate peace, in repudiating Russia's foreign debts, and in preaching a world-wide Communist revolution. Allied intervention in Russia began in March 1918 as a war measure against Germany. Refusing to acknowledge the treaty of Brest-Litovsk, the Allies declined to recognize the government which agreed to it, and enforced an economic blockade against Russia. Moreover, they landed "expeditionary forces" at Murmansk, the single ice-free port of Russia on the Arctic Ocean, at Vladivostok in eastern Siberia, and at Odessa on the Black Sea.

Under protection of the Allied expeditions, various Russian generals collected against the "red" armies of the Communists several "white" armies of the opposition and precipitated civil war within Russia. Thus Allied intervention, beginning as a war measure against Germany, speedily assumed the character of a domestic and foreign crusade against the revolutionary dictatorship.

For a time, toward the close of 1918 and throughout 1919, it seemed as if Lenin's government would be unable to cope with foreign intervention and domestic revolt. Allied troops, reinforced by Russian malcontents, captured Archangel in the north, occupied the Crimean peninsula in the south, and overran the greater part of Siberia from the east. From the Crimea, General Denikin, perhaps the ablest of the anti-Communist leaders, advanced in the direction of Moscow; while at Omsk, in western Siberia, members of the dissolved Constituent Assembly set up an anti-Communist government as the legal successor to Kerensky's "provisional government" of 1917, and this was supported by forces under the command of Admiral Kolchak.

Gradually, however, the Communists got the upper hand. They were favored by personal rivalry of the opposing generals and by chronic dissensions between such of their followers as advocated the establishment of a democratic republic and such as wanted a restoration of the Tsardom. There was no like uncertainty among the Bolsheviks as to what they expected to do, and with singleness of purpose they combined a fanaticism, a ruthlessness, and withal an adroitness of popular propaganda and an adeptness at military organization which were of inestimable advantage to them.

Leon Trotsky, as Lenin's Commissar of War, proved himself the man of the hour. He inflamed the masses of Russian peasants and workers with hatred of the "whites" as agents of "reaction," and though the "red" soldiers whom he rallied to the defense of the dictatorship were often ragged and poorly armed, they were more numerous by the end of 1919, and far more enthusiastic, than their foes.

The Communists were also favored by the fact that foreign

governments, no matter how much they might detest Lenin's Socialist dictatorship, were in no position at the close of the World War to conduct extensive military operations in Russia. Germany certainly was impotent. France, which had most at stake in the way of financial investments, was too war-weary and too occupied with penalizing Germany to undertake forceful debt collection in Russia. Great Britain was restrained by a multiplicity of other imperial concerns and by the pacifist attitude of the rapidly growing Labor party at home. Japan was more interested in obtaining privileges in near-by China than in overthrowing a government in faraway European Russia.

The result was the withdrawal of Allied expeditionary forces, from northern Russia in the autumn of 1919, and from Siberia in the spring of 1920. Then, with the loss of active Allied support, the anti-Communist rebellions in Russia collapsed or were suppressed. Admiral Kolchak had to surrender Omsk in November 1919, and in the following February he was captured and shot at Irkutsk. As for General Denikin, his early successes were followed by reverses and by his flight to Constantinople.

For a while longer, France sought to incite peoples on the Russian border to fight the Communists. In 1920 it abetted an attack by Poland and an insurrection in Ukrainia, and at the same time it encouraged a Russian émigré, Baron Wrangel by name, to raise another "white" army and renew General Denikin's attempt to invade southern Russia.

At first the Franco-Polish effort promised success, but in July 1920 the "red" armies of Communist Russia defeated the Poles and drove them back to the very gates of Warsaw. Here the Poles rallied and defeated the Russians, but they were no longer sanguine of ultimate victory. So Poland agreed to an armistice, and in March 1921 concluded at Riga a peace treaty with Russia.[1] Meanwhile, in the autumn of 1920, "red" armies overwhelmed the "white" forces in the Crimea and obliged General Wrangel to follow General Denikin into exile at Constantinople, while other "red" armies, in conjunction with Ukrainian Communists, put an end to the independence of Ukrainia.

By 1921 the authority of the Communist dictatorship was not seriously disputed in Russia. Domestic opposition was suppressed and foreign intervention stopped. In 1922, moreover, Germany

[1] See above, p. 431.

formally recognized the dictatorship, and presently the Allies followed suit: Great Britain, France, and Italy in 1924; the United States ultimately in 1933.

But if foreign countries failed to destroy the Communist dictatorship in Russia, the latter made little immediate headway abroad. The outbreaks which it inspired in 1919 in Germany and Hungary were quickly suppressed;[1] and for several years none of the Communist parties which it fostered abroad, and which it directed through the Comintern at Moscow, was able to seize power. It did manage, in Asia, to detach Outer Mongolia from China and to install a puppet Communist government there in 1924. Not until sixteen years later did the Russian dictatorship succeed in dominating any other foreign country.

In the meantime, the Communist regime felt obliged to part with certain European territories which had belonged to the Russian Empire and to agree to the series of treaties of 1921–1922 that recognized the independence of Finland, Estonia, Latvia, Lithuania, and Poland; and it offered only formal protests to Rumania's annexation of Bessarabia.[2] Indeed, it seemingly adopted a pacific policy in its foreign relations. It renounced the "spheres of influence" and special privileges which the Tsar's government had obtained in Turkey, Persia, and China; and it made a virtual alliance with Germany in 1922 and renewed it at the time of the Locarno Treaty in 1925.[3]

At home the Russian Communists, in recognition of the principle of nationality, transformed the old Empire into a federal "Union of Soviet Socialist Republics," commonly called the U.S.S.R. This at first comprised four states, and subsequently (in 1936) eleven. Of the eleven, three were wholly or largely in Europe: Russia proper, with its capital at Moscow, and embracing the "Great Russian" nationality; Ukrainia, peopled by "Little Russians," with its capital at Kiev; and Byelorussia, or "White Russia," with its capital at Minsk. The other eight states were in Asia: Georgia, Armenia, and Azerbaijan, in Transcaucasia; Uzbekistan, Turkmenistan, and Tadzhistan, in southern Turkestan; Kirghizia, in eastern

*Marginal notes:* Communist Failure Abroad

Union of Soviet Socialist Republics

---

[1] See above, pp. 412–413, 416–417.
[2] See above, p. 457.
[3] See above, pp. 449–450.

THE SOVIET UNION
IN EUROPE,
1936

TERRITORIES SURRENDERED BY
SOVIET RUSSIA DURING AND AFTER
WORLD WAR I

500 MILES

TRM

Turkestan; and Kazakhistan, stretching through northern Turkestan and southwestern Siberia from the Caspian Sea to Mongolia. Of the eleven, the Russian state was by far the largest and most important; it contained nearly two-thirds of the population and three-fourths of the area of the entire Union. Regardless of size, nevertheless, each of the states was treated as an entity and pledged to accord cultural rights to national minorities within its borders.

The Communist dictatorship functioned under a constitution, which was first adopted in 1918, and revised and expanded in 1923 and again in 1936. Nominally, it was "democratic." Local soviets chose deputies to regional soviets, and these were represented in Congresses of Soviets for the several federated states and also in the All-Union Congress of Soviets for the entire federation. The All-Union Congress, which in theory was the supreme **"Democratic" Constitution and Communist Party Control** governing body of the U.S.S.R., consisted of about two thousand delegates thus indirectly chosen by the majority of the people. The All-Union Congress, however, was too large and unwieldy to exercise real power. Its actual functions were to assemble once in two years, to listen to reports, to ratify acts of government, and to elect a Central Committee to which the cabinet—the Council of People's Commissars—was supposedly responsible.

The organization of the Communist party resembled that of the Union's, with local and regional soviets, with central Congress, Executive Committee, and Council. Each state might enact laws concerning matters of local justice, health, and education, but the Union might annul any state legislation at variance with its own.

In practice, the "democracy" of Communist government, whether of the Union or of its federated states, was a sham. Certain categories of citizens were expressly disfranchised; and for the rest the indirect and highly complex system of voting was so arranged as to discriminate against the peasant majority of the country and in favor of the working-class minority of the cities. But the basic check on any real democracy was the privileged monopolistic position of the Communist party.

No political party other than the Communist might exist in the U.S.S.R., and no person might belong to the Communist party unless he avowed an unquestioning faith in the principles of Marx and Lenin, promised strict obedience to party discipline, and proved his sincerity and zeal during a probationary period. Numerically the party was small. At first it was almost infinitesimal, and, though it gradually grew, it had in 1939 only one and a half million members and less than a million "probationers," out of a total population of 170 million—only about one and a half per cent. And of this very slight fraction, over two-thirds were urban workmen. Peasants (still the large majority of the nation) constituted less than a fifth of the Communist party, and professional men less than a seventh.

The organization of the Communist party resembled that of the Union. Party "cells," in factories, offices, and villages, were represented in regional committees, which sent deputies to an All-Union Party Congress, which in turn elected a Central Committee, with its small supreme "Politburo." This Politburo proposed the major policies and utilized the party machinery to insure their adoption and enforcement by the government. In practice, the party completely dominated the government.

The Communist party was the only group which could put up candidates for government office. It alone had the means of enforcing its will and silencing opposition. It controlled the "red army." It directed a drastic censorship of the press and of public meetings. It had an extraordinary tribunal for the summary trial and execution of its opponents.

The Cheka, as this tribunal was originally styled, put to death some 50,000 persons prior to 1922. Though it was then formally abolished, it was revived the next year, under the initials OGPU, as a "third section of the police," with a staff of 45,000 agents. Under either title, it might arbitrarily seize, imprison, exile, or sentence to death any persons suspected of "counter-revolutionary" (that is, anti-Communist) tendencies in politics or economics. "Shooting," said one of the party leaders, "is the highest measure of social defense." And year after year, thousands were imprisoned without any hearing and other thousands were shot without any public trial. The victims included not only outright and suspected opponents of the regime but also professed Communists who failed to follow the "party line" or lost favor with the dictator.

For there was a supreme dictator—a man who, through his personal influence and with the aid of revolutionary tribunal, red army, censorship, and party discipline, could actually rule as few despots in history have been able to rule. He had to have the support of a compact group, such as the core of the Communist party provided, but, once **Dictators** assured of this, he was in a position to make his will **Lenin and** prevail throughout the huge Russian domain. **Stalin**

First the dictator was Lenin, who held the two posts of President of the Council of Commissars in the government and President of the Politburo in the party. By 1922, however, Lenin was suffering grievously from overwork; he was partially paralyzed and beginning to lose the power of speech. Whereupon ensued a bitter rivalry for the succession between Trotsky, the Commissar of War in the government, and Stalin, the secretary of the Central Committee of the party. Gradually the latter gained the support of the party, which meant the control of the government, so that, shortly after Lenin's death in 1924, Stalin became the acknowledged dictator. Trotsky was immediately dismissed from the Commissariat of War; in 1927 he was expelled from the Communist party; in 1928 he was banished to Turkestan; and in 1929, in danger of his life, he fled abroad.[1] Stalin did not directly preside over the government. He was content to remain as secretary of the Central Committee of the Communist party and chief member of its Politburo, and from these party-posts to exercise his virtual dictatorship over the country.

The avowed central purpose of the Communist dictatorship, whether of Lenin or of Stalin, was to realize in Russia the material and economic millennium promised to the "toiling masses" by Karl Marx. Capitalism would be destroyed. The profit-making motive would be removed. Russian society, instead of comprising a wealthy minority and a poverty-stricken majority, would consist of a single class, all of whose members would enjoy the fruits of their labor and a consequent high standard of living.

To achieve this purpose, a variety of expedients were tried. At first, in 1918, a "war communism" was decreed. Private property was confiscated. Debts, both domestic and **War** foreign, were cancelled. Factories and land were "so- **Communism** cialized"; and a gigantic system of state barter was introduced, whereby the government financed the industries, frequently in kind, while these delivered their products to the state for distribution to other industries, to the countryside, and to the

[1] He was assassinated by a Communist agent at Mexico City in 1940.

army. But the barter system, unworkable in itself, and particularly handicapped by current disorders and civil war, led to a catastrophic decline in production and consumption. Production of large-scale industry dropped in 1920 to twelve per cent of its pre-war level. Net output of coal fell to zero in 1921. Agricultural production declined by a third, and the rationing and distribution of the remainder encountered manifold difficulties. The results in city and country were frightful. Forty million persons suffered from malnutrition and at least five million starved to death. Millions more would doubtless have perished but for the arrival of foreign relief expeditions.[1]

Faced with an impossible situation, Lenin abruptly called a halt on "war communism" in the spring of 1921 and substituted a "new economic policy"—the so-called NEP. This **New Economic Policy** permitted peasants to trade for profit in the open market after turning over a specified percentage of their produce to the government. It also permitted private industry, except that socialization would be retained for banking, transport, and certain large manufacturing establishments. Lenin called it "a partial return to capitalism."

The NEP improved matters somewhat. In 1926–1927 the gross industrial production regained the level of 1913, though the production of iron ore was still only half of what it had then been, and grain production was also below the 1913 level. What improvement there was, however, was along capitalistic, rather than socialistic, lines. It gave a degree of prosperity to independent peasants and private industrialists, the very elements that were apt to be most hostile to Communism and the Communist party.

Consequently, the Communist dictatorship, if it was to remain in power, had to replace the semi-capitalistic NEP with some other policy. On just what this should be, there was protracted and bitter debate in the Communist party and especially within the Politburo. At length, when Stalin was firmly established as **Bureaucratic State Socialism** Lenin's successor, he imposed a system of bureaucratic state socialism, involving a forced advance of industrialization and collective farming through a series of five-year plans. The first of these was put into effect from 1928 to 1933. The production of coal was increased from 42 million tons to 77 million; pig iron, from four million tons to

---

[1] The most notable of these was the American, headed by Herbert Hoover.

seven million; petroleum, from 88 million barrels to 150 million. Besides, new blast furnaces, automobile and tractor plants, and machine-shops were erected, and the supply of electric power was almost tripled. Much progress was made, moreover, in socializing and mechanizing agriculture. More than 200,000 "collective farms" were organized and put into socialized operation.[1] The share of the country's grain production from this type of farming was raised much above the two per cent of 1928, though it fell considerably short of the forty per cent contemplated by the first five-year plan.

From 1933 to 1938 a second five-year plan still further increased the output of coal, iron, petroleum, electric power, and the socialization of agriculture. It also put new emphasis on the improvement of internal transportation and on the manufacture of goods for popular consumption. There followed a third five-year plan, with stress on preparedness for war.

Altogether, under the "state socialism" of Stalin, with its five-year plans, Russia became a more industrialized country than formerly. By 1938 it had advanced to fourth place among the nations of the world in coal production, while it was surpassed only by the United States in the production of iron, steel, and petroleum. At the same time, its private farming was being almost wholly supplanted by socialized collective farming, and it was producing twice as much wheat as the United States, its nearest competitor.

Yet there was not a corresponding rise in the standard of living for the ordinary workman or peasant, nor was there an attainment of promised equality in a "classless" society. The bulk of the peasantry and a majority of the artisans were essentially slaves of the state. What they received from the state in the way of wages hardly sufficed to buy bare necessities, let alone luxuries. There was, moreover, a serious shortage of consumer's goods; and there was inequality of wages. "Equality," as Stalin cynically remarked in 1934, was "a petty bourgeois ideal." Actually, Communist Russia had what amounted to privileged classes in its high government officials, its army officers, its party members, and its bureaucracy.

[1] There was a good deal of resistance from the independent and relatively well-to-do class of peasants known as "kulaks," and many of these, especially in Ukrainia, were "liquidated."

A steady growth of bureaucracy, with special honors and emoluments, was a striking feature of Stalin's dictatorship and his planned economy. By 1939, according to a report submitted by Molotov to the party congress, the bureaucracy numbered close to a million at the top level, about five million at intermediate levels, and five and a half million at the lower level—a total of over eleven million. These, under the rule of Stalin and his Politburo and the scrutiny of OGPU and militant party members, directed everything in the Soviet Union.

Mass propaganda was a prime means which the Communist dictatorship employed to buttress the socialization of the country and to keep itself in power. From the outset it banned **Propaganda** any education or propaganda in Russia which might have purposes at variance with its own. Dissident political groups were dissolved, and the dissemination of their ideas was prohibited and rigorously penalized. Newspapers multiplied in Russia under the Soviet regime, but only approved Communist opinions might be expressed in them. Radios and cinemas spread rapidly, but they too might not be agencies of "reaction." The universities and learned societies of Tsarist times were retained and enlarged, but they were purged of scholars unsympathetic with Communism and newly staffed with persons willing to interpret their subjects according to the "party line." Museums and art galleries and theaters were kept open, and the common people were encouraged to attend them; so as not to cripple them, they were permitted to retain many of their former officials and actors but these were scrupulously watched for any overt hostility to the new order.

The Communist dictatorship was particularly determined to counteract religious influence. The Communist leaders, being **Anti-Religious Campaign** Marxian in philosophy and therefore dogmatically materialist, were not merely indifferent but actively antagonistic to all supernatural religion. To them, historic Christianity of every form was superstitious and worse: it was an instrument of reaction, an "opiate of the people." As early as January 1918 the Communist dictatorship decreed the separation of church and state in Russia, the confiscation of all church property, and the suppression of all church schools. Clergymen were disfranchised, and during the ensuing years, as the dictatorship strengthened its hold on the country, the Orthodox Church and all the other Christian bodies—and Judaism and Islam like-wise—were reduced to the status of barely tolerated private cults. Many clergymen were exiled or put to death. Many church edifices were transformed into national museums or recreational centers. Public teaching of religion was forbidden. While "groups of believers" were empowered in 1929 to contract with the government for the use of church buildings for exclusive purposes of worship, they were estopped from any other religious activity.

The government, while curbing Christianity, gave free rein and active encouragement to atheistic propaganda. A militant "Society of the Godless" arose and throve, establishing permanent exhibitions of anti-religious paintings and cartoons, holding frequent demonstrations, and conducting a systematic campaign of vituperation against priests and of jeering at religious rites and beliefs. To the younger generation of the Russian masses, the so-called "anti-religious front" of the Communist party and the Society of the Godless mainly addressed themselves, and with much success. The older generation was less affected; many of them persevered in their habitual Christian worship. But with the younger generation cut off from Christian religious instruction and simultaneously exposed to the unrestrained counter-propaganda of atheism, the Communist dictatorship had reason for being optimistic about the outcome. It would be miraculous if in the long run historic religion could impede the fulfilment of the Soviet program, and the only miracles in which the Communist put much stock were those of modern technology.

Communism was a kind of religion itself. It was not purely an economic program or a set of political principles. It had a dogmatic philosophy. It promised a millennium—one, to be sure, that was material and secular, but one that was as emotionally attractive as it was problematical. And it inspired its devotees with a faith and an ardor transcending ordinary human experience. Not since the Jacobinism of the French Revolution had there been such an all-compelling non-supernatural religion as was this Russian Communism of the twentieth century. Like the French Jacobins, the Russian Communists evinced the faith within them by a wealth of symbolism and a fever of missionary zeal. They paraded red flags, sang proletarian anthems, addressed one another as comrade, and raised Marx and Lenin to the stature of divinities.

*Making Materialistic Communism a "Religion"*

The city of St. Petersburg, which had been patriotically re-christened during the World War as Petrograd, was renamed Leningrad; and the town of Tsaritsyn, on the Volga, was renamed Stalingrad. In the central "Red Square" of the capital city of Moscow was enshrined in 1924 the embalmed body of Lenin as a perpetual object of public worship. In workmen's tenements and peasants' cottages, lithographs of Lenin and Marx and Stalin were hung, like icons, in the midst of customary candles. The religion of Communism was formal, but it was also very serious and very intolerant.

If Communism was a substitute for other religions, its foremost missionary agency was the Communist party. It eagerly preached the new dispensation throughout the Soviet Union, laboring among the masses and striving particularly to convert the rising generation. It organized a "Communist League of Youth," and for younger children an association of "Communist Pioneers."

In furtherance of its aims, the dictatorship promoted popular education. Elementary schools were rapidly multiplied in town and country, always under strict governmental control and always with teachers and textbooks of Communist sympathies. In 1931 the central government decreed that every child within the Soviet Union must attend a primary Communist school for at least four years, and in 1933 a supplementary decree lengthened the period of compulsory attendance to seven years. For the maintenance and extension of such schools, ever heavier charges were made on the budgets of localities as well as on that of the state. By 1939 Soviet Russia was becoming literate, and able to read, as well as to hear, Communist propaganda.

Another agency of Communist propaganda, as well as of national might, was the Red Army. This had originally been re-

**Red Army** cruited by Trotsky and had been greatly enlarged by him during the trying days of 1918–1920. After the defeat of the "white armies" and the cessation of foreign intervention, the Red Army had been largely demobilized, and Trotsky's scheme for a well-organized professional army, with a territorial militia, was not immediately realized because of shortage of funds. Under Trotsky's successor, however, a decree of 1925 provided for a permanent Red Army on the basis of compulsory military training for all able-bodied men between the ages of nineteen and forty. Practically, a selection was made from those liable to serve in the army, both in order to save expense and in order to assure a preponderance of confirmed Communists. By 1935 the Red Army of the Soviet Union was larger than the army of pre-war Germany. About three-fourths of the officers were members of the Communist party or of its affiliated "League of Youth." And the Soviet government's expenditure on army surpassed its expenditure on education.

The revised constitution which was prepared under Stalin's auspices in 1936 was widely advertised as insuring democracy and personal liberty within the Soviet Union. It did provide for a bicameral parliament (or Council)—one chamber popularly elected, and the other representing the several nationalities—but it left intact the unique position of the small Communist party and the practical domination of the chief of the Politburo; and its pledges of personal liberty were purely verbal. Not only did the dictatorship continue ruthlessly to repress any opposition or dissent, but it carried on a veritable reign of terror **Purges** against "foreign influence" and a systematic purge of the Communist party itself. Charges ranged from sabotage to treason, and court trials, when held, were farcical.

Out of 71 individuals elected to the party's central committee in 1934, only 26 were left in 1939—nine had been certainly executed, twelve had been declared "enemies of the people" and probably executed, and 24 had "disappeared"; and out of 68 alternates chosen in 1934, all but nine were "liquidated." At the same time a considerable number of high army officers were put to death, while the Communist party was purged of almost a fourth of its members and over a half of its "probationers." Apparently Stalin had less faith in the emancipating principles of Communism than fear for his own despotic power. At any rate he was now undisputed master throughout the U.S.S.R. and ready to embark on an ambitious expansion abroad.

## 2. FASCIST DICTATORSHIP IN ITALY

At the close of the World War, Italy seemed to be committed, in common with other nations of central and western Europe, to the perfecting of democratic institutions. In fact, however, Italy was sorely beset with post-war difficulties, more so than any of the other Allies (except Russia). Economic conditions were bad. The country was relatively poor, its industry and trade were disorganized, its agriculture was stagnant, and in the cities unemployment was rife. Public indebtedness had been vastly increased by the war, and post-war budgets showed ever bigger deficits.

**Economic Difficulties and Political Instability**

Such conditions invited a resurgence of Marxian socialism, with its left wing of revolutionary syndicalism. It was newly inspired and rendered more extreme by the example of Lenin and his "dictatorship of the proletariat" in Russia; and the plight of urban workmen in Italy, particularly in the north, afforded to its apostles a favorable seed-ground for their propaganda. Italian Socialists, in the general election of November 1919, secured 156 seats in the Chamber of Deputies (out of a total of 574), and, while they demonstrated in the Chamber against the existing government, they took "direct action" outside parliament against the existing economic and social order. They conducted strikes. They committed sabotage. In some instances they appropriated industrial plants and attempted to operate them.

Another movement, not at all revolutionary in purpose but very troublesome to the government, gathered headway at the same time. This was the rise of a Catholic political party, the so-called Popular party, headed by a Sicilian priest, Luigi Sturzo, and supported by Catholic intellectuals who wished to counteract the traditional hostility of the Liberal regime, and by Catholic peasants who were sympathetic with the party's program of democratic social reform, especially with its project of distributing large landed estates among peasant proprietors. In the election of November 1919, the Popular party secured 101 seats in the Chamber.

Against the Socialists on one side and the Populists on the other, both with fairly well-defined purposes, the middle-class Liberal majority in the Italian parliament could present no united front. Indeed, the factionalism which had characterized Liberal groups in Italy before the war reappeared in an acute form just at the time when unity and firmness were most needed. In June 1920 the veteran Liberal politician Giolitti contrived to form his fourth ministry.[1] He was an old man, however, and either unable or unwilling to press for any real social reform or to employ armed force against lawlessness and disorder. Internal troubles reached

[1] On Giolitti and his earlier ministries, see above, p. 127.

a zenith in the winter of 1920–1921. While Socialist extremists, in imitation of the Russian Communists, warred on capitalists, set up "revolutionary tribunals," and armed themselves as "red guards," while strikes paralyzed the metal industries, the railways, and even agriculture, the government remained irresolute and supine.

In April 1921 Giolitti dissolved parliament and appealed to the country. The ensuing elections only emphasized the radical differences of purpose and method among Italians. The Socialist representation in the Chamber was cut from 156 to 122, but alongside the Socialists appeared a definitely Communist party with 16 representatives. The Populists increased their representation to 107, but a new nationalist group, the Fascist, obtained 35 seats. Liberals were now a quarrelsome minority. In June 1921 Giolitti resigned, but the premiers who succeeded him were mediocre and apparently impotent to halt the growing violence of Communists and Fascists.

The Fascists had abler leadership and larger popular following than the Communists. The latter were becoming too extreme for the majority of Socialists, and they had no leaders of outstanding ability or determination. The Fascists, on the other hand, appeared to a rapidly growing number of Italians as the one bulwark against national disintegration and social chaos, and in Mussolini they possessed a leader both ambitious and unscrupulous.

Benito Mussolini (born in 1883) had been identified during most of his life with left-wing Marxian socialism. His father, a blacksmith, had been a vehement revolutionary and anti-Catholic before him, and he himself had joined the **Mussolini** Socialist party in his late teens while he was studying in a normal school. For a time he lived in Switzerland, engaging in Socialist journalism and organizing Socialist trade unions. Expelled from one canton after another and eventually from the Swiss Confederation, he was patriotic enough to return to Italy for required military training, but his subsequent participation in Socialist agitation cost him an imprisonment in 1908. Shortly afterwards, he betook himself to Trent (then in Austria), where he edited a newspaper in support both of revolutionary socialism and of Italian irredentism, until the Austrian government suppressed the paper and expelled the editor. Returning to Italy once more,

Mussolini espoused revolutionary syndicalism, denounced parliamentary government, and lauded Sorel's advocacy of violence and Nietzsche's plea for the "superman." [1] For opposing the Tripolitan War of 1911–1912, he was imprisoned for five months. This made him a hero in Socialist circles, and at the end of 1912 he became editor of the official organ of the Italian Socialist party.

Mussolini's break with the Socialist party began over the question of participation in the World War. The majority of the party leaders opposed participation, while Mussolini favored it. He argued that Italy was a "proletarian nation," committed by the doctrine of class-conflict to war against the "capitalist nation" of Austria-Hungary, and that the surest way of converting the Italian masses to Socialism was to identify it with a national cause. Forced out of the editorship of the official Socialist newspaper, he established at Milan a "National Socialist" journal of his own, through whose pages he conducted a campaign first for Italy's participation in the war and then for working-class cooperation in winning the war. In 1915 he joined the army and served in the trenches as private and corporal until wounded in 1917. Then, back on his newspaper, he zealously combated pacifism.

For a time Mussolini seemed to think that he could best serve his vaulting personal ambition by winning control of the Marxian movement in Italy and utilizing its rising tide to carry him to a dictatorship similar to Lenin's in Russia. But the large majority of Italian Socialists refused to follow him; and with the termination of the war and the demobilization of the Italian army he found he could make greater headway by attacking Marxian socialism and the existing Liberal government, which appeared unable to cope with economic unrest and violence or to satisfy popular demands for the annexation of Fiume. In this way he enlisted the support of a growing number of ex-soldiers, property owners, and youthful intellectuals; and for his new movement, which he called "Fascism," he borrowed Communist methods.

The word "Fascism" was derived from the "fascio" (or "club") which Mussolini organized among his followers at Milan in **Fascist Movement** March 1919 for the general purpose of propagating his brand of nationalism and for the specific purpose of fighting Communists. During the next two years, a network of similar "clubs" (or "fasci") was spread over the

[1] On Sorel, see above, pp. 219–220, and on Nietzsche, see above, pp. 209–210.

industrial towns of Italy, and the members indulged in counter-violence against the "reds." In April 1921 some 35 Fascists, together with ten Nationalist disciples of D'Annunzio, were elected to the Chamber of Deputies, and in November of the same year the Fascist political party was definitely constituted with a graded hierarchy headed of course by Mussolini, with a rigid discipline, and with a wealth of symbolism and ceremonial. As Garibaldi's volunteers had worn red shirts, so Mussolini's distinguished themselves with black shirts, and as the word Fascist suggested not only the "fasci" of modern Italy but also the "fasces" which officials of the ancient Roman Republic had borne, so Fascism was symbolized by a bundle of rods enclosing a battle axe, and Fascists saluted their chief—"Il Duce"—with the outstretched hand of the old Roman salute.

With mounting enthusiasm and violence and with perfecting organization and resolution, the Fascist movement gathered momentum rapidly during 1921–1922. Simultaneously, the opposing groups in Italy weakened. Giolitti, the most famous of the Liberal leaders, was in his eighties and widely distrusted. The Socialist party lacked competent leadership and at its congress in 1922 it split on the question of cooperation with the Communists. The Communists were a sect, rather than a national party, and they too lacked resourceful leadership. The Popular (or Catholic) party, despite the endeavors of its chief, Sturzo, was also disintegrating: its left wing was too radical to collaborate successfully with the Liberals; its right wing was drawn toward Fascism; and the Pope was becoming sceptical of the official participation of Catholics in Italian politics and distrustful of Sturzo.

In October 1922 the Fascists held a congress at Naples. Forty thousand of them paraded the streets in military formation, and Mussolini, in a grandiloquent speech, declared that "either the government will be given to us or we shall march on Rome." On October 27 the Liberal premier resigned, and the Fascist "army" at Naples moved on Rome. The regular army stood **Fascists** aside, and King Victor Emmanuel III, without a gov- **in Power** ernment and with Fascist fighting men pouring into the capital, sent for Mussolini and asked him to form a ministry.

Thus, at the end of October 1922, Mussolini became prime minister of Italy. From the frightened parliament he at once obtained a grant of dictatorial powers for a year, and then proceeded, on the one hand, to extend and consolidate the Fascist organization throughout the country, and, on the other, to conduct and reform the public administration. With his harsh voice and crisp sentences, with his flashing eyes and magnificent scowl, with his Napoleonic bearing, he mightily impressed the nation, as well as King and parliament; and his energy and attention to details soon produced effects. Order was restored throughout the country. Strikes were suppressed and Socialist agitators punished. Economies were introduced into government. Public works were undertaken and unemployment relieved.

In November 1923, Mussolini persuaded parliament, despite opposition from Socialist and Populist members and from some Liberals, to enact an essentially revolutionary electoral law. Thereby, in the future, the political party securing a plurality of votes in the general election would be entitled to two-thirds of the seats in the Chamber of Deputies, while the remaining third would be distributed among the other parties on a proportional basis. The first election under the new arrangement was held in April 1924. The Fascists, better organized than their rivals and freer to exercise compulsion, obtained four and a half million votes out of a total of seven and a half million and therefore appropriated two-thirds of the seats in the Chamber, leaving the combined Socialists, Populists, and Liberals in a helpless minority.

The kidnapping and murder of a Socialist leader by Fascists, just after the assembling of the new Chamber, temporarily filled many Italians with mingled fear and indignation, and for a time in 1924 the anti-Fascist minority in the Chamber threatened to form a compact group and make some trouble for the Fascist government. Mussolini, however, disclaimed any responsibility for the crime, and by strict censorship of the press and forceful police measures he managed to weather the storm. A reign of terror ensued. Political opponents were imprisoned or intimidated, and critics were silenced. Sturzo escaped into exile, together with some Socialists leaders and a number of Liberals. Others, especially those most nationalistically inclined, espoused Fascism, and still others merely retired into private life and set a seal on their lips. By the end of 1924 Italy was definitely resigned to a dictatorship of Mussolini and the Fascists.

By enactments from 1925 to 1928 the Fascist majority in parliament empowered the government to dismiss "disloyal" officials, to dissolve all political parties except the Fascist, to abolish Freemasonry and all other secret societies, to set up a tribunal of summary justice for the trial of political offenders, to confiscate the property of "seditious" persons, to suppress seditious newspapers, and to centralize the administration. Mussolini, as prime minister, was authorized to initiate all legislation, and offenses against his person were made direfully punishable. The local prefects, whose powers were strengthened, were to be directly responsible to him, and he would appoint governors (or podestàs) of cities and villages. To cap the climax, the popular election of members of parliament was transformed, by a law of 1928, into a mere plebiscite; henceforth, the electorate would simply vote yes or no on a list of candidates approved by the Fascist party. Political democracy, as previously practiced in Italy, was at an end, and liberty was sharply abridged.

Formally, the central Italian government continued to be "constitutional." The King was still the nominal sovereign. The Parliament, composed of Senate and Chamber of Deputies, was still the legal law-making body; and to it was still responsible the ministry (or cabinet). Actually, however, the whole government was dominated by the party organization of the Fascists, just as the contemporary Soviet government of Russia was controlled by a single Communist party. And in Italy, as in Russia, the dictatorial party comprised a small minority of the population. **"Constitutional" Government and Fascist Party Control**

In 1932—ten years after the "March on Rome"—the Fascist party numbered about a million and a quarter. No person was admitted to it unless he had demonstrated his loyalty to its principles and undergone preliminary training. In 1933, out of 600,000 applicants for membership in the party, 200,000 were accepted. The members of the party were distributed among some 10,000 local "fasci," which were federated by provinces and ultimately directed by the party's Grand Council. This Council, as reconstituted in 1928, included the leaders of the "March on Rome," the general secretary and certain other officials of the party, and representatives of Fascist corporations, about twenty persons in all.

The chairman of the Grand Council of the Fascist party was

prime minister of the country. The Council not only ruled the party and shaped its policies, but also nominated candidates for parliament, and inasmuch as no other party existed after 1928 to make nominations or to conduct organized campaigns against Fascist nominees, all the members of parliament were practically certain to be members of the Fascist party, quite obedient to the dictates of the Grand Council. To make doubly sure of the supremacy of the party's Council over the state parliament, it was further provided in 1928 that the Council must be consulted on all matters affecting the constitution, the royal succession, the powers of the prime minister, the relations between church and state, and the ratification of treaties involving territorial changes. And to enforce its will throughout the country, the Grand Council had at its disposal a special body of Fascist militia and a special tribunal of Fascist magistrates.

The machinery of the Fascist party and that of the Italian state were thus closely interlocked, and the supreme manipulator of both was Mussolini, "Il Duce." He was chairman of the Grand Council, and through its discipline, its militia, and its tribunal he was master of parliament and the country at large. He was also prime minister of the state, initiating legislation, appointing officials, advising the King, and directing the whole national administration. No statesman since Napoleon, except Lenin and his successor in Russia, had exercised such wide and dictatorial powers.

Mussolini and his fellow Fascists in Italy sought to gain the support of the working classes by undertaking social reform and substituting a "corporate state" for the previous "liberal state." Individualism would be frowned upon, and the differences between capital and labor minimized. With these ends in view, an enactment of 1926 abolished non-Fascist trade unions, prohibited strikes and lockouts, and at the same time legalized thirteen "syndicates" (six of employers, six of employees, and one of professional men), under whose joint auspices special tribunals should be established for the settlement of labor disputes. In 1927 a "charter of labor" was promulgated: while guaranteeing private property and encouraging private initiative, it forbade employers to work their men more than eight hours a day or six days a week or to discharge them on the score of illness or military service; it obliged employers to contribute

**"Corporate State"**

to the insurance of their men against illness, accidents, old age, and unemployment; and it empowered the labor corporations to train apprentices and maintain employment bureaus. In 1928 the electoral law entrusted the thirteen syndicates with political functions; each would nominate parliamentary candidates to be passed upon and approved by the Grand Council of the Fascist party before a general election. In 1930 the thirteen syndicates were reformed and coordinated as "corporations" under a general Fascist Confederation of Industry, headed by a state Minister of Corporations. In 1934 a National Council was created of deputies from the various corporations in order immediately to advise parliament on economic and social legislation and eventually to supplant parliament as the law-making body of the realm.

Mussolini and his fellow Fascists sought also to secure the support of the Catholic masses by reversing the anti-clerical policies which Liberal governments had pursued since the time of Cavour and reaching a friendly agreement with the papacy on the "Roman question." To Mussolini's overtures, Pope Pius XI responded sympathetically; he was no advocate of Fascism but he perceived an advantage to the Church in ending the conflict which since 1870 had forced Italians to choose between loyalty to their national state and obedience to their religious head.[1] Consequently, the treaty of the Lateran was concluded in 1929. Italy agreed to the sovereignty of the Pope within a small but independent Papal State, embracing the Vatican and St. Peter's (the so-called Vatican City) and also the estate of Castel Gandolfo outside Rome. In return the Pope recognized the Kingdom of Italy, surrendered his claims to the greater part of Rome, and promised to "remain extraneous to all temporal disputes between nations and to international congresses convoked for the settlement of such disputes unless the contending parties make a joint appeal to his mission of peace."

*Lateran Treaty and Concordat with Pope*

Simultaneously with the signing of the Lateran Treaty, a financial agreement and a concordat were concluded between the papacy and the Italian government. The financial agreement provided for the payment to the Pope of a sum of about 100 million dollars in lieu of the annual appropriations which Italy had been making as indemnity for the seizure of Rome in 1870 but which

[1] On the conflict between papacy and Italian government, see above, pp. 126, 246.

the papacy had hitherto refused to accept. The concordat, on the other hand, provided for the future relations of church and state in Italy. The Pope would appoint all bishops in Italy, but before doing so he would communicate each nomination to the Italian government "in order to be sure that the latter has no objection from a political standpoint." The state would continue to pay the salaries of bishops and priests, and bishops, before taking office, must swear loyalty to the state, the King, and the government. Religious instruction would be given in the state schools by persons approved by the church. The church might engage in popular propaganda of a religious nature but not in political activity, and no ecclesiastic might belong to any political party.

This sensational termination of the long feud between the Italian state and the Catholic Church was acclaimed alike by devout Catholics and by enthusiastic Fascists. Some friction continued, nevertheless. In 1931 the dissolution of Catholic clubs by the Fascist dictatorship, and in 1938 its promulgation of anti-Semitic decrees, evoked vigorous protests from the Pope.

The Fascist regime concerned itself with popular education. The number of schools was increased, and the laws providing for **Fascist** compulsory attendance were more rigorously enforced. **Enter-** In 1921, just before Mussolini took office, some three **prises** million children were attending elementary schools in Italy; in 1935, there were four and a half million. In 1921 the percentage of illiteracy in the country as a whole was over a fourth; in 1935 it was less than a fifth, and in northern Italy it was fast reaching zero. The great stress in the schools was on training for Fascist citizenship. The teachers were Fascist in sympathy; and Fascist in principle and aim were the curricula and textbooks. For many children, moreover, Fascist training in the schools was supplemented by similar training in the party's auxiliary organization of youth. For all young men, furthermore, it was supplemented by intensive training in the army, which of course was Fascist in its command and conduct. The Fascist party might be relatively small, but the younger generation of the Italian nation was being educated in Fascism.

Nationalism was emphasized and extolled by Mussolini and his fellow Fascists. Italians were ceaselessly reminded of their past greatness and future destiny as a nation. For patriotic reasons as well as to provide work for men otherwise unemployed, the government fostered a variety of public works. Pride in the past was stimulated by repairing ancient monuments, unearthing and reconstructing the old Roman forum, and erecting memorials to Julius Cæsar and Augustus. Faith in the future was aroused by a host of "modern improvements." The railways were refurbished. Palatial steamships were built for transoceanic service, and the Italian merchant marine, which in 1913 had been hardly a fourth as large as Germany's, or a half of France's, reached in 1935 a tonnage almost equal to either the French or the German. New cable lines were laid. The radio industry was fostered. Airplanes were manufactured and increasingly utilized for passenger and mail service throughout the country. Agricultural works were also undertaken, involving extensive reforestation and the reclamation of swamp lands. Industrially, Italy's lack of coal and iron was partially compensated for by a remarkable development of hydroelectric power, which by 1935 represented a horsepower of almost five million, more than twice the developed water power of any other country.

As far as might be, economic self-sufficiency (or, in other words, economic nationalism) was a Fascist policy and goal. In keeping with it were the hydroelectric developments, the agricultural works, and the national merchant marine. In keeping with it, likewise, were the new national syndicates, the heightening of previous protective tariffs, and the drastic regulation of banking and currency.

Militarism was another conspicuous feature of Fascist Italy. Not only was the army kept on the basis of universal compulsory service, but it was paraded much more frequently in public view and lauded by Mussolini more often and more ostentatiously. The Italian navy was increased, and also the air service of both army and navy.

Imperialism was another aspect of Fascist thought and ambition. The Italian population was growing faster than that of most other European countries. Already it was surpassing the French, and to Mussolini and other patriots it required a commensurate colonial expansion. Hence Mussolini, who as a Socialist had decried the seizure of African territory in 1911, now as a Fascist loudly championed a greater imperial domain for Italy.

For all the enterprises of the Fascist government in Italy— military, naval, and imperial, economic, educational, and ecclesiastical—expenditure was immensely increased. Yet, despite general post-war depression and special economic difficulties in Italy, the increase of expenditure and taxation was made without serious popular murmuring. In appearance, the Fascist dictatorship was becoming solidly entrenched in Italy.

### 3. NAZI DICTATORSHIP IN GERMANY

The German Republic, as established in 1919, was a liberal democracy, supported by Socialists, Catholic Centrists, and Democrats, and, after 1923, by the People's party of Gustav Stresemann. For ten years it seemed to be gathering strength and surmounting the grave economic difficulties which beset it. There was, to be sure, a good deal of dissension within the coalition of governing parties, and a good deal of opposition from without. At the extreme Left, the Republic was denounced by a Communist party, patterned after Russia's and led by Ernst Thälmann. At the extreme Right, it was criticized and reprobated by a Nationalist party of ultra-conservatives who wanted to restore the Hohenzollern monarchy. And it was assailed with peculiar bitterness and violence by the group of National Socialists (or Nazis) which gathered about the fanatical demagogue Adolf Hitler.[1] Yet in the general election of 1928 the Republican coalition polled twenty-three million votes, while the combined opposition polled only eight million.

What eventually created havoc for the democratic Republic and its supporters was the economic depression which began in **Economic Crisis of 1929** 1929. Business "prosperity," which had been artificially stimulated for several years by foreign loans and which had been accompanied by industrial overproduction and financial speculation, came to an abrupt halt. There was disappearance or diminution of profits for middle-class persons as well as for landlords and peasants. For workmen there was decline of wages and rise of unemployment.

Desperately but unavailingly the government sought financial relief. Foreign loans could no longer be negotiated, and yet the Allies were exasperatingly dilatory about lightening the load of reparation payments which Germany was expected to carry. Economies in internal administration only swelled the ranks of the

[1] On the emergence of Hitler and on other developments within Germany between 1919 and 1929, see above, pp. 481–487.

unemployed. Heavier taxation only impeded the recovery of business. And the death of Stresemann in the fateful year of 1929 cost the government a capable Foreign Minister and a statesman who had linked the industrialists with the cause of the Republic. In the circumstances, the democratic majority in Germany was rapidly whittled away.

The Communist party made gains, chiefly at the expense of the Socialists. But principal gains were made by the Nazi party, which now redoubled its propaganda and its violence. To it flocked crowds of emotional youths and the bulk of the lower middle class. Even landed aristocrats of the conservative Nationalist party, though regarding Hitler as a vulgar upstart, were quite willing to climb on his bandwagon, which they fondly thought they could subsequently steer. And industrial magnates commenced to contribute money and votes to him. Altogether, a rapidly increasing part of the German electorate turned to Nazism, as Italians had turned to Fascism, to save them from Communism and to effect a "national regeneration" at home and abroad.

Early in 1930, in a desperate attempt to retrieve the fortunes of the Republic, Heinrich Brüning, a Centrist and one of the ablest men in the Reichstag, was entrusted with the **Brüning's** chancellorship. Brüning was sincere and courageous, **Chancel-** and he succeeded in bringing about a belated revision **lorship** of the reparation arrangements and the withdrawal of foreign troops from the Rhineland. Nevertheless, neither his achievements nor his abilities availed in the internal situation. The Communists assailed him and the "bourgeois" Republic, while from the opposite extreme the Nazis denounced him and the "traitorous" Republic.

Nor could Brüning take energetic measures against the extremes. He was himself a liberally minded person, conscientiously opposed to meeting violence with violence; Socialists on whom he had to rely were tender of the Communists; his more moderate supporters were tender of Nationalists; and both extremes were making dangerous inroads into the electoral strength of democratic republicanism. In vain Brüning appealed to the country in a special election of September 1930. The Communists gained over a million votes and the Nazis almost six million.

The upshot was that the Republican coalition no longer had a

dependable majority in the Reichstag. The Socialists, who held
a balance of power, remained aloof from Brüning's ministry, and
whenever they threatened to withhold parliamentary support he
had recourse to the article in the constitution which empowered
the President to govern by decree. It thus transpired that for two
years, from 1930 to 1932, the government of the German Republic
was perilously carried on by Brüning with the apparently loyal
cooperation of President von Hindenburg.

So convincing was Hindenburg's loyalty and so strong was his
hold on the country at large that Brüning and the Republican
coalition labored manfully in the spring of 1932 to ensure his
reelection to the presidency of the Republic for another term of
seven years. Against him, Hitler was the candidate of the National Socialists, and Thälmann, of the Communists. The results
seemed reassuring. Hindenburg was reelected.

Hindenburg's reelection was hailed alike by Centrists, Socialists, and Democrats as a victory for the Republic. It turned out
**Reelection** to be nothing of the kind, for Hindenburg proceeded
**of** to disappoint his republican supporters in 1932, just as
**Hindenburg** back in 1925 he had disappointed his monarchical sup-
**and Dis-** porters, only now more quickly and more utterly. There
**missal of** is little doubt that at heart the Marshal had always
**Brüning** been unsympathetic with the republican regime which he headed,
and now that he had received a new vote of popular confidence
in himself, he felt free to heed the more congenial advice of
aristocrats and conservatives like himself. These, as we know,
were chiefly identified with the Nationalist party, and they sedulously instilled in the old man—now a very old man—a fear that
Brüning was much too radical and the hope that a Nationalist
government might utilize the numerous Nazis in order to get
rid of radicals and to restore things as they had been in the "good
old days." At any rate, a month after his reelection, Hindenburg
took sudden fright at proposals for breaking up the large landed
estates in his native East Prussia and peremptorily dismissed
Brüning from the chancellorship.

In Brüning's place Hindenburg appointed Franz von Papen,
an aristocrat who had once been a member of the Center party
but who had quarreled with its democratic leaders and had left it
to ally himself with the Nationalists; and with Papen was associated a ministry of ultra-conservatives, including General Kurt

von Schleicher. The new government, though enjoying the confidence of Hindenburg and clothed by him with practically dictatorial powers, was confronted with a hostile majority in the Reichstag and with a threatening situation in the key state of Prussia, where Socialists held the premiership and commanded the police. Furthermore, it had to rely upon the backing of Hitler and the National Socialists as well as upon that of the conservative Nationalists, **Failure of Conservative Nationalists** and between the two groups were notable differences of size and divergencies of aim. The Nationalists, who constituted the government, wanted to use the Nazis for their own ends, but the Nazis, whose following was far more numerous, would tolerate the new government only as a means of enabling themselves to get into power.

In the meantime Papen and Schleicher, with the help of Nazi fury and violence, sought to remove the handicaps which beset the reactionary government. In July 1932, they executed a military *coup* against the Socialist premier and police officials in Prussia. The latter refrained from calling a general strike, such as had defeated Kapp's monarchical *coup* ten years earlier,[1] and meekly surrendered their posts, alleging in justification of their pusillanimous behavior that resistance would have aided the Communists. This collapse of the Socialists overjoyed Papen and his Nationalists, and the Nazis likewise. Then, eleven days after the *coup,* a general election was held in an effort to secure an amenable Reichstag. This effort was not so successful. Papen's party lost seats in the Reichstag, and in carrying on the administration he was more than ever dependent on the friendship of Hindenburg and the favor of Hitler.

In November 1932 Papen had Hindenburg dissolve the Reichstag again, and once more he appealed to the verdict of a general election. This time the conservative Nationalists made some gains, but they were more than offset by gains of the Communists. Disappointed, Papen resigned; and Hindenburg, still averse to turning over the government to the plebeian Hitler, appointed General von Schleicher as Chancellor. For two months longer Schleicher carried on without a Reichstag majority, in the face of open opposition from Hitler, and in the midst of secret intrigues on the part of Papen and influential landlords and busi-

[1] See above, p. 484.

ness men who were now convinced that the conservative cause could best be served through outright collaboration with the National Socialists.

This conviction was finally implanted in Hindenburg, and in January 1933 the senile President dismissed Schleicher and appointed Hitler to the chancellorship, with Papen as vice-chancellor. "And now, gentlemen," declared Marshal von Hindenburg, "forward with God!"

It was really "forward with Hitler." For Hitler was at last in power, and to the discomfiture of his opponents he was in power in accordance with the letter of the constitution.[1] His

**Hitler in Power**

government, to be sure, was not yet a unit; it represented a coalition of Nazis with conservative Nationalists. But the latter were a convenient link with Hindenburg and "respectability," and in view of their relatively small popular following they were less likely to oppose the Nazi phalanx than to be absorbed by it. The important thing was that Nazi members of the government commanded the public police as well as the private "storm troops," and thereby Hitler was enabled to suppress opposition and overawe the country. Moreover, a timely burning of the Reichstag building in Berlin was blamed upon Communists and utilized both to justify strong measures against them and to increase the popular following of the Nazis. Amidst excitement and terrorism, new elections, in March 1933, resulted favorably to the latter. Their popular vote went up to seventeen and a quarter million while that of the conservative Nationalists remained at three million. Of the other parties, only the Catholic Centrist held its own; the Socialist and the Communist both lost ground, and the Democratic and People's parties almost completely disappeared.

President von Hindenburg at once decreed that the Republican

**Third (Nazi) German Empire**

flag of black, red, and gold should be hauled down and replaced by two flags: the black, white, and red of the old Empire, and the swastika of the new nationalism. And on April 1 the Reichstag voted to delegate its powers, for a term of four years, to the Hitler government.

[1] Both the Socialists and the Centrists and also organized labor protested otherwise, but their protests were platonic. Schleicher at first was minded to defy the President, but he hesitated and presently acquiesced. Communist demonstrations against Hitler were suppressed by Nazi storm troops.

Thus the democratic German Republic formally passed away and was succeeded by what was styled the "Third German Empire"[1] and what was essentially a Nazi dictatorship.

The change was not merely one of name. It was a real break with Germany's past, not only with the liberal and democratic traditions of the Frankfurt Assembly of 1848 and the Weimar Assembly of 1919, but also with the conservative traditions of the Hohenzollern Empire from 1871 to 1918. Conservatives who helped Hitler to bring about the change hoped no doubt that it would be but a prelude to the restoration of the former Empire, but in this they were disappointed. Hitler's main backing was popular and radical rather than aristocratic and reactionary, and by means of it he was enabled to overthrow the democratic Republic and to hold conservatives in check and forestall any restoration of constitutional monarchy. The Third Empire was something new; a dictatorship, less evolutionary than revolutionary.

The revolution which inaugurated the Third Empire was attended by a great show of popular enthusiasm, skilfully worked up and exploited by propagandists of the new regime. Press, radio, and cinema were alike utilized to stir patriotic emotions and to direct them into National Socialist channels. For the same purpose was staged a rapid succession of imposing public demonstrations: brown-shirted storm troopers parading and saluting, young people singing and cheering, multitudes listening to inflammatory speeches and waving swastika flags. Such methods were usual with the Nazis, and they were developed to the full and employed with overwhelming effect under the guidance of one of Hitler's chief lieutenants, Joseph Goebbels,[2] who had a genius for showmanship and was given an official post as "Minister of Propaganda and Public Enlightenment."

[1] The "First" had been the Holy Roman Empire, from 962 to 1806; and the "Second," the Hohenzollern Empire, from 1871 to 1918.

[2] Goebbels was born in the Rhineland in 1897 of peasant and artisan stock. Undersized and afflicted from infancy with a club foot, he was rejected for army service in the World War. Endowed with a good mind and aided by scholarships, he attended several universities, eventually obtaining the Ph.D. degree from Heidelberg in 1921. He joined the National Socialist party in 1924, becoming the editor of its Berlin newspaper in 1926 and a member of the Reichstag in 1928. In 1929, as director of the party's propaganda, he found a most congenial field for his talents: his vituperative fanaticism, his cynical lying, his fondness for the spectacular, his great organizing abilities.

The hysteria of the Nazi revolution was heightened and extended by spectacular "drives" of Hitler and his aides against certain groups—notably Jews and Marxists—who were made scapegoats for Germany's misfortunes during and since the World War. On April 1, 1933, the very day on which the dictatorship was formally established, the government sponsored a nation-wide boycott against Jewish shopkeepers and professional men, and shortly afterwards it decreed that only "Aryans" (that is, German citizens who were not Jews and whose parents and grandparents were not Jews) might occupy civil or military posts or serve as judges, policemen, school teachers, or university professors. There followed a wholesale dismissal of Jews (and Christians with Jewish blood) from state institutions and public offices, an active discrimination against them in the learned professions and in business, and spasmodic assaults upon them individually and collectively. Thousands of German Jews fled abroad, and the much larger number who could not or would not flee suffered grievously in mind and estate. Such rabid anti-Semitism evoked indignation in foreign countries, but in Germany it was excused and gloried in as making for national unity and patriotic regeneration.

On May Day 1933, while the anti-Jewish "drive" was still in full vigor, Hitler's government climaxed its parallel campaign against Marxists by staging at Berlin a monster counter-demonstration of "German labor." Hundreds of thousands of Nazis paraded and saluted, sang and cheered, while Nazi storm troops cowed Communist and Socialist workmen into silence. So utterly cowed, indeed, were the latter that the government proceeded promptly and without trouble to ban all Marxian propaganda in the country, to abolish all Socialist as well as Communist trade unions and confiscate their funds, and to substitute a single labor organization, the "German Labor Front," directed and controlled by the National Socialist party.

Taking advantage of the rising popular enthusiasm for the "new Germany" and of the swift and spectacular suppression of Jews and Marxists, Hitler and his Nazi lieutenants moved next to rid themselves of possible political opposition. In May 1933 the parliament of the key state of Prussia was obliged to confer on the local premier dictatorial powers similar to those which the Reichstag had already conferred on the Imperial Chancellor, and to the new dictatorship in Prussia Hitler at once appointed his close friend and associate, Hermann Goering.[1] Simultaneously the other German states were subjected to "governors" named by Hitler and responsible to him. Moreover, leaders of the conservative Nationalist party, and likewise of the People's party, perceiving at last that they were but tails to the Nazi dog (and powerless to wag the dog), were induced to break up their respective political organizations and to accept "guest membership" in the National Socialist party. In June 1933, furthermore, the government decreed the destruction of the Socialist and Democratic parties, and early in July, through a concordat which Papen in Hitler's behalf negotiated with the Vatican, Pope Pius XI agreed to the dissolution of the Catholic Center party in return for a pledge that the Catholic Church should continue to enjoy full religious freedom in Germany. Whereupon Hitler decreed that in the Third Empire there would be but a single political party, and that the National Socialist party.

Thus, within six months of Hitler's advent to the chancellorship, he was the practical dictator of Germany. Hindenburg still remained titular "President of the Republic," but the Republic was dead and Hindenburg was dying. The living state was now the highly centralized Third Empire, and the real power in it was Hitler's. To Hitler, at once Chancellor of the Empire and leader of the sole remaining political party in Germany, had been subjected the central Reichstag, the several state governments, the entire civil and military bureaucracy, the press, the radio, the schools, and all individual liberties. A clean sweep was made of all elements who had opposed the Nazis during recent years. Not only Jews and Marxists suffered, but a large number of other German citizens. Open dissenters who were not hounded into exile were herded into "concentration camps."

By the autumn of 1933 Hitler was ready to seek a national endorsement of the Nazi revolution which he had effected, and in order to obtain the greatest possible endorsement he cleverly

---

[1] Goering, who shared with Goebbels the special confidence of Hitler, was born in Bavaria in 1893, the son of a Prussian army officer and colonial administrator. He had a brilliant record as an aviator during the World War, and his disappointment with the outcome of the war made him a temporary drug-addict and a permanent convert to National Socialism. Goering was wealthy and resourceful, and with energy and ruthlessness he combined a fondness for art and show.

availed himself of an international issue which would appeal to German patriots. At an international conference then pending at Geneva on the limitation of armaments and sponsored by the

**Buttress-**
**ing the**
**Nazi**
**Revolution**

League of Nations,[1] Hitler's representatives had proclaimed the right of Germany, under the Versailles treaty, to rearm itself fully unless the other powers should straightway reduce their armaments to the German level. In October, when the conference failed to reach any agreement about mutual disarmament or to sanction any rearmament of Germany, Hitler withdrew his delegates from the conference and announced Germany's secession from the League. If foreign nations would not recognize Germany as an equal, he said, Germany should go its own way without them. This was the issue which he presented to the German electorate. He called for popular ratification of his action in breaking with the League of Nations and simultaneously he called for the election of a new and "loyal" Reichstag.

The plebiscite and the election of the new Reichstag were held in November 1933. In the former, forty and a half million Germans voted "yes" and two million voted "no." In the latter, thirty-nine and a half million cast their ballots for the list of candidates nominated by the National Socialist party—the only party which could nominate candidates—while three and a half million ballots were "blank" or "spoiled."

With a Reichstag unanimously devoted to him, Hitler buttressed the new regime with two important constitutional laws. The first, adopted in December 1933, provided that the National Socialist party "is inseparably united with the state," and that "its regulations are determined by the Führer" (that is, by Hitler).

The second, ratified by the Reichstag in January 1934 on the anniversary of Hitler's accession to the chancellorship, formally abolished the state parliaments and transformed the several states (Prussia, Bavaria, Saxony, etc.) into mere administrative districts of the Empire, and at the same time empowered the central government to alter the imperial consitution at will.

The Third Empire, then, emerged as a National Socialist dictatorship. It was highly centralized and emphatically national. What neither the Hohenzollern Empire nor the Weimar Republic

[1] See above, pp. 454–455, and below, pp. 608–609.

had ventured to undertake—the destruction of local autonomy and the complete submerging of Prussia and the other historic German states—was now achieved.

As there was only one government in the Third Empire, so there was only one party, the National Socialist. This was splendidly organized, with headquarters at Munich in a famous "brown house," with an intricate hierarchy of departments, vocational, educational, and recreational, with a Political Bureau, with a Labor Front, with a Youth Movement, with an extraordinarily adept Propaganda Agency, with disciplinary courts of its own, and with armed forces of its own—the picked party police (the S.S.) and the more numerous storm troops (the S.A.). Like the Communist party in Russia or the Fascist party in Italy, the enrolled membership of the German Nazi party was relatively small; it was kept down by a system of careful selection and probation, and comprised, in the autumn of 1933, fewer than two million. Nevertheless, it was a militant membership, in close and manifold touch with the masses all over Germany, and disciplined and directed from above.

The dictator of the Third Empire was Adolf Hitler. This he was in virtue of his leadership of the Nazi party, of his official position as Chancellor, and of his own personal qualities. Before his advent to public office there had been a tendency to regard him either as an ignoramus incompetent to rule or as a demagogue whose vogue would be fleeting. After his advent, however, it became apparent, even to his bitterest foes and detractors, that he possessed remarkable qualifications for dictatorship: not only oratory and histrionics, but insight into popular psychology, quickness in making decisions and energy in carrying them into effect, adroitness in managing men and inspiring their confidence, and untiring application to details.

There was some danger of conflict within the National Socialist party. It had a "left" wing and a "right" wing, disposed respectively to stress or to belittle the "socialism" in the party's name and platform, and some of its leading men had rival personal ambitions. To Hitler the danger seemed acute in the spring of 1934, when the ambitious commander of the storm troops, Ernst Röhm, growing critical of the government's economic "conservatism" and indignant at its talk of reducing and reforming his command, was

*Purging the Nazi Party*

suspected of conspiring with the ex-Chancellor, General Kurt von Schleicher, to overthrow Hitler. At any rate, Hitler, in conjunction with Goebbels, Goering, and the secret police, took drastic action at the end of June 1934 to nip any such conspiracy in the bud and to terrorize the National Socialist party into unity and the country at large into obedience. Röhm and several of his aides were murdered at Munich in Hitler's presence. General von Schleicher was dragged from his home in Berlin and slain. Simultaneously, some of Papen's associates were slaughtered, and so too were certain Catholic and labor leaders. Altogether, in the "purge of 1934," several hundred persons were murdered. "Reasons of state" and of "morality" were all that Hitler would advance, and the unquestioning acceptance of his explanation clearly demonstrated the strength of the dictatorship he exercised over the party and the country.

About a month after the "purge," President and Marshal Paul von Hindenburg died on his estate in East Prussia. Then, following grandiose funeral rites on the battlefield of Tannenberg, at which Hitler was chief mourner and orator, he decreed

**Führer and Nazism**

that, subject to ratification by popular vote, he should be President as well as Chancellor under the new official title of Imperial Leader (Reichsführer). Ratification was given in a plebiscite in August 1934. Although four and a quarter million Germans voted "no," thirty-eight and a quarter million voted "yes." At last, by popular will as well as by his own, Adolf Hitler was supreme Führer, real successor of the Hohenzollerns and of Hindenburg and with far more authority than any of them.

Reinforcing the dictatorship was incessant preaching of the philosophy—one might say the religion—of National Socialism. This philosophy was essentially Fascist but more extreme and more devotional. Like Italian Fascism, it taught that people exist for the state, not the state for its people, and that the state must be national and imperial, military and expansive. Like Italian Fascism—and also like Russian Communism—its ideal was the "totalitarian state," a state which should regulate all the activities of its members, political, economic, and cultural. Likewise, after the manner of Italian Fascism and Russian Communism, its program called for an "authoritarian state," in which a single select political party would rule and from which personal dissent and class conflict would be banished.

Ostensibly it differed from Russian Communism and resembled Italian Fascism in that it aspired to a "corporate state," which would retain private property and class distinctions, while subordinating them to national welfare and making occupational groups, rather than individuals, the units of economic and political life. Like Italian Fascism, German National Socialism was the foe alike of liberalism and of Marxian socialism, and also of pacifism and internationalism and of what were deemed the traditional Christian virtues of humility, meekness, and charity. Beyond Italian Fascism went German National Socialism in respect of its distinctive doctrine of racial superiority—that the Germans, being "pure Aryans," are inherently superior in moral virtue and military prowess to all their "Slavic" and "Latin" neighbors and especially to the alien and contaminating "Semitic" Jews in their midst. Fiercer and more evangelical, too, was the ardor with which National Socialism inflamed its votaries. Mussolini had a sense of humor, but not Hitler. Fascism was ceremonial and even theatrical, but the rites of National Socialism were performed with deadly earnestness.

The exposition and inculcation of Nazi philosophy was entrusted to Alfred Rosenberg, "supervisor of the party's educational and spiritual work." [1] Rosenberg was the theorist, expounding the "gospel" and detecting "heretics" among writers, artists, university professors, and intellectuals generally. In collaboration with Goebbels, he "coordinated" with National Socialism the press throughout Germany, the radios, cinemas, and theaters, and the entire school system—the teachers and the textbooks in all educational institutions from kindergarten to university.

Some difficulty was experienced in "coordinating" the Christian churches. Prior to Hitler's appointment to the chancellorship, the bishops of the Catholic Church in Germany had forbidden the faithful to join or support his party on the ground that its incitements to hatred, war, and racial intolerance were

---

[1] So designated by Hitler in January 1934. Rosenberg, born in 1893 in one of the Russian Baltic provinces and educated as an engineer, fled to Germany after the Communist revolution in Russia and joined the National Socialist party in 1919. A prolific writer of brochures and books, and from 1921 the editor of the principal Nazi newspaper, he made amends for his Jewish name and his Russian background by becoming the most rabid anti-Jewish and anti-Russian leader of the party. His main work, published in 1930, *The Myth of the Twentieth Century*, contained a savage attack on Christianity and Judaism.

basically anti-Christian.[1] Then, following Hitler's establishment in office and his apparently conciliatory negotiations of a con-

**Relations with Churches** cordat with the Vatican, promising religious freedom to the Church, the bishops acquiesced in the dissolution of the Center party and withdrew their formal condemnation of National Socialism. The concordat, however, brought about a restless truce rather than real peace between the Catholic Church and the Third Empire. Hitler and his associates, regarding the concordat as a first step in "coordinating" the Church, interfered with Catholic societies and publications of all kinds, compelling them to serve Nazi ends or else suppressing them. Moreover, appropriations for Catholic worship were decreased and a campaign was waged against Catholic schools and religious orders. All this was interpreted in Catholic circles as willful violation of the concordat, and many bishops and priests protested against the "tyranny" and "paganism" of the Nazi regime. Nevertheless, neither Hitler nor the Church was anxious to engage openly in another Kulturkampf.[2] The government preferred a gradual undermining of the Church, and Catholic leaders were apprehensive about losing popular support if an out-and-out conflict was joined with the nationalist government. The uncertainty on both sides made for caution but not for harmony.

German Protestantism had traditionally been allied with secular government and was usually subservient to it. But there were several different Protestant churches in Germany, not only the Lutheran and the Calvinist, but the separate state churches of Prussia, Saxony, etc., and in each were different shades of individual opinion. The problem here, then, for Hitler and his colleagues was twofold: first, to combine all the Protestant churches into one, as the Catholic Church was one; and second, to "coordinate" the unified church with the Empire. They did succeed in effecting a corporate union—in name—under an "Imperial Bishop" warmly sympathetic with National Socialism, but they failed to "coordinate" the whole union or even to hold it together. Before long it was apparent that many Protestants as well as Catholics, though willing to cooperate politically with Na-

---

[1] Hitler in childhood has been baptized and reared a Catholic, but as a youth he had practically repudiated Christianity. National Socialism became his real religion.

[2] On the Kulturkampf of Bismarck's time, see above, pp. 139–141.

tional Socialism, would resist dictation in the field of religion.

On the other hand, extremists among the Nazis pressed for a national repudiation of Christianity altogether and a revival of the pre-Christian tribal and pagan religion of the ancient Germans, with at least symbolic worship of Thor and Woden and veneration of the warrior-heroes of Valhalla. Prominent among such extremists was Alfred Rosenberg, the "philosopher" of National Socialism.

Accompanying the Nazis' forceful campaign to establish uniformity of thought and action in Germany was a remarkable emigration of intellectuals—scholars, scientists, publicists, professors—who would not or could not be "coordinated." Some of these were Jews, but many were non-Jews. Though the government tried to arrest the emigration, thousands managed to get away to foreign parts, spreading hatred of the Nazi regime and incidentally depleting Germany of independent men of genius and reputation.

The chief reason why Hitler kept his hold upon the German masses was the striking success which for several years attended his financial, military, and foreign policies. For a decade before his advent to power he had been an impassioned and much publicized champion of Germany's tearing up *Hitler's Seeming Success* the treaty of Versailles, rearming itself, and recapturing all "German" lands; and during the first five years of his dictatorship he actually achieved an impressive part of this very program—to the delight of Germans and the chagrin of foreigners. Moreover, in preparing for ultimate war, he built up, in conjunction with the capable Goering, huge military industries which provided full employment for German workmen and satisfactory profit for employers. And in Hjalmar Schacht,[1] who was appointed Minister of Economy and president of the Reichsbank in 1934, Hitler had a kind of financial wizard. Schacht initiated a complicated system of currency controls and barter trade with foreign countries, which

[1] Schacht, a Conservative and a capitalist, served the Republican government prior to 1930 and was chiefly responsible for the reorganization of German finances after the ruinous inflation of 1923. See above, pp. 448–449, 482. Though subsequently supporting the Nazi regime, he opposed the elimination of Jews from the country's economic life and gradually withdrew from public office. Goering, already laden with other offices, succeeded him as finance minister in 1937 with the famous slogan, "guns instead of butter."

enabled Germany to secure raw materials for its rearmament without overtaxing its people and which at the same time extended German economic and political influence in central Europe, the Balkans, and South America.

By 1935 the Nazi dictatorship was obviously restoring Germany to the position of a great power, and thenceforth it pursued an increasingly aggressive foreign policy. What this was we shall explain in the next chapter.

### 4. TREND TOWARD DICTATORSHIP IN OTHER COUNTRIES

All the lesser national states in east-central and southeastern Europe issued from the World War as democracies, and most of them as republics.[1] Within them, however, the operation of democratic government soon proved extraordinarily difficult. They were newly created or newly unified states, confronted with the task of getting people to govern themselves who had never done so before or of welding together hitherto disparate populations. They were handicapped, too, by social and economic conditions of the utmost gravity—by losses and costs of the war, by staggering public and private indebtedness, by urgent requirements of reparation or reconstruction, and simultaneously by pressing popular demands for agrarian and other social reform. Moreover, to surmount their handicaps and perform their tasks, the new democracies had to rely upon parliaments whose members were generally inexperienced in the practical conduct of public affairs and split up among a large number of quarrelsome factions. All these conditions were especially favorable for the rapid growth of Communist and Fascist parties modeled after those of neighboring Russia or Italy and contributing to the paralysis of orderly government. The usual result was that, to safeguard themselves against a Communist revolution and dictatorship, which seemed the more threatening, the democratic governments throughout east-central Europe adopted dictatorial methods that savored in greater or lesser degree of fascism.

One notable exception to the general rule was Czechoslovakia. True, it had some very serious difficulties. It was an artificial state, geographically misshapen and ethnically incongruous. Czechs and Slovaks comprised a scant majority of its total population, and between these two peoples, despite a similarity of

[1] See above, pp. 463–464.

language, were significant differences of tradition and ambition. The Czechs, concentrated in the western provinces of Bohemia and Moravia (which had long been associated with **Democratic** Austria), were inclined to look down upon the Slovaks **Czecho-** of the eastern provinces (which had been connected for **slovakia** a longer time with Hungary) and to deny them the autonomy to which they aspired. Moreover, in the western provinces the Czechs were disliked by a large minority of Germans—the so-called Sudeten Germans—while in the east the Slovaks were despised by a minority of Hungarians. To add to the ethnic confusion, the city of Teschen was Polish and the mountainous region in Carpathia was almost entirely Ruthenian (Ukrainian).

Nevertheless, the great prestige of Thomas Masaryk, who in a very real sense had been the "father of his country" and who was its first President, enabled Czechoslovakia to hold together and maintain a liberal democratic government for eighteen years. There were spasmodic conflicts between Socialists and Catholics and between Czechs and Slovaks, and much grumbling by the minorities. Yet noteworthy progress was made in industry and transportation, in education and armament, and at least until 1930 in economic and financial rehabilitation. Until 1935, when Masaryk retired from office on account of age and infirmity, Czechoslovakia appeared to be a solidly established democracy.

Austria was less favored. The peace treaties of 1919 had reduced it to narrowly German confines, and it preserved its independence only on the sufferance of its neighbors and amid a series of economic and political crises. At **Austria** the outset its government was carried on by a coalition of Social Democrats and Christian Socialists,[1] but presently the latter gained predominance under the leadership of a statesmanlike priest, Ignatius Seipel, who was Chancellor of the Republic from 1922 to 1924 and again from 1926 to 1929.

The majority of both Christian Socialists and Social Democrats were loyal to the Republic, but it was difficult for them to cooperate. The former were Catholic and chiefly rural and agrarian; the latter were Marxian and almost wholly urban and wage-earning. The former were jealous of provincial autonomy; the latter were eager to subordinate the countryside to the capital

---

[1] On the democratic constitution of the Austrian Republic, and on the parties of Christian Socialists and Social Democrats, see above, pp. 417–418, 464.

city of Vienna. To complicate matters, the Social Democrats had a left wing, which, under the stress of sorry economic conditions at Vienna, grew more numerous and more inimical to collaboration with any "bourgeois" government,[1] while a right wing of the Christian Socialists was so antagonistic to Marxian Socialists that it stood ready to make common cause against them with extreme Nationalists.

There were two types of Nationalist in Austria. The first, corresponding to the Conservative in Germany, was aristocratic, aiming at a repudiation, so far as possible, of individualistic democracy, a restoration of the Habsburg dynasty, and an alliance or federation with Germany. The second type was more plebeian; it was embodied in a National Socialist (Nazi) party, which, imported from Germany, availed itself of the desperate economic conditions prevalent from 1929 to win converts, especially from the restless youth and the impoverished middle class, to the entire program of Hitler, including the submergence of Austria in a militant German Empire.

When Seipel retired from politics on account of ill health, another Christian Socialist leader, Engelbert Dollfuss, came to the fore. He was of peasant stock, young in years and diminutive in stature, but full of energy. For a time he sought collaboration of the Social Democrats with his Christian Socialists, but it was difficult to obtain, and, as the menace of National Socialism rapidly increased in Austria after its triumph in Germany, he gradually reached the conclusion that democracy must be sacrificed for a dictatorship of his own party. This was accomplished by a new constitution which he put into effect in April 1934, and which set up a "Christian Corporate State."

To the Christian Socialist dictatorship both Social Democrats and National Socialists were violently opposed, and against both the government directed repressive measures. In February 1934, on the eve of the adoption of the new constitution, the proclamation of a general strike by Socialist leaders was answered by an attack of government troops on Socialist strongholds in Vienna, resulting in four days' street fighting, the outlawing of the Social

[1] Social Democrats controlled the municipal government of Vienna, which sponsored expensive public works, including noteworthy construction of model tenements. In July 1927 they organized against the national government a monster demonstration at Vienna, which was terminated by state police and militia.

Democratic party, and the merging of all trade unions in a national union under government guidance and control.

Then, in July 1934, National Socialists attempted a *coup* against the government. Dollfuss was assassinated at Vienna and widespread rioting occurred in the provinces. In the face of threats from Mussolini, however, Hitler did not venture to intervene; and under the leadership of Kurt von Schuschnigg, who succeeded Dollfuss in the chancellorship, order was restored and the peculiar Austrian dictatorship continued on its difficult course for four years more.

Yugoslavia, like Czechoslovakia, was a newly created hybrid state, but the differences between the Serbs and Croats in Yugoslavia were greater and more troublesome than those between Czechs and Slovaks. The Serbs were Orthodox **Yugoslavia** in religion and "backward" in economic development. The Croats were Catholic and "progressive." Furthermore, though both were devoted to the "greater Yugoslavia" which the World War had brought into existence, the former regarded it as a mere expansion of Serbia and insisted therefore upon manning the whole centralized administration of the realm, while the latter strove for a federal state with "home rule" for Croatia. Frequent fights between Serb and Croatian deputies in the Chamber at Belgrade reached a climax in June 1928 with the killing of Stefan Radič, the Croatian leader, and several of his lieutenants. Whereupon, early in 1929, King Alexander, with the support of the army, dissolved the parliament, suspended the constitution, and proclaimed himself dictator. He personally appointed the ministers and all local officials. He exercised a rigorous press censorship and directed a ruthless suppression of dissent.

In 1931 the royal dictatorship was formally ended by the promulgation of a new constitution. Practically, however, the dictatorship continued, for the new constitution was issued by the King, and it enabled him to control both the military and the civil service, to name half the Senate, and indirectly to dominate the elections to the Chamber of Deputies. As was expected, "government candidates" carried the ensuing general election, and for the next three years the ministry was solidly Serbian with no Croatian representation. In 1934 King Alexander, on a trip to France, was assassinated at Marseilles. His son, a boy of eleven years, succeeded as Peter II with a regency which adopted a more conciliatory policy. A separatist movement developed in Croatia, and a Communist party emerged.

**Rumania** managed under parliamentary auspices to unify, politically and administratively, the newly acquired provinces of Transylvania, Bukovina, and Bessarabia, and also to effect an important land reform throughout the kingdom, involving the expropriation of 13,000 landlords and the partition of their combined estates of fourteen and a half million acres among a million peasants. Nevertheless, the agencies of democratic government—elections, parliament, and ministries—continued to be manipulated by cliques of professional politicians, some of whom were notoriously corrupt and all of whom were inclined to be arbitrary if not dictatorial. On the death of the war-King, Ferdinand I, in 1927, his infant grandson, Prince Michael, succeeded to the throne under a regency, but by a *coup d'état* in 1930 Michael's father, who had been legally debarred from the succession on account of his infatuation with a woman of unsavory reputation, deposed the child-King and crowned himself as Carol II. Carol II, in a somewhat mercurial manner, exercised practically dictatorial power, at one time banning a Nazi party known as the "Iron Guard" and at another time entrusting the premiership to a fanatical anti-Semite.

**Poland**, the largest and most populous of the new states of central Europe, achieved a remarkable amount of consolidation and reconstruction, administrative, financial, and educational, but it did so at the expense of liberal parliamentary democracy. From the outset, the Polish electorate, and consequently the Polish parliament, were split into an extraordinarily large number of political factions, the chronic rivalries and intrigues of whose leaders made the successful operation of constitutional government almost impossible. At length in 1926 Marshal Joseph Pilsudski, the Polish hero of the World War and of the ensuing war with Communist Russia,[1] executed a military *coup d'état*, overturning the cabinet of the day, assuming the premiership of a "nationalist" ministry, and becoming virtual dictator. Pilsudski refused to be called a dictator and showed notable reluctance to appear as one. He declined to accept the presidency of the republic, and in 1930 he relinquished the premiership. Nevertheless, with the army in back of him, he

[1] See above, pp. 415–416, 431.

tolerated in the presidency and in the ministry only such persons as would do his will, and shortly before his death in 1935 he compelled a reluctant parliamentary majority to accept a new constitution under which the powers of the President were enhanced and those of parliament curtailed.

In Lithuania, similar political turbulence prevailed, until a similar *coup d'état*, likewise in the year 1926, put General Anton Smetona, an ardent nationalist, into the presidency. Then, in 1928, the adoption of a new constitution provided Smetona with legal basis for his dictatorship. **Baltic States**

In the other Baltic states, Latvia and Estonia, the radically democratic constitutions which had been adopted just after the World War were discredited by the free scope which they gave to conflicting and paralyzing agitation of Communist and Fascist extremists. A dictatorship was maintained in Estonia from 1934 to 1936, and another was established in Latvia in May 1935. In both countries Communist propaganda was outlawed.

Hungary, of all the states of central Europe, was least affected by the wave of liberal democracy which had followed in the wake of the World War. The Magyars, long accustomed to government by the land-owning families of the old **Hungary** aristocracy, looked all the more readily to them for guidance after the partition and humiliation of the country by foreigners and the failure of Béla Kun's Communist efforts.[1] From 1920 onwards, Hungary was nominally a "constitutional monarchy," but really an aristocratic and semi-Fascist state, much as it had been before the World War and with no partition of the large landed estates. Its head, or "Regent," Admiral Horthy, and its successive prime ministers directed public affairs in quite arbitrary fashion, and were sustained in parliament and in the country at large by a well-organized patriotic party—the National Unity party. Not only was revolutionary radicalism suppressed, but agitation of "legitimists" in behalf of a Habsburg restoration was discouraged.

In Bulgaria, under King Boris III, the post-war years were marked by intense party strife and frequent crimes of political violence. In 1923 the able Agrarian premier, Stambulinsky,[2] was deposed by a *coup d'état* and murdered, and dur-

[1] See above, pp. 416–417.
[2] See above, p. 418.

ing the next three years a nominally "democratic" but essentially
reactionary ministry conducted a campaign of terror-
**Bulgaria** ism against "radicals" whether of town or of countryside. A more truly democratic government was installed in 1926,
but before long it felt obliged to manipulate elections and to
stamp out a growing Communist party; and in May 1934 it in
turn was forcefully overthrown by a group of army officers intent
upon transforming Bulgaria into a Fascist state. For a year these
Fascists ruled, only to be supplanted in 1935 by still another
*coup d'état*, engineered this time by the King.

In Albania, the attempt of an Orthodox bishop who had been
educated in the United States, Fan Noli by name, to create an
enduring democratic republic was brought to nought by
**Albania** a young Moslem army officer, Ahmed Zogu, who, becoming President in 1925, had himself proclaimed King as Zog I
in 1928.

As Albania relapsed from republic to dictatorship, so Greece
wavered between monarchy and republic and between dictatorship and democracy. The Greek parliament compelled
**Greece** King George II to quit the country in December 1923,
and in March 1925 it voted the dethronement of the dynasty and
the establishment of a republic, which was promptly endorsed by
popular plebiscite. The change, however, was only one of name;
and under the republic, as under the monarchy, Greek politics
continued turbulent and at times bloody. Venizelos, the country's
veteran statesman, contrived to return to office in 1928, but his
enemies, of whom he had many, combined against him, and in
1933 an acknowledged royalist became premier. In 1935 Venizelos inspired a revolt, which was put down with considerable
bloodshed, and Venizelos fled abroad. There followed immediately
a military and royalist *coup d'état*, and, after the formality of a
plebiscite, the restoration of King George II to the Greek throne.
In 1936 the King sanctioned a dictatorship by an army officer,
General John Metaxas.

From what we have already said in the present section, it must
be apparent that throughout east-central Europe the post-war
political trend was toward dictatorship, while retaining some
parliamentary forms. It was true of the republic of Poland and
the kingdoms of Rumania and Yugoslavia. It was true, too, of the
small republics on the Baltic: Lithuania, Latvia, and Estonia.

It was true, also, of the small states on the Danube and in the Balkan peninsula: the nominal kingdom of Hungary, the actual kingdom of Bulgaria, Greece which was royalist and then republican and then royalist again, and Albania which was republican and then royalist and finally fascist.

It was similar, as we have elsewhere pointed out, in the southwestern peninsula of Europe—in Spain and Portugal. It was similar, too, in the Near Eastern countries of Turkey and Iran, and in the Far Eastern nations of China and Japan. Even in western Europe, where democracy was most firmly entrenched, advocates of a Communist dictatorship were increasing during the 1930's in such an important country as France and were being countered by advocates of a Fascist dictatorship.

By 1935 it was clear that the tide of democracy which had been so wide and full in 1920 was ebbing rapidly. It was also becoming clear that the remaining democracies in Europe were now so absorbed in domestic concerns or so weakened by political strife between extremes of "Left" and "Right" that they were hardly prepared to meet aggression by the totalitarian dictatorships of Germany, Italy, and Russia.

# CHAPTER XIV

## TOTALITARIAN AGGRESSION, 1930–1939

### 1. INTERNATIONAL CHAOS AND JAPANESE AGGRESSION
### AGAINST CHINA, 1930–1934

 EALOUSLY it had been hoped at the time of the Paris peace settlement in 1919–1920 that Europe and the world at large would attain to order and peace through the beneficent functioning of democratic government and the League of Nations. A decade later, events were pointing to quite a different outcome.

By 1930 totalitarian dictatorship had triumphed over liberal democracy in both Russia and Italy and was on the way to triumph in Germany. Moreover, the trend toward some sort of dictatorship was now evidenced throughout east-central and southern Europe, in Latin America, in Turkey and Persia, in China and Japan. Democracy, and the hope attached to it, were ebbing.

At the same time the League of Nations was losing prestige and failing to reconcile international differences. Foremost among **Impotence** these differences was the question of maintaining or **of League** revising the Paris peace settlement. France, together **of Nations** with its lesser allies, such as Belgium, Czechoslovakia, Poland, Rumania, and Yugoslavia, wanted the settlement rigorously maintained. Germany, together with other defeated nations, such as Hungary and Bulgaria, wanted it drastically revised. Italy and Japan, not being satisfied with what they got from the Paris peace settlement, followed independent courses; and Great Britain was willing to compromise. With widely conflicting aims among its chief members, there could be little harmony or effective action within the League of Nations.

What made matters vastly worse was the fact that the totalitarian dictatorships were the very governments not only most anxious to revise the territorial arrangements of 1919–1920 but most willing to employ violence for the purpose. They were accustomed to the use of violence at home; they had no scruple about using it abroad. It was a prime means of securing and strengthening their hold on their peoples. Dictatorships, as they developed in Russia, Italy, Japan, and Germany, were bound to be militantly aggressive.

On the other hand, the democratic peoples were as reluctant to face the threat of outright war as the dictators were bent on committing aggression. While the latter concentrated upon military preparedness, the former pressed their governments to cut expenditure on army and navy and to avoid any step which might lead to war. The United States, throughout the 1920's and 1930's, was popularly pacifist and isolationist to an extreme degree. Its criticism of the totalitarian dictatorships and their aggressions was purely verbal. It persistently held aloof from the League of Nations, even from the World Court. It would not consider any joint action with France or Great Britain. It enacted legislation aimed at maintaining a strict neutrality in the event of any foreign war.

*Pacifism of Western Powers*

Pacifism flourished also in France and Great Britain. Both countries were extremely fearful of undergoing anew the sacrifice of men and money which they had made in the First World War; and in coping with the financial depression of 1929–1930, both countries curtailed their expenditure on armaments. In Britain, the Labor party vied with the majority of the Conservative party under Stanley Baldwin and Neville Chamberlain in seeking to avoid war through a conciliatory foreign policy. In France, any strong or consistent policy was rendered almost impossible by mounting strife between extremes of "Left" and "Right"; and the "Popular Front" ministries of Socialists and Radicals were so intent on labor legislation that they neglected the country's defense.

There was troublesome uncertainty about the Soviet Union. While it professed peaceful intentions, it steadily increased its armaments and pursued a disconcerting policy of intrigue and opportunism. At first, its foreign policy was directed toward cooperation in Europe with Germany, and in Asia with the Chinese Nationalists under Sun Yat-sen and

*Dubious Russian Policy*

Chiang Kai-shek. In the latter case, a break came in 1927 when Chiang Kai-shek repudiated Communism and suppressed a revolt of its Chinese supporters. Whereupon the Soviet Union cultivated friendly relations with Japan and in 1931 proposed a non-aggression pact with it.

Toward Germany, the Soviet foreign minister, Maxim Litvinov, retained the conciliatory policy, even after Hitler and the Nazis came into power in 1933. Not until September 1934 did the Soviet Union join the League of Nations and apparently align itself with the Western democracies in a kind of international "popular front." Yet in the following January the Soviet statesman Molotov indicated at Moscow that Stalin stood ready to reach an agreement with Hitler. As Hitler was not yet ready to reciprocate, the Soviet Union was more or less obliged to stick to the "popular front," but how long it would stick no one knew.

The chaotic international situation favored totalitarian aggression, which was begun by Japan in 1931. Japan had long looked **Japanese** upon China as a promising big field for economic ex- **Policy be-** ploitation, and upon the sparsely settled but naturally **fore 1931** rich Chinese province of Manchuria as an inviting area for Japanese colonization. China's military weakness and its chronic unrest and disorder [1] provided constant temptation and ample opportunity for interference by an ambitious and militarized nation like Japan. Back in 1915, in the midst of the World War, Japan had presented to China "twenty-one demands," calculated to transform the whole country into a Japanese protectorate. There had then been sufficient diplomatic pressure from the United States and other Western powers, and sufficient pacific sentiment in the Japanese government, to bring about a withdrawal of most of the "demands," though Japan did obtain some special economic concessions and police rights in southern Manchuria. Again in 1921 Japan had set up a puppet government in Outer Mongolia, but had soon abandoned it to native Communist forces backed by Russia.

Indeed, in the years immediately following World War I, when Japan was apparently being democratized,[2] its government had been quite conciliatory. At the Washington Conference of 1922,[3]

[1] See above, pp. 295–296, 505–508.
[2] See above, pp. 504–505.
[3] On the naval agreement of this same Conference, see above, p. 453.

it signed with the United States, Great Britain, France, Italy, the Netherlands, Belgium, Portugal, and China, the so-called "nine-power treaties," affirming the independence and territorial integrity of China and prohibiting special agreements "designed to create spheres of influence . . . in Chinese territories."

By 1931, however, the domestic situation was changing in Japan, and bringing about a change of its foreign policy. There was impatience with parliamentary government and civilian political parties, agitation for economic reform through a totalitarian regime, and eagerness of army and navy to exercise dictatorial control. A military *coup* was attempted in March 1931 by General Kuniaki Koiso, the "Tiger of Korea"; and though it failed of its immediate purpose, it was followed by a series of political assassinations which served to transfer authority from pacific civilians to bellicose generals and admirals. In May 1932 the last of the parliamentary prime ministers—the aged Ki Inukai—was assassinated. He was succeeded by Admiral Saito, a protégé of the military. And as the military got the upper hand, they called for an early repudiation of the naval agreements and nine-power treaties which bound Japan and for an aggressive policy toward China.

Change in 1931 and Conquest of Manchuria

Already in September 1931, officers in command of the Japanese troops which were policing the South Manchurian railway had opened hostilities against the Chinese governor of the territory. They did so on their own authority, "to repress banditry," they said. But as soon as Admiral Saito was in power at Tokyo, he committed Japan to the conquest of Manchuria and heavily reinforced the troops in charge of it. Japanese armies speedily overran the entire territory, dispersing the forces of the Chinese governor and putting him to flight.

Both China and Japan were members of the League of Nations, and to it China appealed for help against the obvious Japanese aggression. The League responded by appointing a special commission, which, after six months' investigation, recommended that Japan be censured and Manchuria be given an autonomous government under Chinese sovereignty. Japan ignored the recommendations, and in March 1933 withdrew from the League. The League, unable to agree upon any joint "sanctions" against Japan, contented itself with expressing regret. Unavailing, too, was China's protest to the United States and other signatories of the

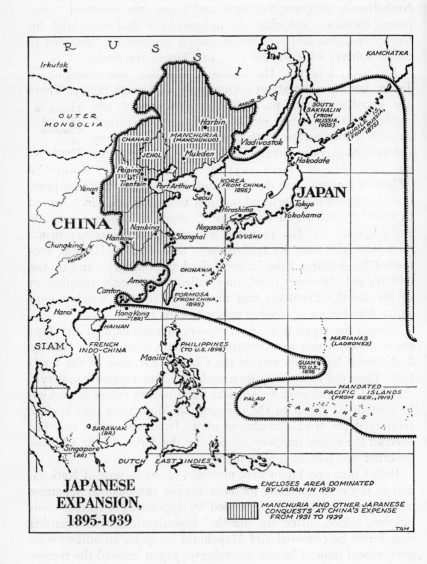

OUTER
MONGOLIA

R U S S I A

Irkutsk

KAMCHATKA

AMUR R.

Harbin

SOUTH
SAKHALIN
(FROM
RUSSIA,
1905)

KURILE IS.
(FROM RUSSIA,
1875)

MANCHURIA
(MANCHUKUO)

CHAHAR

JEHOL

Mukden

Vladivostok

Peiping

Tientsin

Port Arthur

KOREA
(FROM CHINA,
1895)

Hakodate

Yenan

Seoul

JAPAN

CHINA

Nanking

Hiroshima

Tokyo

Yokohama

Hankow

Shanghai

Nagasaki

Chungking

KYUSHU

YANGTZE R.

OKINAWA

Amoy

RYUKYU IS.

Canton

FORMOSA
(FROM CHINA,
1895)

Hanoi

Hong Kong
(BR.)

MARIANAS
(LADRONES)

SIAM

HAINAN

FRENCH
INDO-CHINA

PHILIPPINES
(TO U.S. 1898)

Manila

GUAM
TO U.S.
1898

MANDATED
PACIFIC ISLANDS
(FROM GER., 1919)

PALAU

C A R O L I N E S

SARAWAK
(BR.)

Singapore
(BR.)

DUTCH EAST INDIES

**JAPANESE
EXPANSION,
1895-1939**

ENCLOSES AREA DOMINATED
BY JAPAN IN 1939

MANCHURIA AND OTHER JAPANESE
CONQUESTS AT CHINA'S EXPENSE
FROM 1931 TO 1939

TRM

nine-power treaties and the Kellogg-Briand Pact. None was minded to go to war with Japan or even to take economic measures against it. China, left alone, was powerless.

Already, in February 1932, the Japanese military authorities had installed at Mukden a native but sympathetic "provisional government" and inspired it to proclaim Manchuria *Puppet* an independent state with the name of Manchukuo. *State of* Then in March the ex-Emperor of China, Henry Pu-yi, *Manchukuo* who had been a pensioner of Japan since boyhood,[1] was placed in nominal charge of the new state; and with him Japan concluded in September 1932 a treaty, formally recognizing the independence of Manchukuo. In vain, patriotic Chinese attempted a boycott against the Japanese. A Japanese expeditionary force landed at Shanghai, and Japanese troops occupied the Inner Mongolian province of Jehol, south of Manchuria. At length in May 1933 the Chinese government of Chiang Kai-shek consented to a truce, leaving Manchukuo, with Jehol, in Japanese possession and providing for a demilitarized zone as far south as Peiping and Tientsin.

Within Manchukuo, Japanese arms dictated a political arrangement embodied in a constitution of March 1934. Henry Pu-yi was enthroned as the Emperor Kang Teh, with a native ministry, but with Japanese advisers for foreign affairs, for financial and economic matters, and indeed for the whole central and local administration. Manchukuo was independent in name. In fact, it was a Japanese dependency. All that the United States and the League of Nations did was to withhold official recognition.[2] In December 1934, preparatory to further aggression, Japan denounced the Washington treaty which in 1922 had imposed a limitation on its naval armaments.[3]

## 2. GERMAN REARMAMENT AND ITALIAN CONQUEST OF ETHIOPIA, 1934–1936

Japan's withdrawal from the League of Nations in March 1933 nicely synchronized with the advent of Hitler's Nazi dictator-

[1] See above, p. 295.
[2] The United States, through its Secretary of State, Henry L. Stimson, announced its refusal to recognize the legality of any situation or treaty resulting from action in violation of the Kellogg Pact. This so-called Stimson Doctrine received no general endorsement.
[3] See above, p. 453.

ship in Germany; and Japanese aggression in Asia was soon followed by German aggression in Europe. To prepare for this, Hitler was resolved to rearm Germany, and to do so he had to repudiate the restrictive provisions in the treaty of Versailles.[1]

By that same treaty, the League of Nations had been charged with the responsibility of following up the limitation on German armaments with negotiation of a world-wide limitation; and after protracted delay a "draft treaty" for such general disarmament **Failure to** had been prepared[2] and was submitted to an Inter-**Limit** national Conference convened at Geneva in February **Armaments** 1932 and attended by official representatives of all members of the League (including Germany) and, in addition, by delegates of the United States and the Soviet Union. The task of the Conference was not only to debate and if possible to agree upon the "draft treaty" but also to supply its most glaring omission—the exact specification of the future size of each nation's army and of the future expenditure of each nation on war material. The task was humanly impossible in existing circumstances, and no miracle occurred. From the beginning the viewpoints of France and Germany were diametrically opposite. France would be insecure if it reduced its army to a level with Germany's, and Germany would be insecure if France didn't. Unable to find a way out of the impasse, and yet reluctant to admit failure, the Conference floundered about in a bog of irrelevant discussion.

At length in October 1933, after Hitler had control of Germany, he withdrew its representatives from the Conference and declared that, inasmuch as other nations would not agree to limit their armaments, Germany would no longer respect the limitation upon its armaments. At the same time he denounced the League of Nations in scathing terms and proclaimed Germany's secession from it. This, as we know, was promptly confirmed by a plebiscite of the German people.[3]

For several months longer the International Conference continued at Geneva, but, with Germany gone, the discussions about disarmament grew ever more futile. Finally, in the summer of 1934, Great Britain, the power most interested in limiting armies

[1] See above, p. 425.
[2] See above, pp. 454–455.
[3] See above, pp. 587–588.

(if not navies), acknowledged that this could not be brought about, and indicated its intention of enlarging its own armaments, particularly its air force. The Conference then faded away.

The collapse of the protracted efforts at Geneva in behalf of a general limitation of armaments, in conjunction with the almost simultaneous withdrawal of both Germany and Japan from the League of Nations, was a staggering blow to the League and to any assurance of collective security. And almost immediately, with the obvious intention of isolating France, Hitler made friendly overtures to Great Britain and to Poland. The latter was persuaded in January 1934 to sign a non-aggression pact with Germany, guaranteeing for ten years the existing boundaries between them. Poland imagined that the pact relieved it of the chief threat to its territorial integrity, while Hitler knew he was weaning away an ally of France and removing a serious obstacle to the plans he was maturing for the annexation of Austria and the rearming of Germany. *Germany's Pact with Poland and Attempted Coup in Austria*

The prohibition, in the treaty of Versailles, of Austrian union with Germany was no bar to Hitler. He actively encouraged Nazi agitation within Austria and connived at the attempted *coup d'état* there in July 1934 which was attended by the murder of Dollfuss.[1] The *coup* failed of its primary purpose, however, partly because Hitler and the Nazi cause had as yet too slight a popular backing in Austria, and partly because the Italian government of Mussolini threatened war if Germany should appropriate Austria; and Italy's strong stand was seconded by Czechoslovakia and France. Germany was not prepared for war with all these powers, and so Hitler backed down, disavowing any complicity in the disturbances within Austria and any intention of seizing the country.

To hold Hitler to his disavowals and to keep him out of Austria was, at the time, a cardinal point in Italian foreign policy. Mussolini adopted an attitude of benevolence toward France, and the French government was quite responsive to his overtures. Accordingly, in January 1935, a *Opposition of France and Italy* Franco-Italian pact was signed at Rome. Not only did the two Latin powers mutually pledge themselves to support the independence of Austria, but in return for French concessions to Italy in northern Africa, including secret arrangements about

[1] See above, pp. 596–597.

Ethiopia,[1] Italy promised to join France in opposing unilateral treaty revision in Europe.

Simultaneously, in January 1935, the plebiscite in the Saar, provided for by the treaty of Versailles,[2] was held to determine whether the district should revert to Germany, be annexed by France, or remain under the League of Nations. The outcome was convincing proof of German patriotic sentiment in the Saar. Ninety per cent of the votes favored reunion with Germany, and on March 1 the district was formally turned over to the Nazi Empire.

Elated and emboldened by its success in the Saar—a legitimate success—Nazi Germany strove the harder to "Nazify" other separated districts, preparatory to their annexation, legitimate or otherwise, by the Empire. In the free city of Danzig, Nazi sympathizers gained control of the local parliament. In Memel, they created grave difficulties for the Lithuanian government. Moreover, Nazi leaders in Germany made no bones about their ultimate intention of appropriating Austria, of "redeeming" the large German minority in Czechoslovakia, and even of detaching Ukrainia from Soviet Russia.

**German Rearmament** As if to give speedy effect to this ambitious program Hitler dramatically announced on March 16, 1935, Germany's repudiation of all treaty limitations on its armaments and the reestablishment of universal military service in the Empire. This meant for Germany a standing army of 550,000 men and an aircraft strength superior to that of Great Britain or France.

Hitler's militant policies elicited loud popular applause in Germany, but abroad they aroused resentment and fear. In April **Stresa Declaration of France, Italy, Britain** 1935 at a conference at Stresa (in Italy), Mussolini joined the premiers of France and Great Britain in proclaiming that "the three powers, the object of whose policy is collective maintenance of peace within the framework of the League of Nations, find themselves in complete agreement in opposing, by all practicable means, any

[1] To Italy, France granted special privileges in Tunis and ceded some 44,500 square miles bordering on Libya, a strip of French Somaliland on the Gulf of Aden, and a share in the ownership of the railway connecting the Gulf with Addis Ababa, the Ethiopian capital. By the secret arrangements, Italy would have a "free hand" in Ethiopia, so far as France was concerned.

[2] See above, pp. 424, 438.

unilateral treaty repudiation which may endanger the peace of Europe, and will act in close and cordial collaboration for this purpose."

By this time, the Soviet dictator, Stalin, and his foreign minister, Litvinov, were becoming alarmed about the pro-German, and even pro-Nazi, policy which Russia had been pursuing. They resented the new pact between Poland and Germany, as a possible prelude to German-Polish aggression in Ukrainia. Consequently on May 2, 1935—less than a month after the Stresa Conference—Litvinov signed with Pierre Laval, the French foreign minister, a treaty of mutual assistance between France and the Soviet Union; and this was speedily extended to include Czechoslovakia. For the moment it appeared as though these agreements and alliances in the spring of 1935 would do what the League of Nations had failed to do and would effectually restrain Nazi Germany. *Franco-Russian Pact*

Appearances were deceptive, nevertheless. Great Britain, jealous of the enhanced position of France through its alliance with both Italy and the Soviet Union, and particularly fearful of the effects of the Franco-Italian combination on naval supremacy in the Mediterranean, made an important concession to Germany. In June 1935—only two months after the Stresa Conference—the British government independently sanctioned Germany's repudiation of the naval clauses in the treaty of Versailles in return for a pledge that the German navy should not exceed thirty-five per cent of the British. This alarmed and angered France, and impeded cooperation with Britain, while diminishing the sense of security. *Britain's Naval Concession*

But far more serious in ultimate effects was Italy's imperial ambition in Ethiopia, and its forceful realization. Ever since Mussolini had established his Fascist dictatorship he had been anxious to win for Italy a commanding position in the Mediterranean and particularly to bring the big and backward East African country of Ethiopia under Italian sway. Thereby, painful memories of the disaster inflicted on Italian arms at Adowa in 1896 [1] would be wiped out, and a promising region obtained for Italian colonization and exploitation. For several years Italy sought such imperial sway through diplomatic negotiation. In 1925 an agreement between Italy and *Italian Designs on Ethiopia*

[1] See above, pp. 128-129.

Great Britain, while granting to the latter free water-rights in northern Ethiopia for the benefit of the Anglo-Egyptian Sudan, promised to Italy a free hand in seeking concessions in the rest of the country. Ethiopia promptly protested to the League of Nations (of which it had been a member since 1923) against this foreign partitioning of "spheres of influence" within its territory and against the implied affront to its sovereignty, but the League contented itself with recording "explanations" from Italy and Britain which really did not explain.

Then Italy attempted to ingratiate itself with the native rulers of Ethiopia—the usurping Empress Zauditu, daughter of Menelek II,[1] and her husband, Haile Selassie—and in 1928 agreed to a treaty with them, pledging "perpetual friendship" and arbitration of all disputes. But Haile Selassie, especially after the death of Zauditu in 1930 and his accession as Emperor, doggedly refused the requests of his "friend" for exceptional concessions and favors, and gradually Mussolini reached the conclusion that Italy must use force against Ethiopia, even if it involved violation of existing treaties and a flouting of the League of Nations. He had no conscientious scruples himself, and that Italy could proceed with impunity was evidenced by what both Japan and Germany had recently done. To make doubly sure of success, he got France to agree in January 1935, as we have seen, to his having a "free hand."

Alleging the necessity of suppressing disorder along the undefined Ethiopian border of its colonies of Eritrea and Somaliland, Italy dispatched large forces to East Africa. Against the threatened aggression, Ethiopia appealed to the League of Nations, and the appeal won popular sympathy and presently governmental support in Great Britain, which now perceived in Italy's African ambitions a menace to its own imperial interests and to the cause of "collective security" which it had not perceived, or at any rate acted upon, in the case of Japan's aggression in Manchuria or of Germany's rearmament. Britain mobilized its fleet in the Mediterranean and besought the League to take a strong stand. In

**British Opposition and Failure of League Sanctions**

---

[1] On Menelek II, see above, p. 305. He died in 1913 and was succeeded by his grandson, the Emperor Lej Yasu, a weak youth, who was deposed and imprisoned in 1916 by his aunt, Zauditu, and her ambitious husband, Haile Selassie. There was a good deal of tribal disaffection within Ethiopia.

vain France tried to effect a compromise acceptable to Italy and Britain, if not wholly so to Ethiopia. Italy went relentlessly ahead with military preparations, and in October 1935, disregarding alike the League Covenant and the Kellogg Pact, Italian troops invaded Ethiopia, captured Adowa, and pushed into the interior. Italy and Ethiopia were actually, if not legally, at war.

The military preoccupation of Italy in Africa and the accompanying embitterment of Anglo-Italian relations practically extinguished the hope which the Stresa Conference had given France of United European action against further treaty violations by Germany. France was left an uncomfortable choice: either to continue to support Italy, which would completely discredit the League and probably impel Britain to an accord with Germany; or to stick by the League and effect a rapprochement with Britain, which would undoubtedly antagonize Italy and might lead to a Fascist-Nazi entente. France chose the latter alternative. It joined Britain in backing action by the League of Nations. And most of the other League members fell in line behind Britain and France. Consequently in October 1935 the League formally adjudged Italy an "aggressor" and in November applied economic "sanctions."

The very next month, the French foreign minister, Pierre Laval, still anxious to conciliate Italy, persuaded the British foreign minister, Sir Samuel Hoare, to agree to a compromise whereby Italy might appropriate part, but not all, of Ethiopia. British public opinion, however, was so critical of this Hoare-Laval agreement that the government at London felt obliged to repudiate it. Hoare resigned and was succeeded by Anthony Eden, who would consent to no compromise.

Yet success again attended the scrapping of treaties and resort to violence. Economic sanctions, though causing some distress and much anger in Italy, failed of their purpose. They solidified the Italian nation in support of its Fascist government and in opposition to the League. Moreover, they were imperfectly applied. Requisite war materials which Italy could not import from League members it freely obtained from non-members, most notably from Germany.

And the Suez Canal, under British control was left open to Italian transport of soldiers and supplies for the conquest of Ethiopia.

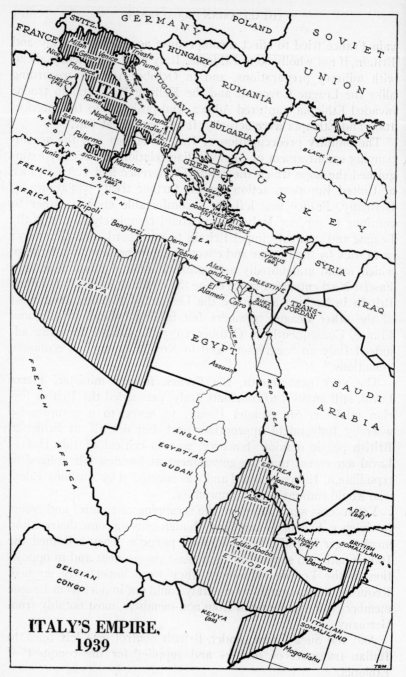

**ITALY'S EMPIRE, 1939**

Besides, the war in East Africa did not last as long as had been anticipated. Italian armies made surprisingly quick work of Ethiopia. Their airplanes and motor trucks surmounted the country's physical difficulties, and they had munitions and supplies, competent generalship,[1] discipline, and morale, which the native tribesmen lacked. Organized resistance was largely overcome by March 1936. Early in May the Emperor Haile Selassie fled abroad and Italian troops occupied the capital city of Addis Ababa. Mussolini proclaimed the annexation of the whole country to Italy, and King Victor Emmanuel III took the additional title of Emperor of Ethiopia.

*Italy's Conquest of Ethiopia*

The results, in international relations, were sorry and far-reaching. Not only had the League of Nations flagrantly failed to preserve the integrity and very existence of one of its members, but the public law of Europe and any effective cooperation among the great powers had been dealt a body-blow. Italy had proved that might made right and that any determined power could exercise its might without let or hindrance on the part of the League. To Italy, therefore, as to Japan and Germany, the League of Nations became a nonentity and its Covenant a garb of hypocrisy. In May 1936 Italy, following the examples of Japan and Germany, withdrew from the League, and in July the League publicly confessed its impotence by rescinding the economic sanctions against Italy.

The attempted utilization of the League of Nations by Great Britain and France to restrain Italy proved worse than a failure. It aroused bitter enmity of Italy toward France and Britain and thereby provided Germany with new and favorable opportunity for unilateral denunciation of treaty obligations.

Already in March 1936, just when the Italo-Ethiopian War was reaching its climax, Hitler ordered German troops to march into the demilitarized zones of the Rhineland which had been provided for by the treaty of Versailles and guaranteed by the Locarno Pact.[2] He did so against the advice of his chief army generals, who feared resistance and defeat by the supposedly stronger forces of France.

*Hitler's Remilitarization of Rhineland*

Such fears proved baseless, however. The French government appreciated that armed resistance on its part was likely to precipitate a war which France would have to wage practically alone

---

[1] The able commander-in-chief of the Italian forces was Marshal Pietro Badoglio.

[2] See above, pp. 425, 449–450.

and in which it would eventually be overborne by the superior industrial resources and man-power of Nazi Germany. Only little Belgium seemed minded to make common cause with France. The Soviet Union was disinterested. Italy was hostile and busy in Ethiopia. Great Britain was deeply pacifist, and its government was more concerned with Italy than with Germany.

France did get the Council of the League of Nations to adopt a resolution that Germany was violating treaties. But this was a mere formality. Actually and without opposition, Germany occupied the Rhineland in force and proceeded to construct there a heavy line of fortifications facing the so-called Maginot Line which the French were building on their side of the frontier from Switzerland to Belgium. Incidentally, Belgium in October 1936 ended its military alliance with France and proclaimed its "neutrality."

### 3. FORMATION OF THE AXIS, CIVIL WAR IN SPAIN, AND JAPANESE INVASION OF CHINA, 1936–1939

In October 1936, Fascist Italy entered into an open accord with Nazi Germany, creating what Mussolini styled the "Rome-Berlin Axis." It was a consequence of the close commercial rela-

German-Italian "Axis" and Japanese Adherence

tions between the two countries during the Ethiopian War, of their common hostility toward Great Britain, France, and the League of Nations, and of their common desire for territorial aggrandizement. In the next month, Germany concluded a pact with Japan, expressly directed against Russian Communism and its international organization, the Comintern,[1] and obviously intended to safeguard Japanese aggression in the Far East and to serve German ambitions in Europe. A year later, in November 1937, this Anti-Comintern Pact was joined by Italy, and a Berlin-Rome-Tokyo Axis created.

A new balance of power was thus set up between Germany, Italy, and Japan, on the one side, and France, Great Britain, and the Soviet Union, on the other. It was a precarious balance,

Precarious Balance of Russia and Western Powers

however, and one that the latter three powers could hardly maintain. Between the Communist dictatorship of the Soviet Union and the democratic governments of France and Great Britain there were basic differences of outlook and purpose which caused mutual suspicion and pre-

[1] See above, p. 549.

vented effective cooperation. The Russian dictatorship had aggressive designs not shared by the French or British, and its recent adoption of a "popular front" foreign policy was merely an expedient by which it hoped to protect itself against Germany and Japan while spreading its influence in the democratic countries and utilizing them for its own ends. France, under its Popular Front government of the time, was more amenable than Great Britain to Communist infiltration and influence; and between the two democracies there was no such solidarity as among the Axis powers. Nor were France and Great Britain devoting themselves wholeheartedly to war preparedness, as were the Axis powers, and yet without comparable military strength they were not likely to restrain the Axis and sustain a real balance of power.

The highly dangerous state of international relations was illustrated during a civil war which raged in Spain from 1936 to 1939. It was a war that was strictly Spanish in origin and that was fought largely by Spaniards. But it incidentally provided the occasion for rival interventions of the Soviet Union and the Axis powers of Italy and Germany and for a test of strength between the opposing coalitions of great powers. How it happened requires some explanation.

The Spanish monarchy of Alphonso XIII had been faced, ever since the close of the First World War, with growing domestic opposition, especially from Republicans and Socialists, and the King's attempt to save the monarchy by entrusting dictatorial powers to General Primo de Rivera had broken down with the General's retirement in 1930.[1] In local elections of 1931, the Republicans secured a large majority, and their leader, Niceto Alcalá Zamora threatened a general insurrection unless the King should immediately abdicate. Alphonso replied by flight.

Alcalá Zamora at once proclaimed Spain a republic; and, putting himself at the head of the "provisional government" of this Second Spanish Republic,[2] he called for the election of a National Assembly to draw up a new constitution. The election, which was held in June 1931, amidst popular commotion and considerable revolutionary violence, returned a majority of Socialists and Radicals, with a sprinkling of such diverse groups as Communists, Syndicalists, **Second Spanish Republic, 1931–1936**

[1] See above, pp. 480–481.
[2] On the First Spanish Republic, see above, pp. 118–119.

Anarchists, Monarchists, and Catalan and Basque Nationalists. In December this body adopted a republican constitution, containing pledges of personal liberty, prescriptions for the "separation of church and state" and the nationalizing of church property, and provisions for democratic government through a single-chamber parliament (or Cortes), with a ministry responsible to it and a President elected by it. Alcalá Zamora was confirmed as President of the Republic; and Manuel Azaña, a literary man, less moderate in his republicanism, became its first constitutional premier with a coalition ministry of Radical Republicans and Socialists.

With the completion of the task for which it had been chosen, the National Constituent Assembly should then have arranged for regular parliamentary elections and adjourned. Instead, being fearful of a Conservative reaction, it continued for two years longer to function as the supreme authority in the country and to adopt some very radical legislation. In 1932, in response to demands of Catalan Nationalists, it enacted a home rule law for Catalonia, delegating certain powers to a local legislature and a local president of its own choice and putting the Catalan language on an equal footing with Castilian. Similar measures of local autonomy were proposed for the Basques and for the province of Galicia. In the same year, moreover, the central parliament authorized the expropriation and partition of large landed estates belonging to the nobility.

Simultaneously, with its strongly anti-clerical majority, the Assembly took severe measures against the Catholic Church. In 1932 the Jesuits were banned and their schools and other property confiscated, and every Catholic clergyman in Spain, whether regular or secular, was deprived of government salary or subsidy. A law in 1933 transferred all ecclesiastical property, valued at half a billion dollars, to the state, and another law of the same year required all Catholic congregations to pay taxes and to report regularly to the government and it forbade them to engage in industry, commerce, or education. The Pope protested against these measures as "infringements on the liberty of the Church," and militant Catholics in Spain began to organize an electoral resistance.

Groups, other than churchmen, were disaffected by the Assembly's radical measures, and by the recurrent disorders which accompanied them. High army officers did not take kindly to being pushed into the background and having their forces reduced. Landlords and business men were aggrieved by the attacks on their property. Monarchists, Moderate Republicans, and a Fascist group—the Falange, founded by Antonio Primo de Rivera, son of the former dictator—all became increasingly critical of the course of events. In August 1932 the government had to use force to suppress a military and monarchist revolt at Seville.

Local elections in the early autumn of 1933 showed a strong popular reaction against the radical, particularly the anti-clerical, policies of the government. Azaña resigned the premiership, and, following the failure of the Moderate Republican leader, Alejandro Lerroux, to command a majority of the deputies, President Alcalá Zamora finally dissolved the Constituent Assembly and ordered the election of a regular Cortes. In this general election, in November 1933, the first under universal suffrage, the masses of the population participated—of twelve and a half million electors, at least eighty per cent voted. It confirmed the conservative trend evident in the preceding local elections. The coalition of Radical Republicans and Socialists was decisively defeated, the representation of the latter being cut in half and the Radical coalition as a whole being outnumbered three to one. The new majority comprised groups of Moderate Republicans, among whom the balance of power was held by a Catholic party, organized and led by José Gil Robles.

With the defeat of the Radicals and Socialists, and with the support of Gil Robles, Lerroux was enabled to form a fairly stable ministry of Moderate Republicans and to hold in abeyance the execution of the land laws and some of the anti-clerical measures previously enacted. But this aroused the active hostility of the revolutionary minority. Terrorism by Communists, Syndicalists, and Anarchists, and an attempted general strike were overcome by the government in December 1933, and in October 1934 a more serious insurrection in which left-wing Socialist miners in Asturias, Catalan Nationalists, and even the Radical ex-premier, Azaña, participated, and which involved considerable loss of life and destruction of property, was crushed by government troops.

The rigorous repressive measures taken by the Moderate government served to alienate some of its supporters and at the same time to unite opposing Radicals, Socialists, and Communists in a so-called "Popular Front." Consequently, in the general election which President Alcalá Zamora ordered in February 1936, though Moderates obtained a popular majority, the Popular Front secured a majority of seats in the new parliament.[1] Alcalá Zamora was forced out of the presidency as being too moderate, and was succeeded by Azaña; and the new Radical government, while announcing its intention to execute earlier social and ecclesiastical enactments, seemed unwilling or unable to prevent its Communist and Anarchist allies from burning churches and monasteries, killing priests, and terrorizing anyone suspected of reactionary sentiments. Spain appeared in the early summer of 1936 to be drifting into anarchy.

The murder of a Monarchist leader on July 13 was the signal for a revolt of several army generals in different parts of the country. One of these, General Francisco Franco, military governor of the Canary Islands, flew to Spanish Morocco and, with troops he gathered there, crossed to Cadiz.[2] The insurrection swept over southern and western Spain during the next few months and enlisted in its support about three-fourths of the regular army and half of the navy. In October the rebellious army generals chose General Franco as their chief, or Caudillo, and presently he set up a provisional government at Burgos.

*Army Rebellion and Civil War*

Meanwhile, early in September, the Republican government had been transformed by President Azaña into a practical dictatorship under a new premier, Francisco Largo Caballero, a former stone mason and a fanatical left-wing Socialist, quite sympathetic with Russian Communism. To offset the desertion of the majority of trained Spanish soldiery to General Franco, Caballero raised

[1] The Popular Front, comprising Socialists, Communists, Syndicalists, and Left Republicans, had 265 seats, while the Center and Rightist parties, comprising Moderate Republicans, Catholic supporters of Gil Robles, Monarchists, and Falangists, had 213 seats.

[2] Franco, born in 1892, was a professional soldier. He became a general at the age of thirty-two after organizing the Spanish Foreign Legion in Morocco and successfully cooperating with Marshal Pétain in suppressing a serious native revolt led by Abd-el-Krim. Franco continued a purely military career, and in 1934 was appointed Chief of the Spanish General Staff by the Moderate Republican government of Lerroux, and as such he put down the Leftist insurrection in Asturias. But afterwards the "Popular Front" government transferred him to the military governorship of the Canaries, a post which amounted to exile.

new levies from among the "Reds" and Radical Republicans, especially in eastern Spain and also from among Catalan and Basque nationalists.[1] He also obtained important help from the Soviet Union and its Comintern affiliates in other countries.

The Russian dictatorship for some time had regarded Spain as a country which might be brought most readily and profitably under its tutelage; and although the number of outright Communists in Spain was relatively small, they were well organized and able to take advantage of the divisions and discords within the Republican government. Now, in 1936, when Largo Caballero, a friend of theirs, was in power, they gained a foothold in his government and got the Soviet Union to supply him with counselors and a steady stream of supplies for his army. Moreover, under Communist auspices, "international brigades" were formed abroad and hurried to Spain "to defend the Republic," [2] while leading Communists, trained at Moscow and including the subsequently famous Tito of Yugoslavia and Dimitrov of Bulgaria, took an active part as aides to Largo Caballero. Besides, the fact that Largo Caballero's government was ostensibly a "Popular Front" government, representing itself as a champion of democracy and social reform, elicited much sympathy for it, and no little support, from the Popular Front government of France, and in only lesser degree from the Labor party in Great Britain and from "liberals" in the United States.

International Complications

On the other hand, General Franco sought and obtained foreign aid from Fascist Italy and Nazi Germany, which were vehemently anti-Communist and which, along with Portugal, recognized his government in November 1936. Mussolini and Hitler loaned him funds; the former sent him several thousand Italian troops, and the latter furnished him with airplanes, pilots, mechanics, and munitions. In this way, the Spanish Civil War, primarily a domestic struggle, gave rise to an international contest between Communist and anti-Communist dictatorships—between Russia on the one side, and Italy and Germany on the other. And as France and Great Britain (and the United States) were preponderantly sympathetic with the Republican regime in Spain, the

[1] The Spanish Republic had granted autonomy to Catalonia in 1932. It did the same to the Basque provinces just after the beginning of the Civil War in 1936.
[2] Including an "Abraham Lincoln" brigade, recruited in the United States.

struggle took on the appearance in those countries of a conflict between "democracy" and "fascism."

In the second half of 1936 and the first half of 1937, the contending forces in Spain were fairly evenly matched. Franco made minor gains but failed to capture the capital city of Madrid. And during this period there was much fear among neutral peoples, and particularly in Great Britain, lest the international complications of the Spanish Civil War might bring on another World War. The British government, in concert with the French, appealed to the other foreign powers to withdraw their "volunteers" from Spain and to agree to joint action against the importation of military supplies into the country. Lip service was paid to the British proposals. An international "blockade" was formally set up, and the United States enforced its "neutrality" legislation. Yet neither the Axis powers nor Communist Russia desisted from continuing to give encouragement and material assistance to the contending armies in Spain.

From the middle of 1937, the tide of the Spanish Civil War turned gradually in favor of the forces of General Franco. This **General Franco's Victory** was the result not only of better generalship on his side and of a superiority in air power to which Germany contributed, but also to a growing popular reaction within Spain against the terrorism practiced by the Communists and Anarchists and a resulting conflict among the supporters of the Republic. In May 1937 President Azaña removed Largo Caballero from the premiership, but his successor, Juan Negrín, was scarcely less radical and considerably less competent.

In the latter part of 1937 Franco accomplished the piecemeal conquest of the Basque provinces, Asturias, and Galicia, in the mountainous north, and in March 1938 he turned east and drove a wedge between the "red" armies in Catalonia and those in the Valencia-Madrid zone. Then, early in 1939, he conquered the whole of Catalonia, including the key city of Barcelona, and remaining Republican resistance rapidly disintegrated. Azaña fled to France in February and shortly afterwards renounced the presidency. General José Miaja, who had successfully defended Madrid for the Republic since the beginning of the Civil War in 1936, now finding his position untenable, prepared to surrender the capital to Franco. In vain Negrín and the Communists urged resistance to the death. Miaja disarmed the Communists and obliged Negrín to flee into exile. By the end of March 1939, Franco was in undisputed control of all Spain, and the tragic Spanish Civil War was over.

The war, lasting for almost three years, cost Spain a million persons, killed, wounded, or exiled, and many millions in property losses.[1] It ended the Second Spanish Republic after eight years of inglorious existence, established a military dictatorship with Fascist trimmings,[2] and left a legacy within Spain of disillusionment, impoverishment, and bitterness.

The Spanish Civil War also had fateful effects on international relations. On one hand, it increased the prestige of Germany and Italy, which had sided with the victorious Franco, and encouraged them in their aggressive policies. Incidentally, they secured from Franco in April 1939 Spain's adherence to the Anti-Comintern Pact and thereby the implied addition of Madrid to the Berlin-Rome-Tokyo Axis. On the other hand, the war registered a distinct setback for the powers which had aided or sympathized with the defeated Republican government—the Soviet Union, France, and Great Britain—and produced a cleavage among them. France and Great Britain made haste in February 1939 to conciliate Franco by extending full diplomatic recognition to his government, and their example was soon followed by the United States and the other democratic powers.

*Increased Prestige of Axis Powers*

The Soviet Union, however, could not forgive Franco for preventing the realization of its hope of establishing a puppet Communist state in Spain; and it was bitterly disappointed with the dubious and half-hearted support it had had from Britain and France. In the circumstances the Communist dictatorship of Russia eventually reached the conclusion that its own aggressive

---

[1] And millions more which the fleeing Republican leaders took with them out of Spain.

[2] In 1937 General Franco, in imitation of the Fascist regime in Italy, decreed the union of the Monarchist and other parties supporting him in a single national party —the Falange. Actually, however, the Spanish Falange, as thus constituted, was no such compact, disciplined party as the Nazi in Germany, the Communist in Russia, or the Fascist in Italy. It was rather a confederation of rival groups, including Monarchists, Carlists, Conservative Republicans, and Falangists proper, all held together by the military and by common repugnance to the revolutionary character of the Spanish Republic.

designs could be better served by collaboration with the Axis dictatorships than with the Western democracies.

Meanwhile, the Spanish Civil War had an important, if indirect, bearing on renewed Japanese aggression in the Far East. Previously, there had been divided counsels among the military masters of Japan. One faction had wanted to confine their conquests to Manchuria and to make it a barrier against the Soviet Union, while a second faction, led by Generals Koiso and Tojo, wanted to conquer all China. After the outbreak of the Spanish Civil War in 1936, the European situation favored this second faction, and it soon got the upper hand. In October of that year Japan signed the Anti-Comintern Pact with Nazi Germany as a kind of insurance against the Soviet Union. In fact the Soviet dictatorship was too engrossed in Spain to devote major attention to the Far East, although it did resume a benevolent attitude toward the Chinese Nationalist leader, Chiang Kai-shek, and encouraged a temporary alliance between him and the Chinese Communist forces which had been fighting him.[1]

With Japan freed from fear of any effective outside interference, and with China struggling to realize an unnatural domestic "union" between Nationalists and Communists, the stage was set for far-flung Japanese aggression. In July 1937, some irregular fighting at the Marco Polo Bridge in the outskirts of Peiping rang up the curtain for full armed conflict between Japan and China.

The Japanese, with superior discipline and instruments of war, won a series of striking successes. They overran northern China, **Japanese Conquests in China** drove the Chinese government from its capital city of Nanking, shelled and seized Shanghai, conquered a large district along the lower Yangtze, and in October 1938 captured both Canton, the great port in the South, and Hankow, the principal city in central China. The Chinese put up what resistance they could, but the destruction of life was appalling both of soldiers on battlefields and of civilians from bombing and famine, flood and pestilence. Chiang Kai-shek, with his Nationalists, was forced to retreat to the remote town of Chungking, while the Chinese Communists were driven far inland toward the Mongolian border. There was no halting of Japan's subjugation

---

[1] The Soviet Union concluded a Non-Aggression Pact with Chiang Kai-shek in August 1937.

of China. Attention of other great powers was concentrated else-where. Eventually, the Japanese War against China would be merged in the Second World War.

## 4. EXPANSION OF NAZI GERMANY AND PARTITION OF CZECHOSLOVAKIA, 1938–1939

While Japan was invading China, Nazi Germany continued with impunity to pile up its armaments and to violate the treaty of Versailles. In November 1936 Hitler repudiated the treaty's provision for international control of German waterways. In January 1937 he denounced its clauses charging Germany with responsibility for World War I. He then definitely set out to expand Germany beyond the restrictive boundaries which the treaty of Versailles had imposed upon it. For this purpose he would commit a series of quick aggressions against neighboring countries. He would do so preferably by means of intrigue and diplomacy, but if necessary by force and even at the risk of a general international war.

By the beginning of 1938 everything seemed to be shaping up most auspiciously for Hitler. His armies, thanks in no small measure to Goering's energy and organizing ability, Circum-were now the strongest in the world, and the best stances mechanized with up-to-date tanks and bombers. His German people, subjected to the incessant outpouring of Goeb-Expansion bels' propaganda machine, were now overwhelmingly in back of him, proud of his past successes, and confident of his unfailing leadership. Moreover, the international situation was favorable. Through the Axis and Anti-Comintern agreements, Germany now had close friendship with Italy, Japan, and Spain, and its non-aggression pact with Poland provided a buffer in the east against the Soviet Union, just as the newly fortified Rhineland furnished a strong line of defense in the west against France. With the Russian setback in the Spanish Civil War, there was lessening chance of cooperation between the Soviet Union and the Western democracies. France, troubled by internal strife, was on the de-fensive. In Great Britain anxiety to keep out of war characterized both the Conservative government of Neville Chamberlain and the opposing Labor party. And the United States was rigidly adhering to "isolation" and "neutrality."

Early in 1938, preparatory to his territorial aggressions, Hitler appointed as his foreign minister the unscrupulous, raucous-voiced Joachim von Ribbentrop, and as Chief of Staff of his armies the Nazi-minded General Wilhelm Keitel. In February he acted. He summoned Schuschnigg, the Austrian prime minister, to his castle of Berchtesgaden and extorted from him a promise to admit Austrian Nazis to his cabinet, including their violent leader, Arthur Seyss-Inquart. Schuschnigg, after his return to Vienna, made a desperate attempt to ward off the Nazifying of Austria. He called for a plebiscite of the Austrian people, urging the Socialists to join his own Catholic party in upholding the country's independence. There is little doubt that if the plebiscite had been freely held as scheduled on March 13, it would have resulted in a two-to-one defeat for the Nazis.

But two days before the scheduled date, Hitler dispatched into Austria a German army, which quickly overran the defenseless country and installed Seyss-Inquart at Vienna as "Governor." Schuschnigg and other patriots were imprisoned, and still others escaped a like or worse fate only by flight. In April, Hitler proclaimed the annexation of Austria to Germany, and this was promptly ratified by a plebiscite which the Nazis directed and controlled. Germany thus increased its population by seven million and extended its territory like a wedge into east-central Europe between Czechoslovakia and Yugoslavia.

**Seizure of Austria**

Hitler's forceful seizure of Austria was a flagrant case of aggression and treaty violation. Yet it met with no serious opposition abroad. Four years earlier, a first attempt of Hitler to seize Austria had been blocked by the firm united stand of Italy, France, and Great Britain.[1] Now none of these powers moved. France was in the midst of a cabinet crisis and feared to act without Italy and Britain. Italy, bound by recent ties to Germany and mindful of its own imperial ambitions in the Mediterranean, was content to receive Hitler's assurance of "eternal" gratitude and cooperation. Already Britain's prime minister, Neville Chamberlain, had dismissed his anti-Axis foreign minister, Anthony Eden, and adopted a policy which he thought best calculated to preserve peace among the great powers but which his later critics dubbed "appeasement." While leaving the dubious Soviet Union out of account, he would strive for a friendly understanding between

[1] See above, pp. 597, 610–611.

Great Britain and France on one side and Italy and Germany on the other.

Hence Great Britain promptly acquiesced in Germany's annexation of Austria in April 1938, and in the same month it signed a set of conciliatory treaties with Italy. In return for Italy's promise to withdraw from Spain "as soon as practicable" and to stop anti-British propaganda in Egypt and Palestine, Britain promised to use its influence with the League of Nations to secure general recognition of Italy's conquest of Ethiopia. Accordingly, Great Britain obtained from the League, amid many recriminations and against the despairing protests of the Emperor Haile Selassie, an authorization for its individual members to recognize, as they pleased, the King of Italy as Emperor of Ethiopia. It was an humiliating desertion of the League in behalf of a hoped-for Concert of great powers.

*British "Appeasement"*

Reassured by Chamberlain's appeasing attitude, Hitler quickly followed up his success in Austria with preparations for aggression against Czechoslovakia. This country, though possessing fairly strong armaments and defensive alliances with both France and the Soviet Union, had certain internal weaknesses resulting from nationalistic differences among its inhabitants.

*Germany and Czechoslovakia*

There was considerable friction between the Czechs of Bohemia and the Slovaks of Slovakia; the former, more industrial and "progressive," and more tinged with Marxian socialism, insisted upon their primacy in a centralized state; the Slovaks, more agricultural and more solidly Catholic, aspired to "home rule" within a federal state. There were also, in Czechoslovakia, minority groups of Poles, Magyars, and Ruthenians (Ukrainians) whose national self-consciousness was at variance with that of the majority, whether Czech or Slovak.

But far more serious were the differences between the Czechs and the large and influential minority of Germans—the so-called Sudetens—in Bohemia and Moravia. These Sudeten Germans, long used to a privileged position in the old Habsburg Empire, were naturally resentful, after the destruction of that Empire, of being subordinated to the Slavic Czechs. Not only did they make nationalistic demands on the Czechoslovak government, but they counted on the sympathy, if not the active assistance, of their kinsmen in Germany.

So long as Thomas Masaryk was President of Czechoslovakia, there was relatively little trouble,[1] but by the time Eduard Beneš succeeded him in 1935, the Nazis were in power in Germany and were fostering the growth of an essentially Nazi party among the Sudetens with Konrad Henlein as its chief. In the parliamentary elections of that year, this violently anti-Czech party polled more votes than any other single party in Czechoslovakia, and, although a coalition of the democratic parties managed to retain control of the government, the country was increasingly disturbed by domestic dissension.

Nazi Germany encouraged the dissension and took full advantage of it to conduct a vigorous diplomatic and press campaign against Czechoslovakia. The Czechs were accused by the Goebbels propaganda machine of harsh mistreatment of the Sudeten Germans and of depriving them of economic and cultural opportunities. The Czechs were also branded as being in league with the Soviet Union to spread Communism. In vain the Czechoslovak government denied the charges and in 1937 promised fuller cultural autonomy to the Sudetens. Henlein, with Hitler's backing, was now demanding political autonomy for them.

After Germany's seizure of Austria in March 1938, the campaign against Czechoslovakia was intensified both by Henlein and his Sudeten following within the country and by Hitler and the German Nazis outside. Matters reached a crisis in September. By this time Henlein was demanding not mere autonomy for the Sudetens but their outright incorporation in Germany, and Hitler was openly declaring that he would use force to "liberate" them if peaceful means failed. And his truculence toward Czechoslovakia was echoed in Poland and Hungary. On its side, Czechoslovakia prepared to resist any dismemberment. It mobilized its army and called upon France and Russia, and also its lesser allies of Rumania and Yugoslavia,[2] for their promised assistance in case of a German attack. For a few days, a vast international war seemed inescapable.

But Neville Chamberlain was resolute for peace, and in this he undoubtedly reflected the prevailing popular sentiment in Great Britain. Dramatically he flew back and forth between England and Germany, beseeching Hitler not to precipitate war,

---

[1] On Czechoslovakia prior to 1935, see above, pp. 408, 414, 594-595.
[2] On these alliances, see above, pp. 444-445, 611.

while, less spectacularly, Édouard Daladier, the French premier, flew back and forth between Paris and London. France was in a peculiarly embarrassing position. It was under treaty obligation to go to war in defense of Czechoslovakia, and yet it dared not go to war without Britain; and the other major guarantor of Czechoslovakian integrity, the Soviet Union, caustically criticized French inaction without taking any action itself.

The upshot was the sacrifice of Czechoslovakia. At a hectic conference at Munich on September 29, 1938, attended by Chamberlain, Daladier, Mussolini, and Hitler, a solemn pact was drawn up and agreed to by the four great powers of Britain, France, Italy, and Germany. It pledged the maintenance of peace among them, but it authorized Germany to occupy and annex the preponderantly German regions of Czechoslovakia. It was another striking victory for Hitler in tearing up the treaty of Versailles and expanding Germany's territory and mili- **Munich** tary resources, and it was followed by Poland's occu- **Pact and** pation of the Bohemian city of Teschen and Hungary's **Partition of Czecho-** appropriation of a strip of Slovakia. Czechoslovakia **slovakia** in the circumstances could do nought but submit to the loss of a third of its area and population and the bulk of its industrial plants.

Chamberlain did succeed in getting Germany and the other signatories of the Munich Pact to include in it a joint guarantee of the independence and territorial integrity of what was left of Czechoslovakia; and on his return from Munich to London a big crowd vociferously applauded his statement that he had assured "peace in our time."

In fact, however, Germany and Italy were in no mood to respect any guarantees, and Britain and France were in no position to enforce them. The latter powers were deficient in military strength, and they lacked allies. The Soviet Union, recognizing the weakness of the Western democracies, veered toward the Nazi and Fascist dictatorships, and the lesser powers in eastern Europe were quite disillusioned by Franco-British failure to prevent the partition of Czechoslovakia.

Germany, on the other hand, was now the largest state in Europe, west of the Soviet Union, with a population of about eighty million, and it was the strongest militarily and industrially. To Hitler, moreover, any treaties or pacts which stood in the way

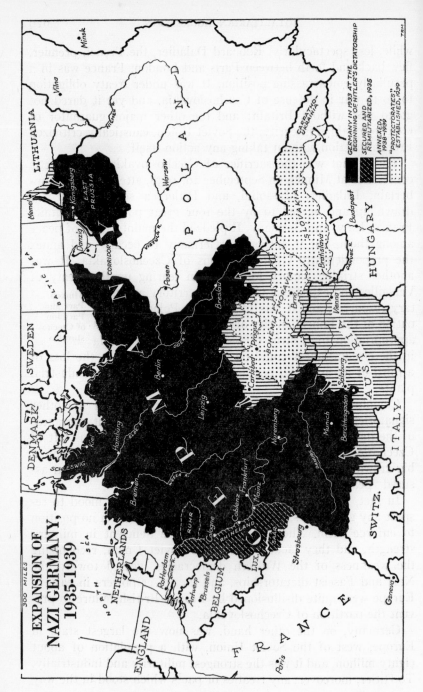

EXPANSION OF
NAZI GERMANY,
1935-1939

300 MILES

GERMANY IN 1933 AT THE
BEGINNING OF HITLER'S DICTATORSHIP

SECURED AND
REMILITARIZED, 1935

ANNEXED,
1938-1939

"PROTECTORATES"
ESTABLISHED, 1939

of its continuing expansion were so many "scraps of paper." He had abundantly demonstrated his contempt for the treaty of Versailles and the pact of Locarno. He speedily showed like contempt for the Munich Pact. If Britain and France could not prevent him from taking a part of Czechslovakia, why should a paper pledge deter him from completing the partition of that country?

Czechoslovakia, after its territorial and industrial losses in September 1938, was reorganized politically. In an effort to conciliate Hitler, Eduard Beneš resigned as President and was succeeded by Emil Hácha, a judge who was less identified with Czech nationalism and presumably more acceptable to Germany. Also, to conciliate the Slovaks, the centralized state was transformed into a federal union of three semi-autonomous states—Czechia (Bohemia and Moravia), Slovakia, and Carpatho-Ukrainia. These changes were made under pressure and amidst partisan strife and difficult economic readjustments, and they actually speeded, rather than retarded, the fulfillment of Hitler's designs.

In March 1939, utilizing as an excuse the complaints which the premier of the newly established state of Slovakia, a priest by the name of Joseph Tiso, made to him against the Czechs, Hitler ordered German troops to occupy Prague and to take possession of the whole country. No resistance could be offered. Czechia was immediately converted into a German "protectorate of Bohemia-Moravia," with Hácha as nominal President but with a German Nazi in actual control. Slovakia, under Tiso, became a puppet state of Germany, like Manchukuo of Japan. And Carpatho-Ukrainia was turned over to Hungary. Thus, despite international guarantees, Hitler did what he pleased, and Czechoslovakia disappeared entirely.

In the same month of March 1939, Hitler bullied Lithuania into surrendering its port of Memel to Germany. Early the next month, Mussolini, emboldened by Hitler's successes **Italian** and perhaps a bit envious of them, dispatched Italian **Seizure of** forces across the Adriatic to Albania, which could put **Albania** up little resistance and was promptly overrun. King Zog fled. Albania was joined to Italy. Victor Emmanuel III added to his titles of King of Italy and Emperor of Ethiopia the title of King of Albania. Mussolini was cheered, and the other powers acquiesced in this latest aggression.

### 5. FRANCO-BRITISH ATTEMPT TO HALT AGGRESSION, AND
### THE STALIN-HITLER PACT, 1939

The dual aggressions of Germany and Italy in the spring of 1939 alarmed both Britain and France and dispelled the dream which Chamberlain and Daladier had entertained at Munich that the four great powers would henceforth collaborate loyally to maintain peace and harmony. Not only did Italy use violence against Albania, but Mussolini followed up his aggression there by inspiring a violent press campaign against France. France, it was declared, had robbed a weak Italy in the past of territories, such as Savoy, Nice, Corsica, and Tunis, which were rightfully Italian, and now that Italy was strong, it should insist upon their restoration by France.

There was a good deal of bombast in the utterances of Mussolini and his Fascist press, and the French and British could safely discount Italy's military strength. Nevertheless they could not discount Germany's military might, and they soon discovered that Hitler would continue to employ it, or the threat of it, for German expansion, regardless of any treaty or pact to the contrary. No sooner had he gotten Franco-British consent to his partial spoliation of Czechoslovakia than his controlled press was demanding of Great Britain and France that they return the overseas colonies they had taken from Germany in the World War. And only six months after the solemn promise he had given Britain and France in the Munich Pact, he glaringly violated it by completing the destruction of Czechoslovakia.

Nor was this all. As soon as Hitler added to his previous conquest of Austria the conquest of Czechoslovakia and the Lithuanian port of Memel, he turned against Poland. **Germany and Poland** True, he had entered into a pact with Poland in 1934, guaranteeing its boundaries and independence for ten years, and the pact still had five years to run.[1] But Hitler was no respecter of treaties unless they served his immediate purposes, and he was now intent upon Germany's expansion at Polish expense. The tactics he adopted were similar to those he had recently used, with such eminent success, against Czechoslovakia. He asked Poland to agree to Germany's annexation of

[1] See above, p. 609.

the internationalized city of Danzig and to German control of a strip of land across the "Polish Corridor" which separated East Prussia from the main part of Germany and provided Poland with a direct outlet to the Baltic Sea. Then, when the Polish government showed an unwillingness to accede promptly to the request, Goebbels' propaganda machine again went into noisy action, this time in behalf of the "liberation" of fellow Germans from Polish "oppression" and "persecution."

This was too much and too hasty for the British prime minister, Neville Chamberlain. It completely disillusioned him about Nazi Germany and its lying Führer, and he suddenly and radically recast Great Britain's foreign policy. Taking advantage of the firm stand of Poland and of the fear in France that unless it now acted it would be completely isolated and become Hitler's next prey, Chamberlain arranged for a triple alliance among Great Britain, France, and Poland, guaranteeing one another's independence and territorial integrity, by war if necessary, against any aggression or threat. At the same time he proclaimed Britain's readiness to enter into a like alliance with Rumania, Greece, and Turkey. At last, Great Britain and France were minded to call a halt to aggression by either Germany or Italy. As a countermeasure, these two Axis powers signed at Berlin in May 1939 a close ten-year alliance, pledging mutual military assistance in case of war and promising that one would not conclude peace or an armistice without the other.

*Change in British Policy: Alliance with France and Poland*

Whether Great Britain and France, with the inferior armaments they possessed in the spring of 1939, could actually restrain Germany from attacking Poland, and thereby precipitating a second world war, was extremely doubtful. Much depended upon the attitude of the Communist dictatorship in Russia, which had a big army and obviously held a balance of power between the Axis and the Western democracies. If it should add its forces to the latter's, Hitler and his General Staff would certainly think twice before plunging Germany into a war that would involve heavy fighting in the east as well as in the west. On the other hand, if the Soviet Union held aloof, German chances of success were excellent.

*Decisive Role of Russia*

For a moment, Stalin seemed undecided. In April, his foreign minister, Litvinov, sounded out France and Britain about a Soviet pact with them, but on the same day the Soviet ambassador at Berlin suggested the possibility of an agreement with Germany. Then, cautiously, Stalin followed up the latter overtures. Early in May he retired Litvinov, the advocate of cooperation with France and Britain, and replaced him as foreign minister with Viacheslav Molotov, who was very suspicious of the Western powers and favorable to a Soviet policy of "realism" and "imperialism."

The next three months were feverish with negotiations and military preparations. France and Britain sent special representatives to Moscow to try to arrange for joint military action of the Soviet Union with them. They naturally expected that Hitler's long-standing hostility to Communism and Communist counter-denunciation of Fascists and Nazis would bar any Soviet aid to Germany and would secure it for themselves. Yet while the Soviet dictatorship continued to beguile the French and British missions at Moscow, it was secretly making serious proposals at Berlin. These, Hitler quickly perceived, provided a golden opportunity for Germany. He easily put aside his earlier scruples about Communism, and with them the anti-Comintern pact, and authorized his foreign minister, Ribbentrop, to make a definite arrangement with Stalin. It proved fairly easy. Germany could promise Russia, for its cooperation, an expansion of its territories which France and Britain, as the upholders of existing boundaries, were not free to offer; and Hitler was always free with promises.

Negotiations culminated on August 23, 1939. On that day, at Moscow, Molotov signed with Ribbentrop a Russo-German non-aggression pact, and at the ensuing festive banquet Stalin drank a toast to Hitler. The pact provided that, for the next ten years at least, the Soviet Union and Germany would not resort to war against each other, would not support any third power in the event it attacked either signatory, and would consult together on all matters of common interest. A supplementary agreement obligated the Soviet Union to supply Germany with certain needful war supplies, and Stalin obtained his reward in a secret protocol which was not made public until 1948. This virtually divided eastern Europe into spheres marked respectively for German and Russian conquest.

**Russo-German Pact: Beginning of World War II**

News of the Russo-German non-aggression pact, even without its secret protocol, created instant consternation in Britain, France, and Poland. It made clear that Poland would be attacked, and that in its defense France and Britain could expect no assistance from the Soviet Union. Events transpired accordingly, and rapidly. On September 1, 1939, only a week after the agreement between Hitler and Stalin, German armies invaded Poland. On September 3, honoring their assurances to Poland, Great Britain and France declared war on Germany. It was the beginning of World War II.

# CHAPTER XV

## WORLD WAR II, 1939–1945

I. INITIAL GERMAN SUCCESSES AND RUSSIAN COOPERATION, 1939–1940

UITE auspiciously did Nazi Germany begin the Second World War. It was splendidly prepared, with superior air and ground forces and extraordinary mechanized equipment and with popular confidence in the vigor and ability of its high command. By its recent pact with Communist Russia it was safeguarded on the East and assured of a speedy victory over Poland. On the West, of course, there would have to be a reckoning with France and Great Britain, and with British Dominions all of which, with the exception of Ireland, followed Britain in declaring war against Germany. But the reckoning could safely be postponed until the conquest of Poland was completed and the whole might of German arms was concentrated in the West.

France and Britain were ill prepared for war. They had fewer available soldiers than Germany and notably inferior equipment. Moreover, they entered the war reluctantly and with misgivings. Especially in France the war effort was gravely impeded by an undercurrent of popular pacifism and by more or less open criticism and opposition. There were Frenchmen of "rightest" and fascist tendency who favored collaboration, rather than war, with Nazi Germany. There were still more "leftist" French Communists who echoed the propagandist contention of the dictatorship at Moscow that the war, so far as the Western Allies were concerned, was "capitalistic" and "imperialistic."

Weakness of France at home was attended by its weakness abroad. Events of the last few years had dissolved or nullified the defensive alliances which it had formed after the First World War with Belgium, Czechoslovakia, Rumania, and Yugoslavia,[1] and none of these countries was now minded to antagonize Germany or Russia by siding with France and Britain. On the other hand, Germany now had an outright ally in Italy and virtually another in the Soviet Union; and it apparently had nothing to fear from the two non-European great powers—the United States and Japan. The militarists in control of Japan were inclined to sympathize with Nazi Germany and to believe that its success in Europe would contribute to the success of their own aggressive designs in the Far East by forestalling foreign interference. In the United States popular sentiment was overwhelmingly pacifist, and though verbally favorable to Britain and France, it was quite opposed to active support of them. In accordance with the strict neutrality legislation then in force, and in unquestioned harmony with public opinion, President Franklin Roosevelt declared on September 3, 1939, that the United States would stay out of the war and remain at peace.

In the circumstances the initial stage of the Second World War—the slashing German attack on Poland, beginning on September 1—proved a very one-sided affair. The Poles, taken by surprise, were unable to effect a full mobilization; and, outnumbered three to one and deficient in equipment, their armies were no match for the *Blitzkrieg* ("lightning war") which the German invaders waged under the brilliant direction of Hitler's Chief of Staff, Marshal Walther von Brauchitsch. It was essentially a new kind of war, and a most terrifying kind. It involved heavy air bombing of fortifications, roads, railways, industrial plants, and power stations, and, amid resulting confusion and destruction, a quick infantry advance spearheaded by a big mobile force of armored tanks. Even the weather helped the Germans, for the clear bright days of that September were ideal for air operations and kept the Polish plains dry and firm for tank maneuvers.

*Conquest and Partition of Poland*

The Poles fought bravely and furiously, but to no avail. Within two weeks their western provinces were overrun and their capital city of Warsaw was surrounded. Then, on September 17, their retreating forces were engulfed from the rear by an invasion of Russian armies. Ten days later, after being reduced to a shambles, Warsaw surrendered to the Germans, and Poland was prostrate

[1] See above, pp. 444–445.

before its conquerors. On September 29 Germany and Russia, through their respective foreign ministers, Ribbentrop and Molotov, partitioned the hapless country. Russia's share, comprising slightly over half the total area of Poland and about fourteen million of its people, was annexed, after farcical plebiscites, to the Soviet states of Ukrainia and Byelorussia. Germany's share, which included the industrialized and more populous western regions, was split into two parts: one half was incorporated outright in the Nazi Empire; the other half, with Cracow as its "capital," was made into a German "protectorate." Everywhere throughout the former Republic, the surviving population was subjected to ruthless exploitation; and in the German-occupied areas this was accompanied by merciless extermination of large numbers of Poles and Jews by firing squads and "gas chambers" directed by the Nazi police chief, Heinrich Himmler.

Remnants of the Polish armies, together with the Polish Republican government, managed to escape capture. The government fled to Rumania and thence established itself as a "government-in-exile" under the premiership of General Sikorski, first at Angers in France and subsequently at London. Escaping Polish troops made their way by devious routes to western Europe where they joined the French and British armies.

With Poland out of the way, Germany could concentrate all its forces against the Western Allies, while Russia felt free to assail countries of eastern Europe which the Russo-German pact had indicated as within its "sphere of influence." The very day after obtaining half of Poland, the Soviet dictatorship, in flat violation of previous pledges, compelled Estonia to grant it naval and air bases and to admit Russian troops. Within the next two weeks it extorted similar concessions from Latvia and Lithuania. The three small Baltic states, utterly powerless to oppose their big neighbor, thus passed under its military control, which was merely preliminary to their extinction as independent republics and their incorporation in the Soviet Union.

**Russian Seizure of Baltic States**

Simultaneously, in early October, the Soviet dictatorship demanded of Finland the dismantling of the strong defensive "Mannerheim Line" which it had built along the Russian frontier, the cession of part of the Karelian peninsula, certain Baltic islands, and the Arctic port of Petsamo, and a thirty-year lease of the naval base of Hangö close to the Finnish capital. Finland, unlike the other Baltic states, did not yield immediately. Though it offered to concede some of the Russian demands, it held out against others. In mid-November, Stalin and Molotov abruptly ended the negotiations, and the Soviet Union went to war with Finland. **Russo-Finnish War**

The Finns, under command of the veteran Marshal Mannerheim, put up a stubborn and valiant resistance. They were adept at winter fighting; and they received considerable material help from Sweden and Norway, and at least moral encouragement from France and Britain and the entire Western world. In mid-December, the League of Nations, in a last gasp of life, pronounced Russia an "aggressor" and expelled it from membership. Yet Finland could not long withstand Russia's overwhelming forces. These breached the Mannerheim Line in January 1940, and a month later they were in occupation of a large part of the country. Finland then sued for peace, and on March 12 the war was formally ended by Finnish acceptance of all the original Russian demands and in addition the cession of the whole Karelian peninsula including the city of Viborg. Altogether Finland was despoiled of over 16,000 square miles of territory and 400,000 inhabitants, and of its principal military and naval defenses. The Soviet Union correspondingly enlarged its own "Karelian-Finnish State."

Meanwhile, nothing was done, and apparently nothing could be done, by France and Great Britain to prevent the defeat and partition of Poland or the despoiling of Finland. The Western Allies were in no position to undertake an offensive against Germany, much less against Germany and Russia combined. They were astounded by the swiftness and terror of the *Blitzkrieg* in Poland and quite unprepared to cope with it. They possessed a wholly inadequate number of planes and tanks, and they recognized that any infantry advance would be stopped by the heavily fortified German "Westwall" (or Siegfried Line) in the Rhineland and might cost them catastrophic losses. Though Britain enjoyed naval superiority over Germany, it had a relatively small and ill-equipped army, the transport of which to the Continent took time. France had a larger army, but its morale was none too good and its commander-in-chief, General Maurice Gamelin, was convinced **Unpreparedness of Western Powers** that it could be preserved and strengthened only by avoiding offensive operations and maintaining defensive positions behind the supposedly impregnable Maginot Line which the French had been building since 1930 along their northeastern border from Switzerland to Belgium and which was now paralleled across the border by the German Westwall.

Thus the land forces of the Western Allies, if seemingly sheltered from German attack by one line of fortifications, was practically prevented by the opposite line from invading Germany, and hence from affording any relief to Poland. This curious situation in the West continued throughout the winter of 1939–1940 with some patrol activity and with occasional airplane dropping of propaganda pamphlets, but without serious fighting. It gave currency to the description of the apparent inactivity as a "phony war."

On the German side, appearances were deceptive. True, the unusual severity of the winter of 1939–1940, and perhaps an overestimate of French strength, militated against Germany's prompt following up of its offensive in the East with one in the West. Yet the Germans were feverishly active. Throughout the winter they were busily building up their forces behind the Westwall and along the Belgian and Dutch borders, speeding the production of planes and tanks and other instruments of mechanized warfare, accumulating munitions and supplies, and preparing for an all-out offensive in the spring. They also launched, as early as October, a vigorous campaign of unrestricted submarine warfare, which, with improved technique, soon proved more destructive of Allied shipping and more menacing to Great Britain than the similar campaign in the First World War.

On the Allied side, Great Britain gave special attention to safeguarding its navy and commerce against German submarines and surface raiders; and in a naval engagement off the coast of Uruguay in South America, a British squadron in December 1939 destroyed the German battleship *Graf Spee*. Moreover, from November onwards, both Britain and France supplemented their stock of munitions and supplies by purchases in the United States under a so-called "cash-and-carry" amendment to American neutrality legislation. Yet neither the British government of Neville Chamberlain nor the French government of Édouard Daladier exhibited any such energy as Lloyd George and Clemenceau had displayed in the First World War or as Nazi Germany was now putting forth. The dispatch of British troops to France was limited and leisurely, and French arming was sluggish and to a large extent outmoded. In vain a French army officer, Charles De Gaulle, urged speedy mass production of tanks and other implements for waging the new type of war which Germany had so successfully demonstrated in Poland. The lessons of this war seemed lost on the Allied governments, which optimistically hoped that their armies could sit indefinitely behind the protecting Maginot Line, while their superior economic and commercial resources, combined with a naval blockade, would gradually weigh against Germany and bring it to terms. They failed to appreciate that what Germany was deprived of by a blockade at sea, it was getting in ample quantity overland from Russia.

In March 1940 a bit more energy was infused into French preparedness by the replacement of Daladier in the premiership by Paul Reynaud, though Daladier remained in the cabinet as minister of war. And in early April the Allied governments pressed Norway to stop the transport of Swedish iron ore through its coastal waters to Germany. Already, however, the Germans had prepared a counter-stroke to obtain control of all Scandinavia. On April 9 they invaded and occupied Denmark against the "protest" of its King, Christian X; and simultaneously they launched an air and naval attack on Norway. Here they met with a declaration of war and an attempt at resistance. This was confused and disjointed, and was interfered with by traitors within the country. The leading traitor, a certain Major Vidkun Quisling, who had once been Norwegian minister of war, was later to enrich modern language with a new word, for "quisling" came to stand for any "fifth-column" betrayer of his homeland to a foreign country. Major Quisling, backed by a small group of Norwegian Nazis, co-operated with the Germans and headed the puppet regime they set up in Norway.

For a short time it seemed as if Great Britain might be able, with its superior naval strength, to free Norway. But German air power drove British ships out of the straits between Denmark and Norway and soon compelled them to quit Norwegian ports from Oslo up to Narvik. The Norwegian King Haakon VII, after being chased about the country by the victorious Germans,

escaped to England and there set up a "government-in-exile."
Most of the Norwegian merchant marine also escaped and became
an important adjunct to Allied shipping in the Atlantic. Yet the
Allies had to face the distressing fact that their naval superiority
was ineffectual without air superiority and that Germany now
had in Norway and Denmark strategically located bases whence
its planes could dominate all Scandinavia and further imperil
North Atlantic shipping and Great Britain itself.

On May 10, 1940, as a result of the British fiasco in Norway,
Winston Churchill succeeded Neville Chamberlain as prime minister. In Churchill the British found a great war leader, capable
of uniting and inspiring them in the face of disaster. Son of an
American mother and a father who was descended from the
famous Duke of Marlborough, Churchill had had a long experience in public affairs. He had consistently warned his country of
the rising menace of Nazi Germany and had severely criticized
Chamberlain's pre-war policy of "appeasement." He now took the
helm in Britain's gravest crisis. For the loss of Norway was only a
portent of much greater loss. On the very day he became British
prime minister the Germans let loose a thunderous *Blitzkrieg*
against the Allies in France.

### 2. FALL OF FRANCE AND ISOLATION OF BRITAIN, 1940–1941

The Germans, instead of making a frontal attack on the Maginot
Line, which would have been much too costly, outflanked it by a
surprise attack through the neutral countries of Holland, Belgium, and Luxemburg. Luxemburg was occupied on the first day of the attack, May 10, 1940, and
its Grand-Duchess and her government fled to France
and thence to the United States. Holland and Belgium declared
war, but the armed resistance they offered was quickly mowed
down by the same tactics as the Germans had employed in Poland
—a skillful use of air power, lightning movements of armored
columns spearheaded by tanks, some "fifth column" work, the use
of parachute troops, and relentless pressure against a disorganized
foe.

In Holland, German paratroopers, wearing Dutch uniforms,
hurtled down from the air, while German ground forces, in rubber
boots, swarmed across canals and flooded fields. The Rotterdam
airfield was captured on the first day, and the city was turned to

rubble by a murderous and unopposed bombing. Armored columns raced across the country, cutting the Dutch army into bits. Within a week all resistance was crushed, and while Queen Wilhelmina and her government took refuge in England, the Germans installed as "governor" Seyss-Inquart whose earlier reputation for Nazi ferocity in Austria he amply confirmed in Holland.

Belgian resistance lasted not much longer. At the very start the Germans captured bridges over the Meuse River and the Albert Canal. All the British forces on the Continent, together with a French army, were pushed northward to help the Belgians hold a second line from Antwerp to Louvain and Namur. But German armored columns swept through the Ardennes, which the Allies had imagined would be impassable, and on May 14 broke into France at Sedan beyond the west end of the Maginot Line. Thence, joined by their forces in Luxemburg, they rushed westward to Boulogne on the English Channel, thus cutting off the main French armies in France from the million Allied troops in Belgium. Against the latter the Germans drove fast and furiously from all directions.

On May 28 the Belgian King Leopold III, in despair, complied with the German demand for "unconditional surrender" of his army, and was placed in "protective custody" near Brussels. He did so against the advice of his cabinet, which escaped to London, and against the bitter protest of France and Great Britain whose troops in Belgium were left isolated along the coast. For a week the British worked manfully with all sorts of water craft to evacuate these troops from Dunkirk. Despite heavy German bombing, they managed to rescue some 225,000 of their own soldiers and about 110,000 others (mostly French) and get them safely to England. They had to abandon, however, all their guns, munitions, and supplies.

**British Evacuation from Dunkirk**

Meanwhile, the same tactics which the Germans employed to cut off Belgium and the British were being used to demoralize, cut through, and overwhelm the several French armies in France itself. In vain the French high command was transferred from General Gamelin to General Maxime Weygand, and De Gaulle was promoted to the rank of general and named under-secretary of war. It was too late. The French armies lacked planes and tanks, and they were confused and blocked not only by the German *Blitzkrieg,* but by enormous

**French Defeat and Italian Attack**

numbers of civilian refugees and, in some instances, by internal Communist and "fifth-column" activity. And, to cap the climax, Fascist Italy seized the opportunity to join its Axis partner in the attack on France, just as Communist Russia had seized a like opportunity to assist in the destruction of Poland.

On June 11, 1940, Italy declared war on France and Great Britain, and its armies were set in motion across the southeastern French border. The next day the Germans crossed the Marne and on June 14 occupied Paris, while the French government moved to Tours and thence to Bordeaux, with German armored columns in hot pursuit. The French armies were already dissolved or taken prisoner by the Germans.

France had promised Britain not to make a separate peace, and on June 11 Churchill flew to Tours in an attempt to persuade the French cabinet to stick to the promise and carry on the war from North Africa in continuing union with the British Empire. Reynaud, the French premier, agreed; but by the time the cabinet reached Bordeaux a majority of its members were so convinced of the hopelessness of the situation that they overruled him and voted to quit the struggle. Whereupon Reynaud resigned, and the French President Lebrun replaced him with the eighty-four-year-old Marshal Henri Pétain, who had won fame as the defender of Verdun in the First World War.[1] The new premier on June 16 obtained Churchill's reluctant consent for the withdrawal of France on the one condition that its navy should not fall into German hands. On the next day Pétain asked Hitler for an armistice.

For the conclusion of the armistice, the Germans brought out of a museum the railway car used for signing the armistice **Armistice** of November 11, 1918, which had registered Germany's **of June** defeat in the First World War.[2] At the same spot, in **1940** the forest of Compiègne, French delegates now signed, on June 21, 1940, an armistice which registered the disastrous defeat of their country. A camera at the scene caught Hitler dancing a little jig. And shortly afterwards, another crestfallen French delegation signed an armistice with Italy in the presence of a puffed-up Mussolini at Rome.

By the terms of the double armistice, France north of the

---

[1] See above, p. 383.
[2] See above, p. 409.

Loire River and its entire Atlantic coast would be occupied and administered by the Germans, and a strip along its southeastern border, by the Italians; the remainder would have a measure of autonomy; the country would have to pay heavy "costs of occupation"; French prisoners of war, numbering almost two million, would be held in Germany as hostages; the French navy, though retained by Pétain's "autonomous" government, would be disarmed. It was a sensational victory for Nazi Germany. France, the one country on the Continent for whose armed forces Hitler had had respect and some fear, was now crushed, and its crushing had been accomplished within six weeks and with almost negligible cost to Germany.

The fall of France had immediate effects of far-reaching importance. First of all, it practically ended the Third French Republic, which had lasted for seventy years, from the military defeat of 1870, through the victory in 1918, to this terrible defeat in 1940—longer than any other government which France had had since the eighteenth century. On the morrow of the armistice with Germany and Italy, Marshal Pétain established his government at Vichy, in the part of France left to him, and the members of the Republican Parliament who could be assembled there voted in July to grant him dictatorial powers as "Chief of the French State." With Pierre Laval as his principal lieutenant, the Marshal proceeded to establish a "rightest" and authoritarian, if not fully fascist, regime. Political parties and trade unions were suppressed, and for the revolutionary watchwords of "liberty, equality, fraternity" were substituted "labor, family, fatherland." For a time, most Frenchmen regarded Pétain as an heroic patriot who only awaited a favorable chance to strike back at the Germans. Actually he proved a more or less innocent tool of Laval and other officials of the Vichy regime who imagined that the salvation of France depended on collaboration with Nazi Germany. This, of course, was encouraged by Hitler, who in December 1940 made a theatrical and somewhat ironic gesture of friendship by having the remains of "Napoleon II" [1] brought from Vienna to Paris and laid alongside the remains of his father, the famous Emperor.

Not all Frenchmen accepted the armistice or recognized the Vichy regime. A leading opponent was General De Gaulle, who

[1] See *Modern Europe to 1870*, pp. 543, 708.

escaped to England, and, with British backing, formed a "Free French" provisional government and enlisted the support of the

**De Gaulle and "Free French"** French soldiers who had been evacuated from Dunkirk. In response, a Vichy court-martial condemned him to death for treason and desertion. Thus began a struggle between "Vichy French" and "Free French" for national predominance, first in the colonies, and eventually in the homeland. The Free French won French Equatorial Africa and some scattered island possessions of France, while the Vichy French for a time retained French North Africa, Syria, Madagascar, and Indo-China. In France itself, where the German police and occupation forces naturally made common cause with the Vichy French, the Free French had to confine their efforts to stimulating an underground resistance movement.

The fall of France, calamitous as it was for the French, threatened equally calamitous consequences for the British.

**Isolation of Britain** Churchill had told Parliament in his first speech as prime minister that all he could promise his fellow countrymen was "blood and toil and tears and sweat." The debacle in Belgium and France gave terrifying significance to his words. Great Britain now stood alone, and from Germany's triumphant forces it was separated only by the narrow waters of the English Channel. The whole Atlantic coastline of Europe from Norway to the Pyrenees was in German hands, and all the resources, factories, and labor of western and central Europe, together with much of Russia's, were at Germany's disposal.

Following the French collapse, the Germans made preparations for the conquest of Britain. They assembled at the coastal ports between Rotterdam and Cherbourg some three thousand barges for a sea-borne invasion, and, to insure its success, they established numerous adjacent bases whence they could intensify their submarine campaign against British shipping and dispatch bombing and fighting planes to destroy British defenses and provide air coverage for the invasion.

The time required for these German preparations was energetically utilized by Churchill and his colleagues to put Britain in the best possible position to withstand the impending onslaught. English factories worked overtime to replace the military equipment which had been lost in the evacuation from Dunkirk, and auxiliary forces were added to the home army. To guard the

surrounding seas, and the ocean routes over which needful supplies were coming from America, special precautions were taken
against German submarines, including installation of British bases
in the Danish dependencies of Iceland and Greenland. Besides,
to forestall possible German appropriation of the French navy,
British squadrons early in July 1940 interned or forcibly disabled
all French warships except the dismantled fleet in the protected
harbor of Toulon. Most important of all, as events proved, was
British attention to air defense. The Germans in 1940 had many
more war planes than the British, but the British planes were
better built and their pilots better trained and they were supplemented by effective anti-aircraft guns.

The "Battle of Britain" really opened on August 8, 1940, with
a mass German air attack on British coastal towns, and for the
next five months wave after wave of German bombers
spread destruction all over Britain. On London, a main **"Battle of Britain"**
target, some fifty thousand high explosive bombs (not
counting incendiaries) were dropped. The city of Coventry was
almost obliterated, and nearly every manufacturing or commercial town was badly battered. Almost 40,000 persons were
killed, and twice as many wounded.

Yet the British held out. Their civilian, as well as military,
morale was excellent, and their airforce performed prodigies
of skill and daring. Not only did the British knock down over
three thousand enemy planes, three times as many as they lost
of their own, but they made counter night raids on German
bases on the Continent and wrought havoc among the German
barges. Although the "Battle of Britain" continued through the
winter of 1940–1941, the chances of Germany's obtaining the
mastery of air and sea essential to a successful invasion of
Great Britain dwindled steadily. For this outcome, Winston
Churchill paid tribute to British flyers: "Never in the field of
human conflict was so much owed by so many to so few."

Meanwhile, Fascist Italy was emboldened by the collapse
of France and by British preoccupation with home defense to
undertake conquests in the Mediterranean area. Italian columns, operating from Ethiopia, overran British Somaliland and
penetrated into Kenya and the Sudan. In September an Italian
army under Marshal Graziani, starting from Tripoli, invaded
northern Egypt and drove back the defending force of

Australians and Poles commanded by the British General Wavell.
Then in October, following the refusal of the Greek government
**Italian** of George II to break relations with Great Britain and
**Attack on** to submit to a virtual Italian protectorate, Italy de-
**Greece** clared war on Greece and attacked it with an army
based on Albania. Mussolini's hopes ran high. Italian victory in
Greece seemed likely, and it might lead, with like victory in
Egypt, to the incorporation of the whole eastern Mediterranean
basin in a Fascist Roman Empire.

Communist Russia likewise took advantage of the fall of France
and of British isolation to forward its imperialist ambitions. On
**Continuing** the same day on which the Germans entered Paris, the
**Russian** dictatorship at Moscow directed the forceful annexa-
**Aggression** tion of Lithuania, and two days later it seized Latvia
and Estonia. From all three Baltic countries, patriots fled
abroad or were committed to Russian prison camps. In the same
month of June, the Russian dictatorship demanded of Rumania
the "return" of Bessarabia and the cession of northern Bukovina.
In vain the Rumanian King Carol II appealed to Germany and
Italy. Hitler and Mussolini advised him to yield, and so Rumania
helplessly surrendered to the Soviet Union 21,000 square miles
of territory and four million people.

As soon as Russia, with Axis cooperation, secured a part of
Rumania, other parts were demanded by Hungary and Bulgaria.
**Partition** And as a result of "friendly intervention" by the Axis,
**of Rumania** unopposed by Russia, a further partitioning of Rumania occurred in August 1940. Bulgaria obtained
3,000 square miles of southern Dobruja, and Hungary got the
northern half of Transylvania, containing an area of 16,000
square miles and a population of two and a half million. Whereupon King Carol II abdicated in favor of his son Michael, who
was obliged to entrust what was left of Rumania to a pro-Axis
fascist dictatorship under General Ion Antonescu.

Japan also turned pro-Axis. Its military leaders were im-
mensely impressed by the display of German might in the spring
**Extending** of 1940, and they perceived in the crushing of France
**Japanese** and the difficulties of Britain an assurance that Japan
**Aggression** could extend its imperial sway in the Far East without
serious danger of foreign interference. In July a definitely pro-
German cabinet took office at Tokyo, under the premiership of

Prince Konoye, pledged not only to vigorous prosecution of the war in China [1] but also to the creation of a Japanese-controlled "Greater East Asia." In September, treaties of alliance were signed with Germany and Italy, making Japan a full-fledged member of the Axis. At the same time Japan extorted from the Vichy governor of Indo-China permission to land soldiers and use airfields in that French dependency, and not long afterwards it brought Siam (Thailand) under its influence by helping that country despoil French Indo-China of some 21,000 square miles of territory.

By the autumn of 1940, Nazi Germany appeared all-powerful. True, it was experiencing difficulty in conquering Great Britain or persuading it to negotiate. But how long could Britain hold out alone against so much of the world that was now cooperating with Germany? The enlarged Soviet Union seemed quite willing to go on cooperating indefinitely; its press was certainly filled with diatribes against British "imperialists" and "war-mongers." And the close Axis alliance of Italy and Japan with Germany was joined in November by Hungary, Rumania, and Slovakia. The Spanish government of General Franco, indebted as it was to Hitler and Mussolini, assured them of its abiding friendship, although its repugnance to Communist Russia and its desire to effect domestic recovery from recent civil war restrained it, at least temporarily, from actual juncture with the Axis.[2]

In the United States, the rapid succession of German victories, culminating in the rout of the British in Belgium and the fall of France, and inciting cooperation with Nazi Germany on the part of Italy, Russia, and Japan, caused consternation and particular alarm lest Great Britain itself might soon fall and its empire be dismembered, in which case America would be the next victim of Axis aggression. Popular sentiment was still averse to active participation in the war, but it was now inclined to back President Roosevelt in taking defensive measures and giving the British "all aid short of war." **United States Aid to Britain**

In May 1940, amid the German *Blitzkrieg* in France, the President called for American production of what then seemed the

[1] See above, pp. 624–625. In March 1940 the Japanese set up a Chinese puppet government at Nanking to collaborate with them in the war.

[2] See above, pp. 620–623. It may be noted that when pressed to go to war with Great Britain, Franco requested military equipment and territorial compensation far in excess of what he could expect that Germany and Italy would provide.

fabulous number of 50,000 war planes. In July, Congress passed a "two-ocean navy bill," authorizing the construction of some two hundred new warships and their distribution so that the United States would possess naval superiority in both Atlantic and Pacific waters. Provision was also made, through a Pan-American Conference at Havana, for cooperation in mutual defense between the United States and the republics to the south of it, and in August a similar agreement was reached with Canada.

In September the United States turned over to Great Britain fifty naval destroyers in return for naval bases in Newfoundland, Bermuda, and the West Indies. In the same month, Congress passed a "selective service act," establishing a system of compulsory military training. The United States also multiplied its production of war material, and in November agreed to share the increase on a fifty-fifty basis with Britain. By the spring of 1941 it was making large loans to Great Britain under a "lend lease act," and its navy was helping the British to patrol the Atlantic against German submarines.[1] The United States was indeed becoming, as its President said, "the arsenal of democracy." Meanwhile it was issuing ever more weighty warnings against Japanese aggression in the Pacific.

Thanks to American aid, as well as to its own heroic efforts, Great Britain was enabled not only to hold out against Nazi Germany but to contribute to Italian reverses in the Near East.

**Italian Reverses**    Fascist Italy in the autumn of 1940 had been too ambitious and had weakened its offensive in North Africa by undertaking another in Greece. Consequently, the Italian invasion of Egypt by Marshal Graziani was arrested and turned back by General Wavell's army in December 1940, and by the following March almost all of Italian North Africa was in British hands. Meanwhile, other British forces were overcoming the Italians in Eritrea and Somaliland, and expelling them from Ethiopia. In May 1941 they restored the Emperor Haile Selassie [2] to his capital of Addis Ababa, thus dispelling Mussolini's dream of a vast Italian empire in East Africa.

---

[1] United States naval forces took over Greenland in April 1941 and Iceland in July, and from these areas, as well as from Continental America, they patrolled the western half of the Atlantic, thereby enabling the British to concentrate their naval forces in the eastern half.

[2] See above, pp. 612, 614.

Nor did Mussolini's hope of subjugating Greece prove less illusory. The Greeks, under the leadership of General Metaxas, put up surprisingly strong resistance to the Italian invaders and in January 1941, after three months' fighting, drove them entirely out of Greece and back into Albania.

Germany was then called upon to pull Italy's chestnuts out of the fire. In February 1941 Hitler sent into North Africa several highly trained and armored divisions under one of his most brilliant and resourceful generals, Erwin Rommel, who replaced Graziani and pushed the British out of Tripoli and Libya and carried the war anew into Egypt. At the same time, to avenge Italian defeat in Greece, Hitler prepared to attack it with German forces. To do so, he demanded free passage for them across Bulgaria and Yugoslavia. Bulgaria readily acceded to the demand and indeed became in March 1941 a seventh member of the Axis coalition.[1]

Yugoslavia hesitated, however, and when its ruler, the Regent Paul, finally decided to negotiate an agreement with Germany, an army revolt at Belgrade on March 27 deposed him and in the name of the youthful King Peter II installed an anti-German cabinet. The outcome was a brief German-Yugoslav war. Within two weeks the Germans, with their terrifying *Blitzkreig*, mowed down all formal resistance and drove King Peter and his cabinet into exile. They then divided Yugoslavia into two parts: Croatia they made into a puppet state, an eighth member of the Axis; Serbia they put under the nominal rule of an Italian prince with themselves in military control at Belgrade. Though guerrilla fighting was continued by the patriotic General Mikhailovich in the mountainous wilds of Serbia, it did not stay the rolling of the German war machine into Greece.

*German Conquest of Yugoslavia and Greece*

The Greeks were now pretty well exhausted by their great effort against the Italians. The death of General Metaxas in January had dispirited them, and they lacked the means of coping with the mechanized warfare of the Germans. In vain the British weakened their own army in Egypt by detaching from it an expeditionary force to assist the Greeks. By the end of April 1941, Greece was overrun by the Germans, and the British saved 44,000 of their force only by another Dunkirk-like evacuation.

[1] Thus joining Germany, Italy, Japan, Hungary, Rumania, and Slovakia.

For another month the Greeks, with British aid, clung to Crete, but this too they had to abandon in the face of overwhelming attacks of German airplanes and paratroopers. The Greek government of King George II became still another "government-in-exile" at London.

Yet the very reverses which Great Britain suffered in the spring of 1941 in North Africa, Greece, and Crete were evidence that Germany was far afield from a knockout blow against England itself. And any such blow was now indefinitely postponed by a break between Germany and Russia.

### 3. BREAK BETWEEN GERMANY AND RUSSIA AND PARTICIPATION OF THE UNITED STATES, 1941

In November 1940 Nazi Germany had sought to supplement the existing Russo-German pact by drawing Communist Russia into full-fledged membership in the Axis alliance along with itself, Italy, and Japan. Hitler and his foreign minister, Ribbentrop, had then welcomed a visit of the Russian foreign minister, Molotov, to Berlin and had proposed to him a general plan for delimiting "spheres of influence" among the four great powers: Japan would have China and southeastern Asia; Italy, northeastern Africa; Germany, central Africa; and Russia, if it should join the Axis, an expansion through Persia into India and an unrestricted outlet **Hitler** through the Turkish Straits. Molotov, after consulting **Angered** Stalin, expressed Russia's willingness to join the Axis, **by Russian** though he required additional pledges that the Soviet **Demands** Union should have a free hand in Finland, Bulgaria, and part of Turkey and that Japan should cede it the southern half of Sakhalin.[1]

If Hitler had accepted these terms, there can be little doubt that Russia would have continued and intensified its cooperation with Germany, with the gravest consequences to the whole world. Hitler, however, was angered by what he deemed the exorbitant demands of Russia, which had already acquired a big extension of territory in eastern Europe without risk or loss to itself while Germany was battling in Poland and in the West; and besides he wanted German, not Russian, domination in the Balkans. Why, with his now proven military strength, should he submit to being "blackmailed" any longer by Stalin?

[1] See above, pp. 288–289.

So in mid-December Hitler gave secret instructions to his chief of staff to prepare the German armies for a surprise attack on Russia. He believed that a mighty *Blitzkrieg,* such as had subdued France and gained him the mastery of western Europe, could almost as quickly overwhelm Russia and insure his domination of eastern Europe. He could then utilize the resources of the entire Continent, and those of Japan too, to defeat Great Britain and dismember the British Empire.

The attack was planned for the early spring of 1941. But delay was occasioned by the need of deflecting German troops for the conquest of Yugoslavia and Greece, and meanwhile the bringing of Bulgaria under German tutelage aroused Stalin's resentment and caused him to take counter-measures. Russia encouraged Yugoslav resistance, and simultaneously in April it negotiated a treaty with Japan, pledging neutrality between them for a minimum period of five years. Thus protected in Asia, Russia could concentrate its armed forces in Europe. Any attack which Germany might now make would not be the surprise which Hitler had planned.

At length in June 1941 the German armies were ready, and on the twenty-second of the month, which happened to be the anniversary of Napoleon's fateful invasion of Russia back in 1812,[1] Hitler sent them across the Russian frontier. The break between the chief, and previously cooperating, European dictatorships was complete. They were at war. And against Communist Russia declarations of war were promptly issued by Nazi Germany's European allies—Italy, Rumania, Hungary, Slovakia, and Bulgaria. Finland seized the opportunity to renew hostilities against Russia. Even Spain, while proclaiming its "non-belligerency" in the West, contributed an armed division to the invaders in the East. Altogether, it was a mighty host that swept into Russia in June 1941.

**German Invasion of Russia**

The bulk of the force was, of course, German, and it gave promise of repeating in Russia in 1941 what had been done in Poland in 1939 and in France in 1940. Using the tactics of the *Blitzkrieg,* with planes and tanks, it rapidly pierced the protective belt of East Poland and the former Baltic republics and pushed deep into Russian territory. In less than a month, German armies hammered into Smolensk. Then as their central thrust slowed

[1] See *Modern Europe to 1870,* pp. 563–564.

# EUROPE IN 1942,
## AT THE HEIGHT OF
# THE NAZI EMPIRE

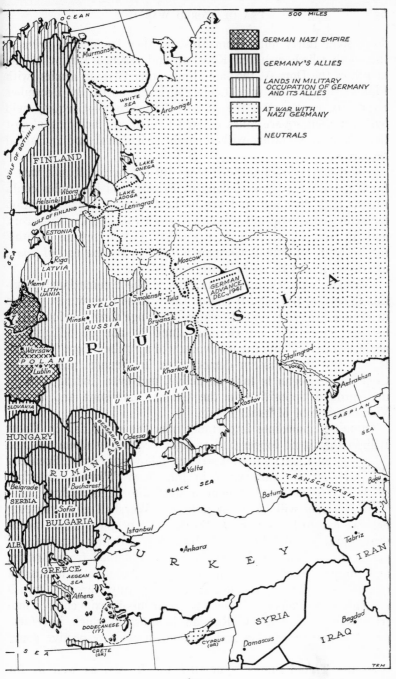

500 MILES

GERMAN NAZI EMPIRE

GERMANY'S ALLIES

LANDS IN MILITARY
OCCUPATION OF GERMANY
AND ITS ALLIES

AT WAR WITH
NAZI GERMANY

NEUTRALS

GERMAN
ADVANCE,
DEC., 1941

OCEAN

Murmansk

WHITE
SEA

Archangel

GULF OF BOTHNIA

FINLAND

LAKE
ONEGA

Viborg

Helsinki

LAKE
LADOGA

GULF OF FINLAND

Leningrad

ESTONIA

Riga
LATVIA

Moscow

Memel

LITH-
UANIA

BYELO-

Smolensk

Tula

Minsk

RUSSIA

Bryansk

R U S S I A

Warsaw

XXXXXX

POLAND

Lublin

Kiev

Kharkov

Stalingrad

Astrakhan

SLOVAKIA

U K R A I N I A

Rostov

CASPIAN

HUNGARY

BESSARABIA

Odessa

SEA

R U M A N I A

Yalta

Belgrade

Bucharest

BLACK   SEA

TRANSCAUCASIA

Baku

SERBIA

Batum

Sofia

ALB.

BULGARIA

Istanbul

GREECE

AEGEAN
SEA

Ankara

Tabriz

IRAN

Athens

T   U   R   K   E   Y

DODECANESE
(IT.)

SEA

CRETE
(GR.)

CYPRUS
(BR.)

Damascus

SYRIA

Bagdad

IRAQ

TRM

down some thirty miles from Moscow, they launched a drive to the south which engulfed Kharkov and reached Rostov at the mouth of the Don. At the same time, other German armies, with Finnish support, encircled Leningrad in the north. By December 1941—six months after the start of the invasion—Germany held half a million square miles of Soviet territory, including almost the whole of Ukrainia with its rich agricultural and industrial resources.

Yet the expected knockout blow did not occur. Russia was a far bigger country than Poland or France, and its armies could retreat long distances and yet be kept intact. It had munition factories and copious oil supplies in the Urals and the Caucasus, and the severity of its winter weather gave it several months' respite from continuous German *Blitzkrieg*. By the end of 1941, moreover, it was receiving foreign assistance.

Germany's attack on Russia altered the international situation in several respects. It caused the various Communist parties in France, America, and elsewhere to change their previous pacifist and essentially pro-German stand to one of belligerency against "fascism" and eager advocacy of a "united front" between Russia and the Western democracies. In France, particularly, Communists began to take an active, and even leading, part in underground opposition to the German garrisons and to the Vichy regime of Marshal Pétain.

Of more immediate importance was the relief felt in Great Britain that it no longer had to fight practically alone but had in Russia a new, if strange, fellow combatant. Speaking for his countrymen in June 1941, Winston Churchill declared: "Any man or state who fights against Nazidom will have our aid. . . . We shall give whatever help we can to Russia and to the Russian people." These words were speedily followed in July by a Russo-British "mutual aid pact," in accordance with which Russia obtained from Britain, and through it from the United States, a gradually increasing quantity of military supplies. Likewise in July, through British mediation, the Polish and Czech governments-in-exile entered into friendly relations with the Russian dictatorship which, in return, promised the restoration and freedom of their respective countries.

In the United States, sympathy for Russia, as well as for

Great Britain, was now marked. To many an American, Russia seemed to be serving the cause of "democracy and freedom" against "fascism and slavery." To promote democratic solidarity, President Roosevelt in August met Winston Churchill on a battleship in the Atlantic and joined with him in issuing a document subsequently known as the "Atlantic Charter." It set forth certain principles which should govern future policy of the democratic countries. The most significant were these: "They seek no aggrandizement, territorial or other; they desire no territorial changes that do not accord with the freely expressed wishes of the peoples concerned; they respect the right of all peoples to choose the form of government under which they will live; and they wish to see sovereign rights and self-government restored to those who have been forcibly deprived of them; . . . they desire to bring about the fullest collaboration between all nations in the economic field with the object of securing, for all, improved labor standards, economic advancement, and social security; after the final destruction of the Nazi tyranny, they hope to see established a peace which will afford to all nations the means of dwelling in safety within their own boundaries, and which will afford assurance that all the men in all the lands may live out their lives in freedom from fear and want. . . ."

*The Atlantic Charter*

This idealistic Atlantic Charter undoubtedly stimulated popular morale among Germany's foes in the Second World War, as Woodrow Wilson's "Fourteen Points" had done in the First World War.[1] But neither Churchill nor Roosevelt overlooked the more earthy need of strengthening Germany's foes, particularly Russia, in material ways. Russia in 1941 was obviously inferior to Germany in military equipment, and supplementary importation from Britain and America was slow and difficult. The ordinary sea routes, through the Baltic, or the Arctic Ocean, or the Mediterranean and Black Seas, were either closed or infested with German submarines and bombing planes. Hence chief reliance had to be placed on a more roundabout route through the Persian Gulf and across Iraq and Iran, and special effort had to be made to prevent its falling into hostile hands.

Already in May 1941 the British had intervened in Iraq and expelled its pro-Nazi prime minister. In June and July, with the help of Free French forces of General De Gaulle, British troops

[1] See above, pp. 405–406.

wrested Syria from the Vichy governor who was collaborating with the Germans. In August, when the ruler of Iran, Riza Shah,[1] adopted a pro-German policy, both British and Russian forces invaded the country and compelled him to abdicate in favor of his son, Mohammed Riza. Whereupon, in September, Anglo-Russian control of Iran was consolidated and a regular transport service was organized across it. To clinch matters, the British army in Egypt was sufficiently reinforced to enable it, in November 1941, to push back the Axis army of General Rommel into Libya and thus to safeguard the area of the Suez Canal and southwestern Asia.

In the meantime, the German attack on Russia provided Japan with what its government, under the premiership of Prince Konoye,

**Japanese Advance in Far East** decided in July 1941 was an extraordinary opportunity to expand its war with China into a drive for supremacy throughout the Far East and the Pacific. There was certainly no danger from Russia, which had promised in April to observe neutrality toward Japan for at least five years, and which must now devote all its efforts to grappling with German invasion from the West. On the other hand, France and the Dutch Netherlands, since their conquest by Germany a year before, were clearly incapable of defending their colonial empires in the Far East; and Great Britain was too heavily engaged in the Atlantic and the Mediterranean to exercise much restraint in the Pacific. Some opposition might be expected from the United States, but the Japanese militarists tended to discount it. The Americans, they imagined, were more concerned with Europe than with Asia or Indonesia and correspondingly reluctant to divert any of their strength to outright war with Japan; opposition from them was apt to be mainly verbal and could probably be overcome by diplomatic means.

The Japanese acted promptly. In July they moved troops into French Indo-China and Thailand, and assumed an aggressive attitude toward British Burma and Malaya and the Dutch East Indies. They professed to be seeking the establishment of a "co-prosperity sphere" which would ensure "Asia to the Asiatics" and rid it of European exploitation.

The United States, which for some time had been protesting against Japanese aggression in China, now became greatly

[1] See above, pp. 498–499.

alarmed about the safety of the Philippines. In conjunction with Great Britain and the Netherlands, and contrary to the hope of Prince Konoye, it shut off export to Japan of all such vitally necessary war materials as oil and metals. In vain, Japan tried to negotiate an agreement with the United States; the latter would not consent to lift the embargo unless the former would withdraw from China and respect the pre-war *status quo* in the Far East.

**United States Embargo and Japanese Attack at Pearl Harbor**

Confronted by this impasse, Prince Konoye resigned the premiership in October and was succeeded by the bellicose General Tojo. Though "peace talks" were continued by a special Japanese agent at Washington, they only veiled the preparations at Tokyo for war; and at the end of November, when Cordell Hull, the American Secretary of State, stiffly reasserted his demands on Japan, General Tojo was already arranging an attack on the United States.

On December 7, 1941, without a prior declaration of war, the attack was made by Japanese warships, planes, and submarines at Pearl Harbor, the great naval base and center of United States sea power in the Pacific. A considerable part of the American fleet was destroyed or badly damaged, and by this one blow Japan won temporary naval supremacy. Against Japan, the United States immediately declared war, followed by Great Britain, the Netherlands, Australia, New Zealand, Canada, and several Latin-American nations. Against the United States, on the other hand, declarations of war were soon forthcoming from Japan's Axis associates: Germany, Italy, Rumania, Hungary, and Bulgaria. The Second World War was now indeed global. Every major power and many a minor one were directly involved.

Fortune smiled on the Axis powers. Just as Germany had recently conquered a vast extent of Russian territory, so now Japan achieved a rapid series of victories in the Pacific. The Japanese immediately captured Guam and Wake Island from the Americans and Hongkong from the British, besides sinking two British battleships off the coast of

**Japanese Conquests in the Pacific**

Malaya. In another month they took Manila and overran most of the Philippines. By early March 1942 they had reduced the great British fortress and naval base of Singapore and were in possession of all of Burma, Malaya, and Dutch Indonesia, together with innumerable small Pacific islands, including some of the Aleutians off Alaska. They had at their disposal the oil and metal resources of the Dutch East Indies and British Malaya, and they were threatening Australia and India. Corregidor, the last American foothold in the Philippines, despite brave resistance, was forced to surrender in May; already in March the American commander-in-chief, General Douglas MacArthur, had barely escaped in a plane to Australia.

## 4. PASSING OF THE AXIS FROM OFFENSIVE TO DEFENSIVE, 1942-1944

On New Year's Day of 1942, twenty-six "United Nations" issued a joint declaration, expressing loyalty to the principles of the "Atlantic Charter"[1] and promising common action against the Axis powers. Yet the United Nations, thus constituted, were then more impressive in number than in military **"United Nations"** strength. They included, in addition to the United States, Great Britain, and the Soviet Union (which, however, continued to maintain friendly relations with Japan), a badly battered China, five British Dominions of limited resources (Australia, Canada, New Zealand, South Africa, and India), nine small republics of the Caribbean area (Costa Rica, Cuba, Guatemala, Haiti, Honduras, Nicaragua, Panama, Salvador, and Santo Domingo), and eight countries occupied by the Germans and represented only by governments-in-exile (Belgium, Czechoslovakia, Greece, Luxemburg, Netherlands, Norway, Poland, and Yugoslavia). The odds at the beginning of 1942 seemed highly favorable to the Axis powers, and neither the declaration of the United Nations[2] nor a formal alliance concluded in May between Britain and Russia materially changed the aspect of affairs.

Throughout the spring and summer of 1942 Axis offensives continued, while the opposing Allies suffered one reverse after **Height of Axis Success** another. In Europe, the Germans, who in 1941 had conquered Ukrainia and gotten to the gates of Leningrad and Moscow, resumed their advance in Russia as soon as the weather permitted in the spring of 1942. Although they still failed to take Leningrad or Moscow, they overran the Crimea and captured Sevastopol. Then in the summer they made two extensive drives. One was southeastward, netting them Rostov and

---

[1] See above, p. 657.

[2] Within the next year, the governments of five other nations adhered to the declaration: Mexico, Brazil, the Philippines, Ethiopia, and Iraq.

carrying them hundreds of miles into the Caucasus with its rich oil fields. The other was eastward between the Donetz and the upper Don, and on to the manufacturing center of Stalingrad on the Volga.

While thus pressing its offensive in eastern Europe, Nazi Germany kept firm military hold on the countries it had conquered in western Europe, compelling them to supply it with money, materials, and labor.[1] "Resistance movements" in these countries were repressed or driven underground; and the Atlantic coastline from Norway to the Pyrenees was so heavily fortified and so dotted with air—and submarine—bases as to render any hostile incursion by sea extremely hazardous if not quite impossible. In vain Stalin begged Britain and the United States to relieve the German pressure on Russia by landing an Allied army in France. The Western Allies were not yet prepared for any such offensive operation, and they recognized that to attempt it would invite disaster. In the spring of 1942 German submarines were sinking Allied ships at an unprecedented rate.

In North Africa also the Axis started a new offensive. German and Italian armored divisions, under General Rommel, captured Tobruk from the British in June and swept on eastward over the desert, recrossing the Egyptian frontier and reaching El Alamein, only sixty miles from Alexandria. Again, Axis conquest of Egypt and the Suez Canal seemed imminent.

Paralleling these Axis successes in Europe and North Africa were the startling Japanese successes in the Far East and the Pacific. By June 1942 Japan was in possession of French Indo-China, Thailand, British Burma and Malaya, the whole of the Dutch East Indian empire, the Philippines, and many lesser Pacific islands. It dominated Manchukuo and all of coastal China. It was clearly threatening both Australia and India, and in the case of India its prospects were brightened by Gandhi's preachment of "non-cooperation with Britain and non-resistance to Japan." [2]

In the latter part of 1942, nevertheless, each of the several offensives of the Axis powers was halted and changed into a defensive operation; and the Allies began important offensives of

---

[1] In April 1942 Marshal Pétain, yielding to German pressure, restored to the chief post in the French regime at Vichy the collaborationist Laval, whom he had dismissed the year before.
[2] On Gandhi, see above, pp. 500–501.

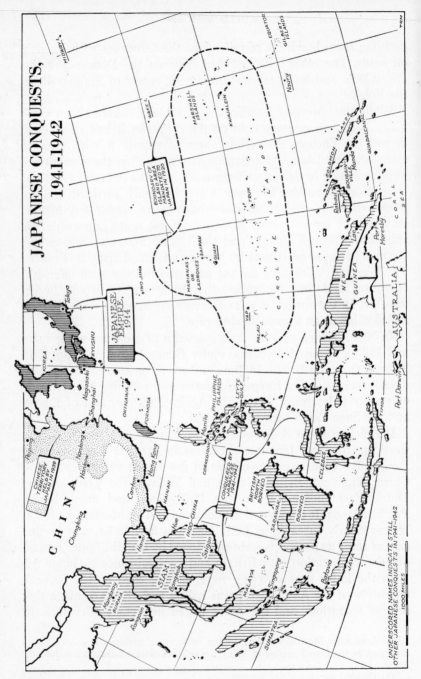

JAPANESE CONQUESTS, 1941-1942

UNDERSCORED NAMES INDICATE STILL
OTHER JAPANESE CONQUESTS IN 1941-1942

1000 MILES

their own. The main reason for this change was that, whereas the Axis had previously been better prepared for war, possessing superiority in planes, tanks, guns, and munitions, and United having more technically trained men, it was now being States and equalled and gradually surpassed in all these respects Fortunes by its foes. Particularly did the United States perform of War industrial prodigies. Once it was tooled up for war production on a mass basis, it turned out a veritable avalanche of weapons of all sorts.

The United States, of course, was faced with war on two different and distant fronts: in the Pacific against Japan; and in the Atlantic and Europe against Germany and Italy. The latter seemed the more immediately urgent, for unless Italy and Germany were defeated, Great Britain and Russia would be overborne and the United States left to fight alone against all the Axis powers. Hence the American strategy was to devote first and major attention to aiding Britain and Russia in their struggle against Germany, while putting into the Pacific only such naval and expeditionary forces as would harass and halt the Japanese and clear the way for later offensives against them. In accordance with this strategy, the United States during the second half of 1942 helped the British to build up a powerful mechanized army behind El Alamein in Egypt, and, in collaboration with Great Britain, to furnish Russia with 4,600 planes, 5,800 tanks, and tens of thousands of trucks and other motor vehicles.

With such assistance from the Western Allies, together with its own expanding war-production and its vast man-power, Russia stopped the German invaders. The decisive contest was Russian at Stalingrad, where for two months the German Gen- Victory at eral von Paulus with an army of 330,000 hammered Stalingrad away furiously but unsuccessfully. In November 1942 Russian forces under Marshal Gregory Zhukov struck back with a well-prepared counter-offensive, which encircled and decimated Paulus's army and brought about his surrender at the beginning of February 1943. The Russian defense of Stalingrad and the succeeding Russian counter-offensive marked a turning point of the war. Henceforth Nazi Germany was on the defensive in eastern Europe.

Meanwhile, the offensive in North Africa was passing from the Axis to the Western Allies. In October 1942 the British, under

command of General Montgomery, engaged the Germans and
Italians in a spectacular battle of tanks at El Alamein. It resulted
**Anglo-American Offensives in North Africa** in heavy losses for General Rommel and his being
driven out of Egypt and thirteen hundred miles back-
ward past the city of Tripoli. This British drive was
part of a larger offensive which the Western Allies had
been planning and which aimed at securing all North Africa and
utilizing it as a base for attack on what Churchill called the "soft
under-belly" of the Axis through Sicily and Italy.

On November 8, 1942, an Anglo-American expedition, carried
by 500 vessels and protected by 350 warships, effected landings
in French North Africa, near Casablanca on the Atlantic coast
and at Oran and Algiers on the Mediterranean. It had been feared
that Spain, under General Franco, might interfere with the operation. This did not occur, however, and what difficulty the landing
forces had was not with Spaniards but with French units loyal to
Marshal Pétain. Even this difficulty was soon surmounted through
special agreement between Admiral Darlan, representing at the
moment the Vichy regime in North Africa, and General Dwight
Eisenhower, the commander-in-chief of the Anglo-American
forces. Subsequently, Darlan was assassinated, and in time a
"Free French" government was established at Algiers under
General De Gaulle.

The Allied seizure of French North Africa had repercussions
within France. Though the Vichy regime of Marshal Pétain denounced the action of the Allies and broke off diplomatic relations
with the United States, it did not prevent the scuttling of most
of the French fleet at Toulon nor did it save itself from German
retaliation. The Germans quickly seized the part of France which
since the armistice of June 1940 had been administered by the
Vichy government, and made Marshal Pétain virtually a prisoner.
All of which gave momentum to the underground resistance movement throughout the country.

For a time, Rommel's army of Germans and Italians, reinforced
from across the Mediterranean, put up a stubborn fight in Tunisia
against the British advance westward from Egypt and Libya, and
the American push eastward from Algeria. At length the Allies
effected a juncture, and on May 6, 1943, they won a decisive
victory. The city of Tunis and the naval base of Bizerte fell to
them, and within a week Axis resistance in Africa ceased.

With North Africa entirely in their hands, the Anglo-American forces prepared for the next operation. On July 10, *Allied* 1943, after prolonged air bombing, they landed in *Conquest* Sicily and rapidly overcame the Italian defense. But *of Sicily, and* German forces, which had been evacuated from North *Italy's* Africa, fought fierce rearguard actions across Sicily and *Surrender* safely reached the mainland. Sicily itself, within forty days, was an Allied conquest.

The defeats in Africa and Sicily produced important results among the Italians, who, as a people, had not been enthusiastic about Mussolini's getting them into the war. There were mutterings even inside the Fascist party. On July 24, 1943, at a meeting of the Fascist Grand Council, a motion was passed asking King Victor Emmanuel III to assume real leadership. The King responded by entrusting the government to Marshal Badoglio. Mussolini was imprisoned, and Fascism outlawed.

Badoglio then opened secret negotiations with the Allies. The Germans still had large forces in Italy, and the Allies demanded "unconditional surrender," as Roosevelt and Churchill had agreed to do at a meeting the previous winter at Casablanca. The negotiations were kept secret until the Allies actually landed on the Italian mainland on September 9, 1943, when it was announced that Badoglio and the King had agreed to an armistice, amounting to unconditional surrender. The Germans, however, were not caught napping. They had already taken over the defense of southern Italy and they moved promptly to seize control of the entire peninsula. Thus Italy was in an odd position. It had signed an armistice, and most of its navy went over to the Allies, but in the country at large it was powerless against German *Continuing* armies of occupation. These were strongly reinforced *German* from Germany, and they disarmed most of the Italians *Resistance in Italy* who opposed them. Indeed, German paratroopers managed to rescue Mussolini from his imprisonment and to take him to the north, where he conducted a sort of phantom puppet government in the service of Germany.

An Anglo-American army, supported by planes from Sicily and by heavy fire from naval vessels, landed on the beaches at Salerno in southern Italy on September 9, but it met strenuous German opposition, and its position was perilous until it was joined by a British army which had disembarked at Taranto, Brindisi, and

Bari. Early in October, Allied forces captured Naples, but not before the Germans had destroyed the port facilities and wrecked much of the city.

Allied advance northward was held up by a strongly fortified "Gustav Line" which the Germans constructed across the mountainous Italian peninsula through Monte Cassino. In January 1944 the Allies tried to turn the Line by landing troops behind it at Anzio. But this maneuver failed of its purpose. The Germans confined the Anzio expedition to the beachhead, and continued to defend the Gustav Line until May, when it was finally breached by a frontal assault of the main Allied army at Monte Cassino. Allied forces then advanced. On June 4, 1944, they entered Rome. Nevertheless, the German General Albert Kesselring dexterously extricated his troops and prepared new defense lines still farther north.

One of the factors which made Kesselring's retreat inevitable, despite his military skill and the advantages of the terrain he defended, was an increasing difficulty of securing supplies from Germany. This difficulty in turn arose not only from the mounting demands of the war in Russia but also from the rising tempo with which Allied bombers were striking at production centers and transportation lines in Italy and more especially in Germany. As early as May and June of 1942 the British staged three raids of a thousand bombers each on Cologne, Essen, and Bremen.

**Allied Air Power**

Afterwards, improved airplane design and increased production, plus the participation of the American air force, rendered such heavy bombing more frequent and more destructive. British bombers specialized in night raids; American, in daytime operations. By early 1943 Germany was subjected on successive days to "round the clock" bombing, and the bomb-carrying capacity of the planes was gradually increased.

The main targets of the Allied air forces were submarine pens and other German installations on the Atlantic coast, industrial plants within Germany, with special emphasis on refineries and synthetic fuel factories, and railways and other means of communication. Germany was not "knocked out" from the air, but the bombing did produce shortages and a creeping paralysis of transport which seriously hampered the German armies.

Growing Allied air power paid another dividend. Air patrols from

Newfoundland, Iceland, North Ireland, and later from the Azores (with Portugal's permission), together with the use of "baby flat top" carriers, checked the submarine menace. In May 1943 the Germans for the first time lost more submarines than they put in operation. Thenceforth the threat to Allied shipping decreased, though it was held in check only by constant vigilance.

While the Western Allies were clearing the Mediterranean, concluding an armistice with Italy, and bombing Germany, Russia was likewise scoring notable successes. At the beginning of 1943, while one German army was being crushed **Russian** at Stalingrad, another was being driven out of the **Offensives** Caucasus. The siege of Leningrad was broken in January, and in early March the threat to Moscow was virtually ended.

Throughout the spring and summer of 1943 there was heavy fighting in southern Russia, with certain towns and areas changing hands several times. Finally, in the autumn, energetic Russian offensives captured Kharkov, the strategic railway junction of Bryansk, and the city of Smolensk, which had been German eastern headquarters in 1941–1942. The Germans were pushed out of the Donetz basin, and in November 1943 they had to surrender the Ukrainian capital of Kiev.

By June 1944 the Russians had cleared the Germans and their Axis allies out of most of the territory held by the Soviet Union in 1938. In the south they had advanced into pre-war Rumanian and Polish territory. In the center they had regained much of Byelorussia (White Russia). In the north they had come nearly to the old Estonian and Finnish borders. They had inflicted on the Germans tremendous losses which could not be repaired. These successes they had achieved by noteworthy strategy, by hard fighting, and by an ability to maintain supply lines with comparatively few railways. This last ability was greatly enhanced by American motor trucks shipped to them by the tens of thousands under the Lend-Lease arrangement and brought in from Arctic Ocean ports or across Iran.

In the Far East and the Pacific, Japan attained the maximum of its conquests in the late spring of 1942. By this time **American** the United States was sufficiently advanced in war **Repulse** preparedness not only to make major contributions to **of Japan** struggle in Europe but also to contest the naval and air superiority which Japan had enjoyed in the Pacific since the attack at

Pearl Harbor. In May 1942, in an air and naval battle in the Coral Sea, the Americans repulsed a Japanese expedition proceeding from New Guinea toward Australia. Less than a month later, in a similar battle off Midway Island, the Americans warded off a threat to Hawaii by destroying four Japanese air carriers at a cost of only one of their own. On Hawaii and Australia, Allied troops were gathered for counter-offensives under the supreme command of the American General Douglas MacArthur, with cooperating naval forces of Admirals Nimitz and Halsey.

Simultaneously the British took special precautions against any Japanese attack on India. They strengthened its army and fortifications, and repressed domestic dissent; in August they jailed Gandhi and other leading nationalists. Also, to safeguard the route through the Indian Ocean, they occupied the large island of Madagascar and ousted its Vichy-French government.

In August 1942 American marines landed on Guadalcanal in the Solomon Islands and after a valiant six months' struggle finally obliged the Japanese garrison to withdraw. During the summer and fall of 1943 American forces extended their hold in the Solomons by taking New Georgia and the air base at Munda, together with adjacent islands. Likewise, airfields were captured on Bougainville, and the Japanese were expelled from the Aleutian Islands.

As a counter-measure against the attacking Americans and their British and Dutch allies, the Japanese government of General Tojo adopted the policy of fostering popular nationalism in the previously colonial countries which it now controlled. It set up native governments which were ostensibly independent, but which would actively collaborate with Japan in the war. Thus the "independence" of Burma and the Philippines was proclaimed, and in November 1943 a conference was held at Tokyo of representatives of the pro-Japanese "governments" of those countries and also of Manchukuo, Nanking-China, and Thailand, and including Chañdra Bose as "head of the provisional government of free India." The conference pledged support of Japan against the Western powers, and shortly afterwards this was endorsed by still another nationalist government which Japan sponsored in Dutch Indonesia.

Meanwhile the American commander, General MacArthur, persevered with his "island-hopping" strategy in the Pacific, securing one key airfield after another in an ever narrowing circle about Japan. In December 1943, Rabaul, the principal Japanese base on New Britain, was reduced. Early in 1944 the Americans struck into territory which had been Japanese before the war. They captured the atoll of Kwajalein in the Marshall Islands and thereby secured a base for bombing the Japanese at Truk in the Carolines and for a farther push which carried them to Saipan in the Marianas by the summer of 1944. They were at length in a position to strike for the recovery of the Philippines and to bring the war to Japan itself.

In July 1944 General Tojo, admitting ultimate defeat, was deposed from the Japanese premiership. Though his successor, General Kuniaki Koiso, promised an "all-out" prosecution of the war, it was increasingly evident that for Japan, as well as for Germany, an expansive offensive was definitely turning into a straitened defensive.

## 5. ALLIED VICTORY, 1944–1945

On June 6, 1944, the very day on which the Germans evacuated Rome, American and British forces under the supreme command of General Dwight Eisenhower landed in France.[1] This was the greatest water-borne invasion of history. It began with air and naval bombardment of fifty miles of Normandy beaches and the dropping of paratroopers behind the coast line; and presently the main forces were put ashore from over 4,000 ships, protected by air coverage of 11,000 planes. Despite stout enemy resistance, the Allies secured a firm foothold in the Cherbourg peninsula, and thence launched an offensive with planes and tanks which beat the Germans at their own *Blitzkrieg* and compelled them, in the latter part of August, to quit both Orleans and Paris.

*Anglo-American Landing in Normandy*

Meanwhile, in mid-August, other Allied forces were landed near Cannes on the Mediterranean coast. These speedily brought about a German withdrawal from southern France; and in mid-September, after capturing Lyons, they effected a juncture with the Anglo-American forces from the west in the vicinity of Dijon. Together, the Allied invaders numbered two and a half million, and before the end of September they had liberated almost all of France,

[1] There were 20 United States divisions, 14 British, 3 Canadian, 1 Free French, and 1 Polish.

pushed into Belgium and Luxemburg, and entered Holland. They were preparing to turn the Westwall and to invade Germany itself.

Already in July a group of German army officers, including General Rommel, who then commanded the armies in the West, had reached the conclusion that Allied victory was inevitable and that the only way of stopping needless carnage and saving something for Germany was to get rid of Hitler. On July 20 an attempt was made to assassinate him. It almost, but not quite, succeeded. Those immediately involved were executed; Rommel committed suicide; and Hitler, now completely crazed, insisted on fighting to a finish.

The Allies were closing in upon Germany from all directions. While the Anglo-Americans were advancing from the west, their **Allied** troops in Italy were passing northward from Rome **Success in** through very difficult mountainous terrain into sight of **Italy and** the Po valley. The Russians, too, were driving forward **Invasion of** **Germany** from the east. In August, Russian armies broke through to the Baltic west of Riga, pushed into East Prussia, overran eastern Poland, and reached the Vistula River both above and below Warsaw. At the same time other Russian forces occupied Bucharest and penetrated into the Balkans. Both Rumania and Bulgaria surrendered to Russia and declared war on Germany. Finland agreed to an armistice on Russian terms. Yugoslavia was cleared of German troops by joint action of resistance forces of General Mikhailovich, representing the royal government-in-exile, and those of a Russian-sponsored Communist leader, Josip Broz ("Marshal Tito"). Greece was freed with British assistance.

In the late autumn and early winter of 1944, Nazi Germany made a supreme effort to hold off the victoriously advancing Allies. Russian advance in the east was almost everywhere checked. Allied advance in the south was halted by a "Gothic Line" defending the Po valley in Italy. Allied advance in the west was arrested and actually turned back in December by the so-called "Battle of the Bulge," in which a German army under Marshal Karl von Rundstedt cut fifty miles through American lines and re-invaded Belgium. Supplementing all this effort on the Continent, Germany employed against Great Britain certain new weapons. First were the pilotless, jet-propelled "robot bombs," of which some 2,300 fell on London in the summer of 1944, killing or injuring more than 20,000 people. Next were the longer-range rockets—so-called V-2's—which caused death and destruction in England during the winter of 1944–1945.

Yet Germany could not maintain for long a counter-offensive, or even a defense, on so many fronts against such a host of enemies. Its war material, its man-power, and its morale were dwindling away. Early in 1945 Allied offensives were resumed and went on unrelentingly. The Russians captured Warsaw in January. In February, following the fall of Budapest, Hungary concluded an armistice with Russia; and Turkey declared war against Germany. In March and April, Russian armies under Marshals Zhukov and Konev entered Danzig and Vienna and overran Czechoslovakia and western Poland. Meanwhile, Allied armies in the west, now including substantial French contingents, wiped out the "Bulge," gained control of the Rhineland and the Ruhr, and on April 25 made first contact with Russian troops at Torgau in Saxony.

Simultaneously the Allied forces in Italy pierced the "Gothic Line," took Bologna, and crossed the Po. On April 28, 1945, Benito Mussolini, fleeing toward Switzerland with his mistress, was caught and shot by Italian communists, and his body was hanged by the heels in Milan. Two days later, as Russian armies penetrated Berlin, Adolf Hitler shot his mistress and himself in a bunker in which he and a few of his fanatical followers [1] had hidden under the Chancery building. Thus ended most miserably the amazing careers of those Axis partners, the Fascist Duce and the Nazi Führer.

*Fate of Mussolini and Hitler*

On May 2 Berlin finally capitulated. The Western Allies might have taken it, but by previous agreement they left it to the Russians, who mowed down the last resistance of frenzied Nazis. On May 7, German military and naval commanders, headed by Admiral Karl Doenitz, met Allied commanders at Reims and formally accepted the latter's demand for the unconditional surrender of Germany. Allied victory was complete in Europe.

*Germany's Surrender*

Victory in the Pacific over Japan was yet to be achieved, but by May 1945 it was in clear prospect. The United States now possessed superabundant naval and air strength, and the end of hostilities in Europe enabled the Western Allies to concentrate

---

[1] Including Goebbels, who stuck to Hitler to the end and similarly killed himself in the bunker.

on the war in the Far East. Moreover, to hasten victory, President Roosevelt and Winston Churchill, at a conference with Stalin at Yalta in February, had secured, for a price, a secret pledge that Russia would denounce its non-aggression pact with Japan and in due course join them in the Far Eastern conflict.[1]

Already in October 1944, in the battle of the Leyte Gulf, the biggest naval action ever fought, American warships and planes had destroyed most of the Japanese fleet and cleared the way for General MacArthur's recovery of the Philippines. This was accomplished during the winter of 1944–1945, and was followed in the spring by American conquest of Iwo Jima and Okinawa, which provided bases for effective bombing and eventual invasion of the Japanese homeland. Meanwhile the British regained most of Burma, the Australians landed on Borneo, and the Chinese, aided by American supplies, were cutting the Japanese off from Indo-China and freeing some of their own coastal territory.

*Final Campaign against Japan*

Faced with these setbacks, the Japanese cabinet of the bellicose General Koiso resigned and was succeeded in early April by another with the aged and more moderate Admiral Suzuki as premier. Worse setbacks followed immediately. Russia denounced its non-aggression pact with Japan; and the last of the Japanese fleet, in a vain attempt to relieve Okinawa, was wiped out by American warships in a battle off Kyushu.

A large-scale invasion of Japan was planned, but it proved unnecessary. By midsummer of 1945, incessant air bombing of the country convinced Admiral Suzuki's cabinet and the Emperor Hirohito that further fighting was futile and that they should sue for peace. The final determinant came in early August. On the sixth, an American plane dropped on Hiroshima a new and most terrible kind of bomb—the atomic bomb—destroying the city and killing some 66,000 civilians. On the seventh, Russia declared war on Japan and ordered an advance into Manchuria and Korea. On the ninth, another atomic bomb laid the Japanese city of Nagasaki in ruins and killed 40,000 inhabitants.

*Use of Atom Bombs*

The next day, Japan offered to surrender, on the one condition that its Emperor was not molested. The condition was accepted,

[1] The price exacted by Stalin was the Southern part of Sakhalin, the Kurile Islands, a lease of Port Arthur, and a free hand throughout Mongolia.

and on September 2, 1945, an armistice was formally signed on the American battleship *Missouri* by Japanese representatives and by General Douglas MacArthur in behalf of the United States, China, Great Britain, the Soviet Union, Australia, Canada, France, the Netherlands, and New Zealand. It marked the end of the Second World War.

**Japan's Surrender**

The costs of the war can never be accurately determined. To the American people alone, the immediate and direct cost was over a million casualties, including nearly 400,000 deaths, and a financial expenditure of something like 350 billion dollars. The direct expenditure of other countries has been estimated at a trillion (1,000 billion) dollars, while loss of property must run to another trillion, and of human lives to at least 22 million dead and 34 million wounded. The indirect and long-range cost to the world is simply incalculable.

From mid-September, totals in numbers was formally situation. The American battleship destroyed by Japanese representatives and by General Douglas MacArthur in behalf of the United States (Chester Nimitz), the Soviet Union, the British, Chinese, French, the Netherlands, and New Zealand terminated the most bitter war in human history.

The costs of the war can never be accurately determined. The direct military expenditures, including military and naval expenditure or economic assistance, are billion dollars. The direct outlay of other countries has been estimated at 1,150 billion dollars. At least 15 million men in uniform were killed, and 25 million were wounded. The battlefield and bombing casualties killed.

# PART V

# TWO WORLDS: COMMUNIST AND FREE, SINCE 1945

# CHAPTER XVI

# THE UNITED NATIONS AND AGGRESSIVE COMMUNISM

## I. FORMATION OF THE UNITED NATIONS

ORLD War II, unlike World War I, was not followed immediately by a general peace congress. The international situation appeared too chaotic in 1945. The vanquished Axis countries, compelled to accept "unconditional surrender," were occupied by foreign armies, and in the case of Germany no government remained with which the Allies could treat. On the Allied side, moreover, numerous countries, including France, Belgium, the Netherlands, Norway, Greece, and the nations of east-central Europe, had only recently been "liberated," and their governments were "provisional" or still "in exile."

Throughout Asia, also, the political order was in extraordinary flux, an object of nationalist or communist agitation. And most unfortunately, though its consequences were not then fully perceived, there was a fundamental difference about peace-objectives among the three major victorious powers—Great Britain, the United States, and the Soviet Union.

It was optimistically believed in 1945 and 1946, at least by the general public in Britain and America, that just as the "Big Three" had cooperated in winning the war, so they would continue to cooperate in restoring and securing peace. Important steps in this direction had been taken while the war was still in progress. As early as August 1941, President Roosevelt of the United States and Prime Minister Churchill of Great Britain had set forth, in the Atlantic Charter, certain principles which should govern the peace. Stalin, the Soviet dictator, raised no objection to the Charter and at the beginning of 1942 it was formally adopted as the platform of twenty-six "United Nations." [1]

Subsequent conferences were held between Roosevelt and Churchill at Washington, at Quebec, and at Casablanca. Chiang Kai-shek of China joined them at Cairo in 1943, and Stalin at Teheran in December 1943 and at Yalta in February 1945. Though for the most part these conferences had to do with matters of strategy and prosecution of the war, some specific agreements were reached looking to eventual peace arrangements.

To Franklin Roosevelt in particular, as to Woodrow Wilson before him, it seemed less urgent to determine precise terms of peace than to organize the world for the maintenance of peace; and American public opinion, under pressure of participation in a second world war, gave Roosevelt the backing which Wilson had failed to obtain. Consequently, prior to the termination of hostilities and apart from any other peace treaty, plans were laid to substitute for the discredited "League of Nations" a new world organization. On this there was agreement among the Major Allies. In November 1943 a meeting at Moscow of the foreign ministers of the Soviet Union, the United States, Great Britain, and China asserted the need for including "all peace-loving states" in such an organization; and at the Teheran Conference, in December, endorsement of "a world family of democratic nations" was given by Roosevelt, Churchill, and Stalin. Then in the autumn of 1944, at the Dumbarton Oaks Conference in Washington, representatives of the Big Three and of Chiang Kai-shek outlined a proposed Charter for a permanent United Nations Organization.

**Plans for World Organization**

Preparatory to ratification of the Charter by all the governments arrayed against the Axis and in order to overcome possible objections to it, President Roosevelt obtained in advance a practical assurance of its ratification by the United States Senate. He also, at Stalin's insistence, agreed at the Yalta Conference in February 1945 that the Soviet Union should have three votes (including those of Soviet Ukrainia and Byelorussia) instead of one in the projected Assembly and also, of course, a right of veto in the Council along with the United States, Great Britain,

[1] On the Atlantic Charter and the origin of the "United Nations," see above, pp. 657, 660.

France, and China. Furthermore, the countries of Latin America were brought into line at a conference with United States representatives at Mexico City in April 1945, which, by the "Act of Chapultepec," pledged mutual defense and aid. Then, from April to June, the Charter was discussed and finally adopted (with minor amendments) by a conference of fifty-one nations at San Francisco. It went into effect on October 24, 1945, just after the surrender of Japan and the end *San Francisco Conference and UN Charter* of hostilities of the Second World War. In the following April the League of Nations at Geneva formally dissolved, and turned over its physical assets to the United Nations.

The United Nations Organization bore a close resemblance to the League of Nations which it superseded. Its initial members were the fifty-one represented at San Francisco, comprising states which had warred against the Axis or broken diplomatic relations with it.[1] The Charter provided that others, including enemy states, might subsequently become eligible for membership. Nevertheless, for a full decade afterwards, friction between the Soviet Union, which vetoed nations unfriendly to it, and the Western Allies, which vetoed Communist satellites of the Soviet Union, permitted admission of only nine additional nations: Afghanistan, Iceland, Sweden, and Thailand in 1946; Pakistan and Yemen in 1947; Burma in 1948; Israel in 1949; Indonesia in 1950. *UN Members*

At the end of 1955, however, a compromise between the Soviet Union and the West permitted the admission of sixteen more: Communist Albania, Bulgaria, Hungary, and Rumania; and non-Communist Austria, Cambodia, Ceylon, Finland, Ireland (Eire), Italy, Jordan, Laos, Libya, Nepal, Portugal, and Spain. In 1956 Morocco, Sudan, and Tunisia were admitted; and in 1957 Japan, Ghana, and Malaya. Thus at length did membership in the United Nations become truly worldwide, the only notable omissions being Communist China and Mongolia and divided Germany, Korea, and Vietnam.

[1] Argentina, Australia, Belgium, Bolivia, Brazil, Byelorussia, Canada, Chile, China, Colombia, Costa Rica, Cuba, Czechoslovakia, Denmark, Dominican Republic, Ecuador, Egypt, El Salvador, Ethiopia, France, Greece, Guatemala, Haiti, Honduras, India, Iran, Iraq, Lebanon, Liberia, Luxemburg, Mexico, Netherlands, New Zealand, Nicaragua, Norway, Panama, Paraguay, Peru, Philippines, Poland, Saudi Arabia, Syria, Turkey, Ukrainia, Union of South Africa, Union of Soviet Socialist Republics, United Kingdom of Great Britain and Northern Ireland, United States of America, Uruguay, Venezuela, and Yugoslavia.

The members, according to the Charter, promise to maintain international peace and to cooperate in establishing political, economic, and social conditions favorable to it, and not to interfere in the internal affairs of one another. The chief agencies of the organization are a General Assembly, a Security Council, and a Secretariat. The General Assembly, composed of one voting representative of each member nation, is empowered to debate and make recommendations on any matter within the scope of the Charter. The Security Council, consisting of five permanent members (United States, Great Britain, the Soviet Union, France, and China) and of six members elected for two-year terms by the Assembly, is charged with primary responsibility for ensuring peace and security, and all member nations are obligated to carry out its decisions. Though any seven members of the Council may decide simple "procedural" questions, every major action is subject to veto by each permanent member. The Secretariat, under a Secretary General chosen by the Assembly upon the recommendation of the Security Council, and with an ever growing staff, performs administrative and technical tasks. In practice, the successive Secretaries General, Trygve Lie of Norway and Dag Hammarskjöld of Sweden, have served as representatives and spokesmen of the whole organization.

*U.N. Organization*

Attached to the United Nations are a number of auxiliary bodies. (1) An *International Court of Justice,* composed of fifteen members elected for nine-year terms by Council and Assembly, decides international disputes of a justiciable nature and offers advisory opinions on other matters submitted to it. (2) A *Trusteeship Council* supervises the administration of colonial peoples transferred from defeated to victorious nations in First and Second World Wars; it comprises, along with the Soviet Union and China, seven administering states (Australia, Belgium, France, Great Britain, Italy, New Zealand, and the United States) and five others elected by the Assembly for three-year terms. (3) An *Economic and Social Council,* consisting of eighteen members elected by the Assembly for three-year terms, has general charge of a wide variety of functional commissions (transport and communications, population, statistics, human rights, status of women, narcotic drugs, etc.), of regional economic commissions for Europe, for Asia and the Far East, for Latin America, and of several specialized agencies: International Labor Organization (ILO), Food and Agricultural Organization (FAO), United Nations Educational Scientific and Cultural Organization (UNESCO), International Civil Aviation Organization (ICAO), World Health Organization (WHO), Universal Postal Union (UPU), International Telecommunication Union (ITU), World Meteorological Organization (WMO), International Monetary Fund, and the International Bank for Reconstruction and Development—commonly called the World Bank. Provision is also made, under the Security Council, for a Military Staff Committee, composed of Chiefs of Staff of the major powers, to plan and direct military action against aggressor nations, and likewise, in 1957, for a special Atomic Energy Agency.

The United Nations Organization established its headquarters in the United States, at New York, although for some of its meetings and auxiliary bodies it has utilized Paris, The Hague, and buildings of the defunct League of Nations at Geneva. Its official languages are English, Russian, Chinese, French, and Spanish. It has a distinctive flag of light blue emblazoned in white with a polar map of the world between twin olive branches.

The Organization has not fulfilled all the hopes of 1945–1946. It has been repeatedly disturbed and on occasion well-nigh paralyzed by disputes between the Soviet Union and the Western powers, particularly by the former's frequent use of its veto in the Security Council. A succession of efforts to reach agreement about a mutual limitation of armaments has failed dismally. It has often seemed as if both Council and Assembly were utilized for propaganda and denunciation rather than for constructive action. Nevertheless, much has been accomplished through the United Nations. It has intervened more or less effectively to prevent or limit strife or aggression in Iran, Greece, Palestine, Indonesia, and India-Pakistan, and to call a halt to hostilities in Korea and in Egypt. But its major importance has not been in settling disputes or preventing conflicts. Instead, it has been chiefly important as a world forum and through the work of its special agencies. It has provided in times of tension a meeting place where small as well as large nations can be heard. It has focused on some problems what amounts to a world opinion, whose weight even the great powers feel.

Yet more important has been the quietly effective work of many

of the United Nations' auxiliaries. An early and temporary one
—the Relief and Rehabilitation Administration (UNRRA)—
distributed in 1945–1946 one and a quarter billion dollars' worth
of aid to war-ravaged countries. The World Bank, beginning operation in 1946, twelve years later had sixty-eight member nations and a capital of nine and a half billion dollars, of which a
third had been supplied by the United States; it had made loans
totalling three and a half billions to forty-four countries or territories. All the other auxiliaries, listed above, have been serving
in unspectacular but vital respects the cause of international cooperation and human welfare.

## 2. FAILURE TO ACHIEVE A GENERAL PEACE

Certain war-time agreements among the United States, Great
Britain, and the Soviet Union looked to a post-war peace settlement. At the Cairo Conference in November 1943, President
Roosevelt and Prime Minister Churchill forswore any territorial
gains for their countries and assured their Chinese ally, Chiang
Kai-shek, that Japan would be stripped of all the territory it had
acquired since 1894, including Formosa which would be returned
to China, and Korea which would become independent.

At the Yalta Conference in February 1945, three significant
agreements were reached. (1) The Soviet Union, as a
price for entering the war against Japan, was promised
the Kurile Islands and the southern half of Sakhalin,
at Japan's expense, and control, at China's expense, of outer Mongolia, Port Arthur, Dairen, and the Manchurian railways; and
the Nationalist Chinese Government of Chiang Kai-Shek would
be induced to acquiesce in the arrangement by regaining sovereignty over Manchuria and having its Communist opponents
disowned by the Soviet Union. (2) In "liberated" countries of
Europe, Stalin agreed with Roosevelt and Churchill to the restoration of independence and the holding of free democratic elections.
Specifically about Poland it was agreed that the Soviet Union
might retain, up to the "Curzon Line," [1] the eastern Polish lands
it had appropriated while an ally of Nazi Germany in 1939; in
compensation, Polish territory would be extended northward and
westward at German expense, the definitive boundaries being fixed

**Agreements of Yalta Conference**

---

[1] See above, p. 431, and below, p. 696.

at a future peace conference; and meanwhile the Poles should choose their own government through free elections with universal suffrage and secret ballot. (3) Germany would be divided into zones for military occupation and administration by the Soviet Union, Great Britain, and the United States, with a possible fourth zone for France, and it would be compelled to dismantle most of its industrial plants and to make heavy reparation payments, half of which would go to the Soviet Union.

To implement the Yalta agreement about Germany, another conference was held at Potsdam in the summer of 1945. By this time President Roosevelt had died (in April) and a general election in Great Britain had turned Winston Churchill out of office and brought the Labor party in. **Agreements of Potsdam Conference** Hence it was a new American President, Harry Truman, and a new British Prime Minister, Clement Attlee, who met and made the decisions at Potsdam with the Soviet dictator, Joseph Stalin. The zones for Allied military occupation of Germany were delimited: the Soviet zone would cover the eastern part of the country, while the western part would comprise zones for Great Britain, the United States, and France.

In each zone, authority was vested in the military commander of the occupying power, and the four commanders together would constitute a "Control Council" for Germany as a whole, with its seat in Berlin, which was itself divided into four sectors for the several powers.

Pending a "final peace treaty," the eastern frontier of Germany was tentatively drawn along the Oder and Neisse rivers, the Soviet Union getting the northern part of East Prussia including Königsberg,[1] and Poland obtaining Danzig, Upper and Lower Silesia, eastern Brandenburg, most of Pomerania, and a southern strip of East Prussia. In addition, of course, Alsace-Lorraine was restored to France; Eupen and Malmédy to Belgium; the Sudetenland to Czechoslovakia; while Austria was detached and divided into zones for Allied military occupation, and the Saar area was put under French rule. Altogether, Germany was condemned to much greater territorial losses than it had suffered after the First World War.

Furthermore, Germany was to be completely disarmed, its war

---

[1] Its name was changed to Kaliningrad, in honor of the titular "president" of the Soviet Union.

plants and "war potential" destroyed, its people "de-Nazified," and its future government decentralized and rendered democratic and liberal. Moreover, rules were agreed upon for the trial of Nazi "war criminals" by a tribunal of Allied judges; and the drafting of definitive peace treaties with vanquished countries was entrusted to a council of foreign ministers of the chief Allied powers.

In accordance with one of the decisions of the Potsdam Conference, a Tribunal of American, Russian, British, and French **Trial of** judges opened at Nuremberg, in November 1945, the **War** trial of leading German Nazis accused of "plotting ag- **Criminals** gressive warfare" and "committing atrocities against any civilian group." The outcome, a year later, was the conviction of twenty-two, of whom eleven were condemned to death. One of these, Hermann Goering, committed suicide just before he was scheduled to be hanged. Included among the other ten were Marshal Keitel, General Jodl, Alfred Rosenberg, Arthur Seyss-Inquart, Julius Streicher, and Joachim von Ribbentrop. Besides, several Nazis were summarily executed for atrocities in concentration camps, especially for slaughter of Jews in frightful gas-chambers.

During 1946–1948 a number of Japanese "war criminals," including General Tojo, were similarly tried and put to death. Subsequent trials were conducted by local or national courts in both Germany and Japan. By 1950 about 8,000 had been tried and 2,000 executed.

Meanwhile, in accordance with another decision of the Potsdam Conference, the foreign ministers of the major Allies met late in 1945 at Moscow. They agreed to proceed at once with the **Peace** drafting of peace treaties with each of the European **Treaties** nations which had fought at one time or another on the **with Italy** **and Minor** side of Nazi Germany: Italy, Rumania, Hungary, Bul- **Axis Allies** garia, and Finland. They also agreed to establish an Allied Council to oversee the administration of Japan in cooperation with the American commander, General Douglas MacArthur.

Drafting of the proposed treaties proved much more difficult than had been expected and was attended by much wrangling among the Allies. Compromises were eventually effected, so that the definitive treaties were signed at Paris in February 1947. All provided for reparations (Italy, 360 million dollars; Bulgaria, 70 million; Hungary, Rumania, and Finland, 300 million each), most of which was to go to the Soviet Union. All provided, too, for drastic limitations of armed forces. Italy relinquished any claim to Ethiopia and Albania, and ceded Fiume, most of Istria, and certain Adriatic islands to Yugoslavia, a few western frontier posts to France, the Dodecanese Islands in the Aegean to Greece, and the island of Saseno to Albania. Italian colonies in Africa were to be placed under United Nations' trusteeship,[1] and Trieste was to be internationalized.[2]

Hungary had to return Transylvania to Rumania and a small area to Czechoslovakia. Rumania, while regaining the whole of Transylvania, had to recognize the incorporation of Bessarabia and Bukovina in the Soviet Union and of southern Dobruja in Bulgaria.

Bulgaria, being particularly favored by the Soviet Union, lost nothing and regained Dobruja. Finland lost the Petsamo province and most of Karelia to the Soviet Union and granted to the latter the lease of a naval base commanding the Gulf of Finland. This base was returned, however, in 1955 in an obvious Russian effort to cultivate Finnish favor.

The foreign ministers of the major Allies, having successfully negotiated a peace settlement with Italy and minor European powers, next discussed the preparation of peace treaties with Germany and Austria. For this purpose they met at Moscow in the spring of 1947 and again at London in the follow- **No General** ing winter. But they reached no agreement, and the **Peace** discussions served only to reveal and to accentuate **Treaty** basic differences in aim and method between the Soviet dictatorship and the Western democracies. Nor could any general agreement be reached at the time concerning a peace treaty with Japan. Hence both Germany and Japan continued under military occupation while their conquerors waged a curious kind of "cold war" among themselves.

---

[1] Eritrea went to Ethiopia; Libya, after brief Franco-British occupation, became independent; and Italian Somaliland was reassigned as a "mandate" to Italy until 1960 when it too would be freed under the name of Somalia.

[2] Following prolonged negotiations, Italy and Yugoslavia reached agreement in 1954 that the former should possess the main part and the port of Trieste, and the latter the adjacent portion of the Istrian peninsula and emergency access to the port.

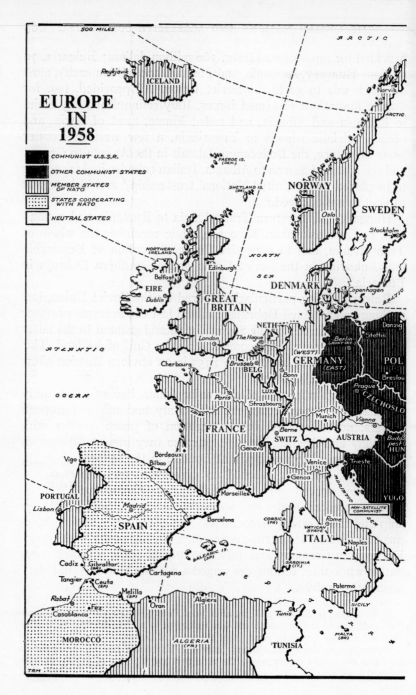

EUROPE
IN
1958

COMMUNIST U.S.S.R.

OTHER COMMUNIST STATES

MEMBER STATES OF NATO

STATES COOPERATING WITH NATO

NEUTRAL STATES

In the case of Germany, conflicts between the Western occupying powers and the Soviet Union culminated in the practical partition of the country. Great Britain, the United States,

**Partition of Germany**

and France authorized the holding of free democratic elections throughout their respective zones, with the result that in 1949 a "Federal Republic" was set up in West Germany, with its capital at Bonn. Almost simultaneously the Soviet Union erected in its zone in East Germany a puppet Communist state entitled "German Democratic Republic," with its capital in East Berlin.

The Western Allies refused to recognize the latter state, or a permanent division between East and West Germany, but they formally proclaimed in 1951 an end to the state of war with Germany, and the Soviet Union did likewise in January 1955. In 1957 by an agreement between France and West Germany, the disputed Saar region was integrated with the latter.

In May 1955, in conjunction with the Western Allies, the Soviet Union finally signed a peace treaty with Austria. This

**Restoration of Austria**

recognized Austria's independence with frontiers of 1938, provided for its disarmament and neutrality, prohibited political or economic union with Germany, and required it to uphold democratic institutions, to dissolve Nazi-type organizations, and to prevent a Habsburg monarchical restoration. Whereupon, foreign troops were withdrawn from Austria (but not from Germany), and Austria was admitted to membership in the United Nations.

Post-war Japan was not divided like Germany, among several occupying powers, nor did it lack a functioning government of its own. The occupation forces were entirely American, and General

**Settlement with Japan**

MacArthur, their commander, managed to ignore any inter-Allied control. At length, in September 1951, failing to get Soviet agreement to peace terms with Japan, the United States sponsored a peace congress of forty-eight other nations at San Francisco. The resulting peace-treaty, in accordance with pledges of the Yalta Conference six years earlier, reduced Japan to its four main islands. It surrendered southern Sakhalin and the Kurile islands to Russia, and Formosa to Nationalist China, and recognized the independence of Korea and the transfer of mandated Pacific Islands (Marshalls, Carolines, and Ladrones) to the United States. The treaty was not signed by the Soviet Union, nor by China or India. However, the latter two negotiated separate peace treaties with Japan in 1952; and in October 1956 the Soviet Union signed an agreement at Moscow formally ending its state of war with Japan, and providing for the restoration of diplomatic relations and the return of Japanese prisoners of war. The next year (1957) Japan was admitted to membership in the United Nations, and elected a member of its Security Council.

Thus it transpired that twelve years after the cessation of the Second World War, a kind of partial and piecemeal settlement prevailed. It seemed in the nature more of a truce than of a real peace. It left Europe—and the world—in a precarious balance between the Soviet Union and its Communist satellites on the one hand and the United States and its democratic associates on the other. To each of these groups in turn, we next give our attention.

### 3. POST-WAR COMMUNIST RUSSIA AND THE SOVIET UNION

The Soviet Union—or, to use its official title, the "Union of Soviet Socialist Republics"—emerged from the Second World War as the largest and (next to China and India) the most populous country in the world. It covered a sixth of the world's land surface and had a population of close to 200 million. Of the sixteen "states" which made up the "Union," Russia was the core and the dominant member. It embraced almost three-fourths of the area and over half the population of the entire Union.[1] Its capital city of Moscow was the Union's capital. Here centered the Communist dictatorship.

The Soviet Union suffered almost as grievously in the Second World War as the old Russian Empire had suffered in the First World War. German invasion penetrated even deeper into it, and its losses in men and property were almost as great. Yet this time, thanks to more effective organization, to better generalship, to an aroused patriotism, and especially to decisive military aid from

[1] Two other members—Ukrainia, with its capital at Kiev, and Byelorussia (or White Russia), with Minsk as its capital—were represented, along with the Union itself, in the United Nations. The remaining states were: in the Caucasus, (4) Azerbaijan, (5) Georgia, (6) Armenia; in Asia, (7) Uzbek, (8) Turkmen, (9) Tadzhikistan, (10) Kazakh, (11) Kirghiz; in Europe, recently annexed, (12) Moldavia, (13) Lithuania, (14) Latvia, (15) Estonia, (16) Karelia. This last, taken from Finland, was incorporated into Russia proper in 1956, thereby reducing the number of constituent states to fifteen.

Britain and the United States, it not only repelled the German invasion but turned it into a victorious counter-invasion of Ger-

**Victory and Annexations**

many. Hence instead of losing territory, as it had done at the close of the First World War, it now, at the close of the Second World War, made remarkable additions and gained enormously in prestige.

The Soviet Union, under its Communist dictatorship, utilized its practical alliance with Nazi Germany from 1939 to 1941 to acquire a big increase of territory in Europe. It then annexed the eastern half of Poland, the whole of the Baltic states of Estonia, Latvia, and Lithuania, and portions of Rumania and Finland. Subsequently, it utilized its collaboration with the Western Allies in war against Nazi Germany (and for a few days in 1945 against Japan) to extend its boundaries and sway much farther.

True, the Soviet Union, by subscribing to the original declaration of the United Nations in January 1942, had endorsed the Atlantic Charter, including its renunciation of "territorial aggrandizement" and its promise to restore complete freedom to all peoples who had been forcibly deprived of it. This was agreed to when the Soviet Union was hard pressed and in dire need of military assistance from Britain and America. When matters improved for the Allies, it was flouted and violated by the Soviet Union.

Nor at the outset did the United States and Great Britain seriously oppose the Soviet Union's violation of the Atlantic Charter

**Allied Appeasement of Soviet Union**

and the Declaration of the United Nations. For a variety of reasons they sought to appease the Communist dictatorship by acquiescing in its aggressive expansion. They raised no question about its keeping the territories it had forcibly seized during the first two years of the Second World War, when it was cooperating with Hitler and was being denounced by the League of Nations.[1] They assured it, as the price for its entering the war against Japan, not only certain Japanese territories, but also bases in Manchuria which rightfully belonged to China. They later acceded to the Soviet Union's appropriation of the chief part of East Prussia from Germany, of Carpatho-Ruthenia from Czechoslovakia, and Bukovina from Rumania. And they entrusted sole military occupation of the

---

[1] See above, pp. 638–639.

"liberated" countries of east-central Europe to the Soviet Union with only its paper promise to permit the people of those countries to hold free elections and to establish independent democratic governments.

Back of this appeasement by the Western Allies was their hope that thereby the Soviet Union could be induced to collaborate loyally with them in hastening the end of the war and securing a firm and durable peace. They optimistically imagined in 1945 that, as a result of companionship in arms, the Communist dictatorship, like their own democracies, was really "peace-loving" and desirous of maintaining a "united front"; and in this idea they were backed by propaganda of Communists and other "leftist" groups.

It should also be borne in mind that at the end of the war the Western Allies were hardly in a position, even if they had been minded, to oppose Soviet ambitions.

After all, Soviet red armies, which the Communist dictatorship kept at war-time strength, were in forceful occupation of almost all eastern Europe as far west as the Elbe and the Adriatic, together with Manchuria and the northern half of Korea in Asia, while the war-weary Western democracies, yielding to popular clamor at home, rapidly demobilized their armies, retaining only minor forces to garrison Germany, Italy, and Japan. In the circumstances it is not surprising that in the early post-war years one concession after another was gained by the Soviet Union from the Western Allies.[1]

The Soviet Union did not stop with outright annexation of the Baltic states of Estonia, Latvia, and Lithuania, half of Poland, the Czechoslovak province of Carpatho-Ruthenia, most of the German province of East Prussia, the Rumanian provinces of Bessarabia and Bukovina, the Finnish provinces of Karelia and Petsamo, and the Japanese Kurile Islands and Sakhalin. Ostensibly to have friendly and peaceful countries on its borders, and actually to build up a subject Communist Empire, it cynically flouted the promises it had made at the Yalta and Potsdam Conferences about the holding of free democratic elections in liberated countries of Europe and about supporting the Nationalist government of Chiang Kai-shek in China.

---

[1] For subsequent stiffening of Allied resistance to Soviet pressure and aggression, see below, pp. 729–737.

Instead, it followed a definite pattern in establishing puppet Communist regimes for countries which its military forces occupied or could influence, and in bringing them under its sway. The pattern was much the same in all cases and was something like this: First, an existing or "provisional" government would be denounced as "fascist" and usually superseded by a "popular front" government in which Communists would hold key positions. Second, the Communist ministers, with direct or indirect military aid from the Soviet Union, and under the leadership of a native who had been trained for his job at Moscow, would oust their non-Communist colleagues and set up a practical dictatorship. Third, this dictatorship would promulgate a constitution modeled after that of the Soviet Union and obtain its ratification by a supposedly democratic but actually controlled and terrorized plebiscite. Fourth, a supporting minority would emerge as a disciplined single party, and dissenting leaders among the majority would be "liquidated."

*Puppet Regimes and Parties*

There were, of course, variations of detail in the manner of building and maintaining the far-flung dependent Communist Empire. These will be indicated in later sections of this chapter. Here it suffices to note that by 1950—less than five years after the cessation of the Second World War—the Soviet Union had Communist satellites and allies in the European countries of Poland, Yugoslavia, Albania, Bulgaria, Rumania, Hungary, Czechoslovakia, and East Germany, and also in the Asian countries of China, Mongolia, North Korea, and North Vietnam. Besides, there were active Communist parties, directed from Moscow, not only in newly independent nations in Asia, but in the democratic West, those of France and Italy being particularly strong and militant.

Already in 1947, the pre-war Communist International [1] was revived at a meeting at Warsaw, under auspices of the Soviet Union, with name changed from "Comintern" to "Cominform." In 1950 the Soviet Union signed a thirty-year "mutual aid" treaty with Communist China, and in 1955, at Warsaw, similar twenty-year military pacts with the Communist bloc in Europe. Thus were Communist parties and states bound in close alliance with the Soviet Union, and local and national dictatorships fettered to the supreme dictatorship at Moscow.

[1] See above, p. 549.

Before the war, Joseph Stalin had been all-powerful in this dictatorship, and after the war he had the added prestige of military victory and imperialist success—the annexation of some 260,000 square miles of territory with more than twenty million inhabitants, the creation of a ring of satellite states in the west, the triumph of Communism in China, and its seeming advance throughout the world. Russian propaganda and folklore naturally made Stalin into an heroic figure, a veritable demigod, who had won the war single-handed and whose every whim was law. What was supposedly a government by a *group* of party leaders was now, more than ever, a tyranny of *one man*.

*Stalin's Apotheosis*

Thanks to forced labor of hundreds of thousands of prisoners of war who were detained in the Soviet Union—Germans, Poles, Japanese, etc.—as well as to careful planning of Stalin's lieutenants, the ravages of war were fairly rapidly repaired. The succession of pre-war "five year" plans [1] was resumed, with a fifth for 1951–1955, and a sixth for 1956–1960. In 1958 the latter was changed into a "seven-year plan," involving administrative decentralization, and aimed at effecting "a massive increase in heavy industrial output and a sharp rise in productivity on farms and in factories." By such means, supplemented by control of resources and trade throughout the expanded Communist Empire, the Soviet Union was enabled to raise the standard of living above the pre-war level, although, relative to that of the Western democracies, it was still low. Military expenditures were a heavy drain on Soviet finances.

The Soviet Union's armed forces were kept at a minimum of three and a half million men. By 1957 it had 20,000 first-line combat planes, and was annually producing 10,000 military planes, of which at least 6,000 were jet-powered. Moreover, it was supplying munitions to other countries, successfully experimenting with atomic weapons and guided missiles, and building up a navy second only to that of the United States. The armament industry was very important in the Soviet Union.

Arbitrary arrests and imprisonments—rigid censorship and wholesale repression—continued, and were even intensified under Stalin. He was the arbiter of art and science, and the merciless executioner of anyone whom he suspected of overstepping the

[1] See above, pp. 564–565.

party line as he drew it. His death from a brain hemorrhage in March 1953 must have been a relief to Communist colleagues in high government circles. It also caused some obvious confusion and undoubted maneuvering among them. Presently it was announced from the Kremlin that he would be succeeded by a five-man group, consisting of George Malenkov as premier and four deputy premiers: Vyacheslav Molotov as foreign minister, Marshal Nicholas Bulganin as defense minister, Laurence Beria as minister of the interior and head of the secret police, and Lazar Kaganovich in charge of economic affairs. At the same time, Nikita Khrushchev succeeded Stalin in the strategic post of Communist party secretary.

**Stalin's Death and Debasement**

Just as Stalin had originally risen to dictatorial power in the 1920's after Lenin's death, through his position as party secretary and by supplanting and liquidating potential rivals,[1] so now did Khrushchev in the 1950's after Stalin's death. First, in concert with colleagues who feared or were jealous of Beria, he had him arrested in July 1953 "as an enemy of the people" and put to death in December along with several aides. Next, following a purge of Beria supporters and Stalin stalwarts in Georgia, Ukrainia, and other states of the Union, Malenkov was compelled in February 1955 to resign the premiership, confessing his "incompetence," and was succeeded by an intimate of Khrushchev's, Marshal Bulganin. Then in February 1956, at the twentieth all-Union congress of the Communist Party at Moscow, Khrushchev in a sensational seven-hour speech assailed the "myth" of Stalin's infallibility and the "cult of personality"; and, while extolling "Marxian-Leninist" Communism, he called for reforms in its tactics and application. He was seconded in speeches by Bulganin and a rising Armenian associate of Khrushchev's, Anastas Mikoyan, and also by Malenkov probably in an effort to regain favor.

Backed by Marshal George Zhukov, the most famous of Russian war-commanders, Khrushchev took the decisive step toward supreme dictatorship in 1957 by attacking and practically exiling the "old guard" of the governing group. The veteran Molotov was ousted from the foreign office and sent off to Outer Mongolia. Malenkov was given a minor

**Khrushchev, Succeeding Dictator**

[1] See above, p. 563.

job, under surveillance, in far-away Siberia, and Kaganovich in a cement factory. Then it was the turn of the too popular Marshal Zhukov; in October 1957 he was denounced and replaced as head of the armed forces by Marshal Rodion Malinovsky. Meanwhile, Khrushchev and Bulganin (amusingly referred to as the "B and K" team) engaged in extensive propagandist visits to Yugoslavia and other Communist states, to "neutralist" India, Burma, and Afghanistan, and to England.

Whatever the shift in leadership at Moscow, it brought no change in fundamental policy. There was evidence of a more subtle conduct of foreign relations and of some willingness to make certain concessions to the satellite states. These will be indicated in the following section. There was likewise considerable new talk about "co-existence." Basically, however, the objective of the Soviet Union remained the same under Khrushchev, as under Stalin and Lenin before him, the creation of a Communist "One World" with its directing center in the Russian Kremlin.

## 4. COMMUNIST SATELLITES IN EUROPE

We have sketched in the preceding section the general pattern followed by Stalin and the Soviet Union in converting the nations of east-central Europe into dependent and "satellite" Communist states. We now take a closer view of what happened in each of these nations, starting with Poland.

Poland, which had been the first nation to defy Hitler and Nazi Germany, was a major sufferer in the ensuing Second World War. Its losses, both human and material, were very heavy. It had been partitioned, we may recall, between **Poland** Nazi Germany and Communist Russia in 1939 and its government had gone into exile at London. Then in 1941, after the break between Germany and Russia, the latter, through British mediation, had resumed diplomatic relations with the Polish government and had promised to restore an independent Poland.

The Soviet Union soon made clear, however, that it meant to retain the part of eastern Poland it had seized while cooperating with Hitler; and, as the exiled Polish government objected, Stalin transferred recognition from it to a handpicked "provisional government" headed by a Moscow-trained Polish Communist, Boleslav Beirut. There is reason to believe, moreover, that Soviet

**PARTITION OF POLAND BETWEEN GERMANY AND RUSSIA, 1939-1941**

Memel
LITHUANIA
Vilna
BYELO-
Minsk
RUSSIA
Gdynia
Danzig
Königsberg
EAST
PRUSSIA
Stettin
Berlin
ODER R.
VISTULA R.
Posen
Warsaw
CURZON
LINE
Lodz
Breslau
Lublin
NEISSE R.
Teschen
Cracow
Lemberg
UKRAINIA
Prague
BOHEMIA
MORAVIA
SLOVAKIA
AUSTRIA
Vienna
HUNGARY
RUMANIA
GERMANY
POLAND
RUSSIA

**POST-WAR POLAND AS SATELLITE OF RUSSIA**

Memel
LITHUANIA
EAST
PRUSSIA
Vilna
BYELO-
Kaliningrad
Minsk
Gdynia
Danzig
RUSSIA
Stettin
Berlin
ODER R.
VISTULA R.
Posen
Warsaw
CURZON
LINE
Lodz
Breslau
Lublin
Prague
Cracow
Lemberg
UKRAINIA
Teschen
CZECHOSLOVAKIA
AUSTRIA
Vienna
HUNGARY
GERMANY
POLAND
RUSSIA

TRM

696

agents, in order to weaken future resistance, massacred several thousand Polish army officers who had been taken prisoner.[1]

At the Yalta Conference in February 1945, Stalin prevailed upon Roosevelt and Churchill to disown the Polish government in exile at London—the government with which they had been allied—and to recognize Beirut's government on condition that this should include some non-Communist members and should hold free, democratic elections. A show was made of adding a few non-Communists to Beirut's regime—for example, Stanislas Mikolajczyk, leader of the Peasants' party and a representative of the government in exile, and Edward Morawski, leader of the Social Democratic party—but they had little influence on their Communist colleagues. These were backed by Soviet armed forces, and elections were postponed.

In August 1945, shortly after the "liberation" of Poland by Russian armies, the Beirut government signed a treaty with the Soviet Union, ceding to it some 70,000 square miles and obtaining by way of "compensation" the promise of some 40,000 square miles to be taken from Germany. In January 1946 a decree abolished the "capitalist system" and nationalized all basic industries. When elections were eventually held in January 1947 they were dominated by a small, but disciplined and terroristic, pro-Communist minority, supported by Russian troops and police. The National Assembly, thus chosen, immediately adopted a constitution patterned after the Soviet Union's, with Beirut as nominal president and actual dictator. Both Morawski and Mikolajczyk were removed from office, the latter escaping execution by flight, and their respective parties, after being severely purged, were merged with the Communists. Even the secretary of the Communist party, Wladyslaw Gomulka, was purged for "submission to nationalist and bourgeois influence, lack of enthusiasm for socialization of agriculture, and failure to appreciate the decisive role of the Soviet Communist Party in the fight against imperialism"! Gomulka was jailed, and so too was the Polish Catholic primate, Cardinal Wyszynski. Indeed, the customary Communist intolerance of religion and denial of personal liberty were duly exemplified.

---

[1] Their graves were discovered at Katyn, on Russian soil, and, though Russia accused German invaders of committing the outrage, later evidence indicated that the responsibility was really Communist Russia's.

In Yugoslavia, rival "resistance movements" had carried on guerrilla warfare against the Germans. One was headed by General Draja Mikhailovich, loyal to the young King, Peter II, and his government-in-exile at London. The other was led by Joseph Broz, a Communist who had been trained in Russia and was popularly known as "Marshal Tito." In 1944 the Soviet Union persuaded Great Britain and the United States to insist on a merger of the two movements, with the result that, following the final withdrawal of German troops, King Peter was obliged to appoint Tito prime minister. Then the Communist leader used his official position and armed forces, together with the acquiescence of the Western powers, to obtain complete control of the country. Through farcical elections in November 1945 a subservient Assembly was chosen which deposed Peter, abolished the monarchy, and in January 1946 proclaimed Yugoslavia a "federal people's republic," with a soviet-like constitution.[1] Any dissent, real or suspected, was sternly crushed. In the summer of 1946 General Mikhailovich was executed at Belgrade, and the Catholic primate, Archbishop Stepinac, was sentenced to sixteen years' imprisonment.

What was done by Tito in Yugoslavia was paralleled in Albania by another Russian protégé, Enver Hoxha. His "provisional government" was recognized by Great Britain and the United States in November 1945, on condition that it would hold free elections, but the election in the next month was anything but "free." King Zog, who had been an exile since the Italian invasion of 1939, was formally deposed and in January 1946 Albania was transformed into a "people's republic," dependent on the Soviet Union. Enver Hoxha was succeeded as local dictator by General Mehmet Shehu in July 1954.

In Bulgaria, George Dimitrov, a Communist and former secretary of the Comintern, returned from Russia, forced his way with the help of Soviet troops into the government and dominated a referendum which in September 1946 dethroned the youthful King Simeon II (who had succeeded his father, Boris III, in 1943) and instituted another "people's republic." A year later, the leader of the democratic Agrarian party was put

*Yugoslavia*

*Albania*

*Bulgaria*

---

[1] The Yugoslav "federal union" comprised six "states": Serbia, Croatia, Slovenia, Montenegro, Bosnia, and Macedonia.

to death, and a constitution of the Communist pattern was adopted. Dimitrov died in 1949, but the succeeding premier, Vassil Kolarov, showed no sign of easing the dictatorship; he too had lived long in the Soviet Union and been duly trained at Moscow.

In Rumania, the pro-Nazi dictator, General Antonescu, had been overthrown and constitutional monarchy restored in 1944. Under Soviet pressure, however, King Michael was compelled to appoint a coalition cabinet including Peter **Rumania** Groza, a pro-Communist, as premier and Ana Pauker, a fanatical disciple of Stalin, as foreign minister. The latter, with the support of Russian troops, got the upper hand. King Michael's abdication was forced in December 1947, and in the following spring a typical Communist constitution was adopted for the Rumanian "people's republic." All dissenting political parties were proscribed, and their leaders were imprisoned or killed.

Despite the presence of Soviet troops and pressure from Communist minorities, both Hungary and Czechoslovakia made valiant attempts to preserve national independence and to pursue democratic policies. A "provisional government" for Hungary was organized in December 1944 by a group of Hungarian Communists who had been living in Moscow, **Hungary** some of them since the fall of Bela Kun's regime in 1919.[1] But democratic elements obtained a large majority in the National Assembly which was elected in November 1945 and which shortly afterwards adopted a liberal republican constitution and entrusted the premiership to Ferenc Nagy, a prominent democrat. Then, gradually, the Communists, who were skillfully led by Matthias Rakosi and assisted by troops and threats of the Soviet Union, infiltrated the government, changing its complexion and subverting it to their own purposes.

In May 1947, while Nagy was in Switzerland on a vacation, the dictatorship at Moscow prompted a coup d'état at Budapest which practically forced him out of office and into exile. Next, one democratic party after another was dissolved or outlawed; and in February 1949 the popular Catholic primate, Cardinal Mindszenty, an outspoken patriot, who had been a consistent opponent of the German Nazis during the war years, was tried for treason and condemned to life imprisonment. And many another

[1] See above, pp. 416–417.

Hungarian patriot suffered a like or worse fate. By the middle of 1949 Hungary had been turned into a full-fledged "people's republic," with a Communist constitution, a single Communist party, intimate ties with the Soviet Union, and a crushing of all domestic dissent.

In Czechoslovakia, the pre-war republican and democratic constitution had been restored in the spring of 1945, with the liberal Eduard Beneš again as President, and with a coalition cabinet pledged to friendly relations with both the Soviet Union and the Western democracies. A general election in May 1946 showed that the majority in the country as well as in the government were clearly non-Communist. Nevertheless, pressure from an increased Communist minority and a desire to please Russia actuated President Beneš to appoint, as premier, Klement Gottwald, a Communist and former member of the Comintern at Moscow. In February 1948 Gottwald, assured of Socialist support and the Soviet Union's backing, executed a coup d'état and established a virtual dictatorship. Jan Masaryk, liberal foreign minister and son of the famous founder of Czechoslovakia, ended his life in mysterious circumstances in March; and in June Beneš handed over the presidency to Gottwald, who at once, with typical coercion, put into effect another typically Communist constitution. Within a year, at least 10,000 persons were seized by the Communist secret police on charges of "sympathy with the West or the Catholic Church" and sent as slave labor to Russia. Antonin Zapotocky, another strenuous Communist, succeeded Gottwald as prime minister in 1949, and as president just before Gottwald's death in 1953.

In East Germany, the occupying Soviet forces sponsored the formation of a single "Socialist Unity Party," comprising Communists and left-wing Socialists, from which was chosen, for the conduct of civil affairs, a "provisional people's council." In October 1949, by proclamation in the Soviet sector of Berlin, East Germany was constituted the "German Democratic Republic," with Wilhelm Pieck as titular president, Otto Grotewohl, as premier, and Walter Ulbricht, deputy-premier and head of the local Communist party. These took orders from Moscow, and no general election was ventured.

It is to be noted that in every one of the countries just mentioned the establishment of a Communist regime and subjection to the Soviet Union were accomplished not by free popular choice but by force or intimidation. It is also to be noted that further extension of such satellites in Europe was halted in the late 1940's, when the United States re-armed, and, in cooperation with Britain and France, adopted measures that prevented the Russians from taking over the whole of Berlin and from turning Greece and Turkey into Communist states. Of these measures we shall treat in the next chapter.

**Factors in Soviet Success**

Meanwhile, in explaining the comparative ease with which the Soviet Union won its European satellites in the two or three years immediately after the war, we should bear in mind not only its use of force but a peculiarly favorable climate of opinion among the peoples affected. The majority in each instance was certainly not Communist, nor, with the possible exception of Bulgaria, Czechoslovakia, and part of Yugoslavia, was it traditionally pro-Russian. Yet in each there was undoubtedly a post-war increase of the number of native Communists and of others who looked to Communist Russia for aid and guidance. In part this was a result of reaction against German Nazi domination and of participation with Communists in wartime "resistance movements." In part it was the result of a feeling of a goodly number of people, especially in Czechoslovakia, Poland, Yugoslavia, and Hungary, that the Western Allies had "sold them down the river" and that no choice was left them but to throw in their lot with Communist Russia. And from the very straitened economic circumstances in which these countries found themselves after the war, Communism promised a way out.

In all the satellites, socialization along Soviet Communist lines was introduced and speeded up. Industrial plants were nation-alized, and their production regulated by governmental planning for five or some other number of years in advance. At the same time, private landed estates were confiscated, and collectivized farms instituted. All this was accompanied, of course, by growth of bureaucracy and police. It was accompanied, likewise, by Com-munist state control of press, meetings, schools, and churches.

Undercurrents of opposition tended to develop, and in time to run stronger, as satellite peoples found that the regulated econ-omy deprived them of open markets, that their increased indus-

trial production accrued less to their own benefit than to the
Soviet Union's, and that their financial plight in many instances

**Satellite Opposition to Soviet Control**    got worse. There was especial trouble about enforced
collective farming and the growing peasant resistance
to it. Then, too, national patriotism cropped up anew
and fed popular resentment at being bossed from Moscow. In addition, peoples who had been traditionally long associated with the West, such as Poles and Hungarians and most
Yugoslavs, did not take kindly to the drastic curtailment of their
personal liberties, or to the persecution of patriotic and respected
clergymen, Catholic or Protestant.

Such undercurrents came to the surface and brought about
alterations first in Yugoslavia. Here, as early as 1948, faced with
rising peasant and nationalist unrest, Tito denounced Stalin's

**Tito and Yugoslavia**    policy of dictating to all Communist nations and refused to obey Moscow's directions about the speedy
socializing of Yugoslav agriculture. The Cominform at
once denounced Tito and expelled Yugoslavia; it instituted an
economic boycott and threatened an armed invasion from neighboring Communist countries. This might have occurred if Tito had
not been the recipient of economic assistance and military equipment from the United States, of concessions in foreign trade from
Britain and France, and of loans from the World Bank. As it was,
Tito remained Communist, though as a peculiar kind of "nationalist" Communist, repudiating satellite status and willing on occasion
to collaborate with the Western democracies. In 1953 Tito sponsored a revision of the Yugoslav constitution, whereby its form
was changed from the Soviet type to one more apparently Western:
a bicameral parliament, consisting of a Federal Council, representing the states, and a Council of Producers, representing the nation;
a President, chosen for a four-year term; and a Federal Executive
Council, selected by the President. Tito was reëlected President in
1954 and again in 1958. Change of form did not change the substance, however. Tito was still a Communist dictator—perhaps
more so, now that he was fairly independent of a super-dictator at
Moscow. At any rate, he had his former chief lieutenant, Milovan
Djilas, imprisoned for daring to publish a book critical of the regime.

The death of Stalin in March 1953 was the signal for anti-
Communist rioting in East Germany and a general strike affect-

ing 200,000 workers. The disturbances were quelled by Soviet troops, and early next year the Soviet Union, as a sop, proclaimed East Germany a "sovereign" republic. The proclamation significantly added that Soviet troops would remain.

As Khrushchev rose to power at Moscow, he assumed a conciliatory attitude toward the satellites. In May 1955, he, with the Soviet premier, Bulganin (that "team of B. and K."), paid a five-day state visit to Belgrade and there offered public apology for Stalin's treatment of Tito and an assurance that there were "different forms of socialistic development." In following months the Soviet Union granted Yugoslavia a credit of 300 million dollars; and in 1956, shortly after Khrushchev's attack on Stalin, the Cominform was dissolved. Then Tito made a return visit to Moscow, though he took pains to pay visits also to London and to Paris.

In 1955 Khrushchev made concessions to Rumania by authorizing the elevation of another national Communist, Chivu Stoica by name, to the premiership. The next year he countenanced the purging of a strait-laced Stalinist dictator of Bulgaria and the substitution of Anton Yugov, a patriotic and somewhat more lenient Communist.

These concessions aroused national ambitions and stimulated popular uprisings in both Poland and Hungary. In Poland, rioting of workmen at Poznan (Posen) in June 1956 was so severe, and the ensuing arrest and trial of more than a thousand participants so inflaming, as to frighten Edward Ochab, the *Gomulka and Poland* Communist party leader, into promising redress of grievances. As a result, Wladyslaw Gomulka, who had been in prison for four years on Stalin's orders as a "Titoist"— a right-wing nationalist Communist—was released and made practical dictator. The Russian general who commanded the armed forces was sent home. The Cardinal Primate was released from jail and permitted to make a long-delayed trip to Rome. All along the line there was at least a temporary abatement of internal repression, and in November 1956 Gomulka signed an agreement at Moscow with the Soviet Union whereby future relations between the two countries were to be based on "complete equality, mutual respect for territorial integrity and national independence, and non-interference in each other's internal affairs;" and the Soviet Union would restrict its troop movements in Poland, cancel past Polish debts of two and a half million rubles, deliver one and a half million tons of grain in 1957 on credit, and grant long-term credits of 700 million rubles. Ties between the outstanding National Communists were confirmed and publicized by a visit of Gomulka of Poland to Tito of Yugoslavia in the autumn of 1957.

The uprising in Hungary had only tragic results. It began in October 1956 with demands of riotous students and workers for **Hungarian Revolt and Repression** the return to office of a former patriot premier, Imre Nagy, and the withdrawal of Soviet troops. This quickly turned into open revolt, which for a few days seemed to be successful. Nagy, installed as prime minister, promised free elections, and Cardinal Mindszenty was released from prison. On November 4, however, Soviet forces unleashed a massive attack on Budapest. Nagy fled and was jailed in Rumania. The Cardinal took refuge in the American legation. Thousands lost their lives, and by the end of the month over 100,000 Hungarians had fled into exile. In vain a majority in the Assembly of the United Nations condemned the Soviet Union for its intervention and use of force. Its veto in the Security Council stopped any effective international action. Apparently, in last analysis, Khrushchev was as determined as Stalin had been to prevent any disruption of the Communist Empire. Yet the Hungarian revolt, failure though it was, together with the obvious show of national self-assertiveness in Yugoslavia and Poland, was evidence that all was not well in that Empire.

## 5. COMMUNIST CHINA

The creation of Communist dictatorships as satellites or allies of the Soviet Union was not confined to Europe. It occurred in China and in Korea and Indo-China.[1]

In China the Soviet Union took advantage of grave weaknesses and difficulties of the Nationalist government of Chiang Kai-shek. **Weakening of Nationalist Regime** Not only had this government had to contend with Japanese invasion and conquest of Manchuria in 1931 and subsequent conquest of all coastal China, but it had had to wage intermittent warfare with armies of domestic Communists commanded by Mao Tse-tung, who had spent several years and been duly indoctrinated in Russia. By

[1] On Korea and Indo-China, see below, pp. 738–745.

1945, as a result, the government of Chiang Kai-shek was in dire need of assistance, both economic and military. And it was being accused in the United States and Great Britain of "incompetence" and "corruption."

The United States and Great Britain still insisted at the Yalta Conference in February 1945 that the Soviet Union, in return for obtaining bases and a privileged economic position in Manchuria, should pledge itself to support the Nationalist government rather than the Chinese Communists. The Soviet Union did give such assurance in a treaty it negotiated with Chiang Kai-shek in August 1945, although it wrested from him recognition of the "independence" of Outer Mongolia, which became merely another Communist satellite. The treaty also provided for joint ownership of the Chinese Changchun railway and for joint use of the ports of Dairen and Port Arthur.

But this was by no means the goal of Soviet ambition. With arms which the Russians captured in Manchuria from the Japanese, the Chinese Communists were plentifully supplied and thereby enabled not only to prevent reconquest of Manchuria by the Chinese Nationalists but to launch an increasingly successful offensive against them in China proper. In vain Chiang Kai-shek appealed to the United States for help. He was told that he must make terms with the Soviet Union and take the Communists into partnership, and when he refused, the American Secretary of State, Dean Acheson, publicly blamed Chiang's "reactionary" clique for his setbacks and gave notice that no further aid would be given his government.

*Communist Conquest of Mainland*

So, in 1949, Mao and his Communist forces, liberally supplied by the Soviet Union, won victory after victory. They captured Tientsin and Peiping in January, Nanking in April, and by December they were in possession of the whole of continental China. Chiang Kai-shek, by means of his superior naval forces, took refuge, with the remnant of his Nationalist troops, on the island of Formosa (or Taiwan), which the Japanese had recently surrendered.

*Nationalist Retention of Formosa*

Meanwhile Mao Tse-tung proclaimed in September 1949 at Peiping the "People's Republic of China"; and in the following February, in company with his chief lieutenant, Chou En-lai, premier and foreign minister of the new regime, visited Moscow and there concluded a treaty

*Communist China in Action*

with the Soviet Union. It was a thirty-year treaty of "friendship, alliance, and mutual assistance," pledging each to join no coalition against the other. To Communist China, the Soviet Union ostentatiously handed back the ports it had exacted from Nationalist China.

Communist China, though not immediately awarded Nationalist China's seat in the United Nations, received prompt diplomatic recognition not only of the whole bloc of Communist states but also of many others, including Great Britain, Sweden, India, Burma, and Israel. Only the United States appeared adamant against its recognition, and that chiefly because of its part in the Korean War. For, as we shall explain later,[1] Communist China, abetted by Communist Russia, forcefully intervened in 1950 to defend and maintain Communist North Korea after the latter's failure to subdue South Korea.

The next year Chinese troops invaded Tibet and compelled its religious head (the Buddhist Dalai Lama) to accept the Communist regime. Similar action was taken in 1953 in the distant Moslem territory of Sinkiang (Chinese Turkestan). Furthermore, as a result of Communist China's military assistance to native Communist rebels, an important part of French Indo-China— northern Vietnam—was erected in 1954 as still another Communist state under the immediate dictatorship of Ho-Chi-Minh.[2] In the same year Communist China concluded an eight-year mutual non-aggression pact with India.

Internally the Chinese regime of Mao Tse-tung followed the usual Communist practices. Large land-holdings were divided, and collective farms organized. Imports and exports were rigidly controlled. Missionaries, Catholic and Protestant, were slain, imprisoned, or exiled, and their schools closed. Marxism was made the key-subject of popular education. Personal liberty of all sorts was repressed, and forced labor camps were set up. In 1953 a first five-year economic plan was instituted with the aid of advisors and technicians from the Soviet Union: it aimed at developing heavy industry and increasing the food supply. Armed forces, estimated at three million, were maintained. In 1956 a party congress, held at Peiping, was attended by Anastas Mi-

---

[1] On the Korean War, see below, pp. 740–743.
[2] For the war in Indo-China, see below, pp. 744, 757.

koyan, official representative of Moscow, who hailed the achievements of Communist China.

China, whose population according to a census in 1953 numbered slightly over 600 million, or a fourth of the whole world's population, was no mean conquest for Communism. Joined with the Soviet Union and the latter's European satellites, it expanded the Communist Empire to almost thirteen million square miles of the Earth's surface, **Communist Empire** embracing a total population of approximately eight hundred million. It was the greatest empire known to history, and one of the two worlds which emerged from the Second World War. It was rich in natural resources and strong in war potential. It was ambitious and aggressive.

# CHAPTER XVII

## THE FREE WORLD AND ITS DEFENSE

### I. POST-WAR BRITAIN AND FRANCE

FTER the Second World War, the swift expansion of Communist Russia and its satellite Empire from Czechoslovakia to China, which we have traced in the preceding chapter, owed much to the absence of any effective balance of power in Europe or in the world at large. In other words, the war produced a kind of power vacuum outside of Russia. Before the war there had been six other great powers—Britain, France, Germany, Italy, Japan, and the United States—

**Upset Balance of Power** and one or another combination among them might suffice to hold Russia in check. Immediately after the war, however, three of them—Germany, Italy, and Japan—were totally disarmed and quite helpless, and two others —Great Britain and France—were so seriously weakened as to offer slight counterbalancing force to Russia's. The United States remained unquestionably a great power, but more so in potential than in actual armed strength, and it was slow to recognize the need of constructing a new balance of power.

Britain and France had indeed made heavy sacrifices in the two world wars of the twentieth century. Britain had been in both from beginning to end, pouring out men and money, and it had borne the brunt of the second. France had bled itself white in the first, and had been overwhelmed and subjected to foreign occupation and dictation in the second. Both were now afflicted with grave economic ills—staggering indebtedness, soaring taxation, threatening inflation. Both, too, were faced at home with insistent demands for socialistic reforms, and overseas with disruption or rebellion of their colonial empires. In the circumstances, neither could maintain the armies or the navy, and hence the international prestige, it had previously had.

Yet Britain and France continued to enjoy and to merit their traditional European leadership in the cause of liberty and democracy. Despite their difficulties and losses, their decline was relative, not absolute. They were still stronger than the rest of free Europe. In combination with the United States, they could still be of incalculable service in upholding a democratic world in competition with the Russo-Chinese Communist world.

In Great Britain, elections were held in July 1945 while the war in the Pacific was still going on. They occasioned some surprise by giving the Labor party 390 seats out of the 640 in the House of Commons, thus pushing Winston **Great Britain** Churchill, war-hero and Conservative, from office and replacing him as prime minister by the Labor leader, Clement Attlee. The new government at once pressed forward the socializing of basic industries. One after another it took from private hands, and nationalized, the Bank of England, the coal mines, communications, the railways and long-distance trucking, the iron and steel industry, civil aviation, electricity and gas. Medicine was also nationalized or socialized, wages were regulated, and an extension of social legislation promised the British "a security from the cradle to the grave."

Emphasis was put on the advancement of social democracy. A "family allowance act" sought to raise the standard of living of the lower classes. Drastic income and inheritance taxes were aimed not only at obtaining needful revenue but also at reducing the wealth and influence of the upper classes. Educational facilities were expanded, and a larger proportion of working-class youth was enabled to attend university or technical school. Britain under the Labor government was clearly becoming a socialist "welfare state."

The new socialization was expensive, and an added burden to the very heavy financial burden left from the war. Yet to bear it Britain no longer possessed the wealth of former days or the leadership of the capitalist world. While the cost of socialized industry was higher than that of private industry, its productivity appeared less. An unfavorable balance of trade prevailed; a decade after the war, imports still exceeded exports in value by 850 million pounds. This was the more serious in that Britain had liquidated most of its foreign investments during the war, and was therefore deprived of income which might have offset the unfavorable trade balance. Correspondingly, its banking profits lessened; New York, not London, was now the financial center of the world. To increase exports and decrease imports, the pound sterling was devalued and a rigid rationing of foodstuffs—an "austerity" of living—was maintained. Expenditure on army and navy was slashed, and yet for several years Britain had big deficits, which were met by loans and subsidies from the United States. In the single year 1946 these amounted to three and three quarters billion dollars.

In wartime Winston Churchill had said he was not in office to preside over the dissolution of the British Empire. But after the war Britain was in no position to resist the demands of major portions of the Empire for practical independence, and the Labor government willingly granted them. Leaving details to the next chapter, it may be noted here that between 1946 and 1958 Great Britain granted full independence to Ireland (Eire), to the bulk of its Asiatic possessions (India, Pakistan, Burma, Ceylon, Malaya), to Ghana and the Sudan in Africa, and to the Caribbean Federation in America. Most of these, though in some cases repudiating the British monarch and becoming republics, retained nominal connection with the British Commonwealth, which, after all, was only a loose alliance with no super-governing authority. India and Pakistan even rejected the word "British" in the title. The nations attached to it and represented at a conference in London in the summer of 1957 were Britain, Canada, Australia, New Zealand, India, Pakistan, Ceylon, the Union of South Africa, and Ghana.

The British people, the masses no less than the classes, met their post-war difficulties with the same stoicism they had exhibited during the war; and the regular functioning of the parliamentary government was untroubled by any large number of extremists, whether Communist or "Rightist," such as troubled the French. There were differences of opinion, of course, and sometimes heated debate about specific questions, especially about the extent of socialization, and no little criticism of particular measures. In the general election of 1950, the Labor party's majority in the House of Commons was reduced to seven out of a total of

625. For a year and a half longer Attlee managed to remain in office, although he was assailed not only by the large Conservative opposition but also by a "leftist" group in his own party led by Aneurin Bevan, who urged a speeding up of socialization and advocated less dependence on the United States and more cooperation with the Soviet Union.

Hoping to enlarge his majority, Attlee had King George VI dissolve Parliament and call for another general election in 1951. But the result was a victory for the Conservatives, though a slender one. Attlee resigned, and Winston Churchill returned to the post of prime minister. Thus the famous war leader was in power again when George VI died in 1952 and was succeeded by his twenty-five-year old daughter, who was crowned with customary medieval pomp as Elizabeth II.

The Conservatives retained all the social legislation enacted by the Laborites. But they returned the iron and steel and trucking industries to private ownership, sought to stimulate private enterprise, reduced Britain's dependence on American financial aid, and in 1954 completely ended food rationing for the first time in more than fourteen years. Prosperity increased, along with full employment and rising industrial production. It is doubtful how much of the betterment resulted from Conservative policies and how much from world conditions. At any rate the Conservatives gained popular votes. For in 1955, when the aging Churchill turned over the premiership to his Foreign Minister and son-in-law, Sir Anthony Eden, and a new general election was held, the Conservatives increased their majority in the Commons from seventeen to sixty. The retiring prime minister, we may add, refused a title of nobility but accepted from Queen Elizabeth a knighthood which gave him the title of Sir Winston Churchill. In retirement he devoted himself all the more assiduously to his avocations of painting and history writing.

Eden's premiership proved brief. Opposition to him developed within his own party as well as in the Labor party over matters of foreign policy, particularly the failure of his armed intervention in Egypt,[1] and he fell seriously ill. Early in 1957 he resigned and was succeeded by a fellow-Conservative, and previous Chancellor of the Exchequer, Harold Macmillan, with Selwyn Lloyd

[1] See below, pp. 765–767.

continuing as Foreign Minister. A reorganization took place also in the Labor party. Clement Attlee retired from its leadership, being made an Earl, and was succeeded by Hugh Gaitskell, while Aneurin Bevan, the "left-winger," became the party's spokesman on foreign affairs in the House of Commons. The House of Lords, we may add, was opened to women holding life peerages.

France emerged from the Second World War in a very weakened condition. Its armed forces were slight, its finances chaotic,

**France**

and its people dispirited and badly divided. It even lacked a regular government, for that of the Third Republic had ended with the military débâcle of 1940, and the ensuing Vichy regime of Marshal Pétain had come to an inglorious end with his internment in Germany in 1944. After Germany's collapse, prominent figures in that regime were brought back to France and tried for treason. Laval was among those put to death, and other "collaborationists" were imprisoned. The aged Pétain was confined to a desolate island where he died in 1950.

Taking charge of affairs in France at the time of its liberation in 1944–1945 were the forces of General Charles De Gaulle, coming from Algeria, and a variety of resistance groups at home, ranging from Nationalists to Communists. Out of these heterogeneous elements, De Gaulle set up at Paris a "provisional government" which authorized the popular election in October 1945 of a National Assembly to draft a constitution for the "Fourth French Republic."

The Assembly elected De Gaulle "Provisional President" of the Republic, but the majority of its members differed with him about the nature of the constitution. They wanted it essentially the same as that of the Third Republic, with an all-powerful parliament and a merely titular President, while he insisted that it should endow the presidency with powers similar to those exercised by a President of the United States. Amid growing party strife, De Gaulle resigned in January 1946 and appealed to the country to reject the kind of constitution favored by the Assembly majority. His appeal bore fruit, for when the proposed constitution was submitted to plebiscite in May 1946 it was rejected by a majority of over a million.

A second National Assembly was then elected to redraft the

constitution. This was done, with only minor changes, and in October 1946 the result was finally ratified by a second plebiscite in which, however, only nine and a quarter million persons voted aye, while over eight million voted no and eight and a half million abstained. The constitution of the Fourth French Republic, thus doubtfully accepted, was much more elaborate than that of the Third Republic, but the actual changes it introduced were relatively few. There was now a detailed declaration of rights of the individual and of labor. In place of the previous Chamber of Deputies and Senate were substituted respectively a National Assembly, elected by universal (including female) suffrage, and a Council of the Republic, chosen by indirect election and having only advisory functions. The President would still be elected by the two bodies for a term of seven years and could still take no action except through cabinet ministers responsible to the Assembly. In the hope of lessening the frequency of cabinet crises which had disturbed the Third Republic, the new constitution empowered the cabinet to dissolve the Assembly and hold new elections if two such crises occurred within eighteen months. The new constitution also provided for an advisory Economic Council, and for a confederation of the colonies with the mother-country in a "French Union."[1]

*Constitution of Fourth French Republic*

The first parliamentary elections under the new French constitution, held in November 1946, gave the Communists almost a third of the six hundred seats in the National Assembly, and "Rightist" followers of De Gaulle (in the "Reunion of the French People," or R.P.F.) half as many. There were, besides, 173 Catholic democrats (of the "Popular Republican Movement," or M.R.P.), 104 democratic Socialists, and 43 Radicals; and these joined in choosing Vincent Auriol, a Socialist, as President of the Republic. The coalition, however, was difficult to maintain. While the parties to it were agreed on upholding the democratic constitution against possible subversion by either Communists or the De Gaullist R.P.F., they differed greatly among themselves. The Radicals disliked the social legislation and taxation measures urged by Socialists and the M.R.P. The Socialists, along with the Radicals, opposed the M.R.P.'s championship of state aid for Catholic schools. Moreover, both Socialists and M.R.P. were re-

[1] On this, see below, p. 750.

luctant to take stands that might lose them followers, the one to the Communists, the other to De Gaulle. The result was much the same instability of government as had characterized pre-war France. There were frequent cabinet crises. The prime minister at the end of 1957 was the twenty-fourth since 1945.

In the general election of 1951, the De Gaullists gained, the Communists declined, while among the coalition parties the Socialists held their own, the M.R.P. lost ground, and the Radical Socialists gained. One of the last-named, René Coty, was elected President in 1953 in succession to Auriol. The next general election, in 1956, returned a larger number of Communists, Radicals, and Conservatives, a reduced number of Socialists, M.R.P., and De Gaullists, and some fifty members of a new right-wing group headed by a youthful anti-tax agitator named Poujade.

Financial and economic problems of the post-war era were even more troublesome in France than in Great Britain, and the difficulty of solving them was enhanced in France, not only by the obstructive tactics of a numerous Communist party and by constant bickering among the governing groups, but also by protracted warfare to maintain French rule in Indo-China and Algeria. This was largely unavailing, as we shall indicate in the next chapter.[1] Yet it was very costly in men and money, and very disturbing to the French ministries that coped with it.

Nevertheless, France succeeded in surmounting some of its difficulties. Currency inflation was temporarily checked, though the value of the franc was only a tiny fraction of what it had been before the war. Thanks to American financial aid, the budget was gradually brought into approximate balance. There was a progressive nationalizing of banks, coal mines, air lines and other utilities, though it was slower and more restricted than in Britain. Industrial production was somewhat increased. Hydro-electric plants were built. Use of agricultural machinery was extended. Public health was bettered. The birthrate rose.

A decade after the Second World War, France, despite the continuing drain of its colonial warfare, appeared to be regaining its previous prosperity. As a whole, too, despite its totalitarian extremists, France remained stalwartly democratic and liberal, an inspiring member of the free western world.

[1] See below, pp. 743-744, 757, 770-771.

## 2. OTHER POST-WAR NATIONS OF WESTERN EUROPE

The nations of Western Europe, other than France and Great Britain, showed similar trends in the post-war period.[1] All faced economic and social difficulties and most of them sought recovery through democratic procedures. Those which had suffered German occupation—the Low Countries of Belgium, Netherlands, and Luxemburg, and the Scandinavian countries of Denmark and Norway—welcomed back their previous independent governments, all from exile except the Danish, and speedily restored their pre-war constitutions.

In Belgium, the two chief political parties, the Christian Social (Catholic) and the Socialist, obtained between them, in elections of 1946, an overwhelming majority in the parliament, and afterwards usually cooperated in governing the country. **Belgium** Temporarily a cleavage developed over the question of restoring King Leopold III who had surrendered to the Germans in 1940. The Catholic party, advocating his restoration, won a majority in the parliamentary election of 1949 and likewise in a popular plebiscite on the question in the following year. But the majority was scanty and the Socialist opposition persistent and threatening. A most serious crisis was finally averted by a compromise, whereby Leopold returned as King, and then abdicated in favor of his son, Baudouin, and again left the country. Belgium fared well economically. It stabilized its currency, checked inflation, and benefited from the post-war prosperity of its African Congo possession, rich in uranium and copper, as well as in rubber.

Belgium likewise benefited from joining with the other Low Countries in a tariff union called "Benelux" (from the **"Benelux"** first syllables in the names of Belgium, Netherlands, and Luxemburg). Woman suffrage was adopted, a good deal of social legislation was enacted, and public education extended.

In the Netherlands, post-war government was similarly conducted usually by a coalition of Catholic and Labor parties. The popular Queen Wilhelmina abdicated, by reason of age **Netherlands** and infirmity, in 1948, and was succeeded by her daughter Juliana. Economic recovery was slower and less complete in the Netherlands than in Belgium, in large part because

---

[1] For Italy and Germany, see the next section, pp. 721–727, below.

of rebellion and loss of its rich East Indian empire. A part of New Guinea was troublously retained; sovereignty over the remainder was transferred to the independent republic of Indonesia.[1] In 1954, furthermore, complete internal autonomy was accorded to Surinam and the Dutch West Indies. By a constitutional amendment, the Netherlands became the first country to provide for ceding national authority to supra-national organizations.

Recovery from the effects of war and military occupation was fairly rapid in both agricultural Denmark and commercial Norway. In Norway the Socialist Labor party carried general elections and manned the cabinet; in Denmark it was a coalition of Socialists and Liberals. The Danish King, Christian X, who had been virtually interned by the Germans during the war, died in 1947 and was succeeded by his son, Frederick IX. The venerable Norwegian King, Haakon VII, who had escaped the Germans and lived in exile during the war, was succeeded on his death in 1957 by his son, Olav V. It is noteworthy that post-war Norway had an advanced system of public health and social welfare, and the world's third largest merchant marine.

**Norway and Denmark**

Denmark's occupation by German troops during the war cost it the final severing of its political ties with Iceland. Until then the King of Denmark had been King of Iceland, but in 1944 a large majority of Icelanders voted to separate their country from the Danish crown and to make it an independent republic. In Denmark a new constitution in 1953 lowered the voting age from 25 to 23, and changed the status of Greenland from colony to self-governing member of a "Danish Commonwealth," with representatives in the Danish parliament.

Finland, though obliged to make important territorial cessions to the Soviet Union and to act very circumspectly in dealing with its powerful Communist neighbor, clung tenaciously to national independence and democratic government. Parliamentary rule was exercised by a coalition of Socialists, Agrarians, and Liberals; and Julio Paasikivi, a Socialist and astute statesman, served as President from 1945 to 1956, when he was succeeded by a former able premier, Dr. Urho Kekkonen.

**Finland**

Greece, though geographically not a part of Western Europe, has shared with it a common cultural heritage and a like devotion

[1] See below, pp. 755–756.

to liberty and democracy. It suffered grievously from both international and civil war. By the end of 1944, the in- Greece
vading and occupying Germans, Italians, and Bulgarians had been evacuated. King George II was recalled from exile
by popular plebiscite, and on his death in 1947 was succeeded in
due course by his brother, Paul. Meanwhile, however, groups of
Greek Communists, abetted and aided by Communist Yugoslavia,
Albania, and Bulgaria, undertook by force of arms to make
Greece another Soviet satellite, and the ensuing civil war was
protracted and costly. The democratic government eventually got
the upper hand, as financial and military assistance arrived from
America,[1] and Tito of Yugoslavia, quarreling with Moscow, cut
off aid to the Greek Communists. Greece adopted woman suffrage
in 1952, and concluded a twenty-year mutual defense pact with
Turkey and Yugoslavia in 1954.

The five countries of Western Europe which had been neutral
during the Second World War—Sweden, Switzerland, Ireland,
Portugal, and Spain—encountered in the early post-war years
somewhat different difficulties from those which confronted the
ex-belligerents. While the ex-belligerents had to shoulder debts
of war and reconstruction, the neutrals were deprived of exceptional profits derived from wartime exports to Axis or allied
powers. Sweden and Switzerland suffered least in this Sweden
respect. Sweden, dubious how to conduct its foreign and
relations between the Soviet Union and the Western Switzerland
democracies, was governed by Socialist cabinets and continued
to develop its democratically planned economy and welfare state.
Its nominal head, King Gustavus V, died in 1951 at an advanced
age and after a long reign, and was quietly succeeded by his son,
Gustavus VI.

Switzerland maintained its traditional federal democracy and
emphasized its traditional neutrality by refusing to have any part
in the United Nations Organization. It applied itself economically
to increasing its peacetime manufacture and export of clocks and
watches, machinery, textiles, and chemicals.

The Irish Republic (Eire) secured its complete political independence from Britain in 1949, on the thirty-third anniversary of
the Easter Rebellion of 1916.[2] Eamon DeValera, leader of the

[1] See below, p. 731.
[2] See above, pp. 387–388, 459.

nationalist Fianna Fail party, alternated with John Costello of the more moderate Fine Gael party as premier in the post-war years. Much was done to improve housing and health and to promote industrial, as well as agricultural, development. But the republic was handicapped by a steady continuing decline of population through emigration and by being deprived of manufacturing and commercial counties in Ulster, which were included in the separate self-governing territory of "North Ireland" united with Great Britain.

The Iberian countries of Spain and Portugal retained, despite foreign criticism and domestic depression, their pre-war military dictatorships. The Spanish regime of General Francisco Franco was the object of special attack alike in Communist Russia and in the Western democracies for its alleged fascist character; and for several years after the war Spain was treated as a kind of outcast among the European countries, being excluded from the United Nations and subjected to partial ostracism, diplomatic and economic. Yet the majority of the Spanish people, fearing a renewal of civil war if General Franco was removed and resenting what appeared to be foreign interference, rallied to his support and there was a gradual easing of his dictatorship. A national parliament, or Cortes, was established in 1942, partly appointive and partly elective. A charter of individual liberties was issued in 1945.

In 1947 a popular referendum endorsed a "succession law," whereby, in case of Franco's death or incapacity, a regency council would propose a King or Regent who must be acceptable to a two-thirds majority of the Cortes; and Don Juan Carlos, a young grandson of Alphonso XIII, was brought from abroad for schooling in Spain. Although the country was afflicted by inflation and a low standard of living, it profited from rebuilding and other public works, from a notable increase of tourist trade, and eventually from an arrangement with the United States involving the grant of military bases and receipt of financial aid. Eventually, too, in 1955 Spain was admitted to the United Nations. It may be added that in 1957 Spain turned over most of its North African territory to newly independent Morocco.[1]

In Portugal, Marshal Carmona, the army officer who had seized power in 1926, remained President of the Republic, through a

[1] See below, p. 770.

series of controlled elections, until his death in 1951, when a successor was chosen in the person of Francisco Craveiro Lopez. Actually, however, the government continued to be directed by Dr. Antonio de Oliveira Salazar. Though constitutional forms were observed, the regime was essentially dicta- **Portugal** torial. Domestic opposition was curbed in part by Salazar's watchful police and in part by his salutary management of public finance and administration. Portugal, alone among European nations except for Belgium, astutely managed to keep intact its important colonial empire.

We should recall that overseas, particularly in America and the Pacific, were a goodly number of nations that derived their languages, population, and cultures primarily from West- **West** ern Europe and shared its ideals of liberty and de- **European** mocracy. They belonged to the Free World, as over **Heritage** against the Communist World, and they at least morally **Overseas** reinforced it. We here make brief mention of them.

Of course, the foremost in population and resources is the United States of America. Indeed, it has played a finally decisive role in both First and Second World Wars, and since 1947 it has been the recognized champion and leader of the West's defense against Communism. Curiously enough, only two really great powers now remain to replace the old European balance: one, the Soviet Union, is only partly in Europe; the other, the United States, is geographically quite outside Europe.

Along with the United States in the Europeanized "New World," are, of course, the twenty Latin-American republics. All have democratic constitutions with guarantees of indi- **Latin** vidual liberty, but most of them have been prey, in **America** greater or lesser degree, to political coups and military dictatorships. These have been latterly accentuated by domestic unrest and foreign propaganda accompanying the Second World War and the economic difficulties and adjustments which followed. Portuguese-speaking Brazil, the largest and most populous, was directed by a semi-dictator, Getulio Vargas, from 1930 to 1945. Reëlected President in 1950, he was deposed by an army coup and committed suicide in 1954. The next year, in a comparatively free election, a professed democrat, with the odd name of Juscelino Kubitschek, succeeded to the presidency. Argentina, in many ways the most important of the Spanish-American states, was subjected to a series of military coups, culminating in the oppressively dictatorial rule of Juan Perón from 1946 until 1955, when a group of army officers, encouraged by church leaders, revolted. Perón fled into exile, Pedro Aramburu assumed a provisional presidency, and a return to liberal democracy was promised. A famous liberal newspaper, *La Prensa,* which had been expropriated by Perón in 1952, was returned and reappeared in 1956. There remained from the dictatorship, however, an unfortunate legacy of financial chaos and army unrest, which gravely troubled the new government.

Dictatorial regimes seemed to flourish especially in the Caribbean states of Haiti, the Dominican Republic (with its Trujillo dynasty), Cuba (with General Batista), Venezuela (with Jimenez, who was overthrown in 1958), and Nicaragua (with the Somoza family). In Colombia, a destructive uprising at Bogotá, abetted by Communists, was put down in 1948, but a semi-dictatorial Conservative regime was followed, through a coup of 1953, by a military regime headed by General Pinilla, who in turn was ousted in 1957.

In Guatemala, unique among American nations, a group of Communists actually got control in 1950 through a sympathetic President, Arbenz Guzman. In 1954, however, an anti-Communist force, organized in Honduras under command of Colonel Carlos Armas, and supplied with arms from the United States, invaded Guatemala and overthrew the pro-Communist regime. Though Armas himself was assassinated in 1957, his policies were continued briefly under democratic auspices and then under military rule. Some of the Latin-American states showed exceptional moderation and stability. This was particularly evidenced in Mexico, Peru, Ecuador, Chile, and Uruguay.

Further evidence of successful operation of democracy is found in the two American members of the British Commonwealth: its **Canada** oldest, the Franco-British "Dominion of Canada"; and its youngest, the largely Negro "Caribbean Federation." Canada experienced in the post-war years a remarkable development industrially and commercially. It gained, too, in international prestige, and played a prominent part in the United Nations. In the general election of 1953, the Liberal party of Prime Minister Louis St. Laurent won its fifth successive victory, obtaining 171 out of 265 seats in the parliament. The tables were turned, nevertheless, in the next general election, that of 1957. The Conservative leader, John Diefenbaker, became Premier, and Sidney Earle Smith succeeded Lester B. Pearson as Minister of External Affairs. Newfoundland, with its Labrador dependency, became the tenth province of Canada by popular referendum of 1949. Arrangements for forming the Caribbean Fed- Caribbean eration were made in 1955, and in 1958 it began func- Confederation tioning as another autonomous and democratic unit in the Commonwealth. It comprises Jamaica, Trinidad-Tobago, Barbados, Windward and Leeward Islands.

In the Pacific, the Europeanized democratic countries are Australia, New Zealand, and the Philippines. In the first two, both members of the British Commonwealth, there has been Australia a recent trend away from the socialistic features which and New characterized them before the war.[1] Australian elec- Zealand tions at the end of 1955 retained Robert Menzies in power as prime minister with a parliamentary majority of cooperating Liberal and Country parties, pledged to encouragement of private enterprise and strengthening of relations with both the Commonwealth and the United States. Corresponding New Zealand elections of 1954 gave the Conservative National party a majority over the socialistic Laborites, although the latter were returned to power in 1957. Of post-war events in the liberated Philippines, and likewise in African members of the British Commonwealth, we defer mention until the next chapter.

## 3. POST-WAR ITALY, GERMANY, AND JAPAN

The hardest hit of all the countries of western (and central) Europe, following the war, were the vanquished nations of Italy and Germany. They were subjected to foreign occupation and dictation, and saddled with the gravest sort of economic and political problems. In the case of Italy, while the course and outcome of the war had discredited Mussolini and his Fascist Italy party, there was conflict between royalists and republicans, and, among the latter, strife of Communists, Socialists, Liberals, and Christian (Catholic) Democrats. With a view to preserving the monarchy, King Victor Emmanuel III was prevailed upon in 1944 to appoint as Regent his son, the Crown Prince,

[1] See above, pp. 64–65, 473.

and in May 1946 to leave the country after installing the Prince as King Humbert II. Meanwhile a provisional coalition government had been formed, and in June 1946 it held a popular plebiscite (including women as well as men) on the question whether Italy should remain a monarchy or become a republic. While monarchy was favored by a majority in the agricultural south, a larger majority in the industrial north voted for a republic. This was accordingly proclaimed, and King Humbert abdicated and followed his father into exile.

The Italian Republic was immediately confronted with the question whether it would follow a democratic course or be subverted into a Communist dictatorship. Many Italians were attracted to Communism because it represented an extreme reaction against discredited Fascism and promised a drastic short-cut to economic betterment. Fortunately for democratic and liberal forces, the foreign occupying troops in Italy, unlike those in Germany and the countries of east-central Europe, were not Russian; they were exclusively British and American. As it was, the Italian Communists under the leadership of Palmiro Togliatti, together with sympathetic Socialists under Pietro Nenni, won 219 of the 556 seats in the Constituent Assembly elected in 1946. The largest party opposing them was the Christian (Catholic) Democratic, which won 207 seats, and whose leader, Alcide De Gasperi, through collaboration with minor Liberal groups and with a number of right-wing Socialists who broke away from Nenni, was enabled to head an anti-Communist coalition cabinet.

The supporting majority in the Assembly was dangerously small and shifting but it gradually achieved its purpose. After reluctantly ratifying the humiliating treaty with the Allies,[1] and securing the withdrawal of the Anglo-American occupying forces, it adopted late in 1947 a democratic republican constitution. This provided for a bicameral parliament, composed of a Chamber of Deputies and a Senate. The Chamber was to be chosen by universal direct suffrage; the Senate, partly by popular vote and partly by regional councils. The two houses were given equal legislative functions, and disagreement between them could be settled by a popular referendum. A President was to be elected for seven years by parliament plus some regional representatives, and was endowed with considerable authority although his cab-

[1] See above, pp. 684–685.

inet, as in France, was to be responsible not to him but to the parliament. Into the constitution was also incorporated the Lateran Accord of 1929 with the papacy.[1]

The first general election under the new constitution was held in April 1948 and resulted in victory for De Gasperi and his Christian Democrats. These won 306 of the 574 seats in the Chamber of Deputies, while the "Popular Front" of Communists and left-wing Socialists secured 182 seats. Then, in May, a prominent Liberal, Luigi Einaudi, was elected President. De Gasperi remained as prime minister until 1953. The general election of that year dangerously increased Communist strength in parliament; while the number of Christian Democrats fell from 306 to 261, that of the Communist-Socialist bloc went up from 182 to 218.

Yet the Christian Democrats contrived, by means of continuing collaboration with Liberal groups, to retain the premiership through a succession of cabinets following De Gasperi's. One of their number, Giovanni Gronchi, was elected President of the Republic in 1955 in succession to Einaudi.

Despite persistent Communist opposition, and of minor opposition from a "rightist" neo-fascist movement, the Italian Republic, under its democratic government, pursued a foreign policy of cooperation with the Western powers, and, in return, these powers helped it to recover from the war and to regain prestige. Restrictions on its armaments in the peace-treaty of 1947 were repudiated by the United States and ten other Western nations in 1951. It was enabled, too, to exercise a trusteeship over its former African colony of Somalia, to get back in 1954 the Adriatic port of Trieste, and next year to join the United Nations. Most important, it was the recipient of American aid in goods, money, and technical skills that contributed to its industrial rehabilitation and to much needed land reform.

Problems remained for Italy—very serious problems. But from 1955 onwards, at any rate, there was a perceptible decline of the number and influence of the Communist following. This was accelerated by Soviet Russia's intervention in Hungary in 1956.[2]

Germany emerged from the war not merely weak; it was prostrate. It was disarmed and dismembered. Large sections of its

---

[1] See above, p. 577.     [2] See above, p. 704.

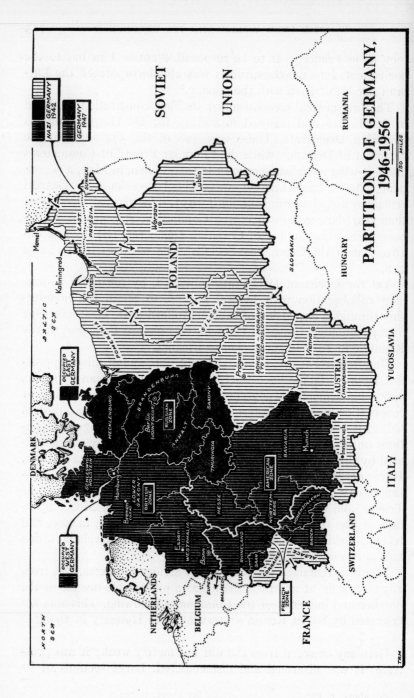

PARTITION OF GERMANY, 1946–1956

NAZI GERMANY 1942

GERMANY 1947

OCCUPIED EAST GERMANY

OCCUPIED WEST GERMANY

150 MILES

SOVIET UNION

RUMANIA

HUNGARY

YUGOSLAVIA

AUSTRIA (INDEPENDENT)

SLOVAKIA

BOHEMIA – MORAVIA (TO CZECHOSLOVAKIA)

Prague

Vienna

Innsbruck

ITALY

SWITZERLAND

FRANCE

BELGIUM

NETHERLANDS

LUXEMBURG

EUPEN

MALMEDY

SAAR

BADEN

WÜRTTEM-BERG

HOHENZOLLERN

BAVARIA

Munich

AMERICAN ZONE

FRENCH ZONE

BRITISH ZONE

RUSSIAN ZONE

RHINELAND

HESSE

THURINGIA

SAXONY

ANHALT

LOWER SAXONY

WESTPHALIA

Essen

Bonn

Bremen

Hamburg

SCHLESWIG-HOLSTEIN

MECKLENBURG

BRANDENBURG

Berlin (JOINT)

DENMARK

NORTH SEA

BALTIC SEA

Memel

Kaliningrad

Danzig

POMERANIA

SILESIA

EAST PRUSSIA

SUWALKI

POLAND

Warsaw

Lublin

TRM

724

chief cities were in ruins. The Russians were dismantling and taking away whatever machinery they could lay their hands on, and the Western Allies appeared at first to acquiesce and to be quite willing that Germany should be kept weak. What remained of the country, after detachment of its eastern **Germany** territory up to the Oder-Neisse rivers, was under continuing military occupation and control of foreigners, and yet obliged to receive and resettle some twelve or thirteen million Germans displaced from their homes in that extensive territory. At the start, the four occupying powers—Russia, Great Britain, the United States, and France—cooperated in trying "war criminals" and "de-Nazifying" Germany. In 1946, they agreed on the abolition of the historic state of Prussia and the division of Germany into sixteen relatively equal-sized states: Schleswig-Holstein, Hamburg, Lower Saxony, and Westphalia, in the British zone; Bremen, Hesse, Württemberg-Baden, and Bavaria, in the American zone; Rhineland-Palatinate, South Baden, and Württemberg-Hohenzollern in a French zone; and Brandenburg, Mecklenburg, Saxony, Thuringia, and Anhalt, in the Russian zone.

But as Russia soon gave unmistakable evidence of its intention to transform its military zone into a Communist satellite [1] and to oppose any general peace treaty except on its own terms, the Western powers began to see in Germany a possible counterweight to Soviet influence in central Europe. Gradually it became their policy to work for a strong and stable Germany. To this end they sponsored democratic constitutions and free elections in the states within their several zones and in 1948 the incorporation of all their zones in a Federal Republic of Germany. A Con- **Federal** stituent Assembly was accordingly elected; and the **Republic** democratic constitution which issued from it provided **of West** for a bicameral parliament, comprising a popularly **Germany** elected Bundestag and a Bundesrat representing the states, for a President, chosen by a special assembly for five years, and for a Chancellor, with a cabinet, responsible to the Bundestag. Theodor Heuss of the Free Democratic party, was chosen first President in 1949 and re-elected in 1954. The first Bundestag, chosen in 1949, contained 139 Christian (chiefly Catholic) Democrats, 131 Social Democrats, 52 Free Democrats, and 80 others including 15 Communists. A coalition cabinet was formed with the sturdy,

[1] On Communist East Germany, see above, pp. 688, 700.

seventy-three-year-old Christian Democratic leader, Dr. Konrad Adenauer, as Chancellor. Adenauer proved to be a truly remarkable statesman, commanding ever greater respect at home and abroad. In the 1953 general election, his coalition won 306 of the 487 seats in the Bundestag, and in the general election of 1957 his own party of Christian Democrats overwhelmed the Socialist opposition and gained a clear majority of the seats.

Meanwhile, under Adenauer's guidance, West Germany made a phenomenal recovery. Relief materials and credits were obtained from America. Bombed areas were repaired. Inflation was checked and the currency stabilized. The big immigration of dispossessed Germans from the East was absorbed. A decade after the close of the war West Germany was the most prosperous and productive country in western Europe. With factories rebuilt and expanded, its industrial output was considerably above that of pre-war years, and its exports were rising. It was foremost in Europe in steel production, and next to the United States and Great Britain in foreign trade.

West Germany was clearly and constructively aligned, moreover, with the Western democracies and the free world. And it was taking an ever more important part in international relations. Diplomatic recognition was accorded it by the Western occupying powers in 1951 and by the Soviet Union in 1957. It was admitted to membership in several auxiliary organizations of the United Nations. It recovered the Saar from France. It was encouraged by the West to rearm. Incidentally, West Germany in 1952 agreed to pay Israel during the next twelve or fourteen years an indemnity of 822 million dollars for losses inflicted on Jews by Hitler and his Nazis. There still remained, of course, a most difficult problem, that of reuniting Russian-held, Communist East Germany with democratic West Germany, and no solution of this problem was in sight.

German-speaking Austria, which had been forcibly annexed to Germany by Hitler in 1938, was separated again in 1945. Though it was divided, like Germany, into four zones for military occupation, it was permitted from the outset to to have a single democratic government of its own. The chief political parties were the People's (Catholic) and the Socialist. Dr. Karl Renner, a veteran Socialist, served as President until his death in 1950; he was succeeded by Theodore Koerner. The

**Austria**

Catholic party supplied the Chancellors: Leopold Figl from 1945 to 1953; Julius Raab afterwards. The latter was continued in office by the victory of his party in the parliamentary election of 1956. This was attributed in large part to his success in negotiating the treaty whereby, in exchange for the country's neutralization, the Soviet Union, as well as the Western powers, made formal peace and withdrew all foreign troops.[1]

In the case of Japan, the third of the vanquished Axis powers, the post-war military occupation was exclusively American, under General Douglas MacArthur, and it was chiefly concerned at the start with democratizing and disarming *Japan* the country. By the terms of the surrender in August 1945 Japan had agreed to a democratic government and free elections; and, before that, the Potsdam declaration had specified that Japan must accord freedom of speech and religion and "respect for the fundamental rights of humanity." Then, under MacArthur, Baron Shidehara, a former ambassador to the United States, was named premier. One of the first acts of Shidehara's cabinet was to grant suffrage to women and to lower the voting age for men from 25 to 20. A new constitution was adopted, becoming effective in 1947. It stripped the Emperor of all claims of divinity and of all but nominal authority, and vested sole law-making power in a parliament consisting of a House of Representatives popularly elected for not more than four years and a House of Councilors elected for six years. It likewise renounced any Japanese resort to war or maintenance of armed forces.

Meanwhile the American occupation was sponsoring the trial of "war criminals," the ousting of right-wing nationalists and militarists from government, education, and business, the break-up of large landed estates and big business combines, and the outlawing of the nationalist Shinto religion and the emperor-worship connected with it. So thorough was the purge of conservative elements in schools, universities, labor unions, and agricultural cooperatives that many of these were left in the hands of Socialists sympathetic with Marxist doctrine. At the same time the United States was aiding the Japanese people by importation of food and raw materials and promotion of public health.

Before long, American policy toward Japan underwent a drastic

[1] See above, p. 688.

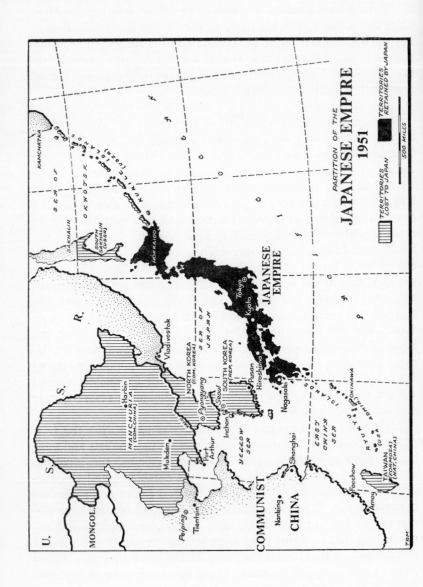

PARTITION OF THE
JAPANESE EMPIRE
1951

TERRITORIES LOST TO JAPAN

TERRITORIES RETAINED BY JAPAN

500 MILES

change. Just as Germany began to seem a bulwark against the advance of Communism in Europe, so did Japan in Asia, especially after the Communist conquest of China in 1949. In 1950 the United States approved the creation of a Japanese "police force" that much resembled an army, and four years later, under American pressure and despite the constitutional prohibition, Japan enacted legislation providing for military, naval, and air "defensive" forces.

Supplementing the peace treaty of 1951,[1] the United States agreed in 1957 to withdraw its main occupying army, while temporarily leaving defensive air forces. Already Japan, through its ingenious and hardworking population, was well on the road to economic recovery. A general election in 1955 returned to the House of Representatives 300 Liberal-Democrats and 154 Socialists out of a total of 467. Shiguru Yoshida had been premier during the six stirring years from 1948 to 1954.

### 4. AMERICAN LEADERSHIP IN DEFENSE OF FREE EUROPE

Following World War II, the United States was not only the foremost world power in material respects, but, in keeping with ideals shared by western Europe, it was a leading champion of liberal democracy, national self-determination, and international cooperation through the United Nations. These principles, most Americans optimistically believed in 1945, would be everywhere acceptable and would provide the spiritual cement for the "one world" of the future. Such popular idealism helps to explain why the United States demobilized and disarmed so quickly and largely after the cessation of active hostilities, and why its government was so trustful, in 1945–1946, of Russian intentions and promises. Stalin and his foreign minister, Molotov, said they were "democratic" and "peace-loving." They endorsed the Atlantic Charter and the United Nations Organization. They pledged the Soviet Union to respect the right of liberated peoples to set up and maintain governments of their own free choice. Why, then, shouldn't the United States (and the European nations) expect to live on friendly terms with Russia, the one other unquestionably great power? To do so, some occasional compromises might be desirable and necessary. Not to do

*American Optimism After War*

---

[1] See above, pp. 688–689.

so, a Third World War might be the alternative, and that was too terrifying to contemplate.

For a brief time, American optimism seemed justified. It was a bit shaken, as early as the autumn of 1945, by Russian aggression against Iran and the occupation of the important oil-producing province of Azerbaijan by Russian troops. But in this instance the Soviet Union yielded to mediation by the United Nations in behalf of Iran; the troops were withdrawn, and optimism temporarily reigned again.

Not for long, however. By the end of 1946 it was becoming quite obvious that the Soviet dictatorship attached quite different
American meanings to "democracy," "free elections," and "self-
Disillusion- determination" from those usual in the United States,
ment and that, instead of adhering to its earlier promises and honestly cooperating for the realization of a free Europe, it was aggressively seeking to transform as much of Europe as possible into a Communist empire dependent on Moscow. It was retaining armies at wartime strength, and using them to impose satellite Communist regimes on country after country in east-central Europe. It was also fostering subversive Communist movements in the West, especially in France and Italy. At the same time it was well-nigh paralyzing the United Nations by frequent use of the veto; and it was directing a continuous and abusive propaganda campaign against the Western democracies and particularly against the United States. These were incessantly denounced as war-mongering, capitalistic countries, trying to bolster up a decaying oppressive economic system, and hence bent on throttling the "homeland of socialism," the Soviet Union.

Although the Soviet Union, for its own ends, did join the United States and the other Western Allies in concluding peace, in February 1947, with Italy, Hungary, Bulgaria, Rumania, and Finland, it definitely refused, two months later, to consider peace terms with Germany. By this time it was quite clear that the Soviet Union was implacably hostile to the democracies and was
"Cold War" in fact engaged in what came to be termed a "cold war"
and "Iron (as opposed to a "hot" or shooting war) against them.
Curtain" Eastern Communist Europe was cut off from the West by what Winston Churchill called an "iron curtain," for the Russian Communists severely restricted travel, trade and communication in the lands they controlled. Historic ties were broken. The

continent of Europe stood divided into two parts, the one free, the other subject to the dictates of Communist Moscow. The free part, if it were not to fall further prey to the Communist part, needed help from America.

The Soviet Union was already preparing to add Greece and Turkey to its Communist empire. After denouncing its non-aggression treaty with Turkey, it demanded in August 1946 a share in the control of the Turkish straits from the Black Sea into the Mediterranean. Simultaneously, it incited its satellite states of Yugoslavia, Albania, and Bulgaria to provide military assistance to a Communist insurrection in Greece against the democratic government of that country. Great Britain, which had helped to free Greece from the Germans in 1944, and to re-establish order there, now lacked the military strength to defend it and so informed President Harry Truman of the United States. **Truman Doctrine: Aid to Greece and Turkey** The President responded by enunciating in March 1947 the so-called "Truman Doctrine," that the United States would use its economic power to arrest the advance of Communism. Then in May the Doctrine was endorsed by the American Congress with an initial appropriation of 400 million dollars for troops and supplies for the defense of Greece and Turkey.

American aid proved sufficient in both cases. It enabled Greece to suppress the internal Communist menace and the guerrillas operating from across the borders, and likewise to improve economic conditions and to maintain an orderly democratic government. In the case of Turkey, it served to halt the Soviet Union's aggressive pressures and to encourage democratic progress.

A second step was taken by the United States in June 1948, when President Truman's Secretary of State, General George Marshall, proposed a plan for extending American financial aid to other European countries in order to **Marshall Plan: Financial Aid to Free Europe** hasten their recovery from the war and thereby to strengthen them. The Soviet Union was invited to participate, but at a conference at Paris the plan was bitterly denounced by Molotov, the Russian foreign minister, and rejected, under orders from Moscow, by the entire Communist bloc [1] and by unhappily situated Finland. Nevertheless it was

---

[1] In addition to the Soviet Union itself: Albania, Bulgaria, Czechoslovakia, Hungary, Poland, Rumania, and Yugoslavia.

gladly accepted by France and Great Britain and by fourteen other European nations, only Spain being expressly excluded.[1] In the United States it was implemented by a Foreign Assistance Act, under which was set up an Economic Cooperation Administration (ECA), headed by Paul Hoffman, to administer the European Recovery Program (ERP). Altogether, between 1948 and the end of 1951 the United States expended twelve and a half billion dollars on the Marshall Plan, and the money and goods thus provided were of incalculable value in rebuilding a prosperous West Europe and greatly lessening the want and misery on which Communism thrives.

The Soviet dictatorship recognized the menace to its own ambitions and to the Communist cause in the strengthening of the European democracies through financial assistance from the United States, and it took a variety of counter-measures. It intensified its propaganda against the United States and against

**Soviet Retaliation**  any country's acceptance of American aid, blatantly proclaiming that while it was the champion of the masses and the foe of imperialism, the United States, besides being "war-mongering," was "imperialistic" and essentially "fascist." The Communist International (Comintern), which had been disbanded in 1943, was now resurrected as the Cominform and used to unify and quicken Communist parties abroad.

In 1948, by a coup d'état at Prague, Czechoslovakia was transferred from democratic to communist ranks, enclosed behind the "iron curtain," and obliged to refuse American assistance. In April 1948, a Communist group, doubtless incited by Moscow, tried to break up a Pan-American Conference then in session at Bogotá in Colombia and attended by the United States' Secretary of State, General Marshall, by precipitating partisan riots which raged for several days and were suppressed only after much destruction in the city.

Apparently the Communist action at Bogotá was intended to distract American attention from simultaneous and more important Soviet action at Berlin. This German capital, we may recall,

---

[1] The fourteen were: Austria, Belgium, Denmark, Greece, Iceland, Ireland (Eire), Italy, Luxemburg, Norway, Netherlands, Portugal, Sweden, Switzerland, and Turkey. Subsequently, Spain became a recipient of American financial aid, as did Yugoslavia. See below, p. 734.

lay deep in the Russian military zone, though Britain, France, and the United States had been guaranteed military occupation of part of it and free access to it from their respective zones in western and southern Germany. In March 1948 the Soviet dictatorship began a series of aggressive activities calculated to force the Western Allies out of Berlin and to humble them in the eyes of all Germany. First its delegates quitted and broke up the joint Control Council which had been provided for at the Potsdam Conference in 1945.[1] Next, in April 1948, it imposed drastic restrictions on land traffic between the Western zones and Berlin. Then, in June, it definitely repudiated its agreement with the Western Allies for joint government of Berlin, and denied them all use of the railroads, highways, and waterways over which they had been supplying their part of the city.[2] The United States, Britain, and France were reluctant to use force and yet they were determined to maintain their position in Berlin. To overcome the "blockade," they resorted to an "airlift." For a year and more American and British airplanes transported into West Berlin, in addition to army reenforcements, over two and a quarter million tons of food and fuel.

Berlin<br>Blockade<br>and<br>Airlift

At length checkmated and realizing the propaganda value of the airlift for the Western democracies, since it was a peaceful yet dazzling display of air power and piloting skill, the Soviet Union in 1949 abandoned the blockade and again opened the roads to Berlin.

Nevertheless the Berlin episode, in combination with the current overthrow of Czechoslovakia's democratic regime, convinced the Western democracies that the "cold war" might at any moment be turned into a hot "shooting war." If and when that occurred, the superior armed forces of the Soviet Union and its satellites could most probably engulf the whole European continent in Moscow's Communist empire. Until 1949 it was presumed that the United States had one great advantage in war weapons —a monopoly of the atomic bomb. In that year, however, President Truman announced that the Soviet Union had exploded one and hence had the secret of its manufacture. Obviously, the de-

---

[1] See above, p. 683.
[2] Their part had a population of two million, while that of the Soviet Union was 1,175,000.

fense of the West had to be military, as well as economic and moral.

Already in the spring of 1948 the United States had inaugurated a program of rearmament, involving an increase of ground and air forces and a stock-piling of atomic bombs. Now, in April 1949, **NATO:** by a pact signed at Washington, it entered into a **Military** twenty-year defensive military alliance with a stra-**Aid to** **Free** tegically placed group of nations astride the northern **Europe** Atlantic: Canada, Great Britain, France, Italy, Norway, Iceland, Denmark, Netherlands, Belgium, Luxemburg, and Portugal. The pact pledged the signatories to regard an armed attack on one or more of them as an attack on all, and it established a North Atlantic Treaty Organization (NATO) with an executive committee of foreign ministers, meeting at least once a year, and, under it, a defense council of war ministers and a military committee of chiefs of staff. To the European members of NATO, the United States granted an initial subsidy of a billion dollars to help them rearm; and supervision of the planning and coordination of mutual defense was entrusted to "Supreme Headquarters, Allied Powers, Europe" ("SHAPE") at Paris, with the American General Dwight Eisenhower in command.

Greece and Turkey were subsequently admitted to membership in NATO, and a Mutual Security Agency (MSA) replaced the ECA (Economic Cooperative Administration) as the chief dispenser of continuing financial grants and loans from the United States. When General Eisenhower returned to America in 1952 to be elected President in succession to Harry Truman, command of SHAPE was entrusted to another American, General Matthew Ridgway, and later, in turn, to still others, General Alfred Gruenther (1953) and General Lauris Norstad (1956).

For further defense of free Europe, the United States cultivated friendly relations with Spain and in 1953 concluded with it a ten-year agreement whereby, in return for financial and economic assistance, the United States obtained use of several strategic naval and air bases in the peninsula. Likewise, in concert with Britain and France, the United States signed at Paris in 1954 an agreement which opened the way to West Germany's joining NATO and furnishing twelve divisions to its armed forces. Moreover, the United States arranged with Denmark for joint defense of Greenland and with Portugal for joint defense of the

Azores; and it established military bases in Morocco and Iceland.[1] It thus ringed the Atlantic periphery of Europe with defensive outposts. And all the while it was making large financial grants to Europe.

Such aid from the United States undoubtedly contributed to the lessening of Communist influence and pressure in western and central Europe. But it should not obscure the important continuing influence, in Europe as well as in America, of traditions of personal and national freedom. Among Western peoples, reaction against Communist Russia was as natural as against Nazi Germany, and it was voiced and reinforced by political parties of liberals and conservatives, laborites and socialists, and also by the churches. Pope Pius XII denounced Communist tyranny and intolerance and called for a united front against it; and Catholic parties and statesmen took a prominent part in post-war defense of liberal democracy in France, Italy, the Low Countries, Austria, and West Germany. Protestant Christians—and Jews also—were similar upholders and preachers of liberty and democracy; and the World Council of Churches, which Protestants formed at Amsterdam in 1948, was outspoken against enslaving Communism.

*Europe's Will to Freedom*

In the trying post-war period, the free nations of Europe drew closer together than ever before. In 1947 the "Benelux" countries of Belgium, the Netherlands, and Luxemburg formed a customs union which abolished tariffs between them. In the same year Great Britain and France signed a fifty-year treaty of alliance, and in 1948, "Benelux" was included and a joint organization set up, with a consultative council "for collaboration in economic, social, and cultural matters, and for collective self-defense." Simultaneously, a protocol was signed at Turin looking toward a customs union between France and Italy.

*West European Coöperation*

Supplementing the Franco-British-Benelux alliance (and NATO), a "Council of Europe" was organized in 1949. In addition to the countries in the alliance, it comprised Denmark, Ireland (Eire), Norway, and Sweden, and it was soon joined by Greece and Turkey, and later by Italy and West Germany. It was directed by a Council of foreign ministers and advised by a Con-

---

[1] Iceland insisted in 1956 on a change in its agreement with the United States, whereby American forces would be withdrawn on six months' request by Iceland.

sultative Assembly of parliamentary representatives of the member nations.

The first session of this Assembly was held at Strasbourg in the late summer of 1949. The optimistic hope was at once voiced that the Council of Europe might foreshadow a federal union of most, if not all, of the free nations on the continent.

Both the Council of Europe and the North Atlantic Treaty Organization (NATO) pledged themselves to function as "regional" bodies within the general framework of the United Nations and in complete loyalty to its principles and purposes. And the United Nations, through its Assembly and Security Council, provided convenient means of broadcasting, not only the propaganda of the Soviet Union, but also the counter-propaganda of the Western democracies. When it came to voting on crucial questions, the latter could usually command a big majority, at first some forty to six in the Assembly and seven to two in the Security Council, but the Soviet Union's veto in the Council could, and frequently did, block action by the majority. To lessen this difficulty, the United States persuaded the Assembly in 1949 to create a standing committee (the "Little Assembly"), which could act for it between annual meetings without being subject to the veto.

In 1950 the French Foreign Minister, Robert Schuman, offered a plan for improving the economy of western Europe by pooling its steel and coal industries. The British Labor **Schuman Plan** government rejected the plan, but it was accepted by six nations on the Continent—France, West Germany, Italy, Belgium, Netherlands, and Luxemburg—and was put into effect in 1953. In 1953, also, a "Nordic Council" was formed by Sweden, Denmark, Norway, and Iceland; and, most significant, the long-standing ill-feeling between France and Germany was notably assuaged. West Germany joined France in the Schuman Plan. France amicably returned the Saar to German sovereignty.

Meanwhile the United States had proposed in 1950 that West Germany be rearmed and that a German army be included in the plans for defense of the West. To this France at first objected and offered a counter-proposal that a "European" army be established with small German units scattered through it. Eventually French objection was overcome when the British Foreign Minister, Sir Anthony Eden, in a surprising reversal of traditional policy, offered to keep British troops on the continent indefinitely if western Europe could agree on an appropriate defense system which would include Germany. Finally agreements were reached at Paris in 1954, by which West Germany was recognized as a sovereign state, given the right to have armed forces, and admitted to NATO. The Franco-British-Benelux treaties of 1948 were to be expanded into a defensive alliance to be called the Western European Union and to include both Italy and West Germany. Ratification of these agreements was secured from the countries concerned during 1955; and arrangements were then made to end the military occupation of Germany (save in divided Berlin) by France, Britain, and the United States, though it was understood that troops of theirs would remain there as part of the European defense system.

*Western European Union*

In 1956 Chancellor Adenauer eloquently urged a closer confederation of western Europe, "to be of some importance in the world." John Foster Dulles, American Secretary of State, at once expressed United States' approval of Europe's uniting to become "a third great power." Significant progress toward this goal was registered at Rome next year, when representatives of West Germany, France, Italy, and the "Benelux" countries of Belgium, the Netherlands, and Luxemburg signed two important additional pacts. One provided for the establishment of a "European Community of Atomic Energy" (Euratom); the other, for the creation of a "European Economic Community" (Euromarket) to form and administer a joint tariff union.

So far as Europe was concerned, the "cold war" by this time was turning distinctly against the Communist Soviet Union and in favor of the Western democracies. This was attributable in considerable part certainly to American economic and military assistance and backing, but also to the stamina and liberal traditions of Western Europe itself, and not inconsiderably to the change brought about in Soviet tactics by the death of Stalin and the growing restlessness and self-assertiveness of such Soviet satellites as Yugoslavia, Poland, and Hungary.[1]

Nevertheless, the prospect of a political confederation or unification of West Europe still appeared far off. Unlike the United States of America, a United States of Europe would be made up of peoples speaking diverse languages—French, Dutch, German,

[1] See above, pp. 702–704.

Italian, etc.—and possessing very divergent historical traditions and no little national distrust of one another.

Nor should we overlook the fact that serious difficulties still confronted the Western Allies in Europe. Alike in Great **Drawbacks** Britain and in France, there was no little jealousy of **to United** the leading role taken by the United States and fear **Action** lest it might lead them into another catastrophic war. They felt they had borne the brunt of two terrible world wars; a third, they thought, would ruin them completely. They were reluctant to rearm, in part because of that fear, and in part because the cost of rearming would necessitate sharp cuts in expenditure for social welfare. Indeed, rearmament of Western Europe was extremely slow, so that the total effective forces which it could place at the disposal of NATO in 1958 were far fewer than they had had before the Second World War or than Russia currently had. Besides, the bulk of the French forces—the most numerous in the West—were engaged in colonial fighting in Indo-China or North Africa.

Then, too, most governments in Western Europe were dependent, in greater or lesser degree, on collaboration with Socialist or Labor parties whose left wings generally favored an "appeasement" policy toward Russia and assumed a very critical attitude toward the United States. And while the countries of Western Europe accepted large sums of money from America, they were apt to be resentful of their benefactor, thereby confirming the old adage that "no debtor loves a creditor."

## 5. KOREAN AND INDO-CHINESE WARS

If the Soviet Union, and the spread of Communism which it promoted, were halted in Europe by 1950, they were not so in Asia. Not only was the whole vast mainland of China conquered by Communist arms, supplied mainly by Russia,[1] but Communist forces waged real "shooting wars" in both Korea and French Indo-China. As in Europe, so in the Far East, the United States gradually became the chief and most active defender of national freedom against Communist aggression.

In the case of Korea, arrangements had been made at the Cairo Conference in 1943, we may recall, that it should be independent.[2] But at the close of the war, it was divided into zones, like Ger-

[1] See above, pp. 704–706.    [2] See above, pp. 678, 682.

many, for military occupation. The part north of the thirty-eighth parallel of latitude (containing most of the country's mineral and industrial resources) was entrusted to the Soviet Union, while the part south of that **Partition of Korea** parallel (containing the best agricultural land and a large majority of the population) was to be occupied by the United States.[1] A "provisional government" was set up in 1946, consisting of five members from the American zone and five from the Russian, but it soon became obvious that the Soviet Union would not permit the representatives from its zone to agree to any permanent arrangement unless it provided for a Communist regime. After protracted but fruitless negotiations, the United States appealed to the United Nations, which directed the holding of free elections in the country.

These were barred in the northern Russian zone, but in May 1948 they were held in the more populous south, with the result that a Republic of Korea was established with Seoul as its capital, a democratic constitution adopted, and Syngman Rhee, a veteran patriot, chosen as president. The Soviet Union responded by proclaiming a "people's republic" for northern Korea with its capital at Pyongyang, with Kim Il-sung, a Communist, as premier, and with a Communist constitution modeled closely after those of the Soviet satellites in Europe.

In December 1948 the Soviet Union withdrew its army of occupation from North Korea. It could afford to do so, because it left there, not only a dependent Communist regime, but also a large native army indoctrinated with Communist ideology and well armed. Moreover, the withdrawal was useful for purposes of Communist propaganda, which acclaimed it as proof of the Soviet Union's respect for the "freedom" of Asian peoples in contrast with the "imperialism" of the Western powers, particularly of the United States.

Not to be outdone in championship of the freedom of Asian peoples, the United States followed the Russian example and in June 1949 withdrew its occupation forces from South Korea. It left there, however, to defend the democratic Republic, only a relatively small and very scantily supplied native army.

---

[1] The Soviet Union's part embraced 48,500 square miles with a population of nine million; that of the United States, 36,750 square miles with a population of twenty-one million.

It was in this same year of 1949 that Mao and his Communists triumphed in China [1] and were soon recognized by the Soviet Union and its satellites, and likewise by Great Britain (anxious over the fate of its important commercial port of Hong Kong) and by other countries, including India. It seemed an auspicious moment for Communist conquest of South Korea.

In the early morning of June 25, 1950, without previous warning, North Korean Communist armies, many thousand strong, **Invasion of** crossed the thirty-eighth parallel and swept into South **Free South** Korea. Taken by surprise and desperately short of **by Communist** weapons, the forces of the republican government of **North** South Korea could not withstand the attack. In four days they lost the capital city of Seoul and were in full retreat. Communist conquest of all Korea appeared imminent. This would doubtless have occurred if the United States had not intervened.

President Truman and his Secretary of State, Dean Acheson, —along with the American public—were now becoming alarmed by the results of the "hands off" policy which they had followed during the Communist conquest of China, and were now ready to try to arrest further Communist advance in Asia no less than in **Support** Europe. Wherefore on the morrow of the Communist **of South** aggression in Korea, President Truman ordered armed **Korea by** American resistance. Troops, planes, munitions, and **U. S. and** **U. N.** supplies were hurried to South Korea from General MacArthur's command in Japan, and these were later increased by direct shipments from the United States.

Also the American government early called the invasion of South Korea to the attention of the Security Council of the United Nations. Since the Russian member had walked out in the preceding January in protest against the Council's refusal to transfer Chinese representation from the Nationalist government of Chiang Kai-shek to Mao's Communist regime, there was no Soviet delegate to exercise the veto. Hence the Council, with Russia absent and Yugoslavia abstaining, declared that North Korea had broken the peace, directed it to withdraw its troops from South Korea, and urged all nation members to help South Korea repel the invasion. Collective action by United Nations' forces was authorized, with General MacArthur in supreme command. In the event, sixteen members sent military forces, though

[1] See above, p. 705.

most of the forces were of merely token size; and thirty-seven others contributed supplies, medical equipment, or the like. The brunt of the defense was borne by soldiers of the United States and South Korea.

During the summer of 1950 the North Korean invaders made steady progress southward. By early September they had pushed the South Korean and American troops into the southeastern corner of the country. But by this time American reinforcements were arriving in sufficient numbers to turn the tide. General Mac-Arthur launched a counter-offensive with surprise landings at Inchon, a hundred miles behind the fighting front. It recaptured Seoul, and at the end of September, in conjunction with the South Koreans, it drove the invaders back over the thirty-eighth parallel. The Allies did not stop here. **Rout of North Koreans** They continued their triumphant drive across North Korea, and on November 21 they reached the Manchurian border. It seemed as if the war was about to end with decisive defeat of Communist aggression and the unification of Korea under democratic auspices.

The Communists of North Korea were indeed routed. But already Chinese Communist armies, with Russian equipment, were massing along the Manchurian border for a second and fiercer offensive. On November 26, 1950, a quarter million men, plentifully supplied with planes and tanks, crossed the frontier and threw back the American and other United Nations' forces with heavy losses. On **Intervention of Communist China** they pressed, conquering all North Korea, capturing Seoul, and carrying the war ever farther into South Korea.

The Korean War, and especially this second phase of it, had peculiar international aspects. There was no doubt that the Soviet Union inspired the aggression and furnished major weapons for it. Nor was there any doubt that the Chinese Communist government of Mao Tse-tung was fighting the United Nations, as well as Koreans and the United States. Yet there was no declaration of war on either side, and little disposition to call the Soviet Union to account.

There was widespread fear lest otherwise the conflict could not be "localized" in Korea but would bring on another world war. It was known that Communist China and the Soviet Union were bound together by a mutual defense treaty, which might be invoked at any time.[1] Besides, the British and certain other European governments wanted, for economic reasons, to trade with China; and the Indian and other newly independent Asian governments, being highly suspicious of Western imperialism, showed an embarrassing tenderness toward both Communist China and Soviet Russia. No government which had previously recognized Mao's Communist regime in China broke off diplomatic relations with it when its armies engaged the United Nations' forces in Korea. Some even supported the Russian contention that Communist China should supplant Nationalist China as member of the United Nations and holder of a veto in the Security Council.

All this influenced and handicapped the United States government in its conduct of the war. General MacArthur was kept strictly on the defensive and debarred from bombing Chinese bases and supply lines in Manchuria and from accepting any assistance from Chiang Kai-shek on Formosa; and when he complained about these and other restrictions, President Truman replaced him with General Matthew Ridgway.

Meanwhile, American reinforcements continued to pour into Korea, and eventually the Chinese invasion into South Korea was halted and turned back. Seoul was again recaptured by the Americans and their allies. By the autumn of 1951 the contending armies faced each other along a battle-scarred and **Korean Deadlock and Armistice** bloodily contested line across Korea near the thirty-eighth parallel, a little north of it in the east and a little south of it in the west. In September, in an effort to stop the carnage and with the sanction of the United Nations, the United States opened truce negotiations with the army commanders of Communist China and North Korea. These, intent upon gaining time, strengthening their forces, and improving the positions they held, greatly prolonged the negotiations. As the discussions dragged on, sporadic fighting continued, and it was not until July 27, 1953, that an armistice was signed at Panmunjom.

One of the difficult questions in the armistice negotiations concerned the repatriation of prisoners of war. The Communists wanted the Chinese and North Korean prisoners turned over to them, but it was clear that many of them did not want to return

[1] On this treaty, see above, pp. 678, 682.

to their Communist-ruled countries. The United States therefore insisted that each prisoner be allowed to choose whether to go home or not. In the end a "neutral" repatriation commission was authorized to take charge of the matter: a handful of American youths, indoctrinated while in prison-camp, chose to settle in China, though most of them later grew disillusioned and went home; on the other hand, some 25,000 Chinese and North Korean prisoners of war refused to return to their Communist countries.

The armistice left the line between North and South Korea approximately where the opposing armies stood at the time, which was not far at either end from the original boundary between Russian and American zones. An attempt to convert the armistice into a more definite and permanent peace was made by a conference of nineteen interested nations, including Communist China, at Geneva in 1954. Regarding Korea, however, the conference proved ineffectual. The Communist powers refused to accept the idea of genuinely free elections throughout the country and argued that not they but the United Nations had been the "aggressor" and was therefore disqualified from supervising any elections there.

The task of rehabilitating war-torn South Korea was formidable. President Rhee, re-elected in 1952 and again in 1956, did what he could to ease it, and the United States provided considerable economic assistance. It should be remembered that the Korean War lasted more than three years and cost the United States more than a third as many casualties as World War II.

Indo-China was another Asian scene of "shooting war" in which the United States became involved. It had comprised for several decades, we know, a number of nominally monarchical states under actual French rule: Annam (including Tonkin and Cochin China), Cambodia, and Laos. The wartime occupation of Indo-China by the Japanese, however, had fostered the development of a native revolutionary movement, called Viet Minh, which in August 1945 dethroned the titular and pro-French Emperor, Bao Dai, of Annam and installed its own leader, Ho Chi Minh, as president of an independent republic to be known as Vietnam. The next month the French succeeded in temporarily re-establishing their protectorate over

*Struggle in French Indo-China*

the two other Indo-Chinese states of Cambodia and Laos; and in March 1946 they induced Ho Chi Minh to "associate with France" his Vietnam Republic.

But Ho Chi Minh, espousing Communism as well as an extreme nationalism, soon took the field against the French, who then disowned him and restored Bao Dai. Bitter fighting ensued between the rival regimes in Vietnam. Ho Chi Minh's, aided by the Chinese Communists, was recognized by the Soviet Union in 1950. Bao Dai's, supported by French troops, was recognized by the United States and Great Britain.

The war in Indo-China flared up with renewed vigor as soon as the cessation of hostilities in Korea in 1953 permitted Communist China to augment its military aid to Ho Chi Minh. Despite increasing assistance against him from the United States, which at one point (April–May 1954) included an airlift of French troops all the way from France to Indo-China, the Communists continued to win victories. In May 1954 they captured the strategic and stubbornly defended fortress of Dienbienphu.

The French, weary of a very costly and seemingly endless and fruitless struggle, backed the efforts of a new premier, Pierre Mendès-France, to bring the conflict to a close; and the United States, less concerned with Indo-China than with Korea, raised no objection. By negotiating with the Chinese Communist leaders present at the Geneva Conference on Korea, Mendès-France obtained an armistice agreement in July 1954. By its terms, Vietnam, like Korea, was split in two. Ho Chi Minh and **Partition of** his Communists secured the northern half, including **Vietnam** the capital city of Hanoi and the seaport of Haiphong. The southern half was left to the French, but the next year it deposed again the pro-French Emperor Bao Dai and became a free republic with its nationalist and anti-Communist leader, Ngo Diem, as first president. We may add that the adjacent states of Cambodia and Laos were recognized as independent and admitted to membership in the United Nations.[1]

The United States continued annually to give to free Indo-China considerable economic aid, reaching a total in 1957 of more than 800 million. More important, by a series of mutual defense pacts, it half-encircled the Communist Asian countries

[1] See below, p. 757.

of China, North Korea, and North Vietnam with democratic allies: with Australia in 1951; with Japan and South Korea in 1953; with a "Southeast Asia Treaty Organization" (SEATO), embracing Australia, New Zealand, the Philippines, Thailand (Siam), Pakistan, France and Great Britain, in 1954; with Nationalist China, that is Formosa, in 1955. The United States was obviously determined to defend democracy and national freedom in Asia, as well as in Europe.

U. S. and SEATO

# CHAPTER XVIII

# WORLD FERMENT AND THE REACTION AGAINST WESTERN IMPERIALISM

### I. GENERAL FACTORS

ONG the seat of a great and distinctive civilization, Europe had become in the nineteenth century the most highly industrialized, the most technically skilled, of all the continents. Its population had multiplied, and its material wealth still more so. Thereby it was enabled to sustain the heaviest armaments, the largest armies and navies, and, through them, to dominate the world.

As we have pointed out in an earlier chapter,[1] not only had Europe colonized the American continents and thereby linked together both sides of the Atlantic, but in the years between 1870 and 1914 it had brought under its tutelage the vast continent of Asia and numerous islands of the Pacific and had effected the conquest and partition of the big "dark" continent of Africa. Empire building was then a nationalistic pursuit of many a European power.

Great Britain could proudly boast that the sun never set on its world-wide empire. France constructed an imperial domain, second only to Britain's. Other extensive oversea empires were held by the Netherlands and Portugal, and still others were newly built by Germany, Italy, and Belgium. The Russian Empire stretched across all northern Asia.

Yet the swift expansion and world triumph of European imperialism up to the First World War was followed, during the next forty years, by its decline and partial extinction, at least so far as Western Europe was concerned. Indeed, a central as-

[1] Chapter VII, pp. 264–306, above.

pect of the period since 1870—the period covered by the present volume—might appropriately be described as the "Rise and Fall of Western Imperialism."

The First World War, from 1914 to 1918, was a factor in the decline, though it was not immediately recognized as such. That war had been waged primarily in Europe, with only incidental campaigning in Asia and Africa; and the only obvious change it wrought outside of Europe was merely the transfer of German colonies (and Turkish dependencies) to other imperialist powers of Western Europe, most notably Great Britain and France. It precipitated no widespread native revolts, and seemingly created no world ferment. Beneath the surface, however, the outcome of the war was not propitious for continuing imperialism. The break-up of imperial dominions within Europe—those of the Austrian Habsburgs and Russian Tsars,—and the recognition of the principle of national self-determination in the European peace-settlement of 1919–1920,[1] served to stimulate nationalistic movements in Near East and Far East, especially among Turks, Arabs, Persians, East Indians, and Chinese. Besides, the victory of France and Britain in that war was more apparent than real. Both emerged from it war-weary, suffering from heavy losses in man power and financial resources; and the successful stand which Russian Communists and Turkish Nationalists made against them was not overlooked by subject peoples.

*Effect of World War I*

By 1939, on the eve of the Second World War, nationalism was becoming a major force throughout Asia and in parts of Africa. It was quickened in native leaders through schooling in Europe or other contact with Europeans, and by such leaders it was preached to the masses. Political parties of nationalists were very active in China and India, in Egypt and the other Arab lands. They spread among the masses the belief that their respective countries, while spiritually and fundamentally superior to Europe, were being exploited and impoverished by Europe, and that, if they were free, they could make the same material progress which the West had made. Gandhi in India might decry the West's mechanized industry and urge his people to cling to their spinning wheels and traditional handicrafts, but in this respect he was unique.

[1] See above, pp. 487–508.

In general, native nationalists welcomed the introduction from Europe (and America) of factories, foundries, railways, airplanes, and technical education. Industrialization, no doubt, might temporarily benefit foreign investors and imperialists. In the long run, however, it gave promise of raising the standard of living and the national pride of "backward" and "dependent" peoples and of enabling them to compete successfully with the industrialized nations of Europe and to cast off Western domination. Japan was a striking example of how an Asian nation, by borrowing the material aspects of Western civilization, could retain its own spiritual and national essence and yet rise speedily to the position of a great world power.

The Second World War, from 1939 to 1945, was the decisive factor in the waning of Western imperialism. This war was more **Effect of** truly a *world* war than the First, and its effects were **World** correspondingly more far-reaching. It was waged all **War II** over the Far East, across the breadth of North Africa, and in strategic spots of the Near East; and the natives in these areas witnessed at close range repeated military setbacks to Western imperialist powers. Arabs were fully aware of French impotence in Syria and North Africa, and of British difficulties and reverses in Palestine, Egypt, and Greece. Peoples of the Far East were especially impressed by the ease with which non-European Japan ousted the French from Indo-China, the British from Burma and Malaya, the Dutch from Indonesia, and the Americans from the Philippines, and installed native governments with the slogan "Asia for the Asians." Eventually, as we know, Japan was defeated and a semblance of order was briefly restored in the Near East and in Africa. But Western imperialism did not benefit. The imperial powers of Western Europe lost too much prestige during the war, and were far too weakened after the war, to cope successfully with persistent and militant demands of subject peoples for national independence.

These demands were supported and utilized by the Soviet Union in order to make trouble for its Western rivals in the "cold war" and to win converts to Communism among the **Soviet** teeming millions of Asia and Africa. Soviet propaganda, **Propaganda** as well as Soviet arms, contributed immensely to the triumph of Communism in China, North Korea, and North Vietnam. Everywhere among "colonial" peoples the propaganda identified Communism with native nationalism and stressed its rôle as the implacable foe of imperialism. To be sure, the Soviet Union by ceaselessly assailing Western imperialism might be masking an ambitious Eastern imperialism of its own, but any such consideration seemed to matter little to peoples absorbed in denouncing and getting rid of the imperialism—the Western—with which they were familiar.

The United States, which had been reacting against imperialism since the First World War, now appeared also as a champion of native rights and native rule. Its pre-war promise of independence to the Philippines was honored in 1946, **American Example** and in 1952 Puerto Rico was made a self-governing democratic "Commonwealth." Sympathy of the United States for "colonial" peoples was strengthened by its desire to counteract Soviet influence on them. Between 1946 and 1957 it made financial grants totaling fourteen billion dollars in Asia and six billion in Africa.

Nevertheless the encouragement given to native nationalists by the United States, important as it might be as defense against Communism, was apt to be a source of resentment in imperial European powers that were America's chief allies.

Great Britain, under the Labor government of Clement Attlee, fortunately and rather gracefully surrendered large segments of its empire, and when the Conservatives returned to office they continued the policy. The mandate over Pales- **British Surrenders** tine and the protectorates of most Arab states were abandoned. Full independence was accorded to India, Ceylon, Burma, Malaya, and the African Gold Coast (Ghana), and self-government was granted to other African possessions and to Caribbean crown colonies. Malta was given direct representation in the British Parliament, and only in Cyprus did Britain forcefully repress a nationalist movement.

Thanks to mutual conciliation, at least a nominal bond of union remains between Great Britain and the chief of its former dependencies. This is the British Commonwealth, comprising now not only Canada, Australia, New Zealand, and South Africa, but India, Pakistan, Ceylon, and Ghana. By most of the members the British monarch is recognized as the titular ruler; and the crown is represented in some of them by an honorary governor-general who since the war has usually been a local dignitary rather than a titled nobleman from Britain. Fairly frequent meetings of Commonwealth prime ministers are held at London for discussion of common problems in economics, trade, and international relations.

Of course members of the British Commonwealth are no longer British "imperial possessions"; they are independent nations merely allied with Britain and free to withdraw from the alliance at any time. Yet bonds of habit and sentiment, as well as nominal ties, still hold the Commonwealth together, as was clearly evidenced at the coronation of Queen Elizabeth II in 1953 and in her enthusiastic reception when she and her husband, the Duke of Edinburgh, made their round of oversea visits.

France pursued a different and less fortunate policy. In an effort to arrest the rising tide of native nationalism and at the same time to provide a greater degree of unity for its colonial empire than the British Commonwealth, the framers of the 1946 constitution of the Fourth Republic established under it a "French Union." This would consist of the mother country; the colonial "départements" of Martinique, Guadeloupe, Guiana, Réunion, and Algeria; the "associated territories" of French West Africa, French Equatorial Africa, Madagascar, Comora, French Somaliland, New Caledonia, and French Oceania; and the "associated states" of Morocco, Tunisia, Vietnam, Laos, and Cambodia. The Union would have a High Council of delegates of France and the "associated states," and an Assembly half representative of the mother country and half of the overseas dependencies. In addition, the colonial "départements" were to have direct representation, as they had had previously, in the French Parliament, while each of the "associated territories" and "states" was to have an elective assembly. The Union, satisfactory as it might be to Frenchmen in the colonies, failed to satisfy the national aspirations of natives; and France, unlike Britain, tried to repress opposition and rebellion by force of arms.

In this, too, it largely failed. It was unable to prevent the secession of the "associated states" or to put down native uprisings in Algeria. The "French Union" proved a failure, as did a similar "Netherlands Union." World ferment and nationalist reaction against Western imperialism were too upsetting in the postwar years.

In successive sections of the present chapter, we shall treat of the disruptive developments in particular areas of the world: (1) in India and southeastern Asia; (2) in the Near and Middle East; (3) in Africa.

## 2. INDIA AND SOUTHEASTERN ASIA

On the eve of the Second World War, native nationalist movements were rampant in Great Britain's huge "Indian Empire," and concessions to them were being made or proposed by the British government.[1] Already in 1937, for example, Burma was detached and made into a self-governing Dominion. Immediately after the war native unrest reached such threatening intensity as to induce the Parliament of exhausted Britain to enact an Indian Independence Act, which became effective in August 1947. This did not provide for a united India, but, recognizing the profound religious differences and prejudices in that Empire, it excluded Buddhist Ceylon as well as Burma from India proper and split the latter between predominantly Hindu India and a mainly Moslem state called Pakistan. The last British Governor-General, Lord Louis Mountbatten, supervised the departure of the last British troops in 1948, and the setting up of provisional governments headed by native nationalist leaders: Jawaharlal Nehru, of the "Congress" party, in India; Mohammed Ali Jinnah, of the "Moslem League," in Pakistan. Both accepted nominal membership in the British Commonwealth, though both favored republican institutions and eventually rejected even a titular connection with the British Crown and, for that matter, the very word "British." Of the two new nations, the Republic of India was much the larger, embracing an area of one and a quarter million square miles and a population of 375 million, while Pakistan covered 365 thousand square miles with a population of 75 million.

In India, a constitution, modeled after that of the United States, was adopted late in 1949. It contained a bill of rights and provided for a democratic and republican federal government, with a President chosen for a five-year term by an "electoral college," for a bicameral parliament consisting of an upper Council of States and a lower House of the People, and for a prime minister appointed by the President but

*End of Britain's Indian Empire*

*Free India*

[1] See above, pp. 499–503.

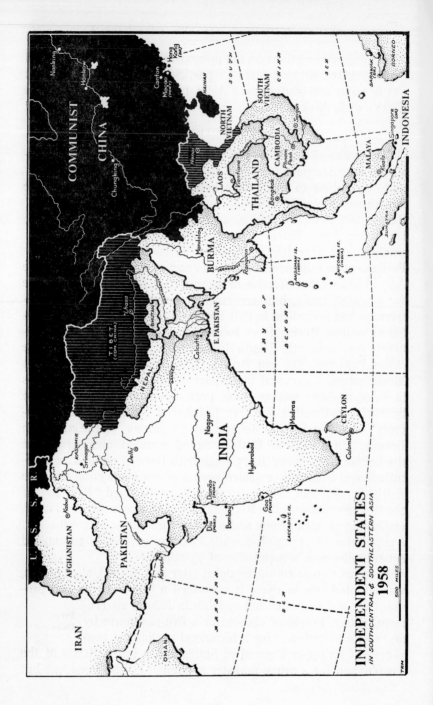

INDEPENDENT STATES
IN SOUTHCENTRAL & SOUTHEASTERN ASIA
1958

500 MILES

(unlike the United States) responsible to the parliament. Some twenty-eight semi-autonomous states originally composed the federation, part of them being former princely dominions, but the number was later reduced to fourteen states and six territories.[1] The constitution also formally abolished "untouchability," the age-old stigma which the Hindu caste system had imposed on an unfortunate racial group and against which "Mahatma" Gandhi had long preached.[2]

The first President of India was Dr. Rajendra Prasad, an ardent nationalist, who was installed provisionally in 1950, and constitutionally elected in 1952 and again in 1957. The real leader, however, continued to be the prime minister, Jawaharlal Nehru, whose Congress party held three-fourths of the seats in both houses of parliament. The government had to cope with grave economic and social conditions and with an extremely low standard of living and a very high degree of popular illiteracy. Moreover, the country was not really a national state. Its provinces differed racially and culturally, and as many as twelve different languages were spoken. Hindi, the "official" language, was familiar to less than half of the population, and in parliament, ironically enough, English was frequently used.

Some notable progress was made, nevertheless, in improving economic conditions through a succession of five-year plans. All public utilities and banking were taken over and operated by the federal government. Industrial development was promoted; India's iron and steel works were the largest in Asia, and its manufacture of cotton goods was comparable with Europe's. Special attention and large sums of money were devoted to the construction of a number of big dams and reservoirs for increasing agricultural production and hydro-electric power.

Pakistan, the lesser of the two major countries carved out of former British India, had to face the same sort of difficulties as Republican India, and, in addition, that of being split into northeastern and northwestern areas which were **Pakistan**

---

[1] The states are Andhra, Assam, Bihar, Bombay, Kerala, Madhya Pradesh, Madras, Mysore, Orissa, Punjab, Rajasthan, Uttar Pradesh, West Bengal, and disputed Kashmir. The territories are Andoman and Nicobar, Delhi (the capital), Himachal Pradesh, Laccadive Is., Manipur, and Tripura.

[2] He had described the "untouchables" as "Harijans," that is, "children of God." Gandhi was assassinated at New Delhi by a Hindu fanatic on January 20, 1948.

separated from each other by a thousand miles of the Indian Republic's territory. Both areas were predominantly Moslem and anti-Hindu, but otherwise they differed widely. The western area was overwhelmingly agricultural, constituting one of the chief granaries of Asia, though the capital city of Karachi was an important seaport and had the largest airport on the Continent; its main language was Urdu. The eastern area, on the other hand, was more industrial and commercial, and its language was Bengali.

Pakistan experienced difficulty and delay in adopting a constitution, in part because of the death of its leader, Mohammed Ali Jinnah, in 1949, and in part because of ensuing partisan strife. At length a republican, democratic constitution was drafted, and in 1956 it was put into operation and General Iskander Mirza, former governor-general, was inaugurated as president. At the same time a five-year development plan was started.

To add to their troubles, Pakistan and India, instead of co-operating, engaged in much bickering and disputing with each other. Quarrels were sometimes accompanied by bloodshed on both sides. For instance, rioting between Hindus and Moslems in Calcutta in August 1946 took a toll of 3,000 dead. Conflict was particularly bitter over Kashmir. This mountainous principality was ceded by its Hindu ruler (maharajah) to India, although three-fourths of its population were Moslem. Hence both Indian and Pakistani troops entered Kashmir. As one of his last acts, the retiring British Governor-General, Lord Mountbatten, proposed in 1947 the settlement of the question by plebiscite, and the proposal was endorsed by the United Nations. Pakistan agreed, but, while Nehru concurred "in principle," India steadily opposed its implementation.

Then, too, while in foreign policy Pakistan leaned toward the West and banned any Communist party, India under Nehru and his chief lieutenant at the United Nations, V. K. Krishna Menon, took a "neutralist" position between the Communist and the Western powers, involving in practice less criticism of the former than of the latter. Incidentally, Nehru succeeded in getting France to surrender the five coastal trading posts it had retained since the destruction of its Indian Empire in the eighteenth century.[1] Portugal, however, was less compliant; it stubbornly refused, despite

---

[1] Pondicherry, Karikal, Mahe, Yanaon, and Chandernagor. See *Modern Europe to 1870*, pp. 353–355.

threats and riots, to hand over its three small sixteenth-century posts of Goa, Damao, and Diu.

Burma and Ceylon, formerly associated with the British Indian Empire, were likewise freed in 1947, and in the next year they organized their new governments along democratic lines. Burma became, under the leadership of the nationalist U Nu, an independent republic completely outside the British Commonwealth. It was seriously disturbed by efforts of Communists to seize power, and of a minority people, the Karens, to **Burma** obtain separate independence; and concessions were made to both Karens and Communists. An eight-year development plan, to cost one and a half billion dollars, was inaugurated in 1953, and elections in 1956 were overwhelmingly favorable to U Nu.

In the case of Ceylon, its constitution was patterned after Britain and at first it appeared content to be simply a self-governing Dominion of the British Commonwealth. But fol- **Ceylon** lowing a general election in 1956, in which Nationalists defeated the Government party, Ceylon transformed itself into a republic, with only nominal connection with the Commonwealth.

The British tried to keep control of Malaya, rich in tin and rubber, but to do so they found themselves obliged to wage protracted and costly jungle war against nationalist and **Malaya** Communist guerrillas. In 1954 they conceded to the natives a larger measure of self-rule, and eventually in 1957 they recognized Malaya as an independent Dominion and withdrew their forces. The strategic and commercially important port of Singapore, with its large Chinese population, was cut off from Malaya, and partial self-government was accorded it in 1958.

Thus within a dozen years after the close of the Second World War, all that was actually left of the once extensive British Empire in India and the Far East consisted of a few minor and scattered spots: Hong Kong off the Chinese coast opposite Canton; North Borneo, and Sarawak. Little Portugal was now not far behind, with its posts in India, with Macao off the Chinese coast, and with half of Timor in the East Indies.

The fate of the Dutch Empire in the Far East was similar to that of the British. Native nationalism, stimulated by the Japanese wartime occupation, became militant **Indonesia** in Java. In August 1945, nationalists, led by Achmed Sukarno, seized power from the Japanese and proclaimed the "Republic of Indonesia" with its capital at Jakarta (the former Batavia) and with a claim of sovereignty over Sumatra and Madura as well as Java. The next year another nationalist government, with its capital at Macassar, was set up for East Indonesia—Celebes, the Moluccas, and the Lesser Surdas. The Dutch sought to oppose these developments with armed force, and at one time they captured the Republican leaders including Sukarno. But the Netherlands was not strong enough to suppress the far-flung rebellion, and in 1949, after four years of intermittent fighting, it accepted intervention of the United Nations and agreed to recognize the practical independence of the "Republic of the United States of Indonesia," including all the former Dutch East Indies except New Guinea.

For five years longer, the Dutch tried to exercise some influence through a Netherlands-Indonesian Union (patterned after the British Commonwealth) with Queen Juliana at its head. The Indonesians, however, would have none of it, and it was finally dissolved in 1954.

The next year, under the presidency of Sukarno, the member states of the new nation agreed to form a strongly centralized union, and consequently its title was changed back to "Republic of Indonesia." The government functioned rather dictatorially and pursued a vigorously nationalist policy. It protested against continuing Dutch occupation of New Guinea. It repudiated over a billion dollars' debt to the Netherlands, and in 1957 began expelling Dutch business-men and settlers and confiscating their property.

In reacting against the old-style colonial imperialism, Indonesia was perhaps too gullible in accepting Communist propaganda and guidance. Certainly, Sukarno followed the Moscow "party line" and was rewarded by subsidies from there; native Communists made notable gains in a general election in 1957.

Yet the forceful expulsion of the Dutch added immensely to the serious economic and financial problems already confronting Indonesia; and large fractions of the country's eighty million Moslems did not take kindly to the centralized government or to its drift toward Communism. Unrest grew prevalent, with attendant riots; and early in 1958 an anti-Communist and anti-Sukarno government established itself in Sumatra and gained a foothold on Celebes. Outright civil war ensued.

French dominion in the Far East also disappeared in the post-war years. Mention has already been made of the surrender of the old French trading posts in India and of the insurrection and warfare which cost France its important dependencies in Indo-China.[1] We may here recall that, according to the "cease fire" negotiated at Geneva in 1954, Vietnam was divided. The northern half, with its capital at Hanoi, formed a Communist "people's republic" under the presidency of Ho-Chi-Minh. The southern half (including Cochin-China) with its capital at Saigon, became a separate state under the guidance of a national leader, Ngo Diem. North Vietnam had an area of 60,000 square miles and a population of twelve million; South Vietnam, with approximately the same area, had a population of ten million, although it received nearly a million refugees, a large proportion of whom were Christians, from Communist North Vietnam. In 1955 South Vietnam, by popular referendum, adopted a democratic republican form of government with Ngo Diem as president. *End of French Indo-China*

The other states of Indo-China—Cambodia and Laos—were recognized as independent in 1955. Both retained native titular monarchs, and Laos was especially troubled by Communist infiltration from North Vietnam and from China.

In the case of the Philippines, the United States fulfilled its earlier promise by formally recognizing them as an independent republican nation on July 4, 1946. It also gave financial and economic aid which helped the native government, under successive presidents—Manuel Roxas, Elpidio Quirino, and Ramón Magsaysay—to repair the extensive war damages and to suppress Communist-inspired guerrilla bands called "Huks." In foreign affairs, the Philippines, being culturally the most Europeanized and Christianized of all Asian countries, cooperated with the Western democracies. *Philippines*

Siam, or Thailand as it has latterly been called, suffered during the war from Japanese occupation and afterwards from a series of palace revolutions and army revolts. A new constitution was adopted in 1952, providing for a National Assembly half of whose members are elected and half appointed. Actually the government has been controlled and directed by a military junta. *Thailand*

[1] See above, pp. 743-744, 754.

Nepal, tucked away in the Himalayas, and the only long-independent country, other than Siam, in southeastern Asia, changed **Nepal** its ruling dynasty and established popular government in 1951. The next year it outlawed the native Communist party, and subsequently, by treaty with Communist China, it surrendered its claim to sovereignty over Tibet and its receipt of annual tribute.

It is to be noted that in India and Pakistan, and in all the countries of southeastern Asia (Ceylon, Burma, Thailand, Malaya, Laos, Cambodia, Vietnam, and Indonesia), the **Democracy** operation of democratic government was rendered peculiarly difficult by lack of native experience with it, by nationalist reaction against the West which stood for it but which stood also, in native minds, for imperialism, and by native illiteracy and poverty on which Communist propaganda flourished. In the circumstances it is truly remarkable—and evidence of abiding Western influence—that all the countries should at least strive to be democratic as well as nationalist and that none of them should voluntarily accept Communism. They were, of course, favored fields for rival propagandist activity of the Soviet Union and Communist China on the one hand and the Western powers, especially the United States, on the other hand. From Moscow, Khrushchev and Bulganin in person ostentatiously toured most of them, only to be followed, from Washington not long afterwards by the American Vice-President Richard Nixon. Incidentally, in the three years prior to 1958, while Pakistan and Thailand relied for foreign subsidies exclusively on the United States, the Soviet Union rivaled America in subsidizing India, Burma, Ceylon, and Indonesia.

The United States, for mutual defense, managed to ring the ocean side of Communist China with a string of allied bastions extending from Japan and South Korea, through Okinawa and the southern Ryukyus, to Formosa and in addition to inspire the creation, in 1955, of a South East Asia Treaty Organization (SEATO). This included the Philippines, Thailand, Pakistan, Australia, and New Zealand, as well as the United States, Great Britain, and France, and was in the nature of a mutual defense pact somewhat like NATO for the North Atlantic area; headquarters for it were fixed in 1957 at Bangkok in Thailand. At the same time, the President of the United States was empowered by

Congress to use American forces to protect Formosa and adjacent islands and to take action if Communist China invaded them. Moreover, the United States, Great Britain, and Canada endorsed the "Colombo Plan," which undertook "to better living conditions, increase food production, and educate the people of underprivileged Asian nations." There were eighteen members in 1958, including the British colonies of Singapore, Sarawak, and North Borneo.

Most of the newly independent countries of southeastern Asia, however, held aloof from SEATO and, like the India of Nehru, pursued "neutralist" policies. Indeed, under the auspices of such dissident countries, a conference of twenty-nine nations of Asia and Africa was held at Bandung in Indonesia in April 1955. Its most prominent speakers were Nehru from India and Chou Enlai from Communist China. It applauded the elimination of colonialism and imperialism and demanded independence, self-determination, and United Nations' membership for all countries. It registered the rise of an interesting and important "Asian-African bloc."

### 3. NEAR AND MIDDLE EAST

Western Asia—the "Near" and "Middle" East—had long had a common Moslem civilization, and in the present century it has assumed a new importance by reason of its being a chief source of the world's oil supply. Since the First World War, too, it has been the scene of nationalist development and rivalry among its peoples: Turks, Iranians, Arabs, and Israelis.

Turkey, which had emerged after that war as a national state out of the ruins of the old Ottoman Empire, grew in strength in the years following the Second World War. It stood off **Turkey** demands of the Soviet Union for territorial and other concessions in 1945–1950, and was supported in the latter years by military and economic aid from the United States. It developed its industry, improved its agriculture, and in 1946 permitted the appearance of a Democratic party opposed to the dominant and essentially dictatorial People's party of Mustafa Kemal (Ataturk) and his successor, Ismet Inönü.[1] In free elections of 1950, the Democratic party won a resounding victory and its leader, Celâl Bayar, became President; he was re-elected in 1954.

[1] See above, pp. 488–492.

In foreign affairs, Turkey, out of fear of its big and powerful Communist neighbor to the north, aligned itself with the Western powers and their allies. It joined not only the United Nations but the Council of Europe and NATO. It made a defensive pact with Greece and Yugoslavia. It signed in 1955 the "Bagdad Pact" with Iran, Iraq, Pakistan, and Great Britain, which created a Middle East Treaty Organization (METO), analogous to NATO and SEATO, except that the United States, while expressing a friendly interest in it, was not a member.

**Cyprus**  The large Near East island of Cyprus, which Britain had taken from Turkey in 1878, was important strategically as a base for safeguarding access to the Suez Canal and also to the oil lines across Syria. Four-fifths of its inhabitants, however, were Greeks, and after the Second World War a patriotic movement, called "enosis," gathered headway among them under the leadership of their Orthodox Archbishop, Makarios, for independence from Britain and union with Greece. The remaining fifth of the island's population was Turkish and Moslem, who greatly preferred remaining under British rule to passing under Greek rule, and in this they were naturally supported by Turkey. Hence to satisfy the Turks as well as to serve its own interests in the Near East, Great Britain clung to Cyprus and heavily garrisoned it. The Greek rebels were adept at guerrilla warfare and terrorism. In 1956 the British offered a measure of partial home-rule, and on its rejection they seized Archbishop Makarios and deported him to Seychelles in the Indian Ocean. They next proposed a Cypriot referendum, but Turkey objected so strongly that they abandoned it. In 1957 the Archbishop was released from confinement though not permitted to return home. Only superior force kept Cyprus in the dwindling British Empire.

**Iran**  Iran (Persia) had been occupied in 1941, during the Second World War, by Russian and British troops, who deposed its nationalist and pro-Nazi Shah, Riza Pahlavi,[1] in favor of his young son, Mohammed Riza Pahlavi. Although the Soviet Union joined Britain and the United States at the Teheran Conference in guaranteeing the independence and territorial integrity of Iran, it did not withdraw its troops when Britain did in early 1946. Already it was inspiring and forcefully backing a revolt and the establishment of Communist rule in the northern

---

[1] See above, pp. 498–499.

province of Azerbaijan. Iran protested to the United Nations, which prevailed upon the Soviet Union to recall its forces.

A revision of Iran's constitution in 1949 made the prime minister and his cabinet responsible to the parliament. Two years later an aged and fanatical nationalist, Dr. Mohammed Mossadegh, became premier and attempted to nationalize Iran's rich oil industry. The great Abadan refinery of the Anglo-Iranian Oil Company, in which Britain had a controlling interest, was closed, and Britain broke off diplomatic relations with Iran, while Mossadegh sought closer relations with the Soviet Union. Production of oil ceased for lack of native technicians, and a financial crisis ensued. A resulting uprising in 1953 enabled the Shah and his royalist supporters to regain the ascendancy. Mossadegh was tried and sentenced to three years' imprisonment, and an agreement was eventually reached with foreign oil companies (British, American, Dutch, and French) whereby they would exploit the country's oil resources for twenty-five years and pay to Iran half of their earnings. Also, a seven-year plan was put into effect for the development of hydro-electric projects, agriculture, and communications; it involved expenditure of a billion dollars, to be derived from oil revenues and loans from the United States and the World Bank.

The Arab states, under the influence of ever heightening nationalism, took advantage of events of the Second World War to reject the tutelage which Great Britain and France had previously exercised over them and to insist on complete freedom. France, following its military collapse in 1941, was unable to enforce its mandate over Moslem Syria or Christian Lebanon, and these countries promptly proclaimed their independence. They secured the withdrawal of the last French garrisons in 1946, and were duly admitted to membership in the United Nations.

**Arab States and League**

Already in 1945, as the Second World War was drawing to a close, an Arab League was formed by a conference and pact at Cairo. The League included Syria and Lebanon and likewise the British-directed or mandated lands of Egypt, Iraq, Palestine, Jordan, Saudi Arabia, and Yemen, all pledged to mutual help in asserting and maintaining their national freedom. They were subsequently joined by the African Arab states of Libya and the Sudan.

Iraq succeeded, after many protests and much pressure, in getting the British to withdraw the troops they had been keeping there for the avowed purpose of protecting their interest in the country's very important and valuable oil resources. Jordan (the former Transjordan) obtained British recognition of its independence as a monarchy in 1946, although it accepted for several years longer a mutual-assistance treaty with Great Britain. Yemen similarly secured recognition of its independence, and admission in 1947 to the United Nations. Saudi Arabia, representing an expansion of the earlier state of Hejaz, continued its free course under King Abdul Aziz and, after his death in 1953, under his son and successor, King Sa'ud. Great Britain did manage to retain considerable influence with chieftains of smaller states in the Arabian peninsula, some of them rich in oil, such as Kuwait, the Bahrain Islands, Muscat and Oman.

In Egypt, the most populous and presumably the strongest of the Arab states, anti-British feeling was rife before the war. Afterwards it took acute form in popular riots against the

**Egypt**

British and demands for their withdrawal from the Suez Canal and from the Sudan. In 1951 the government of King Farouk denounced the Anglo-Egyptian treaty of 1936, and the rioting grew more intense until much foreign property was destroyed in Cairo in January 1952. The King tried to calm the clamor, but he had lost all influence through his government's corruption and its delay in effecting promised reforms and through his own extravagant and scandalous way of life. In July he was dethroned and exiled by a group of nationalist army officers under General Mohammed Naguib, who seized control and in 1953 made Egypt a republic. The next year Naguib was replaced as premier by another army officer, General Gamal Abdel Nasser, under whom an agreement was reached for Britain's evacuation of the Suez Canal zone.

Meanwhile, what most concerned the Arabs and intensified their common nationalism was the situation in Palestine. The

**Palestine and Israel**

"Balfour Declaration" of 1917 had pledged Great Britain to use its "best endeavors to facilitate the establishment in Palestine of a national home for the Jewish people," [1] and in the following years, under a British mandate for the country, the number of Jewish immigrants rapidly in-

[1] See above, pp. 494-495.

creased, especially after Hitler's persecution in the 1930's. The native Arab inhabitants resented the Jewish influx, and riots and bloodshed, spasmodic before the Second World War, became constant afterwards. Unable to maintain order, Great Britain appealed to the United Nations, which voted in November 1947 to partition Palestine into two independent states, respectively Jewish and Arab, and to internationalize the sacred city of Jerusalem under a governor appointed by the United Nations.

But neither Jews nor Arabs would accept the arrangement, and, confronted by their militant rival nationalisms, Great Britain renounced its mandate over Palestine in May 1948. At once the Jewish leaders proclaimed at Tel Aviv the transformation of the country into the independent republic of Israel. Whereupon the neighboring Arab states—Syria, Lebanon, Iraq, Saudi Arabia, Jordan, and Egypt—went to war with Israel in an effort to preserve the Arab character of Palestine. In this, however, they were only partially successful; they were not as well armed or as well organized as the Israelis. In the course of 1949, through mediation of the United Nations, armistices were signed between Israel and the several Arab states. Jordan obtained an eastern strip of Palestine, including the "old city" of Jerusalem. Egypt secured a southeast coastal strip, centering in Gaza. Israel held some 8,000 square miles of Palestine, out of a total of 10,500.

In 1949 the new nation adopted a democratic constitution and elected the veteran Zionist leader, Chaim Weizmann, as President. On Weizmann's death in 1952, he was succeeded in the presidency by Yitzhak Ben-Zvi. The real guiding hand throughout the period, however, was David Ben-Gurion's, the very able prime minister's. Moshe Sharett served as Israel's foreign minister until 1956, when, following a rift between him and Ben-Gurion, he was succeeded by Mrs. Golda Weir, a former school-teacher in Milwaukee, Wisconsin. Israel, it may be noted, was admitted to the United Nations in 1949. And it gained considerable strength and a measure of prosperity through the industry and vigor of its immigrants and the financial and other assistance it received from the United States, Britain, and France.

Yet Israel, in area and population, was like a small island in a big Arab sea. Between them there was no peace but only an uncertain truce. The Arabs were determined that sooner or later they would destroy Israel. The Israelis—backed by majority Jewish

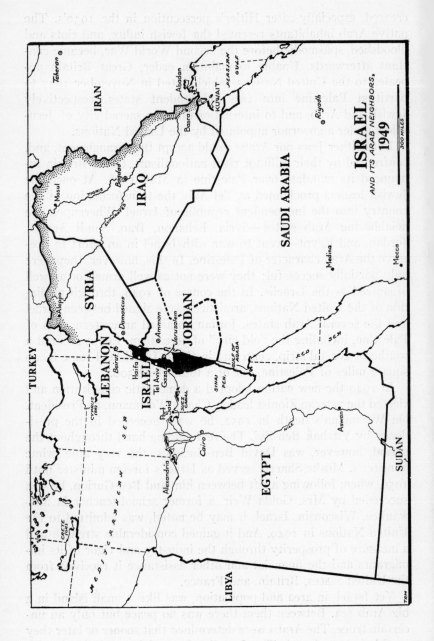

ISRAEL AND ITS ARAB NEIGHBORS, 1949

support abroad—were equally determined to resist any attempt to oust them from Palestine. Indeed, the truce was punctuated by bloody border incidents, for which responsibility seemed to lie with both Israelis and Arabs. Immensely complicating the situation, moreover, was the lot of more than 850,000 Palestinian Arabs who had fled or been expelled from their homes and had become penniless refugees in other Arab lands. Here they were at once a drain on their hosts' resources and an added cause for hostility to Israel.

Matters reached a very serious stage in 1956 in connection with an international crisis concerning Egypt and the Suez Canal. In the previous December Egypt had been offered finan- **Suez** cial assistance by the United States and Great Britain **Canal** toward the construction of a 1.3 billion-dollar high dam **Crisis** at Aswan on the Nile for controlling floods, supplying electricity, and reclaiming two million acres of farm land through desert irrigation. The offer was protested on the ground that Egypt would not use the assistance for the avowed purpose but rather for an attack upon Israel, and Egypt did show signs of anti-Western and pro-Soviet leaning. In May 1956, following an outbreak of fighting in the Gaza strip, it recognized Communist China. In June it imported arms from Communist Czechoslovakia, raised the ultra-nationalist General Nasser to the presidency, and celebrated with loud acclaim the British evacuation of the Canal Zone and a visit by the Soviet Foreign Minister. Then in July, as Nasser joined Tito of Yugoslavia and Nehru of India in a Big Three Neutralist Conference, the United States withdrew its offer to help build the Aswan dam. A week later, Nasser denounced the American action and decreed the nationalization of the Canal and the application of profits from it to the dam's construction.

Vigorous protests were immediately forthcoming from Britain and France, both of which had heavy financial investments and important commercial interests in the Canal. Secretary Dulles of the United States tried to mediate. On one hand, he wanted to maintain American solidarity with Britain and France and to safeguard Israel. On the other hand, he feared to antagonize Egypt lest it and its Arab allies (with their highly strategic oil resources) should pass under Communist influence and control. At a conference in London he proposed the internationalization of the Canal "with due regard for the sovereign rights of Egypt." The proposal met opposition from the Soviet Union on one hand, and from Britain and France on the other. In vain the latter set up a "Canal Users Association"; it was ignored by Egypt, which in September took over full operation of the Canal.

Whereupon, toward the end of October 1956, Israel, undoubtedly through secret agreement with Britain and France, dispatched armed forces across the Sinai peninsula and into the Gaza strip. Two days later Britain and France, without prior knowledge of the United States and despite President Eisenhower's angry protest, began a naval and air attack on Egypt. The Egyptians were simply not prepared for the joint assault. Within a week, Israeli forces completed their lightning conquest of the Gaza strip and the Sinai peninsula and were in sight of the Suez Canal, while Anglo-French forces were in possession of Port Said and a northern section of the Canal. The invaders, with minor casualties of their own, had killed 3,000 Egyptians and captured 7,000 more.

**Anglo-French-Israeli Attack on Egypt**

Meanwhile the Soviet Union was engaged not only in suppressing revolt in Hungary but also in proclaiming its sympathy with the Egyptians and condemning the "imperialism" of France and Britain. Khrushchev announced on November 5th that the Soviet Union was prepared to use force "to crush the aggressors and restore peace," and he proposed joint military action by the United States with backing of the United Nations. The United States rejected the proposal, perceiving in it a maneuver to get Russian Communist forces into the Near East and to separate America from its European allies, and President Eisenhower warned the Soviet Union against any attempt it might make to intervene militarily.

But already on November 2nd, in order to counteract growing Soviet influence in the Near East, the United States presented to the General Assembly of the United Nations a resolution calling upon Israel to withdraw its troops from Egypt, urging Britain and France to halt movement of their forces into the Canal zone, and asking for a "cease-fire" by all engaged in the hostilities. The resolution was adopted by an overwhelming majority; only twelve votes were lacking in its favor.[1] Specific condemnation of "Israeli

---

[1] Only five members voted against it (Great Britain, France, Israel, Australia, New Zealand); six abstained from voting (Belgium, Canada, Laos, Netherlands, Portugal, South Africa); and Luxemburg was absent.

aggression" and demands for complete withdrawal of Anglo-French and Israeli troops were also voiced by the prime ministers of Britain's Bagdad Pact allies (Turkey, Pakistan, Iran, and Iraq); by a conference at New Delhi of the premiers of India, Ceylon, Burma, and Indonesia; and by the entire Arab League. In Britain itself, the Labor party and some Conservatives were critical of the government's action.

On November 7th, under United Nations' auspices, a "cease-fire" was agreed to, and gradually an international police force, recruited from twenty nations and commanded by General Burns of Canada, replaced the withdrawing Anglo-French and Israeli forces and restored order along the Canal and in the Gaza strip.

The repercussions of the affair were many and far-reaching. Britain and France and Israel failed to achieve their objectives. Egypt remained in possession of the Sinai peninsula, the Gaza strip, and the Suez Canal. For a year afterwards, moreover, Britain and France and Western Europe generally suffered a serious shortage of oil; it took that long to repair the pipe lines which Arabs had cut in Syria and to clear the Canal of the sunken ships and other obstructions which Egyptians had put in it. Then, too, the British set-back undoubtedly aggravated an illness of Sir Anthony Eden and brought about his replacement as prime minister by Harold Macmillan. More serious was the cleavage, with mutual recriminations, which the affair caused between the United States and its chief European allies, and which was only slowly mended. Most serious of all was the blow to Western prestige, with corresponding heightening of the influence of the Soviet Union and of the ambition of Egypt's General Nasser.

Nasser sought to head a "neutralist" Arab bloc against "Western imperialism" and particularly against Israel. He cultivated political and military leaders of the other Arab states. He welcomed, if he did not directly inspire, anti-British movements in Jordan and in the principalities of Yemen and Oman, and a development of militant anti-Western, even pro-Soviet, activity in Syria. In January 1957 President Eisenhower, fearful of an increase of the Soviet Union's influence in the Arab states, and desirous of safeguarding Israel, told the American Congress that, because of the "immense importance" of the Middle East to the free world, he wanted authorization (1) to employ the armed forces of the United States to secure and protect the territorial integrity and political independence of nations in that region requesting aid against overt armed aggression from any **"Eisenhower Doctrine"** nation controlled by international communism, and (2) to undertake in the same region programs of military assistance and cooperation with any nation or group of nations which desired such aid. This so-called "Eisenhower Doctrine" was approved by the Congress.

Of all Middle Eastern countries, Syria had the largest Communist party, some 10,000 members, led by Khaled Bekdash, who had been tutored in Moscow. With his support, a group of Syrian army officers, headed by General Afif Bizri, seized power in August 1957 and thereby precipitated a new crisis. **Syrian Crisis** The coup, preceded and followed by the importation of arms from the Soviet Union and Egypt, alarmed not only Israel but the monarchical Arab states of Iraq, Jordan, and Saudi Arabia; and Turkey was frightened by the prospect of being bordered south as well as north by hostile Communist forces. The United States moved a fleet into the eastern Mediterranean, whereupon both the Soviet Union and Communist China proclaimed their determination to defend Syria by force of arms against Turkish "aggression" and American "imperialism." Egypt concurred and sent a token naval force on a visit to Syria's port of Latakia.

Although the immediate crisis was quickly surmounted by mutual reassurances in the United Nations Assembly, it proved the forerunner to close collaboration between Syria and Egypt. At **Union with Egypt** length in February 1958, after preliminary negotiations, the Syrian President, Shukri al-Kuwatly, proclaimed to a cheering crowd in Cairo the union of Egypt and Syria in a United Arab Republic, "with one flag, one army, one people." The Union was promptly approved by the two parliaments, and the choice of Nasser as its President was ratified by popular plebiscites.

Establishment of the "United Arab Republic" gave immediate **Federation of Jordan and Iraq** impetus to conferences of the youthful kings of Iraq and Jordan, the cousins Feisal II and Hussein I, and the creation, in the same month of February 1958, of a rival monarchical "Arab Federation." Toward the Federation gravitated Saudi Arabia, and toward the United Republic the principality of Yemen. The United Republic was "neutralist";

the Federation, pro-Western. Both shared a common Arab nationalism, as well as a common Moslem religion, and a common hostility to Israel.

## 4. RISING NATIONALISM IN AFRICA

Prior to 1935, the only independent states on the African continent, aside from the Union of South Africa which was associated with the British Commonwealth, were the tiny Negro republic of Liberia on the west coast and the "empire" of Ethiopia at the mountainous headwaters of the Nile, and the latter fell victim to Italian imperialism in 1935–1936.[1]

The Second World War and its aftermath changed matters, however. Italy's African empire was broken up and practically destroyed. Ethiopia was freed, and the Emperor Haile Selassie restored to its throne. In 1950 Eritrea was federated with it, and in the same year, to emphasize its national **Ethiopia** independence ecclesiastically as well as politically, the Emperor detached the Ethiopian Coptic Church from the long-standing jurisdiction of the Coptic Patriarch in Egypt and appointed an Ethiopian archbishop to head it. In 1955 the country passed from absolute to limited monarchy under a constitution containing a bill of rights and providing for parliamentary government and democratic suffrage.

Libya, also detached from Italy, was briefly administered by Great Britain and then, in 1949, recognized by the United Nations as a sovereign state. A native prince, Mohammed Idris, **Libya** the spiritual and temporal ruler of the Senussi tribesmen, became constitutional monarch of the country in 1951 under the title of King Idris I.

Libya joined the Arab League and was admitted to the United Nations. Sparse in population, its arid lands lacked natural resources, but from the start it received skilled and devoted technical assistance from the United Nations. Italian Somaliland, with its burning sands, was temporarily left by the United Nations under Italian administration, though it was promised independence as "Somalia" by 1960.

How Egypt cut its last ties with Great Britain and nationalized the Suez Canal, and how it formed with Syria the United Arab Republic, we have noted in the preceding section on the Near East.

[1] See above, pp. 611–615.

**Sudan** The Sudan, lying between Egypt and Ethiopia and centering in Khartoum, had been administered jointly by Egypt and Great Britain, but the latter, as part of its settlement with Egypt, agreed in 1953 to relinquish its share in the government of the Sudan and to let the Sudanese decide on union with Egypt or independence. Accordingly, a plebiscite was held at the end of 1955, resulting in a victory for independence and the establishment of still another free Moslem state. The chief of the Nationalist party, Abdullah Khalil, became the Sudan's first premier.

The ascendant nationalism in the Moslem world from Indonesia and Pakistan through Near and Middle East to Egypt, and the attainment of independence by Moslem Libya and Sudan, had immediate effects on the Moslems in French North Africa, that is, in Morocco, Tunisia, and Algeria. In French Morocco, national-

**Morocco** ists were increasingly rebellious and terroristic, and in 1953 the French government, feeling that they were being egged on by the nominal Sultan, Mohammed ben Youssef, exiled him and replaced him by his more docile uncle, Mohammed ben Moulay Arafa. This only intensified native nationalism and rebellion and rendered French rule practically impossible. At length in 1955 Mohammed ben Youssef was brought back as a veritable conquering hero with the title of Mohammed V, and in the following year the French surrendered to him their protectorate, the Spaniards did likewise with theirs,[1] and a conference of interested powers [2] ended the international rule of Tangier. Thus was Morocco reunited and freed.

In Tunisia, native nationalists similarly agitated and caused more and more serious outbreaks. In vain France tried to pacify

**Tunisia** them by granting various degrees of local self-government. Only full independence would satisfy them, and this they eventually obtained in 1956. The next year the native monarch (the Bey) was deposed as being too favorable to the French; and Tunisia became a constitutional republic, with Habib Bourguiba, the nationalist leader, as its first President.

Against Moslem native unrest and revolt in Algeria, France

---

[1] Spain retained Ceuta and Melilla on the Mediterranean and resisted native armed attempts against its colonial Enclave of Ifni on the Atlantic coast.

[2] Britain, Belgium, France, Italy, Netherlands, Portugal, Spain, and the United States.

was less yielding. After all, Algeria had been longer under French control than Morocco or Tunisia and it was commer- Algeria cially more important to France; it was deemed not a colony or protectorate but an integral part of France; and out of a total population of some ten million, nearly two million were French settlers (or their descendants) who were directly represented in the French parliament at Paris. These settlers were naturally fearful of being subjected to the Moslem majority and hence were especially hostile to any compromise; and naturally the government at Paris was reluctant to abandon them. The result was protracted guerrilla warfare, accompanied by deadly raids and occasional massacres. By 1956 France was maintaining, at heavy cost, nearly 400,000 troops in Algeria, and obviously failing to repress the nationalist movement.

France in 1958 still ruled fairly peacefully the extensive tropical parts of its African empire: French West Africa, French Equatorial Africa, and Madagascar. There was reason to doubt, however, whether this would long endure. Negro peoples of Central Africa were acquiring from closer commercial and cultural contacts with Moslem North Africa as well as with Christian Europe a common aspiration toward national freedom. Natives returning from college in the West, together with Communist propaganda and pressure from the United Nations, provided stimulus and guidance for anti-imperialistic movements. Already in 1957 France felt impelled to grant domestic self-government to the major part of the Cameroons (Kamerun) which it had held as a mandate since taking it from Germany French Cameroons at the close of the First World War. Legislative functions were entrusted to a popularly elected Assembly, and executive authority to a cabinet composed entirely of natives and responsible to the Assembly. The first general election was won by a coalition of three "moderate" nationalist parties—Christian, Moslem, and Independent—although it was significantly attended by violence from a sizable party of extreme nationalists whom the French outlawed and prevented from voting.

The British, too, encountered a rising and frequently militant nationalism in their African possessions, and in most cases made important concessions to it. In their East African colony of Kenya, they had to deal with bloody native terrorism of a secret society called the Mau Mau. This was probably influenced by Communist

as well as nationalist ideas, but more immediate was native opposition to the privileged position of white settlers and
their monopoly of the best land. The Mau Mau leader
was finally captured and put to death in 1956, and, with
Britain's assurance of land reform and eventual home rule, the
movement subsided.

**British Kenya**

In 1953 the colonies of Nyasa and Northern and Southern
Rhodesia were joined in a "Central African Federation" with
virtual self-government, preparatory, it was said, to
attaining independent Dominion status in the British
Commonwealth. In 1955 Britain arranged that Tanganyika, the former German East Africa, should have a Legislative Council, represenative equally of native Negroes, Asian
immigrants, and European settlers. In 1957, most symptomatic
of the post-war trend, a Negro state called Ghana, comprising
an enlargement of the British colony of the Gold Coast in western
Africa, was accorded full independence within the
British Commonwealth and admitted to membership
in the United Nations. To the nationalist leader of Ghana and its
first prime minister, Kwame Nkrumah, the operation of liberal
democracy seemed too sluggish and cumbersome to cope ade-
quately with the many problems facing a new nation of heterogeneous and inexperienced tribesmen. He stood, he said, for "a
new type of democracy with strong leadership just short of despotism."

**Central African Federation**

**Ghana**

Bordering on the Union of South Africa were the three almost
solidly Negro states of Bechuanaland, Basutoland, and Swazi-
land. They were primitive and arid and were ruled by native
chieftains under supreme authority of a British High Commissioner and his deputies. After the war they were grouped together
as "British South Africa" in contradistinction to the "Union of
South Africa."

The Union itself, while retaining a nominal tie with the British
Commonwealth, pursued nationalist policies dictated by its Dutch
(Boer) inhabitants. These constituted a majority of
the three million white settlers in the country, but the
entire white population was greatly outnumbered by
colored people: ten and a half million Negro natives and half
a million East Indian immigrants. General elections of 1948
drove from the premiership the moderate General Smuts and

**Union of South Africa**

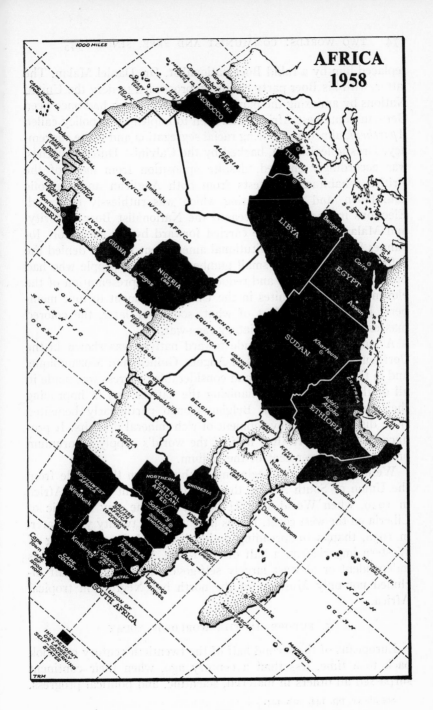

1000 MILES

## AFRICA
## 1958

CAPE VERDE IS.

Madeira Is. (Port.)
Casablanca Tangier Rabat Fez
Canary Is. (Sp.)
Oran Algiers
Rio de Oro

MOROCCO

ALGERIA

TUNISIA
Tunis
Tripoli

MEDITERRANEAN SEA

LIBYA
Bengasi
Port Said
Cairo
EGYPT
Aswan
RED SEA

Dakar
GAMBIA (Br.)
PORT. GUINEA
SENEGAL
FRENCH GUINEA
SIERRA LEONE (Br.)
Monrovia LIBERIA
IVORY COAST
GHANA
DAHOMEY
Accra

FRENCH WEST AFRICA
Timbuktu

NIGERIA (Br.)
Lagos

CAMERUN
FERNANDO PO
RIO MUNI

FRENCH EQUATORIAL AFRICA
UBANGI-SHARI
GABON
Brazzaville
Leopoldville
Loanda

BELGIAN CONGO

ANGOLA (Port.)

SUDAN
Khartoum

ERITREA
Asmara
Addis Ababa ETHIOPIA
SOMALILAND (Fr.)
Berbera

SOMALILAND (It.)
SOMALILAND (Br.)
Derbei

UGANDA
KENYA (Br.)
Nairobi
Mombasa

TANGANYIKA (Br.)
Zanzibar
Dar-es-Salaam

Mogadisho

SOMALIA

SEYCHELLES IS. (Br.)

ATLANTIC OCEAN

SOUTH

INDIAN OCEAN

SOUTHWEST AFRICA
Windhoek

NORTHERN RHODESIA
CENTRAL AFRICAN FED.
Salisbury
SOUTHERN RHODESIA
NYASALAND

BRITISH SOUTH AFRICA (BECHUANALAND)

Kimberley
CAPE COLONY
TRANSVAAL
Pretoria
ORANGE FREE ST.
Cape Town
CAPE OF GOOD HOPE
NATAL
UNION OF SOUTH AFRICA
Lourenço Marques
Beira
MOZAMBIQUE (Port.)

MADAGASCAR (Fr.)
Tananarive

MAURITIUS (Br.)

INDIAN OCEAN

INDEPENDENT OR LARGELY SELF-GOVERNING STATES

TRM

773

replaced him by a rabid Boer nationalist, Dr. Daniel Malan. The latter, with his Boer party majority, proceeded to defy the United Nations by annexing the mandated territory which had once been German Southwest Africa,[1] and then to implement a policy called *Apartheid,* aimed at ensuring racial segregation and white supremacy. Drastic legislation, backed by the Calvinist Dutch churches, was accordingly enacted, despite opposition from most of the British inhabitants, protests from both Anglican and Catholic churchmen, and native rioting which was ruthlessly repressed. Elections in 1954 only increased the Nationalist Boer majority, and Malan's policies were carried forward by his successor, Johannes Strijdom. A constitutional amendment in 1956 denied the suffrage to most of the small number of colored people who had previously exercised it and reduced possible representation of the eleven million non-whites in the Union parliament to four members. Fear was prevalent of what, sooner or later, the colored masses might do in a retaliatory race-war.

A more benevolent attitude toward natives was shown in the Portuguese African colonies of Angola, Guinea, and Mozambique, and in the Belgian Congo; and considerable progress was made in all of them both in Christianizing the natives and in improving their material condition. Belgian Congo particularly benefited from discovery and development of rich mineral deposits. It produced in 1958 more than half of the world's supply of uranium ore, and ninety per cent of the radium.

We have said at the beginning of this section that, aside from the Union of South Africa, the only independent part of Africa in 1939, when World War II began, was the tiny republic of Liberia on the west coast. Let us here add that twenty years later, in 1958, thanks to spreading nationalism and the weakening of Western imperialism, a half of the whole African continent was independent or at least largely self-governing. And this half included not only Moslems in the north but Negroes in tropical Africa.

### 5. EUROPE IN THE WORLD OF TODAY

Europeans of the second half of the twentieth century can look back to a time, less than a century ago, when their continent surpassed all others in material, scientific, and political progress.

[1] See above, pp. 144, 303, 424.

It was first and foremost in industry, in commerce, in capital wealth. It was the source and seat of highest attainments not only in technology but in pure and experimental science, in physics, chemistry, biology, and medicine. It also provided model examples of the national state, and of the practical operation of principles of popular sovereignty and parliamentary government.

*Heritage from Europe*

Since then, Europe has retained importance in all these respects but it has ceased to have any such monopoly or even predominance as it once had. For its very imperialism has helped to spread its science, machinery, and political ideas all over the world and to raise up imitators and competitors. Nowadays, all "backward" peoples aspire to national freedom and some sort of democracy —and to industrialization.

Indeed, so successful has been the export of material features of European civilization—natural science, technology, and mechanics—that now their greatest development is to be found outside of Europe proper, in the United States and in the Soviet Union.

The United States, of course, being a cultural frontier of Western Europe, has long shared and even anticipated Europe's political democracy, and throughout the ninety years since 1870 its material progress has kept pace with Europe's. Latterly, as decisive participant in two world wars, without suffering any destruction at home, the United States has become unquestionably one of two mighty poles about which Europe—and the world— revolves.

The other pole is the Soviet Union. Its predecessor, the Russian Empire of the Tsars, shared to a much lesser extent than the United States in the material progress of western and central Europe, and, despite domestic agitation for democratic government, it remained essentially an autocracy. The Communist revolution, which ushered in the Soviet Union forty years ago, brought no democracy or individual liberty as these are known and practiced in Europe proper and in America, but it did inaugurate a strictly planned economy, which, with the aid of semi-slave labor, progressively industrialized the country to an extent that has enabled it to triumph in the Second World War and to vie with the United States in post-war might and prestige. As the imperialism of Europe proper wanes, that of

*Soviet World Power*

the Soviet Union waxes. The Union now has Communist satellites and allies that reach in Europe from East Germany to Albania and Bulgaria and that in Asia cover Turkestan, Siberia, Mongolia, China, Tibet, North Korea, and North Vietnam. It thus heads an imperial domain the most extensive of any in the world's history. It maintains, moreover, extraordinarily large armed forces, fully equipped with all those weapons which latest developments in science and technology have fashioned. It carries on, too, world-wide propaganda and has numerous followers and advocates not only in "backward" regions of Asia and Africa but in such progressive European nations as France and Italy. Indirectly, at any rate, the apparent achievements of the Soviet Union have helped to concentrate popular attention throughout Europe—and the world—on material concerns and to quicken the rise of the socialist "welfare state."

The United States, which after the First World War spurned the League of Nations and sought to isolate itself from Europe, has emerged from the Second World War twenty-five years later **U. S. World Power** as leading protagonist of the United Nations and most powerful ally and protector of free peoples in Europe —and the world. Against Communist propaganda it conducts farflung democratic counter-propaganda; and against further expansion of the Soviet Union and Communist sway, it directs a many-sided policy. It has a much larger military establishment and a vastly bigger military expenditure than ever before in peacetime. It has ties of mutual security with Latin America, with the members of the North Atlantic Treaty Organization (NATO),[1] with those of the South East Asian Treaty Organization (SEATO),[2] with Far Eastern Japan, South Korea, and Formosa (Nationalist China). It backs the "Eisenhower Doctrine" in the Near and Middle East. It has military bases and forces at strategic points all over the world—in free Europe, in the Far East, in Africa, in the Arctic, on islands of Atlantic and Pacific. Its navy outranks all others. And from its immense financial resources it has expended since World War II, up to 1957, some thirty-seven and a half billion dollars in economic aid and nineteen billions in military aid to its allies and hoped-for friends—

---

[1] Great Britain, France, West Germany, Italy, Canada, Iceland, Norway, Denmark, Netherlands, Belgium, Luxemburg, Portugal, Greece, and Turkey.

[2] Australia, New Zealand, Philippines, Thailand (Siam), Pakistan, France, and Great Britain.

a total in ten years of nearly fifty-seven billion dollars.[1] And this total, it should be borne in mind, does not include American expenditure for waging the Korean War or for maintaining its own armed forces in Europe and at the numerous air and sea-bases outside.

To be sure, the leadership and policing of the free world by the United States is disliked and even resented among its Allies. It appears to some as a scarcely veiled form of imperialism, and it arouses fear lest it hasten, rather than halt, a World War III. On the other hand, the Communist empire looks stronger than perhaps it is. At any rate, an upsurge of nationalism is becoming evident among its European satellites and in China and is promising to loosen control by Moscow. Yet one should not exaggerate such developments. The local dictators of Communist states, no matter how nationally minded they may be, are still Communists, and, as such, almost certain on major matters to see eye to eye with the Russian dictatorship; even Marshal Tito, supposedly the most "independent" of them, has conformed his foreign policy in 1957–1958 with the Soviet Union's in respect of crucial questions in the Near East and in Germany.[2] Likewise, the free democratic nations, no matter how critical on occasion they may be of the United States, are not likely to repudiate their alliance with it and to renounce the protection and help derived from it. Nor, in a real show-down between the Soviet Union and the United States, would the so-called "Neutralist" nations of the Asian-African bloc be apt to preserve neutrality; they would almost certainly side with one or the other of the two big world rivals.

The rivals are reminiscent of those that had anciently warred to the death in Greece. Like Sparta, the Soviet Union is a regimented, militarized, and aggressive land power. Like Athens, the United States heads an oversea confederation, with democratic ideals, greater wealth, and superior naval power. But of course the similarity is qualified by difference of time and degree. The antique classical struggle be-

U. S.-
Soviet
World
Struggle

[1] Broken down by areas, this total consists of 24.6 billion expended for economic aid and 11.6 billion for military aid in western Europe; 8.6 billion and 4.5 billion respectively in India and the Far East; 3 billion and 2.5 billion in the Near East and Africa; and 1.2 billion and 317 million in Latin America.

[2] Tito, contrary to the policy of the Western powers, encouraged pro-Soviet movements in Egypt and Syria; and his recognition of the puppet Communist regime of East Germany ruptured relations between him and the democratic government of West Germany.

tween Athens and Sparta was a narrowly localized struggle, fought
by very small forces and with very primitive weapons. The contemporary struggle that threatens is more than local or European;
it is world-wide, involving everybody on Earth, and the weapons
available for it are a product of marvelous modern progress in
science and technology.

The United States and the Soviet Union run a race in devising
and developing new weapons. Both now have atomic bombs, jet
planes, and guided missiles. The United States launched
the first atomic-powered submarine, the Nautilus, in
January 1954; and in May 1956 on a barren island in
the far Pacific it dropped from the height of ten miles
a hydrogen bomb the explosion of which had the force of ten
million tons of TNT. Then on October 4, 1957, the Soviet Union,
from a point near the Caspian Sea, shot into the sky an artificial
moon, weighing nearly 200 pounds and equipped with radio, which
at an altitude of from 300 to 500 miles started revolving about
the Earth at the terrific speed of 18,000 miles per hour, or five
miles a second, thus circling the Earth in a scant hour.

**Arms-
Race
and
"Sputnik"**

This pioneer man-made moon, which was quickly nick-named
"Sputnik" (from the Russian for "Fellow Traveler"), had a twofold significance. (1) It represented a victory for Soviet scientists
over those of the United States in the keen competition between
them to be first in getting a data-gathering moon into outer space,
and thereby added to Soviet prestige. (2) More important, the
heavy Sputnik's ascent and delicate injection into an orbit indicated that the Soviet Union had rocketry and electronic controls
of superior quality, and that a score of its rockets, equipped with
H-bombs instead of radio, could be so despatched and guided as
to spew their deadly "fall-out" at any time over most of the
United States or Europe.

That was in October 1957. Before the month was over, announcement was made of an American rocket's being shot four
thousand miles into space. In November the Soviet Union put
another "moon" into an Earth-encircling orbit, and in February
1958 the United States performed a like feat with its "Explorer."
There was no doubt of the will of the United States and its European allies not to be surpassed by the Soviet Union in possession
of the latest instruments of death and destruction. No wonder
there is vast dread of what a Third World War might do.

Since 1956 disarmament talks have been going on, mainly at London, between the United States and the Soviet Union, but so far (two years later) without tangible results. More fruitful, if less related to the problem of competitive armaments, has been the formation in 1956–1957, on the initiative of the United States, of an International Atomic Energy Agency of the United Nations to create and utilize a world pool of atomic energy for peace; the United States has made an initial contribution to it of 11,000 pounds of basic uranium.

Doubtless the prospect of the unparalleled havoc and destruction which the new weapons could inflict upon whole nations—indeed, upon all mankind—is the main deterrent to any Third World War. Yet even without the holocaust of ultimate atomic world war, the cost of maintaining a dubious "peace" in existing circumstances is staggering and may prove intolerable. The Soviet Union, to finance its war preparedness and forward its aggressive designs, can hardly attain to the promised goal of Marxian-Leninist Communism; it must impoverish and enslave the millions subject to it. And necessary defense expenditure of the United States and its democratic allies must reach such amounts as eventually to lower their standard of living and to endanger their free institutions.

Europe still counts, not only as a continuing great center of industry and trade, of science and art, but also as a font of liberty and spiritual ideals. No doubt contemporary Europe— **Abiding** and the world around it—faces in the present age one of **Europe** the greatest crises in history: a crisis both material and spiritual. The outcome cannot be predicted with any certainty. But the historian knows that man is a curiously resourceful being who is naturally averse to suicide. He knows also that European and Western civilization, in its long evolution and extension, has repeatedly met crises and suffered seemingly mortal blows—only to undergo resurrection.

# EUROPEAN STATES AND THEIR SOVEREIGNS
## SINCE 1870

### ALBANIA

*Part of Ottoman Empire to 1913*
William of Wied, *Prince*, 1913–1914
*Republic, 1918–1928*
Zog, *King*, 1928–1939

*To Italy, 1939–1944*
Communist "People's Republic,"
1946–

### AUSTRIA

Francis Joseph, *Emperor*, 1848–1916
Charles I, 1916–1918
*Republic, 1919–1938*
*Part of Germany, 1938–1945*

*Republic, 1945–*
Karl Renner, *President*, 1945–1950
Theodore Koerner, 1951–

### BELGIUM

Leopold II, *King*, 1865–1909
Albert I, 1909–1934

Leopold III, 1934–1951
Baudouin I, 1951–

### BOHEMIA

*Part of Austria to 1918*

*Part of Czechoslovakia since 1918*

### BULGARIA

*Part of Ottoman Empire to 1878*
Alexander Cuza, *Prince*, 1879–1886
Ferdinand I, *Prince*, 1887–1908;
  *King*, 1908–1918

Boris III, *King*, 1918–1943
Simeon II, 1943–1946
Communist "People's Republic,"
  1946–

### BYELORUSSIA

*Part of Russian Empire to 1917*

*Part of U.S.S.R. since 1917*

### CROATIA

*Part of Hungary to 1918*

*Part of Yugoslavia since 1918*

### CZECHOSLOVAKIA

*Part of Austria-Hungary to 1918*
*Republic 1918–1939*
  Thomas Masaryk, *President*, 1918–
  1935
  Eduard Beneš 1935–1939

*Partitioned, 1939–1945*
*Republic, 1945–1948*
  Eduard Beneš, *President*
Communist "People's Republic,"
  1948–

## DENMARK

Christian IX, *King*, 1863–1906
Frederick VIII, 1906–1912
Vincent Auriol, *President*, 1947–1954

Christian X, 1912–1947
Frederick IX, 1947–
René Coty, 1954–

### Prime Ministers

Wm. E. Gladstone, 1868–1874
Benjamin Disraeli, 1874–1880
Wm. E. Gladstone, 1880–1885
Marquess of Salisbury, 1885–1886
Wm. E. Gladstone, 1886
Marquess of Salisbury, 1886–1892
Wm. E. Gladstone, 1892–1894
Earl of Rosebery, 1894–1895
Marquess of Salisbury, 1895–1902
Arthur J. Balfour, 1902–1905
Sir Henry Campbell-Bannerman, 1905–1908
Herbert Asquith, 1908–1916

David Lloyd George, 1916–1922
Stanley Baldwin, 1923–1924
Ramsay MacDonald, 1924
Stanley Baldwin, 1924–1929
Ramsay MacDonald, 1929–1935
Stanley Baldwin, 1935–1937
Neville Chamberlain, 1937–1940
Winston Churchill, 1940–1945
Clement Attlee, 1945–1951
Winston Churchill, 1951–1955
Sir Anthony Eden, 1955–1957
Harold Macmillan, 1957–

## GREECE

George I, *King*, 1863–1913
Constantine I, 1913–1917
Alexander I, 1917–1920
Constantine I, 1920–1922

George II, 1922–1924
*Republic, 1924–1935*
George II, *King*, 1935–1947
Paul I, 1947–

## HOLLAND
### See Netherlands

## HUNGARY

Francis Joseph, *King*, 1867–1916
Charles, *King*, 1916–1918
*Republic, 1918–1920*
*Kingdom:* Admiral Nicholas Horthy, *Regent*, 1920–1944

*Republic, 1945–1949*
*Communist "People's Republic," 1949–*

## ICELAND

*Union with Denmark to 1944*

*Republic since 1944*

## IRELAND

*Part of Great Britain to 1921*
*Irish Free State, 1921–1938*
*Republic, as "Eire," 1938–*

Douglas Hyde, *President*, 1938–1945
Sean T. O'Kelly, *President*, 1945–

## ITALY

Victor Emmanuel II, *King*, 1861–1878
Humbert I, 1878–1900

Humbert II, 1946
*Republic, 1946–*
Luigi Einaudi, *President*, 1948–1955

Victor Emmanuel III, 1900–1946
Benito Mussolini, *Dictator,* 1922–1943

Giovanni Gronchi, 1955–

---

### LATVIA
*Part of Russian Empire to 1918*    Republic, *1918–1940*
*Part of U.S.S.R. since 1940*

---

### LITHUANIA
*Part of Russian Empire to 1918*    Republic, *1918–1940*
*Part of U.S.S.R. since 1940*

---

### LUXEMBURG
William III (of Netherlands), *Grand-Duke, 1849–1890*
Adolphus, 1890–1905

William IV, 1905–1912
Adelaide, 1912–1919
Charlotte, 1919–

---

### MONTENEGRO
Nicholas I, *Prince,* 1860–1910; *King,* 1910–1918

*Part of Yugoslavia since 1918*

---

### NETHERLANDS
William III, *King,* 1849–1890
Juliana, *Queen,* 1948–

Wilhelmina, *Queen,* 1890–1948

---

### NORWAY
*Union with Sweden to 1905*
Olav V, 1957–

Haakon VII, *King,* 1905–1957

---

### OTTOMAN EMPIRE
Abdul Aziz, *Sultan,* 1861–1876
Murad V, 1876
Abdul Hamid II, 1876–1909

Mohammed V, 1909–1918
Mohammed VI, 1918–1922
*See Turkey*

---

### PAPACY
Pius IX, *Pope,* 1846–1878
Leo XIII, 1878–1903
Pius X, 1903–1914

Benedict XV, 1914–1922
Pius XI, 1922–1939
Pius XII, 1939–
John XXII - 1959

---

### POLAND
*Part of Russia, Germany, and Austria to 1918*
*Republic, 1918–1940*
Joseph Pilsudski, *President,* 1918–1922
Stanislas Wojciechowski, 1922–1926

Ignace Moscicki, *President,* 1926–1940
*Partitioned between Germany and U.S.S.R., 1940*
*Communist "People's Republic," 1945–*

### PORTUGAL

Louis I, *King*, 1861–1889

Charles I, 1889–1908

Manuel II, 1908–1910

*Republic, 1910–*

Marshal Carmona, *President*, 1926–1951

Francisco Craveiro Lopez, 1951

Antonio de Oliveira Salazar, *Prime Minister*, 1928–

---

### UKRAINIA

*Part of Russian Empire to 1917*     *Part of U.S.S.R. since 1919*

---

### U.S.S.R. (UNION OF SOVIET SOCIALIST REPUBLICS)

*Succession to Russian Empire, 1917*     N. Lenin, *Dictator*, 1917–1924

*Communist Dictatorship, 1917–*     Joseph Stalin, 1924–1953

Nikita Khrushchev, 1953–

---

### UNITED KINGDOM
*See Great Britain*

---

### VATICAN CITY STATE
*See Papacy*

---

### WHITE RUSSIA
*See Byelorussia*

---

### YUGOSLAVIA

Peter I (of Serbia), *King*, 1918–1921

Alexander I, 1921–1934

Peter II, 1934–1945

*Communist "People's Republic," 1945–*

Joseph Broz (Marshal Tito), *Dictator*, 1945–

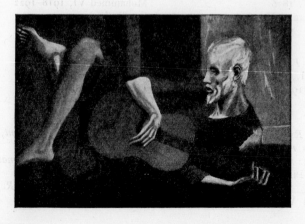

# SELECT BIBLIOGRAPHY

## I. EUROPE AS A WHOLE

**General histories.** Surveys of whole period after 1870: P. W. Slosson, *Europe since 1870* (1935); F. L. Benns, *European history since 1870*, 3rd ed. (1951); Hajo Holborn, *Political collapse of Europe* (1951). Surveys of 20th century: J. W. Swain, *Beginning the 20th century, a history of the generation that made the war* (1933); W. C. Langsam, *The world since 1919*, 7th ed. (1954); C. V. Easum, *Half century of conflict* (1950); W. P. Hall, *World wars and revolutions*, 3rd ed. (1952); R. R. Ergang, *Europe in our time, 1914 to the present* (1951); Geoffrey Bruun, *The world in the 20th century*, new ed. (1952). Select source materials: Columbia University, *Introduction to contemporary civilization in the West*, 2 vols. rev. ed. (1954); Leon Bernard & Theodore Hodges, eds., *Readings in European history* (1958); W. C. Langsam, *Documents and readings in the history of Europe since 1918* (1951).

More detailed or specialized works: *Rise of modern Europe*, ed. by W. L. Langer, an important series of volumes, of which only one has yet appeared treating of Europe since 1870—C. J. H. Hayes, *A generation of materialism, 1871–1900* (1941)—but others are expected shortly: S. B. Fay, *The great illusion, 1900–1914;* Bernadotte Schmitt, *The world in the crucible, 1914–1919;* Raymond Sontag, *Revolt against the old order, 1919–1939;* Harold Deutsch, *The second world war. Cambridge modern history*, ed. by Sir A. W. Ward, Sir G. W. Prothero, & Sir Stanley Leathes, vol. xii, *The latest age, 1870–1910* (1910). *Histoire générale*, ed. by Ernest Lavisse & Alfred Rambaud, 3rd rev. ed., vol. xii, *1870–1900* (1925). *Propyläen-Weltgeschichte*, ed. by Walter Goetz, vols. ix, and x, *Das Zeitalter des Imperialismus, 1890–1933* (1933). C. A. Macartney, *National states and national minorities* (1934). W. F. Dodd, *Modern constitutions*, 2 vols. (1909). A. J. Peaslee, *Constitutions of nations*, 3 vols. (1950). J. C. Adams & others, *Foreign governments and their backgrounds* (1950), on Britain, France, Italy, Germany, Russia, Japan. D. W. Brogan, *The price of revolution* (1952), comparing Russian and Asiatic with earlier American and French revolutions. H. A. L. Fisher, *The republican tradition in Europe* (1911). C. J. H. Hayes, *Historical evolution of modern nationalism* (1931), and *Essays on nationalism* (1926); Hans Kohn, *Prophets and peoples:*

*studies in 19th century nationalism* (1946); B. C. Shafer, *Nationalism, myth and reality* (1955).

For general histories of international relations, of economics, of culture, of the several European nations, and of imperialism and countries outside Europe, see following sections of the bibliography.

**Encyclopedias, biographical dictionaries, and historical atlases.** Much historical information can be obtained from encyclopedias and biographical dictionaries which are published in the major countries of Europe and also in the United States. There are excellent ones, for example, in Italy, Spain, France, and Germany. In English, the best are: *Encyclopaedia Britannica*, 11th ed., 29 vols., and 14th ed., 24 vols.; *Encyclopedia of the social sciences*, 15 vols. (1930); *New international encyclopedia; Colliers' encyclopedia; Dictionary of (British) national biography*, 63 vols. (1885–1900), and many later supplementary vols. Convenient one-volume reference works: *The Columbia encyclopedia*, 2nd ed. (1950); W. L. Langer, ed., *Encyclopaedia of world history*, rev. ed. (1948).

Most textbooks of the period are equipped with maps. These can be supplemented by such atlases as W. R. Shepherd's, 7th ed. (1929); E. W. Fox & H. S. Deighton, *Atlas of European history* (1957); R. R. Palmer, ed., *Atlas of world history* (1957); J. F. Horrabin, *Atlas history of the 2nd world war* (1941–5); *Bartholomew's advanced atlas of modern geography* (1950).

**Bibliographies.** Most of the works cited in the present select bibliography contain bibliographies of their own. In addition, the following are useful: I. G. Mudge, *New guide to reference books* (1929); *A guide to historical literature*, ed. by W. H. Allison & others (1931); B. Sachs, *Bibliography for Europe between 1815 and 1914* (1946); L. J. Ragatz, *A bibliography for the study of European history, 1815–1939* (1942, and later supplements), and *Literature of European imperialism* (1944); F. D. Scott & A. Rockefeller, Jr., *The 20th-century world, a reading guide* (1948); *International bibliography of historical sciences, 1926–1950* (1930–52); E. M. Coulter & M. Gerstenfeld, *Historical bibliographies* (1935).

F. C. Dahlmann & G. Waitz, *Quellenkunde der deutschen Geschichte*, 9th ed. (1931). R. J. Kerner, *Slavic Europe* (1918), bibliography of works in West-European languages. W. B. Walsh, *Russia under tsars and commissars, a readers' guide* (1946). Charles Morley, *Guide to research in Russian history* (1951). *Foreign affairs bibliography*, 3 vols. (1933–52). K. S. Pinson, *A bibliographical introduction to nationalism* (1936). H. Higgs, *Economic bibliography* (1935). Judith B. Williams, *A guide to the printed materials for English social and economic history* (1926).

## 2. INTERNATIONAL RELATIONS, WAR AND PEACE

**General, chiefly for period prior to 1914.** W. L. Langer, *European alliances and alignments, 1871–1890*, and *The diplomacy of imperialism, 1890–1902*, 2 vols., 2nd ed. (1950). R. J. Sontag, *European diplomatic history, 1871–1932* (1933). B. E. Schmitt, *Triple alliance and triple entente* (1934). *Cambridge history of British foreign policy*, ed. by Sir A. W. Ward & G. P. Gooch, vol. iii, *1866–1919* (1923). G. P. Gooch, *Recent revelations of European diplomacy* (1940). A. J. P. Taylor, *The struggle for mastery in Europe, 1848–1918* (1954). P. W. Buck & M. W. Travis, Jr., *Control of foreign relations in modern nations* (1957). F. H. Hartman, *Basic documents of international relations* (1951).

Documents on foreign policy of Germany—*Die grosse Politik der europäischen Kabinette, 1871–1914*, 40 vols. (1922–6); of France— *Documents diplomatiques français, 1871–1914*, 2 series, 24 vols. (to 1952); of Britain—*British documents on the origin of the war, 1898– 1914*, 11 vols. (1926–38); A. F. Pribram, *Secret treaties of Austria- Hungary, 1879–1914*, 2 vols. (1920–2).

T. A. Bailey, *A diplomatic history of the American people*, 4th ed. (1950). S. F. Bemis, *A diplomatic history of the United States*, 3rd ed. (1950). Dexter Perkins, *Evolution of American foreign policy* (1948). L. E. Ellis, *Short history of American diplomacy* (1951). J. F. Rippy, *Latin America in world politics*, 3rd ed. (1938). G. F. Kennan, *American diplomacy, 1900–1950* (1951), and *Realities of American foreign policy* (1954).

Alfred Vagts, *History of militarism* (1937). L. Montrose, *War through the ages*, rev. ed. (1946). E. M. Earle, ed., *Makers of modern strategy, military thought from Machiavelli to Hitler* (1943). E. A. Pratt, *Rise of rail power in war and conquest, 1833–1914* (1915).

**Dismemberment of Ottoman empire, 1875–1913.** Ferdinand Schevill, *History of the Balkan peninsula*, ed. by W. M. Gewehr (1933). J. A. R. Marriott, *The eastern question, an historical study in European diplomacy* (1940). B. H. Sumner, *Russia and the Balkans, 1870– 1880* (1947). David Harris, *A diplomatic history of the Balkan crisis of 1875–1878* (1936), and *Britain and the Bulgarian horrors of 1876* (1939). J. F. Maurice, *Russo-Turkish war of 1877* (1905). R. W. Seton-Watson, *Disraeli, Gladstone, and the eastern question* (1935). W. N. Medlicott, *Congress of Berlin and after, a diplomatic history of the near eastern settlement, 1878–1880* (1938). B. E. Schmitt, *Austria's Annexation of Bosnia, 1908–1909* (1937). T. Barclay, *Turco-Italian war of 1911–1912* (1912). W. E. Askew, *Europe and Italy's acquisition of Libya* (1943). J. G. Schurman, *The Balkan wars, 1912–1913* (1926).

E. M. Earle, *Turkey, the great powers, and the Bagdad railway* (1923).
J. B. Wolf, *Diplomatic history of the Bagdad railroad* (1936).

**Special peace efforts prior to 1914.** R. B. Mowat, *Concert of Europe* (1931). Arthur Nussbaum, *A concise history of the law of nations* (1947). W. I. Hull, *The two Hague conferences* (1908). J. B. Scott, ed., *The Hague peace conferences of 1899 and 1907,* 2 vols. (1909). G. G. Wilson, ed., *The Hague arbitration cases* (1915). Norman Angell, *The great illusion* (1911, 1933), famous attack on war. Merze Tate, *Disarmament illusion, the movement for a limitation of armaments, to 1907* (1942). G. G. Coulton, *Main illusions of pacificism* (1916). M. Margaret Ball, *Problem of inter-American organization* (1944). Clara Barton, *The Red Cross, a history* (1898). P. H. Epler, *Life of Clara Barton* (1915). O. J. Falnes, *Norway and the Nobel peace prize* (1938). A. L. Gúerard, *Short history of the international language movement* (1922). N. M. Butler, *The international mind* (1913).

**Crises in early 20th century.** A. Kuropatkin, *The Russian army and the Japanese war,* 2 vols. (1909). D. Murray, *Official history of the Russo-Japanese war,* 5 vols. (1908–10). P. J. Treat, *Diplomatic relations between the United States and Japan, 1895–1905* (1938). E. B. Price, *Russo-Japanese treaties of 1907–1916 concerning Manchuria and Mongolia* (1933). O. J. Hale, *Germany and the diplomatic revolution, 1904–1906* (1931). M. B. Giffin, *Fashoda, the incident and its diplomatic setting* (1930). E. N. Anderson, *The first Morocco crisis, 1904–1906* (1930). Ima C. Barlow, *The Agadir crisis* (1940). R. J. S. Hoffman, *Great Britain and the German trade rivalry, 1875–1914* (1933). A. S. & H. Castle, *German sea power* (1913).

**World War I.** Diplomacy: S. B. Fay, *Origins of the world war,* 2 vols. (1930); B. E. Schmitt, *The coming of the war, 1914* (1930); Pierre Renouvin, *Immediate origins of the war* (1928); Luigi Albertini, *Origins of the war of 1914,* Eng. trans., 3 vols. (1952–7); H. E. Barnes, *Genesis of the world war* (1926), seeking to absolve Germany of "war guilt"; C. C. Tansill, *America goes to war* (1938), critical of Wilson; Dexter Perkins, *America and two wars* (1944); Charles Seymour, *American neutrality, 1914–1917* (1935), and *American diplomacy during the world war* (1934); H. C. F. Bell, *Woodrow Wilson* (1945); R. S. Baker, *Woodrow Wilson, life and letters,* 8 vols. (1927–39).

The war itself: C. R. M. F. Cruttwell, *History of the great war, 1914–1918* (1934); B. H. Liddell Hart, *History of the world war, 1914–1918* (1935); Winston Churchill, *World crisis, 1911–1918,* 5 vols. (1923–9); *Ludendorff's own story,* Eng. trans., 2 vols. (1920), account by leading German general; N. N. Golovine, *The Russian army in the world war,* Eng. trans. (1931); Viscount Wavell, *Allenby, a study in greatness,* 2 vols. (1945); T. Frothingham, *Naval history of the world war,* 3 vols. (1924–6); Sir W. A. Raleigh, *The war in the air,* 6 vols. (1922–37); R. Gibson & M. Prendergast, *German submarine war, 1914–1918* (1931); F. L. Paxson, *America at war, 1917–1918* (1939); F. P. Chambers, *The war behind the war, 1914–1918, a history of the political and civilian fronts* (1939); G. Bruntz, *Allied propaganda and the collapse of the German empire* (1938). E. L. Bogart, *Direct and indirect costs of the great world war* (1919). A. L. Bowley, *Some economic consequences of the great war* (1930). L. Grebler & W. Winkler, *Cost of the world war to Germany and to Austria-Hungary* (1940). F. W. Hirst, *Consequences of the war to Great Britain* (1934). J. M. Clark, *Costs of the world war to the American people* (1931). S. Kohn & Baron A. F. Meyendorff, *Cost of the war to Russia* (1932).

There are elaborate official military histories sponsored by the several war departments of the major powers participating in the war. There is also an elaborate series of studies of the impact of the war upon various nations, neutrals as well as belligerents, ed. by J. T. Shotwell under the auspices of the Carnegie Endowment for International Peace, *Economic and social history of the world war,* 150 vols. (1919–29).

**Paris peace settlement of 1919–1920.** H. W. V. Temperley, ed., *History of the peace conference at Paris,* 6 vols. (1920–4). Harold Nicolson, *Peace-making, 1919* (1939). G. B. Noble, *Policies and opinions at Paris, 1919* (1935). E. M. House & Charles Seymour, eds., *What really happened at Paris* (1921), story by American delegates. T. A. Bailey, *Wilson and the peacemakers* (1947). A. S. Baker, *Woodrow Wilson and the world settlement,* 3 vols. (1922–3). René Albrecht-Carrié, *Italy at the Paris peace conference* (1938). Alma Luckau, *The German delegation at the Paris peace conference* (1941). N. Almond & R. H. Lutz, eds., *Treaty of St. Germain* (1934), on settlement with Austria. Francis Deák, *Hungary at the Paris peace conference, the diplomatic history of the treaty of Trianon* (1942). C. A. Macartney, *Hungary and her successors, 1919–1937* (1937). F. M. Russell, *The Saar, battleground and pawn* (1951). A. Cobban, *National self-determination* (1944).

Paul Birdsall, *Versailles twenty years after* (1941), a critical summation. Stephen Bonsal, *Unfinished business* (1944), reflections of Wilson's interpreter at Paris. W. E. Stephens, *Revisions of the treaty of Versailles* (1939).

**League of nations.** F. P. Walters, *A history of the league of nations,* 2 vols. (1952). C. K. Webster & S. Herbert, *League of nations in theory and practice* (1933). M. Beer, *The league on trial* (1933). M. O. Hudson, *Permanent court of international justice* (1934).

J. T. Shotwell, ed., *Origins of the international labor office*, 2 vols. (1934). F. G. Wilson, *Labor in the league system* (1934). P. de Azcárate, *League of nations and national minorities* (1946). Quincy Wright, *Mandates under the league of nations* (1930). D. F. Fleming, *The United States and the league of nations, 1918–1920* (1932). C. A. Berdahl, *Policy of the United States with respect to the league of nations* (1932). Hans Aufricht, *Guide to league of nations publications* (1951).

**Towards World War II.** B. E. Schmitt, *From Versailles to Munich, 1918–1938* (1939). G. M. Gathorne-Hardy, *A short history of international affairs, 1920–1939*, new ed. (1942). F. Gilbert & G. A. Craig, eds., *The diplomats, 1919–1939* (1953). Maurice Beaumont, *La faillité de la paix, 1918–1939* (1945), in *Peuples et civilisations* series ed. by Halphen & Sagnac, an economic and social interpretation. W. E. Rappard, *Quest for peace since the first world war* (1940). Arnold Wolfers, *Britain and France between two wars, conflicting strategies of peace since Versailles* (1940). J. M. Keynes, *Economic consequences of the peace* (1920). H. G. Moulton & Leo Pasvolsky, *War debts and world prosperity* (1932). C. Bergmann, *History of reparations* (1927). J. W. Wheeler-Bennett, *Wreck of reparations* (1933).

M. W. Boggs, *Attempts to define and limit "aggressive" armaments* (1941). R. L. Buell, *The Washington conference* (1922). D. H. Miller, *The Geneva protocol* (1925). J. W. Wheeler-Bennett, *Disarmament and security since Locarno* (1932). L. G. Cowan, *France and the Saar* (1950). R. Machray, *Polish-German problem* (1942). R. H. Ferrell, *Peace in their time* (1952), on the Kellogg-Briand pact.

Sara R. Smith, *The Manchurian crisis, 1931–1932* (1948). W. W. Willoughby, *Sino-Japanese controversy and the league of nations* (1935). F. C. Jones, *Manchuria since 1931* (1949). H. S. Quigley, *Far Eastern war, 1937–1941* (1942). A. W. Griswold, *Far Eastern policy of the United States* (1938). P. Badoglio, *The war in Abyssinia*, Eng. trans. (1937). Elizabeth Wiskemann, *Rome-Berlin axis, a study of the relations between Hitler and Mussolini* (1949). J. W. Wheeler-Bennett, *Munich, prologue to tragedy* (1948). Max Beloff, *Foreign policy of Soviet Russia, 1929–1941*, 2 vols. (1947, 1952). U. S. Dep't of State, captured *Documents on German foreign policy*, covering years 1933–1941 in 11 vols. to date (1948–1958). R. J. Sontag & J. S. Beddie, eds., *Nazi-Soviet relations, 1939–1941* (1948). L. B. Namier, *Diplomatic prelude, 1938–1939* (1948), and *Europe in decay, a study in disintegration, 1936–1940* (1950). Gerald Freund, *Unholy alliance, Russian-German relations from the treaty of Brest-Litovsk to the treaty of Berlin* (1957); A. Rossi, *Russo-German alliance, 1939–1941* (1951). H. Seton-Watson, *Eastern Europe between the wars, 1918–1941* (1945).

**World War II.** C. G. Haines & R. J. S. Hoffman, *Origins and background of the second world war* (1943). H. C. O'Neill, *Short history of the second world war* (1951). J. F. C. Fuller, *The second world war, 1939–1945, a strategic and tactical history* (1949). For Britain's crucial part in the war, reference should be had to Winston Churchill's charming and monumental memoirs: *The second world war*, 6 vols. (1948–1953). B. H. Liddell Hart, *The revolution in warfare* (1947). Harold & Margaret Sprout, *Toward a new order of sea power* (1940).

On how the United States became involved in the war, conflicting interpretations have been made, depending upon whether the authors favored or opposed Roosevelt's foreign policy, whether they were "internationalist" or "isolationist." Outstanding works of the former kind: W. L. Langer & S. E. Gleason, *The challenge to isolation, 1937–1940* (1952); Walter Millis, *This is Pearl!, the United States and Japan, 1941* (1947); Herbert Feis, *The road to Pearl harbor* (1950); Basil Rauch, *Roosevelt, from Munich to Pearl harbor, a study in the creation of a foreign policy* (1950). So-called "revisionist" works, critical of the policy pursued: C. A. Beard, *American foreign policy in the making 1932–1940, a study in responsibilities* (1946), and *President Roosevelt and the coming of the war, 1941* (1948); C. C. Tansill, *Back door to war, the Roosevelt foreign policy, 1933–1941* (1952). On American foreign policy during the war: Herbert Feis, *Churchill-Roosevelt-Stalin, the war they waged and the peace they sought* (1957); R. E. Sherwood, *Roosevelt and Hopkins*, rev. ed. (1950); Walter Millis, ed., *The Forrestal diaries* (1951); W. L. Langer, *Our Vichy gamble* (1947); C. J. H. Hayes, *Wartime mission in Spain* (1945); Herbert Feis, *The Spanish story* (1948); S. F. Bemis, *The Latin American policy of the United States* (1943). See also Toshikazu Kase, *Journey to the "Missouri"* (1950), Japanese account of Japan's foreign policy, 1937–1945.

On special campaigns: C. Hollingsworth, *The three weeks' war in Poland* (1940); T. Draper, *The six weeks' war in France, May–June 1940* (1944); A. D. Divine, *Dunkirk* (1945); J. H. Wuorinen, *Finland and World War II, 1939–1944* (1948); D. D. Eisenhower, *Crusade in Europe* (1948); O. N. Bradley, *A soldier's story* (1951); Raymond de Belot, *Struggle for the Mediterranean, 1939–1945*, Eng. trans. (1951); P. Badoglio, *Italy in the second world war*, Eng. trans. (1948); Desmond Young, *Rommel the desert fox* (1950); L. E. O. Charlton, *The royal air force and the United States A. A. F., 1943–1945*, 2 vols. (1946–7); A. Guillaume, *La guerre germano-soviétique, 1941–1945* (1949); W. E. D. Allen & P. Muratoff, *Russian campaigns of 1944–1945* (1946); R. Merriam, *Dark December* (1947), battle of the Bulge.

S. E. Morison, *History of United States naval operations in World War II* (1947 ff.), important "official" history in numerous volumes. Other official histories of military operations are emanating from the United States, Great Britain, and Russia. Of special interest: P. O'Sheel & G. Cook, eds., *Semper fidelis, the United States marines in the Pacific, 1942–1945* (1947); J. Hersey, *Hiroshima* (1946), on first use of the atom bomb.

**After World War II.** E. P. Chase, *The United Nations in action* (1950), non-technical survey. Amry Vandenbosch & W. N. Hogan, *The United Nations: background, organization, functions and activities* (1952). C. E. Toussaint, *Trusteeship system of the United Nations* (1956). P. Calvocoressi, *Nuremberg, the facts, the law, and the consequences* (1948), on the trials of German Nazis accused of war guilt. Hajo Holborn, *American military government, its organizations and philosophy* (1947). W. H. Chamberlin, *The European cockpit* (1947).

L. Fischer, *The Soviets in world affairs*, 2nd ed. (1951); H. Seton-Watson, *The East-European revolution* (1950), important for construction of Communist Empire. R. Bishop & E. S. Grayfield, *Russia astride the Balkans* (1948). J. R. Deane, *The strange alliance* (1947), Soviet suspicions of Western powers, especially the United States. W. B. Smith, *My three years in Moscow* (1950), revealing memoirs of American ambassador to Russia. J. F. Byrnes, *Speaking frankly* (1947), memoirs of American secretary of state in crucial period.

E. M. Markham, *Allied occupation of Japan* (1948). D. J. Dallin, *Soviet Russia and the far east* (1948). J. K. Fairbank, *The United States and China* (1948), critical of Chiang Kai-shek's nationalist regime. Department of State, *United States relations with China, with special reference to the period 1944–1949* (1949), a "white book" of documents intended to justify American policy toward China. Herbert Feis, *The China Tangle* (1953), based on official record. Frieda Utley, *The China story* (1951), highly critical of American policy. K. S. Latourette, *The American record in the far east, 1945–1951* (1952), factual. R. T. Oliver, *Why war came in Korea* (1950). J. C. Campbell & others, *The United States in world affairs, 1945–1949*, 3 vols. (1947–9).

### 3. Industrial and Social History

**"Industrial revolution."** On its beginnings: T. S. Ashton, *The industrial revolution, 1760–1830* (1948), in Home university library; H. L. Beales, *The industrial revolution, 1750–1850* (1938); S. T. Mc-Cloy, *French inventions of the 18th century* (1952).

A. P. Usher, *History of mechanical inventions*, 2nd ed. (1954). E. Cressy, *Discoveries and inventions of the 20th century* (1930). J. K. Finch, *Engineering and western civilization* (1951). D. L. Burn, *Eco-*

*nomic history of steel-making, 1867–1939* (1940). Rollo Appleyard, *Charles Parsons, his life and work* (1933). C. E. Gibson, *Story of the ship* (1948). D. B. Tyler, *Steam conquers the Atlantic* (1939). F. E. Bowen, *A century of Atlantic travel* (1930). A. Berglund, *Ocean transportation* (1931). M. Luckiesh, *Artificial light* (1920).

S. J. C. Nixon, *Invention of the automobile* (1929). R. C. Epstein, *Automobile industry, its economic and commercial development* (1928). C. L. M. Brown, *Conquest of the air* (1927). C. R. Gibson & W. B. Cole, *Wireless of today* (1923). Martin Quigley, Jr., *Magic shadows, the story of the origin of motion pictures* (1948). V. Rose, *Evolution of the oil industry* (1920).

See also works on science in Section 4, p. 795, below.

**General economic history.** S. B. Clough and C. W. Cole, *Economic history of Europe*, new ed. (1952). H. Heaton, *Economic history of Europe* (1936). E. L. Bogart, *Economic history of Europe, 1760–1939* (1942). Witt Bowden & others, *Economic history of Europe since 1750* (1937). J. H. Clapham, *An economic history of modern Britain:* vols. i, *Early railway age, 1820–1850* (1936), ii, *Free trade and steel, 1850–1886* (1932), iii, *Machines and national rivalries, 1887–1914, with an epilogue, 1914–1929* (1938). J. H. Clapham, *Economic development of France and Germany, 1815–1914*, 3rd ed. (1928), and *The Bank of England, a history*, 2 vols. (1944). L. C. A. Knowles, *Economic development in the 19th century: France, Germany, Russia, and the United States* (1932). P. Benaerts, *Les origines de la grande industrie allemande* (1933). Thorstein Veblen, *Imperial Germany and the industrial revolution*, new ed. by J. Dorfman (1939). S. B. Clough, *France, a history of national economics, 1789–1939* (1939). G. R. Porter, *Progress of the (British) nation in its various social and economical relations, from the beginning of the 19th century*, rev. ed. by F. W. Hirst (1912), statistical data of wide range.

Percy Ashley, *Modern tariff history: Germany, United States, France*, 3rd ed. (1920). A. Plummer, *International combines in modern industry*, 2nd ed. (1938). L. H. Jenks, *Migration of British capital to 1875* (1927). Herbert Feis, *Europe, the world's banker, 1870–1914* (1930). G. W. Edwards, *Evolution of finance capitalism* (1939). Wesley Mitchell, *Business cycles, the problem and its setting* (1927). Joseph Schumpeter, *Business cycles, theoretical, historical and statistical analysis of the capitalist process*, Eng. trans., 2 vols. (1939). A. C. Pigou, *Aspects of British economic history, 1918–1925* (1947). H. V. Hodson, *Slump and recovery, 1929–1937* (1938). S. E. Harris, *European recovery program* (1948), after World War II.

**General social history.** A. F. Weber, *Growth of cities in the 19th century* (1899). R. E. Dickinson, *The West European city, a study in urban geography* (1951). National Bureau of Economic Research, *Inter-*

*national migrations*, 2 vols. (1931). J. P. Schechtman, *European population transfers, 1939–1945* (1946).

Sidney and Beatrice Webb, *History of trade unionism*, rev. ed. (1920). C. R. Fay, *Cooperation at home and abroad*, 4th ed. (1939), a history of workers' cooperative movement. S. Perlman, *Theory of the labor movement*, new ed. (1948). W. Galenson, ed., *Comparative labor movements* (1952). Sir William Beveridge, *Unemployment, a problem of industry*, 4th ed. (1930). E. Varga, *The great crisis and its political consequences* (1935). Dixon Wecter, *The age of the great depression, 1929–1941* (1948), vol. xiii in *History of American life* series ed. by A. M. Schlesinger & D. R. Fox.

C. W. Pipkin, *Social politics and modern democracies*, 2 vols. (1927). D. O. Wagner, *Social reformers* (1934). José Ortega y Gasset, *The revolt of the masses*, Eng trans. (1932). G. A. Briefs, *The proletariat, a challenge to western civilization* (1937). J. U. Nef, *War and human progress, an essay on the rise of industrial civilization* (1950). W. F. Ogburn, ed., *Technology and international relations* (1949).

**Marxian socialism and its variants.** Isaiah Berlin, *Karl Marx, his life and environment*, new ed. (1948), best critical biography. H. J. Laski, *Life of Karl Marx* (1922), highly laudatory. Jacques Barzun, *Darwin, Marx, Wagner* (1941), brilliant criticism. Karl Kautsky, *Economic doctrine of Karl Marx*, Eng. trans. (1925), exposition by "orthodox" disciple. Karl Federn, *Materialistic conception of history* (1939), a critique. Sidney Hook, *Towards the understanding of Karl Marx* (1933), and G. D. H. Cole, *What Marx really meant* (1934), attempts to explain and reconcile Marx's inconsistencies. Solomon Bloom, *Marx and the society of nations* (1941), on Marx's attitude toward particular countries and nationalities.

G. M. Stekloff, *History of the first "International"* (1928). Eduard Berstein, *Evolutionary socialism, a criticism and affirmation*, Eng. trans., 2nd ed. (1912), on "reformist" or "right-wing" socialism. L. L. Lorwin, *Syndicalism* (1914), and R. D. Humphrey, *Georges Sorel, prophet without honor* (1951), on "direct-action" or "left-wing" socialism. E. H. Carr, *Michael Bakunin* (1937), on founder of dissident anarchism. D. Footman, *The primrose path, a life of Ferdinand Lassalle* (1946), on founder of German socialist party. M. Beer, *History of British socialism* (1940). E. R. Pease, *History of the Fabian society* (1916). G. D. H. Cole, *Socialism in evolution* (1938). Waldemar Gurian, *Rise and decline of Marxism* (1938). R. N. Carew Hunt, *Marxism, past and present* (1954). P. Gay, *Dilemma of democratic socialism* (1952).

M. Salvadori, *Rise of modern communism* (1952), a brief survey. R. N. Carew Hunt, *Theory and practice of communism* (1951). J. Plamenatz, *German Marxism and Russian communism* (1954). J. E. LeRossignol, *From Marx to Stalin, a critique of communism* (1940).

Waldemar Gurian, *Bolshevism* (1932), excellent analysis. F. Borkenau and others, *World communism, a history of the communist international* (1939). Mario Einaudi, ed., *Communism in western Europe* (1951), in contemporary France and Italy. Milovan Djilas, *The new class, an analysis of the communist system* (1957), critique by a prominent Yugoslav Communist, for which he has been jailed. See also works listed under Soviet Russia, pp. 804–805, below.

## 4. CULTURAL HISTORY

**Science.** F. S. Taylor, *Short history of science and scientific thought* (1949). Sir William C. Dampier, *A history of science in its relations with philosophy and religion*, 3rd ed. (1942), and *A shorter history of science* (1944). *Scientific American*, vol. 183, no. 3 (September 1950), survey of the several sciences, 1900–1950.

Charles Singer, *A history of biology* (1950). G. G. Simpson, *The meaning of evolution* (1949). Geoffrey West, *Charles Darwin* (1938). Hugo Iltis, *Life of Mendel* (1932). Charles Singer, *A short history of medicine* (1928). R. H. Shryock, *Development of modern medicine*, new ed. (1947). C. D. Haagensen & W. E. B. Lloyd, *Hundred years of medicine* (1947). P. H. DeKruif, *Microbe hunters* (1926), and *The fight for life* (1938). R. J. Dubos, *Louis Pasteur, free lance of science* (1950). W. W. Cheyne, *Lister and his achievements* (1925). Hans Zinsser, *Rats, lice, and history* (1935). H. C. Sherman & S. L. Smith, *Vitamins* (1931). I. Galdston, ed., *Social medicine* (1949). E. E. Slosson, *Creative chemistry* (1930).

F. Cajori, *A history of physics*, new ed. (1938). C. T. Chase, *Evolution of modern physics* (1947). A. S. Eddington, *Nature of the physical world*, new ed. (1937). Sir James H. Jeans, *This physical universe* (1930), *Through space and time* (1934), and *Growth of physical science* (1948). Bertrand Russell, *The a. b. c. of relativity* (1925). L. Infeld, *Albert Einstein, his work and its influence* (1950). N. M. Bligh, *Evolution and development of the quantum theory* (1926). Selig Hecht, *Explaining the atom* (1947). D. J. Hughes, *On nuclear energy, its potential for peacetime uses* (1957).

E. Boring, *History of experimental psychology* (1929). Sigmund Freud, *General introduction to psycho-analysis*, Eng. trans. (1935). E. Jones, *Life and work of Freud* (1953). J. P. Baxter, *Scientists against time* (1946), on contribution of scientists to World War II.

**Philosophy.** Egon Friedell, *A cultural history of the modern age*, vol. iii (1932). C. Brinton, *Shaping of the modern mind* (1953). J. T. Merz, *History of European thought in the 19th century*, 2nd ed., 4 vols. (1912–28). Jacques Barzun, *Darwin, Marx, Wagner, the fatal legacy of "progress"* (1941). F. A. Lange, *History of materialism*, 3rd ed. (1925). Karl Federn, *The materialistic conception of history* (1939).

H. A. Reyburn, *Nietzsche, the story of a human philosopher* (1948).
Sir James H. Jeans, *Physics and philosophy* (1942). Arnold Lunn &
J. B. S. Haldane, *Science and the supernatural* (1935), a debate.

G. H. Sabine, *A history of political theory*, new ed. (1950). Crane
Brinton, *English political thought in the 19th century*, new ed. (1949).
Y. R. Simon, *Philosophy of democratic government* (1951). J. R. Pen-
nock, *Liberal democracy, its merits and prospects* (1950). Feliks Gross,
ed., *European ideologies, a survey of 20th-century political ideas* (1948).
P. A. Sorokin, *Social philosophies of an age of crisis* (1950). Bertrand
de Jouvenel, *On power, its nature and the history of its growth*, Eng.
trans. (1949), a critique of state power. Barbara Ward, *Faith and freedom* (1954). G. W. F. Hallgarten, *Why dictators?* (1954). P. Geyl,
*From Ranke to Toynbee* (1952), on modern philosophies of history.
George Orwell, *1984* (1954), a contemporary's dread prophecy of future
"progress."

On "racialism" of the period: C. S. Coon, *Races of Europe* (1939);
Jacques Barzun, *Race, a study in modern superstition* (1937); L. L.
Snyder, *Race, a history of modern ethnic theories* (1939); Ruth Bene-
dict, *Race, science, and politics* (1940).

**Religion and the churches.** *Catholic encyclopedia*, ed. by C. G.
Herberman, 15 vols. (1907–12), supplemented by *New Catholic dictionary*, ed. by J. J. Wynne (1933). Protestant *New Schaff-Herzog
encyclopedia of religious knowledge*, ed. by S. M. Jackson, 16 vols.
(1907–14), and *Encyclopædia of religion and ethics*, ed. by James
Hastings, 12 vols. (1908–27), supplemented by Vergilius Ferm, *A
Protestant dictionary* (1950). *Jewish encyclopedia*, ed. by Cyrus Adler,
12 vols. (1901–6). *Encyclopedia of Islam*, ed. by M. T. Houtsma, 4
vols. (1908–34).

Christopher Dawson, *Progress and religion* (1931), *Religion and the
modern state* (1935), and *Religion and culture* (1948). E. Troeltsch,
*Protestantism and progress* (1912). J. N. Figgis, *Churches in the
modern state*, 2nd ed. (1914). G. B. Smith, ed., *Religious thought in
the last quarter century* (1927). C. H. Cotton, ed., *Has science discovered God?* (1931). J. H. VanderVeldt & R. P. Odenwald, *Phychiatry
and Catholicism* (1952). A. E. Haydon, ed., *Modern trends in world
religion* (1934). K. S. Latourette, *History of the expansion of Christianity*, vol. iv, *The great century, 1800–1914* (1941), on Christian missions. M. P. Fogarty, *Christian democracy in Western Europe, 1820–
1953* (1957). Albert Galter, *The red book of the persecuted church*
(1957), behind the "iron curtain" since 1939.

Philip Hughes, *A popular history of the Catholic church* (1949).
Josef Schmidlin, *Papstgeschichte der neuesten Zeit*, vols. ii, *Pius IX,
Leo XIII* (1934), and iii, *Pius X, Benedict XV* (1935). L. P. Wallace,

*The papacy and European diplomacy, 1869–1878* (1948). Charles Pichon, *The Vatican and its role in world affairs, 1878–1946*, Eng. trans. (1950). J. J. Wynne, ed., *Great encyclical letters of Pope Leo XIII* (1907). V. A. Yzermans, ed., *All things in Christ* (1952), encyclicals and other documents of Pius X. J. H. Ryan, ed., *Encyclicals of Pius XI* (1934). Oscar Halecki, *Eugenio Pacelli, pope of peace* (1951), on Pius XII. W. Gurian, ed., *The Catholic church in world affairs* (1954).

S. Chestham, *History of the Christian church since the reformation* (1907), Protestant. A. C. McGiffert, *Rise of modern religious ideas* (1915). William Cunningham, *Christianity and the social question* (1910). F. W. Cornish, *History of the English church in the 19th century*, 2 vols. (1910). D. O. Wagner, *Church of England and social reforms since 1854* (1930). H. L. Stewart, *A century of Anglo-Catholicism* (1929). Harold Begbie, *Life of William Booth, founder of the Salvation Army*, 2 vols. (1920).

Adrian Fortescue, *Orthodox eastern church*, 3rd ed. (1911), and *Uniate eastern churches* (1923). G. P. Fedetov, *Russian church since the revolution* (1928). S. W. Baron, *A social and religious history of the Jews*, vol. ii (1937). D. Philipson, *Reform movement in Judaism* (1931). L. Cohen, *Jewish life in modern times* (1929). N. Sokolow, *History of Zionism*, 2 vols. (1919).

**Literature and art.** G. Brandes, *Main currents in 19th-century literature*, 6 vols. (1901–5). *Cambridge history of English literature*, ed. by Sir A. W. Ward & A. R. Waller, vols. xiv–xv (1931). E. Wilson, *Axel's castle, a study in the imaginative literature of 1870–1930* (1931). G. K. Chesterton, *Victorian age in literature* (1913). Joseph Bédier & Paul Hazard, *Histoire de la littérature française contemporaine*, rev. ed. (1931). D. S. Mirsky, *A History of Russian literature* (1927). E. J. Simmons, *Outline of modern Russian literature, 1880–1940* (1943). Aylmer Maude, *Life of Tolstoy*, rev. ed., 2 vols. (1930). Halvdan Koht, *Life of Ibsen*, Eng. trans., 2 vols. (1931).

Joseph Pijoan, *History of art*, vol. iii (1928). E. Faure, *History of art*, Eng. trans., vol. iii (1930). André Michel, ed., *Histoire de l'art*, vol. viii (1929). Thomas Craven, *Modern art, the men, the movements, the meaning* (1934). Ulrich Thieme & Felix Becker, eds., *Allgemeines Lexikon der bildenden Künstler*, 33 vols. (1907–35), biographical dictionary of artists. F. M. Simpson, *History of architectural development*, vol. iii (1909). H. R. Hitchcock, *Modern architecture* (1929). Talbot Hamlin, ed., *Forms and functions of 20th-century architecture*, 4 vols. (1952). W. H. Wright, *Modern painting* (1930). M. Raynal, *The 19th-century, Goya to Ganguin* (1951). Alfred Leroy, *Histoire de la peinture française, 1800–1933* (1934). G. G. Dehio, *Geschichte der deutschen Kunst*, 2nd ed., vol. iv (1934). P. H. Láng, *Music in western civilization*

(1941). *Grove's dictionary of music and musicians*, ed. by H. C. Colles, 5 vols. (1927–8).

## 5. NATIONAL HISTORIES

**Great Britain.** R. C. K. Ensor, *England, 1870–1914* (1936). D. C. Somervell, *British politics since 1900* (1950). G. M. Trevelyan, *British history in the 19th century* (1922). Sir Spencer Walpole, *History of twenty-five years, 1856–1880*, 4 vols. (1904–8). R. H. Gretton, *A modern history of the English people, 1880–1910*, 2 vols. (1913). Sir John Marriott, *Modern England, 1885–1932, a history of my own times* (1934). E. C. Wingfield-Stratford, *History of British civilization*, vol. ii (1928), *The Victorian sunset* (1932), and *The Victorian aftermath, 1901–1914* (1933). G. A. N. Lowndes, *The silent social revolution, an account of the expansion of public education, 1895–1935* (1937). J. M. Gaus, *Great Britain, a study of civic loyalty* (1929).

C. R. Fay, *Great Britain from Adam Smith to the present day*, 3rd ed. (1933), on relationship of economics to politics. F. C. Dietz, *Economic history of England* (1942). J. H. Clapham, *Economic history of modern Britain*, vols. ii–iii (1932–8). Helen M. Lynd, *England in the 1880's* (1945), on socializing drift. G. D. H. Cole, *Short history of the British working-class movement*, vols. ii–iii, 1848–1927 (1927). B. L. Hutchins & Amy Harrison, *History of factory legislation*, 3rd ed. (1926). E. P. Cheyney, *Modern English reform, from individualism to socialism* (1931). C. F. Brand, *British labour's rise to power* (1941). R. E. Prothero (Baron Ernle), *English farming, past and present*, 5th ed. (1936).

D. C. Somervell, *Disraeli and Gladstone* (1926). Hesketh Pearson, *Dizzy, life and personality of Benjamin Disraeli* (1951). W. F. Monypenny & G. E. Buckle, *Life of Benjamin Disraeli, Earl of Beaconsfield*, 6 vols. (1910–20). P. Magnus, *Gladstone, a biography* (1955). John (Viscount) Morley, *Life of William Ewart Gladstone*, new ed., 3 vols. in 2 (1911). G. M. Trevelyan, *Life of John Bright* (1914). Lady Gwendolen Cecil, *Life of Robert, Marquess of Salisbury*, 5 vols. (1921–35). Winston Churchill, *Lord Randolph Churchill*, 2 vols. (1906). Janet H. Robb, *The Primrose league, 1883–1906* (1942). J. L. Garvin & Julian Amery, *Life of Joseph Chamberlain*, 4 vols. to 1903 (1932–51). Thomas Jones, *Lloyd George* (1951). J. H. Edwards, *David Lloyd George, the man and the statesman*, 2 vols. (1929). Keith Feiling, *Life of Neville Chamberlain* (1946). Lytton Strachey, *Queen Victoria* (1921). Hector Bolitho, *Reign of Queen Victoria* (1948), *King Edward VIII* (1937), and *King George VI* (1938). C. Brinton, *The United States and Britain*, 2nd ed. (1948).

For British empire and commonwealth, see Section 6, p. 807, below.

**Ireland.** Francis Hackett, *Ireland, a study in nationalism* (1918). Sir James O'Connor, *History of Ireland, 1798–1924,* 2 vols. (1925). J. C. Beckett, *A short history of Ireland* (1952). G. J. Shaw-Lefevre (Baron Eversley), *Gladstone and Ireland, the Irish policy of parliament, 1850–1894* (1912). J. E. Pomfret, *Struggle for land in Ireland, 1800–1923* (1930). J. D. Clarkson, *Labor and nationalism in Ireland* (1925). Denis Gwynn, *The Irish free state* (1925), and *History of partition, 1912–1925* (1950). R. S. Kelly, *Ireland's bloodless revolution, 1932–1936* (1936). R. B. O'Brien, *Life of Charles Stewart Parnell,* 3 vols. (1899). F. Sheehy-Skeffington, *Michael Davitt, revolutionary, agitator, and labour leader* (1908). M. J. McManus, *Eamon de Valera* (1946).

**France.** D. W. Brogan, *France under the republic* (1940), fairest political narrative. J. P. T. Bury, *France, 1814–1940* (1949), good brief survey. J. B. Wolf, *France, 1815 to the present* (1940). R. W. Hale, Jr., *Democratic France, the third republic from Sedan to Vichy* (1941). Jacques Bainville, *The French republic, 1870–1935,* Eng. trans. (1936), "rightist" in outlook. Ernest Lavisse, ed., *Histoire de France contemporaine* (1922) vols. vii, *1859–1875,* and viii, *1875–1914,* by Charles Seignobos; vol. ix, *La grande guerre,* by H. Bidou & others. W. R. Sharp, *Government of the French republic* (1938). R. H. Soltau, *French parties and politics, 1871–1921* (1922), and *French political thought in the 19th century* (1931). S. B. Clough, *France, a history of national economics, 1789–1939* (1939). F. A. Haight, *History of French commercial policies* (1941). V. R. Lorwin, *The French labor movement* (1954).

Gabriel Hanotaux, *Histoire de la fondation de la troisième république,* 4 vols. (1925–6), "moderate republican." Emile Simond, *Histoire de la troisième république, 1887–1906,* 4 vols. (1913–22), "rightist." F. Jellinek, *The Paris commune of 1871* (1937). E. Mason, *The Paris commune* (1930). J. M. S. Allison, *Monsieur Thiers* (1932). Paul Deschanel, *Gambetta* (1920). T. F. Power, Jr., *Jules Ferry and the renaissance of French imperialism* (1944). S. H. Roberts, *History of French colonial policy, 1870–1925,* 2 vols. (1929). Evelyn Acomb, *French laic laws, 1879–1889* (1941). E. O. Golub, *The Méline tariff, French agricultural and nationalist economic policy* (1944).

Armand Charpentier, *Dreyfus case,* Eng. trans. (1935). D. C. McKay, ed., *The Dreyfus case* (1937). Charlotte T. Muret, *French royalist doctrines since the revolution* (1933). W. C. Buthman, *Rise of integral nationalism in France* (1939), on Charles Maurras and his "Action française." C. S. Phillips, *The church in France, 1848–1907* (1936). P. T. Moon, *The labor problem and the social Catholic movement in France* (1925). Mildred J. Headings, *French free-masonry under the third French republic* (1949). E. M. Carroll, *French public opinion and foreign affairs, 1870–1914* (1931). C. W. Porter, *Career of*

*Théophile Delcassé* (1936). H. R. Weinstein, *Jean Jaurès, a study of patriotism in the French socialist movement* (1936). Geoffrey Bruun, *Clemenceau* (1943). C. J. H. Hayes, ed., *Social and economic studies of post-war France*, 5 vols. (1929–31): i, *Public finances*, by R. M. Haig; ii, *Process of inflation*, by J. H. Rogers; iii, *Economic development*, by W. F. Ogburn & William Jaffé; iv, *Labor movement*, by D. J. Saposs; v, *France, a nation of patriots*, by C. J. H. Hayes.

E. J. Knapton, *France since Versailles* (1952), good brief survey. Alexander Werth, *Twilight of France* (1942). A. Rossi, *Les communistes français pendant la drôle de guerre* (1951). Paul Farmer, *Vichy, political dilemma* (1955). Gordon Wright, *Reshaping of French democracy* (1948). Dorothy Thomson, *Democracy in France, the 3rd and 4th republics*, 2nd ed. (1952). P. Williams, *Politics in post-war France* (1954). François Goguel, *France under the fourth republic* (1952). E. M. Earle, ed., *Modern France, problems of the third and fourth republics* (1951). D. C. McKay, *The United States and France* (1951).

**Belgium, Netherlands, Luxemburg, and Switzerland.** J. A. Goris, ed., *Belgium* (1945). T. H. Reed, *Government and politics of Belgium* (1936). Henri Pirenne, *Histoire de Belgique*, vols. vii–ix (1932). S. B. Clough, *History of the modern Flemish movement in Belgium* (1930). B. H. M. Vlekke, *Evolution of the Dutch nation* (1945). A. J. Barnouw, *Holland under Queen Wilhelmina* (1923), *Making of modern Holland* (1948), *Pageant of Netherlands history* (1952). B. Landheer, *The Netherlands in a changing world* (1947). P. J. Blok, *History of the people of the Netherlands*, Eng. trans., vol. v (1912). H. Brugmans, *Geschiedenis van Nederland*, vols. vii–viii (1936). Ruth Putnam, *Luxemburg and her neighbors*, 2nd ed. (1919).

W. Oechsli, *History of Switzerland, 1499–1914* (1922). W. Martin, *History of Switzerland*, Eng. trans. (1931). W. E. Rappard, *Government of Switzerland* (1937). D. de Rougemont & Charlotte T. Muret, *Switzerland, the heart of Europe* (1941). André Siegfried, *Switzerland, a democratic way of life*, Eng. trans. (1950).

**Scandinavia (Denmark, Sweden, Norway, Iceland).** B. A. Arneson, *The democratic monarchies of Scandinavia* (1939). P. Drachmann & H. Westergaard, *Industrial development and policies of the three Scandinavian countries* (1915).

J. H. S. Birch, *Denmark in history* (1938). J. Eppstein, ed., *Denmark* (1945). J. C. Moller & K. Watson, *Social Denmark, a survey of Danish social legislation* (1946).

A. A. Stromberg, *A history of Sweden* (1931). Carl Hallendorf & Adolf Schück, *History of Sweden* (1929). M. Blomstedt & F. Böök, *Sweden of today* (1929).

Karen Larsen, *A history of Norway* (1948). Knut Gjerset, *History of the Norwegian people*, vol. ii (1915). O. J. Falnes, *National romanticism in Norway* (1933). T. Blegen, *Norwegian migration to America* (1931). Björn Collinder, *The Lapps* (1949). Knut Gjerset, *History of Iceland* (1924).

**Spain and Portugal.** H. D. Sedgwick, *Spain, a short history of its politics, literature, and art* (1925). Louis Bertrand & Sir Charles Petrie, *History of Spain*, rev. ed. (1952). Salvador de Madariaga, *Spain* (1930). Ramón Menéndez Pidal, *The Spaniards in their history*, with introd. by Walter Starkie (1950). Rafael Altamira, *A History of Spain*, Eng. trans. (1949), and *A history of Spanish civilization*, Eng. trans. (1936). C. E. Chapman, *A history of Spain*, new ed. (1948), based on Altamira's six-volume "liberal" *Historia de España* (1900–30). Antonio Ballesteros y Beretta, *Historia de España y su influncia en la historia universal*, vols. vii–ix (1934–41), most thorough and scholarly.

J. A. Brandt, *Toward the new Spain* (1933), a monograph on the revolutionary years 1868–1874. Charles Benoist, *Cánovas del Castillo, la restauration rénovatrice* (1930). E. A. Peers, *The Spanish tragedy, 1930–1936, dictatorship, republic, chaos*, 3rd ed. (1936); *Spain in eclipse, 1937–1943* (1943); *Spain, the church, and the orders* (1939). Gerald Brenan, *The Spanish labyrinth, an account of the social and political background of the civil war*, 3rd ed. (1950), and *The face of Spain* (1951). Richard Patee, *This is Spain* (1951), favorable to the "nationalists" and General Franco in the civil war and after. C. J. H. Hayes, *The United States and Spain* (1951). Most judicious account of rival partisanships during the civil war is to be found in the novel by José Maria Gironella, *The cypresses believe in God*, Eng. trans., 2 vols. (1956).

H. V. Livermore, *A history of Portugal* (1947). V. D. Braganca Cunha, *Revolutionary Portugal, 1910–1936* (1939). Richard Pattee, *Portugal and the Portuguese world* (1957).

**Italy.** René Albrecht-Carrié, *Italy from Napoleon to Mussolini* (1950). L. Salvatorelli, *A concise history of Italy*, Eng. trans. (1940). Benedetto Croce, *A history of Italy, 1871–1914* (1919), philosophical. Alfredo Comandini, *L'Italia nei cento anni del secolo XIX*, vol. v, *1871–1900* (1939). H. R. Spencer, *Government and politics of Italy* (1932). F. Foerster, *Italian emigration* (1919). A. W. Salomone, *Italian democracy in the making, the political scene in the Giolittian era, 1900–1914* (1945).

George Seldes, *Sawdust Caesar* (1935), unflattering account of Mussolini. Gaudence Megaro, *Mussolini in the making* (1938). H. W. Schneider, *Making the fascist state* (1928). G. Prezzolini, *Fascism* (1927). H. A. Steiner, *Government in fascist Italy* (1938), C. T.

Schmidt, *The corporate state in action, Italy under fascism* (1939). J. Meenan, *The Italian corporative system* (1945). M. H. H. Macartney & P. Cremona, *Italy's foreign and colonial policy, 1914–1937* (1938). Luigi Villari, *Expansion of Italy* (1930). S. W. Halperin, *Italy and the Vatican at war, 1870–1929* (1939). Wilfred Parsons, *The pope and Italy* (1929), on the Lateran treaty and concordat. D. A. Binchy, *Church and state in fascist Italy* (1942). M. Grindrod, *The new Italy, transition from war to peace* (1947). Mario Einaudi & François Goguel, *Christian democracy in Italy and France* (1952). H. S. Hughes, *The United States and Italy* (1953).

**Germany.** K. S. Pinson, *Modern Germany, its history and civilization* (1954). Veit Valentin, *The German people, their history and civilization from the Holy Roman empire to the third Reich*, Eng. trans. (1946). W. H. Dawson, *The German empire, 1876–1914*, 2 vols. (1919). F. K. Krüger, *Government and politics of the German empire* (1915). Adalbert Wahl, *Deutsche Geschichte, 1871–1914*, 4 vols. (1926–36). Johannes Ziekursch, *Politische Geschichte des neuen deutschen Kaiserreiches*, 3 vols. (1927–30).

Erich Eyck, *Bismarck and the German empire*, Eng. trans. (1950), summary of author's monumental *Bismarck, Leben und Werk*, 3 vols. (1943). Otto von Bismarck, *Reflections and reminiscences*, Eng. trans., 3 vols. (1898–1922). Arthur Rosenberg, *Birth of the German republic, 1871–1918*, Eng. trans. (1931), highly critical of Bismarck and William II. Erich Brandenburg, *From Bismarck to the world war, 1890–1914*, Eng. trans. (1927). Erich Eyck, *Das persönliche Regiment Wilhelms II, politische Geschichte des deutschen Kaiserreiches von 1890 bis 1914* (1948). L. L. Snyder, *From Bismarck to Hitler, background of modern German nationalism* (1935). Georges Goyau, *Bismarck et l'église, le culturkampf, 1870–1887*, 4 vols. (1911–3). Mary E. Townsend, *Rise and fall of Germany's colonial empire* (1930). Mildred S. Wertheimer, *The pan-German league, 1890–1914* (1925). R. W. Tims, *Germanizing Prussian Poland, 1894–1919* (1941). G. D. Crothers, *German elections of 1907* (1941).

Gustav Stolper, *German economy, 1870–1940* (1940). W. F. Bruck, *Social and economic history of Germany, 1888–1938* (1938). R. H. Bowen, *German theories of the corporative state, with special reference to the period 1870–1919* (1949). W. H. Dawson, *Social insurance in Germany* (1911). Sarah R. Tirrell, *German agrarian politics after Bismarck's fall* (1951). E. Anderson, *Hammer or anvil, the story of the German working-class movement* (1945).

R. H. Lutz, *The German revolution, 1918–1919* (1922). S. W. Halperin, *Germany tried democracy, a political history of the Reich from 1918 to 1933* (1946). A. Rosenberg, *A history of the German republic* (1936). A. J. Berlau, *German social democratic party, 1914–1921* (1949). R. Fischer, *Stalin and German communism* (1948). J. W. Angell, *Recovery of Germany* (1932). R. T. Clark, *Fall of the German republic* (1935). J. W. Wheeler-Bennett, *Wooden Titan, Hindenburg in twenty years of German history, 1914–1934* (1936).

Konrad Heiden, *Hitler's rise to power* (1944). A. L. C. Bullock, *Hitler, a study in tyranny* (1952). Adolf Hitler, *Mein Kampf*, Eng. trans. (1939), the Nazi "bible." Peter Viereck, *Metapolitics, from the romantics to Hitler* (1941). Theodore Abel, *Why Hitler came into power* (1938). R. H. Lutz, *Reichstag election of March 1933* (1943). C. B. Hoover, *Germany enters the third Reich* (1934). G. N. Shuster, *Strong man rules* (1934), and *Like a mighty army* (1935). F. L. Neumann, *Behemoth, the structure and practice of national socialism* (1942). Eva G. Reichmann, *Hostages of civilization, a study of the social causes of anti-semitism in Germany* (1951). M. Power, *Religion in the Reich* (1939). N. Micklem, *Assize of arms, story of the disarmament of Germany and her rearmament, 1919–1939* (1945). Willi Frischauer, *Rise and fall of Hermann Goering* (1951). Hans Rothfels, *German opposition to Hitler* (1948). A. W. Dulles, *Germany's underground* (1947). H. R. Trevor-Roper, *Last days of Hitler* (1947). Friedrich Meinecke, *The German catastrophe, reflections and recollections*, Eng. trans. (1950). Proceedings of Nuremberg trials are published as *Nazi conspiracy and aggression*, 8 vols. (1946). Lucius D. Clay, *Decision in Germany* (1950), with documents on Allied occupation 1945–1949. J. B. Conant, *Germany and freedom* (1958).

**Austria, Hungary, and Czechoslovakia.** A. J. P. Taylor, *The Habsburg monarchy, 1809–1918*, 2nd ed. (1948). A. J. May, *The Hapsburg monarchy, 1867–1914* (1951). R. A. Kann, *The multinational empire, nationalism and national reform in the Habsburg monarchy, 1848–1918*, 2 vols. (1950). Richard Charmatz, *Österreichs äussere und innere Politik von 1895 bis 1917* (1918). Joseph Redlich, *Emperor Francis Joseph of Austria*, Eng. trans. (1929). Louis Eisenmann, *Le compromis austro-hongrois de 1867, étude sur le dualisme* (1904). Oscar Jászi, *Dissolution of the Habsburg monarchy* (1929). Leo Pasvolsky, *Economic nationalism of the Danubian states* (1928). R. Hertz, *Economic problem of the Danubian states, a study in economic nationalism*, Eng. trans. (1947).

W. A. Jenks, *Austrian electoral reform of 1907* (1950). C. A. Gulick, *Austria from Hapsburg to Hitler*, 2 vols. (1948). O. Bauer, *Austrian revolution* (1925). Kurt von Schuschnigg, *Austrian requiem*, Eng. trans. (1946).

D. G. Kosáry, *A history of Hungary* (1941), brief survey. Louis Eisenmann, *Le Hongrie contemporaine, 1867–1918* (1921). Oscar Jászi,

*Revolution and counter-revolution in Hungary* (1924). C. A. Macartney, *Hungary and her successors, 1919–1937* (1937), and *A history of Hungary, 1929–1945*, 2 vols. (1957). Ferenc Nagy, *Struggle behind the iron curtain,* Eng. trans. (1948), how Communists took over Hungary. M. J. Lasky, ed., *The Hungarian revolution* (1957), documented accent of 1956 uprising.

S. H. Thomson, *Czechoslovakia in European history* (1943). R. J. Kerner, ed., *Czechoslovakia* (1948). R. W. Seton-Watson, *Slovakia then and now* (1931). Elizabeth Wiskemann, *Czechs and Germans, a study of the struggle in Bohemia and Moravia* (1938). J. W. Wheeler-Bennett, *Munich, prologue to tragedy* (1948). Hubert Ripka, *Czechoslovakia enslaved, the story of the communist coup d'état* (1950).

**Russia (and Union of Soviet Socialist Republics).** On the Russian empire to the revolution of 1917: A. Kornilov, *Modern Russian history from the age of Catherine the great to the end of the 19th century,* Eng. trans., new ed. (1943). George Vernadsky, *History of Russia,* new ed. (1951). Michael Karpovich, *Imperial Russia, 1801–1907* (1932). H. Seton-Watson, *Decline of imperial Russia, 1855–1914* (1952). Karl Stählin, *Geschichte Russlands,* vols. iii–iv (1935–9), covering reigns of Alexander II, Alexander III, and Nicholas II. P. N. Miliukov, *Outlines of Russian culture,* ed. by Michael Karpovich, Eng. trans., 3 vols. (1942), topical treatment. T. G. Masaryk, *Spirit of Russia, studies in history, literature, and philosophy,* Eng. trans., 2 vols. (1919). E. J. Simmons, *Outline of modern Russian literature, 1880–1940* (1943).

Maxime Kovalevsky, *Russian political institutions,* Eng. trans. (1902), of tsarist Russia. Richard Hare, *Pioneers of Russian social thought, studies of non-Marxian formation in 19th-century Russia and of its partial revival in the Soviet union* (1951), chiefly on "slavophiles" and "westernizers." G. T. Robinson, *Rural Russia under the old regime* (1932). M. S. Miller, *Economic development of Russia, 1905–1914* (1926). B. H. Sumner, *Russia and the Balkans, 1870–1880* (1937), and *Tsardom and imperialism in the far east and middle east, 1880–1914* (1943). Hans Kohn, *History of pan-slavism* (1955). S. M. Dubnow, *History of the Jews in Russia and Poland,* Eng. trans., 3 vols. (1916–20).

On Communist Russia (U.S.S.R.) since 1917: W. H. Chamberlin, *The Russian revolution, 1917–1921,* 2 vols. (1935), critical. E. H. Carr, *A history of Soviet Russia* (1950 ff.), projected elaborate work, of which first four volumes cover years to 1924, partisan and should be used with caution. B. D. Wolfe, *Three who made a revolution—Lenin, Trotsky, Stalin* (1948). David Shub, *Lenin, a biography* (1948). Eugene

Lyons, *Assignment in Utopia* (1937), and *Stalin, czar of all the Russias* (1940). J. W. Wheeler-Bennett, *Brest-Litovsk, the forgotten peace, March 1918* (1939). George Stewart, *The white armies of Russia, a chronicle of counter-revolution and allied intervention* (1933).

Waldemar Gurian, *Bolshevism, theory and practice* (1932), and ed., *The soviet union, background, ideology, reality* (1951). M. T. Florinsky, *World revolution and the U S S R* (1933), and *Towards an understanding of the U S S R*, rev. ed. (1951). Barrington Moore, *Soviet politics, the dilemma of power* (1950). M. Fainsod, *How Russia is ruled* (1953). Maurice Dobb, *Soviet economic development since 1917* (1948). Harry Schwartz, *Russia's soviet economy*, 2nd ed. (1954). D. J. Dallin & B. L. Nicolaevsky, *Forced labor in soviet Russia* (1947). R. Pipes, *Formation of the Soviet Union* (1954), relating to national minorities, 1917–1923. G. P. Fedetov, *The Russian church since the revolution* (1928). D. F. White, *Growth of the red army* (1944). M. Beloff, *Foreign policy of soviet Russia, 1929–1941*, 2 vols. (1946–9). D. J. Dallin, *The new soviet empire* (1951). Hugh Seton-Watson, *The east European revolution* (1951). D. J. Dallin, *Soviet Russia and the far east* (1948). J. P. Nettl, *The eastern zone and soviet policy in Germany* (1951).

J. S. Reshetar, Jr., *Ukrainian revolution, 1917–1920* (1952). W. E. D. Allen, *The Ukraine, a history* (1940). C. A. Manning, *Story of the Ukraine* (1947). A. Yarmolinsky, *Jews and other minor nationalities under the soviets* (1929).

**Poland and East Baltic countries (Finland, Estonia, Latvia, Lithuania).** Oscar Halecki, *History of Poland* (1942). George Slocombe, *A history of Poland* (1939). W. F. Reddaway & others, eds., *Cambridge history of Poland*, vol. ii, *From Augustus II to Pilsudski* (1941). R. Machray, *The Poland of Pilsudski, 1914–1936* (1937). W. F. Reddaway, *Marshal Pilsudski* (1939). K. Symonolewicz, *Studies in nationality and nationalism in Poland between the two wars* (1944). R. L. Buell, *Poland, key to Europe* (1939). B. E. Schmitt, ed., *Poland* (1945). Stanislaw Mikolajczyk, *Rape of Poland, pattern of soviet aggression* (1948). A. B. Lane, *I saw Poland betrayed* (1948), by former American ambassador at Warsaw.

J. H. Wuorinen, *Nationalism in modern Finland* (1931), and *Finland and World War II* (1948). K. R. Pusta, *Soviet union and the Baltic states* (1942). Alfred Bilmanis, *A history of Latvia* (1951). Arnolds Spekke, *History of Latvia* (1951).

**Ottoman empire and Turkey.** William Miller, *The Ottoman empire and its successors*, 3rd ed. (1934). A. La Jonquière, *Histoire de l'empire ottoman depuis les origines jusqu'à nos jours*, vol. ii (1914).

E. Pears, *Life of Abdul Hamid II* (1917). D. C. Blaisdell, *European financial control in the Ottoman empire* (1929). A. J. Toynbee, *The western question in Greece and Turkey*, 2nd ed. (1923). L. Ostroróg, *The Angora reform* (1928), on rise of Turkish nationalism. A. O. Sarkissian, *History of the Armenian question, 1869–1885* (1938). H. N. Howard, *Partition of Turkey, 1913–1923* (1931). P. Paneth, *Turkey, decadence and rebirth* (1945). Eleanor Bisbee, *The new Turks, pioneers of the republic, 1920–1950* (1951). H. C. Armstrong, *Gray wolf, Mustapha Kemal* (1933). D. E. Webster, *The Turkey of Atatürk* (1939). B. Ward, *Turkey* (1942).

**Greece and Balkan countries (Rumania, Yugoslavia, Bulgaria).** R. W. Seton-Watson, *Rise of nationality in the Balkans* (1917). W. M. Gewehr, *Rise of nationalism in the Balkans* (1931). Ferdinand Schevill, *History of the Balkan peninsula*, rev. ed. by W. M. Gewehr (1933). J. S. Roucek, *Politics in the Balkans* (1939).

William Miller, *A history of the Greek people, 1821–1921* (1922). E. S. Forster, *A short history of modern Greece, 1821–1940* (1941). Nicholas Kaltchas, *Introduction to the constitutional history of modern Greece* (1940). H. A. Gibbons, *Venizelos* (1923). J. A. Levandis, *The Greek foreign debt and the great powers, 1821–1898* (1944).

R. W. Seton-Watson, *A history of the Roumanians* (1934). D. Mitrany, *The land and peasant in Roumania* (1930). J. S. Roucek, *Contemporary Roumania and her problems* (1932). H. L. Roberts, *Rumania, political problems of an agrarian state* (1951).

H. W. V. Temperley, *History of Serbia* (1917). S. Graham, *Alexander of Yugoslavia* (1939). R. J. Kerner, ed., *Yugoslavia* (1949). H. F. Armstrong, *Tito and Goliath* (1951). Josef Korbel, *Tito's communism* (1951). C. Fotitch, *The war we lost, Yugoslavia's tragedy* (1948). C. E. Black, *Establishment of constitutional government in Bulgaria* (1944). H. R. Madol, *Ferdinand of Bulgaria* (1933).

6. European Imperialism and Countries outside Europe

**General.** P. T. Moon, *Imperialism and world politics* (1926). Mary E. Townsend, *European colonial expansion* (1941). L. J. Ragatz, *March of empire* (1948). E. M. Winslow, *Pattern of imperialism* (1948). J. A. Hobson, *Imperialism, a study*, 3rd rev. ed. (1938), an economic interpretation. Arthur Salz, *Das Wesen des Imperialismus, Umrisse einer Theorie* (1931), nationalist interpretation, questioning the economic. G. W. F. Hallgarten, *Imperialismus vor 1914*, 2 vols. (1951). T. F. Power, *Jules Ferry and the renaissance of French imperialism* (1938). S. H. Roberts, *History of French colonial policy, 1870–1925*, 2 vols. (1929). Mary E. Townsend, *Rise and fall of Germany's colonial empire, 1884–1918* (1930). André Siegfried, *Suez and Panama*, Eng.

trans. (1940). H. D. Hall, *Mandates, dependencies, and trusteeship* (1948).

R. Linton, ed., *Most of the world* (1949), interesting survey of non-European peoples. K. S. Latourette, *A history of the expansion of Christianity*, vol. vi. (1945). E. Fischer, *The passing of the European age, a study of the transfer of Western civilization and its renewal in other continents*, new ed. (1948). Arnold Toynbee, *The world and the west* (1953).

**British empire and commonwealth.** Paul Knaplund, *Britain, commonwealth and empire, 1901–1955* (1957). Howard Robinson, *Development of the British empire*, rev. ed. (1936). J. A. Williamson, *Short history of British expansion*, 2nd ed., vol. ii, *The new empire* (1930). *Cambridge history of the British empire*, ed. by J. H. Rose, A. P. Newton, & E. A. Benians, vols. iii–viii (1929–52), including vols. v, *Indian empire, 1858–1918*, by H. H. Dodwell; vi, *Canada and Newfoundland*, by W. P. M. Kennedy; vii, pt. 1, *Australia*, by Ernest Scott; vii, pt. 2, *New Zeland*, by J. Hight; viii, *South Africa, Rhodesia, and the protectorates*, by E. A. Walker. Sir Reginald Coupland, ed., *British empire history* (1950): *India*, by C. H. Philips; *New Zealand*, by Harold Miller; *South Africa*, by Arthur Keppel-Jones; *Burma*, by D. G. E. Hall. L. C. A. Knowles, *Economic development of the British overseas empire*, 2 vols. (1924–36).

R. M. Dawson, *Development of dominion status, 1900–1936* (1937). G. Grady, *Democracy in the Dominions*, 2nd ed. (1952), a comparative study. K. C. Wheare, *Statute of Westminster, 1931* (1933). R. Briffault, *Decline and fall of the British empire* (1938). Edgar McInnis, *Canada, a political and social history* (1947). G. P. de T. Glazebrook, *History of Canadian external relations* (1951). C. H. Grattan, ed., *Australia* (1947).

**America.** J. F. Rippy, *Historical evolution of Hispanic America*, 2nd ed. (1940), and *Latin America in world politics*, 3rd ed. (1938). J. F. Bannon, *History of the Americas*, vol. ii (1952). A. B. Thomas, *Latin America, a history* (1956). W. C. Gordon, *The economy of Latin America* (1950). P. V. Horn & H. E. Bice, *Latin-American trade and economics* (1949). R. A. Humphreys, *Latin America, a selective guide to publications in English* (1949).

S. F. Bemis, *Latin American policy of the United States* (1943). Dexter Perkins, *Hands off, a history of the Monroe doctrine* (1941). Walter Millis, *The martial spirit* (1931), on Spanish-American war of 1898. D. C. Miner, *The fight for the Panama route* (1940). W. H. Callcott, *Caribbean policy of the United States, 1890–1920* (1942). A. P. Whitaker, *United States and South America, the northern republics* (1948). C. H. Haring, *South America looks at the United*

*States* (1928). Carlos Davila, *We of the Americas* (1949). Dexter Perkins, *Evolution of American foreign policy* (1948). G. H. Stuart, *Latin America and the United States,* 4th ed. (1943).

For bibliographies of United States history, consult recent college textbooks.

**Far East, general.** K. S. Latourette, *A short history of the far east,* new rev. ed. (1951). J. Pratt, *Expansion of Europe in the far east* (1947). P. H. Clyde, *The far east, a history of the impact of the West on Eastern Asia,* new ed. (1952). A. W. Griswold, *Far eastern policy of the United States* (1938). F. R. Dulles, *America in the Pacific, a century of expansion* (1932). B. H. Sumner, *Tsardom and imperialism in the far east and middle east, 1880–1914* (1943). D. J. Dallin, *Rise of Russia in Asia* (1949), and *Soviet Russia and the far east* (1948). Malcolm Kennedy, *A history of communism in East Asia* (1957).

**Japan.** E. O. Reischauer, *Japan, past and present* (1946). K. S. Latourette, *History of Japan* (1947). Sir George Sansom, *The western world and Japan, a study of the interaction of European and Asiatic cultures* (1950). Arthur Walworth, *Black ships off Japan, the story of Commodore Perry's expedition* (1946). Chitoshi Yanaga, *Japan since Perry* (1949).

E. H. Norman, *Japan's emergence as a modern state, political and economic problems of the Meiji period, 1868–1904* (1940). W. W. McLaren, *Political history of Japan, 1867–1912* (1916). Seiji Hishida, *Japan among the great powers, a survey of her international relations* (1940). J. E. Orchard, *Japan's economic position* (1930). Hugh Borton, *Japan's modern century* (1956). Toshikazu Kase, *Journey to the "Missouri"* (1950), domestic politics and foreign policy, 1937–1945. E. O. Reischauer, *United States and Japan,* new ed. (1957), postwar.

**China.** L. C. Goodrich, *A short history of the Chinese people* (1951). K. S. Latourette, *The Chinese, their history and culture,* 2 vols. (1934). E. R. Hughes, *Invasion of China by the western world* (1938). Henri Cordier, *Histoire des relations de la Chine avec les puissances occidentales, 1860–1902,* 3 vols. (1901–2). A. W. Hummel, ed., *Eminent Chinese of the Ch'ing period, 1644–1912,* 2 vols. (1943), a biographical dictionary. J. O. P. Bland & E. Backhouse, *China under the Empress-dowager,* new ed. (1939). P. H. Clements, *Boxer rebellion* (1915).

A. N. Holcombe, *The Chinese revolution* (1930). S. Chen & R. Payne, *Sun Yat-sen, a portrait* (1946). L. S. Hsü, *Sun Yat-sen, his political and social ideals* (1933). R. H. Berkov, *Strong man of China* (1938), on Chiang Kai-shek. H. F. MacNair, ed., *China* (1946), a symposium. B. I. Schwartz, *Chinese communism and the rise of Mao* (1951). F. C. Jones, *Manchuria since 1931* (1949). J. K. Fairbank, *The United States and China* (1948), in support of contemporary

SELECT BIBLIOGRAPHY 809

American policy. Freda Utley, *The China story* (1951), in criticism of that policy.

**Southeastern Asia.** Virginia Thompson, *French Indo-China* (1937), and, with Richard Adloff, *The left wing in southeast Asia* (1950). A. Vandenbosch, *Dutch East Indies* (1934). C. Wolf, Jr., *The Indonesian story* (1948). G. M. Kahin, *Nationalism and revolution in Indonesia* (1952). J. A. Le Roy, *Americans in the Philippines, a history of the conquest and first years of occupation*, 2 vols. (1914). G. A. Grunder & W. E. Livezey, *The Philippines and the United States* (1951). W. C. Forbes, *The Philippine islands* (1945). D. L. Oliver, *The Pacific islands* (1951).

**India.** G. Wint, *The British in Asia*, rev. ed. (1954). W. H. Moreland & A. C. Chatterjee, *Short history of India* (1936). *Cambridge history of India*, vol. vi, *Indian empire, 1858–1918*, ed. by H. H. Dodwell (1937). Louis Fischer, *Life of Mahatma Gandhi*, new ed. (1954). J. Coatman, *India, the road to self-government, 1908–1940* (1943). T. W. Wallbank, *India, a survey of the heritage and growth of Indian nationalism* (1948), and *India in the new era, a study of the origin and development of the Indian union and Pakistan* (1951). Sir George Dunbar, *India and the passing of empire* (1952). V. P. Menon, *Transfer of power in India* (1957). N. Ahmad, *Basis of Pakistan* (1947). Richard Symonds, *The making of Pakistan* (1950). T. G. Spear, *India, Pakistan, and the west*, 2nd ed. (1952). L. A. Mills, *Ceylon under British rule, 1795–1932* (1933). D. G. E. Hall, *Burma* (1950). Other works relating to India are listed under British empire and commonwealth, p. 807, above.

**Middle and Near East.** Royal Institute of International Affairs, *The middle east, a political and economic survey* (1950), on the Arab countries, and on Turkey, Cyprus, and Israel. W. C. Smith, *Islam in modern history* (1957). H. A. R. Gibb, *Islamic society and the West* (1951). A. J. Arberry & R. Landau, eds., *Islam today* (1943). Percy Sykes, *A history of Persia*, 2 vols. (1952). L. P. Elwell-Sutton, *Modern Iran* (1941). E. G. Brown, *Persian revolution of 1905–1909* (1910). George Lenczowski, *Russia and the West in Iran, 1918–1948* (1949), and *Middle east in world affairs* (1952), treating of period since World War. J. C. Hurewitz, *Diplomacy in the near and middle East, a documentary history, 1914–1956* (1957). L. V. Thomas & R. N. Frye, *The United States and Turkey and Iran* (1951).

P. K. Hitti, *History of the Arabs*, 5th ed. (1952). George Antonius, *Arab awakening* (1939). Elizabeth McCallum, *Nationalist crusade in Syria* (1928). P. K. Hitti, *History of Syria* (1951). A. H. Hourani, *Syria and Lebanon, a political essay* (1946). H. A. Foster, *The making of modern Iraq* (1935). K. S. Twitchell, *Saudi Arabia* (1947).

P. L. Hanna, *British policy in Palestine* (1942). E. Sereni & R. E. Ashery, *Jews and Arabs in Palestine* (1936). J. Garcia-Granados, *Palestine, a study of Jewish, Arab, and British policies,* 2 vols. (1947), and *Birth of Israel* (1948). I. F. Stone, *This is Israel* (1948). J. C. Hurewitz, *The struggle for Palestine* (1950).

For Turkey, see pp. 805–806, above.

**Africa.** Sir Harry Johnston, *History of the colonization of Africa by alien races,* rev. ed. (1930). Sir Charles Lucas, *Partition and colonization of Africa* (1922). S. E. Crowe, *The Berlin West African conference, 1884–1885* (1942). H. L. Hoskins, *European imperialism in Africa* (1930). R. L. Buell, *Native problem in Africa,* 2 vols. (1928). W. E. B. DuBois, *The world and Africa* (1947). J. A. Noon, *Labor problems of Africa* (1944).

Lord Cromer, *Modern Egypt,* new ed. (1916), classic apology for British occupation and rule. W. S. Blunt, *Secret history of the English occupation of Egypt* (1907), antidote to Cromer. C. W. Hallberg, *The Suez canal, its history and diplomatic importance* (1931). Victor Piquet, *La colonisation française dans l'Afrique du nord: Algérie, Tunisie, Maroc,* 2nd ed. (1914). M. M. Knight, *Morocco as a French economic venture* (1937). W. C. Askew, *Europe and Italy's acquisition of Libya* (1943). P. Badoglio, *The war in Abyssinia* (1937). Christine Sandford, *Ethiopia under Haile Selassie* (1946).

H. R. Rudin, *Germany in the Cameroons, 1884–1914* (1938). F. M. Bourret, *The gold coast, a survey of the Gold Coast and British Togoland, 1919–1946* (1949). C. H. Huberich, *Political and legislative history of Liberia,* 2 vols. (1947). Sir Reginald Coupland, *Exploitation of East Africa, 1856–1890, the slave trade and the scramble* (1939). Zoë Marsh & G. W. Kingsnorth, *An introduction to the history of East Africa* (1957). L. S. B. Leakey, *Mau Mau and the Kikuyu* (1954). Guillaume Grandidier, *Quarante années de l'histoire de Madagascar, 1880–1920* (1923). Lois A. C. Raphael, *The Cape-to-Cairo dream* (1936).

J. H. Hofmeyr & J. P. Cope, *South Africa,* 2nd ed. (1952). Sarah G. Millin, *Cecil Rhodes* (1933). Basil Williams, *Botha, Smuts, and South Africa* (1948). C. W. de Kiewiet, *A history of South Africa, social and economic* (1941). L. Marquard, *Peoples and policies of South Africa* (1952). G. H. Calpin, ed., *The South African way of life: values and ideals in a multi-racial society* (1953). Alan Paton, *Cry, the beloved country* (1948), for psychological insight into racial situation.

## 7. CURRENT HISTORY AND HISTORICAL CRITICISM

**Nature and methods of history.** Louis Gottschalk, *Understanding history, a primer of historical method* (1950). G. J. Garraghan, *A guide to historical method,* ed. by Jean Delanglez, S. J. (1946). Allan

Nevins, *Gateway to history* (1938). Jacques Barzun & H. F. Graff, *The modern researcher* (1957). G. P. Gooch, *History and historians in the 19th century*, new ed. (1952). Herbert Butterfield, *History and human relations* (1951). Benedetto Croce, *History*, Eng. trans. (1939), a neo-Hegelian view. H. E. Barnes, *The new history and the social studies* (1925), and *A history of historical writing* (1937). Reinhold Niebuhr, *Faith and history, a comparison of Christian and modern views of history* (1949). A. J. Toynbee, *A study of history*, ed. by D. C. Somervell (1947, 1957). Christopher Dawson, *The dynamics of world history* (1956). Jacques Maritain, *Philosophy of History* (1958).

**Current journals with historical articles and book reviews.** *American historical review*, official publication of American Historical Association, Washington, D. C. *American Catholic historical review*, published at Catholic University of America, Washington. *Journal of modern history*, University of Chicago. *Foreign affairs*, organ of the Council on Foreign Relations, New York. *American journal of international law*, Washington, D. C. *Political science quarterly*, Columbia University, New York. *American political science review*, official publication of American Political Science Association. *American economic review*, official publication of the American Economic Association. *Journal of economics and business history*, published at Harvard University, Cambridge, Mass. *Economic history review*, organ of Economic History Society. *Journal of the history of ideas*, published at City College, New York. *Thought*, published at Fordham University, New York. *The Yale review*, published at Yale University, New Haven, Conn.

Chief historical reviews published in Europe: *English historical review; History today; Revue historique; Historische Zeitschrift; Hispania; Journal of world history*, beginning in 1953 under auspices of UNESCO. Reviews of special areas: *Hispanic American historical review; Slavonic review; Russian review; Journal of central European affairs; Far eastern quarterly; Middle East journal*. The London *Times* has by far the best weekly book-review supplement of all newspapers; in the United States, the book-review supplement to the *New York Herald Tribune* is somewhat superior to that of *The New York Times* in the field of European history. Some good reviews may also be found in *The Saturday review of literature* of New York, and in *The critic* of Chicago.

**Records of current events.** Containing much reliable and useful data: *The statesman's year book*, published in England; *The world almanac*, published annually by the *New York World-Telegram;* the United Nations' *Yearbook;* and the *Political handbook of the world*, sponsored by the American Council on Foreign Relations. In addition: *The new international yearbook*, ed. by H. E. Vizetelly; *Survey of* *international affairs,* published by the Royal (British) Institute of International Affairs; *The annual register* (British); *La vie politique dans les deux mondes,* and *Europäischer Geschichtskalender,* two famous Continental annuals.

There are, of course, frequent governmental publications which are usually catalogued under particular nations, and many of which are important to the historical student. There are likewise numerous publications of the League of Nations, continued by the United Nations.

# INDEX

ENGLISH-SPEAKING AREAS

ROMANIC-SPEAKING AREAS (SPANISH, PORTUGUESE, FRENCH, OR ITALIAN)

TEUTONIC-SPEAKING AREAS

SLAVIC AND OTHER EAST-EUROPEAN-SPEAKING AREAS